P9-DVK-745

Betwixt &
Between

Betwixt & Between:

Patterns of Masculine and Feminine Initiation

Edited by Louise Carus Mahdi
Steven Foster and Meredith Little

OPEN COURT
LA SALLE, ILLINOIS

THE REALITY OF THE PSYCHE SERIES

General Editor:
Louise Carus Mahdi

Advisory Board:
Gerhard Adler, Ernest Bel, Michael Fordham, Marie-Louise
von Franz, Marco Gay, James Hall, Joseph Henderson, Elie
Humbert, Thomas Kapacinskas, Thomas Lavin, John
Mattern, William McGuire, C. A. Meier, Lee Roloff, Jeffrey
Satinover, June Singer, Murray Stein, Jane Wheelwright,
Joseph Wheelwright, Edward Whitmont, Harry Wilmer,
Beverly Zabriskie.

This book has been reproduced in a print-on-demand
format from the 1994 Open Court printing.

Open Court Publishing Company is a division of
Carus Publishing Company.

© 1987 by Open Court Publishing Company

First printing 1987
Second printing 1987
Third printing 1988
Fourth printing 1993
Fifth printing 1994

All rights reserved. No part of this publication may be
reproduced, stored in a retrieval system, or transmitted, in any
form or by any means, electronic, mechanical, photocopying,
recording, or otherwise, without the prior written permission
of the publisher, Open Court Publishing Company, 315 Fifth
Street, P.O. Box 599, Peru, Illinois 61354-0599.

Library of Congress Cataloging-in-Publication Data

Betwixt and between.
    Filmography: p.
    Includes bibliographies and index.
    1. Initiation rites. 2. Rites and ceremonies.
3. Developmental psychology. I. Mahdi, Louise Carus.
II. Foster, Steven, 1938– III. Little, Meredith, 1951–
GN473.B47 1987   392'.14   86-31271
ISBN 0-8126-9047-8
ISBN 0-8126-9048-6 (pbk)

**To order books from Open Court,
call toll-free 1-800-815-2280.**

EDITOR'S ACKNOWLEDGMENTS

I want to thank many generous and deeply interested people, many more than I can mention individually, for their contributions to making this book a reality. Meredith Little and Steven Foster, co-editors, worked over the book and were adventurous companions on the way at the edge of the desert in Big Pine, California, where they write and function as vision quest guides. We want to express our special appreciation to Edith Turner for permission to name this *Betwixt and Between* after Victor Turner's important chapter at the beginning of the book. Each of the authors has been patient and helpful beyond measure. We are very grateful to each one. Susan Sack has been my great aide at home base in Peru, Illinois, providing a lively dialogue through the final stages of getting *Betwixt and Between* finished, as well as helping at the typewriter, creating the index and assisting with countless details. Dennis Merritt, Jennette Jones, Robert Moore, James Hall, Russell Lockhart, Murray Stein and Thomas Kapacinskas have all been valued counselors. Vera Bührmann in South Africa has been inspiring in her pioneer work combining skills in both analytical psychology and anthropology. C. A. Meier in Zurich has been a mentor through crucial stages and I am very grateful. Mircea Eliade was graciously available for consultation. Edith Sullwold has been a great friend on the by-ways of initiation. Arnold Bergstraesser first introduced me to the works of C. G. Jung at the University of Chicago. Dieter Baumann provided important perspectives. Arnold Mindell has opened channels. Paul Carus and Blouke Carus have supported this book since they were convinced of the value of a new discussion of the practical significance of rites of passage and initiation in our times. Particular thanks go to Teresa Gibbs, Eleanor Schmitz, LeRoy Ceresa, Todd Sanders, Connie Terselic, Linda Frederick, Jaci Hydock, David Ramsay Steele, and Lisa Zimmermann, all of whom were very generous with their time and contributions. Cara and David Knudsen, Tom Kapacinskas, and Barry Williams have been unselfish and inspiring companions in the practical application of the ideas in *Betwixt and Between* at our wilderness island refuge in Temagami, Ontario. In this book, we are building on what we have learned with and from each other, and from participants who have shared so much.

Louise Carus Mahdi
La Salle, Illinois
February 1987

You see, in the image of Aquarius, it's a man who pours water into the fish. Now the fish is the unconscious. It's not enough to just have it. We have to actively turn towards it [the unconscious] and support it so that it then helps us.

—MARIE-LOUISE VON FRANZ (1983)

CONTENTS

INTRODUCTION

Louise Carus Mahdi

It is increasingly clear that our cultural values have been undermined, so that even among the masses, and especially among today's youth, there are individuals who are seeking, not so much the destruction of the old, as something new on which to build. And because the destruction has been so widespread and has gone so deep, this new foundation must be located in the depths in the most natural, the most primordial, most universally human core of existence.

—Marie-Louise von Franz (1975)

Betwixt and Between: Patterns of Masculine and Feminine Initiation is an interdisciplinary study with an accent on individual as well as more social issues. Victor Turner's important chapter, "Betwixt and Between: The Liminal Period in Rites of Passage," presents characteristic basic patterns in initiation practices in several cultures from the author's perspective as a social anthropologist. Throughout the book, we take Turner's view that the "betwixt and between" times, the threshold transition times, deserve special attention as constructive "building blocks" for change, or possibly transformation and initiation to another level of consciousness. These liminal or threshold times have a power of their own for both the individual and the culture at large. The authors of this book focus on these key times of what one might call "betweenness" or liminality and their positive potential for each of us at significant stages of life, at the crossroads.

Our book is essentially practical, applying basic ideas and patterns of initiation for several age groups. Since so-called puberty rites in most societies were the major rites of passage and initiation throughout history, we move from Turner to very practical issues in our own society. We open the section on the initiation of youth with a chapter by John Allan and Pat Dyck who use these ideas for youngsters approaching puberty in the public school system, providing a new approach to the curriculum.

In order to get into the subject of initiation, we present a "case study," Harold Schechter's chapter on Huckleberry Finn's journey down the Mississippi. The trip floating down the river on the raft is a liminal experience *par excellence*, Huck Finn's individual response to the "call to adventure," to use Joseph Campbell's phrase to describe the heroic journey. As a metaphor within the individual as well as in outer reality, the heroic journey is important for both masculine and feminine initiation. We all have something of Huck inside us, something of Ulysses on our own individual odyssey. The journey is, of course, the great metaphor for the initiation and individuation process.

Although the vision quest journey presented here by Meredith Little and Steven Foster is for young people, it is an ancient procedure used by adult men and women in various cultures, but called by different names such as "incubation" in ancient Greece (see the chapter by C. A. Meier). The vision quest, however, has deep roots in North America. In his books, the visionary Black Elk said that "everyone" in the Sioux culture was going on the vision quest when he was young (Neihardt 1932 and Brown 1971). Among the Ojibway Indian people, the dream or vision quest was considered "the most crucial experience of a man's life" (Hallowell 1966). We have evidence that these practices were widely used by young people, supported and encouraged by their communities and elders among the first Americans. Since constructive rites of passage and initiation are not functioning for vast numbers of people nowadays, we need a comparative cultural perspective to find the patterns most suited for us. Useful here is the work of Stephen Bacon, *The Use of Metaphor in Outward Bound* (1983).

Some sense of the need for a book like *Betwixt and Between* grew out of my own involvement with initiation while I was teaching in a four-year college in the 1960's. A small group of graduates of this school wanted to "re-search" practical ways and means of initiation and extending consciousness without the use of drugs. 1970 was the year of our first project, "Camp Re-Search," just before these students entered their first professional positions. The students organized the camp to search together for new forms of initiation. During this camp I experienced the practical value of a conscious approach to initiation and rites of passage in our project that we later called a "vision quest," the first of many similar adventures. Since 1979 we have had summer programs on a wilderness island in Ontario led by a team from the Chicago Jung Institute located in Evanston, Illinois.

Each year since 1970, I have continued to take small groups camping in the wilderness. We have found that focused group experience is necessary to create a small community where people can begin to support each other in their individual transition tasks (see Jung 1964, Ch. III by M. L. von Franz). Working in groups, in addition to one-on-one dialogues, is needed today to compensate for what modern civilization has lost: a *social* way to experience life-transitions through rites of passage and initiation. As Eric Neumann (1973, p. 186) points out,

> . . . in modern man [where] collective rites no longer exist, and the problems relating to these transitions devolve upon the individual, his responsibility and understanding are so overburdened that psychic disorders are frequent. This is the case not only in childhood but also in puberty, in marriage and mid-life, at the climacteric, and in the hour of death. All these stages in life were formerly numinous points at which the collectivity intervened with its rites; today they are points of psychic illness and anxiety for the individual, whose awareness does not suffice to enable him to live his life.

In recent years widespread "initiation hunger," particularly at mid-life, has become so great that psychologists working in private practice have begun to combine forces with scholars and teachers from other fields. *Betwixt and Between* presents relevant works not only of Jungian analysts but also of anthropologists, vision quest guides, poets, theologians, and scholars of popular culture. Extending consciousness is the task in our quest for wholeness (see Edinger 1984) and is discussed throughout the book, as are various detailed approaches to initiation at major crossroads for both men and women.

There is evidence that initiation and rites of passage have been widely practiced throughout human history in small societies because of a psychological/social need with a biological foundation, particularly around the time of puberty.

> If we measure a culture's worth by the longevity of its population, the sophistication of its technology, the material comfort it offers, then many [so-called] primitive cultures have little to offer us, that is true. But our study of the life cycle will show that in terms of a conscious dedication to human relationships that are both affective and effective, the primitive is ahead of us all the way. He is working at it at every stage of life, from infancy to death, while playing just as much as while praying; whether at work or at home his life is governed by his conscious quest for social order. Each individual learns this social consciousness as he grows up, and the lesson is constantly reinformed until the day he dies, and because of that social consciousness each individual is a person of worth and value and importance to society, also from the day of birth to the day of death. It all begins in childhood. (Turnbull 1983, pp. 21-22)

Only one or two generations ago, certain institutions like the church, even the army, were facilitating initiations more successfully than today. Regardless of one's profession or age, all adults are somehow involved in initiation issues nowadays, whether we like it or not, even if only as taxpayers supporting overcrowded prisons—that is, houses of failed initiation. As A. Stevens says (1982, p. 159), it appears to be

> . . . society at large that has abdicated responsibility for initiating the young. Traditional initiatory procedures have been allowed to atrophy with disuse because our 'elders' have lost confidence in the values of which they are the custodians and no longer possess any certain knowledge as to what it may be that they are initiating young people for. Ultimately, it is the fault of neither teacher nor pupil, elder nor novice, but the consequence of a *collective crisis of confidence in our culture*. The loss of respect for traditional values, the progressive relativisation of all canons and ethics, results in a conceptual miasma in which one television interviewee's opinion is as good as another. So far, all attempts to replace traditional procedures with pragmatic ones has met with little success, largely, I believe, because they are based on a shallow, one-sided and biologically ignorant view of human nature . . . they fail to take into account those fundamental archetypal determinants which demand that religious forms of experience, family integrity, stability and continuity in relationships between the generations, hierarchical social structures, gender differences, initiatory procedures, and so on, be respected and allowed expression. [italics added]

With terrorism on the international scene, crime in our local neighborhoods or even next door, trouble in our own families and in ourselves, there are many transitions needing more conscious attention. Since our highly industrialized and technological society has lost touch with our heritage of initiation, we must now re-examine these subjects.

Where have all the elders gone? We cannot provide initiations at puberty—or earlier, or later—unless we have elders with some knowledge of these processes and what aspects of initiation could be applicable today (see the chapter by C. A. Meier, "Ancient Incubation and Modern Psychotherapy," Vera Bührmann's "Xhosa Healers," Claire Farrer's chapter on girls' puberty rites among the Mescalero Apache, as well as Searle and Lavin on Christian initiations).

Carlton Coon, a Harvard anthropologist who devoted fifty years to the study of traditional cultures, concluded that in contemporary America,

> . . . unlike the children of [traditional] hunters, . . . boys and girls [today] have no adults to guide them through the puberty ordeals that they need in order to maintain social continuity. It is no wonder that they create age-graded microsocieties of their own. The secrecy that once formed a vital part of puberty rites is transferred to their parents, to whom they will not reveal what they have been doing . . .
>
> Saving our planet from human destruction, and from the destruction of life itself, is only half of our problem. The other half is for us to learn how nature intended human beings to live and to reestablish continuity with those who may still be alive after the rest of us are dead. (1971 pp. 392-3) [brackets added]

In other words, we badly need qualified adults to guide our young people through contemporary initiation ordeals and later transitions. First we need "elders" who themselves have been initiated. Our age offers new ways of being for women and men, with new challenges. Some of the chapters of this anthology present a new approach to initiation from within using creative and active imagination in relation to an inner guide. We can report that the psyche continues to offer initiatory direction and insight. It is no wonder that thresholds, bridges, and crossings in the past have been so carefully guarded in fact and in myth. These places, both in the outer world as well as within, can be difficult, even dangerous. As Marie-Louise von Franz has said in describing contemporary initiation (1972, p. 64), as it is experienced by individuals,

> . . . The first step is generally falling into the dark place, and usually appears in a dubious or negative form—falling into something, or being possessed by something [and then you have to work out of it]. The Shamans say that being a medicine man begins by falling into the power of the demons; the one who pulls out of the dark place becomes the medicine man, and the one who stays in it is the sick person [but the first step was the same, both were possessed by the dark thing]. *You can take every psychological illness as an initiation.* Even the worst things you fall into are an effort of initiation, for you are in something which belongs to you, and now you must get out of it. [brackets and italics added]

The need for some kind of initiation is so important that if it does not happen consciously, it will happen unconsciously, often in a dangerous form.

Fulfillment of the deep need for initiation in our world today seems to have gone "underground." In other words, our attempts at initiation now appear in less conscious forms than they have in the past. Today images and symbols of ancient rites of passage are frequently found in dreams, fantasies, and in unconscious acting out by people of all ages. Anthony Stevens writes of the persisting psychological and social need to be initiated, and provides many examples of this in his recent *Archetypes* (1982, p. 164):

> This need is very evident in patients undergoing analysis; archetypal symbols of initiation arise spontaneously in dreams at critical periods in the life-cycle—at puberty, betrothal, marriage, childbirth, at divorce, separation, or death of a spouse, at the betrothal and marriage of one's children, at the approach of old age and death. Campbell (1949) and Henderson (1967) give many striking instances of this, all of them examples of that mysterious and fascinating process which Neumann calls "the personal evocation of the archetype." It seems that the attainment of a new stage of life demands that the *initiation symbols appropriate to that stage must be experienced*. If culture fails to provide these symbols in institutional form then the Self [within] is forced to provide them *faute de mieux*. [italics added]

Symbolic death and rebirth were the elements of traditional initiations. The elders were key figures during the passage from one stage of life or status to the next as guides through dangerous ritual passages. But what was symbolic in the practices of traditional small societies is sometimes taken literally or acted out in concrete detail today, in our society in which the elders are missing. Our youth are unconsciously trying to tell us something. In some traditional societies, for example, there are initiations where the initiate is painted with white clay to indicate that he is ritually dead (see the chapter by Schechter on *Huckleberry Finn*). For our adolescents in transition today, however, *actual* suicide has become epidemic (see the chapter on teenage suicide, "Suicide's 'Unanswerable Logic'," by Alina Tugend and M. Sandra Reeves). Claude Brown, author of *Manchild in the Promised Land* (1965) recently wrote,

> The present day manchild is a human paradox. . . . he is a considerably more sophisticated adolescent. He is more knowledgeable, more sensitive, more amicable—and more likely to commit murder. . . .
> I had been talking to young men in the prisons and on the ghetto streets—prisons with invisible bars—but I wasn't comprehending what they were telling me. Perhaps what I was hearing was too mind-boggling, "Murder is in style now . . . " (1985)

It is for the alienated and the unclaimed of modern society that initiation is particularly important. Since traditional classroom forms of education are not working for many, we need to explore alternatives. Vision Quest, Inc., for example, with national headquarters in Tucson, Arizona, offers a practical program using rites of passage and initiation concepts in working with delinquent adolescents. Most interesting are their mule-drawn covered wagon trains traveling the back roads across the United States. They also run various homes and schools across the country in different states. This is just one of several functioning newer approaches based on an appreciation of rites of passage in working with alienated youth. It is an unusual program for liminal persons, that is, delinquents who are learning to change their lives.

I once had some long talks with an old American Indian medicine man who had been taken out on a vision quest initiation for several months when he was 16. His uncle and his father took him up a wooded mountain trail in the wilderness. These elders then sang appropriate traditional songs and marked the tree where they left him for the initial part of his training, that is, for his initiatory journey. He remembers their ancient advice: "Listen," they said. "Even the message of the smallest mosquito must be heard. Listen." (See Mary Griffin's *Cry for Help* 1983). The contributors to this book offer a way to begin listening with a new awareness to the warning signals and alarms at the various turnings and twists in the life cycle. Traditionally, initiation and rites of passage trained the members of a given society for survival of their own group. Humanity itself is in transition on such a large scale that our survival depends on the consciousness of each and every individual. These basic and traditional tools of learning for survival, i.e. initiation and rites of passage, must now be used for the larger task at hand—that is, for the very survival of humankind.

Louise Carus Mahdi, M.A., is a graduate of the University of Chicago and a diplomate of the Jung Institute in Zürich. She is editor of The Reality of The Psyche Series of the Open Court Publishing Company. She is a member of the Chicago Society of Jungian Analysts and is in private practice. Currently she is doing research on children's dreams and fantasies about war and peace.

REFERENCES

Bacon, S. 1983. *The use of metaphor in Outward Bound.* Denver: Colorado Outward Bound School.

Brown, C. 1984. Manchild in Harlem. *New York Times Magazine.* September 16, 1984.

Brown, J.E. 1971. *The sacred pipe: Black Elk's account of the seven rites of the Ogalala Sioux.* New York: Penguin.

Campbell, J. 1949. *The hero with a thousand faces.* New York: Pantheon.

Castandea, C. 1974. *Tales of power.* New York: Simon and Schuster.

Coon, C. 1971. *The hunting peoples.* Boston: Atlantic, Little Brown.

Deren, M. 1952. *Divine horseman: The living gods of Haiti.* New York: Book Collectors Society.

Edinger, E. 1984. *The creation of consciousness: Jung's myth for modern man.* Toronto: Inner City Books.

Eliade, M. 1958. *Birth and rebirth: The religious meanings of initiation in human culture*. New York: Harper.

Erikson, E. 1950. *Childhood and society*. New York: Nortin.

Fox, R. and Tiger, L. 1974. *The imperial animal*. New York: Dell.

Franz, M.L. von. 1971. *C.G. Jung und die theologen: selbsterfahrung und götteserfahrung bei C.G. Jung*. Stuttgart: Radius Verlag.

―――― 1975. *C. G. Jung: His myth in our time*. New York: G.P. Putnam's Sons.

―――― 1972. *The feminine in fairy tales*. Dallas: Spring Publications.

―――― 1983. In film text: *Matter of heart*. Los Angeles: C. G. Jung Institute.

Gennep, A. 1960. *The rites of passage*. Chicago: University of Chicago.

Griffin, M. and Felsenthal, M. 1983. *Cry for help*. New York: Doubleday.

Hallowell, A.I. 1966. The role of dreams in Ojibwa culture; in *The dream and human societies,* ed. von Grünebaum and Cailloio, Berkeley: University of California Press.

Henderson, J.L. 1967. *Thresholds of initiation*. Middleton, Conn.: Wesleyan University Press.

Jung, C.G. 1964. *Man and his symbols*. New York: Doubleday.

Lincoln, B. 1981. *Emerging from the chrysalis*. Cambridge: Harvard University Press.

Macy, J. 1982. *Despair and empowerment in the nuclear age*. Philadelphia: New Society Publishers.

Neihardt, J. 1932. *Black Elk speaks*. New York: William Morrow.

Neumann, E. 1973. *The child: Structure and dynamics of the nascent personality*. New York: Putnam.

Paz, O. 1961. *The labrynth of solitude*. New York: Grove Press.

Stevens, A. 1982. *Archetypes: A natural history of the self.* New York: William Morrow.

Turnbull, C.M. 1983. *The human cycle*. New York: Simon and Schuster.

Wilhelm, R. *I Ching. Book of changes.* New Jersey: Princeton University Press.

As their flesh once labored to bring forth flesh,
  so the minds of the elders labor,
  with like passion,
    to bring forth a mind.
By rites of initiation
  they would accomplish
  the metamorphosis of matter into man,
  the evolution of a mind for meaning in the animal
    which is the issue of their flesh.
By this
  they would insure that the race endure
    as a race of men.
The rites of this second birth
  into the metaphysical cosmos,
  everywhere mime the conditions of
    the first physical birth.
The novice is
  purified of the past,
  relieved of possessions,
  made innocent,
    placed nascent in the womb solitude . . .
The matter,
  which is man himself,
  and the myth of a race
    are joined.
His solitary meditation
  is a gestation
  and, in the end,
  a man emerges by ordeal,
    to be newly named, newly rejoiced in.

—Maya Deren (1952)

THE REALITY OF THE PSYCHE SERIES

BETWIXT
AND
BETWEEN

PART ONE

$$\mathcal{C} \; 1 \; \mathcal{D}$$

BETWIXT AND BETWEEN:
THE LIMINAL PERIOD IN RITES OF PASSAGE

Victor Turner

No recurrent events in human culture give clearer evidence of the archetypal structure of the human psyche than the initiation rituals or ceremonies that accompany the transition from one social status to another. In 1909, Arnold van Gennep first identified the common structure which underlies virtually all such "rites of passage." Since then, his schema has informed every cross-cultural study of the initiation process. However, it was not until Victor Turner focused scholarly attention on the "betwixt and between" (transition) period of initiation rites that the richness and coherence of the liminal or transitional phase became apparent.

Turner's classic essay, "Betwixt and Between: The Liminal Period in Rites of Passage," is generally conceded to be the seminal statement on the subject of ritual liminality. Yet this essay is important for other reasons as well. It sheds light on the broadly-shared, recurrent, "archetypal" aspects of rites de passage. The innate predispositions of the human psyche to think and act in certain ways, regardless of culture or race, are surely implicit in the forms of ritual behavior he so aptly describes.

In this keynote introduction by Victor Turner, we see initiation, a social and cultural event of great, even paramount importance, as a means of tribal survival and self-nurture. We also find here a pattern for understanding initiation as an individual and inner process of growth and individuation. Even as the initiate in a tribal culture must relinquish former structural ties, undergoing nakedness, poverty, and complete submission to the terms of the liminal passage in order to attain the next life stage, so the individual in our own culture must leave old ways behind, divesting oneself of ego's claims to rank and social function, in order to attain a more highly individuated stage of growth.

At the time of his death in 1983, Victor Turner, Ph.D., was Professor of Anthropology and Religion at the University of Virginia. Born in Scotland, he

*received his B.A. from the University of London and his doctorate from the
University of Manchester. Formerly chairman of the Committee on Social
Thought at the University of Chicago, Turner studied extensively in the fields
of literature, folklore, drama, psychology, and neurobiology, and did
fieldwork in Zambia, Uganda, Mexico, Ireland, Italy, France, Brazil, Japan,
and Israel. He published numerous articles and lectured widely on a variety of
subjects bearing on initiation. His books include* The Forest of Symbols
(1967), The Ritual Process: Structure and Anti-Structure *(1969),* Dramas,
Fields, and Metaphors *(1974), and* Image and Pilgrimage *(1978).*

IN this paper, I wish to consider some of the sociocultural properties of the
"liminal period" in that class of rituals which Arnold van Gennep has
definitively characterized as *"rites de passage."* If our basic model of society
is that of a "structure of positions," we must regard the period of margin or
"liminality" as an interstructural situation. I shall consider, notably in the case
of initiation rites, some of the main features of instruction among the simpler
societies. I shall also take note of certain symbolic themes that concretely
express indigenous concepts about the nature of "interstructural" human
beings.

Rites de passage are found in all societies but tend to reach their maximal
expression in small-scale, relatively stable and cyclical societies, where
change is bound up with biological and meteorological rhythms and
recurrences rather than with technological innovations. Such rites indicate and
constitute transitions between states. By "state" I mean here "a relatively
fixed or stable condition" and would include in its meaning such social
constancies as legal status, profession, office or calling, rank or degree. I hold
it to designate also the condition of a person as determined by his culturally
recognized degree of maturation as when one speaks of "the married or single
state" or the "state of infancy." The term "state" may also be applied to
ecological conditions, or to the physical, mental or emotional condition in
which a person or group may be found at a particular time. A man may thus be
in a state of famine or of plenty. State, in short, is a more inclusive concept
than status or office and refers to any type of stable or recurrent condition that
is culturally recognized. One may, I suppose, also talk about "a state of
transition," since J. S. Mill has, after all, written of "a state of progressive
movement," but I prefer to regard transition as a process, a becoming, and, in
the case of *rites de passage,* even a transformation—here an apt analogy
would be water in process of being heated to boiling point, or a pupa changing
from grub to moth. In any case, a transition has different cultural properties
from those of a state, as I hope to show presently.

Van Gennep himself defined *"rites de passage"* as "rites which accompany every change of place, state, social position and age." To point up the

contrast between "state" and "transition," I employ "state" to include all his other terms. Van Gennep has shown that all rites of transition are marked by three phases: separation, margin (or *limen*), and aggregation. The first phase of separation comprises symbolic behavior signifying the detachment of the individual or group either from an earlier fixed point in the social structure or a set of cultural conditions (a "state"); during the intervening liminal period, the state of the ritual subject (the "passenger") is ambiguous; he passes through a realm that has few or none of the attributes of the past or coming state; in the third phase the passage is consummated. The ritual subject, individual or corporate, is in a stable state once more and, by virtue of this, has rights and obligations of a clearly defined and "structural" type, and is expected to behave in accordance with certain customary norms and ethical standards. The most prominent type of *rites de passage* tends to accompany what Lloyd Warner has called "the movement of a man through his lifetime, from a fixed placental placement within his mother's womb to his death and ultimate fixed point of his tombstone and final containment in his grave as a dead organism—punctuated by a number of critical moments of transition which all societies ritualize and publicly mark with suitable observations to impress the significance of the individual and the group on living members of the community. These are the important times of birth, puberty, marriage, and death" (Warner 1959). However, as van Gennep and others have shown, *rites de passage* are not confined to culturally defined life-crises but may accompany any change from one state to another, as when a whole tribe goes to war, or when it attests to the passage from scarcity to plenty by performing a first-fruits or a harvest festival. *Rites de passage,* too, are not restricted, sociologically speaking, to movements between ascribed statuses. They also concern entry into a new achieved status, whether this be a political office or membership of an exclusive club or secret society. They may admit persons into membership of a religious group where such a group does not include the whole society, or qualify them for the official duties of the cult, sometimes in a graded series of rites.

Since the main problem of this study is the nature and characteristics of transition in relatively stable societies, I shall focus attention on *rites de passage* that tend to have well-developed liminal periods. On the whole, initiation rites, whether into social maturity or cult membership, best exemplify transition, since they have well-marked and protracted marginal or liminal phases. I shall pay only brief heed here to rites of separation and aggregation, since these are more closely implicated in social structure than rites of liminality. Liminality during initiation is, therefore, the primary datum of this study, though I will draw on other aspects of passage ritual where the argument demands this. I may state here, partly as an aside, that I consider the term "ritual" to be more fittingly applied to forms of religious behavior associated with social transitions, while the term "ceremony" has a closer bearing on religious behavior associated with social states, where politico-legal institutions also have greater importance. Ritual is transformative, ceremony confirmatory.

The subject of passage ritual is, in the liminal period, structurally, if not physically, "invisible." As members of society, most of us see only what we expect to see, and what we expect to see is what we are conditioned to see when we have learned the definitions and classifications of our culture. A society's secular definitions do not allow for the existence of a not-boy-not-man, which is what a novice in a male puberty rite is (if he can be said to be anything). A set of essentially religious definitions co-exist with these which do set out to define the structurally indefinable "transition-being." The transitional-being or "liminal *persona*" is defined by a name and by a set of symbols. The same name is very frequently employed to designate those who are being initiated into very different states of life. For example, among the Ndembu of Zambia the name *mwadi* may mean various things: it may stand for "a boy novice in circumcision rites," or "a chief-designate undergoing his installation rites," or, yet again, "the first or ritual wife" who has important ritual duties in the domestic family. Our own terms "initiate" and "neophyte" have a similar breadth of reference. It would seem from this that emphasis tends to be laid on the transition itself, rather than on the particular states between which it is taking place.

The symbolism attached to and surrounding the liminal *persona* is complex and bizarre. Much of it is modeled on human biological processes, which are conceived to be what Levi-Strauss might call "isomorphic" with structural and cultural processes. They give an outward and visible form to an inward and conceptual process. The structural "invisibility" of liminal *personae* has a twofold character. They are at once no longer classified and not yet classified. In so far as they are no longer classified, the symbols that represent them are, in many societies, drawn from the biology of death, decomposition, catabolism, and other physical processes that have a negative tinge, such as menstruation (frequently regarded as the absence or loss of a fetus). Thus, in some boys' initiations, newly-circumcised boys are explicitly likened to menstruating women. In so far as a neophyte is structurally "dead," he or she may be treated, for a long or short period, as a corpse is customarily treated in his or her society. (See Stobaeus' quotation, probably from a lost work of Plutarch: "initiation and death correspond word for word and thing for thing" [James 1961]). The neophyte may be buried, forced to lie motionless in the posture and direction of customary burial, may be stained black, or may be forced to live for a while in the company of masked and monstrous mummers representing, *inter alia*, the dead, or worse still, the un-dead. The metaphor of dissolution is often applied to neophytes; they are allowed to go filthy and identified with the earth—the generalized matter into which every specific individual is rendered down. Particular form here becomes general matter; often their very names are taken from them and each is called solely by the generic term for "neophyte" or "initiand." (This useful neologism is employed by many modern anthropologists).

The other aspect, that they are not yet classified, is often expressed in symbols modeled on processes of gestation and parturition. The neophytes are likened to or treated as embryos, newborn infants, or sucklings by symbolic means which vary from culture to culture. I shall return to this theme presently.

The essential feature of these symbolizations is that the neophytes are neither living nor dead from one aspect, and both living and dead from another. Their condition is one of ambiguity and paradox, a confusion of all the customary categories. Jakob Boehme, the German mystic whose obscure writings gave Hegel his celebrated dialectical "triad," liked to say that "In Yea and Nay all things consist." Liminality may perhaps be regarded as the Nay to all positive structural assertions, but as in some sense the source of them all, and, more than that, as a realm of pure possibility whence novel configurations of ideas and relations may arise. I will not pursue this point here but, after all, Plato, a speculative philosopher, if there ever was one, did acknowledge his philosophical debt to the teachings of the Eleusinian and Orphic initiations of Attica. We have no way of knowing whether primitive initiations merely conserve lore. Perhaps they also generated new thought and new custom.

Dr. Mary Douglas, of University College, London, has recently advanced (in a magnificent book, *Purity and Danger* [1966]) the very interesting and illuminating view that the concept of pollution "is a reaction to protect cherished principles and categories from contradiction." She holds that, in effect, what is unclear and contradictory (from the perspective of social definition) tends to be regarded as (ritually) unclean. The unclear is the unclean: e.g., she examines the prohibitions on eating certain animals and crustaceans in Leviticus in the light of this hypothesis (these being creatures that cannot be unambiguously classified in terms of traditional criteria). From this standpoint, one would expect to find that transitional beings are particularly polluting, since they are neither one thing nor another, or may be both; or neither here nor there; or may even be nowhere (in terms of any recognized cultural topography), and are at the very least "betwixt and between" all the recognized fixed points in space-time of structural classification. In fact, in confirmation of Dr. Douglas's hypothesis, liminal *personae* nearly always and everywhere are regarded as polluting to those who have never been, so to speak, "inoculated" against them, through having been themselves initiated into the same state. I think that we may perhaps usefully discriminate here between the statics and dynamics of pollution situations. In other words, we may have to distinguish between pollution notions which concern states that have been ambiguously or contradictorily defined, and those which derive from ritualized transitions between states. In the first case, we are dealing with what has been defectively defined or ordered, in the second with what cannot be defined in static terms. We are not dealing with structural contradictions when we discuss liminality, but with the essentially unstructured (which is at once de-structured and pre-structured) and often the people themselves see this in terms of bringing neophytes into close connection with deity or with superhuman power, with what is, in fact, often regarded as the unbounded, the infinite, the limitless. Since neophytes are not only structurally "invisible" (though physically visible) and ritually polluting, they are very commonly secluded, partially or completely, from the realm of culturally defined and ordered states and statuses. Often the indigenous term for the liminal period is, as among the Ndembu, the locative form of a noun meaning "seclusion site" *(kundunka, kung'ula).* The neophytes are sometimes said to "be in another place." They have physical but not social "reality," hence they have to be hidden, since it is a paradox, a scandal, to see what ought not to be there! Where they are not removed to a sacred place of concealment they are often disguised, in masks or grotesque costumes or striped with white, red, or black clay, and the like.

In societies dominantly structured by kinship institutions, sex distinctions have great structural importance. Patrilineal and matrilineal moieties and clans, rules of exogamy, and the like, rest and are built up on these distinctions. It is consistent with this to find that in liminal situations (in kinship-dominated societies) neophytes are sometimes treated or symbolically represented as being neither male nor female. Alternatively, they may be symbolically assigned characteristics of both sexes, irrespective of their biological sex. Bruno Bettelheim (1954) has collected much illustrative material on this point from initiation rites. They are symbolically either sexless or bisexual and may be regarded as a kind of human *prima materia*— as undifferentiated raw material. It was perhaps from the rites of the Hellenic mystery religions that Plato derived his notion expressed in his *Symposium* that the first humans were androgynes. If the liminal period is seen as an interstructural phase in social dynamics, the symbolism both of androgyny and sexlessness immediately becomes intelligible in sociological terms without the need to import psychological (and especially depth-psychological explanations.) Since sex distinctions are important components of structural status, in a structureless realm they do not apply.

A further structurally negative characteristic of transitional beings is that they *have* nothing. They have no status, property, insignia, secular clothing, rank, kinship position, nothing to demarcate them structurally from their fellows. Their condition is indeed the very prototype of sacred poverty. Rights over property, goods, and services inhere in positions in the politico-jural structure. Since they do not occupy such positions, neophytes exercise no such rights. In the words of King Lear they represent "naked unaccommodated man."

I have no time to analyze other symbolic themes that express these attributes of "structural invisibility," ambiguity and neutrality. I want now to draw attention to certain positive aspects of liminality. Already we have noted how certain liminal processes are regarded as analogous to those of gestation, parturition, and suckling. Undoing, dissolution, decomposition are accompanied by processes of growth, transformation, and the reformulation of old elements in new patterns. It is interesting to note how, by the principle of the economy (or parsimony) of symbolic reference, logically antithetical processes of death and growth may be represented by the same tokens, for example, by huts and tunnels that are at once tombs and wombs, by lunar symbolism (for the same moon waxes and wanes), by snake symbolism (for the snake appears to die, but only sheds its old skin and appears in a new one), by bear symbolism (for the bear "dies" in autumn and is "reborn" in spring), by nakedness (which is at once the mark of a newborn infant and a corpse prepared for burial), and by innumerable other symbolic formations and actions. This coincidence of opposite processes and notions in a single representation characterizes the peculiar unity of the liminal: that which is neither this nor that, and yet is both.

I have spoken of the interstructural character of the liminal. However, between neophytes and their instructors (where these exist), and in connecting neophytes with one another, there exists a set of relations that compose a "social structure" of highly specific type. It is a structure of a very simple kind: between instructors and neophytes there is often complete authority and complete submission; among neophytes there is often complete equality. Between incumbents of positions in secular politico-jural systems there exists intricate and situationally shifting networks of rights and duties proportioned to their rank, status, and corporate affiliation. There are many different kinds of privileges and obligations, many degrees of superordination and subordination. In the liminal period such distinctions and gradations tend to be eliminated. Nevertheless, it must be understood that the authority of the elders over the neophytes is not based on legal sanctions; it is, in a sense, the personification of the self-evident authority of tradition. The authority of the elders is absolute, because it represents the absolute, the axiomatic values of society in which are expressed the "common good" and the common interest. The essence of the complete obedience of the neophytes is to submit to the elders but only in so far as they are in charge, so to speak, of the common good and represent in their persons the total community. That the authority in question is really quintessential tradition emerges clearly in societies where initiations are not collective but individual and where there are no instructors or *gurus.* For example, Omaha boys, like other North American Indians, go alone into the wilderness to fast and pray (Hocart 1952). This solitude is liminal between boyhood and manhood. If they dream that they receive a woman's burden-strap, they feel compelled to dress and live henceforth in every way as women. Such men are known as *mixuga*. The authority of such a dream in such a situation is absolute. Alice Cunningham Fletcher tells of one Omaha who had been forced in this way to live as a woman, but whose natural inclinations led him to rear a family and to go on the warpath. Here the *mixuga* was not an invert but a man bound by the authority of tribal beliefs and values. Among many Plains Indians, boys on their lonely Vision Quest inflicted ordeals and tests on themselves that amounted to tortures. These again are not basically self-tortures inflicted by a masochistic temperament but due to obedience to the authority of tradition in the liminal situation—a type of situation in which there is no room for secular compromise, evasion, manipulation, casuistry, and maneuver in the field of custom, rule, and norm. Here again a cultural explanation seems preferable to a psychological one. A normal man acts abnormally because he is obedient to tribal tradition, not out of disobedience to it. He does not evade but fulfills his duties as a citizen.

If complete obedience characterizes the relationship of neophyte to elder, complete equality usually characterizes the relationship of neophyte to neophyte, where the rites are collective. This comradeship must be distinguished from brotherhood or sibling relationship, since in the latter there is always the inequality of older and younger, which often achieves linguistic representation and may be maintained by legal sanctions. The liminal group is a community or comity of comrades and not a structure of hierarchically arrayed positions. This comradeship transcends distinctions of rank, age, kinship position, and, in some kinds of cultic group, even of sex. Much of the behavior recorded by ethnographers in seclusion situations falls under the principle: "Each for all, and all for each." Among the Ndembu of Zambia, for example, all food brought for novices in circumcision seclusion by their mothers is shared out equally among them. No special favors are bestowed on the sons of chiefs or headmen. Any food acquired by novices in the bush is taken by the elders and apportioned among the group. Deep friendships between novices are encouraged, and they sleep around lodge fires in clusters of four or five particular comrades. However, all are supposed to be linked by special ties which persist after the rites are over, even into old age. This friendship, known as *wubwambu* (from a term meaning "breast") or *wulunda*, enables a man to claim privileges of hospitality of a far-reaching kind. I have no need here to dwell on the lifelong ties that are held to bind in close friendship those initiated into the same age-set in East African Nilo-Hamitic and Bantu societies, into the same fraternity or sorority on an American campus, or into the same class in a Naval or Military Academy in Western Europe.

This comradeship, with its familiarity, ease and, I would add, mutual outspokenness, is once more the product of interstructural liminality, with its scarcity of jurally sanctioned relationships and its emphasis on axiomatic values expressive of the common weal. People can "be themselves," it is frequently said, when they are not acting institutionalized roles. Roles, too, carry responsibilities and in the liminal situation the main burden of responsibility is borne by the elders, leaving the neophytes free to develop interpersonal relationships as they will. They confront one another, as it were, integrally and not in compartmentalized fashion as actors of roles.

The passivity of neophytes to their instructors, their malleability, which is increased by submission to ordeal, their reduction to a uniform condition, are signs of the process whereby they are ground down to be fashioned anew and endowed with additional powers to cope with their new station in life. Dr. Richards (1956), in her superb study of Bemba girls' puberty rites, *Chisungu*, has told us that Bemba speak of "growing a girl" when they mean initiating her. This term "to grow" well-expresses how many peoples think of transition rites. We are inclined, as sociologists, to reify our abstractions (it is indeed a device which helps us to understand many kinds of social interconnection) and to talk about persons "moving through structural positions in a hierarchical frame" and the like. Not so the Bemba and the Shilluk of the Sudan who see the status or condition embodied or incarnate, if you like, *in* the person. To "grow" a girl into a woman is to effect an ontological transformation; it is not merely to convey an unchanging substance from one position to another by a quasi-mechanical force. Howitt saw Kuringals in Australia and I have seen Ndembu in Africa drive away grown-up men before a circumcision ceremony because they had only been circumcised at the Mission Hospital and had not undergone the full bush seclusion according to the orthodox Ndembu rite. These biologically mature men had not been "made men" by the proper ritual procedures. It is the ritual and the esoteric teaching which grows girls and makes men. It is the ritual, too, which among Shilluk makes a prince into a king, or, among Luvale, a cultivator into a hunter. The arcane knowledge or *"gnosis"* obtained in the liminal period is felt to change the inmost nature of the neophyte, impressing him, as a seal impresses wax, with the characteristics of his new state. It is not a mere acquisition of knowledge, but a change in being. His apparent passivity is revealed as an absorption of powers which will become active after his social status has been redefined in the aggregation rites.

The structural simplicity of the liminal situation in many initiations is offset by its cultural complexity. I can touch on only one aspect of this vast subject matter here and raise three problems in connection with it. This aspect is the vital one of the communication of the *sacra,* the heart of the liminal matter.

Jane Harrison (1903) has shown that in the Greek Eleusinian and Orphic mysteries this communication of the *sacra* has three main components. By and large, this threefold classification holds good for initiation rites all over the world. *Sacra* may be communicated as: (1) exhibitions, "what is shown"; (2) actions, "what is done"; and (3) instructions, "what is said."

"Exhibitions" would include evocatory instruments or sacred articles, such as relics of deities, heroes or ancestors, aboriginal *churingas,* sacred drums or other musical instruments, the contents of Amerindian medicine bundles, and the fan, cist and tympanum of Greek and Near Eastern mystery cults. In the Lesser Eleusinian Mysteries of Athens, *sacra* consisted of a bone, top, ball, tambourine, apples, mirror, fan, and woolly fleece. Other *sacra* include masks, images, figurines, and effigies; the pottery emblems *(mbusa)* of the Bemba would belong to this class. In some kinds of initiation, as for example the initiation into the shaman-diviner's profession among the Saora of Middle India, described by Verrier Elwyn (1955), pictures and icons representing the journeys of the dead or the adventures of supernatural beings may be shown to the initiands. A striking feature of such sacred articles is often their formal simplicity. It is their interpretation which is complex, not their outward form.

Among the "instructions" received by neophytes may be reckoned such matters as the revelation of the real, but secularly secret, names of the deities or spirits believed to preside over the rites—a very frequent procedure in African cultic or secret associations (Turner 1962a). They are also taught the main outlines of the theogony, cosmogony, and mythical history of their societies or cults, usually with reference to the *sacra* exhibited. Great importance is attached to keeping secret the nature of the *sacra,* the formulas chanted and instructions given about them. These constitute the crux of liminality, for while instruction is also given in ethical and social obligations, in law and in kinship rules, and in technology to fit neophytes for the duties of future office, no interdiction is placed on knowledge thus imparted since it tends to be current among uninitiated persons also.

I want to take up three problems in considering the communication of *sacra*. The first concerns their frequent disproportion, the second their monstrousness, and the third their mystery.

When one examines the masks, costumes, figurines, and such displayed in initiation situations, one is often struck, as I have been, when observing Ndembu masks in circumcision and funerary rites—by the way in which certain natural and cultural features are represented as disproportionately large or small. A head, nose, or phallus, a hoe, bow, or meal mortar are represented as huge or tiny by comparison with other features of their context which retain their normal size. (For a good example of this, see "The Man Without Arms" in *Chisungu* [Richards 1956], a figurine of a lazy man with an enormous penis but no arms.) Sometimes things retain their customary shapes but are portrayed in unusual colors. What is the point of this exaggeration amounting sometimes to caricature? It seems to me that to enlarge or diminish or discolor in this way is a primordial mode of abstraction. The outstanding exaggerated feature is made into an object of reflection. Usually it is not a univocal symbol that is thus represented but a multi-vocal one, a semantic molecule with many components. One example is the Bemba pottery emblem *Coshi wa ng'oma,* "The Nursing Mother," described by Audrey Richards in *Chisungu.* This is a clay figurine, nine inches high, of an exaggeratedly pregnant mother shown carrying four babies at the same time, one at her breast and three at her back. To this figurine is attached a riddling song:

> My mother deceived me!
> *Coshi wa ng'oma!*
> So you have deceived me;
> I have become pregnant again.

Bemba women interpreted this to Richards as follows: *Coshi wa ng'oma* was a midwife of legendary fame and is merely addressed in this song. The girl complains because her mother told her to wean her first child too soon so that it died; or alternatively told her that she would take the first child if her daughter had a second one. But she was tricking her and now the girl has two babies to look after. The moral stressed is the duty of refusing intercourse with the husband before the baby is weaned, i.e., at the second or third year. This is a common Bamba practice (Richards 1956).

In the figurine, the exaggerated features are the number of children carried at once by the woman and her enormously distended belly. Coupled with the song, it encourages the novice to ponder upon two relationships vital to her, those with her mother and her husband. Unless the novice observes the Bemba weaning custom, her mother's desire for grandchildren to increase her matrilineage and her husband's desire for renewed sexual intercourse will between them actually destroy and not increase her offspring. Underlying this is the deeper moral that to abide by tribal custom and not to sin against it either by excess or defect is to live satisfactorily. Even to please those one loves may be to invite calamity, if such compliance defies the immemorial wisdom of the elders embodied in the *mbusa.* This wisdom is vouched for by the mythical and archetypal midwife *Coshi wa ng'oma.*

If the exaggeration of single features is not irrational but thought-provoking, the same may also be said about the representation of monsters. Earlier writers—such as J. A. McCulloch (1913) in his article on "Monsters" in *Hastings Encyclopaedia of Religion and Ethics*—are inclined to regard bizarre and monstrous masks and figures, such as frequently appear in the liminal period of initiations, as the product of "hallucinations, night-terrors and dreams." McCulloch goes on to argue that "as man drew little distinction (in primitive society) between himself and animals, as he thought that transformation from one to the other was possible, so he easily ran human and animal together. This in part accounts for animal-headed gods or animal-gods with human heads." My own view is the opposite one: that monsters are manufactured precisely to teach neophytes to distinguish clearly between the different factors of reality, as it is conceived in their culture. Here, I think, William James's so-called "law of dissociation" may help us to clarify the problem of monsters. It may be stated as follows: when *a* and *b* occurred together as parts of the same total object, without being discriminated, the occurrence of one of these, *a,* in a new combination *ax,* favors the discrimination of *a, b,* and *x* from one another. As James himself put it, "What is associated now with one thing and now with another, tends to become dissociated from either, and to grow into an object of abstract contemplation by the mind. One might call this the law of dissociation by varying concomitants" (James 1918).

From this standpoint, much of the grotesqueness and monstrosity of liminal *sacra* may be seen to be aimed not so much at terrorizing or bemusing neophytes into submission or out of their wits as at making them vividly and rapidly aware of what may be called the "factors" of their culture. I have myself seen Ndembu and Luvale masks that combine features of both sexes, have both animal and human attributes, and unite in a single representation human characteristics with those of the natural landscape. One *ikishi* mask is partly human and partly represents a grassy plain. Elements are withdrawn from their usual settings and combined with one another in a totally unique configuration, the monster or dragon. Monsters startle neophytes into thinking about objects, persons, relationships, and features of their environment they have hitherto taken for granted.

In discussing the structural aspect of liminality, I mentioned how neophytes are withdrawn from their structural positions and consequently from the values, norms, sentiments, and techniques associated with those positions. They are also divested of their previous habits of thought, feeling, and action. During the liminal period, neophytes are alternately forced and encouraged to think about their society, their cosmos, and the powers that generate and sustain them. *Liminality may be partly described as a stage of reflection.* In it those ideas, sentiments, and facts that had been hitherto for the neophytes bound up in configurations and accepted unthinkingly are, as it were, resolved into their constituents. These constituents are isolated and made into objects of reflection for the neophytes by such processes as componental exaggeration and dissociation by varying concomitants. The communication of *sacra* and other forms of esoteric instruction really involves three processes, though these should not be regarded as in series but as in parallel. The first is the reduction of culture into recognized components or factors; the second is their recombination in fantastic or monstrous patterns and shapes; and the third is their recombination in ways that make sense with regard to the new state and status that the neophytes will enter.

The second process, monster- or fantasy-making, focuses attention on the components of the masks and effigies, which are so radically ill-assorted that they stand out and can be thought about. The monstrosity of the configuration throws its elements into relief. Put a man's head on a lion's body and you think about the human head in the abstract. Perhaps it becomes for you, as a member of a given culture and with the appropriate guidance, an emblem of chieftainship; or it may be explained as representing the soul as against the body; or intellect as contrasted with brute force, or innumerable other things. There could be less encouragement to reflect on heads and headship if that same head were firmly ensconced on its familiar, its all too familiar, human body. The man-lion monster also encourages the observer to think about lions, their habits, qualities, metaphorical properties, religious significance, and so on. More important than these, the relation between man and lion, empirical and metaphorical, may be speculated upon, and ideas developed on this topic. Liminality here breaks, as it were, the cake of custom and enfranchises speculation. That is why I earlier mentioned Plato's self-confessed debt to the Greek mysteries. Liminality is the realm of primitive hypothesis, where there is a certain freedom to juggle with the factors of existence. As in the works of Rabelais, there is a promiscuous intermingling and juxtaposing of the categories of events, experience, and knowledge, with a pedagogic intention.

But this liberty has fairly narrow limits. The neophytes return to secular society with more alert faculties perhaps and enhanced knowledge of how things work, but they have to become once more subject to custom and law. Like the Bemba girl I mentioned earlier, they are shown that ways of acting and thinking alternative to those laid down by the deities or ancestors are ultimately unworkable and may have disastrous consequences.

Moreover, in initiation, there are usually held to be certain axiomatic principles of construction, and certain basic building blocks that make up the cosmos and into whose nature no neophyte may inqure. Certain *sacra,* usually exhibited in the most arcane episodes of the liminal period, represent or may be interpreted in terms of these axiomatic principles and primordial constituents. Perhaps we may call these *sacerrima,* "most sacred things." Sometimes they are interpreted by a myth about the world-making activities of supernatural beings "at the beginning of things." Myths may be completely absent, however, as in the case of the Ndembu "mystery of the three rivers." This mystery *(mpang'u)* is exhibited at circumcision and funerary cult association rites. Three trenches are dug in a consecrated site and filled respectively with white, red, and black water. These "rivers" are said to "flow

from Nzambi," the High God. The instructors tell the neophytes, partly in
riddling songs and partly in direct terms, what each river signifies. Each
"river" is a multivocal symbol with a fan of referents ranging from life values,
ethical ideas, and social norms, to grossly physiological processes and
phenomena. They seem to be regarded as powers which, in varying
combination, underlie or even constitute what Ndembu conceive to be reality.
In no other context is the interpretation of whiteness, redness, and blackness
so full; and nowhere else is such a close analogy drawn, even identity made,
between these rivers and bodily fluids and emissions: whiteness = semen,
milk; redness = menstrual blood, the blood of birth, blood shed by a weapon,
etc.; blackness = feces, certain products of bodily decay, etc. This use of an
aspect of human physiology as a model for social, cosmic, and religious ideas
and processes is a variant of a widely distributed initiation theme; that the
human body is a microcosm of the universe. The body may be pictured as
androgynous, as male or female, or in terms of one or other of its
developmental stages, as child, mature adult, and elder. On the other hand, as
in the Ndembu case, certain of its properties may be abstracted. Whatever the
mode of representation, the body is regarded as a sort of symbolic template for
the communication of *gnosis,* mystical knowledge about the nature of things
and how they came to be what they are. The cosmos may in some cases be
regarded as a vast human body; in other belief systems, visible parts of the
body may be taken to portray invisible faculties such as reason, passion,
wisdom and so on; in others again, the different parts of the social order are
arrayed in terms of a human anatomical paradigm.

Whatever the precise mode of explaining reality by the body's attributes,
sacra which illustrate this are always regarded as absolutely sacrosanct, as
ultimate mysteries. We are here in the realm of what Warner (1959) would call
"nonrational or nonlogical symbols" which

> arise out of the basic individual and cultural assumptions, more often unconscious
> than not, from which most social action springs. They supply the solid core of
> mental and emotional life of each individual and group. This does not mean that
> they are irrational or maladaptive, or that man cannot often think in a reasonable
> way about them, but rather that they do not have their source in his rational
> processes. When they come into play, such factors as data, evidence, proof, and
> the facts and procedures of rational thought in action are apt to be secondary or
> unimportant.

The central cluster of nonlogical *sacra* is then the symbolic template of the
whole system of beliefs and values in a given culture, its archetypal paradigm
and ultimate measure. Neophytes shown these are often told that they are in
the presence of forms established from the beginning of things (see Cicero's
comment [*De Leg.* II. 14] on the Elusianian Mysteries: "They are rightly
called initiations [beginnings] because we have thus learned the first principles
of life."). I have used the metaphor of a seal or stamp in connection with the

ontological character ascribed in many initiations to arcane knowledge. The term "archetype" denotes in Greek a master stamp or impress, and these *sacra,* presented with a numinous simplicity, stamp into the neophytes the basic assumptions of their culture. The neophytes are told also they are being filled with mystical power by what they see and what they are told about it. According to the purpose of the initiation, this power confers on them capacities to undertake successfully the tasks of their new office, in this world or the next.

Thus, the communication of *sacra* both teaches the neophytes how to think with some degree of abstraction about their cultural milieu and gives them ultimate standards of reference. At the same time, it is believed to change their nature, transform them from one kind of human being into another. It intimately unites man and office. But for a variable while, there was an uncommitted man, an individual rather than a social *persona,* in a sacred community of individuals.

It is not only in the liminal period of initiations that the nakedness and vulnerability of the ritual subject receive symbolic stress. Let me quote from Hilda Kuper's (1947) description of the seclusion of the Swazi chief during the great *Incwala* ceremony. The *Incwala* is a national First-Fruits ritual, performed in the height of summer when the early crops ripen. The regiments of the Swazi nation assemble at the capital to celebrate its rites, "whereby the nation receives strength for the new year." The *Incwala* is at the same time "a play of kingship." The king's well-being is identified with that of the nation. Both require periodic ritual strengthening. Lunar symbolism is prominent in the rites, as we shall see, and the king, personifying the nation, during his seclusion represents the moon in transition between phases, neither waning nor waxing. Dr. Kuper, Professor Gluckman (1954), and Professor Wilson (1961) have discussed the structural aspects of the *Incwala* which are clearly present in its rites of separation and aggregation. What we are about to examine are the interstructural aspects.

During his night and day of seclusion, the king remains, says Dr. Kuper, "painted in blackness" and "in darkness"; he is unapproachable, dangerous to himself and others. He must cohabit that night with his first ritual wife (in a kind of "mystical marriage"—this ritual wife is, as it were, consecrated for such liminal situations).

> The entire population is also temporarily in a state of taboo and seclusion. Ordinary activities and behavior are suspended; sexual intercourse is prohibited, no one may sleep late the following morning, and when they get up they are not allowed to touch each other, to wash the body, to sit on mats, to poke anything into the ground, or even to scratch their hair. The children are scolded if they play and make merry. The sound of songs that has stirred the capital for nearly a month is abruptly stilled; it is the day of *bacisa* (cause to *hide*). The king remains secluded; . . . all day he sits naked on a lion skin in the ritual hut of the harem or in the sacred enclosure in the royal cattle byre. Men of his inner circle see that he breaks none of

the taboos . . . on this day the identification of the people with the king is very marked. The spies (who see to it that the people respect the taboos) do not say, "You are sleeping late" or "You are scratching," but "You cause the king to sleep," "You scratch him (the king)"; etc. (Kuper 1947)

Other symbolic acts are performed which exemplify the "darkness" and "waxing and waning moon" themes, for example, the slaughtering of a black ox, the painting of the queen mother with a black mixture—she is compared again to a half-moon, while the king is a full moon, and both are in eclipse until the paint is washed off finally with doctored water, and the ritual subject "comes once again into lightness and normality."

In this short passage we have an embarrassment of symbolic riches. I will mention only a few themes that bear on the argument of this paper. Let us look at the king's position first. He is symbolically invisible, "black," a moon between phases. He is also under obedience to traditional rules, and "men of his inner circle" see that he keeps them. He is also "naked," divested of the trappings of his office. He remains apart from the scenes of his political action in a sanctuary or ritual hut. He is also, it would seem, identified with the earth which the people are forbidden to stab, lest the king be affected. He is "hidden." The king, in short, has been divested of all the outward attributes, the "accidents," of his kingship and is reduced to its substance, the "earth" and "darkness" from which the normal, structured order of the Swazi kingdom will be regenerated "in lightness."

In this betwixt-and-between period, in this fruitful darkness, king and people are closely identified. There is a mystical solidarity between them, which contrasts sharply with the hierarchical rank-dominated structure of ordinary Swazi life. It is only in darkness, silence, celibacy, in the absence of merriment and movement that the king and people can thus be one. For every normal action is involved in the rights and obligations of structure that defines status and establishes social distance between men. Only in their Trappist sabbath of transition may the Swazi regenerate the social tissues torn by conflicts arising from distinctions of status and discrepant structural norms.

I end this study with an invitation to investigators of ritual to focus their attention on the phenomena and processes of mid-transition. It is these, I hold, that paradoxically expose the basic building blocks of culture just when we pass out of and before we re-enter the structural realm. In *sacerrima* and their interpretations we have categories of data that may be handled usefully by the new sophisticated techniques of cross-cultural comparison.

REFERENCES

Bettelheim, B. 1954. *Symbolic wounds.* Glencoe, Ill.: Free Press.
Cicero, M. 1959. *De legibus,* ed. de Plinval. Paris: Les Belles Lettres.

Douglas, M. 1966. *Purity and danger.* London: Routledge & Kegan Paul.

Elwin, V. 1955. *The religion of an Indian tribe.* London: Geoffrey Cumberledge.

Gennep, A. van. 1960. *The rites of passage.* Chicago: University of Chicago Press.

Gluckman, M. 1954. *Rituals of rebellion in south-east Africa.* Manchester: Manchester University Press.

Harrison, J. E. 1903. *Prolegomena to the study of Greek religion.* London: Cambridge University Press.

Hocart, A. M. 1952. *The life-giving myth.* London: Methuen.

James, E. O. 1961. *Comparative religion.* London: Methuen.

James, W. 1918. *Principles of psychology,* vol. 1. New York: H. Holt.

Kuper, H. 1947. *An African aristocracy.* London: Oxford University Press, for International African Instute.

McCulloch, J. A. 1913. Monsters. In *Hastings Encyclopaedia of Religion and Ethics.* Edinburgh: T. & T. Clark.

Richards, A. I. 1956. *Chisungu.* London: Faber & Faber.

Turner, V. M. 1962. *Chihamba, the White Spirit.* Rhodes-Livingstone Paper 33. Manchester: Manchester University Press.

Warner, W. L. 1959. *The living and the dead.* New Haven: Yale University Press.

Wilson, M. 1959. *Divine kings and the breath of men.* London: Cambridge University Press.

Reprinted from *The Forest of Symbols* (Ithaca: Cornell University Press, 1967), by permission from Mrs. Victor Turner and Cornell University Press.

THE
INITIATION
OF
YOUTH

PART TWO

TRANSITION FROM CHILDHOOD TO ADOLESCENCE: DEVELOPMENTAL CURRICULUM

John Allan and Pat Dyck

The transitional guidelines for adolescents presented in this article by John Allan and Pat Dyck have been valuable not only for the youngsters themselves but for teachers, parents, and other educators as well. Allan and Dyck have discovered first-hand some of the most effective ways to foster in our youth a deeper understanding of the behavioral as well as psychological changes that must inevitably take place in their lives as they grow into the new responsibilities of early adolescence.

Although their curriculum focuses on boys and girls just entering puberty, Allan and Dyck clearly demonstrate the ability and readiness of young people even at this early age, to absorb "mature" concepts such as the meaning of life transitions, the function of fear, how to face new challenges and social responsibilities, and how to communicate effectively with parents, teachers, and friends.

One of the most valuable aspects of their program is that it teaches young people the method of thoughtful introspection as an essential tool with which to develop individual yet well-reasoned attitudes and values concerning themselves and others.

To supplement the specific, day-by-day program set out in their article, the authors have supplied a fine bibliography of stories about transitions appropriate for young adolescents. They also include valuable feedback and assessments of several aspects of the curriculum by the students who participated in it as well as their parents.

Psychological research of a theoretical nature concerning the problem of how we can best "initiate" our young children into adulthood is certainly of great importance today; yet here, Allan and Dyck show us from a down-to-earth, "hands-on" perspective, how to achieve more conscious rites of passage into early adolescence.

John Allan, Ph.D., is Associate Professor of Counseling Psychology in the School of Education, University of British Columbia, and, in private practice, a Jungian analyst. As a specialist in the application of Jungian concepts to education, he is the author of three books and numerous articles on symbolic therapies with children. He serves on the editorial board of Journal of Analytical Psychology *and* Elementary School Guidance and Counseling.

Pat Dyck, M. Ed., Head Counselor at Abbotsford Junior Secondary School, Abbotsford, British Columbia, specializes in preventative and developmental aspects of school counseling and is particularly interested in issues relating to student-parent-teacher cooperation, positive learning climates, cross-grade peer interaction, and the childhood to adulthood passage. He has published articles in Elementary School Guidance and Counseling and School Guidance Worker.

MANY parents and teachers are concerned about the lack of adequate educational and psychological preparation our children have for their transition into adolescence and later into young adulthood. Frequently one sees on television and in the newspapers concern over the "troubled" youth of today—their drug problems, unwanted pregnancies, cult involvements, suicides and delinquent acts. One also hears about violence, fear and destruction in the schools. Obviously there are many causes for such behavior, but the question that arose in our minds was: what, if anything, can the public school system do to help in the transition from childhood to young adulthood so that some of these problems might be reduced?

Transition from one developmental phase to another usually involves changes in personal awareness and necessitates the learning of new behavior. Any major change in our life pattern seems to require shifts in our identity and in the way we function. Jung (1969) said this quite poetically in 1931 when he wrote that what is true in the morning of our life is often a lie by the afternoon. On a psychological level, change often involves pain and ambivalence, confusion and dismemberment as the old identity dies and the new one emerges. At times there needs to be a hiatus, an empty period, a period of incubation between the death of the old and the birth of the new.

Recently, counseling psychologists have written quite extensively on transitions (Adams & Hopson 1977) and on the need for intervention strategies to cope with them (Brammer & Abrego 1981). While most of this material has focused on mid-life crises, divorce and career change, the transition from childhood to young adolescence has been largely neglected. School counselors have written about transition from elementary to junior high school and have developed some useful coping strategies (Bent 1976; Childress 1982; Friedman 1976; Nisbet & Entwistle 1969). However, these researchers did not address the deeper developmental issue of change of identity from child to young adolescent.

While working in the public school system as counselors and teachers, it occurred to us that children need to understand and be prepared for this change. To meet this need we set about designing a developmental guidance curriculum on transition for grades six, seven and eight. This paper provides the background to our thinking, the methodology and some of the children's responses to the material. Specific objectives, materials and 12 lesson plans are contained in our manual (Allan and Dyck 1984).

BACKGROUND

In many ways our present day Western civilization is an exception in the history of man because of its lack of rites of passage for the young adolescent. Though some formal rites still do exist (Confirmation, Bar Mitzvah, graduation and the driver's license) most young people are left to make or discover their own challenges or rites of initiation. Historically, this is unusual, for in other cultures the rites of passage involved all levels of the community, from the elders who steered the process, to the very young who joined in the celebrations.

On account of this lack we turned to other cultures for an understanding of some of the psychological principles embedded in the rites of passage. In particular, we examined the work of such anthropologists as Van Gennep (1960), Turner (1967), Freed and Freed (1980), Lincoln (1981) and to writers of stories about initiation and transition (Neihardt 1972; Salerno & Vanderburgh 1980; & Waldo 1980). From these works we tried to identify some of the key components involved in transition so that we could use these in designing a curriculum of transition for today's youth. For example, certain patterns stood out:

- Just before puberty, children are aware of bodily changes and the impending change of status from child to young adult.
- The times or moments of transition were occasions for specific and vital learning, frequently for *groups* of boys or *groups* of girls.
- There were three clearly defined stages: separation and preparation, test or ordeal and celebration with a change of status and re-incorporation.
- All of the phases involved the use of "significant others" from the family and community around.
- The preparation phase often involved separation into single-sexed groups, the learning of new knowledge and skills and actual preparation for a test or challenge.
- The activities were different for each sex. The boys needed the formal break from mothers while girls needed the involvement of the whole community, especially women and men.
- A celebration, or recognition ceremony, was held. This often provided an experience of renewal for the whole community.

- The psychological effects of the rite seemed to result in the internalization of a positive self-concept for each initiate as a competent and capable young adult, ready for new responsibilities.
- The rites helped the young adolescent become a responsible carrier of the culture.

Though we could not incorporate all of these principles into our guidance curriculum, we attempted to adapt some of them for the current times. We did involve parents in the project and the grade 7 classroom became the "community."

Broadly speaking, some of the psychological functions of rites of passage include the act of separation from the family of origin, coming to terms with childhood fears, learning new coping skills, dying psychologically to the childhood identity, and the re-emergence of a new outer and inner identity. The outer identity of a competent young man or young woman is established by passing tests and challenges while the new inner identity occurs through receptivity to the dream or vision process. The dream or vision often provides both the sacred totem or personal guardian spirit and a new name to reflect the new status.

In designing the curriculum we thought it was important first to show the students how other cultures handled transition and then to include units which dealt symbolically with some of the major themes: i.e., the journey, childhood fears, and the devising of a modern rite of passage. We saw as new coping skills (a) awareness and understanding of the process of transition, (b) learning about fear and how to overcome it, (c) devising and passing their own tests, and (d) communicating their thoughts and feelings to their parents. We hoped these processes might help strengthen the new emerging self-concept.

METHOD

The curriculum consisted of three major units: Awareness, Understanding and challenge. Each unit was composed of three or four lessons which involved the presentation of stimulus material, class discussions, written activities, and sharing of individual projects.

Unit 1—Awareness

The purpose of this unit was to help the students become aware of the concepts of transition: rites of passage, death-rebirth and psychological transformation. The goal was to give them a cultural perspective and a frame of reference to help them understand that the changes they are going through (or were about to make) were universal and a normal part of life.

In this unit, the students were introduced to the words: "anthropologist" and *rites de passage,* shown slides of Australian aboriginal puberty rites (*National Geographic Magazine* 1980), and read excerpts from *Nkwala* (see

"Transition Stories," end of chapter). The unit closed with a discussion of the theme of life as a journey.

Unit 2—Understanding

The goal of this section was to facilitate a deeper understanding of the process of change for each of the students. The unit focused on memories from childhood, signs that indicated they were growing up, and past, present and future fears. Part of this understanding of change concentrated on their life-line by helping them see where they have come from, where they are now, and what they hope to achieve in the future.

Unit 3—Challenges

A critical component in becoming a successful young adolescent is the ability to face difficulties and to overcome them. In this unit we set about designing simple challenges and providing students with a structure for handling and mastering certain developmental tasks. The unit starts with the students developing their own modern rites of passage and ends with a "Declaration of Dependence." Many of the challenges in this unit relate to communicating and sharing certain thoughts and feelings with parents. One of our goals was to increase the communication flow between young adolescent and parent, realizing that this can be a very difficult task for some adolescents and for some parents.

After each written activity, time was set aside for students to read and discuss their work with the class. Though this activity was optional, many students volunteered to participate.

The project was introduced as part of guidance to a regular grade seven class and the students were informed that for the next twelve weeks (April, May and June) they would have the opportunity to learn about themselves and the stage they were in, and that this work would help prepare them for adolescence and young adulthood.

RESULTS

Though space does not permit a detailed analysis of each session, a brief overview utilizing the student's written reactions will be provided.

1. Australian Aboriginal Rites of Passage. The focus here was on the concepts of "death-of-childhood" and "re-birth-into-adulthood." Photographs and slides were shown of young aboriginals with their faces painted white, lying as if dead, in shallow graves. There was a stunned response: "Are you for real!" "This is a joke, right?" and "You're making this up!" However, when asked to list the similarities between the initiation ceremony and a North American funeral, they drew several comparisons: "They lie still in a shallow

grave, like a coffin; their faces are white or grey like a dead person's and have no expressions and the relatives come to see them—the last look." Slowly the students came to understand the symbolic act of "dying one's childhood" in order to release new energy for growth.

The last slide showed bodily tatooing given as preparation for acceptance as an adult. The concept of having the adults in a society look physically different from children was initially hard to understand. However, some children commented that in our culture we can tell differences between the two groups based on looks (i.e., looking older), clothes and the driving of cars.

2. Vision Quest. The second, third and fourth sessions focused on the vision quest experience of the North American Indians. The children's story, *Nkwala*, was read to the class and questions were asked regarding key concepts involved in this rite of passage. Nkwala is a young Native American Salish Indian boy who at the time of puberty must make a solo journey to the mountains to attain his manhood and to find his guardian spirit. The journey involves physical tests, self-discipline, fasting, overcoming childhood fears, and the finding of his own personal symbol or totem through the dream process. Once this has been achieved, the youth returns to the tribe and is welcomed with a ceremony marking the young adulthood status. The failure to pass the tests simply means the youth must try again. This process may occur several times over a two or three year period and no social stigma is attached to not passing the tests the first few times around.

The unit led to many interesting class discussions. The idea of "proving oneself" and passing tests to be an adult intrigued some of the students. When tradition was mentioned, several students shared their experiences with Confirmation or Bar Mitzvah. Other students were surprised by the length of time the preparation took (a year or more) for these experiences. Fear of failing was discussed and this led into a discussion of other fears. Though the concept of rites of passage was new to the students they quickly grasped the idea and could draw parallels between Nkwala's culture and their own.

3. Journeys. The last session in this section dealt with the theme of Journey. The word "Journey" was written on the chalkboard and students were asked to share their first thoughts. Their free associations were listed on the board. Later they were asked to study the list and to note the underlying theme. They noticed that a journey involved going somewhere and one child commented that life was like a journey.

Examples of their first thoughts about the word "Journey" were:

Trip I went on	Center of earth	Travelling
Time machine	Space	Going someplace
Camping	Someone's life	Hiking trip
Train ride	Rock group	Adventure

Students were then asked to focus on themselves and write a story: "My Journey." The story could be real or imaginary but would need a beginning, a middle and an end. This section also generated much excitement and interest. Many very touching stories were written. One girl wrote:

> When someone mentions the word journey many thoughts and words come to mind. In my case it reminds me of life.
>
> Life is to me a journey made up of many other smaller journeys, that go on until you breathe your last breath. My journey started almost 13 years ago, and as far as I'm concerned, it will last many, many more years.
>
> Throughout my short journey, I've taken a lot of paths that I've regretted taking, but couldn't retrace. All I could do was hope to do better in the future, and not to make the same mistake again.
>
> Life is sometimes a journey filled with disappointment and unfulfilled expectations, but in the long run, it is a journey much appreciated.

There were surprises too. Several of the very "tough" boys wrote extremely sensitive stories, reflecting pain and aspects of their self-concepts. A brief excerpt from one is given below:

> Milleniums from now a small girl named Serena would sit crying softly as the rays from the moon danced through the window. The door to her room opened, a tall man who wore a blue suit with gold stripes down the side walked in. 'What is the matter child?' said the man. The body looked up. 'I'm a Freak,' she said, 'I'm like no other person. Why was I bestowed with these awful powers?' she sobbed. 'You are not grateful for your powers?' said the man. 'No, I hate them. My parents bug me all the time, kids stare at me like . . . like . . . like . . .' the girl started crying again. 'It was me who bestowed you with those powers. I thought that you with your powers could save your planet from disaster.' 'Disaster?' thought the girl. . . .
>
> 'You see, many years from now your planet could possibly die from pollution and nuclear waste. You see, many people call me Starlord. I can see into the future and have any other power imaginable. To you I gave the power to alter forces and change their course and to change into any shape as a chameleon would change color; therefore I gave thou the name Chameleon girl.'
>
> 'You mean of all the people in the universe you picked me?' 'Yes, I picked you because you already had a certain power that no one else on this unholy planet has!'
>
> 'And what is that?' 'Love.' 'Love?' 'Yes, I scanned your mind and noticed that you loved your planet and people.' 'Yes, but how do you know I love my planet?' 'Because years ago, as you may well remember, you could have gone to live on Mars but your love for this world helped you to stay.' 'But why did you pick this universe to look for someone like me?' 'I was on a journey through the universes when my powers started to fade. I landed on this planet and used the last of my power to turn you into what you are.' 'I'm beginning to understand,' said Serena. 'I am grateful to you. Is there any way I can help you?'
>
> 'Yes, you can use your power to alter forces and send me back to my world.' 'Very well, that is what I shall do,' said Serena as she lifted her finger, sending the Starlord spindalling through space back home that he left eons before.

A girl who had been very withdrawn wrote the following story and later read it to the class:

> I'm going away from home with a friend on my summer vacation; we go to a quiet place where no one can bug us. We get there by bus and walk into a quiet place; all we can hear is birds whistling and singing, and we can see squirrels running down and up the tree. We lay our things on the ground and take out our tents. When we've done that we make our food and later clean up.
>
> We have a lot of fun by seeing a lot of things in the woods and going swimming. A couple of days later we have to go home but we don't want to leave our animal friends or the woods where there's a lot of things to enjoy. We tell our little friends that we'll be back.
>
> My Mom's calling me and I find myself on my bed. I was only daydreaming. I'd like my dream to be true some day.

An important component of the journey discussion occurred when part of the class time was set aside for the students to read their own stories to the class. Attention was riveted to the story and a strong supportive group bond was formed. It was as if they were listening to one of the great mysteries and wonders of life.

4. Past Experiences. The lesson was introduced by writing the word "Metamorphosis" on the board, and leading questions were asked about the life cycle of various insects, animals, plants and trees. Students were then asked to provide evidence of their own metamorphosis, to identify changes in the way they were treated. Some examples were:

You are punished physically less often.

You have more responsibilities.

Bedtime comes later.

You have more say in the clothes you wear.

Parents don't hug and kiss you as often.

Parents stop fighting your battles.

When asked about situations when they felt most like a young adult, the common responses were:

When Dad lets me help him at work.

When Mom leaves me alone without reminding me to . . . .

When my parents let me sit in on adult conversations.

When adults ask for my opinion.

Students stated they wished there more times when parents treated them like adults. Two boys admitted they lost their parents' trust by abusing some privileges.

5. Anticipated Experiences. Students then responded to the question: "What events might you experience in the next ten years that will cause you to feel more like an adult?" Some suggestions were:

You may drive a car.

You may move out of the house.

You may look for a job.
You may go out on your first date.
You may travel alone.
You may graduate from high school.

When the list was completed (28 ideas) the class was asked how they felt while focusing on future experiences. Two-thirds reported feeling anxious and nervous, especially regarding high school, job seeking, graduation, and travelling alone, while less than one-third felt excited about adulthood. This led into the next discussion unit on fears.

6. Fears. The acceptance, understanding and mastery of fear is an important component in growing-up. In order to help the students deal with this developmental task they were asked to brainstorm (a) childhood fears and (b) present fears. Examples of these are given below:

Childhood	*Present*
Getting lost	*Older teenagers*
Doctors/dentists	*Getting beaten up*
Ghosts	*Failing school*
Lightning	*The future*
Dogs	*Arguing parents*

They were also asked to write a short story about what life would be like without fear. The purpose of this activity was to help them see that fear can be useful to them. Examples of this are as follows:

'Life would be sad without fear because it would be like missing an arm or part of your body because you need fears in life; it's part of what you do. Also without fear you would figure you'd be macho or tougher than others.'

'If I had no fears in the world it would be fun because I could walk anywhere I wanted to go and do anything I wanted to do. I would be like a king walking around and when I did something it would be fun getting chased by the cops or the guy I bugged. . . .

When I did do something wrong it wouldn't be fun because I would just walk around as if it was my own world. No one would like you because they would think you a Mr. Macho.'

This second story presents an obvious shift in thinking processes, going from the first shallow reaction to a deeper intuitive level, demonstrating some empathy and understanding of human interactions.

The initial discussions on fear revealed that typically most students do everything they can to avoid or run away from fear and painful situations. Such comments were made as: "Hide it, run away, avoid it, fight it, cry and pretend it doesn't exist." We tried to help them see that some fearful experiences are best overcome by talking with others, by assertive behavior and by problem solving techniques.

A class discussion was held on problem solving techniques for dealing with fear (Allan 1983) and the students were shown how to (a) list facts, (b) identify feelings, (c) define the problems, (d) develop solutions, (e) note possible blocks to solutions, and (f) evaluate the outcome.

This unit ended with a writing project where they had to describe a fearful situation that turned out to be positive. One girl wrote:

Arguing Parents

One night I was at home doing my homework and all of a sudden I heard someone arguing. I went out into the kitchen and saw my parents. I don't know why they were arguing.

I was kind of scared but I didn't say anything to them. I thought to myself I better just go in my room and finish my homework while they work it out. A thought came that I am going to leave this place and never come back if they don't stop it. They were constantly fighting, it seemed they would never stop.

I wished we were a family again but I really felt like getting up and leaving, going anywhere just to get away from here. I yelled at them to stop fighting for once and then left for my sister's for weekend. It would show them how ridiculous they looked when they were fighting.

The fighting decreased a lot after that because my parents knew that I knew. I was happy with my Mom and Dad because they quit fighting. And now we are like a family again.

7. Challenges. A critical component in becoming a successful young adult is the ability to face difficulties and to overcome them. In this unit we set about designing simple challenges and providing students with a structure for handling and mastering certain developmental tasks. The unit starts with the concept of advice, moves to the developing of modern rites of passage, and ends with a "Declaration of Dependence," an idea first proposed by the poet, Gary Snyder. Many of the challenges in this unit relate to communicating and sharing certain thoughts and feelings with parents. One of our goals was to increase the communication flow between young adolescent and parent, realizing that this can be a very difficult task for some adolescents and for some parents.

The advice unit consisted of two main components: giving advice to oneself and giving advice to one's parents. These tasks took the form of written activities in class. An optional challenge was offered whereby they could give these written assignments to their parents or to their teacher.

(a) Advice to Myself

The purpose of this session was to help the student develop ability to use introspective analysis. Students had to write a letter of advice to themselves.

The lesson is introduced by the sharing of times when advice is given and when advice is needed. This is followed up by: "Knowing yourself better than anyone else does, write an honest letter of advice to yourself."

During the discussion, the students became aware of the many times in their lives when advice is both given and needed:

When I do something bad	*Advice is needed*
Report card time	*When I'm depressed or sad*
Before parents go out	*Funerals*
Before day or over night	*When I'm confused*
trips with friends	*When I'm really angry*
When I do something bad	*When I'm screwing up*
Before a game or concert	*Before a game or concert*
Birthdays	*Which courses to take in school*

When the students were asked to write advice to themselves the results demonstrated honesty, accuracy and good intentions. One boy in the class, particularly noted for his denial of any blame or fault, wrote:

> *Advice to Myself*
> Get involved in more activities
> Improve my behavior at school
> Work better with others
> Be more patient at times
> Do the things I don't want to do
> Be more active in events.

This boy's behavior was characterized by impatience, disinterest in many activities during school and difficulty working with peers. If a teacher had questioned him verbally, it probably would have been difficult for him to have accepted any responsibility for his actions.

The results of this activity were refreshing and awakening for the teacher because most of the students were far more aware of their weaknesses and shortcomings than often given credit for.

(b) Advice to my Parents

The students were keen to contribute their own ideas on this topic but had to be reminded of the three criteria of advice (honesty, accuracy, and meaning to help, not harm).

Some students took the opportunity to "get even," thus reflecting unexpressed hostility and perhaps a need for some brief family counseling. However, many of the statements were well-intentioned, and one example is given below.

> *Advice to my Parents*
> Sometimes
> You worry too much
> About me

And the things I do
But relax
Don't worry
I'm grown up
And I know
What's right and wrong.
You brought me up
To be a good person
And I'll do my best
Not to let you down.

Many of the letters and poems reflected themes of worry and trust. In essence the students told the parents to worry less and trust them more. This was done in the context of love: "Look, you've brought me up well."

(c) The Challenge

Once both these activities were finished, the students were challenged to share both sets of advice with their parents. Initially, this challenge was soundly rejected. The fear of a few vocal objectors, who stated they would not do this, exerted a definite pressure on many of the other students. This led into a discussion of fear, the acceptance of how frightening it is to share certain feelings and the value of not being afraid to be what you are. In the end, 14 out of 24 students accepted the challenge, and seven gave the letters to the teacher.

In the follow-up discussion a week later all but one were glad that they had done it. Most students reported that their parents really appreciated the insight the letter gave them. Two parents actually telephoned to mention how informative the letters were and how they were unaware that their children had such "deep" thoughts.

8. Modern rites of passage. Using classroom discussion procedures again (Allan & Nairne 1984), and with the knowledge gained about rites of passage, students discussed what tests they might like to design for themselves. In order to activate ideas for tests or challenges, a brainstorming session was held and the following themes developed:

- *Plan and prepare a meal for the family or grandparents*
- *Learn a new skill, i.e. baking bread or changing the car oil*
- *Do the weekly shopping for the family*
- *Dig up the garden and prepare it for planting*
- *Do your own washing and meals for a week*
- *Sleep without a night light*
- *Teach a class for a period*
- *Wash and clean the family car without being asked*
- *Plan a family outing and make all of the arrangements*
- *An over-night bike hike*

Though all of the children took on a challenge, the greatest degree of success occurred with parent involvement. We also noticed the students needed help in focusing on fears or worries that they wished to overcome. An example of two tests are given below. The first test reflects a girl's experience with overcoming her fear of sleeping in the dark. This fear was an old fear from childhood. She felt that as a young adolescent she should be able to sleep in the dark. This test, then, represented for her a symbolic step into adolescence.

Name of the Test: *Taming my Fear of the Dark*

Preparation: I will need my Dad to help me with this test. I plan on being able to sleep without the hallway light on. Dad will have to put a dimmer switch on the hallway light. This test should take ten days to finish.

Action: With the dimmer switch in place, each night I plan on turning the dial slightly so that the light becomes gradually dimmer. I think by gradually turning down the light until it is off, I won't notice the change and I'll be able to sleep in the dark. Success happens when I've made it without a light for a week.

Reward: My Mom and Dad will appreciate this because they think I'm too old for a light and beside it wastes electricity.

Parent Comment: We've tried to turn the light off for years and nothing has worked. It has been weeks now and she hasn't had the light on or even mentioned it. My husband and I said we're taking her to her favourite restaurant to celebrate. Thank you!

The girl's test possessed all the essential ingredients for a meaningful rite of passage. She designed and prepared herself mentally for the test. She arranged and set up the necessary environment. The parents were involved in supporting the activity and recognized the feat as a meaningful growing-up experience.

Two boys worked on a challenge together:

Name of Test: *Biking and Camping*

Test: We will bike to our property (six hours), camp for the night and bike back home the next day.

Preparation: We will fix our bikes up, get in shape by riding one hour a day for two weeks, map out our route on country roads before we go, take along camping gear and food for meals. We will do it on a weekend in June.

Completion: The test will be passed if we do it all without any help from any adults. That means no phoning home like E.T.

Reward: Our parents will give us a barbecue party at the beach.

This test turned out to be quite a feat. The boys got stuck in a heavy rain storm and found they had to walk their bikes up some long hills. It took them eight hours to get there instead of six. They could hardly sleep at night because of strange sounds (trains, animals). However, they arrived home by four p.m. on Sunday, feeling very proud of themselves. Later one of the mothers telephoned to say the two families (nine people) got together for the beach barbecue at which there had been "speeches" to honor the two "adventurers."

When students devise their own tests, there is increased motivation and commitment to pass the tests. The test of these boys contained many of the essential components of a meaningful rite of passage: preparation, separation, challenges, and celebration with family members.

For the last test, the class was challenged to plan, organize, and run a year-end class graduation party. The teacher provided the structure: "What factors must you take into consideration while organizing a party?" while the students planned the agenda and organized the decorations, food, speeches and awards (every class member got one award), music, and dance. Needless to say it was a great farewell celebration.

9. Declaration of dependence. Another closing activity in the curriculum focused on drawing an analogy between the life cycles of countries and humans. Using the Declaration of Independence as a model, the teacher shifts the students' thinking from gaining independence to recognizing and appreciating dependence. During this stage the students were asked to "brainstorm a list of things adolescents depend on or need from their parents."

After a slow start and many groans, the list grew quickly to 33 items, surprising most of the students. Among these items were the following:

- *to encourage you when you are down*
- *to give you advice when you need it*
- *to love you no matter what you do or look like*
- *to wake you up*
- *to help you remember things*
- *to feed and clothe you*
- *to look after you when you are sick*
- *to drive you places on the spur of the moment (even when they are busy)!*

Once the list was completed, the students were challenged to let the parents know how they felt about them and what they would probably still need them for during their adolescence. The document was called "The Declaration of Dependence" and was to be sent as a letter.

A follow-up discussion allowed the students to share both their reactions and their parents' to this task. Responses varied widely. Most felt nervous and awkward just before giving the letter and greatly relieved afterwards. Common comments were: "My Mom felt privileged when I told her what I needed her for," and "I learned how much my Mum needs me and how much I love her." The parents also responded positively, thanking their son or daughter for sharing their feelings. One mother, who had been in a difficult phase with her daughter, was deeply touched and cried when she read the letter. One father, who had been over-protective, after reading the letter approached his son and told him he deserved more responsibility and freedom now that he was growing older. To sum it up, this activity seemed to help both students and parents be aware of the changing nature of their roles and their interdependence.

DISCUSSION

In many ways, the curriculum passed our expectations of what it could achieve. There were more worthwhile benefits than we planned, especially in the extent of both student and parent involvement. By the end of the school year most students felt challenged by their next developmental task and believed that they would have some support for this from their parents. We felt that they did have an understanding of the changes they were going through and what might be expected of them as a young adult.

The identification of their needs and the communication of these to their parents seemed to be a big step through fear into responsibility and honesty. Students wrote in their journals of changes in themselves and of improved relationships at home and with friends.

> 'I felt good about the sharing time with my Mom. I learned how much she cared about me when I was young. I knew my Mom felt privileged when I told her what I needed for her.'
> 'I really liked the activities. They showed me how much my parents love me. I really like the Declaration of Dependence.'

Several parents telephoned the teacher and thanked him for the sharing activities (i.e., the Advice and Declaration of Dependence challenges). One particular parent sent the following note to the school:

> I thought the activities were very worthwhile and beneficial. They put us more in touch with our children's feelings, made us think and remember.

Another commented on how pleased he and his wife were that the school system was apparently finally changing with the times to meet the needs of the children.

There was also an increased parental awareness of the students' needs to participate in some of the family decision making processes.

One girl in the class was very upset by her parents' decision to send her to a private school the following year. After participating in the sharing activities, the girl proudly announced that her Mom and Dad would allow her to make the decision as to which school she would attend next year. It is interesting to note that the girl eventually chose the private school.

Many of the activities contributed to an improved understanding of the adolescent by the parent. A frequent comment, during the last parent-teacher conference of the year, made mention of how the parents never knew their children had such "deep" thoughts. One mother was "astounded" that her daughter could be so sensitive. She went on to thank the teacher for creating such a meaningful experience.

We felt good about the program in that it attempted to integrate the developmental needs of the students, especially their social and emotional concerns, into the regular school curriculum. The students had an opportunity to share their thoughts and feelings about current issues in their lives and to understand these in the broader context of growth and development of society as a whole. As the program involved considerable writing and sharing, the skills involved in oral presentation, listening, spelling, sentence structure and grammar were constantly being strengthened and reinforced.

We noticed the class became more manageable and the atmosphere more cooperative. A deep sense of trust developed between students and teacher. Trust between student-to-student also improved. Clearly, though, these were just our evaluations. More informal, independent evaluation and follow-up must be conducted to ascertain more precisely the nature of change. Plans are underway to do this and to add a unit for parents and students on the physiological and psychological aspects of puberty.

IMPLICATIONS

Rites of passage, whether formal or informal, are an essential aspect of education. Though our culture seems to have dropped many of the formal aspects, the process of initiation continues to occur in the psyche and lives of our adolescents. Some of this is seen in their peer group activities, their escapades, athletics, music, and in their creative writing projects (Allan 1978).

Our argument is that so much more can be done by parents, teachers and church groups. Our experience is that adults want to do more, feel something is missing, but are not sure where or how to start. The key issue is consciousness—of being aware of the need and the importance of initiation. The second component is awareness of the right time, and the third component is helping to provide an appropriate structure or container for the experience.

Based on some of the principles mentioned in this project, we have found that other parents, teachers and adolescents have been able to devise some of their own rites and celebrations. For example, on reading this material, one father set about designing a small family celebration for his daughter's tenth birthday. First, the girl designed her own party for her girlfriends. This included the food she wanted, the special activities (roller skating and "sleep over"), the type and order of games, how the presents would be opened, a timetable of events, and the sleeping arrangements. Second, the father planned another party just for the extended family (14 members). During coffee and cake, the father said:

> I'd like to spend a few minutes talking about Larissa and the changes she has made over the past year because she was nine and now she is going to be ten. During the year I've been aware of her changing and growing up. I remember she failed one swimming test, but worked hard at it and later in the summer she passed it. She was very brave when she had two teeth pulled. She became a seconder in her Brownie pack, went away to camp and loved it. She started gym and ice skating lessons, . . .

Following this, the other family members spontaneously added their images and memories of Larissa in the past year. There was no flattery, rather statements of what occurred and humorous anecdotes. The following morning, the daughter came to the breakfast table and announced this dream:

> *I lost my bag at Zellers. I couldn't find it so I came home and told Daddy and Daddy said, 'Come with me in the camperbus and I'll help you find it.' But we couldn't find it. So Daddy bought me a new, bright red one, then we went home. Mummy said, 'What a lovely new bag you have. Since you've been so good I'll buy you a pair of new roller skates.' Then we went out for an ice cream and in the ice cream parlour we met Nanny and Nanny said, 'Larissa, I have a surprise for you. Here it is.' 'Oh, goody,' I said, 'it's $500.00. Let's go to Hawaii.' Then we all went to Hawaii and I woke up with a happy feeling inside.*

This dream reflects loss, newness, excitement and affirmation of self. Successful rites usually results in a release of energy and a sense of renewal for all.

Transition Stories For Young Adolescents

There are many activities for teachers and parents to facilitate an understanding of change and transition. Various activities can be built on the rituals that already exist within the family or school environment. For children, an important adjunct to understanding this process of transition can come from reading and discussing stories. Probably most benefit accrues when the stories are read aloud to the child. Probably most benefit accrues when the stories are read aloud to the child. A list of appropriate late childhood-early adolescent stories is provided below.

Blach, F. 1959. *Brave riders.* New York: Thomas Crowell. With an accurate portrayal of Indian culture, this book describes a young boy's initiatory journey into manhood. Ages: 10-13.

Barnouw, V. 1966. *Dream of the blue heron*. New York: Dell. Set in northern Wisconsin in the early 1900's, this story relates the identity struggle of a Chippewa Indian boy, caught between his forest dwelling grandparents and his father who works in a lumbermill. A resolution is achieved through his own vision quest experience. Ages: 10-13.

Bates, B. 1978. *The ups and downs of Jorie Jenkins*. New York: Holiday House. Through parental illness, a young adolescent girl begins to make important decisions for herself and becomes aware of her importance to the family. Ages: 10-14.

Brochman, E. 1980. *What's the matter girl?* Don Mills, Ontario: Fitzherery and Whiteside. A young girl's love for her wounded uncle is challenged when he arrives home from the war. Scarred both mentally and physically from the effects of battle, the man finds it difficult to adjust. The durability of love, the painful process of growing up, and the complexity of family relationships all highlight a poignant and sensitive novel. Ages: 12-14.

Carig, J. 1969. *No word for good-bye*. Toronto: Peter Martin Associates Limited. The painful adjustment of a loss of a close friend is made by a young teenager after efforts to save the aboriginal land of an Ojibway group in Manitoba fail. The entire band disappears and the young protagonist realizes that in the Ojibway language, there is no word for good-bye. Ages: 12-15.

Cate, D. 1976. *Never is a long time*. London: Thomas Nelson. Set in an extended family situation, a twelve year-old boy becomes aware of the rythms of death and birth and sees himself as an emerging adult. Ages: 10-12.

Cooper, S. 1974. *Greenwitch*. New York: Atheneum. A contemporary fantasy story set in Cornwall, England where a young girl, Jane, is asked to take part in a traditional, night-long spring renewal ceremony with the other women of the village. Jane's sensitivity and compassion results in a great gift. Ages: 11-13.

Distad, A. 1977. *The dream runner*. New York: Harper & Row, 1977. A contemporary story of a young boy who sets off on his own vision quest and finds "something to live up to." Ages: 10-13.

Frank, A. 1952. *Anne Frank: The diary of a young girl*. New York: Doubleday. The maturation of a young girl over a two-year period. Describes her relationship to her changing body, her parents and her first love. Ages: 11-14.

Haig-Brown, R. 1962. *The whale people*. London: Collins. A young man of the Hotsath tribe, Atlin, receives both practical and spiritual guidance to prepare him to take his father's place as the whale chief. The daily activities of life on the West Coast of Vancouver Island before the English settlers came is highlighted by magnificent whaling scenes. Ages: 12-14.

Houston, J. 1967. *The white archer: An Eskimo legend.* Toronto: Longman. A young Eskimo boy trains himself for an act of revenge. His transition from an agent of violence to that of a mature, understanding individual is brought about by the wisdom and kindness of an elderly couple who befriend him. Ages: 12-15.

Jones, W. 1968. *Edge of two worlds.* New York: Dial Press. Set in 1842, this beautiful story describes a mentor relationship between a fifteen year-old white boy and an Indian silversmith-teacher. Ages: 10-14.

L'Engle, M. 1980. *A wrinkle in time.* New York: Dell. A young adolescent girl, struggling with feelings of hopelessness, plays a key role in helping her family. Ages: 10-14.

McDermott, G. 1974. *Arrow to the sun.* New York: Puffin. A beautifully illustrated book which shows, symbolically, the transformation process of a Pueblo Indian youth. Ages: 10-14. There is a fine film, as well as film strips by the same artist.

McKenzie, J. 1971. *Rivers of stars.* Toronto: McClelland & Stewart. Fifteen year old Andy, a West Coast Indian boy, takes his injured father's place on a fishing boat for the summer. He meets with hostility from some crew members and is aided in coping with prejudice with the help of an elderly fisherman. Ages: 12-15.

Major, K. 1978. *Hold fast.* Toronto: Clarke, Irwin. Michael's parents are killed in an automobile accident and he is sent from his Newfoundland outport home to live in the city. Local bullies at the new school attempt to terrorize him and Michael's opposition to their threats creates moments of conflict and suspense. (A sensitive exploration of early adolescence by an author who was a teenager when it was written.) Ages: 12-16.

Mildiner, L. 1981. *Getting the eagle.* London: MacMillan. A contemporary story, set in the East End of London, describing a failed vision quest. Ages: 12-16.

O'Dell, S. 1980. *Island of the blue dolphins.* New York: Dell. A young Indian girl is stranded alone on an island off the coast of California in the mid 1800's. This poetic tale records her struggle to survive (building a shelter, making weapons, finding food, fighting wild dogs) and her own personal discoveries. Ages: 12-16.

O' Dell, S. 1981. *Sing down the moon.* New York: Dell. A fourteen-year-old Navaho girl is captured by Spanish slavers. She escapes only to be evicted from her homeland. A poignant tale of Navaho life, including rites of passage. Ages: 10-14.

Peck, R. *A day no pigs would die.* NY: Dell, 1979.

Sharp, E. 1978. *Nkwala*. Toronto: McClelland & Stewart. An accurate and exciting description of a Salish Indian boy's vision quest and of persistence through failure. Ages: 10-14.

Shura, M. 1976. *Seasons of silence*. New York: Atheneum. A young adolescent girl comes to terms with family problems, painful feelings, death, loss of friendship, the beauty and healing powers of nature, life, and love. Ages: 12-16.

Sperry, A. 1940. *Call it courage*. Toronto: MacMillan. The solo journey by boat, of a fifteen-year-old South Sea Island boy who survives a terrible storm and wins his manhood. Ages: 10-14.

Stolz, M. 1977. *Ferris wheel*. New York: Harper & Row. This book is about growing up and a young girl's attempts to adapt to the changes that come with it—her uncontrollable rages, spells of brooding and the move of a best friend. Ages: 11-14.

Stren, P. 1979. *There's a rainbow in my closet*. New York: Harper and Row. A young girl feels abandoned when her mother announces that she is going off on a European holiday. Emma is to be left in the care of her grandmother whom she deems to be "old and not with it!" As time progresses and Emma reveals her uncertainties through her drawings, she is impressed to find that grandmother becomes "the first person to really understand my drawings." Ages: 11-14.

Sutcliff, R. 1982. *Warrior scarlet*. London: Puffin Books. After three years in the Boys' House, Drem must kill his own wolf to prove his right to wear the warrior's scarlet. But how can he do this when his right arm is useless? Ages: 10-13.

Wojciechowsak, M. 1964. *Shadow of a bull*. New York: Atheneum. Using the metaphor of bullfighting, the psychological struggle of a young boy, separating his identity from that of a famous father, is described. Ages: 10-14.

REFERENCES

Adams, J., and Hopson, B., eds. 1977. *Transition: understanding and managing personal change*. Montclair, N.J.: Allenhald & Osmund.

Allan, J. 1978. Serial storywriting. *Canadian Counselor* 12:132-137.

————. 1983. Scapegoating: help for the whole class. *Elementary School Guidance and Counseling* 18:147-151.

Allan, J., and Dyck, P. 1984. *Transition: a developmental curriculum for "growing-up."* Vancouver, B.C.: Faculty of Education, University of British Columbia.

Allan, J., and Nairne, J. 1984. *Class discussions for teachers and counsellors in the elementary school*. Toronto: University of Toronto Guidance Center.

Bent, A. 1976. Orientation and the transfer student. *Clearing House* 49:350-352.

Brammer, L. and Abrego, P. 1981. Intervention strategies for coping with transitions. *Counseling Psychologist* 9/2:19-36.

Childress, N. 1982. Orientation to middle school: a guidance play. *Elementary School Guidance and Counseling* 17:89-93.

Freed, M., and Freed, M. 1980. *Transitions: focus rituals in eight cultures.* New York: W. W. Norton.

Friedman, J. 1976. Introduction to a special project on pre-orientation of sixth grade students to seventh grade and junior high school. *Elementary School Guidance and Counseling* 11:152-155.

Gennep, A. van. 1960. *Rites of passage.* Chicago: University of Chicago Press.

Jung, C. G. 1969. Stages of life. In *Dynamics and Structure of the psyche.* Princeton: Princeton University Press.

Lincoln, B. 1981. *Emerging from the chrysalis: studies in women's initiation.* Cambridge, Mass.: Harvard University Press.

National Geographic, 1980. 158/5.

Niehardt, J. 1972. *Black Elk speaks.* New York: Pocket Books.

Nisbet, J., and Entwistle, N., eds. 1969. *Transition to secondary education.* Edinburgh: University of London Press.

Salerno, N., and Vanderburgh, R. 1980. *Shaman's daughter.* New York: Dell.

Sharp, E. 1978. *Nkwala.* Toronto: McClelland & Stewart.

Turner, V. 1967. *Forest of symbols.* Ithaca: Cornell University Press.

van der Post, L. 1972. *A story like the wind.* New York and London: Harcourt Brace Jovanovich.

Waldo, A. 1980. *Sacajawea.* New York: Avon.

Copyright AACD. Reprinted with permission. No further reproduction authorized without written permission of AACD, 5999 Stevenson Avenue, Alexandria, VA 22304.

3

SUICIDE'S 'UNANSWERABLE LOGIC'

M. Sandra Reeves and Alina Tugend

In the following chapter, M. Sandra Reeves and Alina Tugend draw our attention to a remarkable comment made by Jean Baechler in his study of suicides: that the problem of death is a "favorite" theme, one of great interest, for today's adolescents. The reason for this, says Baechler, is that underlying the theme of death are all the most important fundamental questions facing our young people—questions such as "Who am I?" "Where am I going?" "What can I do [with my life]?" (Suicides, 1979).

It is interesting to notice that functionally successful initiations or rites of passage address the very same questions; thus, suicide might even be viewed as a kind of negative rite of passage, a rite of passage 'gone wrong,' as contrasted with normal, health-giving initiations whose goal it is to address the questions mentioned above in a positive and productive way.

The chapter you are about to read on adolescent suicide calls parents, teachers, and all elders with forceful urgency to devote more attention to our youth in order to help them face the problems of growing up in a better way. This article also levels a severe and frightening warning: if today we persist in ignoring the immediacy of the problem of adolescent suicide, it is unquestionably certain that for many of our youngsters, tomorrow will be too late.

M. Sandra Reeves, senior editor of Education Week, *has written extensively on issues in science, medicine, and education. Alina Tugend, former staff writer for* Education Week, *is a 1986-87 Fellow in Law for Journalists at the Yale University Law School.*

WHEN you turn off the main road from Denver, on your way to Golden High School, you pass Christ the Answer Church and Golden Cemetery before hitting a line of fast-food restaurants on the "main drag" of this new-old town in the foothills of the eastern Rockies.

Almost every liquor store along the way advertises Coors beer, Golden's main industry since the turn of the century. The Coors plant, touted as the largest single brewery in the world, spews smoke from the middle of the business district. A street over, where Coors "hospitality buses" run, is an arch bearing the proclamation, "Howdy Folks—Welcome to Golden, Where the West Lives."

At Golden High, a squat, sprawling structure built in the shadow of Table Mountain, the marquee has a different message: "I'm okay, you're okay."

The school's 1,150 students come from a region encompassing both $500,000 homes and trailer parks. Its assistant principal, John Vidal, describes it as "a small-town school with a whole gamut of big-city problems."

One of those problems is suicide.

In the past 13 months, three Golden High students have taken their own lives. None of the three—two boys and a girl—were close friends. Nor were there any striking similarities in their personalities. Yet all three chose suicide as the only solution to the unknown pressures in their lives—leaving behind families, friends, and school staff members to deal with a tangle of unanswered questions and lingering feelings of sorrow, guilt, and anger.

And Golden High is not an aberration in this scenic stretch of Colorado. Eighteen teen-agers in surrounding Jefferson County have killed themselves since January 1985—the 18th just two weeks ago.

Nationally, about 5,000 young people between the ages of 15 and 24 now commit suicide every year. Often, as in this Colorado county, they do it in so-called "clusters," with one youthful suicide seeming to trigger several others in the area over a relatively short span of time.

Experts recognize this clustering phenomenon, but are uncertain about its dynamics. "It is not clear how the suicide of one person might affect that of another," write researchers from the federal Centers for Disease Control in a recent paper on patterns of youth suicide. What is clear, they say, is that "when there is one suicide death within a school district, other· students are immediately put at high risk."

At Golden, the first suicide death sent shock waves through the student body and the community. It was Jim's, and he had been the quintessential "all-American boy."

"I had one parent who told me that after the suicide his son had asked, 'If Jim can't make it, how can I?'" Mr. Vidal recalls. "Here's a kid who had everything. Suddenly, all the kids who had looked up to him were wondering about their own survival."

Jim was fifth in his class academically, a three-letter athlete, and the winner of an "outstanding student of the month" award. He had won a scholarship to attend Brigham Young University that fall. Yet in April of 1985, he put a gun to his head and pulled the trigger.

"I always secretly idolized Jim," says Molly, a junior at Golden High. "He was kind of like a god to me. My first reaction when I heard the news was that he must have been murdered. I just didn't believe it."

Karen, another junior at the school, says the news "scared" her. "Before

Jim," she says, "you heard about suicide but it never touched you. Then with Jim, it hit you."

"Every time I go by his house," Molly adds, "I think, 'What a neat guy.' And I feel regret. He could have been so helpful."

Aaron's suicide last January, Golden High's second in nine months, was a different matter. Where hundreds of students had attended Jim's funeral, relatively few went to Aaron's. The local newspaper, which had run a picture and story on Jim, downplayed Aaron's death.

Aaron was not as popular as Jim, not athletic, and, according to students at the school, lacked the self-confidence that Jim seemed to have.

"He was the kind of kid that always said, 'Hi,'" Molly recalls. "He got an award in the 9th grade for 'The Kid Who Always Tries.' He was so proud of that."

"Hearing about Aaron's suicide was like hearing the latest gossip," says Karen. "I had a lot of problems dealing with it. He was a person, too."

Aaron had gone to an open field, found a ditch, and shot himself, leaving behind four suicide notes on the windshield of his best friend's father's car.

And though the aftermath of his death was more subdued than what followed Jim's, it was no less disturbing to school officials. To them, it meant that—at least for one student—the suicide-prevention program they had put in place had failed.

There were indications, in fact, that one of the school's preventive measures may have added further stress to Aaron's life. Friends say that on the day Golden High held a series of workshops of self-destructive behavior, Aaron had become so "shook up" that he seriously contemplated suicide that evening. He killed himself a month later.

By last month, when a third suicide—the victim's depression kept secret by friends—came to light, there was beginning to be, Mr. Vidal reports, "real anger and frustration" at the school.

"It reminded us that more needs to be done—on everyone's part," he says.

Inexplicable youth suicides—whether by seemingly well-adjusted high-achievers like Jim, or shy, earnest teen-agers like Aaron—have become an almost common occurrence in America. The C.D.C. researchers call the current self-destructive bent of American youths "an epidemic."

People closer to the phenomenon—the parents, school officials, and young people of towns like Golden—might call it, as the author A. Alvarez does, a tragedy with "the unanswerable logic of a nightmare."

Only 30 years ago, suicide among the young was relatively rare. As the French social philosopher Jean Baechler explains in his book *Suicides,* "Retreat into death to escape an intolerable situation" has traditionally been rare at this time of life because "youth is synonymous with a wide range of opportunities."

But since the mid-1950's, something has reversed the picture. The suicide rate for the 15-to-24-year-old age group in America has tripled over the last 30 years, and doubled since 1960. In 1960, suicide was the fifth leading cause of death for this age group; today, it is the third, trailing only accidents and homicides.

A definitive answer to the question "why?" has been slow to emerge. But current research is probing a combination of factors that may be involved, from genetic susceptibility and demographic pressures to social changes and disrupted family relationships.

But to Frederick Goodwin, director of the division of intramural research at the National Institute on Mental Health, "the single most explanatory factor for suicide is depressive illness." This is as true for teenagers, he says, as it is for adults.

Fifteen percent of those who suffer from major depression, Dr. Goodwin says, will die of suicide. And of those who commit suicide each year, between 60 percent and 80 percent have some type of depressive disorder.

Clinical depression differs in both intensity and duration from the occasional bouts of "the blues" everyone experiences, physicians note. And until recent decades, its most severe forms were thought to begin after the age of 20.

Today, however, doctors are recognizing serious medical depression in children and adolescents. According to Elva Orlow Poznanski, a professor of psychiatry at the University of Illinois Medical Center, "about 80 percent of adolescent suicide attempts are made by depressed adolescents."

Unlike other psychiatric illnesses that can afflict adolescents, she says, there is no hard-and-fast profile of the teen-ager who will become depressed.

He or she may be popular or withdrawn, a straight-A student or a dropout. The depressed teen-ager, she notes in a 1982 review for the American Psychiatric Association, has usually been able to develop friendships and interests at a time when he was not depressed.

And although most depressed teen-agers do poorly in school, Dr. Poznanski adds, "occasionally, a strong student will continue to do well academically, studying compulsively with little pleasure."

"It is the latter type of student—such a 'good' boy or girl—who surprises the community when he or she commits suicide," she writes.

Other psychiatrists point out that the particular type of depression adolescents experience has a potentially lethal combination of characteristics: the distortion of time and a bent toward impulsivity.

Jules R. Bemporad, director of children's services at the Massachusetts Mental Health Center and associate professor of psychiatry at Harvard University, writes eloquently of these characteristics in the A.P.A. *Psychiatry '82* review:

The depressive episodes of adolescents are infused with a sense of time: the feeling that things can never change, the idea that a trivial frustration or humiliation will have lasting effects, the dread of the future. A social rebuff means eternal alienation, a disappointment on a date portends perpetual loneliness, or a bad mark on a test ensures academic failure.

Dr. Bemporad adds that the "particular intensity of adolescent depression" springs from the fact that teen-agers have mastered the adult ability to project themselves into the future, without having acquired the moderation of thought and action that comes with age and experience.

According to the N.I.M.H.'s Dr. Goodwin, this may match precisely the suicidal equation. "The way to conceptualize a completed suicide," he says, "is as the intersection of a depressive state with a personality that makes you vulnerable to impulsive or aggressive behavior."

Like much of the West, northern Colorado seems an unlikely setting for suicide. Its broad, blue horizons and majestic mountain vistas seem to symbolize the American Dream of unbounded opportunity. For more than a century, people from other parts of the country have gravitated here seeking a better life.

Yet, historically, suicide rates have been higher in the West than in other, older sections of the country.

In 1984, Colorado's overall suicide rate was 16.2 per 100,000, compared with a national rate of 11.6 per 100,000. The state's youth suicide rate—15.1 per 100,000—is also well above the national average. Suicide, in fact, is the second leading cause of death among 15-to-24-year-olds here.

Some have theorized that the West's greater population mobility may influence its suicide rate. When people uproot themselves they leave behind family and friends, cutting off their support systems. There is less sense of a common past, of belonging to a community.

In addition, some theorists say, the very promise of the West, of more opportunity, better living conditions, and greater freedom, may lead, in some cases, to disappointment and depression.

There are no scientific studies proving such theories. But it is apparent in talking to youths here who have tried, but failed, to kill themselves that affluence and opportunity are not safeguards for the suicidal teen.

What is most striking in conversations with these high-school students is how well most of them conform to the stereotype of the happy, upwardly mobile American teen-ager. They are, by and large, not the victims of poverty, but products of that mythical American Dream. They wear designer jeans, often drive their own cars, congregate in shopping malls, and have both ambitions and fears that are sometimes larger than life.

Scott, for example, is a tall 18-year-old student from Boulder with Nordic good looks and a love of books and music. He wanted to be a pilot, he says, but when he learned that his eyesight was too poor for flight school, he decided he would be an artist.

For several months last year, Scott would regularly slash his arms with a razor blade, sometimes lifting weights afterward to "make the blood flow." He would tell his friends at school about the cuts, hoping, but also fearing, that they would tell an adult. Finally, in a desperate attempt to seek help, he showed the slashes to his mother.

"I wanted to die, but I didn't," he says now. "When you're alone, thoughts begin to build up in your head. I'd think, 'Why do I have to go through this? Why do I have to be so lonely?'"

Erica, a plump, sweet-faced 17-year-old from Boulder, says she used to take bottles of Bacardi rum to school in the 6th grade, because "most of the kids thought it was pretty cool." She graduated to marijuana and cocaine in high school, then swallowed half a bottle of pills last year before seeking help for her depression.

Erica worries about nuclear war, the situation in the Middle East, and whether "everything will come down" when someone her own age becomes President. Two of her friends have died in car accidents, one considered a possible suicide.

"I used to go to church every week until about a year ago," she says. "Then I kind of came to the conclusion that God had messed me up. I can't grasp the concept of religion anymore. I can't understand how people can say, 'God does this, God does that.' I look at it like, 'God hasn't done this, God hasn't done that.'"

Jennifer, a junior at Golden High School, looks like the kind of teen-ager who never sits home on a Saturday night. She could easily be the girl elected homecoming queen or a cheerleader, with her blonde good looks and slim, miniskirt-clad figure.

"Everyone thought, 'Jennifer has it all,' and I would say, 'No I don't'." Jennifer says this as she talks of being "obsessed with dying" before a suicide attempt last year that resulted in a month-long hospitalization.

She read poems about death during that period, she says, and drew "weird" death-related pictures. And on many nights, she retreated to her room to engage in a private ritual of lighting candles and cutting her arms with scissors and knives.

"It felt really good in a way," she recalls. "I have a hard time letting my feelings show. I don't cry. Every time you cut, you let something out. It's like an escape."

"I didn't want to die. I don't think anyone my age who tries it wants to die. I just wanted to go to sleep and wake up and everything would be okay."

Denise, smoking a cigarette while she eats a serving of Oreo-cookie ice cream, could be any jeans-clad teen-ager in America. She attends a high school in Boulder that she describes as a "rich school" where "kids have everything."

Denise talks of her difficulties with her parents, of fits of rebelliousness, stays in a residential child-care facility for disciplinary reasons, and, finally, two suicide attempts. She swallowed bleach two years ago; this year, she slashed her wrists.

"I wanted people to know I was hurting," Denise says, adding that "sometimes, physical pain is easier to deal with than mental pain."

Not all of the suicidal behavior in American young people is occurring in the white, middle-class segment of society. "Depression knows no class or economic boundaries," the N.I.M.H.'s Dr. Goodwin notes. White males may have a much higher suicide rate than black males, he says, but blacks have a much higher homicide rate. And many of those homicides, he asserts, may represent reckless, self-destructive behavior that is being outwardly, rather than inwardly, directed.

And in the adolescent years, says Carol L. Huffine, director of research for the University of California at Berkeley's school of professional psychology, even minority-group suicide rates are high.

"It is only in adolescence and young adulthood that suicide rates of blacks approximate those of whites," she writes in a paper delivered in May at a special National Institutes of Health conference on youth suicide.

The pattern is similar for Hispanics and American Indians, she says, noting that the "relative parity" in suicide rates at this time of life suggests an underlying social dynamic that is affecting all groups of young people.

But the fact that young male suicides—which account for the bulk of the youth-suicide increases in recent years—are now almost 90 percent white suggests to some that the social factors involved may be especially pertinent to the middle class.

To some social scientists, a partial answer to why teen-agers like Scott, Erica, Jennifer, and Denise attempt suicide lies in the narrowing range of opportunities they see for their age group. Having grown up in reasonable affluence, these young people may have very high expectations for what they should or would like to accomplish in life, the experts point out. Yet the chances of their fulfilling those expectations are diminishing.

Two factors are involved: the decline of the U.S. economy and the impact of the postwar baby boom.

Paul Holinger, associate professor of psychiatry at Rush-Presbyterian-St. Luke's Medical Center in Chicago, says that statistical studies confirm a direct connection between increases in the adolescent suicide rate and increases in the size of the adolescent population and its proportion within the total population.

He says that as the number of young people rises—as it did from the 1950's on—the suicide rate for that group seems to increase.

"Not just numbers, as you would expect," he notes, "but rates per 100,000. It's the opposite of what is found in higher age groups."

In the mid-1950's, there were about 11 million 15-to-19-year-olds, he says, a figure that increased to 21 million in the mid-1970's. The proportion of adolescents in the population also rose steadily over this period, peaking in the late 1970's.

The growth curve in the youth-suicide rate conforms closely to this pattern of population change, Dr. Holinger says. As the baby-boomers began to leave the 15-to-19-year-old age group in the late-1970's, the teen-suicide rate began to decline.

Using such trends as a guide, he predicts a continuous decrease until the 1990's, when the rate will again start to climb.

Social scientists suggest that among the reasons for this correlation between population density and suicide may be the strain placed on such institutions as schools and the decreasing availability of counseling services. Also, they say, more peers mean increased competition and greater chances for failure.

Writes Kim Smith, director of research at the Menninger Clinic in Albuquerque, N.M.: "There are still only so many slots on the football team. Levels of excellence and acceptance rise. College entrance becomes more difficult, as does obtaining desirable employment."

"The message implicitly given by society's institutions is more likely experienced as, 'There may be too many of you; you are expendable,' rather than 'Welcome, we need you.'"

Colorado's teens echo these sentiments when they speak, almost in one voice, of a vaguely defined "pressure" that they feel is responsible for the suicides of their friends and, perhaps, for their own self-destructive acts.

Says Jennifer: "There is so much pressure and I think, 'I'm 16 and I can't handle it. When I'm 30, the pressures will be how much more intense?'"

Erica adds that "so many adults are laying it all on our generation; a lot of people don't think they can handle that. The world's going to be in your hands when you get older. Parents have always said that. But I think we're going through a lot more now."

Molly, who has not attempted suicide, feels the pressure, too. "It's a competitive world," she says. "You've got to do well. Parents think they're putting on positive pressure, but what they're doing is damaging. In 8th grade, I was worried about money for college—that's ridiculous."

Karen, who has also rejected suicide as an option, adds that "because the world is moving so quickly technologically, there's less hope of fitting in. I get overwhelmed with that," she says. "A lot of us are afraid that when we get out of college there won't be anything." Adds the troubled Denise: "Most people in the olden days were used to a regular life—grow up, get married, have kids. Now it's different. A lot of times, I wish I had been born back then; it seems a lot simpler, like there was more control over things."

Because suicide is an individual act, its "causes" in any single instance can be as varied as the human condition.

In antiquity, the subject of "self murder" was left to the church and the philosophers. Today, it is being tackled not only by psychologists, psychiatrists, and medical scientists, but also sociologists and other social scientists. Most of them agree that there is no single road leading to suicide, but many converging pathways.

One of the many being examined in current medical research, for example, is the link between genetic and biological factors and suicide.

Susan Blumenthal, chief of the behavioral-medicine program at the N.I.M.H., says that there is now strong evidence to support the notion that something in the suicidal impulse—whether it is a certain type of depression or the trait of impulsivity itself—is inherited. Those with a family history of suicide, she says, are at a six times greater risk of committing suicide themselves.

Medical researchers have also found that people with low levels of a certain brain chemical—the neurotransmitter serotonin—often tend to be impulsive and given to antisocial behavior. Men generally have lower amounts of serotonin than women, Dr. Blumenthal notes.

Fluctuating levels of all of the neurotransmitters, which help dispatch messages between brain cells, have been implicated in various forms of depression. Most of the drugs successful in treating depression replace or balance the levels of these neurotransmitters.

Another theory being tested is that children who suffer some sort of "birth trauma" may be more susceptible to suicide. Such individuals, scientists say, may have a more fragile "inner time-clock" that makes them susceptible to depression. Or, the researchers add, the children may have parents who, because of the difficulties at birth, have been "more protective and indulgent," not allowing their child "the right to struggle and survive."

Dr. Goodwin of the N.I.M.H. notes that because medical advances have allowed many of the infants who might not have lived in another era to survive, there may be more "fragile people" in the population. He calls this "one of the side effects of our increasing ability to save lives in infancy."

Since the publication in 1951 of Emile Durkheim's classic work, *Suicide: A Study in Sociology,* however, researchers have been looking more closely at the social environment to find keys to unlock the mysteries of such large-scale suicidal phenomena as the recent wave of teen-age suicides.

The N.I.M.H. research director says that medical factors alone are not the answer; they must be viewed in their social context. And for today's adolescents and young adults, he says, that context has often included instability and isolation.

"Since the mid-1960's," Dr. Goodwin says, "we have had a major erosion in our external sources of self-esteem. There has been increased disruption in families; people's identification of being part of a family has been threatened."

"Beginning with the Kennedy assassination, there has also been a deterioration in the image of national leaders," he adds. "As leaders get shot, people tend to withdraw their emotional attachments. There's been a decrease in national pride; one has less a sense of identity based one's own country. There has also been a decreasing sense of identity through religious groups, communities, neighborhoods."

"People's faith in the future has become shakier since the mid-1950's," he concludes.

As Jennifer, the Golden High School junior hospitalized after shashing her wrists, puts it: "You feel like there's no hope for the future. You worry about blowing up. I don't like to read the newspapers."

Developmental psychologists say that such social disruption has a greater impact on the adolescent than on any other age group, because adolescence is the time of life when crucial coping skills must be developed and the difficult psychological tasks of separating from parents, forming a sense of identity, and integrating into the "real world" of social relations must be faced.

It is a time of high risk and many "firsts" for the child, says the University of California's Ms. Huffine, and often the lack of support systems can signal a retreat into isolation and depression.

"During times marked by social change, such as we experienced in the 1960's, there is confusion about customs and moral codes," she says. And this confusion, coupled with the diminishing role of religion in American lives, may deprive today's young of the secure touchstones they need in plotting their own sense of place in the world.

"The degree of stress is not as important as an adolescent's belief that he or she possesses strategies to deal with the stress," says William Porter, director of mental health for Colorado's Cherry Creek school district and the developer of one of the nation's first school suicide-prevention programs.

"The fear of not being able to handle losses or disappointments, even in successful adolescents, concerns them greatly," he says.

Parents have a vital role to play in helping teen-agers develop such coping skills, the experts say. And today's troubled families do not bode well for the psychic integration of this generation.

To the psychiatrist Herbert Hendin, the author of *Suicide in America,* and to many others, the trend of growing suicide rates among the young "is rooted in the diminishing cohesion of the family."

Those intimately connected to the recent surge of teen suicides in northern Colorado communities agree that family relations play a large role. But their comments indicate that not one, but many faulty patterns may be involved.

"There are two extremes," says Craig Rupp, whose youngest daughter, Stacy, killed herself three years ago. "There is the extreme of trying to protect your child too much, and then there is the other side, where there isn't a lot of caring—that can be a hell of a burden, too."

For Kris, a Boulder high-school junior who made a suicide attempt last year, the problem is uncertainty. "Life is such a roller coaster," she says. "My parents—now they're getting back together, now they're not."

She says it would be easy to think of suicide as a way out, but she doesn't anymore. "I believe there's somebody in this world you will make you very happy—even if it's yourself," she says.

Scott, who slashed his wrists last year, grew up with his grandparents in Boulder, but moved to Denver to live with his mother, a single parent, when he was 15.

"It was an atmosphere where there was no one to talk to," he says. "My mother would come home around 10 P.M. My friends were scattered all over the place. School was the only place I had to talk to someone."

Other young suicide attempters in this area also relate stories of disturbed family relations. Jennifer says her father "hit on her" when her mother left home. Denise's parents placed her in residential-care facilities because they could not deal with her behavior problems.

But it is the parents of those who have actually killed themselves who shed the most light on the complicated dynamics of love and separation.

"Jim and I were very protective," says Mary Ann Fisher, whose son Chris killed himself at the age of 14. "That can be a blessing, but it can also be a curse. When you are confronted with a problem, being protected like Chris was, maybe means that you can't deal with it."

"He was our only child. I think he must have felt stifled sometimes. It wasn't that I didn't trust Chris. I guess I didn't trust the rest of the world."

Craig Rupp says that, with the benefit of hindsight, he would have "emphasized the negatives as well as the positives" for his daughter and run less interference for her.

"When I had a problem in school, I had to solve it," he says. "Today, a kid comes home from school with a problem—and this happened many times in this kitchen—and the first reaction is to solve it for them. For example, there's a test with a word that's right marked wrong. What do you do? I would get on the telephone and call the teacher, and that's what most parents do."

"Instead of sending the child back to negotiate with the teacher, we say it isn't fair and try to do something. Hell, they're going to run into unfair things all their lives."

Many other social trends—such as increasing drug use and the growing access to firearms—may have increased the likelihood of suicide among the young, researchers say.

But, to Mr. Rupp, the problem seems more fundamental. "If I could have done one thing differently," he says, "I would have programmed some failure into Stacy's life."

When officials from other schools ask those at Golden High School how to cope with a student suicide, they are told, among other things, to avoid public-address announcements and school-wide assemblies.

It is good advice, says the Cherry Creek school district's Mr. Porter. And he suggests that families be asked not to schedule funerals on a weekday, if that can be avoided.

"We don't want kids to get the notion that the person who committed suicide had the power to stop school," he says. "We've even talked with clergy about not making death seem beautiful in eulogies of young suicide victims."

There is much concern here about "glorifying" suicide—and about making it more, not less, likely by talking about it.

"There is a notion, going back to the original counseling movement, that to get things out in the open is good," says the N.I.M.H.'s Dr. Goodwin, "that if people have more information, it is an unambiguously good thing. This is not invariably true."

But others argue that, when done properly, suicide-prevention programs help far more students than they hurt.

"If we say that suicide is terrible and evil and bad without telling people how to have control, then that can be dangerous," says Brian Brody, a social worker actively involved in Jefferson County's suicide-prevention effort. "If we give awareness with education, then it's beneficial."

Craig Rupp, who, with his wife Joyce, runs a prevention program for Denver-area students, says there continues to be a "myth that if you talk about it, you're going to plant the idea in someone's head."

That myth may have its roots in the well-documented phenomenon now known as "clustering."

The sudden rash of teen suicides in this area and other parts of the country, such as Plano, Tex., have many historical antecedents, according to those familiar with suicide studies. Suicide has often attained an almost cult-like mystique, they note.

There was an outbreak of youthful suicides in Europe following the publication of Goethe's *Sorrows of Young Werther* in 1774, for example.

And in late-19th-century Vienna, reports Frederic Morton in his book *A Nervous Splendor,* suicide became almost fashionable, a factor that perhaps led to the famous double suicide in 1882 of Austria's Crown Prince Rudolf and his young sweetheart at Mayerling.

"Death was an eternally great occasion and Vienna knew how to abandon itself to its ceremonials," Mr. Morton writes. Newspapers, he says, even carried regular reviews of the floral arrangements at funerals.

Later, in the 1920's, a similar death cult grew up around an unknown French girl, a suicide who was fished out of the Seine and never identified. A. Alvarez relates in his book *The Savage God* that a death mask made of the girl's "peaceful smile" was copied and distributed throughout the continent. "Nearly every student of sensibility had a plaster cast of her death mask," he writes, and suicide among the young increased.

Hundreds of people in Japan threw themselves into a volcanic crater in the 1930's after a 19-year-old girl took a boat to the small volcanic island of Mihara-Yama, climbed the mountain to the crater's edge, and jumped. In 1935, the Japanese government stopped the fad by screening boat passengers to the island.

To some who are trying to understand the current clustering phenomenon among young suicide victims in America, the excessive attention given to such deaths seems to have been one factor that precipitated the string of imitators.

Marcia Wenger, a Colorado mother whose daughter killed herself last year, wonders in fact whether a highly publicized television movie on teen suicide may have played a role in the suicide decision. The girl had watched the movie shortly before she killed herself.

"The first hour showed the kids and their deaths, and the last hour was about the families and the devastation the death caused," Ms. Wenger recalls. "Keri sat there enthralled with the first hour, but she tuned out the second hour totally. She was fascinated with the death and with the kids. I think it was almost like her life; it was giving her the O.K."

Ms. Wenger adds that her daughter left her suicide note inside a *People* magazine article on the television movie.

Studies on the impact of the media on suicide are still in the preliminary stages, but the Menninger Clinic's Kim Smith says television may contribute in ways that are not quantifiable.

The increase in youth suicide began to be noticeable in the late 1950's, he notes, adding that "the two most significant events that occurred in the formative years of those who were 15 to 20 years old in the 1960's were the mass availability of television and the birth of the nuclear age."

"Could the vivid images portrayed on the home television screen exacerbate tendencies to have unrealistic hopes for relationships, high expectations for one's self, and a lowered frustration tolerance?" he asks.

But television, Dr. Smith adds, "like the 'broken home,' can be blamed for all manner of social and psychological problems."

Dr. Norman Farberow, co-director of the Los Angeles Suicide Prevention Center, says that studies of the media's impact on suicide show that when suicides go unreported over a period of time—such as in the case of a long newspaper strike—a significant drop in the suicide rate occurs.

Research has also shown a significant rise in suicide deaths, he says, when a relatively prominent person's suicide is publicized. One of the most well-known examples of this, he notes, was the worldwide rate jump that followed the death of Marilyn Monroe.

And research at the federal Centers for Disease Control is finding that the type of reporting may affect the suicide rate. Lucy Davidson, a medical epidemiologist, says that negative press portrayals, such as those following the Jonestown cult suicides in 1978, usually do not trigger imitators.

But Dr. Davidson cautions that although imitation and victim-identification may play a role in suicide deaths, emphasizing these factors exclusively—as in the term "copycat suicide"—trivializes the many other factors contributing to suicide.

"Imitation alone cannot account for the susceptibility and stresses each victim brings to that final pathway," she says.

For Colorado's Marcia Wenger, keeping other teen-agers from walking that "final pathway" is now the prime concern. She says she told the minister who conducted Keri's funeral to "get through to the kids."

"It was probably the hardest thing I ever sat through in my life," she says now. "He basically said, 'This was wrong. Keri made the wrong decision.' But I think at that point maybe some of them got the idea that she wasn't coming back. It was almost as if they thought she'd be back in school the next week."

"The problem of death is a favorite theme of adolescence," writes the philosopher Jean Baechler, "because in that theme all the fundamental questions may be found: Who am I? Where am I going? What can I do?"

But for countless American young people, the theme has turned deadly serious.

Even as the overall suicide rate for adolescents drops, there is fresh evidence that suicidal behavior that does not result in death may be more prevalent in the young than previously assumed—and perhaps increasing.

Already, says Pamela Cantor, a developmental and clinical psychologist and the president of the American Association of Suicidology, the picture is grim enough. In a speech last month to Pennsylvania community leaders, she painted its stark dimensions:

"One American teen-ager commits suicide every 90 minutes; one attempts suicide every minute."

But some researchers insist that because health statistics on suicide attempts include only those who have been hospitalized or have sought professional help, the true extent of the problem may be unrecorded.

Researchers at the Menninger Foundation, in a paper entitled "Suicidal Behavior Among 'Normal' High-School Students," say, in fact, that the expanding suicide rates of the young represent "only the most visible tip of an 'iceberg'-like problem of depression and self-destructiveness."

In research that involved the extensive interviewing and testing of some

300 Kansas high-school students chosen at random, they found that "suicide is a personal concern of most high-school students and a serious concern of one out of four of these students."

Their findings, they write, indicate that as many as 1 of every 8 to 12 American high-school students may have engaged in some kind of suicidal behavior.

The findings are supported by several other studies showing a high percentage of suicide attempters among high-school students in various U.S. cities.

A study of 120 California students, for example, turned up a 13 percent suicide-attempt rate. In a New York study of 113 students, the rate was 10 percent. And in a larger study of 293 new college students in Detroit and Boston, the rate was 15 percent.

"It has become clear that if we wish to help the troubled adolescent," the Menninger researchers write, "we need not target our efforts solely at the seriously suicidal. It seems that most high-school students may need our attention.

In Colorado, Craig and Joyce Rupp are devoting most of their time these days to that task. They conduct workshops in schools, temples, churches, and other places where young people gather. And they have helped found Suicide Prevention Allied Regional Effort (SPARE), a coordinated outreach program of parents and professionals in Denver.

Although they say they are often frustrated, the Rupps continue their work because they believe intervention is crucial—and that making parents, teachers, and other adults aware of suicide's warning signs can save lives.

"If we had known then what we know now, Stacy would be alive today," says Craig Rupp.

But in the schools of troubled Jefferson County, Colorado, where an 18th suicide victim was recorded just this month, many teachers say they feel as if they are the unarmed front line in a never-ending battle.

"I think we're doing as much at Golden as anyone can," says the high school's assistant principal, "but sometimes I think people believe kids are T.V. sets and they give them to us to fix."

"We are not in the therapy business," he says. "Parents have to do it, churches have to do it. To think for one second that we're going to solve this problem on our own is ludicrous."

Cherry Creek's Dr. Porter agrees. "The role of education is not intervention," he says, "it's identification. The role of the mental-health center is intervention."

"These groups have got to give up their turf battles," he argues. "Educators have got to sit down and talk with mental-health people."

But Scott, one of Boulder's recent suicide attempters, says, "I don't really think it's up to the teachers anymore." What suicidal teen-agers need most, he says, is "to listen to each other."

"Around suicidal people, there's a tremendous amount of secrecy," says Gary Borgeson, director of the peer-counseling program at Columbine High School in the Denver suburb of Littleton. "The number one prevention is when people can share."

"My philosophy," he adds, "is to get to the family. With almost all parents whose children are involved in some aspect of suicide—completed or not completed—the openness is not there, even if they love their children."

In Washington, the N.I.M.H.'s Dr. Goodwin says that only if school and community suicide-prevention programs "address the question of depression and teach kids to recognize its signs and seek treatment" will they "have a chance" of turning the picture around.

Clinical depression is the most treatable of all psychiatric disorders, he says, yet only 40 percent of those suffering from it seek help.

For its part, the N.I.M.H. has continued, in austere budgetary times, to fund 10 research projects seeking more information on the causes of teen-age suicide.

And last June, former Secretary of Health and Human Services Margaret Heckler created a National Task Force on Youth Suicide, which will convene three national conferences on the subject this year, before issuing a final report next January.

Meanwhile, one of Colorado's youthful would-be suicides gives this prescription for ending America's youth-suicide crisis: "They need to relay the message that suicide is final. Once that's made clear, there will be less and less."

The names of students who attempted suicide have been changed.

Reprinted with permission from *Education Week*, June 18, 1986, Volume 5, No. 39.

4

JUNG'S FIRST DREAM

Anne Maguire

C. G. Jung's earliest remembered dream presented here had meaning for him throughout his long life devoted to the question, "What is man?" The earliest remembered dream often suggests the structure of the dreamer's later life. In other words, such early dreams can be initiatory. Jung recorded his dreams, lived with them, studied so as to try to understand them and integrate their meaning in his life.

Anne Maguire, M.D., is a Fellow of the Royal College of Physicians of London, and is a Consultant Physician practicing in the specialty of Dermatology. She is also an Analytical Psychologist holding the Diploma of the C.G. Jung Institute of Zurich. Dr. Maguire works in London and in Lancashire, England, both as a Consultant Physician-Dermatologist and a practicing Analytical Psychologist. Over the years she has made an intensive exploration of the psychic significance of physical disorder and disease, and is an acknowledged authority on psychosomatic medicine. She lectures regularly at the Zürich Jung Institute as well as in England and America.

CARL Gustav Jung was born on July 26, 1875, at Kesswil, in Canton Thurgau in Switzerland. He was destined, to be initiated, to use his own phrase, into 'the realm of darkness' by way of a dream which he had at the age of three or four years. It was this initial dream by which he was led eventually to a confrontation with the unconscious, which, after years of study and devotion, enabled him to realize the reality of the creative spirit and thus he came to understand and later interpret this childhood dream as his first initiatory experience.

It was said of Jung that "facts first and theories later" was the keynote of his work—that he was an empiricist first and last (Jung 1976b, par. 1502, p.664). Jung himself said that his principal activity consisted in collecting factual information to describe and explain the reality of the psyche, which was his working hypothesis (*Ibid*. par. 1507, p. 666). He formulated auxiliary concepts which served as tools, as is customary in scientific research. Throughout his life he applied all his creative energy to the exploration of the psyche, using these concepts to elucidate it.

Once such concept was that of the *archetypal image*. Although archetypes are themselves irrepresentable, they have effects which enable us to visualize them in terms of images. Only when the archetype is expressed in individual psychic material and takes on the form of an image does it enter the area of conscious awareness. Thus, as soon as an archetype is spoken of, referred to or described, it has already become an *image*, a *revealed* archetype. To reiterate, the archetype as such is completely unknowable and can only be dimly perceived and partially comprehended by its image, which reaches consciousness. In the particular instance where initiation into another aspect or facet of a human life is required by the unconscious, one can speak of the archetype of initiation. Whatever the archetype itself is belongs to the realm of darkness but the image which human consciousness perceives is quite simply in the life of an individual an initiation into a new area of the vastness of the life process itself which in the course of time confronts or besets the being.

In a letter written in 1934 Jung said, "The exploration of the unconscious has in fact and in truth discovered the age-old timeless way of *initiation*." (Jung 1973, p. 141) Later he added that it was not merely his "credo" but the greatest and most incisive experience of his life that "this door, a highly inconspicuous side door on an unsuspicious-looking and easily overlooked footpath narrow and indistinct, because only a few have set foot on it leads to the secret of transformation and renewal." (*Ibid.*, p. 141)

For thousands of years rites of initiation have been teaching rebirth from the spirit, yet man has forgotten the meaning of divine initiatory procreation in our times. This forgetfulness causes him to suffer a loss of soul, a condition which sadly is everywhere present today.

Whatever the outcome of an initiatory rite enacted in a specific culture, performance of such rites always had tremendous impact upon ego-consciousness, with subsequent far-reaching and fateful effects on the lives of the individuals concerned. These ceremonies affected not only the initiand himself but they also frequently affected the lives of his entire tribe. The initiand had been afforded a view, as through a window of the vast and remote eternal world. However, more than that, he had been touched and made aware of his own self before the objective numinous presence of the Other. This is the real meaning of initiation.

As a child Jung lived in the parsonage at Laufen on the Swiss side of the Rhine River, where his father was the pastor. He lived close to the ever present muted roar of the Rhine falls, and early in his life he was oppressed by the somber atmosphere around him. He describes it as follows (Jung 1963, p. 24):

> All around lay a danger zone. People drowned, bodies were swept over the rocks. In the cemetery nearby the sexton would dig a hole . . . Black solemn men in long frock coats with unusually tall hats and shiny black boots would bring a black box.

He goes on to describe how his father would speak in a resounding voice, whilst women wept. As a small child, he realized that certain persons suddenly disappeared, were put into holes in the ground and were buried. He learned further that the Lord Jesus had taken them to Himself. This inalienable fact together with a misconception regarding a child's prayer in which children as chicks were eaten by Lord Jesus before Satan could get them, gradually brought him to the point where he began to distrust Lord Jesus. He lost the aspect of afforded comfort in the combination image of the gloomy black men in black hats with their shiny boots and black boxes. He gradually became convinced that Jesus was a man-eater.

This was the immediate background of Jung as a child, in a pastor's household in central Europe, two decades before the end of the nineteenth century. Jung tells us that it was about this time that he had the earliest dream he could remember, the dream we mentioned above, which was to preoccupy him all his life. It is an immense dream, and extraordinarily mysterious. Traditional or tribal people call such dreams "big" dreams and consider them of tribal significance, of meaning for the whole community. The same belief was found in Greek and Roman civilizations where such dreams were reported to the Areopagus or to the Senate. Jung himself describes his dream as an initiation into the realm of darkness in which he underwent a confrontation with a subterranean god, "not to be named." He writes:

> *The vicarage stood quite alone near Laufen castle and there was a big meadow, stretching back from the sexton's farm. In the dream, I was in this meadow. Suddenly I discovered a dark rectangular stone-lined hole in the ground. I had never seen it before. I ran forward curiously and peered down into it. Then I saw a stone stairway leading down. Hesitantly and fearfully I descended. At the bottom was a doorway with a round arch closed off by a green curtain. It was a big heavy curtain of worked stuff like brocade and it looked very sumptuous. Curious to see what might be hidden behind it I pushed it aside. I saw before me in the dim light, a rectangular chamber about thirty feet long. The ceiling was arched and of hewn stone. The floor was laid with flagstones and in the centre a red carpet ran from the entrance to a low platform. On this platform stood a wonderfully rich golden throne. I am not certain but perhaps a red cushion lay on the seat. It was a magnificent throne, a real King's throne in a fairy tale.*

Something was standing on it, which I thought at first was a tree trunk, twelve to fifteen feet high, and about one and a half to two feet thick. It was a huge thing, reaching almost to the ceiling. But it was of a curious composition. It was made of skin and naked flesh and on the top there was something like a rounded head with no face and no hair. On the very top of the head was a single eye, gazing motionlessly upward.

It was fairly light in the room although there were no windows and no apparent source of light. Above the head, however, was an aura of brightness. The thing did not move, yet I had the feeling that it might at any moment crawl off the throne like a worm and creep towards me. I was paralysed with terror. At that moment I heard, from outside and above me, my mother's voice. She called out, "Yes, just look at him. That is the man-eater!" That intensified my terror, still more, and I awoke sweating and scared to death. For many nights afterwards I was afraid to go to sleep, because I feared I might have another dream like that. (Ibid., pp. 25-26)

Jung explains that it was years before he knew that the terrifying object was a phallus, and decades before he realized it was a ritual phallus having symbolic meaning.

It is impossible to read this dream without being moved by the extraordinary portentious numinous presence of the mysterious upright ritual phallus. How the awesome, imponderable majesty of this dream must have touched the child! It is understandable that Jung would forever be haunted by this great and terrifying dream.

In his explanation Jung says that he was not sure whether his mother meant, "*That* is the man-eater" or "That is the *man-eater*." In the first case, it would have meant not Lord Jesus or the Jesuit (the idea of whom he was also afraid in reality), but the phallus as the devourer of children. In the second case, if the man-eater in general was symbolized by the phallus, this would seem to indicate that the dark Lord Jesus, the Jesuit and the phallus are identical. These are all dark but equivalent images representing the archetype.

Since the phallus is in the icthyphallic upright position it has an abstract significance. Jung says "The eye which the child found so fearful was the orificium urethrae with the source of light apparently above it pointing to the etymology of the word 'phallos' meaning 'shining,' 'bright' " (*Ibid.*, p. 27).

Jung realized that the phallus of the dream was a subterranean god, "not to be named." He adds,

This image always returned throughout my youth when anyone spoke too emphatically about Lord Jesus, who never became quite real for me, never quite acceptable, never quite lovable, for again and again I would think of his underground counterpart with a frightful revelation which had been accorded me without my seeking it. (*Ibid.*, p. 27)

The symbolism of the phallus is boundless and its worship widespread and immensely old. The mystery of the ritual phallus is unexplainable, but it represents an extremely ancient god. Primitives do not confuse the phallus with the membrum virile. This ancient god embodies the creative, the idea of penetration, and discernment. It also enfolds the principle of Eros, so that the idea of creative Eros is held in its meaning. Thus, together with the former there occurs not only the idea of birth, but rebirth, transformation and renewal, key elements of initiation.

It seems pertinent at this point to recall that throughout the ancient world until the early centuries of our own millenium, there was universal worship of a little phallic god, a veiled Kabir, known as Telesphoros. His meaning was naturally bound up with the Kabiri of Samothrace, and the Dactyloi. He was, however, a unique and potent god, and his name means 'the finisher,' 'the accomplisher,' and 'the one who brings to completion or to the goal.' He was hooded and wore a cloak, a bardocucullus. This implied invisibility. In human thought his appearance was reminiscent of the membrum virile, when the foreskin concealed the glans penis.

Worship of Telesphorus started in Pergamum but rapidly spread and became widespread through the entire ancient world. His appearance implied the 'invisible' phallus. He was in reality worshipped in the form of a human child but the hidden creative god was always concealed in the outer image.

Telesphorus was the companion of Asklepios, the Greek god of medicine, and as the worship of Asklepios gave way eventually to Christianity, the continued worship of the little god extended well into the early centuries of the present era. He signified the mystery of the sexual union, and he was the god of inner transformation. Telesphorus also played a role in Jung's life, when he was a child and again in old age, when he chiselled its image as a small homunculus from a large square stone. He dedicated a few words to him there:

> This is Telesphorus, who roams through the dark regions of this cosmos and glows like a star out of the depths. He points the way to the gates of the sun and to the land of dreams. (*Ibid.*, p. 215)

In her extraordinarily informative and revealing analysis of Jung's great childhood dream, von Franz (1975, p. 19) writes that Jung "saw the dream as a birth, a birth of his intellectual life." She also states that for the ancient Romans, the phallus symbolized "a man's secret 'genius,' the source of his physical and mental creative power, the dispenser of all his inspired or brilliant ideas and of his buoyant joy in life." She says further that

> . . . this joy radiated from Jung in the cheerfulness and openness to any and every kind of joke, in his enormous vitality, and above all in his lifelong commitment to the inner creative spirit . . . which drove him relentlessly to ever more research and creativity. The spirit was also the source of an unusually large capacity for love, which both enlivened him and burdened his existence. (*Ibid.*, p. 19)

In the dream, the phallus was situated on a throne in an underground temple, and was therefore a grave-phallus. Von Franz says that this indicated that "it was a symbol of the *after life of the spirit* and a guarantor of the dead man's resurrection" (*Ibid.*, p. 24). She conjectures that the dead man had obviously been a king, and now as a grave phallus awaited resurrection.

Finally in her analysis, von Franz has this to say of the dream:

> But there is something even greater about the mysterious phallus of Jung's great dream, something of a transpersonal nature behind the surface, for that first dream also contains an answer to the problem of the death of God, the problem of the age into which Jung was born. (*Ibid.*, p. 24)

This dream which came to the child Jung also has a message for mankind because it shows that the image of the god which has disappeared from above, abides below in the form of a ritual phallus, representing an exceedingly ancient god. At the same time it also symbolizes creation, love, healing, transformation, rebirth, and renewal, all essential components of the initiation process.

The idea is already contained in the Christian myth itself, and as Jung himself says,

> . . . the death or loss must always repeat itself, Christ always dies and always he is born, for the psychic life of the archetype is timeless in comparison with our individual time-boundedness . . . The myth says he was not found where his body was laid. 'Body' means the outward visible form, the erstwhile but ephemeral setting for the highest value. The myth says the value rose again, in a miraculous manner and transformed. (Jung 1976a, par. 149, p. 90)

In a letter written in 1952, Jung wrote,

> God has indeed made an inconceivably sublime and mysteriously contradictory image of himself, without the help of man, and implanted it in man's unconscious as an archetype, "the archetypal light": . . . in order that the unpresumptious man might glimpse an image in the stillness of his own psychic substance. This image contains everything which he will ever imagine concerning his god or concerning the ground of his psyche. (1976b, par. 1508, p. 667)

Finally, von Franz has this to say:

> Little by little there was being prepared . . . a fundamental transformation of outlook which is in fact nothing more nor less than a new image of God and man, an image which brings the official Christian image of God and man into a new fullness and greater completeness. This transformation is a process in the collective psyche which is a preparation for the new aeon, the Age of Aquarius. (von Franz 1975, p. 36-37)

In these difficult days of great change when the power of the bureaucratic state assumes the mantle of omnipotence, the individual is devalued. No longer is the individual human being considered to be of consequence. As the light of consciousness darkens, the demons of panic and fear freely enter the twilight zones; obfuscation has always permitted their presence. Yet already, as Jung's great dream has revealed to us, a new image of God in the form of an underground phallic god king is awaiting its eventual resurrection, illuminated with its own aura of light, which implies a potentially greater and wider consciousness for man.

The mysterious dream image which was presented to Jung at so early an age contained the secret instruction whereby he was initiated into a life of creative work in which it was his task to confront, to explore and finally to substantiate the vast collective unconscious world.

REFERENCES

Jung, C.G. 1963. *Memories dreams and reflections.* London: Routeledge & Kegan Paul.
_____1973. *C.G. Jung letters 1906-1950,* Vol. I. G. Adler, ed. Princeton: Princeton University Press.
_____1976a. *Collected Works.* Vol. 11. Princeton: Princeton University Press.
_____1976b. *Collected Works.* Vol. 18. Princeton: Princeton University Press.
von Franz, M.-L. 1975. *C.G. Jung, his myth in our time.* New York: C.G. Jung Foundation for Analytical Psychology, Inc.

SYMBOLS OF INITIATION IN
ADVENTURES OF HUCKLEBERRY FINN

Harold Schechter

In his essay, "Symbols of Initiation in Adventures of Huckleberry Finn," *Harold Schechter finds striking similarities between traditional rites of passage and the many adventures of Huck Finn. Not only does this chapter offer evidence of Mark Twain's sense of patterns of initiation, but Schechter identifies basic aspects of an American male initiatory journey, with numerous amplifications from other cultures. After Huck's passage down the Mississippi in the company of shaman Jim and various other "initiators," Schechter concludes, "the young hero seems to have found true masculine maturity despite Twain's attempts to have him yet remain a child." Schechter demonstrates how* Huckleberry Finn *can be read as a story of male initiation. Most Americans have some knowledge of the* Adventures of Huckleberry Finn *and this chapter adds a new dimension to our understanding of its meaning and fascination.*

Harold Schechter, Ph.D., is Associate Professor of English at Queens College, City University of New York. He has written extensively on the relationship between archetypal myth and the popular arts. He is author of numerous articles and several books, including The New Gods: Psyche and Symbol in Popular Art *(1980) and* Patterns in Popular Culture *(1980). His current project is a book-length study of folklore and film.*

IT is interesting—and a little curious—that, while many critics see *Huckleberry Finn* as the story of an initiation, of a boy's "growth . . . to manhood, and his final acceptance of adult moral responsibilities" (Adams 1957), no one has ever examined the book in relation to any actual initiation ceremonies. And yet, when we compare Twain's novel to those rituals whose function is to transform the adolescent male into an adult, we discover a number of astonishing parallels.

In his "Remarks on the Sad Initiation of Huckleberry Finn," James M. Cox (1954) contends that "the whole initiation and rebirth theme is launched on a tragicomic note" in a chapter "significantly entitled 'Pap Starts in on a New Life.' " To be sure, Pap's avowal that he is beginning "a new life, and'll die before he'll go back"* is the first of several humorous references to death and rebirth in the novel. But in order to trace the initiatory pattern that underlies *Huckleberry Finn*, we must turn back to the very beginning, before Pap even appears—for Huck's situation in the opening chapters is very close to that of the uninitiated males of certain primitive communities.

Extreme sexual segregation is characteristic of many tribes. Men are, to a very large extent, isolated from the world of the women. Only the male children who have not yet been initiated, who have yet to pass through their puberty rites, are in constant interaction with the women of the tribe. In their studies of primitive secret societies, both Robert H. Lowie (1920) and Hutton Webster (1908) discuss the "men's house"—that ubiquitous institution "within [whose] precincts, women and children and men not fully initiated members of the tribe . . . never enter." Note that, in many societies, young boys and females "eat, live, and sleep apart" from the initiated males. This is certainly true of the Arunta of Australia, whose puberty ceremonies are more extensively documented than those of any other Australian tribe. Spencer and Gillen (1899) report that, up until the time of their initiation, Arunta boys live away from the men's camp, or *Ungunja,* and reside with the women and girls. Thus—as Géza Róheim (1950) explains—the Arunta youth is raised "in a state of communal motherhood." Discussing the psychological development of these Central Australian boys, Róheim writes that "they grow up . . . the way all children grow up—through playing at being grown up. . . . the children played at performing ceremonies like the men. . . . "

At the beginning of Twain's novel, Huck too resides in a world dominated by women—Aunt Polly, the Widow Douglas, Miss Watson. Within this "maternal and female world" (Eliade 1965), Huck lives with other boys his age—"thirteen or fourteen or along there" (319)—boys who are ripe for, and play at, initiation. For it is not as Cox maintains, Chapter Five which "launches" the theme of initiation in the novel, but Chapter Two—"Our Gang's Dark Oath." In the blood ritual which Huck and his friends must perform in order to join Tom's outlaw band, we have a comic foreshadowing of the initiatory ordeals which Huck will later undergo. And the oath of secrecy which the gang members swear is a burlesque version of the vow of silence that is a central feature of many actual initiation ceremonies. As Huck explains,

---

*Mark Twain, *Adventures of Huckleberry Finn. The Portable Mark Twain,* ed. de Voto (New York: Viking Press, 1968), p. 217. Further page references to the novel are incorporated into the text.

> if anybody that belonged to the band told the secrets, he must have his throat cut and then have his carcass burnt up and the ashes scattered all around and his name blotted off the list with blood and never mentioned again by the gang, but have a curse put on it and be forgot forever. . . .
> Some thought it would be good to kill the *families* of boys that told the secrets. Tom said it was a good idea, so he took a pencil and wrote it in (201).

During the puberty rites of the Arunta, Spencer and Gillen (1899) report, the novice is told that "on no account must he ever tell any woman or boy of what he was about to see. Should he reveal any of the secrets, then he and his nearest relatives would surely die." It is worth noting that in his *True Adventures of Huckleberry Finn,* John Seelye retitles the second chapter "Nitiation night, and the morning after." Clearly, Seelye (1970) also recognized that it is this, and not the later chapter, that announces the theme of initiation in Twain's novel.

"Puberty institutions for the initiation of young men into manhood," writes Hutton Webster (1908), "are among the most widespread and characteristic features of primitive life. . . . Though varying endlessly in detail, their leading characteristics reproduce themselves with substantial uniformity among many different peoples and in widely separated areas of the world." Jungian psychologists, of course account for this uniformity by explaining that initiation rites "are based, with small variations, on the same . . . archetypal ground-pattern" (Jacobi 1967). Now, the first step in the transformation of the male adolescent into an adult—and this is universal—is to separate him "from his previous environment, the world of women and children"—to sever his childhood domestic ties. The way in which this is accomplished is often "by a violent action"—i.e., the abduction of the novice (van Gennep 1960). Discussing Australian initiation ceremonies, Mircea Eliade (1965) notes that "the scenario is the same" everywhere among the aborigines: "the novices are seized by their guardians and carried off to the forest." The elders who perform this ritual kidnapping, moreover, are terrifying figures, for they are usually colored white—smeared with white clay or ashes or covered with bird down (Campbell 1969). While the novices regard them as "bogeymen" (van Gennep 1960), they are actually meant to represent the Ancestors—"mythical, primal, titanic men who walked the earth in former times" (Henderson 1967a)—temporarily resurrected in order to participate in the ceremonies. "What we have here," writes Eliade (1965), "is . . . a periodic return of the dead among the living for the purpose of initiating the youth." Speaking of these "white clay men," Henderson (1967a) explains that "although impersonating death in its ghostly aspect, they are also harbingers of that life which springs anew from the original source of all things. It is significant that those men are represented as being white. . . . This white is an ambiguous color and would seem to embody just that spirit of paradox which is the essence of the death and rebirth experience. . . . " What we find at the beginning of the puberty rites, then, is the boy being torn from the maternal sphere—from the control of the women—and spirited off to the forest by a "resurrected," deathly white bogeyman.

This, of course, is precisely what happens to Huck. Pap—supposedly "drownded"—appears one night in Huck's room at the widow's. He is a frightening figure: "There warn't no color in his face, where his face showed; it was white, not like another man's white but a white to make a body sick, a white to make a body's flesh crawl—a tree-toad white, a fish-belly white" (214). Then, "one day in the spring" (the traditional time for the performance of many rebirth ceremonies), he "lays for" Huck, seizes him, and rows him across the river "to the Illinois shore where it was woody and there warn't no houses but an old log hut in a place where the timber was so thick you couldn't find it if you didn't know where it was" (219). At first, Huck enjoys himself, but "by and by Pap got too handy with his hick'ry and I couldn't stand it. I was all over welts. He got to going away so much, too, and locking me in. Once he locked me in and was gone three days. It was dreadful lonesome. I judged he had got drownded and I wasn't ever going to get out any more. I was scared" (220). Things get even scarier, though, when Pap returns. Drinking himself blind after dinner, he has a violent attack of delerium tremens and, "looking wild," begins chasing Huck "round and round the place with a claspknife, calling me the Angel of Death, and saying he would kill me and then I couldn't come for him no more. I begged, and told him I was only Huck, but he laughed *such* a screechy laugh and roared and cussed and kept on chasing me up." Finally, though, Pap tires himself out and—telling Huck that he will "rest a minute and then kill" him—falls asleep. Huck crouches down behind a turnip-barrel to keep watch over Pap with a gun: "And how slow and still the time did drag along" (225-26).

Now, a feature that is common to nearly all primitive puberty initiations is the "period of containment" which the novice must undergo, often in a "secluded . . . hut, far away in the forest" (Henderson 1967b). Within this hut, the boy is subjected to a variety of ordeals, symbolic of the initiatory death that is the prerequisite for rebirth. Describing the puberty ceremonies of certain Melanesian tribes, Arnold van Gennep (1960) notes that "the novice is taken to a sacred place. There, he is beaten with more or less heavy sticks . . . by the *tubuan,* a sort of divine bogeyman." Webster (1908), speaking of puberty rites in general, refers to "the brutal beatings received by the novices." Eliade (1965) describes the initiation rites of the Yamana tribe of Tierra del Fuego: "The boys are segregated in a cabin, and an evil spirit, the Earth Spirit Yetaita, plays an important role. . . . During the ceremony Yetaita is represented by one of the instructors, painted . . . white. Springing from behind the curtain, he attacks the novices, e.g., maltreats them. . . . " Another ordeal which these novices undergo, "documented more or less all over the world," is the ordeal of sleeplessness. The Yamana youth is required to "keep long vigils."

The most prevalent of all initiatory ordeals, however, and the most terrifying, is circumcision. Eliade observes that the circumcision of the novice typically symbolizes his ritual murder by a demonic Being. Among certain tribes, in fact, "circumcision is expressed by the verb 'to kill.' " In Australia and elsewhere, the operation is usually performed by an elder who wields a small flint knife and whose attitude "is that of a furious father attacking his son's penis" (Roheim 1950). Paul Radin (1957) describes the circumciser: "Finally, the operator appears, his eyes rolling and his whole behavior indicative of a madman. As he seizes the prepuce of the young boy, the audience of older men shout in chorus: 'Behold the maddened one!' " Thus, Huck's terrifying experiences in Pap's log cabin parallel in a really remarkable way the series of initiatory tortures that is a central feature of the puberty rites.

On the day after Pap's seizure, Huck determines to escape, and stages an ingenious mock murder of himself, leaving a bloodied ax in the cabin as evidence of the crime. The whole community believes that he has been killed, and—as James Cox (1954) points out—he remains "dead throughout the entire journey down the river." Here, too, Huck's story is closely analogous to certain primitive rites. Once a boy has undergone the circumcision ceremony, "he is considered dead, and he remains dead for the duration of his novitiate" (van Gennep 1960). Webster (1908) observes that "almost universally, initiation rites include a mimic representation of the death . . . of the novice." Eliade (1965), discussing the elaborate "scenarios of initiatory death" which characterize so many puberty rites, reports that in certain tribes "the women are shown the bloody lances with which the spirit is supposed to have killed the novices."

At this point in many puberty ceremonies, the neophyte goes off to live for an extended period in the bush. Generally, he is placed "under a number of dietary prohibitions"—certain foods are forbidden to him. He is accompanied by an older man, often a shaman, whose duty is to tutor him in tribal morality and show him "the secrets and miracles of the medicine man" (Eliade 1965). Describing the initiation ceremonies of the Yuin tribe of Australia, for example, A. W. Howitt (1909) writes that, after the ordeals, the novices had "to go and live by themselves in the bush, on such food as they could catch, and which might be lawful for them to eat. They were . . . under the charge of the *Kabos,* who would . . . instruct them." Webster (1908) discusses "the instruction received by candidates during their initiatory seclusion" at some length:

> . . . being cut off from all the interests of the outer world, the lads had an opportunity for . . . meditation, which must have tended to mature their minds, especially as they were at the same time instructed in a good code of morals.
>
> Each lad is attended by one of the elders who instructs him . . . in his duties and gives him advice to regulate his conduct through life—advice given him in so kindly, fatherly, and impressive a manner as often to soften the heart. . . .

It should be noted that, while the elders do indeed serve as "spiritual fathers" to the boys, there is something distinctly maternal about them. "The male shaman or seer," writes Erich Neumann (1952) "is in high degree 'feminine' . . . [and] often appears in woman's dress." And Henderson (1967b) maintains that the master of initiation "is both mother and father" to the novice. It is his function to bring the boy to a second birth, to "continue and consummate his post-uterine gestation, the long process of his growth to a fully human maturity" (Campbell 1969).

Once Huck has "died," he too goes off to live by himself, and "in the thick woods" of Jackson's Island meets Miss Watson's Jim (238). Enslaved in St. Petersburg, Jim is a caricature, a comical witch doctor performing mumbo jumbo with a hair ball. But as soon as he is "free of the corruption of civilization," he becomes a genuine magus, a priest of the river god—"seer and shaman, interpreter of the dark secrets of nature" (Schmitz 1971).

> Some young birds come along, flying a yard or two at a time and lighting. Jim said it was a sign when young chickens flew that way, and so he reckoned it was the same way when young birds done it. I was going to catch some of them but Jim wouldn't let me. He said it was death. . . .
>
> And Jim said you mustn't count the things you are going to cook for dinner, because that would bring bad luck. The same as if you shook the tablecloth after sundown. And he said if a man owned a beehive and that man died, the bees must be told about it before sun-up next morning, or else the bees would all weaken down and quit work and die. . . .
>
> I had heard about some of these things before, but not all of them. Jim knowed all kinds of signs (244).

Jim's function, however, is not merely to instruct Huck "in the lore of weather . . . the omens of luck . . . [and] the talismans of death." Like the primitive masters of initiation, he is also "a source of moral energy" (Hoffman 1961): "the dark tutor who helps unlock the 'sound heart' imprisoned in Huck's breast" (Schmitz 1971). Nurturing and protective, standing watch over Huck while the boy gets some extra sleep, and yearning for his own children, he is both spiritual father and Good Mother. James M. Cox (1954) comments perceptively on Jim's "ambivalent nature":

> It is to Jim that Huck retreats as if to a savior; he it is who mothers Huck as they travel down the big river; and he it is who, knowing secretly that Huck's Pap is dead forever, takes Huck to his own bosom to nourish him through the ordeals of being lost. Acting as Huck's foster father, Jim brings to that role a warmth and gentleness which Huck had never known under the brutal masculinity of his real father. Near the end of the novel, after Jim has accompanied and protected Huck on their perilous journey, how appropriate that he should be led back to the Phelps plantation, following his temporary escape with Tom, arrayed in the dress which the boys had stolen from Aunt Sally. The incident points up . . . [Jim's] role of motherly father to Huck.

Just before the flight from Jackson's Island, Huck also "dress[es] up like a girl," disguising himself in a calico gown and sun-bonnet so that he can sneak ashore and "find out what was going on" (254). This incident, too, has an interesting analogue in the puberty initiations, for "the novice's ritual transformation into a woman" is an important part of many of these ceremonies. Eliade (1965), Bettelheim (1962), Lowie (1920), and Henderson (1976b) all discuss this ritual transvestism. According to Henderson, the purpose of the practice is to "mobilize a bisexual response as an act of integration in the formation of the new man. This is . . . acted out in certain tribal societies in which both novice and tutor (and/or master of initiation) play maternally supportive and sometimes actively homosexual roles." The homoerotic element in Huck and Jim's relationship was pointed out long ago, of course, by Leslie Fiedler (1955).

Another incident, common to initiation rites, takes place while the boy and Jim are still living on Jackson's Island. One night, while Huck and Jim are paddling over the flooded island in their canoe, a two-story frame house comes floating by—the "House of Death." Climbing in "at an up-stairs window," they see "something laying on the floor in the far corner" of the room (249). Jim walks over and finds that it is the naked body of a murdered man, his face "too gashly" to look at. Huck doesn't "want to see him" and turns away (250). Eliade (1965) records a number of puberty ceremonies involving "death houses" and one of them, a Fijian ritual, is strikingly similar to the episode in Twain's book:

> On a particular day the novices, led by a priest, proceed to the Nanda [a stone enclosure]. . . . They are then taken [inside]. There lie a row of dead men, covered with blood, their bodies apparently cut open and their entrails protruding. The priest-guide walks over the corpses and the terrified novices follow him to the other end of the enclosure, where the chief priest awaits them. Suddenly he blurts out a great yell, whereupon the dead men start to their feet, and run down to the river to cleanse themselves from the blood and filth with which they are besmeared.

The resurrection thus enacted is meant to represent the novice's own approaching rebirth. The dead man whom Huck and Jim discover does not, of course, spring back to life. Nevertheless—like the Nanda—this house of death contains the promise of rebirth. For among all the trash "scattered around over the floor," the "greasy cards" and empty whiskey bottles and "masks made out of black cloth"—images of decay and dissolution—Huck finds "a bottle that had milk in it and . . . a rag stopper for a baby to suck" (250)—a symbol of new birth.

In some puberty ceremonies, Eliade explains, the novices actually undergo a ritual "return to earliest infancy"—i.e., they are symbolically transformed into babies: forced to live naked for long periods, forbidden to speak or to use their hands to feed themselves. At one point in his journey, Huck also is assimilated into a baby, for in the so-called "Raft Passage," as Kenneth S. Lynn (1958) has perceived, he identifies himself with the infant in the raftsman's tale:

> Crouched in the darkness, naked and afraid, Huck seems utterly apart from the coarse, rough men, but the fantasy of violence and terror which the raftsman has spun for the scoffing delight of his fellows nevertheless vitally involves the runaway boy, for the story tells, after all, of a man who locked up his son, and of a naked child floating down the river in search of its father. That Huck has escaped to his fabulous voyage by making his Pap think he has been murdered only completes his identification with this dead baby who was somehow "reborn" in the river, an identification which he makes explicit when, suddenly seized from his hiding place and surrounded by strange men demanding to know his name, Huck jokingly replies, "Charles William Albright, sir." Always in Twain the best jokes reveal the profoundest connections, and with the release of laughter triggered by Huck's superbly-timed joke the chapter not only reaches its humorous climax, but we are suddenly made aware that through Huck we have been eavesdropping on a parable of . . . death by violence and rebirth by water which takes us to the very heart of the novel.

As Huck and Jim journey down the river towards Cairo, the relationship established on Jackson's Island remains the same: Huck's situation continues to parallel that of the primitive neophyte during his period of isolation from society, and Jim's that of the attendant shaman responsible for the boy's moral education. Even their self-imposed restrictions on food-stealing are the comic equivalent of the dietary taboos that are part of a novice's ritual seclusion:

> Mornings before daylight I slipped into corn-fields and borrowed a watermelon or a mushmelon or a punkin, or some new corn or things of that kind. Pap always said it warn't no harm to borrow things if you was meaning to pay them back some time, but the widow said it warn't anything but a soft name for stealing and no decent body would do it. Jim said he reckoned the widow was partly right and Pap was partly right, so the way would be for us to pick out two or three things from the list and say we wouldn't borrow them any more—then he reckoned it wouldn't be no harm to borrow the others. So we talked it over all one night, drifting along down the river, trying to make up our minds whether to drop the watermelons or the cantelopes or the mushmelons, or what. But towards daylight we got it all settled satisfactory and concluded to drop crabapples and p'simmons (267).

As Neil Schmitz (1971) points out, however, once the raft has drifted beyond Cairo, Jim becomes, in a very real sense, a "supernumerary." Huck's education passes out of his hands (following the Shepherdson-Grangerford episode) into those of the duke and dauphin. These con men who fleece the folks at a revival meeting, "sell" an entire town with their ridiculous tragedy, cheat orphans, and betray Jim, seem ill-suited for the roles of shaman and tutor. Nevertheless, they embody certain qualities that are characteristic of the primitive medicine man, and their manner of "teaching," while diametrically opposed to Jim's, parallels an instructional method that is common to puberty rites.

Discussing the phenomenon of shamanism in *The Masks of God* (1969) Joseph Campbell quotes from the account of various missionaries, who describe the medicine men as "humbugs," "actors," "creature[s] apart from the honest hunters," men who, "accustomed to [holding their] own against many . . . had to have [their] tricks." Campbell then goes on to examine the shaman as an archetypal trickster figure, an incarnation of "the chaos principle, the principle of disorder, the force careless of taboos and shattering bounds." According to Jung, the function of the trickster is to ritually enact, and thereby hold "before the eyes of the more highly developed individual," different forms of bestial behavior, and to represent a rudimentary level of consciousness which "should never be forgotten for long." This "therapeutic anamnesis," writes Jung (1959), is the most effective method in primitive cultures for keeping the inferior traits of character "conscious and subjecting [them] to conscious criticism." Thus, during certain puberty rites, the medicine men—the masters of initiation—perform "pantomimic representations" that are "intended to teach the novices in a vivid fashion what things they must in future avoid. . . . Various offences against morality are exhibited, and the guardians warn the novices of their death or of violence should they attempt to repeat the actions they have just witnessed" (Webster 1920). Howitt (1909) describes some of these performances in detail:

> The pieces of buffoonery are perhaps some of the most remarkable features of the proceedings. If one were to imagine all sorts of childish mischief mixed up with the cardinal sins represented in burlesque, and ironically recommended to the boys on their return to camp and afterwards, it would give a not inapt representation of what takes place. But there is the remarkable features that at the end of almost every sentence, indeed of every indecent, immoral or lewd suggestion, the speaker adds "Yah!" which negates all that has been said and done. . . . This gave to the whole proceedings . . . a sort of Carnival and April fool aspect. . . .
>
> [One] pantomime represents a number of very old men who came up, following each other, out of the forest, and circled round the fire . . . swaying from side to side at each step, and each holding his head with both hands, one at each temple. After going round the fire several times, the chain broke up into individuals, who began tickling each other, finally falling down into a heap, screeching with laughter. Such an exhibition of childishness in venerable old grey-beards was ridiculous, and this was impressed on the novices by going up to them and saying, "When you go back to camp do like that—yah!" by this warning them not to be guilty of such childish acts in their characters of men.
>
> Other pantomimic representations were to impress rules of tribal morality by visible instances. [Howitt goes on to give examples of two more pantomimes, one dealing with adultery, the second with "the offences for which, it is said, the cities of the plain were destroyed by celestial fire."]

"In all these performances," Howitt points out, "the men are naked"— though they are usually decorated with circles, stripes, and corkscrew lines of white pipe-clay.

What I am suggesting then, is that the duke and dauphin function as shamanistic tricksters, acting out "various offences against morality," instructing Huck by negative example. Both of these "humbugs" (350) are medicine men: the duke dabbles "a little in patent medicine" (346) and occasionally travels around "dissipating witch spells" (354), while the dauphin admits to having "done considerable in the doctoring way. . . . Layin' on o' hands is my best holt—for cancer and paralysis and sich things; and I kin tell a fortune pretty good when I've got somebody along to find out the facts for me. Preachin's my line, too . . ." (346). And their performance of "The King's Cameleopard" is strikingly similar to the scene described by Howitt (the antics of the clay-painted elders):

> . . . the next minute the king come a-prancing out on all fours, naked; and he was painted all over, ring-streaked-and-striped, all sorts of colors, as splendid as a rainbow. And—but never mind the rest of his outfit; it was just wild but it was awful funny. The people most killed themselves laughing, and when the King got done capering and capered off behind the scenes, they roared and clapped and stormed and haw-hawed till he came back and done it over again, and after that they made him do it another time. Well, it would a-make a cow laugh to see the shines that old idiot cut (379).

The ritualistic nature of this scene has been recognized by Robert Tracy (1968), who finds "overtones of a ritualized sexual indecency" in it. As we have seen, the pantomimes performed for the novice often do, in fact, include representations of "heterosexual debauchery [and] sodomy" (van Gennep 1960). By exposing Huck to different forms of immorality and human weakness, then, "the duke and dauphin help to complete his education" (Adams 1957).

In most primitive societies, on completing their passage to adulthood, the novices are given new names to symbolize their second birth. Among the Arunta, Radin (1957) points out, the boy who has successfully passed through the initiation ceremonies is reborn as "The-Morally-Good-One." In *Huckleberry Finn*, the rebirth imagery that signifies the culmination of Huck's initiation into manhood begins with the Phelps farm episode in a chapter aptly entitled "I Have a New Name." By this time, too, Huck has certainly earned the right to be known as a "morally good one." And although this episode is followed by a sequence of events in which the author portrays Huck as failing to bring his passage into adulthood to a satisfactory conclusion, the young hero seems to have found true masculine maturity despite Twain's attempts to have him yet remain a child. For here at Phelps farm, after all the ordeals he has braved and after all the trials, mishaps, and victories through which he so clearly has learned what it means to "grow up," we have it in Huck's own words: "But if they was joyful, it warn't nothing to what I was; for it was like being born again. . . ." (461).

REFERENCES

Adams, R. P. 1957. The unity and coherence of Huckleberry Finn. In *The Norton critical edition of Adventures of Huckleberry Finn*, pp. 342-357. New York: W.W. Norton, 1961.

Bettelheim, B. 1962. *Symbolic wounds.* New York: Collier Books.

Campbell, J. 1969. *The masks of God: primitive mythology.* New York: The Viking Press.

Cox, J. M. 1954. Remarks on the sad initiation of Huckleberry Finn. *Sewanee Review,* vol. 62, pp. 389-405.

Edinger, E. F. 1973. *Ego and archetype: individuation and the religious function of the psyche.* Baltimore: Penguin Books.

Eliade, M. 1965. *Rites and symbols of initiation,* trans. William H. Trashk. New York: Harper and Row.

Henderson, J. L. 1967a. *The wisdom of the serpent: The myth of death, rebirth and resurrection.* New York: Collier Books.

――――― 1957b. *Thresholds of initiation.* Middletown, Conn., Wesleyan University Press.

Hoffman, D. G. 1961. *Form and fable in American fiction.* New York: Oxford University Press.

Howitt, A. W. 1909. *The native tribes of south-east Australia.* London: Macmillan.

Jacobi, J. 1967. *The way of individuation,* trans. R.F.C. Hull. New York: Harcourt, Brace and World.

Jung, C. G. 1935. Psychological commentary on the Tibetan Book of the Dead. *Psyche and symbol,* pp. 283-301, ed. Violet S. de Laszlo. New York: Anchor Books, 1958.

――――― 1928. The relations between the ego and the unconscious. In *Collected works,* vol. 7, 2d ed., pp. 121-241. Princeton: Princeton University Press, 1966.

――――― 1931. The structure of the psyche. *Collected works,* vol. 8, 2d. ed., pp. 139-58. Princeton: Princeton University Press, 1969.

――――― 1944. *Psychology and alchemy. Collected works,* vol. 12, 2d ed. Princeton: Princeton University Press, 1968.

――――― 1959. The psychology of the child archetype. *Collected works,* vol. 9, Part I, 2d ed. Princeton: Princeton University Press, 1968.

Lynn, K. S. 1958. Huck and Jim. In *Yale review,* vol. LXVII, pp. 421-31.

Neumann, E. 1952. *The great mother: An analysis of an archetype,* trans. Ralph Manheim. Bollingen Series, vol. XLVII. Princeton: Princeton University Press, 1972.

Radin, P. 1957. *Primitive religion: Its nature and origin.* New York: Dover Publications, Inc.

Róheim, G. 1950. *Psychoanalysis and anthropology: Culture, personality and the unconscious.* New York: International Universities Press.

――――― 1969. *The eternal ones of the dream: A psychoanalytic interpretation of Australian myth and ritual.* New York: International Universities Press.

Schmitz, N. 1971. The paradox of liberation in Huckleberry Finn. *Texas studies in literature and language,* vol. 13, pp. 125-36.

Seelye, J. 1970. *The true adventures of Huckleberry Finn.* Evanston: Northwestern University Press.

Spencer, B., and Gillen, F. J. 1899. *The native tribes of Central Australia*. London: Macmillan.

Tracy, R. 1968. Myth and reality in The Adventures of Tom Sawyer. *Southern review,* vol. 4, pp. 530-41.

Twain, M. 1884. *Adventures of Huckleberry Finn. The portable Mark Twain,* pp. 193-537, ed. Bernard deVoto. New York: The Viking Press, 1968.

Van Gennep, A. 1960. *The rites of passage,* trans. Monika B. Vizedom and Gabrielle L. Caffee. Chicago: University of Chicago Press.

Webster, H. 1980. *Primitive secret societies.* New York: MacMillan.

6

THE VISION QUEST: PASSING FROM CHILDHOOD TO ADULTHOOD

Steven Foster and Meredith Little

In this practical participation guide for high school students, "The Vision Quest: Passing from Childhood to Adulthood," Steven Foster and Meredith Little have placed this traditional rite into the context of the modern adolescent's experience. "Are you ready to leave mother, father, and the childhood security of home in order to face the future as an adult?" they challenge their young reader. Those who accept the necessary risks of the vision quest rite are asked to study and prepare, to seek their parents' support, to examine their own values and belief systems, and to consciously commit themselves to the three phases of the ceremony: severance, transition, and return.

The particular vision quest model presented here is pan-cultural and nondenominational. In effect, the students are given a make-it-yourself skeleton which they flesh out with their own religious or ethical orientation. The liminal phase includes a three day and night solo fast in a wilderness place. The authors do not delude participating youth into thinking that the vision quest will automatically confer adult status. "You probably will not return to a confetti parade. At the present time modern culture does not honor the vision quest as a valid means of formalizing your attainment of adulthood." Nevertheless, useful guidelines are provided for the use of the vision quest ceremony as a formal means of taking a big step toward eventual emancipation. Educators and therapists (see Sullwold and Allan and Dyck) who have long lamented the absence of such initiatory growth events in the lives of adolescents may be encouraged by the practical applicability of the model discussed here.

Steven Foster, Ph.D., is Co-Director of the School of Lost Borders. With his wife Meredith Little, he trains lay people and professionals in vision quest methodology and dynamics. He taught in the humanities at the University of Washington, the University of Wyoming, and San Francisco State University.

Fifteen years ago he resigned his professorship and began vision quest work. He and his wife cofounded and directed Rites of Passage, Inc., Novato, CA., a non-profit educational organization providing vision quest experiences for youth and adults. Both are members of the Association of Indian Psychologists and the Xat Medicine Society.

Meredith Little, Co-Director of the School of Lost Borders, Big Pine, CA, is a graduate of Antioch College West, a former Suicide Prevention and Crisis Intervention trainer, and has conducted vision quests for youth and adult individuals and groups for many years. With her husband, Steven Foster, she has written The Book of the Vision Quest: Personal Transformation in the Wilderness *(1980),* The Vision Quest: Passing from Childhood to Adulthood *(1983),* The Sacred Mountain: A Vision Quest Guide for Adults *(1984), and* The Roaring of the Sacred River: Modern Apprenticeship to an Ancient Ceremony of Passage *(1986).*

THIS guide was written to meet a need created by the re-introduction of the vision quest as a modern rite of passage for youth entering adulthood. As time passes, the subjects addressed here will assume greater significance. Interest in and application of these concepts will become widespread.

More and more people are saying that the health of our culture depends on our ability to provide a "growth context" in which our young people can mature and find meaning and purpose. Many say that the current cultural means of providing growth and learning experiences are inadequate, that the children are growing up as spectators rather than participants, that too many are content merely to dream the dreams of others instead of acting on their own. There are also many people who are saying that the times are critical, not only for America, but for the world. They say that America needs young men and women of imagination and commitment who are not afraid of the challenge of the future. The vision quest addresses that need.

The vision quest guide is the result of fifteen years of experience adapting traditional life passage ceremonial forms to the cultural biases of nearly a thousand young men and women of various ethnic, religious, and cultural backgrounds. Many of them were seniors seeking a meaningful way to celebrate their commencement from the childhood world of high school. Others were at variance with their society. We found them in juvenile halls or "special schools" or group homes. They were looking for ways to "test" or to "prove" themselves. Still others were students from alternative or private high schools who were enrolled in courses which included the study of ethnology, anthropology, social science, or religion. These students kept journals and discussed their experiences with their instructors. Because of their feedback, this book was possible.

This guide is not theoretical, hypothetical, or figurative. Although it contains some "academic" language, the subject is not academic. It was written from the guts and the hearts of high school students who were afraid— but they went and did it anyway. Probably all of them would say, in retrospect, that participation in the vision quest was one of the most important experiences of their lives.

As it is discussed in the following pages, the vision quest is a learning "form" or process. You volunteer to put yourself through it. A good deal of what you experience is related to your childhood, to your mother, father, and family. You also experience yourself, as you are when nobody sees you, as you are when you are hungry and afraid. In an unforgettable way, you *know* yourself. In this *knowing* there is understanding and a clue as to how you will make it as an adult. Here is how you can do it. Here are the nuts and bolts.

The three phases of the vision quest, as discussed here, can be completed in two months or in a school quarter or semester. At the School of Lost Borders, where we conduct vision quest courses, the usual time is two months. More benefit is derived from more extended study and preparation. Ideally, the vision quest is an exercise offered to graduating seniors, the last semester of high school. Ideally, the courses are instructed by school teachers trained in the vision quest form. As more teachers are trained, the high schools of the community will be able to provide this educational service. Self-instructional methods and procedures are discussed at length in our book, *The Roaring of the Sacred River: Modern Apprenticeship to an Ancient Ceremony of Passage* (1986).

If you are a parent who wants to further explore the subject of the vision quest, you are invited to consult the suggested readings in the Appendix and to read the "Note to Parents." If you are a student, you might also want to read "Returning Early from the Threshold Time" (Appendix).

Introduction

'Father, Oh father! I hear weeping. Is it my mother I leave in grief?' 'Have courage, my son . . . . In your mother's womb you were conceived. From an individual human womb you were born to an individual human life. It was necessary, it was good. But individual human life is not sufficient to itself. It depends upon and is a part of all life. So now another umbilical cord must be broken—that which binds you to your mother's affections, that which binds you to the individual human life she gave you. For twelve years you have belonged to your lesser mother. Now you belong to your greater mother. And you return to her womb to emerge once again, as a man who knows himself not as an individual but a unit of his tribe and a part of all life which ever surrounds him.'
—Frank Waters, *The Man Who Killed the Deer*

Coming of Age in America

Begin with a question. Ask yourself this question. Imagine how those closest to you might answer it:

"Is he/she (meaning *you*) ready to leave mother, father, and the childhood security of home in order to face the future as an adult?"

Before you answer too quickly, you might consider your own "growing up experiences," including those which modern American culture has made available to you. Have these experiences demonstrated (validated) your readiness to step across the threshold into the adult world? With the help of your life, have you been able to prepare yourself? Resist the temptation to consider your life pessimistically. Surely there are plenty of people who have had it worse than you. It may be that you are more prepared than you think.

Let's list the formal "growth experiences" or life passage ceremonies provided for you by our culture. These "tests" or "landmarks" are the means by which our social order guarantees that you are an "adult."

Preparing for and obtaining a driver's license

Attending and graduating from high school

Attaining the age of eighteen (legally no longer a "minor")

Getting a full-time or part-time job

Getting married

Attaining the age of 21

Perhaps there are also certain formal graduations which have been provided for you by your church or synagogue. Among these are baptism, confirmation, bar-mitzvah, batz-mitzvah, etc. There are also other "graduations" provided by various ethnic minority groups and families, not to mention initiations into organizations and clubs.

Has your experience of these ceremonies demonstrated (validated) your readiness to step across the threshold into the adult world? Are you ready to leave childhood behind?

Roget's Thesaurus lists the following adjectives with the word *childhood*: "juvenile, immature, raw, green, sappy, unripe, callow, unfledged, budding, tender, underage, childish, adolescent, pubescent, beardless, maidenly, etc." Presumably, you are at an age when you prefer not to be associated with such terms. The adult world which lies before you, so complicated, so alluring, must seem infinitely preferable. Yet, even yesterday, your own mother or father may have labelled you with one of the above adjectives. You may even sometimes wonder if, in fact, some of these labels still apply.

The same *Thesaurus* also lists the following adjectives with the word *adulthood*: "adult, mature, of age, out of one's teens, of full or ripe age, grown-up, full grown, in full bloom, ripe, mellow, marriageable, nubile, maturescent, manly, womanly, etc." Such terms may seem infinitely preferable. But they may also seem like ideals, difficult to attain, and only partly true when applied to yourself. Perhaps you wonder why you just can't remain in an "in between" state, suspended between the innocent days of your youth and the impossible demands of adult life.

Deep down you know the truth. You must cross over the border. You must take the step. You must inherit your life. You must grow, because growth is required in order for you to survive. In a way, there are only two phases in life: youth and age. The first seems painfully short. The second unwinds like a crooked path through the wilderness of the future. You know that you must put your feet on your Way, knowing that its destination will come clear. You ask yourself: am I ready?

St. Paul defined the cultural process of growing up: "When I was a child, I spake as a child, I understood as a child, I thought as a child; but when I became a man [woman], I put away childish things." We do this because we all must survive and each must contribute his/her part and bear responsibility for his/her actions. We grow up physically. We become strong and capable of being mature. As we grow we become older. We pass from childhood to adulthood. Even then we do not cease to grow. We pass through levels of maturation and completeness until we finally reach the end of our life path. The end represents our final act of life—our death. Shakespeare put it succinctly: "Golden lads and girls all must / As chimneysweepers, come to dust."

If you feel fear in the pit of your stomach when you contemplate your future and your own preparedness to face it, you must not interpret this as a sign that you are not ready. Indeed, the adult world you are inheriting has been described by modern poets as a "wasteland" or a savage jungle. Crime, violence, over-population, poverty, starvation, genocide, political corruption, dwindling energy sources, pollution and contamination, and the fear of nuclear holocaust stalk the streets of the adult world. You can no longer hide your eyes from it. You are no longer innocent about what life is all about. The grim truth is you must find a way to survive in it.

You have the right to feel fear and to seriously question your own ability to survive as an adult. But fear and doubt won't get you to where you must go. You must begin to prepare. You look around at your life, at the ways and the means you have acquired to help you make it through. Are your "means" sufficient to the task? What are your gifts? What are your insights or convictions about the meaning of life? Are they strong enough to get you through some of those long, dark nights lurking up ahead? What are your values about your relationship to others? Will you be self-sufficient or will you be a parasite? Will you be an asset and a source of strength to your people, or will you become "part of the problem?"

Look honestly at your physical and emotional sources of support. In a year's time, will these sources still be there? Where would you go if you needed help? Is your conscience clear about asking these sources for help? What about your parents? Where do they fit into your life plan? How do they feel about continuing to support you? Do you have a job? What means do you have (or plan to have) for maintaining yourself? Are you just deluding yourself or can you live independently of your childhood home?

As you attempt to answer, you may feel justifiable confusion. Modern American culture does not provide meaningful "commencement exercises" for young men and women who are ready to leave childhood behind. Part of the difficulty has to do with the sheer surface complexity and multiplicity of modern life. There are so many definitions of what is "adult," so many roles, so many traps, so many forms of "truth." Whereas Jonathan Swift would say: "No wise man ever wished to be younger," a modern T.V. commerical's message is: "*Stay* young, *feel* young, *be* young." Many laws in the adult world seem contradictory and hypocritical—such as those which prohibit "minors" from doing what adults are doing until the minor "attains" (not earns) these adult rights at age 21.

If you really consider yourself to be prepared, then you are probably even now talking with your parents about leaving home. This communication takes many forms and is not always sweetness and light. Emotion invariably surrounds the discussion of such subjects as your personal habits or friends, your values or lack of them, your plans to get a job, your ability to be self-reliant and responsible, etc. The storms you find yourself in are not unique to your experience. Emancipation from childhood is traditionally a stormy time.

You may consider yourself ready but they (your parents) may not. They may be "pushing you out the door" when you may not feel quite ready, or they may be "holding on" more than they'd like to admit. Your passing into adulthood is almost as important an event for them as it is for you. They must let you go knowing they prepared you as best they could. Their fears for you are magnified at this time. They are looking for concrete evidence that you are ready. Once you are gone, they will turn their attention to a life without your constant presence. This in itself may be difficult for them.

The Need for Rites of Passage

Anthropologists and social scientists generally agree that modern human life is composed of seven major passages: birth, childhood to adulthood, marriage (sometimes), divorce (sometimes), midlife (reaching middle age), aging, and death. In traditional cultures, these life passages (with the possible exception of divorce), were marked by ceremony and ritual. These ceremonies of passage did not exist because of superstition or ignorance. They existed as a means of culturally guaranteeing that each person who passed from one stage to the next was ready to do so and that everyone around understood and consented to the step being taken. We see the ghost of this in the modern world. When you graduate from high school you have presumably prepared yourself to do so and are ready to step into the adult world. All your close relatives and friends have been invited to be the "witnesses" to your taking of that step.

Times have changed. If you were a young man of the Cheyenne nation, facing manhood, your rite of passage into the adult world (your graduation from high school), would have been a ceremony similar in some respects to the vision quest. From your boyhood you would have studied and prepared yourself to pass the test—to live alone for four days and nights without water or food on the sacred mountain. A respected older man, perhaps an uncle, would be your "sponsor" and teacher, helping you to prepare. Finally the long anticipated day would come. You would say goodbye to your mother and father, knowing that when you returned from the mountain you would never live as a child in their lodge. Then you would go with the medicine chief to the sacred mountain, where you would be given a buffalo robe to wrap around you if it got cold. The medicine chief would leave you there and you would remain for four days and nights, facing your childhood fears, your loneliness and boredom, your hunger and thirst, seeking a vision for yourself and for the people of your community. When your quest ended, you would return to the medicine chief who would take you to the council of elders. There you would tell the story of your vision quest and the meaning of your experience would be interpreted by the wise ones. You would receive a new name, a "medicine name," based on your vision quest. Your own private symbols or insignia would also be revealed to you. Afterward, you would not live at home. Henceforth you hunted and rode with the men and became eligible for marriage.

If you were a young woman of the Washoe nation, facing womanhood, you would have prepared for the onset of your first period from the time you were a little girl. Your mother, your mother's relatives, and the grandmothers of the village would have already instructed you in the roles, responsibilities, required skills, and privileges of womanhood. At the first sign of your period, you would withdraw from the village and be taken to a sacred fasting lodge by the medicine grandmother. For four days and three nights, without eating, you would remain in the dark lodge, a symbol of your Grandmother Earth. Late in the fourth day the medicine grandmother would summon you from within the lodge and you would run to the top of the nearby sacred mountain carrying a basket of live coals.

At the top of the mountain you would find four kindling piles of cut fir, placed at the four directions to symbolize the four dimensions of yourself, and a brightly painted stick, symbolizing your heart path. With the coals you would ignite the piles of fir, praying for strength and guidance. The straighter the smoke rose toward the sky, the better your life would be and the more blessings you would bring to your people. Then, with the painted stick in your hand, you would race down the mountain to the village, where everyone was waiting to welcome you as a woman (not a girl any more) and celebrate your "graduation" with the all-night Woman Dance. The next morning, at sunrise, everybody would go down to the stream. There you would wash yourself and emerge as a woman of the village. A great feast would be held in your honor.

The traditional ways differ markedly from modern high school commencement exercises. Nowadays, the requirements for graduation are academic. If you have demonstrated a certain degree of mastery of subject matter and have been in attendance, then you are eligible to take part in the ceremony.

The ceremony itself requires up to a month of occasional practice sessions where the candidates practice their marching, order their caps and gowns, learn to switch their tassels, and make certain they know where to sit. Formal invitations are issued to parents and significant others. Yearbooks appear— one last wistful look at "the way it was." Reservations are made for special clothing (tuxedos, gowns) and "all-night parties." Other ceremonies, some of them formal (giving of gifts, conferring of honors), some of them informal (beer busts, beach parties, cruises, pranks, etc.) precede, and sometimes follow, the commencement ceremony itself.

On the long anticipated day, the students march to solemn music while their loved ones look on. They find their place in the rows and hear speeches made by school, civic and student leaders. A religious official often gives an interdenominational prayer. The moment finally comes to graduate from the childhood world of high school. As the music sounds triumphantly, the graduates switch their tassels to the other side.

Afterward, when the graduates return home to live, it is not clear that they have become adult, nor do many of them claim to have attained adulthood. Their parents also may not be convinced any social change has taken place. Warfare may continue on such issues as keeping a clean room, being financially responsible, etc.

A similar fate has befallen other ceremonies that attend major life passages. Childbirth, having been removed from the home and the neighborhood midwives, is now ordinarily conducted in a sterile, antiseptic hospital room. The doctor and the anesthesiologist are the officials and the witnesses.

The traditional ceremony of marriage seems to have lost much of its power in this age of mutual co-habitation and divorce. The modern life passage of divorce, equally as meaningful a passage as marriage, is often celebrated in the courtroom or in a lawyer's office.

The transition into middle age, according to the commercial media, is almost a disgrace, and certainly a misfortune. Evidence indicates that most adults, when facing middle age, undergo a crisis in personal value and beliefs. No formal ceremonies exist by which adults can mark their passage into middle age and continue to find meaning in their growth.

The passage into old age, often called "retirement," has also lost its cultural meaning. It is often said that in America we have ceased to honor our elders, that we retire them, put them "out to pasture," instead of incorporating their wisdom and energy into our communities.

American ceremonies of passing into death have been aptly described by Jessica Mitford in *The American Way of Death*. American culture as a whole tends to ignore the reality of the final life passage. We don't like to be reminded. Our funeral ceremonies and grieving ceremonies do not necessarily make death meaningful for those who are dying, nor do they inspire the living.

There are many reasons why traditional life passage ceremonies have ceased to be a required part of the education of the young (or the adults). The subject is worth several books. As the human habitat became less and less a part of the natural world and more and more a part of the technological world, human beings tended to place less emphasis on their traditions. In the melting pot of Modern America, traditions have merged and become mixed even as material wealth and technological convenience became available to many. The rush toward "modernization" left thousand year old traditions in the dust of libraries and archives. Not too many people looked back to see what it was they were leaving behind.

Now it would seem that too many of us are growing up limited by fears of what is outside the artificial environment called home. We are fast becoming victims of the apparent meaninglessness of the habitat we built for our own survival. Our life passage ceremonies reflect this. The fast on the sacred mountain has "developed" into the switching of a tassel.

If you persist in feeling that you are ready to undertake a traditional life passage ceremony that has been adepted for use in the modern world, then you must also realize that you could fly to the moon and back and society at large would not confer full adult status on you—not until you were twenty-one. If you fully realize this fact, and persist in wanting to undertake the vision quest, read on.

By now you can obviously see that the vision quest is not for everyone. The idea of it appeals to certain individuals who, by virtue of their life experiences, innate intelligence, and upbringing, see the value of it. Because this ancient ceremony is no longer a means by which *all* the youth attain adulthood, the value that comes from study, preparation, and participation in a *modern* vision quest is largely personal. You could also say that society at large is benefitted, whether or not it recognizes the step you have taken.

The Vision Quest

What *is* the vision quest? On a mythical level, the vision quest is a story about a hero or heroine (in other words, *you*), who leaves everything behind, including the childhood home, and goes off alone to seek vision, insight or meaning. Alone, fasting, in a state of expanded awareness, the hero/ine endures through a long, dark night, facing the monsters of childhood. At the darkest time of the night, supernatural power confers a gift, or a boon, on the seeker. This gift is of great use to the hero/ine and to the people. The hero/ine returns to the community and "performs the vision on earth for the people to see" (Black Elk).

On the practical level, the "candidate" studies and prepares with a group of other candidates. This preparation involves reading, obtaining proper equipment, preparing to get the most from a three or four day fast, communicating with parents and friends regarding intent, learning about survival in a wilderness place, studying the weather, the terrain, the flora and fauna, and learning emergency field procedures. The candidates also study ceremony and their own personal use of symbolism. Each candidate tries to learn as much as possible about his/her value system and its relationship to modern adulthood.

Then the group travels to the wilderness for a week, during which time each candidate lives alone, without eating, for three or four days and nights, and seeks a vision in his/her own way. At the end of this period of solitude, the candidates return to "base camp" and are met by those who instructed the vision quest course. In honor of the candidates, a feast is held. Then the group returns to civilization and each vision quester goes his/her separate way until the reunion (usually a week later), attended by parents, vision questers and the course instructors. A talking stick is passed around and each person in attendance has a chance to speak from the heart.

If something within you leaps up with excitement and fear at the idea of actually taking up the challenge of the vision quest, you must remember that of every ten who respond inwardly to the challenge, only one actually steps across the line and does it. There is a great difference between wanting to go (flirting with the idea) and going ("putting your money where your mouth is"). The difference may have to do with your actual readiness to leave home.

Nowadays, people who are conditioned by the ease of modern American living tend to be appalled by the idea of going without food for three or four days, living alone on the hard ground, surrounded on all sides by dirt and "creepy crawlies." They might see the vision quest as cruel and harsh and certainly not for them. There are plenty of high school students who would consider the idea insane.

In other words, should you decide to go without food for a few days and live alone on your sacred mountain, you probably will not return to a confetti parade. At the present time, modern culture does not honor the vision quest as a valid means of formalizing your attainment of adulthood. More likely, you will return to vast incomprehension.

Self-Generated Ceremony (Doing it Your Own Way)

There are so many different kinds of vision quest ceremonies that it would be foolish to insist that there is only one, proper way. Nevertheless, there are certain basic themes or patterns common to all vision quests. Recognition and understanding of these patterns are a necessary part of your preparation.

Of great use to you will be the study of your own way, i.e., your own value or religious system—your beliefs, your symbols, your childhood teachers and experiences, and the particular methods you use to find your way through crises. You will note how important a role your parents and family life have played in your personal development and growth. You may want to investigate how your parents and their parents acquired their belief systems.

Severance—Threshold—Return

All ceremonies or rites of passage follow the same pattern. Without this pattern, the ceremony lacks meaning. If you decide to become a candidate of the vision quest, you will be led through the three steps of this classic pattern. The first step is called severance. This refers to the time of preparation during which you ready yourself to *sever* from mother, father and home, to cut the umbilical cord tied to your childhood.

The second step is called "threshold" or "the sacred world." This happens when you "step across the threshold" of your former life and its limits, when you voluntarily take on the time of testing, when you "make your last stand" on the sacred mountain and seek insight and vision for yourself and your people.

The third step is called return. Among anthropologists, it is often referred to as "incorporation" (literally, "taking on the body"). When you return, you step across the threshold of adulthood and are reunited with the world you left behind—no longer the child you formerly were. You take on new responsibilities and privileges as befits your life station.

In the modern world, these three stages are not well-defined, understood, or marked by ceremony. Therefore, it will be necessary for you to make the taking of these steps meaningful to yourself. Your instructors can help you to clearly see these three phases and to plan simple but effective actions to focus your energy and attention as you pass from one phase to the next.

PHASE ONE: SEVERANCE

Risk! Risk! Care no more
for the opinions of others,
or for those voices.
Do the hardest thing on earth for you.
Act for yourself.
Face the truth.

—Katherine Mansfield, *Journals*

Preparation for Severance

All ceremonies of passage involve some sort of hardship, risk or trial. As a vision quest candidate, you must prepare youself to meet and learn from whatever the experience holds in store. You may feel some anxiety, especially if you have never been alone in the wilderness before. Even if you are an "old hand," you will probably feel the same apprehension that the seasoned sailor feels, before a long voyage. After all, nature is unpredictable. Her power is beyond imaging. Yet, as a vision quester, you are placing yourself in her hands. By preparing yourself to surrender to whatever she has to teach you, you are confronting childhood fears. Fear itself can be a teacher of clarity and wisdom. "The body likes fear," says the legendary Don Juan. "The body likes the darkness and the wind."

In other words, it is perfectly O.K. to be scared. As the moment to depart for the wilderness approaches, you may feel like the young man who confessed to us (after he had returned from his quest) that three days before he was scheduled to leave he prayed he would break his leg. This same young man ultimately became an experienced and skilled vision quest instructor who helped hundreds of young people take the same step across the threshold of fear.

Prepare carefully and well. Your life or death may hinge on how thoroughly you take the steps that lead to severance. Those who will help guide you through these steps (this can include your parents) can best be seen in the classic definition of what true teachers are: servants who teach as Socrates did, saying, "Know thyself." They do not tell you what to do. They want you to see how you can do it yourself. They are especially interested in how you will apply what you have learned to the realities of your life experience. Utilize their counsel. You may not agree with them on all subjects, but remember that above all they seek your safety, well being, and educational growth. They cannot and will not take steps for you or follow you across the threshold.

Study the following information carefully.

Telling your Parents and Friends

If you have decided to become a vision quest candidate, the first step is to inform your parents and close friends. This step may be the most difficult to take. Many vision questers have spoken of powerful peer pressure against doing something as insane or stupid as the vision quest. You may want to be quite selective about which friends you tell. There will also be those who will understand and even respect you for your decision. They may even express the desire to participate.

From the beginning, your parents must be kept well-informed. If they are not allowed to be a part of your candidacy, they will neither be able to approve nor understand. Regardless of your current standing with them (it could be very stormy) the situation can improve if they are allowed to participate, in their own way, throughout your vision quest experience. This is an important time for them as well. Even as you leave them and your childhood behind, so they are leaving you and their active parenting behind. During the threshold time, they will be invited to attend a meeting with the other parents of vision questers in your group. They will discuss parenting issues and share their experiences. If they attend this meeting, they will be better prepared to understand you when you return.

Encourage your parents to contact the school or agency where the vision quest is conducted, to satisfy their curiosity and anxieties regarding your safety. Give them an opportunity to read this course guide. If you experience difficulty obtaining their consent, maybe your aunt, uncle, teacher, or counselor will help arbitrate.

Saying Farewell to Chidhood

When you say goodbye to your childhood, you have an opportunity to practice your own dying. Even as you say farewell to your former life as a child, so someday you will say farewell to your entire life. It is not "morbid" to think about this. If you care to look, the fact of death exists everywhere and in everyone. Have you ever watched the elderly peopole around you and wondered if you will live long enough to be as old as they? And once you have attained old age, what then? Have you ever thought about how you will die? Will you die with bitterness and feelings of defeat or will you die nobly, feeling complete?

Now is a good time to review your life, to remember fondly or with regret the events, persons, teachers, stories, loves, lovers, inspirations, defeats, lessons and dreams of your childhood. There is a kind of knowing that comes from imagining that your life is coming to a close, that you are about to leave it all behind. Look around at the people in your life. Are you ready to leave them behind, to sever from all that has come to pass between you? Is the air clear between you? Have you made your peace? What would you say to them if you were never going to see them again?

By looking at your life from this perspective, you are better able to see clearly which "childish things" you are putting away. Anyone who is dying must do the same.

Preparing for Your Own Ceremony

Preparation for the vision quest includes the learning of how different peoples vision quested and what their ceremonies were like. You will also study the symbols of various modern religions. This will help you to identify your own cultural roots and to see how they are related to other cultures. You will be provided with a basic skeleton which you will flesh out with your own values or belief system. You are not being asked to follow one way. Rather you are being asked to respond to the challenge of finding in yourself and the circle of your family, friends, teachers, and guides, the way that is uniquely your Way.

Webster defines the word "symbol" as "A visible sign or representation of an idea . . . an emblem; a representation . . . as, the lion is the *symbol* of courage; the lamb is the *symbol* of meekness or patience." What symbols are important to you? What symbols are now part of your past? Are there symbols of the adult world that you want to appropriate and use for your own? Which symbols will you take with you on your vision quest?

The following series of questions will lead you to an understanding about your relationship to the ceremony of the vision quest and an idea of what symbols you want to use. It may be that you view yourself as a "non-ceremonial" person and have little intention to "perform ceremony" on your vision quest. Do it your own way. At any rate, your life is filled with ceremonies and rituals that you unconsciously perform every day. These questions may help you to see meaning in them.

1. What is the main reason why I want to perform the ceremony?
    a. Is it a SEVERANCE? (A saying goodbye, a letting go of, a termination, a parting, a separation)
    b. Is it a THRESHOLD? (A transition, a change in significant behavior, an adjustment, a shift in role, a new job, a move, a personal transformation)
    c. Is it a RETURN? (Taking on civilization again, coming together, a re-establishing of harmony, a joining after a separation, a taking on of new responsibility, a reaffirmation)
2. What "symbolic actions" would express (mark) my intent most meaningfully?
   Examples of "symbolic actions": burying, burning, smashing, changing your name, bathing, using masks, making vows, drawing blood, cutting hair, heaping stones, chanting, rattling, dancing, singing, tying knots, untying knots, lighting candles or a fire, going nude, giving gifts, using incense, praying, kneeling, etc.
3. What symbols or objects do I want to use? This entails a review of your personal life and the objects or symbols that have power and meaning to you.
4. What, if anything, do I want to say during my ceremony—and to whom?
5. In what order do I want to do all these things I plan to do?
6. Do I want any one else there (in spirit or in person)? Do I want witnesses?
7. Where do I want to perform this ceremony and when?

Do not hesitate to get help and consultation from those who will serve as your vision quest guides and instructors. They can help you suit your intent to a ceremony which is appropriate to your value or belief system.*

The Medicine Walk

The following account might help you prepare for the vision quest. It is based on an American Plains Indian model but is adapted and synthesized for modern use.

The medicine walk is a day's journey upon the face of the earth. As a ceremony of preparation for the vision quest, the medicine walk is a mirror in which signs and symbols of your inward journey are reflected. The walk is a highly distilled form of the threshold phase of the vision quest.

During the medicine walk, certain spirits or powers of nature, which typify the nature of your own "medicine power," are attracted by you and reveal themselves to you. With your help, they weave an allegorical or symbolic story which indicates future life direction, your inherent gifts, and the kinds of ceremonies that you might perform during the vision quest.

The medicine walk is customarily made one month before the actual vision quest commences. You prepare the night before by packing an emergency kit and a few other items you might need for a day's journey. Remember to carry water. Inform someone of the location and duration of your walk—in case you don't return. Get a good night's rest. An important dream may arise on this night.

You begin at sunrise and you walk in some natural place. If you must drive, try to get there before dawn. No food is taken on this day—until after the sun has set. Set forth on a wandering, "intuitive" course, without consciously attempting to reach any goal. As you wander, keep your eyes open. Be aware if you are feeling "drawn" in any direction or to any thing. Listen to and sense the consciousness of all that is around you.

At a certain moment on your walk, you will find one thing—a symbol of meaning and importance to you. This one thing must return with you and become a symbol of your vision quest.

The beginning and the end (the "thresholds") of your medicine walk must be marked by ceremony. The ceremony that you perform at these points may be elaborate or simple, but it must involve your focused attention and your gratitude to your Mother Earth for her teaching and safe-keeping.

---

*The above "process actions" are derived from an unpublished manuscript, *Rites of Passage for Our Time*, by Virginia H. Hine (see her examples of self-initiated ceremony in this volume).

It is wise to keep a journal account of your medicine walk and to be familiar with its basic plot—for it is a kind of "life story" and you are its hero/ine. Like your life, this story has a beginning and an end. Be prepared to share this adventure with those who will help you with your preparation for the vision quest. They may be able to point out salient features of the story you may have overlooked or forgotten.

The medicine walk, like the vision quest, is an exercise of balance and attunement. It is not a challenging of the elements or heights nor is it an endurance contest. The medicine walker maintains connection with the beauty of life and the reality of death as both are reflected by the world of nature.

Pay special attention to loved ones and friends who call strongly to you as you walk. Some of these individuals may have already died. Indeed, some of those who call to you are your "spirit guides"—teachers, heroes, and helpers, who will watch as you grow and help to strengthen the circle of your purpose.

PHASE TWO: THE THRESHOLD

'Would you like to have some Medicine Power?' Frog asked.

'Medicine Power? Me?' asked little Mouse. 'Yes, yes! If it is possible.'

'Then crouch as Low as you Can, and then Jump as High as you are Able! You will have your Medicine!' Frog said.

Little Mouse did as he was Instructed. He crouched as Low as he Could and Jumped. And when he did, his Eyes Saw the Sacred Mountains.

Little Mouse could hardly Believe his Eyes. But there they were! But then he Fell Back to Earth, and he Landed in the River!

Little Mouse became Frightened and Scrambled back to the Bank. He was wet and Frightened nearly to Death.

'You have Tricked me!' little Mouse Screamed at the Frog.

'Wait,' said the Frog. 'You are not Harmed. Do not let your Fear and Anger Blind you. What did you See?'

'I,' Mouse stammered, 'I, I Saw the Sacred Mountains!'

'And you have a New Name!' Frog said, 'It is Jumping Mouse.'

—Hyemeyohsts Storm, *Seven Arrows*

The Threshold World

When you cross over into the threshold world, you will enter a time/space continuum where there will be nobody else to define your sense of reality for you. Nature will teach you, care for you, and serve as a mirror of your own awareness. William Bridges calls this threshold time "the fallow chaos." In this world you will be alone and vulnerable to insight and illumination. The threshold is comparable to the time when the seed detaches from the mother plant and rides the winds that carry it to birth.

Classic anthropology sometimes uses the French word, *marge* (margin) or the Latin word, *liminal* (limit) instead of the English word, threshold. At this phase of the vision quest, the candidate encounters the margin or "limit" of him/her self and formally steps beyond into the unknown. You have come as far as you can with your childhood life. You are at the limit of its growth. Now it is time to step across the "child boundary" and enter the passage to the boundary of a new country marked "adult."

In almost all cultures and religions, the threshold is a "sacred world." Your "spirit" or "soul" is awake and aware and is capable of communicating with other spirits, powers, animals, other humans living or dead, God, or the Great Spirit of the Universe. For thousands of years, ceremony enabled our ancestors to orient and ground themselves to the sacred world of the threshold, making it possible to establish a physical, emotional, and spiritual relationship with it.

You are offered ten components to be used as you see fit to make your own ceremonies as you pass through the threshold world. These ten basic elements (with the probable exception of the "Buddy System") are found in rites of passage throughout the human world and are particularly associated with the vision quest. Study them; combine them; change them to suit your own needs.

1. Finding Your Place on the Earth

You are given one day, from the rising to the setting of the sun, to find a "place of power" where you will stay during the threshold time. This usually happens the day before you go out alone. You will have a companion, a buddy, who will be your unseen partner during the time you are alone. Your buddy will be close enough to help you if you are in trouble and you will serve in the same capacity for him/her (see "The Stonepile"). The two of you will find separate places of power situated within walking distance of each other. This is sometimes a little difficult and requires friendly, responsible coordination between the two of you.

There is no one way to find your place. You might consider it as having always been there, waiting for you. Perhaps you will hear it calling to you. Signs may lead you there. On the other hand, your discovery of it might be quite by accident. When you reach the place, relax and spend some time there. Consider it closely. Does it have all the prerequisites for your safety and well-being? Does it "feel" good to be there? If you were a warrior fighting your last battle, would you choose to make your "last stand" here?

There are many different kinds of power places. Some are high and exposed. Some are low and protected. Usually, there is something distinctive about them—a cliff, a face in a boulder, a special tree, a strangely cleared area, a spring, a cave, or a hollow. Certain survival considerations must also be a part of your search. Responsibility to others begins with your ability to take care of yourself and not pose a threat or unnecessary risk to your buddy or to base camp personnel. Aside from responsibility to your buddy, other factors in your choice of a power place are possible exposure to weather, distance from base camp, and accessibility of your place to anything but a mountain goat.

There is an old formula to the vision quest that goes: "The student finds his/her place of power even as he/she finds her place in life." Watch yourself as you search for, and then find, *your* place. Then accept what has been given you.

2. The Stonepile ("Buddy System")

The buddy system requires each of two partners to be responsible for the other during the threshold time. Though they never see each other (unless an emergency arises), they check on each other's condition each day by visiting a stonepile that they erect in a prominent place midway between their respective places. There they leave a sign that they are all right. If a sign is not left at the appointed time and place, the other buddy must go and find out what, if anything, is wrong. If the buddy cannot be found, base camp is notified.

The buddy system is not foolproof. Should there be an accident, its discovery could possibly take up to 36 hours. This is one of the basic risks of the vision quest. It is impossible to remove this risk if your intention is to be alone. Any fear that you may feel regarding this risk must be honored and respected by the impeccability of your performance as a buddy.

The stonepile is a symbol of love and caring for our people. Though we are born and die alone, our life is interconnected with many others, and often what we do affects them: "No man is an island entire of itself." The stones are erected in a place that is easy to find.

3. The Threshold

The time comes when you leave everyone else behind, including your buddy, and face the "sacred world" of the threshold time. All around you will be the features of the natural world, the "faces of the Great Mother." At this moment you will become aware of your loneliness, your seeming insignificance in the immensity of the cosmos, and the thunder of silence. You are at the turning point. Either you can return to base camp (and not accept the challenge) or you can proceed into the unknown future. You are at a limit, at the margin of your childhood. You stand at a major threshold of your life.

The fear or loneliness that you might feel at this moment is a significant adult emotion. You may feel similar emotions at the time of your death. Traditional peoples always performed a simple celebration or ceremony at this point. They constructed a visible sign or symbol of the threshold or boundary they were stepping across. Sometimes it was a line of stones, with a door left open in the middle (closed again after they stepped through); sometimes it was a branch, broken in the middle in order to step through, then closed again. Sometimes they said a prayer to the Great Spirit or God and left an offering there: a piece of their baby clothing, a lock of hair, a few drops of blood, etc. Almost always, they asked for divine guidance and aid as they took this significant step across the threshold.

When you have celebrated your crossing of the boundary, you have entered the "passage" that is meant by the term, *rites of passage.* Some ancient peoples considered this passage to be symbolic of *the journey toward rebirth of the spirit of a human being who has just died.* As you turn your back on your childhood days and begin walking toward your place of power, you are symbolically being carried along in the current of the river of life, the same river that flows in your veins. The river carries you to the place where you will conduct your lonely vigil. There you, your ancestors, and all those who you call on to join you, will await your rebirth into a new life, the life of adulthood.

4. The Fast

Fasting is a traditional act of self-empowerment. The practice of fasting is found in every belief system in the world. In more modern terms, fasting is a natural way to "get high." The hollow sensation you feel in the pit of your being is more than physical hunger. You become aware of a vast "spiritual" hunger within you. You feel at one with all those who have already walked the path of the vision quest before you.

Fasting does no harm to a person who is prepared and who has dedicated the fast to some purpose other than personal weight loss. Fasts up to a week long are possible and even medically beneficial to many individuals who might not ever consider it. Judging from its distinguished history among the peoples of the world, fasting is neither foolish nor weird. Nor is it a form of masochism or self-abuse. Fasting is a time-honored tool, a means of attaining clarity.

The physical effects of a fast are usually far less upsetting than the psychological effects. With no meals to organize your day, you are going without modern life's most common security blanket. You will find out how much of physical hunger is really just social programming. Medically speaking, most persons can go for several weeks without food—and live— but only a few days without water. A belly full of water allays hunger, and is the antidote to a number of fast-related sensations.

The second day of a fast is often the hardest. You may feel weak, dizzy, and experience nausea or vertigo. These symptoms are rarely strong. Most people report feelings of weakness or tiredness which are overcome by modest physical exertion. By the third day, physical hunger seems of less importance. The stomach's cry for food becomes feelings of loneliness and desire to be filled with insight and illumination.

Should you have further concerns regarding your ability to fast for three or four days and nights (because of your physical or psychological makeup) be sure to consult with your parents, your physician, and your vision quest instructors.

5. *The Name You Give Yourself*

The vision quest is traditionally a time when a "medicine name," i.e., a name descriptive of the nature and abilities of a person, is acquired or conferred. This name is carried through life, either as a secret, or as an "adult" name. Such names would reflect a person's personal "myth" or story about him/herself. With this name the individual lives well and dies nobly.

At birth, your parents gave you a name. Now, by virtue of your passage, you are entitled to name yourself, or to be given a name by your Mother Nature. The ancients believed that nature communicated with them via animals, birds, plants, insects, the wind, the stars, and other agencies or creatures. LISTEN and WATCH. A frog may tell you your name, or a raven, or an ant. Perhaps the still, small voice inside all human beings (spirit guide, inner light, God, Great Spirit) knows your name and will tell it to you on your vision quest.

If, despite your attempts, you do not obtain a name, you must not consider yourself unworthy or bad of hearing. You are being taught the virtue of patience. As a well-known Christian hero once said: "Seek and ye shall find." Keep seeking until the perfection and quality of your search defines a name for you. Then others will honor your name though it never is spoken.

6. *Listening with an Intuitive Ear*

Being able to listen to the earth around us is an ancient practice which has largely been lost to humans living in the modern world. Cut off from our natural habitat, aided by the miracles of modern technology, we have developed alternate methods of communication. Despite our miraculous artificial habits of communication, we tend to forget the ancient truth that all things are alive, that they are repositories of consciousness and intelligence, and that human beings have access to these repositories.

Being able to listen—to the wind, for example—has little to do with your ears. It has to do with being able to hear an inner voice which all too often modern humans tend to denigrate or ignore. Many of us have been taught from childhood to doubt what we cannot directly sense and to devalue intuitive voices as nonimportant or of dubious origin. Too many of us learned to underestimate ourselves and the seemingly limitless capacity of our minds to perceive, create, and know.

The wind speaks. If you do not believe this, ask it a question. You must hold your mind steadily on the subject at hand and you must be willing to accept the answer, even if the answer is "what I already know." In the deepest sense, it is true that the wind, the sun, or God himself cannot tell us anything about human life and destiny that we do not already *know*. Look at it this way. You can hear the wind even if your ears are stuffed with cotton. Traditional sorcerers and medicine teachers would be quick to point out that any answer you get should be attributed to the wind, and not to yourself.

It would be helpful to keep in mind that our ancestors held all things in Nature to be sacred. By "sacred" they meant that everything created by the Great Spirit had the Great Spirit in it. Thus they honored all forms and manifestations of nature. All the plants and animals were brothers and sisters and lived cooperatively together for the welfare and survival of all. Awareness of the old ways of your ancestors may help you to listen with an intuitive ear to what Mother Nature has to tell you.

7. Dreaming

Dreams of exceptional power and clarity may occur during your participation in the vision quest. Traditionally, dreams of the threshold period were considered to be sacred. It is important to be attentive and to record your dreams, for their wisdom has much to do with how you grow and change.

Some dreams contain transformational power. In such dreams, the meaning is apparent to the dreamer. There is an unmistakable directive, a definite sign. Other dreams seem less clear, or more complicated, with shifting, vague symbols. Yet they cling heavily to the waking consciousness. Some dreams are downright disturbing; others are profane or seemingly inconsequential. All forms of dreaming (including fantasies, daydreams and wool gatherings) compose a tapestry into which are woven the currents, plots, symbols, and colors of your picture of yourself. The dreams of your vision quest are maps upon which are inscribed the trails through the terrain of your life.

One way to read a dream map is to place yourself as the dreamer in each detail of the dream: "And then the old man (of me) walked across the bridge (of me) that was stretched across the chasm (of me) and embraced the little boy (of me) while the wind (of me) rose up and tore away the bridge (of me) and the old man (of me) held tight to the little boy (of me)."

Day dreams may arise in which you are the "star" or "hero/ine" and you play a super-human or uncharacteristic role as a hero/ine or savior. Do not discourage such dreaming, for it is the stuff of human growth. Like all dreams, however, these kinds of dreams are to be held and learned from, and then let go. If a particular dream returns unbidden again and again, then you can begin to see a trail that leads into the realities of your life. If the trail is of benefit to your people and to Mother Earth, it could be a trail worth walking.

You may wish to use elements of particular dreams within your vision quest ceremony. In so doing, you formally bring the dream into your sense of reality and act at least part of it out. You also bring into your perceived world of the present the wisdom from the dreamtime of human beginnings.

8. Fire

In almost every mythology, fire is represented as belonging to the gods, and was either given as a gift to humans or stolen by a Promethean hero. Truly, the ability to make fire is a god-like attribute, and defines humans as distinct from other animals. As you sit alone in the darkness, sensing the movements of plant, animal and insect life, you will know yourself to be both animal and a special kind of animal: a human being.

On the Sun Dance medicine wheel, fire is in the east, where Grandfather Sun rises at dawn to bring light and life. Fire, then, is symbolic of birth. Paradoxically, in Hindu thought, fire is Shiva, the Destroyer, symbolic of death and destruction. The very fire that burns in our veins consumes us—and so it is with all things in the universe. The knowing of this somehow enhances the living of our lives.

Should you feel the need to perform a ceremony with fire, you must be aware that there may be rules and restrictions regarding the gathering of firewood or the lighting of fires. In many of the national parks, fires may not be set except in certain designated areas. If you are not in a restricted area, then your fire must be arranged in such a way as to minimize any fire hazard. There is no need to build a big fire. Gather fuel sparingly, and from separate areas. You do not need logs. A small bundle of dead and down wood will suffice for your purpose—which is to build a *small* fire for only one person.

When you leave your place, there should be no sign that a fire was ever built there. Widely scatter your hearth stones and re-cycle the wood you never used. Seal up the ashes in the fire pit with the same soil you scooped out for the pit. Make sure the ashes are dead. Give some of your water back to the coals, in appreciation for the fire. Pray that the rains will come soon and erase any indication that you were ever there.

9. The Purpose Circle

The most ancient and widely-used vision quest symbol is the Purpose Circle, or "Circle of the Self." Depending on culture and tradition, this simple yet sophisticated symbol has been variously called the Sacred Enclosure (Australian Aborigine), the Medicine Wheel (American Indian), the Sun Dance Wheel (American Plains Indian), the Round Table (Anglo-European), the Cross (Judeo-Christian), the Mandala (Hindu/Buddhist), and the Kiva (American Hopi Indian), to name a few. Usually, this circle is alligned to the four directions, or powers, as represented by the four cardinal points of the compass. These four directions represent the four seasons, the four ages of man, the four quadrants of the heavens, the four dimensions, etc. The four directions circle, like the Judeo-Christian cross and the Hindu mandala, is a whole, balanced, symbolic representation of the psyche, or self, in harmonious relationship to the cosmos. The Purpose Circle is brought to life when the vision quester builds and then takes possession of it.

Whenever possible, the circle is made by first laying the north stone and the south stone in line with the North Star. If the night is cloudy, approximations will suffice. But the building of the circle is a meaningless gesture unless you plan to take possession of it. By entering and "owning" your Purpose Circle or Circle of the Self, you enter the passage that leads through the long, dark night to your rebirth at dawn. You walk this passage alone, and always will. Yet others will be with you in spirit. Teachers, parents, loved ones, ancestors, gather around you in a "witness circle." To celebrate their presence in your life to come, you will incorporate them into your Purpose Circle. They will stand with you in your hour of need as you "cry for a vision" for yourself and for your people.

The Purpose Circle is built near your place of power. It is composed of stones or material from that place. Other symbolic objects, such as those you brought from home or your medicine walk, may be added. Build the circle with care. Think about what you are doing. It is best to work slowly, feeling the weight of your fast, sensing yourself to be in harmony with your environment. The symbol you are building is a universal symbol of the unity of all beings. It will enclose you, protect you, and awaken you. As a symbol of your purpose, it will follow you through the wilderness of your life. The circle is usually built on the last day of the threshold period, and is entered at sunset of that day. The candidate remains in the circle throughout the night and tries to stay awake so as not to miss insights or illuminations that may come.

Your vision quest instructors will be pleased to consult with you regarding the many ways in which you can use your Purpose Circle as a ceremonial tool. Once the circle is built, it becomes a focal point, a ring of attraction or power, that you cannot ignore. Hence, the circle is built with the sole intention to *occupy* it and to use it in a ceremonial fashion.

The people of the Sioux nation called the vision quest the *hanblecheyapi*, or "lament for a vision." Within his power circle the "lamenter" or vision quester "walked to the four corners of the earth" and cried the following cry: "O Great Spirit, be merciful to me, that my people may live." The Sioux way teaches us much about the meaning of the Purpose Circle and the intent of the prayer or cry for a vision. We do not leave our childhood behind to seek a vision merely for ourselves. If, as adults, we have nothing to bring back for the wellbeing of our people, then we have no reason to vision quest, or claim to be adults.

The act of crying for a vision has no specified form. You can scream or you can pray quietly from the heart. Songs, chants, dances, silence, tears—all are prayers. The Being or Powers to whom you address your prayers may be considered to be inside your Purpose Circle, or outside it, or both. Indeed, you will begin to see that there is really no circumference to your circle, no inside or outside. The six directions (east, south, west, north, earthward, and skyward) which make your circle like a sphere or gyroscope, are symbolic inlets or outlets through which power and influence flow back and forth unimpeded.

If your parents have taken an interest in your vision quest and have committed themselves to attending the parent meetings, then they are probably meeting the same night you enter your Purpose Circle (see APPENDIX: Note to Parents). From your circle, you will remember them, love them, and pray for them, no longer as their child, but as a mature individual who knows them well and respects them for giving nearly 20 years of their life to you. You may want to ask that your friendship with them will grow as they also pass through the life changes that await them.

10. *Emergence (Giving Birth to Yourself)*

During that last night, as you stand watch and cry for a vision, you will symbolically pass through the "contraction field" of your own birthing. As the first light of dawn reaches your eyes, you will realize that the passage from childhood is ending. Soon you will emerge into a world that demands the attributes of maturity from you. You have come to another limit, or boundary—the boundary of adulthood.

When you step out of the circle of your purpose, you will emerge from the threshold world as though you were newly born. But this time you are not innocent, naked or helpless. This time you are walking tall and carrying yourself with balance and purpose. Before you leave your circle, you must ask yourself a very important question: "For what purpose am I entering this new world?" If your answer is not yet clear, allow it to be unclear. What feelings do you feel? What emotions? If you did not experience the illumination and insight you hoped to gain, remember that much of what you have done comes to you after you return. A seed has been sown in you—a knowing about yourself that cannot be forgotten.

As you cross the new threshold, you may want to mark it with another simple ceremony, to thank Mother Nature for keeping you safe, for teaching you, and to offer prayers for her continued wellbeing and the wellbeing of your place of power. Perhaps it will be a place, as Don Juan says, "where you will come in your dreaming," where you will make your "last stand." One thing you must do is erase every sign of your stay there, with the possible exception of your Purpose Circle. This monument to your vision quest can be preserved for a long time to come by removing all but the stones representing the four directions, and a stone representing your self at the center.

The act of shouldering your pack symbolizes the taking on of new privileges and responsibilites. Survey the scene once more for any sign of yourself you may have left behind. As you head for a stonepile meeting with your buddy, you acknowledge that your people wait for you. They will see the purpose dancing in your eyes. Now is the time to remember how much you love them.

PHASE THREE: THE RETURN

I think I have told you, but if I have not, you must have understood, that a man who has a vision is not able to use the power of it until after he has performed the vision on earth for the people to see.

—Black Elk, *Black Elk Speaks*

The Return Home

Meeting the group. Your vision quest guides and instructors did not follow you across the threshold. Though they cared for you from a distance and sought your safety and wellbeing, they have gone about their own business. Now you must come into the body of their company and again be one of the group. At this time a ceremony may be performed which welcomes you back into the "secular" world of basecamp.

The give-away. The next event in your return is the symbolic enactment of your willingness to share your vision, whatever it might have been. Some people bring back a tiny stone or a twisted piece of wood or something they have made to give away to others. Some bring back a song or special words, poems, etc. However you conceive it, try to plan and enact a personal ceremony of giving, for it is dangerous to receive illumination without channeling it to others. You may feel neither powerful nor holy. You may feel completely bushed. It is the *willingness* to be a channel, to give away, that matters.

Eating (Communion). While you were alone, you did not eat. Now that you are together with the others, there is an opportunity to eat. It is fitting that those who have vision quested should share a simple meal together while they feel the onrush of high spirits that is typical of basecamp after the return. Some feel little hunger. Others are ravenous. It is good to eat at least a little, to share with the others the bounty of the earth. Beware of eating too much when your stomach is in a shrunken condition.

Farewell to the sacred mountains. The time comes to consciously turn your back on the sacred mountains, to let go, finally, knowing that they will always be there waiting. It helps to tell yourself that you will never see them again—to make the break final and complete. Then they will haunt you more powerfully. Say to them what you need to say.

Washing away the dust of the Sacred World. By symbolically washing hands, feet, hair, or entire body, you can effectively signify your resolution to return and not to linger in the threshold world. This ceremony is enhanced by the changing of clothes.

Entering a motor vehicle. An automobile is not only a small, enclosed, necessarily social space, but it is a dangerous machine. It is one of the deadlier symbols of the world of modern civilization that you return to. Be aware (on a deliberately conscious level) that you are entering it, trusting it, submitting to its environment, and/or driving it. Once you enter it, there is no turning back. You are committed to the long road home, to the return.

Drivers must pay particular attention to the "vehicle threshold." Driving takes a completely different set of perceptions and reactions than those of Mother Nature. You must pay attention to the matters of driving safely.

Entering buildings, encountering strangers, buying things, eating. One fact becomes quite apparent on the journey home. No one else in the world at large seems to know or care about what you have just done. Everyone is scurrying about, intent on their own quest. All the symbols of civilization come rushing back: advertising, places to dine or sleep, drugstores, freeways, subdivisions, thousands upon thousands of cars, lights, and sounds.

How easy it becomes to overload, to eat too much, to want too much (because everything is offered), to obey the call of old addictions, to buy what isn't needed, etc. A balanced vision quester is wary of the plenitude but does not fall into deep remorse if he/she makes a mistake. You must not fall into the trap of feeling disgust at everything civilized. Loved ones, friends, and family live in this world. Though it seems "artificial," it has thus far been the source of your livelihood. The trail leads into it, to where the vision waits to be "demonstrated" for the people to see.

Home. The threshold of your home represents another important landmark in your return. Try to give yourself at least 24 hours before you tie into the world outside. Kick back. Give yourself time to remember, to integrate, to reconnect with your immediate family, to orient yourself to your surroundings. Though it all looks the same, you are now seeing it with the eyes of a person who has demonstrated his/her readiness to enter adulthood. Which symbols around you are really important to you?

Your parents and other family members may or may not be interested. If they have been active in the parent meetings, then they will want to hear about your adventures. Perhaps they will be curious to see if any changes have been wrought in you by your experiences. Of course, it is up to you as to how you deal with their interest, curiosity, and pride.

This is a good time to speak with your parents about taking on new responsibilities and accepting new privileges. In this way you and they mark a significant shift in your life status. It could very well be that in exchange for certain privileges, it will be necessary for you to demonstrate your readiness to undertake new responsibilities. At any rate, you are probably not about to leave home, at least for a while. If your life situation is like that of most American young adults, it will be necessary for you to accept the reality of your domestic existence until you are truly on your own. This means making mature judgments regarding your behavior within the all-so-familiar procedures and regulations of home life. If you are determined to "perform your vision on earth for the people to see," then you must first perform this vision for the people who are closest to you, your childhood family. But this family no longer belongs to your childhood. Your years as an "adult" in the family have begun, regardless of your legal status.

The reunion. Within two weeks of the return, a vision quest course reunion will be held. You may be asked to fast during that day, in remembrance of your vision quest experience. The reunion will give you an opportunity to be with the group again and to see the experience in retrospect.

Your parents will also be invited to attend. Slide pictures of the wilderness phase of the course will be shown. The meeting will also include a council circle. A "talking stick" will be passed around and each person in attendance will be given a chance to speak. Then you will break your fast by sharing a pot luck feast with the others.

The reunion is merely another step taken in a reincorporation ("taking on the body of your world") process that can extend for many months after your return from the threshold. At the reunion you will have a chance to ask your vision quest instructors for further information about other courses, classes, programs, experiences, offered in your community which are related to the vision quest, and which provide you with the chance to further explore feelings or emotions which have arisen since you returned.

Revisiting your place of power. Within a year of your return, you must go back to your place of power. This is the last formal step of the return, and with this visit, your vision quest ceremony officially ends.

This return to your power place is undertaken on your own initiative and is not a group activity or a party. As a pilgrim you go alone to your place, performing whatever ceremony seems appropriate to your life at that time.

This last step can be a considerable undertaking. Nevertheless, it is important that you demonstrate to yourself that you have acquired self-reliance, independence, and the maturity necessary to make this visit. It may be that another vision quester from your group will buddy up with you and the two of you can go together. No matter how you get there, or with who, you must go *alone* to your power place and stay there for at least one night. When you leave your place, make certain, as you did before, that you have left no evidence of your stay there—with the possible exception of the cardinal stones of your purpose circle.

The Trail Ahead

Usually, by the time of the reunion, the flush of strength and insight that is a by-product of the vision quest experience has worn off and you are facing your future and all its demands without rose colored glasses. By this time there have been numerous opportunities to "test yourself" against the "monsters" of the vision quest of your life. You might be feeling defeated, fearing that you have fallen back into childish habits of doing or being. This, of course, is to be expected. No one can stay "high" forever. Nor can you expect a free ride. As you learned from the vision quest experience, insight and illumination are won by endurance and hard work. There was no easy path through those days and nights of the threshold.

Wisdom tells us that we experience life in rhythms of high and low, that the ascent of every mountain top is followed by a descent, that highs and lows are interdependent and absolutely necessary for the growth of the self. Every spiritual tradition reminds us of the inevitability, even the *necessity,* of the darkness that follows illumination. The yogi teaches his disciples to expect depression when he says: "After Samadhi, we sweep the floor." One can go around with his head in the clouds, but that does not keep the dust from seeping in through the cracks. Dreams and visions will not sweep your floor.

The true measure of the vision of a man or a woman is time. "Flash in the pans" come and go. They expend their energy in one great burst and then they burn out. Many of these burnouts inhabit the bars and drug stores of our time. Likewise, others burn themselves up in remorse or self-disgust because they keep falling short of an impossible goal they have set for themselves. The trail ahead can be taken at your own speed. You don't have to have everything figured out. Your ability to pursue your vision for your life does not depend on how fast you are or how resolved your picture of the universe is. What *does* matter is your ability to persevere. The threshold time was a test of your ability to persevere.

Another measure of the vision of a man or woman is balance. This balance can be expressed in several ways. One way is to accept, and learn from, the highs and lows of your life and to see them as the necessary rhythms of living. Another way is to live in harmony with the natural world, your Mother Earth. Another way is to live in balance with the "smorgasbord" of modern living. Another is to survive, not as a *victim,* but as a *learner.*

If you are certain, deep inside, that you have a vision "to demonstrate on earth for the people to see," then you will not reject the trail that lies ahead. Indeed, it is *your* trail. You have chosen it. You have also learned that you walk this trail alone. Though others may accompany you, in the end, they must be left behind. Therefore, in the deepest sense, you seek clarification, not self-validation. Many times in the years ahead it will be necessary to hold to your vision and continue despite what others are saying.

If you are being assailed by doubts, consider that these are the same doubts that have confronted all those who went before you, including all the saints and hero/ines. Your first challenge is to survive these doubts. In the classic vision quest story of "Jumping Mouse," the hero returns to the world of mice and faces scorn, ridicule, and disbelief. All his old friends think he is crazy and weird. He tries to be accepted again and goes back to living his life among them, as though he were just another mouse. But he is haunted by the memory of the sacred mountains. He can no longer be satisfied with the old life. He finally sets forth on his inward journey to find them. The journey is long and fraught with peril. He does not go unscathed. Before he reaches his destination, Jumping Mouse has given away his two eyes so that his people can be healed.

Consider what you must give away—before you reach the shining, sacred mountains. The crucial question of your life is: Am I ready to begin this, the most perilous of vision quests? Ask your heart.

APPENDIX

A Note to Parents

The enrollment of your son/daughter in the vision quest course is a sign that he/she is serious about the future and his/her impending emancipation from the home you have provided for so many years. In a true sense, the decision to participate in the vision quest is a measurement of your ability as parents to prepare your child for maturity. Without your nurturing and guidance, your child might not have contemplated living alone for three or four days and nights and testing him/herself in this way. You might want to take a bow.

Nevertheless, you may experience some justifiable anxiety regarding this venture, particularly if it is announced "from out of the blue" and you are asked to give your consent to it. You may have a multitude of questions that need answers. You may want to participate in some way. Certain fears may require that you take a cautious approach to the question of participation.

It is important that you satisfy any fears that you entertain and obtain answers to your questions. A certain amount of risk is involved. The amount and extent of that risk must be viewed clearly. Experience with over a thousand modern vision questing youth has shown that they are remarkably careful about their own safety and the safety of their buddy while they are fasting and living alone. Not a single one sustained a serious injury.

There is, of course, always the exception. The amount and nature of the risk in a vision quest course depends not only on the level of preparedness of your son/daughter, but on the competence and skill of the course and its instructors. Hence, you might find it beneficial to discuss any fears or questions with those who will be responsible for the safety of your son/ daughter in the field. Furthermore, you might want to attend some of the course meetings to satisfy your curiosity. Your participation can only enhance your understanding of the course and your involvement with your son/ daughter as he/she undertakes the three phases of the course experience.

Most vision quest courses provide for parents of vision questers to meet twice during the course. The first time they meet together is when their sons/ daughters are in the last day or night of their threshold trial. While their children are alone and hungry on their "vision mountain," the parents meet together to send love to their children and to share their own experiences as parents. This meeting is usually facilitated by a vision quest course instructor or a parent whose son/daughter has already participated in the vision quest.

The second meeting takes place at the Reunion, when the students and parents all meet together for a council and a pot luck feast. The talking stick is passed from person to person. Each is encouraged to speak his/her heart.

Your involvement as a parent depends on a variety of factors, including your own schedule. Our experience has shown that the more interested the parents become, the more benefits are accrued by the entire family. You may find yourself being drawn into the flurry of activity that precedes the threshold phase, as your son/daughter prepares for the time of aloneness and fasting. When your son/daughter returns, you will probably be there to welcome him/ her back and to help them face the demands of their future.

Many parents have given new privileges and responsibilities to their son/ daughter upon completion of the vision quest course. Many have seen it as an important step towards maturity and expect more mature attitudes and behavior. This is a reasonable expectation, although allowances might be made for a certain amount of slipping into old habits. As long as he/she remains in the same environment it may be difficult to make dramatic changes in his/her behavior. In more traditional societies, life passage ceremonies like the vision quest marked the time when the child no longer lived at home. The returning young man or woman faced the realities of living according to a new set of personal and social roles.

The return is a good time to talk with your son/daughter. It is a good time to talk about when and how he/she will actually leave home and start life as an adult. It is a good time to express love and other feelings that have wanted to come forth. It helps to realize that you, as parents, will soon relinquish the role of full-time parents and that there will be an empty bedroom in the house.

Do not expect a miracle or a thorough transformation of character. Storms that existed before the vision quest may also break afterward. These storms may not be calmed until the severance process is complete and your son/ daughter is living elsewhere. The vision quest, however, may bring insight into why these storms exist and how their force might be mitigated. The person who returns to you from the sacred mountains of Mother Earth is more open and vulnerable to you, and certainly more aware of the important part you have played in his/her growth into maturity. Most youth returning from the vision quest speak of feeling great love and respect for their parents and for the home which they provided.

Even as your son/daughter participates in the vision quest you might take the opportunity to reconnect with your own "vision." There was a time when you were not a parent. Did your sense of what life held for you include other ingredients than parenthood? Take a moment to reflect on the meaning and direction of your life, irrespective of your role as a parent.

Returning Early from the Threshold Time

If you return before the threshold time is over—what does this mean? Does it mean you have failed? On the contrary, there is no success or failure in the self-measurement of the vision quest. Because of your experiences you may have attained a greater clarity in terms of your picture of yourself than those who do not return early. In fact, it may be that you returned at precisely the right moment in order to survive and continue your growth.

There are many good reasons for returning early. Foremost among these reasons is your own personal assessment of your health, mental condition and spiritual wellbeing. Don't allow yourself to be caught in the trap of being afraid to terminate what you set out to do if your own self-concept says otherwise. Many have spoken of the fear that others might "look down on them" if they came back early. Many adults have also expressed this fear. Remember that it takes courage to act against peer pressure. This is not the first or only time that you will have to face this fear.

Your instructors will welcome you back and help you define clearly to yourself and to others why you decided to return, and what lessons you have learned through participating in this experience.

REFERENCES

Andrews, L. 1981. *Medicine woman.* New York: Harper and Row.
Bridges, W. 1980. *Transitions: making sense of life's changes.* Boston: Addison-Wesley.
Brown, J. E. 1971. *The sacred pipe: Black Elk's account of the seven rites of the Oglala Sioux.* New York: Penguin Books.
Brown, V. 1974. *Voices of the earth and sky.* Happy Camp, Cal.: Naturegraph.
Cameron, A. 1981. *Daughters of Copper Woman.* Vancouver, B.C.: Gang Press.
Campbell, J. 1968. *Hero with a thousand faces.* Princeton: Princeton Univ. Press.
Castaneda, C. 1971. *A separate reality.* New York: Simon & Schuster.
———. 1972. *Journey to Ixtlan.* New York: Simon & Schuster.
———. 1975. *Tales of power.* New York: Simon & Schuster.

Foster, S. and Little, M. 1987. *The book of the vision quest.* Englewood Cliffs, New Jersey: Prentice Hall.

———. 1986. *The roaring of the sacred river: Modern apprenticeship to an ancient ceremony of passage.* Big Pine: Rites of Passage Press.

Gennep, A. van. 1960. *The rites of passage.* Chicago: University of Chicago Press.

Harner, M. 1980. *The way of the shaman.* New York: Harper & Row.

Jung, C. G. 1964. *Man and his symbols.* New York: Doubleday.

La Chapelle, D. 1981. *Earth wisdom.* Silverton, Colo.: Finn Hill Arts.

Pinkson, T. 1976. *A quest for vision.* Novato, CA.: Free Person Press.

Salerno, N., and Vanderburgh, R. 1980. *Shaman's daughter.* New York: Dell.

Storm, H. 1972. *Seven arrows.* New York: Harper & Row.

Waters, F. 1972. *The man who killed the deer.* Athens, Ohio: Swallow.

Reprinted from *A Vision Quest Handbook for Youth,* with permission of Rites of Passage Press, Box 55, Big Pine, CA 93513. Portions of this guide have appeared in *The Pacific Sun* and *Mothering Magazine.*

$$\mathcal{C}7\mathcal{D}$$

THE RITUAL-MAKER WITHIN AT ADOLESCENCE
Edith Sullwold

In her essay, "The Ritual-Maker Within at Adolescence," Edith Sullwold describes the function of spontaneously created ritual action in helping adolescents make the transition to adulthood. In addition, she describes the appearance of initiatory material to be found in the products of the adolescent psyche, such as in dreams and other forms of creative expression. She points to the necessity of "initiatory education" in the schools which could "lead young persons to their own inner resources." Pointing to the importance of secrecy in the initiatory process of adolescents, as well as the need for elders to help guide this process, she concludes that proper "initiation of the adolescent points to the initiation of the culture into its larger human potentialities."

Edith Sullwold, Ph. D., founded the Hilde Kirsch Children's Center at the C. G. Jung Institute of Los Angeles. A graduate of the University of Chicago, she helped found the Center for Healing Arts in Los Angeles and was Director of Turning Point, a professional group working with children with serious illnesses. She now teaches and supervises therapists in various parts of the United States and Europe.

IT was autumn in Los Angeles, and out in the courtyard of a children's clinic a few leaves were swirling in the brisk wind. Something in the air called for a bonfire in the imagination of the nine year old boy with whom I was spending an hour. The boy, whom I will call Peter, had been suffering from explosive flare-ups of temper at home and at school that seemed to erupt suddenly and without any apparent external cause. On this day Peter led me outside to see what we could construct on the only available inner city space, a large concrete area. A few sticks and some brown leaves served and soon a small fire was crackling.

As I watched, I saw that Peter's interest was not so much in the fire itself, but in his ability to control it—ignite it, fan and feed it, check its boundaries, and eventually put it out. It was as though Peter was acknowledging the fire as a force in itself with its own life, his work being to relate to this dynamic force with careful attention and skill. This process of building the fire, controlling, and extinguishing it was repeated many times.

My concentration on his work was so intense that I didn't notice two other boys joining Peter. They had been in rooms also opening on the courtyard and were fascinated by this fire-making process. Quietly, and without discussion, they entered the scene. At one point when it seemed a satisfactory blaze, one of the new attendants at this fire-becoming-ritual went inside and brought out an empty coffee can. He turned it upside down and began hitting it in a steady, rhythmic beat. Again without a word, the other new boy went to one side of the courtyard and made a stunning leap over the fire. Invited, Peter also went to the beginning place, hesitated a moment, and leapt over. For almost an hour, the three took turns beating the drum, tending the fire, and jumping over it. Then seeming satisfied, they together put out the fire with sand, swept the courtyard and returned to their rooms.

The event was followed by two other appearances of fire as a symbol in a ritual action for young boys or adolescents. A week later another boy, aged twelve, shared a dream in which he found himself with friends at a beach at night. In an area of big sand dunes his friends dug a deep pit in which they carefully built a fire, asking him to leap over it. He did this with both fear and the excitement of victory. A few days later another adolescent boy entering a private school described an actual event in which the new students were accepted by the older classmates only after having successfully leapt over a big bon-fire which he had helped them build.

These events point to the reality of the spontaneous emergence of ritual action in puberty and adolescence. Ritual action acknowledges a major event in the life of the individual or the group for us today as well as in traditional cultures. Like habit, it is action that may be repetitive, but unlike habit is beyond ordinary, everyday behavior. Most often the event which the ritual celebrates is transitional, marking a stage in an individual life such as birth, puberty, marriage or death, or a change affecting a group, such as the seasonal cycles or a new leadership. The action is initiatory in intent, helping to bring the individual or the group into a new state of being. The ritual actions are symbolic of such transitions and are intended to effect a real transformation in the participants.

The experience which I observed raises the possibility that the need for such ritual actions is so profound that it is in the very nature of the human being to create forms for them. In the traditional societies, societies which are cohesive in social structure, the honoring of such transitions generally took the form of elaborate rituals with strict procedures in which the individual and often the whole society took part. In a society such as ours, which is not cohesive, the external individual and collective rituals are becoming more and more neglected. However, the emergence of the fire-building ritual indicates that even without previous instruction or experience these ritual forms and symbols can be created from within the psychic structure of the individual.

It was of course important that I, as a witness to this event, carried a sense of its significance for the boys—a sense of its meaning—and a sense of awe surrounding its intensity. This support provided an atmosphere of safety and understanding that honored their creative and dynamic process of ritual making.

THE ADOLESCENT PASSAGE

What could be the meaning of such a fire-building event? If one is sensitive and knowledgeable about the changes that are going on internally in a boy or girl in puberty, it becomes clear that the preparation for the transformation of the body from the child to the adult has begun. There are often great surges of physical energy, frequently sexual. The biological forces which are involved in this change are powerful, and frequently seem out of control. I often think of how difficult it must be to be a boy of nine required to 'sit still' for six hours of the school day with all this going on inside of him. Often the adults in the children's life do not understand and acknowledge the natural energies which are emerging, and provide few channels for their expression. In such cases, the energy can become destructive. Sometimes the destruction is internal and the child begins to have trouble learning, or begins to have disturbing fantasies or nightmares. Often it is external as in this boy's extreme temper outbursts.

With the event of the fire-building, this boy began to be able to control the temper outbursts. As he was exercising control over the fire, so he learned also to control the emotional fire. However, he needed more space and time for active physical play than had been available to him. When this was understood and provided, he began to move more easily and with less anger both at home and school.

In addition, he needed, as do all boys and girls in this stage of puberty, knowledge of the physical and emotional facts of sexuality including conception. But this knowledge alone is not sufficient preparation for this life transition. Some direct experience and experiment with the handling of these energies is necessary. Ritual action allows for such experiences in a metaphorical manner. In the case of these boys, the initiation into the mysteries of the fire beginning to burn in the body could be experienced by dealing with the outer fire—an equivalent to this inner fire. Here the boys provided for themselves a particular task of courage—to be able to jump over the fire without getting burned. This action, a stretching and testing of their physical agility and awareness, becomes a paradigm of the energies and qualities needed for entering manhood.

This cooperative creation of the fire-building ritual by the boys points to another essential aspect of adolescent transition, the entry into a larger sense of community. The movement begins to shift from identification with the immediate family to the peer group, the school, the culture. In early tribal cultures puberty rites were often given to the boys and girls as a group, already signifying their responsibility to a larger sphere. As Peter and the boys join to create the ritual the effectiveness is increased not only by new ideas, but by community support. The rhythmic beating of the drum invokes and focuses the energy of the group into a single force which supports the courage needed for facing their test of jumping the fire—of crossing the threshold.

In addition to the communal nature of this action, it surrounds as in most rituals, a powerful symbol. The symbol of fire has greater meaning than just that related to the physical and sexual energies of puberty. In all historical times and in all stages of our life we have been attracted to fire, literally and symbolically. It represents life-giving warmth and light of night, promising survival in the cold and dark. But it also destroys. The wood is now ash, and all that enters the fire is also changed. In its destructive aspect, the symbol of fire touches upon the knowledge that in the time of transition the old must be destroyed in order for a full transformation to take place. In the case of adolescence, the physical and emotional 'child' is ultimately to be given up in order that the full adult can emerge. This 'giving up', the destruction of the old, is at the heart of all transition initiations.

This renewal through ritual act was recognized by tribal societies as meaningful not only for the individual child or group of children but for the whole society. In *Rites and Symbols,* Mircea Eliade describes such initiation as a "recapitulation of the sacred history of the world and its tribe. On the occasion of puberty rites, the entire society is plunged back into the mythical times of origin and therefore emerges rejuvenated." (1958, p. 128) All members had an opportunity to relive their own initiation and thereby to strengthen the deeper significance of such rites, which is transformation. What was witnessed was a particular instance of the continuous process of change—of destruction, chaos, and creation. What was celebrated was new life.

There are also of course other symbolic metaphors for the dissolving of the old form other than fire. There is, for example, a rite for girls among the Nootka people of Vancouver Island, B.C., in which each emerging young woman is left far out in the ocean alone to swim to shore by herself. During this test she gives up her form as a child. Through this act of courage she is 'purified' and 'reborn' from the water as a woman. Here the water is the element of transformation. Anne Cameron (1981, p. 52) related one Nootka woman's remembrance of this event.

'And you had to learn or you weren't a woman. It isn't easy becomin' a woman, it's not somethin' that just happens because you've been stand' around in one place for a long time, or because your body's started doin' certain things. A woman has to know patience, and a woman has to know how to stick it out, and a woman has to know all kinds of things that don't just come to you like a gift. There was always a reason for the things we hadda learn, and sometimes you'd been a woman for a long time before you found out for yourself what the reason was. But if you hadn't learned, you couldn't get married or have children, because you just weren't ready, you didn't know what needed to be known to do it right. . . .

When you'd learned everythin' you had to learn, and the Time was right, and you'd had your first bleedin' time and been to the waitin' house, there was a big party. You were a woman. And people would come from other places, uncles and aunts and cousins and friends, and there'd be singin' and dancin' and lots of food. Then they'd take you in a special dugout, all decorated up with water-bird down, the finest feathers off the breast of a bird, and you'd stand up there so proud and happy. And they'd chant a special chant, and the old woman would lead them, and they'd take you a certain distance. When the chant ended the old woman would sing a special prayer, and take off all your clothes and you'd dive into the water, and the dugout would go home . . . And you'd be out there in the water all by yourself, and you had to swim back to the village.

The people would watch for you, and they'd light fires on the beach, and when they finally saw you they'd start to sing a victory song about how a girl went for a swim and a woman came home, and you'd make it to the beach and your legs would feel like they were made of rocks or somethin'. You'd try to stand up and you'd shake all over, just plain wore out. And then the old woman, she'd come up and put her cape over you and you'd feel just fine. And after than, you were a woman, and if you wanted to marry up with someone, you could, and if you wanted to have children, you could, because you'd be able to take care of them the proper way.' (Cameron 1981, pp. 101-103)

In playing with the fire, or swimming in the cold ocean, the child opens itself to being touched indirectly by the deep forces and mysteries of transformation. In such times of transition there is often an experience of being "betwixt and between" when one is neither here nor there, neither child nor adult. Into this open, undefined space of adolescence, other dimensions of reality enter, often of a spiritual nature. Turning away from personal family identity and not yet having formed a new and independent identity, there is a turning toward the Other for meaning and stability, whether this is called God, or the larger Self, or some supportive life source such as Nature itself. Historically, adolescence was the age of entry into the spiritual teaching, initiated by priests and elders.

Eliade, in *Rites and Symbols of Initiation*, describes the rituals of initiation as the "puberty rites by virtue of which adolescents gain access to the sacred, to knowledge, and to sexuality, by which in short, they become human beings" (1958, p. 132). To become human means in this context to begin a process of conscious awareness of our nature—what we are as sexual, emotional, mental and spiritual beings with responsibility to the larger cosmos to which we belong. It means to question or search for the vocation or work that allows us to contribute to this larger whole.

In cultures which had traditional forms for such entry into the adult world, the teaching and testing of the initiates was the responsibility of the elders in the society. The teachings were based on collectively recognized and accepted beliefs concerning issues of creation and birth, sexuality, death and its relation to life. A relation to spirit, or some sense of the Other was found in religious practices, myths and tales. The mystery of sexuality revealed in adolescence was placed in the context of social and spiritual law. Ethical prescriptions were taught regarding individual behavior. It is evident that the single and cohesive view of such strongly united cultures as were existent in times of greater isolation and less cross-pollination is becoming more difficult to maintain even in those societies which were built primarily of social and sacred law.

Consequently, adolescents of our time do not find such collective rituals offered by the elders to support and facilitate their transition. Our cultures have become much more complex and the teenager does not cross the threshold into a clearly defined form of adulthood with its prescribed set of beliefs and skills. No cohesive forms of instruction or initiation into the adult world exist in our culture except certain academic expectations and the development work skills. The deep, natural instinctive and spiritual changes which give meaning to the passage of our lives are generally ignored. Many of the religious forms have lost their significance in favor of materialistic values and this potential opening to deeper meaning in life finds little cultural support either within the family or the educational system. Some of the investigators who are concerned with the rapidly increasing suicidal rate of adolescents, especially those from fifteen to nineteen years of age, speculate that this lack of spiritual sustenance may be one of the complex factors leading to despair and suicide for the teenager.

The trend of the Western culture has been toward the development of the individual—an individual who is seen as having full freedom of choice to fulfill his own destiny, whether that is within the bounds of his collective or not. One consequence of this development has been the continued breakdown of collective forms. Such seems the case surrounding adolescent ritual in our time. There is almost no social form other than the giving of a license to drive a car, or the privilege of voting and drinking, to mark the passage to adulthood by civil society. Meaningful Bar Mitzvahs and Confirmations carry some of the elements of initiation, but are available to only a few whose family and personal belief systems make that possible for them.

Because of the complexities of our culture, not only is there a lack of formal initiators, but in general the model for adulthood is not always clear for adolescents. Outside of an occasional teacher, the primary source of modelling for many young people is in the figures of mass media—sport heroes, musicians, film stars, figures of science fiction. These mass media figures tend to constellate archetypal images for the adolescent of the conquering hero or herione, whether it be through the path of stardom, competitive sports, sexual conquest, or the war against "evil forces." For some the identification with these images is only passive. Others actively search for a test of courage, reminiscent of the demands in earlier adolescent initiation. But there is no content of instruction, discipline, and meaning formerly given by the adult in traditional initiation ceremonies. These adolescents thus turn to their own peer group to create acts of daring, such as car-racing, drugs, sexual promiscuity, and the acts of violence now common in urban areas.

Longing for a collective support they turn to each other for instruction about the issues of life, but lack of experience and knowledge limit the possibility of a true initiation. The high incidence of teenage pregnancies (one out of every five births in 1984) is one current result of lack of real instruction for girls, not only about the facts of sexuality, but also about the realities of conception, pregnancy, and child care. Many girls, not having direct experience of younger children in the community have no vision of these realities. Without this foreknowledge or training, child care can become frustrating. The fantasy of having an object to love becomes tarnished as the life demands of the child emerge, creating impossible situations for unititi-ated, non-instructed girls, who in addition are usually isolated from any larger, extended family or community that might assist them and give them advice.

Modelling for the adolescent in the past when there were small communities or even extended families was multiple. All older females were aunts and grandmothers for a girl in the Native American culture. Her experience of woman was varied therefore, within the limits of the cultural mores. Because of this the girl was not limited in her sense of womanhood by the personal characteristics of her mother, or by the way in which the latter related to marriage and child-rearing. She could experience in this way the more general characteristics of being a woman, physically, culturally, and spiritually. Instruction about these essential qualities of womanhood and the responsibility consequent to them were ideally the focus of initiation rites as well.

In our culture, as the sense of the individuality and freedom of movement has increased many family units have become isolated from this sense of extended family. Paradoxically, although the choices are greater and more varied in our culture, it may be more difficult for a girl or boy to find a sense of the essential nature of adulthood. The choices are there, but on what basis are these choices to be made?

As early as 1926, Margaret Mead wrote about this problem in her book, *Coming of Age in Samoa*. In a final chapter she compared the life of the adolescent in the American culture to that of the Samoan girl. Having described the education of the Samoan girls, she concludes that in that simpler culture adolescence was not necessarily a time of stress, as it so often appears in contemporary America. She sees as the principle cause of our adolescents' difficulty "the presence of conflicting standards and the belief that every individual should make his or her choice, coupled with a feeling that choice is an important matter" (1928, p. 234).

Her suggestion is not that we can or should return to the form of the simpler culture, but that we should more consciously educate to these values within our culture. She says, "We must turn all of our educational efforts to training our children for the choices that will confront them. The child of the future must have an open mind . . . must be taught how to think, not what to think. They must be taught that many ways are open to them and upon them alone lies the burden of choice. Unhampered by prejudices, unvexed by too early conditioning to any one standard, they must come clear-eyed to the choices that lie before them." (1928, p. 246)

INDIVIDUATION AND SECRECY

That this process of choice-making is inherent in the very nature of the adolescent experience is clear. The adolescent begins the separation from childhood, and from an image of himself which has been determined primarily by his particular family. He moves into an in-between time which presents him or her with many adult possibilities, as yet unknown and unexplored. This potential, defined quite specifically in older cultures in terms of spiritual traditions and social needs, is open to many options in our time.

I remember a scene in which this was vividly acted out. Waking early one morning at the beach where I lived, I saw a young adolescent girl walking up and down the sand. Each time she passed by she tried another walk—a strut, a languid flow, a wiggle,—one after another invention for at least an hour. In a moment of privacy, she was experimenting with as many possibilities of woman as her body and her imagery could create. It was a moment in which the essential nature of the emerging woman allowed her freedom to explore outer shape and style without being fettered or identified with personality or culture.

This experiment, when seen at a deeper level, touches a question of our ultimate reality. Although our multi-culture, multi-image time has the disadvantage of lack of cohesion for the adolescent—a lack of specific modelling, it has the advantage of providing a greater freedom of choice in answering the ultimate question, "What am I?" It is this question, emerging at this time, which makes the adolescent open to spiritual matters. As a part of the old person is dying or has died, what is left? What will be created or recreated? These ultimate questions of reality come up since the quality of one's essential self is in question. C. G. Jung tells in his autobiography, *Memories, Dreams and Reflections,* of a question which he often asked as a boy while sitting on his favorite rock. He puzzled over, "Am I the one who is sitting on the stone, or am I the stone in which *he* is sitting?" (1963, p. 20)

Beyond the ambiguity of this question must have been a state of feeling that was also ambiguous. Because these questions and feelings can be so intense and can create a great vulnerability, it seems important that adolescents have a way of finding privacy and protection during this time. When I first worked with adolescents I observed and was concerned that they were not sharing from as deep a place as adults or small children. Then one day I looked at some of the images they were producing in their dreams, writing, painting and clay. Here I saw a clue to the reason for secrecy. I remember especially one painting which seems clear as a metaphor. There was a ship—on a calm sea—itself becalmed. From the ship a long line descended down to an oyster shell on the bottom of the ocean. The picture was entitled, "Waiting for the Pearl." It was clear that the oyster was not yet ready to be opened—it was still in the process of forming the pearl. This seemed to be that pearl which in many cultures symbolizes the Self—the pearl of "greatest price." I realized then that many adolescents consciously or unconsciously were protecting a premature exposure of that deeper Self. It was the essential quality which could provide a basis for new reentry into the world, but it was not yet fully formed, and consequently not ready to be shared. Another image which frequently emerged in the work of these adolescents was a symbolic representation of cell-division. It was as though a new body was being developed, a body which could house the newly developing self. However, the body as well as the ego or new personality was still not fully formed, and consequently not ready to be shared.

The movement from child to adult, between the dying of the old form and emergence of the new, the time of "betwixt and between," can be an experience of non-existence, or "no-form," even invisibility. It is an ambiguous, vulnerable period. Because of this vulnerability, it is important to respect the privacy of the adolescent, providing a container for this secret place of growth.

On the outer level, this period of time is extended in our modern culture long beyond that of the traditional time of initiation. Then the initiate was removed from the family setting and returned as a full member of the larger tribe. Our adolescents remain dependent financially on the family until finishing high school, if not throughout college. This dependence makes it difficult to claim full adulthood and therefore an independent self. This sense of secretive protection may be an important way to keep in reserve a sense of self which does not have full range of expression within the nuclear, restricted family setting.

A Swiss psychologist, Paul Tournier, speaks of this need in his book, *Secrets*.

> The years pass. The child grows. He will have to free himself little by little from his mother, from his parents, in order to become an individual. And his secrets are going to be the indispensable instruments of this emancipation—it is to the extent that he becomes free to keep his secrets from his parents that he gets an awareness of being distinct from them—of having his own individuality, of being a person. One cannot become a person without first being an individual, without freeing himself from the clan, from parental domination, without becoming aware of his own individuality with a right to secrecy. (1963, p. 6)

C. G. Jung also tells of several profound secrets of his childhood, certain dreams and visions and creative actions. He says of these "The possession of a secret had a very powerful formative influence on my character and I consider it the essential factor of my boyhood." One such secret was, for example, a dream that he had when he was very small of an underground chamber in which he saw a phallus on a golden throne. He says, "through this dream I was initiated into the secret of the earth, and many years were to pass before I came out again." What happened then was a kind of burial in the earth, an initiation into the realm of darkness. He could thus say, "I know that it happened in order to bring the greatest possible amount of light into the darkness. My intellect had its unconscious beginning at that moment." (1963, pp. 22-23) Some six years later he formed a little figure, reminiscent of this dream and hid it secretly away, almost a totem which kept alive his connection to this individual revelation of the dream. This early secret, well protected, clearly was a dream of initiation for Jung that presaged his life's vocation, his individual path that was to lead him far beyond the parochial boundaries of his family.

This secret time, this sense of the non-formed, all-potential state, was formalized in tribal and ancient ritual passage. Since the rite of initiation was accepted as a form of death, a period of gestation was provided before the new birth. This was clearly and literally expressed in such action as the isolation of the young in a special cabin, sometimes even shaped like a tomb. In some places they were hidden in seclusion in the forest. In others they were "buried" underground, or covered by leaves. In some instances they were put into a clay vessel shaped like an egg or a womb. They were kept until they emerged "re-created". During this period of isolation the initiates might fast, be blindfolded, or might wander around stumbling and awkward. They might be dressed in clothes of the opposite sex, indicating the ambiguity of the state. All these were outer manifestations of the process of transformation to a new, not yet experienced state.

Trust that a new form would emerge came from the presence of those who had already crossed the bridge and who were carrying the model of adulthood. These elders had of course gone through their own essentially similar transformation. The structure of the ritual form gave shape to the process of transformation itself. The imparting of knowledge regarding the social structure into which the initiant was to move provided a situation of stability and security. The puberty initiation of the Apache girl described in this volume gives a sense of this structure provided by myth and ritual.

In our culture, there is a minimal amount of outer structure to guide this process. However, the transitional movement from child to adult is itself a structure to be discovered in the body and psyche of the individual. It is, in other words, archetypal. The process is like the caterpillar in the cocoon that is no longer recognizable as a caterpillar. It has disintegrated into an unrecognizable mass until in its own organic timing the butterfly emerges. The formal rituals emphasize the importance of a time of reconstruction, in the dark secret place in which the work of change in the new takes place. But this archetypal process can also appear in the psyche of the child, experienced alone, and remembered as an adult as a powerfully formative time.

A friend recalled recently that at nine she withdrew into herself totally—to ask about the meaning of life and death. From a very extraverted, active child, she suddenly became quiet, shy and almost non-verbal for several years. Now, in her mature work as a musician and composer, she considers that much of her music was seeded at that time. It was a time of voluntary removal from the extraversion of her family and cultural surroundings. She had, in essence, created her own isolation into her internal "special cabin." In another such recalled memory, Jung describes his own private, personal and spontaneous discovery of himself when he was twelve. "I was taking the long road to school, when suddenly for a single moment I had the overwhelming impression of having just emerged from a dense cloud. I knew all at once; now I am *myself*. It was as if a wall of mist were at my back, and behind that wall there was not yet an "I." But at this moment, *I came upon myself*. Previously I had been willed to do this and that, now *I* willed. This experience seemed to me tremendously important and new; there was "authority in me." (1963, pp. 32-33)

THE ROLE OF ELDERS

These were ultimately successful experiences, initiatory in content, which clearly moved these adolescents forward in the creative expression of their adult lives. But for many others these experiences are aborted by the lack of understanding in the adult community toward which these adolescents are moving. What can we do as adults in this time to facilitate for our children this transition into adulthood? First of all, an understanding of the natural aspects of this transition is fundamental. Here even a simple grasp of the elements of adolescent initiation ritual form is helpful, since it is based on deep understanding of the processes of this transition. Perhaps these steps can best be seen in an example from our own Native American practices.

A biographical description of the life of Plenty Coup, a Crow chief, tells of his entry into the male world. It began when he was nine. He was taken from the world of women, his mother, aunts and grandmothers, as was traditional at his age. He was given into the care of the grandfather, a tribal elder. The grandfather gave him tasks, such as the exercise of catching butterflies. Imagine the incredible training for alertness, watchfulness, stillness and agility that would have been. In the evenings the grandfather would tell tales, stories of creation and the history of the tribe, probably imparting some mysteries as well. When the boy was judged to be ready for the test, he was invited by his uncles and father to join a buffalo hunt. The men would stir up a buffalo herd attempting to isolate one buffalo that would come close enough to pierce with their arrows. The boy was asked to stand in front of the buffalo, facing it as it was coming toward the group of men. If he was not able to do so at this time, he was given as many chances as he needed without judgement or a sense of having failed. When he did pass this trial successfully, he was awarded his first 'coup'—a notch in a wooden stick, to which would be added many other coups during his life time. He was then taken in as a full member of the adult male community and a celebration was held in his honor. (Lindemann 1963, p. 29)

In this example of initiation ritual there are clearly a series of phases through which the elder led the boy. First he experiences the stage of separation, secondly he is led through a transitional time of instruction and trial, and finally he begins his celebrative integration into the total community as an adult. These stages are well described in Van Gennup's classic work, *The Rites of Passage* (1960), Victor Turner's *The Ritual Process* (1969), Eliade's *Rites and Symbols of Initiation* (1958), and in the article by Stephen Foster and Meredith Little in this volume.

Sensing the reality of life experience symbolized in these ritual elements, an adult may help support an adolescent through this time of transition in a simple offering of compassionate understanding. In a poem addressed to her thirteen year old daughter, the poet Maxine Kumin (1982, p. 223) writes:

> in that uncharted sea
> where no one charts the laws
> of course you do not belong to me
> nor I to you . .

This clear understanding of the necessary separation and the period of uncertainty for both the mother and daughter instructs us all, reminding us of the necessity of releasing our adolescents from a sense of possession so that they do not remain too long in childhood.

But can we, as elders, also help in the second phase of this passage—the time of instruction? Since our culture has belief systems and social forms that are both complex and fluid, no fixed or collective form of instruction seems possible. Although the primary requirement of adulthood in any culture is responsibility to a collective larger than the individual person or family, in this culture this responsibility should be carried out in such a way that the development of the particular character and quality of each individual is not lost. This requires skill in making choices that support both individual development and social concern. Instruction for the adolescent should therefore include awareness of choices that are available, and a sense of the consequences which follow from such choices. In the same chapter in which Mead advocates teaching the child *how* to think in order to make unprejudiced choices, she concludes that such an education would preserve a primary value of this culture as "the primacy of the individual choice and universal toleration within a heterogeneous culture" (1928, p. 234).

By learning to think, Mead did not of course only mean the development of the mind through the exercise of abstract rational tools. In order to become more aware of the 'unprejudiced choices,' a curriculum could be developed which included courses in psychology. A discussion, for example, of the theory of psychological types as well as the various stages of life might help the adolescent become more aware of individual differences and their source. As a consequence, the adolescents might have some basis for tolerance of such differences and a greater sense of acceptance. Especially useful would be reflection about their own individuality, and of the emotional and physical changes which occur during adolescence.

In traditional societies a fundamental form used for achieving a sense of self and one's place in the community was the telling of the myths of origin— "how it was in the beginning." This story gave meaning to the context of everyday life. In order to find such a myth of our time, courses in comparative religion, mythology and anthropology could be taught with a focus on increasing awareness of the collective consciousness of our present culture. Through contrast, the beliefs and value of this system could be examined in order to offer greater freedom of choice for behavior.

The most effective mode of any training is by example. The more adults come to be aware of their own choices and their responsibility in choosing them, the clearer the process will be for adolescents. In addition to the formal courses suggested, adults then need to share their own life experiences, pointing out the negative and positive consequences of their own choices. This honest sharing would maintain the sense of freedom and exploration the adolescent needs for his own development, but it would also give a sense of the fundamental values which have been important to the adult generation.

Beyond such instruction, I believe that individual and collective rituals can also be provided that are relevant to the complexity of our time and conducive to individual development. That fall afternoon in Los Angeles taught me that the ritual maker is alive in us, and if trusted, knows how to create or re-create forms through which adolescents can be honored in their move across the threshold. As an example of such a simple spontaneous ritual a group of women met for dinner to celebrate the approaching twelfth birthday of one of their daughters. During the evening they began to share with each other their memories of being twelve, and what their lives as women had meant to them since that time. In this relaxed context, the girl began to ask questions about their lives and to share her fantasies of becoming a woman, filled with both fear and hope. That night she had her first menstrual period. This event seems to have strongly supported her entry into womanhood through the mutual sharing and instruction which belongs to the second phase of the initiation process.

The last phase of the transition in ritual form is the celebration of the re-entry of the adolescent into the community. As a simple ritual, it has always seemed to me that the least that could be done to honor a girl's passage would be to send her a dozen roses on the occasion of her first menstruation. This bouquet, or a new article of clothing or jewelry, could mark and honor this event as a birthday of the child-becoming-woman. A gesture such as the offering of the roses can be a cue to our inner knowledge of the elements of initiation, stimulating the development of new, relevant and simple forms which satisfy the requirements of a contemporary initiation.

I once attended such a satisfying ceremony of celebration which followed a traditional Bat Mitzvah in a synagogue. The initiated girl returned home with a group of female friends and relatives and received from each of them a gift in the form of a poem, song, or prayer which told of their hopes for her future. Then her mother, aunt and grandmother led her out the back door. After remaining alone for some time she came to the front door asking to be admitted as a woman. Entering, she told of her personal hopes, making as well a commitment to the world as a caring woman. This moving statement was celebrated by feasting, singing and dancing.

In creating rituals, it is important to be cautious and sensitive in bringing them to the adolescents. We may be imposing our form on to a form already emerging in their life experience, and our forms may not have meaning for them. Adolescents can be embarrassed and awkward with a form that does not fit them individually or that is not acceptable to their peers.

There are some adolescents who need to be supported in their passage by a larger collective event. Very important work in this direction is being done by several groups throughout the country combining experiences in wilderness areas with the vision quest ritual derived from the Native Americans. These vision quests contain essential elements for adolescent transition. They are special events away from the old environment, they demand courage and some survival skills in a strange place, and perhaps more importantly provide a time of aloneness, a secret time, in which each individual can find his or her own symbolic, metaphoric images and experiences. It is a time for the dream, the vision, the deeper confrontation with the self and the forces of nature.

Importantly, there is an opportunity for sharing these individual experiences with a group of peers and their guides—the elders—in this ritual. Sharing, the adolescent begins to participate in the last phase of this transition, the movement into larger community. The larger community itself becomes changed by the sharing of the secrets. The individuality of each person is valued as an essential part of the whole and a sense of individual responsibility for the whole is strengthened.

Paul Tournier underscores this in his book. "Keeping a secret is an early assertion of freedom, telling it to someone that one chooses is going to be a later assertion of even greater value. By opening out, by telling one's secrets—but freely this time, one becomes personally linked with others, and becomes fully a person thereby." (1963, p. 25)

For this reason, there is a tremendous need for the creation of groups for adolescents in which they can share their secrets safely. Some innovative teachers have been able to create such a group within the public school system (Bacon, 1982), while others have done so in a therapeutic outreach for such groups as teenage mothers (Homstead, 1985). The support of such groups led by an adult helps in completing the final stage of the adolescent passage, which is the connection to the larger whole.

In the context of this aspect of the passage, it is important to take note of the appearance in the West of spiritual leaders from Japan, India, Tibet and the Sufi traditions. Native American elders are also beginning to share their teachings. The spiritual tenets of these teachings emphasize in varying ways a view of reality that sees the individual not as an isolated entity, but as part of a cohesive totality. Many young people have been attracted to these teachings for their paths of initiation. They offer a traditional form which provides them one of the few options to join a group which has initiation as its focus.

For many, the attraction to the disciplines is not the fact that they are traditional and collective but that the teachings may offer some answers to their question concerning meaning and the nature of reality—the answers to "What am I" and "What am I doing here?"

There are other collective groups, however, which are based on power and conformity, and this is the situation within some of the cults that have attracted some young people. They are here denied the possibility of individual choice and individual morality. This is the advantage of groups whose leadership provides energy for a collective experience but ensures that the experience itself safeguards the individual, and does not bind the adolescent to a particular group after the experience.

THE INNER RESOURCES OF ADOLESCENTS

One of the greatest protections for the adolescent's individuality is when the work allows for them to touch upon their own inner resources, including the realm of dream and image. The inner vision, when capable of being interpreted and integrated into the personality and its work in the world, can become a true source of initiation and guidance. In this sense the psyche becomes the teacher, the guru, the guide through the images it brings to the ordinary conscious mind. The dream of the boy in which he experienced the fire-jumping ritual is an example of this inner instruction by the psyche.

It is important as adults to be sensitive to the content of dreams, fantasies, stories, music and the art products which are created or enjoyed by the adolescents in order to hear and see the statement which they are making about their lives and often about the adult world as well. These products often reveal confusion and pain as well as deep knowledge. Often they are a cry for help. Often they are an inspiration.

It would be of great help to the adolescent process if teachers and counselors were given training in understanding and interpreting these statements from adolescents, not only to be able to offer additional guidance and help, but to support the adolescent's belief in the strength and meaning of his own inner resources (Griffin 1983).

The encouragement of the use of creative forms as vehicles for the imagination is vital. For the contemporary adolescent the pressure of academic requirement, sports competition, and social demands of their peers leaves little, if any, room for the expression of the images which are at the base of all our action. School programs should include theater projects where the adolescents are allowed to create their own story, and classes in which they could make their own music, art and dance not on a competitive basis but as a way of reflecting inner movement. The use of journal writing and the recording of dream material are a few of the many possible ways of supporting and integrating this deeper source of the imagination into the adolescent's life.

In a time when the collective community is providing images of increased materialism and of the threat of nuclear annihilation, it is essential that our imagination be tapped for its deep wellspring of creative life-renewing solutions. To revalue and reactivate our own imagination as adults may be the greatest inheritance we can give to adolescents.

In addition to the statements revealed in these creative forms, aspects of adolescent initiation are frequently expressed outwardly in the actual process of daily living, in the solitary place where the child is alone or with its peers, or in the more dramatic forms of adventure, rebellion or creative action. The rebellion and rejection of the family, so often painfully experienced by both adolescent and parent is an example. The ritual separation from the family is seen in primitive tradition as a necessary step in initiation. In our culture the adolescents are left to provide the separation for themselves, and often use the rebellion and rejection as the only available separating-emotional wedge.

If it is so that the psyche already creates ritual action in the lives of adolescents through dreams, images and outer action, why bring consciousness to the ritual form itself? The answer to this involves issues of life and death. The ritual forms may, in fact, be re-enacted in a way which distorts the ultimate purpose of transition and expansion to a larger form. For example, Eliade says, "Initiation implies an existential experience, basic to the human condition, that is, the experience of ritual death" (1958, p. 19). Such ritual death is real in a symbolic way, but it is now being played out in physical reality by many adolescents. The rate of teenage suicide has increased dramatically in the last years. Here such deaths may occur because of an intense desire for change—a hopelessness in life as it is. But the death is achieved literally, not ritually or symbolically. In her important book on teenage suicide, *Cry for Help,* Mary Griffin (1983) calls for the use of more conscious rites of passage.

For other adolescents, the phase of separation or isolation that belongs to a period of adolescence extends far beyond its time. It may seem that there is no one to relate to in the adult world so that adulthood is without meaning or enticement. There may be violence and destruction in the breaking away from the old, but not always with a sense of the new. We could quote Wordsworth's line from his Ode on Intimations of Immortality, "shades of the prison house begin to close upon the growing Boy." Wordsworth here refers to the growing personality that the adolescent may take on in a culture which may remove him from his deeper nature. The prison house is thus a culture that is too narrow for our full humanity—a culture whose values are too self-centered to provide meaning and community. If the process of death of the old leads only to a hopelessness, we must look for a place of inspiration.

Is it possible that adolescents are playing out the destructive parts of the old ritual form beyond that which is needed to leave the personal childhood—going beyond this to also destroy a form of cultural childhood? If so, it is the responsibility of those who claim adulthood to recognize this, and help to balance this work of the adolescents by understanding and supporting a more complete transformation in themselves and in the world. In this sense, the initiation of the adolescent is the initiation of the culture into its larger human potentialities.

We can perhaps look to processes of the adolescent not only for their perception of what is lacking in our culture, but also for inspiration and solution. I would like to share a final story of a fire-builder whose inner work carries a deep message for change, not only within himself, but within the culture.

This was an eleven year old boy, unusually bright and creative. However, he was becoming increasingly withdrawn from his peers and was suffering from tension headaches and severe muscle pains. It was as though his musculature was holding in some tremendous energy. In my office there was an opportunity for him to work in sandplay. This technique involves the use of many miniature figures which can be placed in a tray of sand, either wet or dry. In this way the inner story of the child can be told. Creative solutions to life situations can emerge in the tray. It was so for this boy who was approaching adolescence and the sandtray was his place of passage.

His first scene showed a pile of airplanes that had crashed. The sense was that his intellect and his creative fantasy, the source of bright, highflying ideas, were not serving his life process at this time. However, one large plane was still there on the ground, an indication that the essential quality of this boy was still intact and there in reserve. In addition there was a place in the center in which some of the crashed planes were being repaired. This indicated that the healing factors in his psyche were already at work. To summarize, this first statement was that his individual gifts were in the keen intellect and creative and probably spiritual insights, but that these had not found a balance in his life.

The next tray began to tell why this was so. It was a zoo in which all animals were in fenced cages. There were extra empty cages, "just in case." In the center was an even more amazing part of the scene—a fence was around the tropical red-flame tree. There was one animal, however, that was free. An old tortoise was following the zoo keeper as he inspected the cages. We can see here a personal but also collective issue. All the animal energies were fenced in, away from their natural setting. Even the red 'tree of life,' with its vitality, was caged. Looking at this boy's rigid use of his body, it was easy to imagine it as the zoo-keeper of his own animal forces. But the tortoise was free—the tortoise who carries its own protection on its vulnerable body is also the primitive long-living animal which in many ancient myths is seen holding up the world, or in some Native American creation myths, as bringing up the earth from the bottom of the deep waters.

For this boy, then, although the tortoise indicated vulnerability and a need for protection, it also brought hope of some ancient sense of stability, the strength and foundation of the earth.

But what of all those other vital animals, and the tree that is fenced in? In a stunning act of courage, in the next sandtray, this boy built some fences out of matches in the center, lit the matches, and destroyed those barriers with a blazing fire. In the tray he had placed fire-trucks with their hoses out—"just in case," an action reminiscent of the boys who spontaneously built the fire in the courtyard. There was a sense of control and caution, but willingness to allow the fire to do its destructive work, destroying forms too limited for the next stage of growth.

Not surprisingly, the next tray showed all the animals who had been caged in the second sandtray were now in their natural setting—free in a jungle of green. And most thrilling was that all these animals were facing toward the center, where the red-flame tree was standing, also naturally free. Only two animals faced outwards,—an adult giraffe and a baby giraffe. Looking at this boy, tall for his age, with his head high and active, but at this time so disconnected to his body, one could easily imagine him as a cousin to the giraffe. The baby giraffe suggests that some new possibilities were coming to him.

His action of lighting the fire symbolically released the animal energies needed for his adolescent transition. Not long after this the headaches disappeared, and he began to play soccer with a few of his former friends. His body regained some fluidity. If one sees the release of these personal energies as the end of such an inner, symbolic ritual-action, this would have been the completion of the transitional process. But, as we understand in ritual, the process is not complete until this new energy carried by the individual—the new 'giraffe'—is brought back into the community, and consequently changes the community.

And so it did, in a most amazing way. In the middle of the next tray he placed a large church. Again he made a fence around it with matches, and burned it down. The fire trucks were there to control the spread of the fire, but the church itself was completely destroyed.

In this courageous action, a clear statement is made. As the zoo had restrained the animals, so the church had restrained the spirit. We know that many old forms in this culture no longer have the vitality to inspire a life of action, to deepen morality, or to instruct us in the mysteries of reality. Deep from within the psyche of this boy came his answer to the proper foundation for the spirit. In the next, most beautiful tray, he used black sand. Here in this dark world, as in a cave or womb, a union takes place. The image shows a body of blue water surrounded by black sand. There is a peninsula jutting into a womb-shaped body of water, very much like the union of male and female. This vision of union in nature is celebrated by angels singing and playing instruments. The black earth is rich with the growth of trees and bright flowers, and there are paths made of naturally polished rocks and shells. In the water are swans, and a peacock, symbolic of transformation and of the presence of the deeper self.

Standing back and looking at this tray, he said quietly, "It is nothing but Nature." At moments like this one experiences a numinosity not only in the tray, but in the energy which was invoked for its creation. Traditional societies understood that to be effective a ritual needed the invocation of greater energies to take the participants out of their ordinary awareness to a place of greater understanding—to a place of original creative source.

C. G. Jung calls this source the Self, not seen as external to the individual but as residing within him, a source greater than the confines of personality and culture which can create new or expanded forms for life. It is the "Nothing but Nature" behind the outer form of the "church."

When both the boy and I had stood silently for a few minutes, celebrating this vision he said, "I must bring something back." He placed a boat on the water, with an image of himself as the driver holding a huge piece of bark from one of the trees in this paradise-like land. He said then, "I'll need this for the building." As in traditional ritual, he was ready to bring back something of his individual transformative experience to the ordinary community in which he lived.

The next tray showed what the particular work was to be. He began to rebuild the church, placing it within an ordinary city. Work trucks, including fire trucks which he had used before, were there to begin the reconstruction. As he put the rebuilt church in its place he said, "Now we know its true foundation." Here was a remarkable insight. This boy, in the midst of his own inner transitional work, understood that the outer forms of our culture were restrictive to the body and the spirit when they lost their connection to a fundamental experience of nature and its creative forces.

This is wisdom much needed in our time when cultural forms have little respect for nature, the earth and all its creatures. The hope which the imaginative work of this boy gives is that the forms can be transformed and rebuilt through such a connection, and need not be destroyed permanently. In the rebuilding of the church, this adolescent pointed a way to the harmonious integration of nature and culture. If societal forms are not transformed on this basis, there is great danger that, as in adolescent suicide, the destructive conflagration will be externalized and total.

But what of this individual boy and his own adolescent crossing? From his last tray it was clear that he had returned from the experience not only with wisdom for the larger collective, but even with his own new possibilities. In this tray he placed the airplanes with which he had started this inner journey. Two were in fine shape, poised upward for the flight. The large plane which had never been damaged was there still in the background. A few were still in need of repair. Here it was clear that his return to the place of original nature and its creative source had strengthened and healed his individual nature and gifts.

But the tray also showed a freight train going over a track through a bridge. The track made an arc far beyond the limits of the tray. Here we see that he had added symbolically a sense of responsibility to the whole, helping to carry to the collective 'on the ground,' close to the foundation: those perceptive insights which he will find in his gifted flights of imagination.

In a time when we cannot easily turn to collective rituals traditionally used to create the energy needed for personal and collective transformation, it is essential to fully recognize that these energies can be found within the individual, in our own inner "Nothing but Nature" sources—in the imagination which shapes our actions.

This boy's story supports the hope that in our individual nature there is a deep knowledge of the process of transformation and the sources of energy to support it. What we as adults can provide is the receptivity to such processes within ourselves, in other adults, and in our children. Then the children-turning-adults whom we call adolescents can share with us their individual concerns and insights which we need to hear, and the vision of the future we need to see, so that our own sense of responsibility for the world is awakened and inspired. Only then will we be able to call them across the threshold with the true wisdom of elders.

REFERENCES

Bacon, G. 1982. *Essential education.* Palo Alto, California: Rainbow Bridge.
Cameron, A. 1981. *Daughters of Copper Woman.* Vancouver: Press Gang Publishers.
Eliade, M. 1958. *Rites and symbols of initiation.* New York: Harper and Row.
Griffin, M. and Felsenthal, M. 1983. *Cry for help.* New York: Doubleday.
Homstead, K. 1985. *Group experience for sexually abused adolescents.* Unpublished dissertation, University of Massachusetts.
Jung, C. G. 1963. *Memories, dreams and reflections.* London: Collins and Routledge and Kegan.
Kumin, M. 1982. *Our ground time here will be brief.* New York: Penguin Books.
Lindemann, F. 1963. *Plenty-coups, chief of the Crows.* Lincoln: University of Nebraska Press.
Mead, M. 1928. *Coming of age in Samoa.* New York: William Morrow and Co., Inc.
Tournier, P. 1963. *Secrets.* Atlanta: John Knox Press.
Turner, V. 1969. *The ritual process.* Chicago: Aldine.
Van Gennep, A. 1960. *The rites of passage.* Chicago: University of Chicago Press.

THE
INITIATION
OF
MEN

PART THREE

THE DECLINE OF MASCULINE RITES OF PASSAGE IN OUR CULTURE: THE IMPACT ON MASCULINE INDIVIDUATION

Jerome S. Bernstein

In this article, "The Decline of Masculine Rites of Passage in our Culture," Jerome Bernstein explores the depths and dimensions of the predicament in which many modern males find themselves:

> *It is not (as many men seem to feel) so much that the man is losing his power to women. Rather, it is that women are taking back power which previously they have used to support and carry the male's feeling side for him. As a result, the contemporary male increasingly experiences uncertainty, depression, dependency, loneliness, despair—feelings which have been there all along.*

He examines the reasons for the decline and considers means by which men might rectify imbalances within themselves caused by the absence of meaningful male rites of initiation. Contrast his treatment of the "Devouring Mother" archetype with that of Marion Woodman in her essay on the emergence of the feminine. Note also his development of the concept of "the male participation mystique." Whether or not the reader agrees with the author on every point, he/she will nevertheless be conducted on a provocative and sometimes controversial view of the psyche of the modern male.

Jerome S. Bernstein, M.A., a clinical psychologist and Jungian analyst practicing in Washington, D.C., received his training at George Washington University and the C.G. Jung Institute of New York, where he presently serves as Vice Chairman of the board. He has lectured on the archetypal dynamics of the nuclear threat and is currently working on a book concerning archetypal and clinical dynamics of masculine individuation and another on the return of the magical level of consciousness.

THE evolution of civilization and modern technology has brought about the progressive weakening of masculine rites of passage and initiation in our culture. Most of the rites which used to carry archetypal value in supporting positive masculine ego development have atrophied or vanished altogether. As Sol Kimball puts it in his introduction to the English edition of Van Gennep's classic, *The Rites of Passage* (1960):

> The continued expansion of an industrial-urban civilization has produced extensive changes in our social system. Prominent among these have been increased secularization and the decline in the importance of sacred ceremonialism . . . . There is no evidence that a secularized urban world has lessened the need for ritualized expression of an individual's transition from one status to another. Obviously, ceremonialism alone cannot establish the new equilibrium, and perfunctory ceremony may be pleasant but also meaningless.

It is clear that "industrial-urban civilization" has been changing even more rapidly since the first publication of this important book in 1909, thus accelerating the decline of essential rites of passage in Western civilization.

Over the years and particularly since the advent of the twentieth century, what was and remains a function of the masculine archetype, i.e., rational science, has become identified with man's ego, intellect, and the power principle. This identification has led to a strong ego inflation and an over-identification with the intellect (to the impoverishment of the spirit and soul) and an over-dependence on science as omniscient. Modern man's rationalism led us to dismiss the psychic dimension. As a result men are at the mercy of the psychic underworld of which they are largely unconscious (Jung 1964). With regard to rites of passage, this inflation of the intellect has led to excessive secondary personalization of transpersonal material—i.e., the reduction of transpersonal contents to personal factors (Neumann 1954). The result has been to further weaken those rituals and rites of passage extant in modern culture, with a drastic depotentiation of the power of the archetype of initiation.

Prior to World War II, for many young men in this country, the high school diploma constituted a major confirmation of passage into manhood. Completion of high school often meant leaving the parental home, becoming self-supporting, and getting married. But since the end of the second World War, the value of a high school diploma has rapidly and consistently declined due to increased technology, rendering high school graduation almost useless as a sure ticket to self-supporting employment. Without the earning capacity the high school diploma used to confer, the male graduate's ability to leave home and live self-sufficiently has been curtailed. The need for higher education in order to compete in the labor market has made many young men more dependent on their parents for financial support. Sometimes it becomes impossible for them to sever from their childhood home while they are still being educated.

Similarly, in times past, the Bar Mitzvah used to represent a true rite of passage for Jewish males. With his Bar Mitzvah, the young man would undergo a dramatic separation from the overt domination of his mother and would take his place in the community of men, having been given the full rights and respect conferred on male adults in the Jewish community. Having become a Bar Mitzvah, he would participate with the men in the study of the law and traditions and would partake of masculine activities and rites from which women were assiduously excluded.

Today, the Bar Mitzvah all too often represents a celebration for the parents who mark *their* achievement in raising a fine young man. The boy performs the "rites" of the modern Bar Mitzvah in the name of his parents and has little knowledge of the meaning of the rite as a celebration of his own passage. This type of Bar Mitzvah has almost no transformative power. It is worth noting, however, that there appears to be an upsurge in the number of Jewish families choosing to follow the more orthodox religious practices, including the traditional Bar Mitzvah. This may be in part a compensatory response to the decline of ritual in American Jewish culture.

Profound isolation, fear, and the threat of death have been a part of masculine initiation rites for thousands of years. The army, until the 1950's, represented another major source of masculine initiation. In the army, the young man would encounter all of the awesomeness of a masculine initiation, including confrontation with death itself. In recent times, however, the character of warfare has radically changed. Since Vietnam, it appears that war will be waged more by machines than men. Recruits for the modern armed forces are sought more for the purposes of maintaining and servicing automated instruments of warfare than for the purposes of man-to-man combat.

In the age of the "volunteer army," the awesomeness and fear formerly inspired in youth by the armed forces (the bastion of masculine power and rule), has degenerated considerably, and with it the army's power to effect the transformation from boyhood to manhood. The military draft, a kind of violent wrenching away of the boy from his childhood home and the dominance of his mother, is gone. Also lost is much of the sense of mysterious awe that the father archetype, as represented by military authorities, held for the new recruit. Whereas before he might have been unavoidably drafted, now he is given the choice, and is allowed to make that choice on the basis of his own assessment of the degree to which the army meets *his* needs![1]

Although the armed forces remain probably the single most potent institutional source of legitimate masculine initiation in our culture, there is a growing decline in its power to bring about a complete separation from the archetype of the mother. For many men, it represents as secure a hiding place as they can find from the power of the feminine, rather than a place where a man learns the heroic art. Even here, where the feminine heretofore was contained rigidly in the model of the officer's wife who centered her life around the manly activities of her husband, women have now infiltrated the military academies themselves. Some even participate in combat training jointly with the men and exercise command authority by rank over them. This kind of "archetypal contamination" represents yet another sign of the inability of the military to provide an effective initiatory experience for the modern male.

The decline of rites of passage in American culture has been universal and rapid. What has been observed about the role of the high school diploma, the Bar Mitzvah and the armed services might also be said of numerous other masculine rites of passage such as college education, competitive athletics, the driver's license, the first job, the bachelor party, the marriage ceremony, the first shave, moving into one's own home, the initiation into the union or guild, and even the first night drunk with the boys.

THE MALE GROUP

Most of the development of the young male's heroic identity takes place during the transition from adolescence to young adulthood. It is particularly at this transition stage that the archetype of initiation breaks down in American culture. Since primitive times, in order to permit the emergence and development of the *individual* ego and differentiation of the *individual* self, group ritual and ceremony has degenerated and been supplanted by rituals of the individual. Over the centuries a split probably occurred between the priest-mediators and those on whose behalf the priest-mediators functioned. The latter progressively ceased to be direct participants in the rites and increasingly became observers of the rites (cf. Neumann 1976). This resulted in a corresponding loss of *participation mystique*[2] on the part of the observers, and led to the loss of a direct, living relationship with the archetype of initiation. Over time, the loss of group identification with archetypal energy has left the individual fascinated with and gripped by the symbols of the archetype, but ignorant of their meaning and value and often untransformed by them.

Outer acts derived from rituals in man's past are now all too often replaced by *inner* symbols and rites within the individual psyche (e.g. dreams, obsessive behavior, etc.). However, the crucial factor in bringing about a true psychological transformation through inner ritual is the individual's consciousness of the process itself. Without some level of ego participation, either through enactment[3] and or self-reflection, ritual becomes ritualism. And herein lies the dilemma, since consciousness tends to be biased against the "intrusion" of unconscious contents, especially the sort that characteristically emerge through ritual behavior (Campbell 1949). With regard to the archetype of initiation, then, the ego is biased against those very practices which would further its own development and evolution.

In a society like ours which places enormous value on the individual, the value and status of the group-Self has progressively declined over the years. At the same time, historically speaking, the group has played a crucial role in masculine individuation and has been the single most powerful source of rites of passage in the psyche of man. Henderson (1967) postulates three conditions necessary for male individuation: 1. separation from the original family or clan, 2. commitment to a meaningful group over a long period of time, and 3. liberation from too close an identity with the group. In primitive times, the group was a powerful entity and males emerging from matriarchal dominance identified themselves with a clearly defined male group to which they owed total allegiance, often for many years. The separation of the sexes in many primitive cultures was usually total, often with severe taboos and sanctions (sometimes death) against the intermingling of the sexes in other than a tightly prescribed manner.

Andrew, a twenty-four year old youth, the middle of three sons, sought my analytic help. He was a middle level staff member in a federal government agency. His complaint was that he was experiencing a high degree of anxiety about being an outsider. He felt like he had missed his social and sexual life as a teenager by trying to play out an idealized, "mature," masculine role based on intellectual ideas prescribed by his parents. He complained of intense jealousy of contemporaries who led a more mature life than he, and of obsessive thoughts about whether or not his lovers had more sexual encounters. He admitted to feeling inadequate and humiliated as a male, which sometimes resulted in situational impotence. He had obsessive fears of impotency. He feared that his penis was abnormally small. Sometimes it shriveled when he was very anxious. He had a violent temper with active fantasies of violence, mostly towards men whom he felt threatened by or who might humiliate him. Often he felt the need to challenge authority figures, male and female. He had invested an enormous amount of energy into containing his anger. This sometimes left him feeling psychically and physically debilitated.

Andrew's parents separated and divorced when he was nineteen. He "remained" with his mother but was away at college for the year. He described his mother as a "pure idealistic, intellectual, castrating bitch," noting that he resembled her most emotionally. He described his father as a man who wanted to appear as big and macho, but who in effect was weak and pathetic. Andrew expressed both pity and rage at this father and had little respect for him.

In our initial session Andrew stated, "I've got to quick get over being a teenager—I've got to hurry up and be a teenager [live it through]. I guess I need some kind of rite of passage." It was my view that Andrew was stuck at the adolescent stage of ego development. Instead of being initiated into his manhood by his father, Andrew had been abandoned by him.

After working with him for a few months, it became apparent to me that Andrew had never really physically or psychically left his mother's home and that although he perceived himself as being financially independent and self-supporting, he had no home of his own. At the time he entered analysis he had half of his clothes and other possessions at his current girl friend's apartment and the other half at his mother's house, his childhood home. He would sleep at his girl friend's several nights during the week and would spend a night or two at his mother's, particularly if the relationship with his girl friend became difficult, which it did with some regularity. He used his mother's address as his legal address.

Andrew had divided his time like this since completing undergraduate school. He would always have a girl friend with whom he would be "kind of" living, but without any formalization of the relationship and no stated commitment to it. He counted on his "other home" at his mother's house as a back-up when things got rough with his girl friend or when he was experiencing other insecurities. It was clear that he had never psychically severed from his mother. Indeed, by his own acknowledgement, he tended to treat his girl friends as he had idealized his mother should be treated when he was younger.

A man's capacity to be related to a woman is, in part, a function of his capacity to live alone, to bring his own inner mother, his own capacity to next, to an internal "home." To the extent that he cannot, he remains dependent in a maternal sense upon a woman. Without the ability to live alone he remains mother-bound and will project the maternal into his relationships with women.

I suggested to Andrew that it was important for him to separate completely from his mother and to claim his own life space. I also suggested that since he was not prepared to commit himself to an exclusive relationship with his current girl friend, he might consider admitting it to her rather than behaving as if he was both independent and exclusively committed to her. I suggested that getting his own apartment, something he had never had in his life, would constitute an important rite of passage and would help to separate him from his mother-bound state. After a few sessions around this issue he did find and move into his own apartment. Exactly four weeks to the day that he moved into his own apartment he had the following dream:

> *I was in a house or apartment. It may have been my brother's or my house or both. It seemed like it wasn't mine. Anyway, I felt ill at ease there. There were people there, a party, and I had only gym shorts on.*
>
> *I remember feeling very anxious and rushing around like I had chores before the party began. The people didn't feel like friends, but like strangers or friends of friends or people I had to be false with.*

I went outside. It was afternoon, Saturday or Sunday. There was a big playing field, like the back of the house opened on to a college campus.

There were people milling around the field, mostly young boys dressed to play soccer or some other sport. I still felt threatened. They seemed to be linked with those in the party—cool, cruel, mocking, frightening.

I felt like I was so insecure I had to be their target. They had lots of balls. They began pitching them to me—from all directions. First came a little rubber ball like we used to have at school. I had to do something with the balls but something was on my mind and for whatever reason I felt like I was in a no-win situation. I had to return the balls and not bobble them, but these kids were threatening me with their leers and I had something on my mind keeping me from playing.

But I got into it. First came the small ball and I was amazed that I kicked it, accurately and low, with my left foot. I kicked a couple of others with my left foot—again, surprisingly accurately.

I thought, throw the balls back to them. Then it will be accurate. They came rapidly, and from all directions; in all only five or ten. Finally came a white soccer ball. I put a little into this kick. The ball soared. A huge kick—tremendously high and far. The power, the wham! when my foot met the ball was surpassed by the distance of the kick. I actually had not put everything into it, just something. But the kick was superior, grand, amazing, powerful, and supremely satisfying. The kids watched with awe, respect, and joy. They felt how powerful I was, but weren't afraid and were getting off on it.

Then I remembered the joy of kicking balls, how I loved to distance them, how I loved to hit home runs, how I could play goalie in soccer and kick the ball to the other goal. Power, joy, exhilaration, expression.

I wanted to kick more, just like I always used to want to kick more back then. The feeling of my power and joy had suddenly broken the hold of my insecurity. I was almost in a trance, a reverie. I wanted to be free and to demonstrate my power.

I woke up.[4]

The dream reflects the culmination of a psychic progression from the dominance of the archetype of the mother, to the archetype of the father and finally to the archetype of the male group. It reflects Andrew's site of separation from his mother and girl friend by claiming his own life space. In the dream he moves from the psychic realm of the mother and the father into the all-male group, an essential step in his journey towards masculine self-hood. The dream itself was a rite of passage; Andrew's dream-initiation into this male group was attended by all of the anxieties involved in leaving a familiar realm for a new and unfamiliar one. But Andrew's initiation was more than successful—he triumphantly passed the trials to which he was submitted and clearly connected with his masculine power. Indeed, he outplayed all the other males on the field (in the group) once he had lived through his fear and dread concerning separation from the mother and his insecurities about his capabilities to survive on his own and compete with other males. Andrew had not yet really begun his hero's journey. But with his dream-entrance into an all-male group, where he could explore his own masculine power, he had taken his first psychic steps in that direction.

In a psychological sense, the masculine mysteries are learned in the male group. With the assistance of the powerful libido of the group, the individual male is helped to pull free from strong, regressive Oedipal forces. The group serves as a kind of second parent (Henderson 1964). It is a way-station for the developing male from which he goes on forays in the fearsome world of adult power. Here in the group he can relax, so to speak, while he builds up his strength and courage for the next, and more difficult, steps in his individuation journey—separation from the mother *and* father archetypes, the male group itself, and finally, encounter with his individual Self. Neumann (1954) states that, "The male group is the birthplace not only of consciousness and of the 'higher masculine,' but of individuality and the hero. . . ."

Some of the "masculine mysteries" performed in modern male groups involve such activities and behaviors as: exclusion of women from membership in the group, collective rites where the feminine is literally or figuratively overpowered and conquered by the masculine (e.g. bachelor parties, or porno movies), sharing with each as a group their individual sexual exploits with women, bragging about power confrontations and sexual conquests, elder-teacher/novice-apprentice relationships between older and younger members of the group, body building, phallic play as reflected in group showers, exploratory homosexual behavior, portrayal of masculine and heroic attributes in posters and art, esoteric language peculiar to the group, group athletic competition, and other kinds of positive or negative group/gang behavior. All of these activities aim at protecting the fearful ego from the negative power of the feminine, depotentiating it while building masculine libido. These behaviors provide training programs for the development of masculine prowess, and, importantly, establish a masculine ethos other than that of the father.

The male group has steadily weakened in American culture, particularly since the early 1960's. With the advent of a stronger social emphasis on individuality, civil rights and feminine individuation, and with the penetration of male groups by women and their disenchantment with the group's excessively patriarchal character, the male group has lost much of its cohesiveness. Many exclusively male fraternities have disappeared altogether, or nearly so—e.g., the all-male army, male athletic teams in some communities, the private men's clubs, the men's barber shops, even the all-male YMCA, among others. Many of those male groups that do remain intact have lost their purpose. They no longer serve as secret societies where masculine mysteries are shared and learned. Many have degenerated into hiding places where men gather to socialize as they hide from the Devouring Mother, rather than to gear up for a final wrenching free of her.

Some surviving forms of the male group include athletic teams, college fraternities, Lions Clubs, and other more loosely formed groups such as can be found in health clubs and gyms (those that practice sexual segregation), men's poker clubs, and the like. It is worth noting, however, that male groups can affect all levels and strata of society. For example, the membership of the segregated, exclusively male Bohemian Club of San Francisco has included U.S. presidents, senators, and supreme court justices. The club became a focused point of controversy in the 1981 confirmation hearings of Attorney General William French Smith (who also has been a member). There were formal charges of sex discrimination by the State of California, allegations of homosexual behavior between guests and staff, descriptions of "bizarre" rituals and ceremonies, and accounts of members dressed as women and portraying female roles performing in various dramas. In its defense, the club's secretary stated that, "The intrusion of women into this atmosphere would destroy that special environment by their presence." Members complained that they would not be able to urinate in the open if women were admitted.[5]

On the other end of the spectrum, those men who use the male group primarily as a place to hide from women and who never consciously deal with their fear of them, may find themselves stuck in the group. The 1960's film *Marty* depicts this dilemma well. Its chief figure, Marty, a man in his thirties, used the group to hide from his fear of women. As the story unfolded, it became clear that the prime factor which held the group together was its fear of women and its refusal to deal with them. As Marty moved towards a meaningful relationship with a woman, he encountered enormous resistance and ridicule from the group. His struggle to break away from his bond with the group in order to relate more freely to his woman resulted in a resumption of his individuation and his eventual departure from the group.

However, not all such situations turn out as positively as with Marty. A negative example of male bonding to the group can be seen in some of the motorcycle gangs where the primary identity of the male is, and remains, with a group from which the female either is excluded or ruthlessly controlled by being treated as if she were group or individual property. As Henderson points out, "The main feature of those who [successfully] undertake the initiation journey is that they have exhausted the absolutism of their group identity—

temporarily, if they are young; more or less permanently, if they are older" (Henderson 1967).

Since passage through the male group is an integral part of the transition from the adolescent to the man-hero stage of ego development, the archetype of initiation still strives for incarnation—even though the male group has significantly atrophied. As a result, many young American males have regressed to a primitive form of *participation mystique*. With the decline of the male group and its associated ritual, the masculine psyche nonetheless seeks connection with a group-Self and will sometimes project that need misguidedly onto "groups" which will give it definition, support, and guidance on its quest for individuation. We can see this today, in sects and cults, in the fanatical followers of Reverend Moon, Scientology, and in other such groups which stand ready to use such youth for their own purposes. The awesome archetypal power of the group-Self as expressed through *participation mystique* can be seen readily in the absolute allegiance of members of these cults no matter how repressive and regressive the group may become. We have witnessed the dramatic results of unconscious projection of this archetype in its most fanatical form with the mass suicides of the followers of Jim Jones in Jonestown, Guyana.

In addition, the mass media, by appropriating the modern ritual medium of male youths, e.g. rock and folk music, team sports, etc., have substituted themselves as oracles for the male group. Through advertisements which project a static image of the "healthy" male in our society, the media have exerted a powerful influence on the determination of modern standards for the masculine group. Ads tell the adolescent and young adults in our society that he is a true hero if he drinks Coke or smokes Marlboro cigarettes or if he treats girls as though they were mindless maidens in distress. The message is that he need only identify (by imitating their personal habits) with the heroes of the mass media to become a hero. He doesn't have to do the work himself by performing his own heroic deeds or experiencing his own rites of passage. These ads systematically undermine the process of self-reflection crucial to masculine ego development. In place of self-reflection is "being cool," i.e. identification with artificial and distorted images of the heroic.

Given the universal decline of the male group and of rites of passage in our culture, the contemporary male is left essentially with three alternatives: 1. to connect up consciously with those legitimate outer rites of passage which survive (or to create new ones), 2. to become aware of the inner rites of passage which take place symbolically within his own psyche and to consciously enact them, or, 3. to pay the price for his unconsciousness and disconnectedness from the archetype of initiation with stunted ego development and the risk of falling into a regressive *participation mystique*.

RECENT DEVELOPMENTS IN THE ARCHETYPE OF THE FEMININE
AND THEIR IMPACT ON THE MALE

Because the atrophy of masculine rites of passage in our culture has left modern man more susceptible to the regressive power of the Great Mother, a look at recent developments in the archetype of the feminine is necessary to assess the present state of the masculine ego in our culture. Since the 1950's, the archetype of the feminine has emerged from what appeared to be a long and quiet "sleep" and has become probably the most dynamic archetypal energy prevalent in our midst today. Although the roots of the current freeing of feminine archetypal energy can be traced back to the suffrage movement after World War I, the "Women's Movement" has become a universal aspect of our culture only in the past two decades. It seems evident that a psycho-evolutionary drama is taking place in our culture, as manifested by a resurgence of the feminine (Whitmont 1982).

Emergence of the Feminine Hero[6]

In the past two decades we have seen the woman emerge from the home and take her place as a competitive member of the labor force. Nowadays, women are represented in almost every occupation which heretofore was the exclusive domain of men. Not only have women entered a number of professions previously unavailable to them, but their mere presence has resulted in changes in the very nature of some jobs (Brenton 1966). This assertiveness on their part is not limited to the type of jobs they hold. Not-withstanding the defeat of the Equal Rights Amendment (ERA), women are winning legal and social victories concerning their right to live and function as more complete women in our society.

Many women no longer see their primary role as being the kind of women their husbands would have them be. They no longer have to choose between being a career woman or a mother. It has become increasingly possible for them to be both—each role representing true and legitimate expressions of their femininity. Women have come to respect their own intellects and to value their contributions to society. In so doing, they have demanded and won male respect for their skills and achievements.

Women appear to be more consciously active in their individuation process than men are at this point in history. The long-time suppression of the feminine ego and the absence of avenues for outer expression gave rise to considerable frustration, resentment, anger, longing, and fantasy. Over time, the resulting tension has tended to stimulate positive animus growth, which in turn has fostered feminine assertiveness—in many instances spurring healthy ego development. The negative, defeminizing side of the Women's Movement is a result of an over-identification with the animus, i.e. the inner masculine component of women.

Rather than being inactive over the centuries, the archetype of the feminine has been incubating and gestating. Its incubation period seems to have ended around the beginning of the decade of the 1960's. Because women were forced to protect and nurture their egos through deep inner reflection and self-awareness (rather than in a more extraverted manner, like men), they tended to focus on their state of being and became more psychically active in their own growth and development. It appears that this introverted process has peaked in the past fifteen years and, with considerable help from the animus, is becoming more outwardly manifested. Sleeping Beauty has finally awakened, if not leapt out of bed!

As the "feminine hero," the woman is one who breaks the bonds of her need for connectedness with a man when those bonds impede her self-realization. The woman is the one who pursues the uncertain path toward her own individuality, often at the cost of intense loneliness and pain. Increasingly, women seem to be forced to separate from emotionally stagnant and dependent attachments with men in order to pursue their lives. The persistently high divorce rates and frequent incidence of female head-of-household families seem to support this impression.

The growing independence and assertiveness of women has put tremendous pressure on the male. This is evident in the labor market and, increasingly so, in the political arena. Most significantly, it has put psychological pressure on men to relate meaningfully with women. There can be little doubt that much of the "encroachment" by women into the masculine domain is resented by men (Brenton 1966). Women are claiming their femininity, not as reflected by men, but as they experience it in themselves. They are insisting that men relate to them as individual women. Women are rejecting the inclusive role of "server" to their husbands, and are seeking true companionship in their relationships with husbands and lovers—both as companion to the man and as recipient of companionship from the man (de Castellejo 1973).

Large numbers of women are now putting considerable sexual pressure on the male to satisfy his partner, as well as himself. Women have assumed an equal status with their sexual partners. This new sexual pressure on the man often leads him to be primarily concerned with his "performance" at the expense of intimacy. In my practice, I have encountered a rash of complaints from both men and women regarding problems of impotency on the part of the man when intimacy and sex must be addressed in the same woman. It is as if many men cannot tolerate expression of their eros and emotional vulnerability in the same relationship. Depersonalization of the woman, i.e. impersonal sex on the part of men, appears to be a way of avoiding the perceived-to-be threatening power of the feminine, a power which, in many men, evokes sexual impotency. Thus, many men who have not fully attained sexual maturity find themselves compulsively pursuing simultaneous relationships with women—one relationship where the man finds emotional security and support (often with a mother surrogate), and another type of relationship (primarily sexual) with one or more women. In the former, often with his wife, the man finds emotional security, which may or may not include intimacy, but is sexually insecure and sometimes impotent. In the latter, the man is sexually active and feels potent, but there is a noted insistence by the man on an absence of emotional commitment to the relationship.

The primary response of many men to their fear of an emancipated woman appears to be a form of escapism involving repression, denial, and sublimation. Many men use work to avoid family life and involvement with their wives and lovers (Brenton 1966). Others escape into affairs with "understanding" women (to whom they have no obligations or responsibilities), or they have multiple marriages. Others find haven in men's groups and "secret societies" where women are excluded, etc. (Tiger 1970, also Ruitenbeck 1967). Homosexuality is another avenue of escape for men fearing intimacy with women (Kettner 1967). Psychotherapy can provide another means of avoidance for the man who wishes to turn his problems over to a father or mother surrogate who, he hopes, either will work it out for him or tell him that his on-going pattern is really okay.

Modern man often reacts to the feminine hero as if she were the Devouring Mother herself. Her assertion of independence and her claim of individuality is perceived as a threat by many men. This is understandable. Men have had nothing in their experience and training to prepare them for this social and psychic revolution, and experience their loss of power over women as an absolute loss of masculine power. On the other hand women have been waiting for centuries for their emancipation and the resumption of their individuation as women. While women find new life meaning and an increasing sense of empowerment, men often experience a loss of power which for them is tantamount to a humiliating defeat for the masculine ego. They face a threatening future which has less and less clear definition for them in relation to women and their own masculinity. This largely unconscious fear of women is amply reinforced by some women, who, when a man does permit himself to be emotionally vulnerable with her, often will attack and humiliate him for not being macho enough to fight her. In this regard, women must face their own reluctance to give up their need for macho men.

For centuries men have romanticized the plight of the woman in distress. They have nurtured the myth of the masculine hero as one who saves the woman from her plight. The net result has been the oppression of women and men's continuing alienation from their own feminine side—from their own feelings and soul. It is their own distressed, feeling side—the anima—which they project unconsciously onto women and which they are continually trying to "save." But with the emergence of the feminine hero—the self-assertive, individuating woman—the male is confronted with the fact that the woman is in less distress than his own anima. The feminine hero is no longer a convenient hook for masculine projections of feminine weakness and dependency. She is giving his distressed anima back to the man, and along with it his insistence that women take care of him. Engaged with her own self-development, she is much less inclined to take responsibility for nurturing the male's anima for him. She is too busy with her own individuation to play the game of "rescue" with a man who would rather project his feminine side onto her than own it himself.

It is not (as many men seem to feel) so much that the man is losing his power to women. Rather, it is that women are taking back power which previously they have used to support and carry the male's feeling side for him. As a result, the contemporary male increasingly experiences uncertainty, depression, dependency, loneliness, despair—feelings which have been there all along. Thus, it is not women in distress that is the primary issue in masculine development, but rather the condition of the man's inner feminine, feeling side. Men can't save women. To the extent that women need to be "saved," they will have to do that for themselves. Likewise, when women stop saving men, i.e. stop trying to hold men's heads above the waters of their own insecurity and depression, men will have to directly address those issues in themselves.

A willingness to engage the feminine hero enables a man to rely, to "depend" on the feminine. But "dependency" does not mean that the woman carries the man's burden for him, not does it mean castration or surrendering masculine power. Rather it means learning to rely on a helper (by definition someone with a commitment to the man) to engage his feelings when necessary. By permitting his feelings and emotions to be engaged, the man is enabled to search within himself for the wherewithal to respond. Through this conscious search he contacts his own inner feminine and explores the depths and strengths of his own psyche.

It is also through this inner quest that he will encounter his inner "Athena-helper." Mythologically, as the goddess born of the masculine (she was birthed live from the swollen head of Zeus) Athena represents the feminine contained in the masculine. She represents a different and crucial dimension of the feminine from that which man typically encounters in women. The inner Athena embodies principles of moral and psychic courage essential to a full realization of masculine power (Whitmont 1976). It is the realization of his inner Athena-helper that will give the male the psychic resources which he has sought erroneously from women.[7]

The Modern Devouring Mother

Concomitant with the emergence of the feminine hero, a powerful and destructive aspect of the mother archetype has been manifesting itself in the form of giant corporations and big government. This modern Devouring Mother appears in the guise of a benevolent, nurturing, protective mother, rekindling images in men of the most nurturing aspects of the maternal. But too often she is one which seeks to hold men to her breast with a stranglehold, opposing their masculine individuation at every turn in the name of fostering and protecting it.

Neumann's (1954) description of the positive aspect of the Great Mother is helpful here:

> . . . [She] is life and psyche in one; [she] gives nourishment and pleasure, protects and warms, comforts and forgives. [She] is the refuge for all suffering, the goal of all desire. For always this mother is she who fulfills, the bestower and helper. This living image of the Great and Good Mother has at all times of distress been the refuge of humanity and ever shall be; for the state of being contained in the whole, without responsibility or effort . . . is paradisical.

For a child, this mother is essential and fosters his psychic and emotional well-being. But for the adult male striving to attain his herohood, she can be deadly and can hold him bound, aborting his hero's journey. As Whitmont (1976) puts it, "There is no freedom possible except by virtue of losing the containedness in the mother and developing a consciousness that is separate."

Today, giant corporations and big government have become the Devouring Mother for many men. Over 38.4 percent of males age sixteen and over work either for one of the Fortune 500 corporations or for the government (U.S. Dept. of Labor 1979). In our society there is chronic unemployment and increasing competition for what jobs are available. Rising inflation increasingly pressures male wage earners to earn more to retain what they now have. The viability of the small employer is shrinking and along with him job security in any context other than in the giant corporation or big government. The concentration of dollars rests overwhelmingly with giant corporations and government which alone can afford to guarantee employment during frequent cycles of economic downturn and provide a viable retirement plan—which for more and more American men and their families means survival in their later years. From the perspective of economic peace of mind, one can see how corporations and government can appear to be a warm, nourishing breast.

A closer look at one giant corporation (International Business Machines), may be helpful in perceiving how the giant corporation is a modern version of the Devouring Mother. IBM offers the following benefits to its employees: up to five weeks vacation; twelve paid holidays per year; 100 percent reimbursement for courses approved by IBM taken outside of working hours; tuition up to a total of $2,500 for courses which will help employees (or their spouse if the employee is deceased) prepare for retirement; competitive scholarships of up to $6,000 annually for as many as four years, and a total of $24,000 per child for dependents of IBM employees to participate in programs of higher education; paid sick leave; a family hospitalization plan; a family surgical plan; a family major medical plan, including psychotherapy; a family dental plan; financial assistance for employees with mentally, emotionally, or physically handicapped children or stepchildren up to age twenty-three to a maximum benefit of $50,000 per child; financial assistance towards expenses incurred in the adoption of children; leave of absence and financial assistance when an employee enters the armed forces, including an induction payment, monthly leave payments and up to twenty-four months of comprehensive medical coverage for children not covered by the U.S. Government; group life insurance and survivors income benefit plan; a total and permanent disability income plan where the disability does not have to be job related; a retirement plan; and a group life insurance plan after retirement—*all of which is 100 percent paid for by IBM*.[8] Other large corporations, as well as the government, offer similar benefits, as well as automatic pay increases, cost-of-living increases, "merit" increases, and the like.

The male who is stuck at the adolescent level of ego development is in a state of constant struggle against the regressive pull of the matriarchy. As he gets older and begins to pass into his mid-thirties, he can almost feel the Devouring Mother at his heels. In addition, the pressure put on him from the newly emerging feminine hero often serves to intensify his sense of powerlessness and heightens his sense of despair.

Government and the giant corporations provide a tantalizing haven for him. Within the bosom of this modern Devouring Mother he feels he can find safety. She will nourish him, protect him, take care of him and his family even unto retirement and death, promise not to throw him out into the cold where, he unconsciously fears, the Terrible Mother awaits him in the form of the feminine hero. The giant corporation will confer power upon him and make him feel manly by giving him constant reinforcement for his activities within her realm. One of the strong appeals of government and giant corporations is that they provide an artificial sense of rites of passage through promotions, new titles, large and more elaborately decorated offices, fancier company cars, and the like. On the very day an analysand who felt creatively stagnant in his work resigned from corporation employment (one of the top ten) in order to become a private consultant in his field, he reported:

> I trembled as I gave notice to [them]. I felt as if I was saying, 'Mother, I don't need you anymore, I'm leaving home.' I have a fear of rejecting my mother and a fear of her rejecting me. At worst, I've told mother I don't need her anymore and I feel I will be punished for that.

In this context, however, government and giant corporations are anonymous, depersonalized, autonomous entities, more a manifestation of the

Devouring Mother through the collective unconscious than a creation of man. They have no clear identity. No "one" controls them. They operate on a principle of anonymous collective "control" and *participation mystique*. The men who "operate" and "control" them are more controlled by them and often are the unwitting agents for agendas which are less designed by the egos of male managers than by the powerful forces of the collective unconscious.

Although many giant corporations (government less so) in fact do carry out many of their promises to their male employees, there is nonetheless a subtle shift from working under the mandate of one's own ego to working for the Great Mother. The very benefits that are provided may create a dependency on the part of the individual worker which subtly but inexorably erodes his masculine self-esteem.

The Stuck Hero

In our culture there is enormous confusion in masculine identity due to the absence of adequate confirmation and validation of the male's hero role. At the same time the complexity of modern-day society, particularly economic competition, has extended the length of the adolescent period. At the turn of the century and up through the 1920's the male in our society was expected to live through his adolescence by the end of high school. Now we have the not unusual phenomenon of men reaching the age of thirty and beyond before completing school and venturing forth into the world on their own (Greene 1967). This tends to confuse the boundaries between the various stages of masculine ego development, most particularly between the adolescent and adult hero stages. Consequently, initiation rites between these stages lose their focus and meaning, archetypal power is lost, and the archetype of initiation itself is weakened.

The fact that one matures physically despite economic necessity and other exigencies has resulted in a psychological crisis in the lives of many men and is most dramatically depicted by stuck middle-aged men still trying to achieve true initiation into their herohood through compulsive competition of all types while the aging process moves them beyond their boyhood dreams. In many instances, our culture tends to produce Willie Lomans and Caseys at the Bat instead of legitimate heroes who mature and individuate.

Archetypally, masculine maturity becomes the focal point at the adolescent stage of ego development. However, at this stage it lacks sufficient libido to pull away and sever fully from the mother. The emerging masculine ego needs the strong positive support of the father to help make this awesome psychic separation and ultimately to enter into apprenticeship with the male group. However, a sign of the times is the divorce that shatters the nuclear family, leaving young boys to arrive at their adolescence not only without the presence of a strong father advocate, but often with their mothers as the primary, if not only, advocate on the scene. No matter how positive and supportive a mother she may be to the adolescent boy, the process of masculine initiation is archetypally inverted.

It is less important that a man experience himself as having lost crucial battles in his attempt to individuate than that he try. Mythology is full of heroes who have lost many a battle with the dragon of life, e.g. Odysseus, Gilgamesh, and Hercules, among others. But most have won in the end. We live in an era of scientific and technological inflation and a collective identification with power. Struggle, as such, has lost much of its virtue. In the modern age only the outcome counts, regardless of personal meaning to the individual man. But the struggle itself is the true heroic deed that strengthens man's ego. At the same time it protects him from an inflating hubris which could destroy him. In the last analysis, if man struggles for his individuation, more likely than not he will attain it to some significant degree.

RITES OF PASSAGE IN THE CONTEMPORARY CONTEXT

The decline of rites of passage in our culture, and thus the weakening of the archetype of initiation, has resulted primarily from the progressive split and alienation between the matriarchal and patriarchal archetypes over the past two thousand years. Over-identification with patriarchal consciousness disintegrates reality and experience and leaves out the reality of the unconscious. Patriarchal consciousness exalts the individual above the group and tends to deny to the individual the reality of his/her growth as a function of a group-Self. It ranks the feeling function as inferior and of a lower order of experience—especially to be avoided when dealing with problem-solving. It is a consciousness which results in massive secondary personalization of transpersonal contents, particularly of ritual. Thus patriarchal consciousness has tended to undermine the archetype of initiation, particularly in boys and men, blocking their ego development.

There is a profound difference between an ego that is inflated from the collective patriarchal power complex, and one that is centered in a meaningful connection to the hero aspect of the individual Self. The former leads to a negative power complex and a loss of individual self, and the latter leads to positive relationship to power which serves legitimate ego needs and a claiming of masculine selfhood and individuation.

The rapid and continuing resurgence of the archetype of the feminine over the past fifteen to twenty years has significantly challenged the patriarchal status quo and is bringing about a necessary deflation of a vastly over-inflated masculine ego. At the same time, the crisis of deflation has provided men with an opportunity to reconnect with their personal individuation process, and opportunity to redeem and claim their heroic selves. For such men, there is little focused assistance in our society to help them negotiate these crises. Many simply weather the storm and struggle, often with considerable help from family, friends and employers, attempting to regain the status they feel they have lost. They see themselves as having gone through a "mid-life" crisis, or having experienced a "nervous breakdown" or some other "breakdown" which calls for re-establishment of the *status quo ante*. They do not see their deflation and depression for what it often is—a restorative attempt on the part of the Self to compensate for a developmental block which is stunting their masculine individuation. If such men succeed in reclaiming their previous status without undergoing a meaningful emotional and psychic transformation, they will have lost the struggle to redeem their herohood and resume their individuation. They will be the stuck heroes of the modern age. Many will repeat old patterns of depression, "nervous breakdown" or divorce into their old age. And as fathers they will fail their sons.

It would appear that, for the present, the primary means for converting such crises into meaningful growth processes is the analytic/therapeutic process. In therapy the inner psychic rituals and dreams of the erstwhile hero can be brought to conscious light and guidance can be provided in identifying the rites of passage necessary for formalizing changes in life station. Some examples of such rites of passage might be: changing a marital relationship which is nothing more than a mother-son marriage; leaving a group living arrangement and learning to live by one's self; standing up to a humiliating supervisor, even at the risk of losing one's job; leaving a boring job which offers tenure and material security in order to reclaim one's creativity and ingenuity in other works; or acting on a homosexual obsession (putting a man in touch with a dimension of his masculinity which he might not gain in any other way) or leaving the security of a homosexual relationship for a needed, albiet unsettling, encounter with a woman.

This last point is crucial. Contrary to considerable psychological theory, insight and an understanding of the meaning of a symbol are not always sufficient to bring about psychic and emotional transformation and to release archetypal libido. To a large extent, the symbol merely points the way. Enactment is necessary to release archetypal libido.[9] For intra-psychic (i.e. symbolic) rites of passage to generate transformative potential, they must be enacted.

Similarly, compulsive behavior must be symbolized, i.e. the archetypal meaning interpreted to the individual, so that the behavior can be seen as symbolic of something beyond itself. At this level, interpretation, although necessary, will not always sufficiently effect emotional and/or behavioral transformation. A further step, a formalized enacted ritual(s) may be necessary. For example, a man of small stature compulsively avoided gyms because of paranoid feelings that he would be thought "queer"; i.e., he had a desire to look at men's crotches in the shower room and to have his own phallus seen. After he was enabled to see that he was afraid his phallic endowment was not up to that of the other men, or that his masculinity would be ridiculed, he was urged to go back to the gym and to make a point of comparing his penis with other men's. When he actually did so, he concluded that he "held his own" better than 50% of the time and that his overall physique was better than that of a vast majority of men (Vangaard 1969). The "enactment" of this phallic exhibitionism resulted in an empowering experience for him. Interpretation in and of itself was not transformative, but pointed the way to transformative enactment.

The resurgence of the archetype of the feminine has refocused a new interest in rituals per se. Fresh attention is being given to fraternities and their "initiations," marathon races, Olympics and other athletic games, vision quests, shamanistic apprenticeships, and the enactment of other primitive rites and seasonal ceremonies. The popularity of certain relevant organizations such as Outward Bound, the National Outdoor Leadership School, or the advanced Boy Scouts testify to the resurgence of interest in the boy to manhood passage. Men's consciousness groups also show promise. None of these movements appears to be strong enough to turn the tide. Rather they attest to a process which has begun rumbling around in the collective unconscious of our culture and in the individual unconscious of many men—a psychic need for rites of passage and a true initiation into manhood.

The revival of the archetype of the feminine would seem to hold most promise for the younger generation(s) of men. I am beginning to see the emergence of young men who are much more in touch with their feeling side, viewing this aspect of themselves as more legitimate and important in their lives than did their forebears. These men, by and large, seem to be split between their feeling and rational sides and are more aware (intuitively if not consciously) of their need for relationships based as much on the eros principle as on the logos. They appear to have greater need to express their love for each other. Sometimes the eros connection between males is mistaken for homosexual leanings. But what we are witnessing is instead a deeper masculine connection between men, a regeneration of a manifest and much needed male *fraternité* (Vangaard 1972). Moreover, these younger men appear to be less afraid of women and the feminine. Their deeper understanding of their own femininity makes possible more realistic and viable relationships with women. As they relate to girls and women as individuals and less as projections of their mothers, they develop non-maternal relationships to the feminine and are more open to outer support as well as inner counsel from the "Athena-helper."

Given the future prominence of the archetype of the feminine, I would predict a revival of interest in the male group, the emergence of new organizations and mechanisms for enactment of rites of passage appropriate to life stage, a greater respect by males for the feminine, the appearance of concepts of masculine power which value feelings and relatedness (rather than excluding them), and the increased manifestation of eros in relationships between men. Significant numbers of men graduating from colleges and universities will be less focused on materialistic aspects of their careers, and more interested in the qualitative aspect of their lives (notwithstanding the "Yuppie" wave of the 1980's), particularly in their intimate interpersonal relationships. In short, there will be some redressing of the imbalance.

At the same time, negative, regressive, patriarchal and matriarchal forces will continue to persist—particularly in large corporations, government agencies, unions, trade associations, educational institutions, and political groups, and will be evident in technological "advances" that mechanize and depersonalize masculine power. These forces will continue to exert considerable pressure on individual men, fostering the supremacy of the group-Self over the individual Self and undermining masculine self-esteem to the overall detriment of the masculine ego. Another, probably temporary, regressive influence is women who are angry at men for not being macho enough in their eyes.

In the interim, for those of us who are aware of the problem and are willing to invest some energy in the process, there are significant remedial measures that can be undertaken. Organizations and groups exist which offer initiatory-type experiences for men of all ages. Some of these experiences are patterned after American Indian vision quests or dream quests, others are based on mythological "underworld journeys" or pilgrimmages. The vision quest holds considerable psychological potential, for American Indian heritage is very much a part of our collective unconscious. Mahdi has demonstrated the value and feasibility of a group initiatory experience patterned on the Plains Indian vision quest for young males and females at the high school and college levels.[10] The reinstitution of dramatic initiatory experiences, particularly during the latter part of adolescence, can do much to reconstitute the natural psychic boundaries which delineate the various stages of masculine ego development.

Although rites of passage have lost much of their archetypal value in modern culture, it would not be too difficult, given a focused effort, to reanimate them with a measure of archetypal libido. A conscious father can assist his son through various stages of growth by applying the archetypal power of rite and ceremony to these growth-events. Any activity can be lifted from the ordinary and given special ritual attention. The ritualizing process can be employed with virtually any activity valued by the boy, such as his first handling and firing of a gun, the first time he kills another creature for its meat, the first time he shaves, the first time he drinks, the first time he stands up to the men's urinal, the first time he gets a bike, a girl friend, a varsity letter, or the keys to the family car.

In the end, what is called for is considerable consciousness raising regarding the crucial importance of rites of passage and initiation for men in our culture. Hopefully, in time, groups offering initiatory, experiential education will become more deeply involved in public education—as well as provide their services to all those who have a conscious need for them. Public education itself must face this issue and open its curriculum to education involving rites of passage. Physical education departments already carry out a quasi-role, albeit a not very conscious one, in so far as competitive athletics are concerned. It would seem appropriate and feasible for organized initiatory experiences to be conducted through physical education programs at the junior and senior levels of high school, for all students, not just those who help the school win the trophy in competitive sports.

The problem of uninitiated men in our culture carries import that reaches beyond the development of the individual man and affects the well-being of our culture as a whole. A healthy transition from a culture that has been dominated by the patriarchy to one which reflects a new integration of feminine with masculine values is dependent on the freeing of the masculine psyche from its adolescent-bound state. In this mission, women have no less stake than men, for the lesson to be learned in the new age is that the individuation of the one is dependent on the individuation of the other.

NOTES

1. Masculine initiation represents a wrenching free of the boy from the mother (and the mother archetype) and an act of *incorporation* on the part of patriarchal authorities, the elder conferring the status of manhood on the younger. Archetypally, *all* authority must reside with the patriarchial initiators, including how and when the boy is initiated. To the extent that the boy has choice—the right to choose the times and terms of his joining the group—patriarchal authority is weakened and the natural flow of libido disrupted, resulting in a loss of psychological, even archetypal power.

2. Unconscious individual and/or group identification with archetypal energy.

3. "Enactment" here means the outer re-construction of symbolic material *because* the behavior involved is recognized (intuitively if not consciously) as having some import above and beyond the symbolic material or the specific acts themselves, i.e., a "numinous experience." Enactment involves a *conscious living through* and claiming of the archetypal meaning (goal) to which symbolic material (i.e., dreams and compulsive behavior) may point, as opposed to "acting out" which represents an unconscious behavior without meaningful self-reflection.

4. I have reported the dream exactly as Andrew recorded it himself, including underlinings.

5. Anderson 1981. Note: I have added the sentence about men urinating in the open in order to point out the degree to which primitive impulses of the male group are manifest in all strata of society, including those males who reach the highest rungs.

6. I use the term "feminine hero" here instead of the standard term "heroine" because often the latter has been used inappropriately to depict the feminine as weak, dependent, and passive instead of emphasizing the phallic aspect of feminine power—the heroic aspect of the feminine.

7. For a full development of the Athena-helper archetype, see Homer, *The Odyssey*.

8. IBM, 1984. The family major medical plan is a supplementary plan and covers 80% of expenses.

9. See above, note 3, re. "enactment."

10. Mahdi 1976. [Editor's note: See also Pinkson 1976, and Foster and Little 1983, in this volume.]

REFERENCES

Anderson, J. 1981. Is trouble brewing for the paradise of the rich? *Parade*, Feb. 22, 1981.

Brenton, M. 1956. *The American male*. New York: Coward-McCann.

Campbell, J. 1949. *Hero with a thousand faces*. Princeton: Princeton University Press.

Castellejo, I.C. de 1973. *Knowing woman: A feminine psychology*. New York: Harper & Row.

Deal, T. E. and Kennedy, A. A. 1982. *Corporate cultures: The rites and rituals of corporate life*. Reading, Mass.: Addison-Wesley.

Edinger, E. F. 1967. On being an individual. *Spring*. Dallas: Spring Publications.

Eliade, M. 1958. *Rites and symbols of initiation*. New York: Harper & Row.

Foster, S. and Little, M. 1980. *The book of the vision quest*. Spokane: Bear Tribe Publications.

————. 1983. *The vision quest: Passing from childhood to adulthood*. Big Pine, CA: Rites of Passage Press.

Franz, M. L. von. 1972. *Patterns of creativity mirrored in creation myths*. Zurich: Spring Publications.

Gennep, A. van. 1960. *The rites of passage*. Chicago: University of Chicago.

Greene, R. K. 1978. Problems in masculine aggression. Thesis written for C. G. Jung Training Center, New York.

Greene, T. A. 1967. *Modern man in search of manhood*. New York: Association Press.

Harding, M. E. 1971. *Women's mysteries*. New York: Harper & Row.

Henderson, J. 1964. Ancient myths and modern man. In *Man and his symbols*, ed. C. G. Jung. Garden City, NY: Doubleday.

————. 1967. *Thresholds of initiation*. Middletown, Conn.: Wesleyan University Press.

Herdt, G. H. 1981. *Guardians of the flutes*. New York: McGraw-Hill.

Hillman, J. 1975. The masturbation inhibition. In *Loose ends: Primary papers in archetypal psychology*. Zurich: Spring Publications.

Jung, C. G. 1964. *Man and his symbols*. Garden City, N.Y.: Doubleday.

Kettner, M. 1967. Some archetypal themes in male homosexuality. *Professional Reports*. San Francisco.

Layard, J. July, 1959. Homo-eroticism in primitive society as a function of the self. *Journal of Analytical Psychology*.

Levinson, D. J. 1978. The seasons in a man's life. New York: Ballantine.

Mahdi, L. 1976. Contemporary aspects of the North American Indian vision quest. Unpublished thesis, C. G. Jung Institute, Zurich.

Neumann, E. 1973. *The child.* New York: G. P. Putnam and Sons.

_____. 1954. *Origins and history of human consciousness.* New York: Pantheon Books.

_____. Winter, 1976. The psychological meaning of ritual. *Quadrant.*

Ruitenbeek, H. 1967. *Male myth.* New York: Dell.

Shorter, A.W. 1937. *The Egyptian gods.* London: Routledge and Kegan Paul.

Steinman, A. and Fox, D. J. 1974. The male dilemma. New York: Jason Aronson.

Stern, J. 1966. *The flight from woman.* New York: Noonday.

Thayer, E.L. 1971. Casey at the bat. In *Sports,* ed. R. R. Knudson and P. D. Ebert. New York: Dell.

Tiger, L. 1970. *Men in groups.* New York: Vintage Books.

U.S. Department of Labor, Bureau of Labor Statistics, U.S. Census. 1979. *General social and economic characteristics, employment and earnings,* 1979. Washington, D.C.: Government Printing Office.

Vanggaard, T. 1972. *Phallos: A symbol and its history in the male world.* New York: International Universities Press.

Whitmont, E. C. 1976. The momentum of men: The cultural evolution of the masculine and feminine. *Quadrant,* Summer 1976, vol. 9, no. 1.

_____. 1969. *The symbolic quest.* New York: C.G. Jung Foundation for Analytic Psychology.

_____. 1982. *Return of the goddess.* New York: Crossroad Publishing Co.

9

FATHERS, SONS AND BROTHERHOOD

Fred R. Gustafson

In his essay, "Fathers, Sons and Brotherhood," Fred Gustafson explores the meaning of the Iron Hans fairy tale (Grimm's Fairy Tales) *within the context of his practice and his life as a modern man. His remarks, drawn from his experiences with his male clients, point out the relevance of Robert Bly's work (see "The Erosion of Male Confidence") with emerging male consciousness in the contemporary world, and are summed up in the words of Laurens van der Post (1985):*

> *We cannot, today, recreate the original "wilderness man" . . . But we can recover him, because he exists in us. He is the foundation in spirit or psyche on which we build, and we are not complete until we have recovered him.*

Fred Gustafson, D. Min., graduated from the Lutheran School of Theology at Chicago and is an ordained minister in the Lutheran Synod. He earned a Doctor of Ministry degree from Andover-Newton Theological School and a diploma in Analytical Psychology from the Jung Institute in Zurich. He is a pastoral counselor and Jungian analyst for the Lutheran Social Services of Wisconsin and Upper Michigan. His special interests include the psychology of the Black Madonna and the spirituality of Native American Indians.

MY Great Uncle Frank was born in 1888, nearly two years before the Battle of Wounded Knee. He spent most of his life hunting, trapping and fishing along the Rock River of Illinois (and Canada). Only dimly aware of his existence until I was 40, I began to feel the need to meet this 95 year old uncle, a need that came from a deep force within me, a force I could not deny. I know it had something to do with being in the presence of not just the "old *one*" but the "old *man*." It was a good meeting. When he played chess with my eleven year old son I felt as though I were in the presence of a mystery. Eighty-four years separated, and united, them through the ancestral root. I felt this mystery of unity within me, and pride in my manhood and in my masculine forebears. Uncle Frank gave new meaning to all I had been trying to understand about the masculine ground upon which I stand.

In the last several years, I have been led to reflect on my attitudes and prejudices toward men, including myself. Earlier in my professional career, I harbored a lot of anger towards men. Like many therapists and analysts, most of my clients were women. Many told devastating stories about men which proved, for the most part, to be true. When these men came reluctantly into therapy, they claimed that either it was their wives' problem or that, if they did have any problems of their own, they could solve them alone. These were men who were battering their wives and putting their fists through walls, men who had lost significant connections with their children. Often they were unaware of all feelings except anger. I began to feel an inner sense of empathy and sadness for these men. I began to see through the exterior veneer of arrogance and hardness. Beneath their unfeeling and arrogant behavior lay the reality of the severely wounded male.

Hidden behind the granite-like exterior of such men there is (often to the embarrassment of the man himself) a vulnerable interior of suffering and grief. Their stories, words and appearances are deceptive, for they do not convey this inner tragedy. Why are there so many rapists, batterers, and chemically addicted men? Why do so many succeed in killing themselves? Why do so many men believe they must keep their feelings hidden and end up burning out at forty and having coronaries at sixty? The answers are many and complex, requiring the combined efforts of men and women to sort through the projections, defenses, hurts, and accusations.

As I pondered these questions, I read an interview with the American poet, Robert Bly (*New Age Journal,* May 1982). Through him I met "Iron Hans" (Brothers Grimm), and through this old fairy tale some of the larger pieces of the puzzle began to fall into place. Old dreams began to make sense. I began to understand the source of that curious blend of sadness and rage in men. The story of Iron Hans awakened in me a deeper sense of compassion towards my sex, a resolve to see more clearly what lies beyond the smokescreens they put up, and a commitment to seek out new rites of reconciliation for the brotherhood of men that has turned against itself.*

IRON HANS

There was once a king who had a great forest in which he mysteriously lost all of his huntsmen. For years he allowed no one to enter until one day an unknown huntsman appeared and persuaded the king to let him and his dog enter. The request was granted, and the young man entered the forest with his dog. The dog came to a deep pool and was instantly seized and pulled under water by a naked arm. The huntsman got a pail to bail out the pond, only to discover a wild man

*The complete, unexpurgated tale of Iron Hans can be found in *The Complete Grimm's Fairy-Tales* (New York: Pantheon Books, 1972).

whose body was brown like rusty iron and whose hair hung over his face down to his knees. He was then bound, put in an iron cage, and placed in the court-yard of the king, who forbade anyone to open the door on pain of death.

The king had an eight year old son whose golden ball rolled into Iron Hans' cage one day. Iron Hans would not give it back unless the boy opened the cage. He continually refused until one day, his parents were gone and Iron Hans persuaded him to get the key from under his mother's pillow. Forgetting everything, the boy got the key, opened the door (pinching his finger in the process) and set Iron Hans free. In fear of what he had done, he cried to Iron Hans for help, whereupon the wild man picked him up and carried him off into the forest. His parents later assumed him to be dead.

Iron Hans told him he would never see his parents again but that he would take care of him. He said he had gold and silver enough, and that the boy was to guard a gold well as bright and clear as a crystal and permit nothing to fall in it. The boy failed three times at his task—first by unconciously dipping his sore finger into the pool, then a hair fell in from his head, and finally, all of his long hair fell into the pool as he was looking at his reflection. Both his finger and his hair turned to gold.

He wandered about and came to a great city, where he got work with a cook who set the royal table for the king of that land. He always wore a hat to hide his golden hair, but was ordered to take it off when once he brought food to the king. The boy claimed to have a sore on his head, which cost him his job. He then worked for a gardener. One day the king's daughter saw his golden hair, and asked him to bring her some flowers. The boy insisted on bringing her wild flowers. That day and the next two days she tried to pull his hat off to see his golden hair as he struggled to prevent her from doing this. She gave him money, which he gave to the gardener's children, for he cared nothing for golden coins.

Some time later a war broke out. The young man was left behind with a lame horse. He called Iron Hans, and received a great troop of warriors equipped with iron and a strong horse of his own. With these he saved the day for the king but quickly left the victory before he could be recognized. He returned his army and horse to Iron Hans.

The king decided to proclaim a great feast for three days and that his daughter should throw a golden apple with the hope of discovering who the mysterious savior was. The young man wanted to catch the golden apple. He went to Iron Hans, who equipped him with a chestnut horse and gave him a suit of red armor. With this he caught the golden apple and rode mysteriously away. The second day Iron Hans gave him a white horse and a white suit of armor. Again he caught the golden apple and rode away. The king was now angered and said that next time he should be stabbed if he didn't come back of his own free will. The third day, he came as a black knight on a black horse, caught the apple and, in the act of getting away, was stabbed in the leg. Though he got away, his helmet fell off and his golden hair was revealed. The king's daughter asked the gardener about the youth and saw his children playing with the three golden apples. Now all was revealed, and the king offered his daughter to the young man as his wife. His parents realized their son was alive and came to the wedding as did a stately king from another place. This king embraced the prince and said, "I am Iron Hans. I was by enchantment a wild man, but you have set me free. All the treasures which I possess shall be yours."

We gain further insight into the significance of the Wildman motif by appreciating its position in European folklore, art and literature. Wildman stories and imagery were popular in the Middle Ages. These hairy men (and women) were said to live in primitive, remote places. They came to embody brute strength, irrational and emotional forces, courage, and lascivious sexuality. They were despised in the early Medieval period as man aspired toward cultural development and sought to differentiate himself from his more primitive, cthonic nature. As religious and cultural forms ossified and cities became larger, the Wildman was thought of in more positive terms as a Dionysian loosening and a return to nature.

The tale of Iron Hans has had a moving affect on many men since its reintroduction by Robert Bly in North America. Bly's article has been xeroxed and passed from man to man with a "you *must* read this" sense of urgency. His thesis is that within every male is an Iron Hans—psychic territory as extensive and threatening as the king's great isolated forest. Men are cut off from large portions of their natural, inner, instinctual world. Their Iron Hans energies are forgotten, never called upon, or repressed. Bly notes that many men are now thoroughly engaged in getting in touch with their feminine side—a discovery that brings relief and renewal at one level, but leaves them disturbed at another. They are afraid of uncovering this Iron Hans side of themselves for fear of being called *macho*. "Many of these men are unhappy," says Bly. "There's not much energy in them. They are life-preserving, but not exactly life-giving." These men often give up their male energy for fear it will offend women. Consequently, they create little, and get caught in that familiar male syndrome of trying to "please Mother," who reappears in their relationship to their wives.

The drama of Iron Hans brought fresh insight to a dream of an analysand in his late 20's:

> *I was in a house by myself, going from room to room. Someone had been murdered and it had been made to look as though I had done it. I was terrified. A fierce wind began to blow, which scared me all the more. I closed the windows and lit a light to protect myself. I now saw a very large man with red hair, named Benjamin. I called to him with a high voice and said I did not do it; I was innocent and had no intention of doing it. He came toward me and I said, "I am a dead man." He then put his arms around me and embraced me lovingly, and I knew I was saved. I saw coffee and refreshments before me, presented as though I had overcome a terrific obstacle.*

This large, red-haired Benjamin can be seen as a modern variant of Iron Hans, also described as having rusty brown hair. The light of the dreamer's unconscious reveals a masculine power stronger than his confidence in dealing with it. The dream speaks well of the gracious quality of Benjamin/Iron Hans and the renewing quality of his environment. Like an initiate, the dreamer has "overcome a terrific obstacle" and now it is time to celebrate. Moving from room to room in the dreamer's interior psychic house and being implicated in some internal murder is an ordeal in itself. But the "terrific obstacle" that is overcome is more a matter of experiencing and enduring an incredible terror rather than conquering it. It is an experience based more on the gracious ability of this Benjamin/Iron Hans power to hold the ego than on the ego's ability to subdue it. In many traditional primitive cultures it was common for male initiates to be subjected to and endure terrifying experiences which in themselves were quite harmless as, for example, the sound of the bullroarer in Australian aboriginal rites. In the fairy tale, the terrifying Iron Hans showed great compassion and concern for the boy and constituted no threat to his life.

We must not forget that Iron Hans was also a king with great treasures. He was able to work wonders even in his unmanifested state. The union of Iron Hans of the woods and Iron Hans the king seems nearly impossible today because of fear of his power. Few fathers in our culture would dare claim connections with Iron Hans. Although he still lives in the unconscious of many men today, he is seen only from time to time in their dreams. Yet the ancient Greeks knew of Iron Hans. Zeus and Hades, the upper and lower gods, were brothers.

Iron Hans, in both his woodland and kingly form, recently emerged in one of my own dreams:

> *I dreamed I was in a church. I had been wearing deer antlers though I now did not have them on. Without a shirt, I had wrapped a vision questing blanket around myself. The pastor of the church, in full clerics, came to me and said he was angry and that I knew why. He said he did not need to say anything else. I said, "Yes, I know." He responded that he wanted it changed right away. He was referring to the issue of my dressing more appropriately. As I emerged from sleep, a last dream thought came to me: "He is not my boss and I must indeed tell him that."*

This dream reveals the collision of two forces within my psyche: collective Western Christianity and natural, inherent spirituality. Although I was identifying with the latter, I was trying to align with *both* in the dream, i.e., a vision quest blanket in a Christian church. The dream task was not to let either force dominate the other but to bring together the truths of what both systems represent. The Native American blanket, a symbol of that part of the psyche that is "wild" is redeemed from the forest of the unconscious and given royalty, a place of honor in church, that is, given a place in the individual and collective psyche. Iron Hans becomes the king, who offers us honor and dignity by rooting us spiritually to the power of the earth, our bodies, and our souls. The earth does not need to be repressed, as in Western Christianity. Iron

Hans does not need to lie at the bottom of a pond or be locked in a cage. He can reign as a king because the earth is sacred. Just as the young hero in the fairy tale was clothed by Iron Hans, so I was clothed in the garments of earth spirituality and "crowned" with antlers, a symbol of woodland royalty. The vision question blanket speaks of my continual personal search to harmonize these forces.

Several years ago I worked with an unmarried twenty-six year old male who was searching for deeper self-understanding. In analysis, he had this dream:

> *I am in a foreign country, touring. I come to an open space where there is a building of some sort. It is of black marble, very tall, with a portion supported by columns. There is a huge crowd seated on rows of benches in front. I begin to walk down one of the aisles. Then I turn and see an enormous door slide to one side which reveals, in what appears to be the vestibule, the statue of a man. It is gigantic and gleams with some kind of light. It seems to have been carved from a crystal. The face is featureless but the statue is alive or animated in some way because I can see it move. A voice declares, "This is Goliath!" and repeats that twice more.*

The dreamer was an intelligent, sensitive man with a high degree of integrity. He was "touring," searching through, his interior, unconscious world—the "foreign country." What was "revealed" to him was an undifferentiated, "featureless," archetypal image of the masculine. It was as though the whole of the unconscious was waiting for this momentous revelation: "This is Goliath!" The defined temple-like structure added dignity to the event and lent credibility to the dreamer's efforts to understand the epiphany of Goliath in his life. The name 'Goliath' (Heb. "to reveal") refers to strength on the surface opening to strength within. The dreamer's Goliath represented strength revealed at the most obvious physical level, and this power came alive before and within him. The dream ended abruptly, but its culmination lay in the dreamer's ability to integrate this power into his conscious life.

Men have been terribly cut off from consciousness of their own "Goliaths" who have either been cursed to remain in the deeper layers of the psychic pool, or kept contained in a personal and cultural cage. We get a sense of this from a dream of a man in his mid-twenties whose complaint was that he lacked energy in his outer life:

> *I am walking along the southern shore of a lake where I live. I see some Blacks and they scare me. I begin to climb a cliff nearby. As I do so, I see an old man from the East, meditating. I climb higher. From this vantage point I see a bull in a boat, battering against its side.*

This dream reveals one man's terror of the dark, instinctual, masculine energy in his soul. His terror is matched only by the urgency of the situation—the angry bull battering the boat. A student of Eastern meditation, the dreamer needed to forego the 'old man from the East' at this point in his life, and face first his own inner, primal masculine power. The bull, psychically contained in a feeble boat structure, was only temporarily afloat on the lake of the unconscious. This bull in him was angry and badly in need of attention. He could not be forgotten, no matter how high the man consciously climbed or how far into the East he might have attempted to flee.

Few have compassion for this side of their psyche. The wildman appears demonic to many because they do not know how to relate to him or for various reasons feel that repression is necessary. As in relating to loved ones, neglect or putting these needs off does not make them disappear; it only turns these forces against one. Jung pointed out that the face we turn towards the unconscious is reflected back towards us. If we react harshly towards our inner needs, we get harsh treatment in return. Iron Hans, Goliath, or the bull do not disappear by being cut off or neglected, but lurk at the bottom of the male psyche, ready to pull the man under by getting him in the grips of a complex (acting out, etc.).

Iron Hans needs to be understood and related to in a feelingful manner. Because of his neglect, like any shadow figure he remains primitive, childish and often brutal. This frightens the man away. He wants to have nothing to do with the shadow. But by paying conscious attention to the dark, shadow side, both ego and shadow are transformed by the interaction. The hero in the fairy tale can be seen as integrating Iron Hans energy by proper use of his power in war and contest. He becomes king by uplifting his Iron Hans energies. In other words, Iron Hans is revealed in his kingly status.

In his inner, woodland form, Iron Hans represents the unintegrated, undirected yet dynamic movement of natural masculine energy. In its somatic form, this energy is felt as the body erupting at a moment's notice to create or to destroy. It is not "body beautiful" but "body powerful," ready for battle with little awareness of its own limitations. At the psychic level, it is experienced as a crude determination to succeed in the face of overwhelming odds. Because the modern male has not served him honorably nor consciously called upon him, Iron Hans withholds his treasures, sending instead only curses. He is lived out unconsciously in a variety of violent activities, or else he abandons a man, leaving him to feel in complete, sad, and empty. Men can dishonor themselves by living out this primitive Iron Hans energy rather than working on its transformation. Out of the difficulties and frustrations of being a "good boy," or from the emptiness of the wildman's absence, a man may revert to the unconscious expression of the good boy's opposite.

For many men, dishonor lies in claiming as their own treasure that belonging solely to Iron Hans. Yet, in the fairy tale, all the powers given to the young man were also eventually conferred on this archetypal force within him. If a man selfishly takes these treasures as his own, he becomes inflated with the sense of power belonging only to the archetypal realm. He may convince himself that he has the right to control the world around him. If this state of self-inflation continues to exist, it becomes dangerous for the man himself and unnerving for those in contact with him. The heroic task, successfully performed by the boy in the tale, is to learn how to use this power when needed and to exercise its energies with force, focus and direction. Both the power and the man are transformed through the experience, practice, and interaction of conscious ego and primitive Iron Hans energy.

MOTHER AND SON

As the fairy tale reminds us, the key to Iron Hans' cage is under the mother's pillow. The feeling that mother "is around somewhere" is quite common whenever a man starts intimately relating to a woman. For mother is the one who initially holds and guards the key to this earthly, creative male energy so necessary to his development. Her level of control and influence can be subtle and unconsciously exerted—the key is under a very private, feminine place, her pillow. The control is felt in the disapproving looks, silent reproofs, outright condemnations, or in the withholding of love if the son behaves like a "bad boy." Just begin to let a little of this wild man energy out around some mothers, and their sons will feel their disapproval. At some levels, the son will get the message. Perhaps one day he will realize just how well his mother helped to keep Iron Hans locked up in him. Even after he has left his mother, his introjection of her and her values and responses may be even more subtly and unconsciously felt.

Sometimes a woman's power is expressed primarily through her use of guilt or rejection. Whether or not a woman actually does this, a man might tend to see her as having this power, thereby giving it to her. Many men express a feeling of responsibility for the woman's well-being, a feeling often tainted with a degree of childhood anxiety: "I must not let mother down." Historically, many women have given men this responsibility outright, and men, all too unwittingly, have tended to pick it up. If they think they have failed in their task of caring for their women, it is a terrible blow to their own sense of destiny, their "God-ordained" role as a man. While today's women are consciously attempting to break this destructive alliance, men are just beginning to realize how much it has worn them down and kept them from discovering themselves.

Unbeknownst to himself, modern man often harbors an unconscious hatred of women. Because the man was never formally severed from the mother, something deep within him knows she must be dealt with if he is to be a man. Psychologically, he must leave her. The over-nourishing mother takes on a devouring aspect that unconsciously prevents the man from standing on his own. Even if mother was simply "good enough," a man is likely to be lulled back into letting her provide for him unless he has been properly severed. I am convinced that much of the violence done by men toward women occurs because the women in their lives unknowingly failed to be nourishing, and instead aroused in the male's unconscious the negative "witch mother" who must be slain and transformed. Many of these men are themselves in agony over the violence they create, and feel they are in the grip of a force over which they have little control.

Women are growing weary of the unresolved mother complex that has been projected into them. I recently had a mother and her fourteen year old son in my office. She was at her limits over his cockiness and acting out. After a few sessions, I found myself forcefully but kindly saying to the boy, "I have an urge to kidnap you from your mother." I had no antagonism toward her. Indeed, I had a strong feeling she would understand and not take offense. Her reply was fitting and without sarcasm: "I wish you would." That exchange set the stage for future sessions with the boy alone. It was time for *his* departure from childhood and *her* letting go. I might add that the boy also suffered from the lack of a father in his life.

FATHER AND SON

I believe that one of the reasons why there are so many angry men today (the one feeling many men permit themselves) is not only because they have been discouraged from having or expressing feelings, but also because they have not felt a significant loving father presence in their lives. Beneath the anger lies feelings of loss and betrayal. The father, who so often in our culture is absent from the parenting process in order to support the family, is often coupled with a woman who compensates for this absence to the point of over-nurturing her male children. That is, the mother complex will manifest itself in a nurturing manner. Even if a woman has no experience raising sons, the males in her life often expect her to conform to the traditional model: to nurture and receive the male.

For many men, the father complex is manifested consciously on a negative level. Years ago a prison chaplain told me that of all the holidays in the year observed by the male prisoners, Mother's Day was the most celebrated. More cards were sent on that day than at any other time. In contrast, very few Father's Day cards were sent. Many of the men in whom this kind of contrast is seen had fathers who were not taken seriously or who were looked down upon. These men saw their fathers as competitors and authorities with whom they must contend. These feelings of competition and of vying for equal authority are too often governed by power tactics which alienate men from each other. Father/son relationships cease to be energized. Creative male qualities are no longer passed on from generation to generation. A father may not pass on to his son the power of his authority. The emerging male then grows up weak or defiant. It is difficult for such a man to know and trust an inner authority grounded on his own individual identity. As a consequence, he often over-compensates for what authority he has, or gives it away through projection to some dominant male or to a corporation.

In today's culture, the father-son relationship is in terrible condition. It is both wounded and wounding. It is armoured with a rage that rarely gets defined and tightly conceals a pain and a sadness that, once touched, usually brings tears or uncontrolled weeping. When the father-son bond is not intact in a way that nourishes the son's growth, and when the father does not act as a vehicle for transmitting some of the masculine mysteries to the son, that child will grow up with a limited and crippling sense of his masculinity. Several impediments to masculine individuation can transpire:

1. The son may get caught living out his father's unlived shadow side or be pressured to duplicate the father's way of doing things. His individual male identity will then be too limited and confined by reactions to the father. This can lead to feelings of emptiness, depression, or open rebellion.

2. Without a healthy masculine identity, the son's anima is likely to dominate the empty spaces created by a weakly-defined male ego. This leaves a man feeling driven by and infatuated with self-importance, or depleted of energy and creativity. Without a solid father figure to relate to, the son's anima, like any woman he might meet, will "lose respect" for him and will counter him with ridicule, provocation, seduction, and insatiable demands.

3. The son will often be controlled by women through guilt or a sense of duty. The power to impose such guilt is one of the strongest weapons a woman (or a man) has, whether she realizes it or not. This power can be unwittingly bestowed on her by the immature male through his projection of the mother complex onto her. This complex escalates in the absence of a "good enough" father bond. As Jung (1953) asserts, in a marital situation,

> . . . . the anima, in the form of the mother-image, is transferred to the wife; and the man, as soon as he marries, becomes childish, sentimental, dependent, and subservient, or else truculent, tyrannical, hypersensitive, always thinking about the prestige of his superior masculinity. . . . his ideal of marriage is so arranged that his wife has to take over the magical role of the mother. Under the cloak of the ideally exclusive marriage he is really seeking his mother's protection, and thus he plays into the hands of his wife's possessive instincts. His fear of the dark incalculate power of the unconscious gives his wife an illegitimate authority over him, and forges such a dangerously close union that the marriage is permanently on the brink of explosion from internal tension—or else, out of protest, he flies to the other extreme, with the same results.

4. If the father's influence is weak, the son may get caught in the force field of the mother's animus, especially if the mother-son bond is strong (as it so often is). The mother will unconsciously project her own animus into the son. He will feel responsible for living out her animus drive—pushed to achieving, perhaps successfully, in any given field. But he will never quite be fulfilled because the animus is the woman's inner male image whose superman nature may be debilitating and impossible to live up to.

This theme can be seen in the dream of a 31 year old man with a strong, positive mother complex and little connection to his father. He saw his father as being weak and ineffective, a perspective shared and reinforced by his mother. Mother felt unfulfilled in her life becuase she was unable to attend college to train for a profession she desired. Her family told her that "women just get married when they get out of college." The analysand was an over-achiever in school, and worked hard in his profession in a manner that gave his mother pride. He had the following dream one year into the analysis:

> *I am talking to my sister in her (upstairs) bedroom. Mother is downstairs somewhere. There are pieces of flesh and blood splattered over the walls. Superman has exploded.*

This dream prompted a re-examination of his relationship to his mother and his almost fanatical desire to succeed.

In the modern male psyche, the mother must be "defused" and the father "infused" with a nurturing authority. This has become increasingly possible in a contemporary society where women are gaining a greater sense of themselves and are not resigned to living out their lives through their children. Woman are helping men to be more conscious of their need as fathers to nurture their children. And though woman are generally far ahead in realizing the importance of fathers in parenting, men are also beginning to discover this and to make attempts to relate more closely to their children. Some fathers, if they hug at all, find it much easier to hug their daughters than their sons. In the privacy of a consulting room, many fathers will declare that they just *do not* hug their sons or even put an arm around their shoulders, and that their fathers never did that to them. But the absence of the father's touch creates a hunger among men for other men, even though there may be little consciousness of it. How important it is that the father start early expressing his affection for his children instead of being so often "absent" even when he is physically present!

The Initiation of the Son

How does a man in our culture relate to his Iron Hans side and still maintain respect as a responsible member of the collective? How does he use his primal masculine energy without getting inflated with its power? How does he keep himself from repressing this force or blindly acting it out? And how can a man attain the necessary separation from the mother in order to develop his masculinity? Primitive peoples knew of these problems and took care of them through elaborate and thorough initiation rites. In male initiations, the fathers, the brotherhood and the Ancestors were called upon to bring the initiate into a full awareness of the powers within and without him. Transition from boyhood to manhood was a most serious matter. It required complete separation from the mother and prolonged isolation in an area accessible to men only.

> Because the mother is the first bearer of the soul-image, separation from her is a delicate and important matter of the greatest educational significance. Accordingly among primitives we find a large number of rites designed to organize this separation. The mere fact of becoming adult, and of outward separation, is not enough; impressive initiations into the 'men's house' and ceremonies of rebirth are still needed in order to make the separation from the mother (and hence from childhood) entirely effective. (Jung 1953)

In "primitive" rites of passage, young male initiates confronted transcendent, sacred, and sometimes demonic forces. They relived the primordial events, the mythic history of their tribe, away from the familiar ground of their childhood homes. It was important to root them in their collective history, to show them the archetypal grounds upon which they could live their lives with meaning and honor. Powers greater than the individual needed to be honored, placated, and experienced in the context of a living mythology (Eliade 1958).

During their time of separation from the community, the initiates experienced a ritual death and rebirth. Boys passed away and men emerged. In order to evoke the virtues of courage and strength, this transition involved ordeals of danger and self-denial. In psychological terms, the ordeal served to evoke the archetype of the hero in the young men. Primitive men knew that the Iron Hans energy needed to manifest itself; yet they were also taught how to control this power. Random courage and strength would be dangerous to the welfare of others, especially on hunting and warring expeditions. It was necessary to learn how to wait for the right moment and work in harmony with the collective. Initiates were also taught how to relate to women, children, and domestic affairs. They were personally directed to seek a dream or vision binding them to the transcendent powers. Their initiation was performed in a sacred manner and was acknowledged as having important consequences for the renewal and welfare of the large community.

Today, initiations into manhood are conducted, if at all, in a limited fashion, and often in an unconscious manner. Young men unthinkingly try to initiate themselves by the way they drive, drink, rebel against their parents or society, or treat women. Others "get initiated" after a thorough round with alcoholism, divorce, critical accident, or a crippling depression at mid-life.

These are like initiatory experiences in that they bring a man to his knees and leave him feeling helpless, broken, and dead. Life crises become the critical and necessary wounds that are essential for psychic transformation. For males so afflicted, such wounds hold the promise of renewal through the birth of a more humane and sensitive view toward themselves and the world around them.

It seems that the male psyche begins to require initiations for itself in the pre-adolescent and early adolescent years. At this time, parents should be encouraged to stop "doing things" for their sons. They should begin to assume that their boys can take care of themselves. If they do not assume this, their sons will continue to allow themselves to be cared for. This means the boys must learn how to make their own beds, do their own laundry and ironing, cook, and pick up after themselves. If the parent imagines the son can only carry five logs to the fire place, he/she might add a sixth one. If the parent thinks that making him clean the garage is about as much as can be expected, he/she might have him clean the basement also. In previous years there was a parental need to protect the young child, but now conscientious effort should be given to counter the inertial force of the childhood years.

The parents' "letting go" of the need to protect their son means that they must become attuned to his need to be severed. They must follow the ancient custom of allowing their son to be forcibly ripped away from the parental home as it exists with the boy himself. For the young man, the process of severance from his boyhood years takes two forms: the mother's role diminishes and the father's role becomes very important. Now the father must move toward a level of honesty and open discussion with his son as never before. The time has come for the revelation of the masculine mysteries in an unabashed, straightforward and loving manner. It is important that the father actually take his son aside more than once as the boy moves into these later years, and share his thoughts and feelings about his view of himself, his experiences with life, his religious views, his attitudes about woman and sexuality, and his relationships to family, work, and friends. Now he can non-judgmentally share his perception of his son's strengths and weaknesses, share his memories of the past, and encourage his son to envision possibilities for his future. In every possible way he must pass on the power he possesses to his son, allowing the son to become strong and psychologically to step beyond him without counterattack, when the time is right. In the end, the father will bequeath a paternal blessing that the son will remember decades after the fact. To fail to do this is tantamount to pronouncing a paternal curse. On the other hand, to succeed in breaking the old and forging these new parental bonds is to duplicate as closely as he can those ancient initiatory rites that proved so effective for our ancestors.

It is quite possible that initiation rites can be restyled and enacted by modern fathers. One man told me he is thinking that when the time is right he will take his son on a two week wilderness outing away from everyone and tell him as much as he knows about life. Another man suggested that since his son and mine are about the same age, we could switch sons for a month and instruct each other's son on growing into manhood. Such a proposal reflects the primitive practice of not allowing the father to be the principal initiator of his son. However a modern initiation might be performed, intentionality and originality are needed to make this rite a viable process for channelling the archetypal energy behind it. Its power would be enhanced if the boy himself helped to plan it.

A young man needs to look imaginatively into the face of his father and see his sacred ancestors living there. "Old Men" need to appear in his life as reminders of the elderly character of the masculine archetype as a mature and refined source of wisdom. He also must be able to look forward through his own sons and the sons around him and at all that is new and possible in him whether he sires a child or not. This new consciousness, which is part of the initiation process, is essential for a view of what, in the profoundest sense, the "masculine" is.

During an analytical process with a male analysand, a dream appeared that illustrates the psyche's need to link the individual male with male generations past and future. In his thirties and twice married, "John's" first wife died of cancer, leaving him with a daughter. This Vietnam veteran had experienced first-hand the horrors of that war. At his age, he had lived more than most people, yet something in him still needed to be initiated:

> I was training a young man (about sixteen) in something. We came to a blocking place where he would not (or could not) go any further. We were then on a bus going somewhere. We stopped in a town in the middle of an arid land. It was about night. All the people got off the bus as if this were a rest stop. The young man and I walked around and the thought came to me that if he could speak to the old man, the boy would be able to complete his training. The boy went into the house of the old man and came out a few minutes later. Somehow I knew that the old man would not say anything different than I did but that the young man would listen to the old man. My job was to convince the young man to complete his training. It was as though he had to go out and learn how to complete his training by risking himself in this arid land.

In his dream, John appears to be on a quest to unite the younger part of himself with the older—for the sake of masculine completeness. The younger man must "complete his training" with the older man and go out and "risk himself" in an "arid land." John did not stand alone. He was heir to a lineage that supported him psychically and held him responsible for the emerging generation. This lineage, represented by the young and old personae of himself, was activated by the linking of generations and the solitary quest of the young trainee. John needed to put his conscious views aside and discover that his psyche had roots that were nourished by the ancient collective unconscious.

Fathers, Sons and Brotherhood

There are many stories from the past that capture the drama between fathers and sons and the need for connection with the brotherhood of men. Take, for example, the Old Testament saga of the patriarch Isaac and his twin sons, Jacob and Esau. Jacob betrayed his blind and dying father by stealing the birthright of his first-born brother, hairy Esau. Fleeing for his life, Jacob went to the land of his uncle, Laban, and lived there for twenty years. Finally, in the time of his greatest prosperity, he knew he must return to the land of his father, meet his brother, and effect a reconciliation. Like Jacob, the modern male feels deeply within himself a need for reunion with his twin—the wild, hairy, instinctual side of himself—and yet he is at a great distance from the psychic ground of his fathers and the brotherhood. He must return to his own country and be reconciled in brotherly love with his wild twin, as did Jacob, and realize the fruits of that union.*

Nevertheless, it is not always possible for a man to physically connect with his actual father. He then faces the awesome but not impossible task of becoming the father to his own neglected inner boy and healing himself. He begins by encouraging an imaginal relationship between himself and his inner child. Can he envision himself sitting next to or walking with the little boy he once was and has long neglected? What would he say to this boy? What would he do? What would be the boy's response?

"Andrew," a thirty-five year old man, had been severely abused as a child by his stepfather. He grew up hating this man, and once strongly considered killing him. As he grew into manhood, what later tortured him most was his hatred toward himself and his explosive anger at his own little son. Through a long and painful process he was able to rediscover within himself his own long forgotten, hurt little boy. He sat with his inner boy and allowed himself to hear what the child was saying. But in order to do this he had to silence the negative stepfather within him that all too easily took over. Ultimately, he was able to psychologically embrace the little boy of himself. His self-hatred disappeared; he was able to forgive his stepfather, and he began to work toward a closer relationship with his son.

---

*Note that Jacob also had to face the consequences of his deception of Esau when, many years later, ten of his sons sold their brother Joseph into slavery—so wounding their father even as he had wounded Isaac.

Because every man has a father and a son within himself, he is a member of a great brotherhood of ancestors, grandfathers, fathers, sons, uncles, brothers, and nephews who all possess the same inner knowing. Though today the concept of "brotherhood" is all too often limited to the local bowling team or to the guys in the office or shop, the concept itself is still powerful enough to collectively support the masculine archetype in any individual man. Brotherhood enables men to see a bit of their own masculine identity in every male they see or experience. When they fail to recognize themselves in other men, they project their own incompleteness on other men, and turn brother against brother. A woman active in the feminist movement told me she works hard to remind women not to despise one another, for they are all sisters and must work for mutual growth and liberation. In the same way, all men need to risk opening themselves and to assist one another in the expansion of their understanding of what being male actually means. No one man can do this comprehensively by himself.

I believe that men are hungry for intimate, brotherly connections with other men, even as now they are becoming more aware than ever of their inward weeping for the fathers they hardly knew. It has become quite clear to me why I have such an intense need to strengthen my bonds with my older relatives and to connect my young son with his father's ancestry. I am seeking to understand in the deepest sense what it is to be a man. Other men are learning to liberate Iron Hans from the swamp in the forest of their masculine unconscious, learning how to revoke his curses and uncover his treasures. Only then will they be the men that women truly want them to be, as well as men who can rightfully gain integrity and spiritual value in each other's eyes.

REFERENCES

Bly, Robert. The Wild Man, *New Age* (May 1982).
Eliade, Mircea. 1958. Rites and symbols of initiation. New York: Harper & Row.
Jung, C. G. 1953. *Two essays on analytical psychology.* Princeton University Press.
van der Post, Sir Laurens 1985. Wilderness—A way of truth, in *A testament to the wilderness.* Santa Monica, CA: The Lapis Press.

THE SPLIT SHADOW AND THE
FATHER-SON RELATIONSHIP

Donald F. Sandner

Donald Sandner's chapter deals with the weak as well as the strong father-son relationship in discussing masculine initiation "into the power of life and death." With pertinent references to related questions in the Navaho culture, the reader is given new insights into inner dilemmas facing men and "why men love war." In the research he presents in this chapter, Sandner shows that "a crucial governing factor in determining how much of the masculine shadow will be expressed and how much will remain unconscious is to be found in the quality of the father-son relationship." This paper will be included in the forthcoming proceedings of the 10th conference of the International Association for Analytical Psychology, Daimon Verlag, Einsiedeln, Switzerland.

Donald Sandner, M.D., is a member of the Society of Jungian Analysts of Northern California and maintains a private practice in the San Francisco Bay Area. He is president of training of the C. G. Jung Institute of San Francisco and has been a member and chairman of the certifying board. A graduate of the University of Illinois College of Medicine, he served his psychiatric residency at Stanford University Medical Center, where he was chief resident in 1960. Dr. Sandner is the author of Navaho Symbols of Healing *(1979); his papers on healing methods have appeared in* Spring *(1972),* Human Nature *(1978), and as a chapter in* Ways of Health, *edited by David Sobel (1979) as well as in* Jungian Analysis, *edited by Murray Stein (1982).*

The Initiatory Stage

Although the boy's initiation reaches its peak in adolescence, in the first part of a boy's life it is the mother, or her substitute, who plays by far the most important role. She is the archetypal center, and the home is her symbolic womb. When the father shares in early maternal care, plays his part in the oedipal romance, and labors in the outside world, he only supports this pattern.

If we follow Erik Erikson's psychological stages of ego development (1950 and 1980), we find the first three stages based primarily on the maternal archetype as expressed through the personal mother. The first stage involves the balance of *trust vs. mistrust,* the basis of comfort in the world. It depends, as Erikson says, "on the quality of the maternal relationship" (1950, p. 221) and the inner assurance that basic needs will be met. One of these needs is the experience of meaning in life. Erikson says: "[The parents] must be able to represent to the child a deep, and almost somatic conviction, that there is meaning to what they are doing" (*Ibid.,* p. 221).

In the next stage, *autonomy vs. shame,* the boy encounters authority. Society demands that he regulate his bodily functions. This is his first encounter with the outside father-world of law and order, though still actively mediated and ameliorated by the mother. There is special somatic concern for the backsides of the body, the buttocks and the anus. As Erikson cogently puts it:

> This reverse area of the body with its aggressive and libidinal focus in the sphincters and in the buttocks, cannot be seen by the child, and yet it can be dominated by the will of others. The 'behind' is thus the individual's dark continent, an area of the body which can be magically dominated and effectively invaded by those who would attack one's power of autonomy and who would designate as evil those products of the bowels which were felt to be all right when they were being passed . . . this finds its adult expression in paranoid fears concerning hidden persecutors and secret persecutions threatening from behind and from within the behind. (*Ibid.,* p. 224)

In these first forceful impositions of authority lie the seeds of the sadomasochistic aspect of the boy's relationship with the father to which we will return.

In the third phase, *initiative vs. guilt* (the phallic phase), the hegemony of the maternal archetype is challenged. Having accepted the first great imposition of authority, mainly through the mother's animus, in the preceding stage of *autonomy vs. shame,* the boy can now identify with it and begin his struggle for individual assertion. The incest taboo is activated and the masculine ego begins its long climb to autonomy. Archetypally, this is the beginning of the hero's journey.

Ego development steadily continues throughout the next stage, characterized as *industry vs. inferiority.* Through enhanced mastery, the ego assimilates its heritage. The boy receives, somewhat passively, the learning and culture accumulated by his society. This encourages a certain separation from the matriarchy, and the beginning of a decade-long confrontation with the father-world as conveyed by the personal father and other representatives.

If he fails here he will bear the onus of inferiority which will handicap him in the ensuing masculine initiation.

Now the boy enters adolescence. His sexuality emerges and he enters into the struggle with what must appear to be ungovernable instinct on one hand and unyielding authority on the other. In the struggle the boy will be molded by the initiatory archetype into the kind of man his culture determines him to be.

This is not a clean and well-defined effort. There is a split in the psyche, an unavoidable wound which has been there from the beginning. Erikson characterizes his stages as essentially either-or: *trust vs. mistrust, autonomy vs. shame, initiative vs. guilt, industry vs. inferiority,* but they may be alternatively viewed as pairs of opposites to be negotiated in childhood, and not essentially different from those encountered later in adulthood. In the early stages, if the experience is 'good enough,' then the trust and autonomy predominate but mistrust (suspicion) and shame maintain their underground existence by means of split-off feeling-toned complexes. Erikson says of the stage of *initiative vs. guilt:*

> Here the most fateful split and transformation in the emotional powerhouse occurs, a split between the potential human glory and potential total destruction. For here the child becomes forever divided in himself. (*Ibid.,* p. 225)

Viewed from another standpoint, the child has been divided against himself from the beginning. The psyche is fundamentally split, and the seeds of what we know as the shadow are laid down in earliest infancy. First there is a split between the essentially good and unsuitably bad breasts (to speak in somatic symbolism), then there is a turning against parts of the body and its products as nasty and repulsive, and finally the incest wound in which the part of the psyche that wants to stay protected, gratified, inflated, rebellious, and unconscious is at war with the part that wants to be independent, assertive, productive, admired, and conscious. The stage is set for the emergence in adolescence of the archetypal opposition of the trickster vs. the hero (characterized by Erikson as *identity vs. role diffusion*) and its resolution in an encounter with the father, the laws of society and the "tribal gods."

A Navaho Myth

To illustrate a psychological parallel from American Indian mythology, let me give a brief example of the hero-trickster myth from the Navaho healing ceremony Big Star Way.[1] I will give a shortened version of the myth of this rite as related to me by Natani Tso, a medicine man, at his ceremonial hogan on the Navaho reservation in northeastern Arizona. In the myth, Badger is the cultural hero and Coyote the Trickster.

> Badger was the one who started this chant (Big Star Way). Coyote came to Badger and said: "Come on, let's go to the top of these cliffs. There are some young eagles up there." Coyote was interested in Badger's wife and hoped to play a trick on him. Coyote persuaded him to climb up the cliff while Coyote stayed down below. When Badger got to the top he was disappointed because he saw no eagles, only grasshoppers.

Coyote plays on Badger's greed to get him to make this strenuous and dangerous climb which results in an almost fatal inflation.

> While Badger was on the top, Coyote blew on the butte from each of the four directions and it started rising up in the air until it almost reached the sky. Badger had no way to get down so he had to stay up there for four nights. There was nothing to eat or drink, so I don't know how he got by.

Coyote traps Badger in his own inflation, in order to get him out of the way so Coyote may seduce his wife. But there is a spiritual dimension with which Coyote has not reckoned.

> Four racer snakes saw Badger from the sky. These racer snakes were divine beings. They were like sentries in the upper world. The Holy people told the racer snakes to get Badger and bring him up the cliffs to the upper world.

> When he got into the upper world Badger saw that the divine beings there were living together in a community. They gave him deer meat and he told them all about himself. The Star People, for that is who they were, then gave him secret knowledge concerning dead people. Badger stayed up there for four years learning different branches of the Big Star Way until he knew everything perfectly. Then he was told to return taking his healing knowledge back to his people.

There is a large part of the myth omitted here in which Badger undergoes various ordeals in the sky world. He becomes stronger after each ordeal until finally he is able to help the Star People against their enemies.

> Finally the racer snakes crisscrossed again and took Badger down to his earthly home. Then they disappeared into the sky. It was four years since he left, and his home was abandoned. He found out from the poker that Coyote had kept his family here for a year and then moved on to the east. This happened four times. When Badger came to the fourth hut, he found his wife and children in a pitiable condition. His wife was thin and sick, and his children were dressed in rags. They didn't even recognize him because he'd been away so long. He gave them all deer meat from the Holy People, and this made them stronger.

> Then he heard Coyote howling outside. He was returning with an old flea bag full of rabbits. Coyote called Badger's children beggars and commanded them to come out and welcome him home as they were supposed to do. As he came in he was startled to see that they were with their father, Badger.

Once more Badger and Coyote meet; this time Badger is much stronger and less easily tricked. He is a spiritual person, and Coyote is at the disadvantage.

> When Coyote came in he immediately saw the deer meat which Badger brought from the upper world. It was much better than the skinny rabbits he caught. He said: "Cousin, give me a piece of that deer meat for taking care of your family while you were gone." Badger gave him a piece of meat, but wrapped in it was a piece of star from the upper world. Coyote ate it all down ravenously. All of a sudden Coyote gave a loud yelp and took off around the house. You could hear his footsteps as they ran; all of a sudden they just stopped. Badger went out and saw that Coyote was dead. The star had burned his throat. Then Badger saw that his wife was sick because of her long stay with Coyote, so he determined to perform his new ceremony over her and the children.

Here the spiritual principle triumphs, but only for the moment. The Holy People decide that Coyote is indispensable and must be brought back to life again.

> A little inch worm came and dragged the dead Coyote to the North, the place of evil. There he was revived again. Meanwhile Badger went out to the woods to find some special berries for his wife's ceremony. As he was looking all around, Coyote's skin came over him. It covered his whole body and his eyes so he couldn't see. It was Coyote back again as full of lust for the woman as before.

Where lust is concerned Coyote never stops, but the sudden covering of the hero with Coyote's skin reveals their hidden identity. Badger, the hero, is also Coyote and even though as the hero he has attained his spiritual quest, the trickster in him is never dead.

In a further part of this account Natani Tso tells how Badger, covered with Coyote's skin, spent four nights blindly crawling around the forest. Finally he asked Big Fly, who was a spiritual messenger, to call the Holy People. They came and held a Big Star ceremony in which Badger crawled through five special wooden hoops. As he passed through each one, the skin came off him a little further until at the last one he was free.

Here the archetypal split in the Navaho psyche is clearly revealed. Coyote is the forbidden instinctual side, closely connected with what is repulsive and repressed in the Navaho culture. As an archetypal trickster, he bears a close relationship to the Freudian id and the Jungian shadow. Reading the Coyote stories, we can recognize, all too easily, our shadowy likeness.

Opposing him, and yet in a certain complementary relationship with him, is the hero, Badger, who is idealistic, sensitive, spiritual and able to learn divine secrets of healing. But the hero is also easily inflated, cut off from his natural base in the earth, forgetful of his humanity, and too much concerned with his own spiritual welfare to care about his wife and children. While he is on his transpersonal quest he leaves his family with Coyote—a pointed critique of spirituality.

The archetypal dimension of the split psyche is outlined in the development of the Navaho culture hero, but the split must in some way be resolved by every young man as an initiatory stage leading to maturity and marriage. Let me bring this into clinical focus, and put the split psyche with its hero and its trickster into a psychological perspective.

The Split Shadow

The concept of the split psyche suggests an extension of the Jungian idea of the shadow, especially in regard to its clinical manifestation. The shadow can be seen as a bipolar or split complex, characterized in the myth as trickster vs. hero, which expresses itself on the personal, cultural and archetypal levels. This view of the bipolar nature of the shadow was presented in an early form by John Perry (1970) and expanded by John Beebe and myself in Murray Stein's *Jungian Analysis* (1982). In a specific culture one side is always bad or undesirable, something to be hidden or repressed, but still containing vital instinctual energy, and the other is good or ideal, something to be encouraged and developed. In the developmental process the masculine ego integrates as much of each side into itself as it can, leaving parts of both unintegrated, unexpressed and unconscious. These unintegrated parts become the adult split bipolar shadow complex.

On the personal level, the negative pole of the complex contains culturally undesirable qualities that have been repressed. These are usually primitive, lustful, aggressive, hateful, envious and anti-social qualities—the familiar shadow material. Theoretically, and actually, in other cultures almost any qualities, including those we idealize, could be considered undesirable and repressed and vice versa. In dreams and other unconscious fantasies these repressed qualities are usually represented by toughs, murderers, sinister figures, aggressive animals, menacing intruders, etc. Though always seen negatively by the particular culture, this pole contains great instinctual vitality.

The opposite pole, the relatively positive side, carries idealized qualities represented by superior, noble, heroic, spiritual or religious figures. These qualities always tend to inflate the ego, though they also carry genuine spiritual values.

In adulthood both poles of this complex are still available to the ego for further efforts at integration, most notably in analytic work. Both poles are rightful extensions of the ego's domain and may be designated as ego-aligned. This designation does not mean that these complexes cannot be projected, which of course they frequently are; it only indicates their natural connection to the ego.

This concept of the bipolar shadow differs from the Freudian concept of id and superego (which derives from the same clinical data) in seeing these components not as separate institutions but as a dynamic, polarized entity (the complex) containing energy and specific qualities, complementary to each other as well as in opposition, and rooted in *both* biological and spiritual archetypes.

The bipolar shadow complex and the ego complex together contain the full range of masculine qualities in any cultural pattern. Any quality not expressed by the ego is held in potentia by the complex. Thus, no matter what the overall pattern, there is a resulting conservation of overall qualities.

I have illustrated one cultural pattern in the Navaho hero-trickster myth. In Balinese culture (Indonesia), for another example, the qualities of close group cooperation, detailed orderliness, and highly developed spiritual refinement are idealized while any gross, animal-like, disorderly or idiosyncratic behavior is, sometimes violently, discouraged. This differs sharply from the American cultural ideal of rugged individualism; thus what is idealized in the United States is shadowy in Bali. Every culture has its own pattern which extends to the formation of masculine identity in its own unique way.

A crucial governing factor in determining how much of the masculine shadow will be expressed and how much will remain unconscious is to be found in the quality of the father-son relationship. I will describe two examples, one a weak father-son relationship involving a boyish (puer) son, and the other a strong father-son relationship involving an aggressive (warrior) son to show how they differ functionally.

The Weak Father-Son Relationship

My first example is a clinical one of a young man in therapy. He was single, in his early thirties, and a teacher. He was born and raised in the Southwest, and retained a deep love for the deserts and mesas of Arizona and New Mexico.

He was bisexual in his instinctual orientation. In his early twenties he had been both emotionally and sexually in love with a young woman, but he also retained a strong and very compelling attraction to men. The aspect especially interesting to us is that one of his sexual fantasies, containing a great deal of energy, was tied to his father, as we shall see in a moment.

The predominant conscious feeling of this young man for his father was one of disgust and disappointment. He thought "the old man" stupid, vulgar and mean. Far from appreciating the comfortable lifestyle his father's labors had procured for him, he saw it all as money-grubbing pretentiousness. All through his adolescence the patient was aloof and inflated. His father treated him superficially with some tolerance and consideration but an overall indifference masked his deeper feelings of jealousy and anger. There was bitter rivalry for the mother-wife, but this was never made conscious and they never confronted each other. Thus the negative father archetype was never fully invoked and mediated by the personal father, and the son was never initiated into manhood. He remained at the threshold, unable to proceed further without help. There is an old saying that what the father has spoiled, only the father can repair, and his father did spoil him by never forcibly claiming the son as his own, by never risking a display of intense love or anger that would have gripped the son and pulled him into the process. Now the initiatory father for this young man can only be found in the symbolic transference-father of analysis, and that is where he came for help.

But the initiatory process has not been entirely absent. There was an unconscious fantasy which was a very important part of his erotic life. He fantasized that his father, in a surge of anger, would take him out to the woods alone, bend him over, and beat him until he promised to be respectful and obedient. This had never happened to him, but by means of the fantasy he preserved his connection to the chthonic, instinctual masculinity that can only be transmitted by the father. He is obsessively fixated on an essentially initiatory ritual. But it is a solitary fantasy, not sanctioned by the society of men (the outer collective). It is an unconscious product of the trickster, and the trick is on him (as it was on Badger in the Navaho myth). Although he outwardly professes that he abhors the act of submission, within he is erotically bound to this very act. As long as the meaning of the fantasy remains unconscious he is doomed like Tantalus to strive, without resolution.

For the initial elucidation of a fantasy of this type we must first turn to Freud who wrote a paper in 1919 entitled "A Child is Being Beaten." Freud comments that to the young male, being beaten stands for being loved (Freud 1950). The boy's beating fantasy is passive and is derived from a feminine, incestuous attachment to the father which has remained unconscious. This is on the mark, but what Freud did not indicate was that this incestuous fantasy is also a part of the archetypal initiatory process. It is the necessary submission to the father, the necessary endurance of pain as an act of masculine love, and the acceptance of symbolic death of the mother's child (unconscious identification with the mother) as a prelude to rebirth into manhood.

In an early dream the patient reported: "I was walking down a dark, deserted street with three black guys. They were intent on destruction. Then I was on a motorcycle being pursued by three tough characters. One was an older man. I threw the emergency switch and was able to speed away up a hill."

Here as in other dreams he is in close contact with the aggressive aspect of his (ego-aligned) shadow complex, but there is danger from the tough characters, and he can escape only by using his emergency energy (motorcycle). The older man may be an early appearance of the therapist in his dreams.

In a second dream he is in the Palace of Fine Arts (his inflated side) being attacked on all sides by blacks who are intent on killing every white in the building.

The shadow complex is full of murderous rage. Only an appeal to the inner father who is also tough can lead him out of this mortal danger. At this time in therapy the patient was suicidal; all his efforts to change were failing. In one dream:

> *I was trying to cross the Golden Gate Bridge, but it collapsed. I was underneath. It started sagging down. Water started to come in. Finally it was like a tunnel, and I just got out to the other side before the water flooded in. Lots of people were killed.*

In spite of such repeated attacks the ego was still able to identify with the inflated heroic pole of his bipolar shadow:

> *I was in a big opera house singing an important aria. The stage began slanting down like the leaning tower. I was quite high up. I had to sit down and block myself from sliding, but I was still slipping. Someone, maybe the stage manager, on the left was bracing me. Thousands and thousands of people were waiting for me to sing the Etruria. I did get through and it was very well received.*[2]

In a dream he tried to get help from his father:

> I went on vacation and left my parakeet in a cage. I asked my father to take care of it but when I got back he hadn't taken care of it at all.

Then the patient dreamed that he saw his father dressed in leather pants and boots. He was having an affair with a 19-year-old boy. His father was whipping the boy with a leather belt. The feeling of the dream was mixed disgust and jealousy of the boy.

The dreams in this case show the typical pattern of the weak father-son relationship. The dream ego, as well as the actual ego, identifies itself with inflated heroism, ready to sing for "thousands and thousands of people." But it is under attack by the instinctual shadow complexes symbolized by the blacks and the toughs. There were many other similar dreams. In the last two dreams cited, the father complex is activated again and though at first there is the expected betrayal, in the sadomasochistic dream the father becomes an ambivalent figure that fascinates the son; my patient thought the boy might be a younger version of himself.

Of the over-riding inflation prominent in the opera dream, and also in the patient's life, Henderson in his important work on the initiation archetype said:

> Every educated person comes out of childhood with the impossible expectation of achieving some kind of godlikeness. I have already called attention to the immense social danger of this illusion unless it is corrected. What we can excuse in a boy and even admire, because of the enthusiasm with which he may enliven his elders with his divine discontent becomes both a private and public danger in a grown man." (1967, pp. 130-131)

Here the transference comes into play, as Henderson says once more:

> The patient's acceptance of his therapist as both trustworthy and humane suggests that in his transference of feeling from mother to father, he accepts the role of the doctor as a transitional figure, a master of initiation, who is both mother and

father, firm and skillful in the use of his instruments, but also compassionate.
(*Ibid.*, p. 97)

The therapeutic initiation process means grounding the godlike expectation. To do that requires activating symbolically an inner archetypal structure
consisting of submission, fusion (in the transference-countertransference),
and re-emergence as a man. This structure is the basis for every initiatory
therapy for which, in the case of a young man, an older man would seem the
most appropriate therapist. In such therapy the inflation of meaning over
substance, and the hegemony of the spirit, is sacrified for substance,
grounding and energy for life itself.

If however, the above process is obstructed, as in our clinical example,
then the symbolic substratum might surface as a sexualized compulsion for
male-male sadomasochistic acts. Many of these acts, submission to the father-
master, the posture of humiliation, being bound or immobilized, the infliction
of physical pain, and even penetration by the stronger masculine phallus,
originally represent necessary stages in the flow of initiatory symbolism. All
of them can be found as parts of initiation rituals in tribal cultures.
Symbolically, every part or product of the father's body becomes an avenue
for longed-for fusion by means of which the transfer of genuine masculine
power takes place. But if there is an obstruction in the process and the libido is
caught in the repetition-compulsion of a specific sadomasochistic act, then it
will remain in that form until the libido is once more restored to the
underlying, initiatory process.

Here caution is necessary on the part of the therapist. No therapist can
know the true relative strength of the contending complexes, nor can one in
any particular case know how far the initiatory process can and should go.
Every part of the initiatory archetypal way is sacred in its own right and
contains a secret symbolism of its own which binds the devotee to a way of
life, both sexually and emotionally, which has its own divine patronage and
fatefulness. Individuation does not demand perfection. In all these secret
scenarios, if they are genuinely experienced, the sacrifice of godlikeness,
hubris and youthful inflation is performed, and that is the all-important step.
Then—and only then—the sacrifice of the spirit can be made which leads of
its own accord to moderation of the flesh.

The Strong Father-Son Relationship

In the strong father-son relationship the son readily accepts psychological
fusion with the father, the deflation of his childhood divinity and his own
identity as an ordinary instinctual man. Then he becomes the father's son, the
culturally approved man; often this also means becoming the patriotic warrior.
He has undergone the initiatory process, and accepted the currently official
form of manhood for his society. But this does not mean that his problems are
over. Far from it. If he is aware he will become conscious that not only his own

masculine identity, but also the culture that shaped it is seriously flawed. Then he, too, must bear the burden of individuation. This situation is well described in an essay by William Broyles, Jr., founding editor of Texas Monthly and past editor of Newsweek, which is entitled "Why Men Love War" (1984). The article is unflinchingly honest and describes his own wakening to consciousness. He says:

> It is no mystery why men hate war. War is ugly, horrible, evil and it is reasonable for men to hate all that. But I believe that most men who have been to war would have to admit, if they are honest, that somewhere inside themselves they loved it, too, loved as much as anything that has happened to them before or since. And how do you explain that to your wife, your children, your parents, or your friends? [He is speaking here only of father's sons]. (*Ibid.*, p. 55)

Of course, it never was explained because, as he says:

> We were mute, I suspect, out of shame. Nothing in the way we were raised admits the possibility of loving war. It is at best a necessary evil, a patriotic duty to be discharged and then put behind us. To love war is to mock the very values we supposedly fight for. It is to be insensitive, reactionary, a brute. (*Ibid.*, p. 56)

Here he describes the very split which is the main theme of this paper. On the one side is the idealism which is publically approved by the outer culture, and to which we must all appear to conform; on the other side is the nakedly aggressive shadow rooted firmly in the dark primitive side of the masculine (father) archetype.

Broyles goes on to describe the dynamics of that archetype:

> Part of the love of war stems from its being an experience of great intensity; its lure is the fundamental human passion to witness, to see things, what the Bible calls lust of the eye, and the Marines in Vietnam called eye-fucking. War stops time, intensifies experience to the point of terrible ecstasy. (*Ibid.*, p. 56)

Finally with relentless self-analysis he concludes:

> The love of war stems from the union, deep in the core of our being, between sex and destruction, beauty and horror, love and death. War may be the only way in which most men touch the mystic domains of our soul. It is for men, at some terrible level, the closest thing to what childbirth is for women: the initiation into the power of life and death. (*Ibid.*, p. 61)

In many tribal cultures, the love of war is openly and unashamedly displayed. War is part of life, but it is often ritually regulated. The Navaho again offer a prime example in the War Ceremony collected and presented by Maud Oakes in "The Two Who Came to Their Father" (1943). This was a ceremony given for young men going to or coming home from war. It provided a path for the return of the warrior to peaceful life. It also lays out the archetypal path of initiation in the clearest possible way.

This is the story of the Navaho warrior twins, Monster Slayer and Child Born of Water, and their journey to find their father. They are born of the great Navaho fertility goddess, Changing Woman. She carefully protects them from the monsters, but when they are twelve years old they can no longer be prevented from setting off to find their father, who is the Sun, giver of all warmth and life.

The basic split I have described is echoed in its Navaho form even in the twinship of the heroes. Monster Slayer is bolder and more aggressive, while Child Born of Water is softer and more gentle, the favorite of the mother. When they left he was the one for whom she wept. Their journey is fraught with the most terrible dangers which are described in great detail in the myth. Before they go far they come upon the house of Spider Woman. She is the Navaho version of the wise old woman, always shrewd and sometimes helpful. She has a very small house, but they find they can enter it nonetheless. One of the things she gives to each of them is a sacred feather which she had obtained secretly from Father Sun himself. These feathers represent the secret, spiritual connection with the father, and in spite of the many terrible ordeals the twins must undergo, the feathers keep them safe. Finally they come to the trackless ocean (what better symbol for the boundless collective unconscious) and with the help of the feather find their way to Sun's house.

Sun's daughter tries to hide them in the cloud coverings, but when the Sun comes home he is very angry, because he has seen from the sky strange men approaching his house. He hunts until he finds them, and then, appearing to disbelieve their claims to be his sons, puts them through a series of ruthless tests.

The first is a sweathouse heated to an unendurable temperature until the rocks inside are so hot they explode. This would have killed the twins except that Sun's daughter helps them. She digs deep pits inside the sweathouse and in these the twins hide themselves to escape the heat and flying rocks. Sun is surprised to find them still alive, but he devises another test. He offers them poisoned mush. Only half of it has the poison. Little Wind, their spiritual advisor, tells them which part to eat. There are several other ordeals, but finally Sun takes them to a high platform placed over sharp, out-thrusting flint knives, and pushes them off. They are sure to be killed, but the feather guides them safely down past the blades. Then Sun relents and recognizes them as his sons. He changes completely, becomes very generous, and offers them all the bounties of his earthly domains. But all they want are his terrible arrow weapons to kill the monsters who are ravaging the earth. Sun is sorry to hear this because the monsters are also his sons, but he does give the twins the arrows. One by one they slay all their enemies, but when the task is accomplished, and the earth is free from the oppression of the monsters, they cannot stop. They want to go on killing so they must be restrained. Sun takes back his powerful arrows because the twins can no longer handle them. War chant ceremonies are held to cleanse them of the blood they have shed.

In this part of the Navaho myth the core of the initiation archetype relating to the father is laid out. The hero(s) must leave the land of the mother. This leaving itself means going outside of time and space which is fraught with strong obstacles. They must finally penetrate into the objective (collective) psyche (the trackless ocean) and there they find the father's house. At first he is the terrible father and he meets them with suspicion and hostility. He subjects them to tests they could never survive if they did not have secret connections to his other spiritual side. These are the feathers from Spider Woman (the feathers represents a spiritual connection between the earth and the upper world), Little Wind—another such spiritual connection—and Sun's daughter who, like Brunhilde, knows the father's tender heart. When they pass his tests he *knows* they are his sons and all the bounty of the earth and heaven is open to them. They choose weapons. Their lust is to kill and nothing else interests them. Even after the monsters threatening civilized progress are dead, the heros cannot give up the lust to kill. Finally the first performance of the War Ceremonial is given on earth to cleanse them of the killing, to renew contact with the peaceful, spiritual father who dwells in the upper reaches of the psyche, and to return to the ways of peace. It is that ceremony for which the whole world now, it would seem, stands in need.

Conclusion

We are in a crucial world situation. The split between instinct and ideal is strained to the utmost. In a world threatened by total nuclear destruction on the one hand and relentless overpopulation on the other, the core relationship to instinctual experiences of life and death involving waging war and childbirth will have to be changed if we are to survive. For a genuine transformation to take place, a sacrifice is necessary on both sides of the bipolar shadow. If man is to sacrifice the intensity of his animal nature he must also sacrifice his divine pretensions. His sacrifice will not be, as in the past, for the perfection of Christian virtue or Eastern enlightenment, but rather to become a more complete human being, consciously aware of both unattainable idealizations as well as instinctual temptations. His path is a narrow one between the opposites, but it is his nature to be at home with (to paraphrase John Gower [Jung 1954]) "this warring peace, this sweet wound and this enjoyable evil."

NOTES

1. A published version of this myth can be found in McAllester, David P., ed., "The Myth and Prayers of the Great Star Chant." *Navajo Religion Series,* Vol. IV. Santa Fe, N.M.: Museum of Navajo Ceremonial Art, 1956.

2. "Etruria" here means "Tuscany"; the word is a dream combination of "erotic" and "Etruscan."

REFERENCES

Broyles, W. Jr. 1984. "Why men love war." *Esquire,* Nov. 1984.

Erikson, E.H. 1950. *Childhood and society.* New York: W. W. Norton and Co., Inc.

———— 1980. *Identity and the life cycle.* New York: W. W. Norton and Co., Inc.

Freud, S. 1950. *Collected papers,* Vol. II. London: The Hogarth Press.

Henderson, J. L. 1967. *Thresholds of initiation.* Middletown, Conn.: Wesleyan University Press.

Jung, C. G. 1954. *The practice of psychotherapy.* Vol. 16, Bollingen Series XX. New York: Panther Books.

Oakes, M. 1943. *Where the two came to their father, a Navaho war ceremonial.* Bollingen Series I. Princeton, N.J.: Princeton University Press.

Perry, J. W. 1970. Emotions and object relations. *Journal of Analytical Psychology,* 25:125-40.

Stein, M. 1982. *Jungian analysis.* LaSalle and London: Open Court.

THE EROSION OF MALE CONFIDENCE

Robert Bly

Robert Bly's essay, "The Erosion of Male Confidence," is edited from a speech given at a symposium, "Understanding Vietnam," Salado, Texas, October 29-31, 1982. Sponsored by the Texas Committee for the Humanities, the symposium included other presentations by historian George C. Herring, General Douglas Kinnard, presidential advisor Walt W. Rostow, psychiatrist Harry Wilmer, and journalist Philip Geylin. In his address, Bly holds up the Vietnam War as a symbol of the betrayal of the young men by the older, that is, a sign of the failure of the older generation to provide meaningful values and models of manhood for their sons. His remarks are pertinent to any socio-political study of modern rites of passage for men. Indeed, as the poet remarks, "When men lose their confidence in older men, what happens then?"

Robert Bly graduated from Harvard and resides in his native state of Minnesota. His collections of poetry include Silence in the Snowy Fields *(1962),* The Light Around the Body *(1968 National Book Award),* The Teeth Mother Naked at Last *(1970),* Sleepers Joining Hands *(1973),* The Morning Glory *(1975),* The Kabir Book *(1977), and others. His poetry journals,* The Fifties, The Sixties *and* The Seventies *published many European and South American poets for the first time in the United States. Today, "He is one of the leaders of a poetic revival which has returned American literature to the world community" (Kenneth Rexroth). In 1966, Bly and David Ray founded an organization called American Writers Against the Vietnam War, a series of readings in which most of the poets in this country took part. He has published other articles on issues of masculine initiation.*

MY subject is the erosion of male confidence in general during the last thirty years, and, specifically, the part the Vietnam War has had in that erosion. Everywhere I go in the country I meet men roughly twenty to forty years old who live in considerable self-doubt. Many of them have few or no close friends. I meet young fathers who do not know what male values they should attempt to teach their sons. These men, often separated from their own remote fathers, and out of touch with their grandfathers, do not feel they belong to a community of men. When they reach out toward truly masculine values, they find nothing in their hand when it closes.

The old anger against the father, so characteristic of the nineteenth century and earlier centuries, has been replaced in many men by a kind of passivity and remoteness, which springs from a feeling that the father has abandoned or rejected them. In some cases, the father lost his sons in divorce proceedings, and many sons interpret that event to mean that men are untrustworthy. Still other sons have lived with remote, overworked, impassive, silent, controlling or condemnatory fathers; and one feels in these men a longing for male values mingled with a kind of helpless bitterness. Some men in recent years admire only certain values which they associate with women—tenderness, concern for the environment, nurturing, the sense of cooperation, ability to feel deeply. These men characteristically confide during a crisis only in women. That is fine; what is missing is the confiding in men. We could conclude by saying that women came out of the sixties and seventies with considerable confidence in their values, but men lack this clarity and belief. We all know many exceptions to this statement, and yet we sense a significant alteration in male confidence since, say, 1950 to 1960.

Because men of all social classes have lost confidence, it's clear that many forces affect this change. The Industrial Revolution has sent the father to work many miles from the home, and given him a work that he cannot teach his son. Male societies have disappeared, along with opportunities for older and younger men to meet each other and to do ordinary physical work together. The mythological layer, with all its models of adult male energy—Apollo, Dionysius, Hermes, Zeus—collapsed long ago, as have models of adult female energy for women. More recently, the relatively humane, or human-ized, male battle disappeared, destroyed by machine-gun slaughter and bombing from the air. In old Irish and Greek stories we meet men who obey the rules of combat and honor their male enemy.

We all notice that suburban life gets along without male community. My parents brought me up on a Minnesota farm during years in which men lived in a community. My father ran a threshing rig, and all through the threshing season the men—young, old and middle aged—worked together, doggedly and humorously, in a kind of high-spirited cooperation at its best. I felt a confidence in the male community and I felt the goodness of it. But for men living in the suburbs all that is gone. We can all suggest many other forces and events that have contributed to erosion of male confidence. I would say that the two major causes for erosion are the attacks launched against men by the separatist part of the women's movement and the Vietnam War.

The women's movement has brought considerable psychic health to women, but we need to distinguish the women's movement from its separatist component: the attacks that heap together virtually all male values and condemn them as evil, and that locate the source of women's pain entirely in men. At a seminar three days ago a woman said to me, "Since all good poetry comes from our reaction to oppression, and since white males are not oppressed in any way, then how could they possibly write poetry?" So I asked, "Does your mother oppress you?" "Oh, not at all," she said. "Women don't oppress, men oppress." So I said, "How do you feel about the matriarchies?" She said, "Oh, there was no oppression in the matriarchies." I said, "Read Margaret Mead sometime." Some feminists are determined to save men even if they have to destroy them to do it.

An ancient story from north England about the ugly dragon-man called the Lindworm says that the transformation of the Lindworm to a man takes place in four stages. The Lindworm's "bride," rather than fighting the Lindworm, asks him to take off one of his seven ugly-skins, and she agrees to take off one of her seven blouses if he does that. After he has removed all seven skins, he lies helpless and white on the floor. She then whips him with whips dipped in lye, then washes him in milk, and finally lies down in the bed and holds him a few minutes before falling asleep. Connie Martin, the storyteller, has suggested that women in the seventies got the whipping part down well, but did not wash the man or hold him. They were too tired after the whipping to do the last two steps.

Let's turn now to the Vietnam War and its influence on men's confidence. That subject is what concerns us here. To introduce the subject, I'll tell two stories that I heard. A friend in Boston told me the first story. He stems from an old and wealthy family that carries a lot of military tradition and so much emphasis on male virtues that even civilians in his family receive a sort of military burial, with only the men present. My friend, whom I will call John, entered, as one would expect, the military service during the Vietnam War willingly, trustingly—became an officer and served in the field. After some duty in the field, he returned to Saigon on leave. One day he found himself by the river talking to an old captain, both of them speaking French. The Vietnamese river captain told him, in the course of many anecdotes, that the American soldiers were not welcome here, any more than the French. John had experienced inconsistencies in the field, but at that instant he felt a terrific shock. He understood that he had been lied to. The men who had lied to him were the very men that his family had respected for generations—military men and men in responsible government positions. Last night we saw a section of the new PBS documentary of the war. In that section one can watch McNamara and McGeorge Bundy lying about the Tonkin Gulf incident. I said to John, "What did you do then when you realized that you had been lied to about the major issues of war?" "Well," he said, "a strange thing happened. A female anger rose up in me." I said, "Why do you use the word 'female'?" He said, "All at once I understood how a single betrayal could being a woman to furious anger. The Greeks talked about that. I understood the female anger, and I felt it." I said, "What happened next?" He said, "Well, the anger continued and turned into rage and I had to live with that the rest of the time I was in Vietnam, and I'm still living with it." He is a friend of John Kerry, who organized the Vietnam Veterans against the War. He remarked that John Kerry has entered politics in Massachusetts—holds a high office—and Kerry still has a nightmare every night. Not one night goes by that he does not have it.

I know anecdotes don't prove anything; they only suggest. To me they suggest that a new situation evolved during the Vietnam War which amounts to older men lying to younger men. This is the grief I want to discuss.

I enlisted in the Second World War when I was seventeen and I, like most of the men I knew, did not feel that older men lied to me during the war. The older men, I felt, were aware of the younger ones, and though many younger men died, the older men died as well. There was a certain feeling of camaraderie and trust all up and down the line. My friend John emphasized that the military and civilian leaders this time did not labor to awaken the sense of patriotism that gives battle labor some meaning. That sense of meaning bound old and young together in the Second World War. Johnson didn't declare war because to do so would have necessitated a full congressional debate. Did you see Dean Rusk lie about that point last night in the documentary? He said, "Well, we didn't try to declare war because, you see, we were afraid that it would be, you know, you mustn't when you have nuclear arms, you mustn't make people angry." Dean Rusk was lying. As the Vietnam War went on, Walt Whitman Rostow, McGeorge Bundy, Dean Rusk, all lied. And I felt lied to by them. But at the time, I didn't fully realized how the soldiers and officers in the battlefield would feel when, their lives at stake, they recognized the same lies.

I will tell a second story. I met recently in San Francisco a veteran who had been an ordinary draftee. When I told him I would be attending a conference in Texas about the war, he looked interested, and I asked him how he felt about the war. He said, "Well, I must tell you that I still feel tremendous anger." I said, "What about?" "Well," he said, "I've been thinking about it, and it has to do with my background. At the time I was a young Catholic boy from Pennsylvania. I had taken in certain moral values, simply through being in that background. One was that killing was wrong. A second was respect for women. We still believed some of the moral declarations that racism was bad. All at once we were out in the jungle, and told to shoot at anything that moves. We couldn't tell if the people we were killing were men or women, let alone Communists or peasants. Moreover, everyone, officers included, called them 'slopes' and 'gooks.' The older men never mentioned this nor told us what we were to do with the ideas we had taken in during Catholic grade school. After a month or so in the field suddenly I was shipped for R and R to a whorehouse in Thailand. Something was wrong with that. A lot of us still had feelings toward women. We had feelings about respect for women and what a woman means in this way. Something got broken in me, and I'm still angry about that."

So the question we have to ask ourselves is, Who made that decision? I remember that during the Second World War the army supported the USO, where one went and danced a little with a woman, who was equally shy. It was very square, but nevertheless, the whole thing helped to preserve some continuity between civilian life and war life. Older men like Eisenhower supported such arrangements. The older men in the Vietnam War led the way to the whorehouses and made no attempt to preserve the continuity between civilian life and war life for these young males. It was a violation of trust. To repeat: when I came out of the Second World War there was a bond between younger and older men and it helped all of us who served to move through our lives.

Let's turn now to body counts. The army didn't announce body counts of Germans during the Second World War. As a speaker mentioned yesterday, we measured our progress in Vietnam not by land taken but by lives taken. "Attrition" is the sugar-coated way of putting it. But the fact is that counting dead bodies is not a way for civilized human beings to behave, especially when your culture emphasizes the dignity of life. How can the same culture that prides itself on respecting the dignity of human life be in favor of body counts? The counting of bodies and the release of that information daily was approved by the Joint Chiefs of Staff, and agreed on by the generals. You can't tell me that they didn't know the implications of this. Even worse, the generals and the Pentagon began to lie about the number of bodies. As we now know, the staff often doubled the count from the field. General Shoemaker, who led the incursion into Cambodia, is present, and several speakers have addressed polite questions to him during their talk here. I'd like to ask him a question also. General Shoemaker, I would like to ask you now: "Were you aware of the false body counts being passed through you?"

"Yes, I was aware that some of them were inflated."

"Have you apologized to the young men in the country for this lie?"

"Well, I would prefer to listen to you."

"All right. Thank you."

You heard the answer General Shoemaker just gave us, "No, I have not apologized to the young men in the country." And we can add that he doesn't intend to.

Our subject here is the bad judgement of older men that resulted in damage to younger men or death of younger men. John mentioned one more decision. The generals decided to have a 365-day field term rotation. Such a plan broke with the traditional situation in which a company lives and dies together as a unit. The company learns to act as a unit; and each man learns to trust, or whom to trust. But the 365-day rotation breaks all that. Everyone is thinking, as John mentioned, about his own survival, and then suddenly the others can't depend on him, or he on them. I think the average age of the soldiers in Vietnam was around eighteen years old; in the Second World War it was around twenty-six. The average age of the company commanders in Vietnam was twenty-two years old; in the Second World War, thirty-six. The decision for rotation was a bad one, and I think General Westmoreland made it; others here would know. General Westmoreland throughout did many stupid things, and his advisors showed a specialist mentality, and a massive insensitivity to the needs of the younger men. The use of Agent Orange is a perfect example. Our first step in recovering from the war, I think, is simply to say this.

So the eighteen-year-olds were out in the jungle with men only two or three years older, and these eighteen-year-olds felt completely isolated and separated. Who made the decision that led to this isolation? Did everyone approve of the public body counts? I will recite to you a poem I wrote in the spring of 1966 about those body counts. It's called "Counting Small-Boned Bodies."

>   Let's count the bodies over again.
> If we could only make the bodies smaller,
> The size of skulls,
> Maybe we could get a whole plain white
>   with skulls in the moonlight!
>
> If we could only make the bodies smaller,
> Maybe we could get
> A whole year's kill in front of us on a desk!
>
> If we could only make the bodies smaller
> We could fit
> A body into a finger ring, for a keepsake forever.

I always thought that we never made good enough use of the Vietnamese heads. Maybe the Pentagon should have encased them in plastic and put them up on motel walls around the United States. Couldn't American men and women make love well below those heads?

Walt Rostow made a remark this morning which you all heard. I don't want to single him out above the others of his sort—it happens he is the only one here representing that group of advisors, and it is brave of him to come. But I could hardly believe my ears this morning when he declared that the true brutality in this war was the brutality of Congress when it refused to vote more money toward the end. Did you hear that one? It was marvelous. Our feelings get damaged when we misuse our own language. All through the war, men like Rostow refused to use language in a clear and honest way. "Brutality" comes from the root, "brute"; and "not voting funds" comes from a decision based on rationality and debate. Words and phrases like "friendlies," "incursion," "Communist infrastructure," and "strategic hamlets" testify to a time in American history when language failed. And it was the older men who brought in that language, and led the movement toward failure of language. They had the responsibility to keep the language clear. The young men can't do that. They are helpless. They believe the older men when they called a dictatorship "democratic," or when they called a certain liquid "Agent Orange" rather than "Poison no. 465." Doesn't "Orange" imply nourishing?

We can say then that when the Vietnam veteran arrived home he found a large hole in himself where his values once were. What is the veteran going to do about that? Many veterans I meet say they still cannot find any values to put in there. The earlier values were blown out, the way acid blows out the brain. Harry Wilmer moved me tremendously when he talked about the dreams of Vietnam veterans yesterday. The dreams of certain veterans, he said, repeat events in exact detail, endlessly, meaninglessly. Only when the veteran is able to find a possibility of meaning—what a wonderful word that is—meaning, meaning, meaning—can his dreams begin to change. Then a veteran can begin to put something into this hole. But most veterans are not receiving help in moving toward meaning; they have not succeeded in finding a man like Harry Wilmer. They live in rage and in a sense of betrayal.

It is clear that this issue is a very serious issue, and the implications go far beyond the mistakes of the Vietnam War. When men lose their confidence in older men, what happens then? When older men betray younger men, and lie to them, in government and in the field, what happens then to male values? What happens to a society in which the males do not trust each other? What kind of a society is that? Do you feel it coming now? That mood in the country? Do you feel how the distrust erodes the confidence that males have in themselves? Did you know that the practice of "fragging," that is the killing by enlisted men of their own sergeants and lieutenants, was statistically not a factor until the Vietnam War? And I feel the poison of that distrust moving through the whole society now. The older men associated with the Vietnam War continue to lie to Vietnam veterans about chemical poisoning and birth defects. Every man in the country knows that. It is no wonder that in Comtrex advertisements on television men are always presented as weak. What does the army's constant lying about Agent Orange do to our respect for men and for male values?

Our general subject is the Vietnam War and its effect on the erosion of male confidence. How can this nightmare end? What healing can take place? Harry Wilmer suggests, and I utterly agree, that no healing can take place until we decide to take in the concept of the dark side, or the shadow. Each of us has a dark side. If I shout at my small sons, I can say that I have a fatherly duty to discipline them, but we know that this shouting has a dark side. When so many whites moved to the suburbs during the fifties, wasn't that a simple longing for open space? But it had a dark side. The dark side was that we let the center of our psyche disintegrate. When entertainment, in the form of television, floods our house every night, we are only sitting and listening— this is a simple thing surely, isn't it? But it has a dark side. It has a very strong dark side, in that we don't have to entertain others, or enter any larger sort of community to be entertained. Why don't we ever talk about that one? Well, when Johnson decided to raise troop levels sneakily, without public debate, that looked like a simple act, perfectly reasonable under the circumstances, as Dean Rusk says. But we know that it had a dark side. The decision to send eighteen-year-olds to whorehouses, whether they wanted to go or not, has a dark side, and the cool dryness with which Robert McNamara and McGeorge Bundy and Dean Rusk discussed hideous realities has a dark side. Have you ever noticed that? How calm the older men are? Some rationalists don't want to get into feeling at all. Did you notice how boyish McNamara looked in the documentary last night? I was shocked. Probably he looked that way because he was a boy. What is a boy? A boy is a person who takes an act and does not think about the dark side of it. An adult is a person who takes an act and remains aware of its dark side. What happens in the psyche when Reagan repeats over and over that we fight our wars with noble purpose while the other side fights its wars with evil purpose? What happens when we say that Russia is an "evil empire"?

Some Europeans studied the dark side of colonial wars, and Joseph Conrad studies it marvelously in his story, *The Heart of Darkness*. We have to think of the possibility that we are adopting European diplomatic phrases and adopting European global responsibilities, but adopting them not as adults but as boys. When we decisively entered Vietnam culture around 1966, we had virtually no one in the State Department who spoke Vietnamese, and very few in the academic community who had close knowledge of Vietnamese culture. Do you think that deterred our people? Not a bit. We invaded a nation and made decisions for it when we had only two or three scholars who could speak the language. That is not adult behavior. Our behavior in Central America is not adult behavior either. Reagan is another boy, an aged boy. How to embalm a boy so he always smiles forever? How could we be so lucky as to find a president who never sees the dark side of anything he does? These boyish men—so cheerful—are among the most dangerous men on earth. One group of Americans carries the knowledge of their danger: the Vietnam veterans. They carry that knowledge for all of us.*

---

*Mr. Bly concluded his remarks by reading selections from a long poem he wrote during the Vietnam War called *The Teeth-Mother Naked at Last* (City Lights Books, 1970).

Reprinted from *Vietnam in Remission*. ed. James Veninga and Harry Wilmer (College Station, Tex.: Texas A&M University Press, 1985), by permission of the author.

THE
INITIATION
OF
WOMEN

PART FOUR

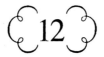

FROM CONCRETE TO CONSCIOUSNESS:
THE EMERGENCE OF THE FEMININE

Marion Woodman

Marion Woodman examines the process of feminine self-transformation in her essay, "From Concrete to Consciousness: The Emergence of the Feminine." She raises the very pertinent question: "What can modern women do to redeem their unconscious from the compulsive, materialistic ethos of our capitalist society?" Rather than to berate men for their traditional suppression of feminine energy, she challenges modern women to resist the demands of the negative aspect of the Devouring Mother and to raise their consciousness of themselves—"resonating with their own femininity." Within all women, "the Great Mother wants to be brought to consciousness."

Acknowledging the need for women to express their own femininity through genuine relationships, she examines the passage dreams of women in the process of self-transformation and demonstrates how such dreams connect women to their own inner masculinity: "When the ego and the inner partner are working together, the masculine nurtures the feminine." Hence, Woodman advises women to avoid either the unconscious "Daddy's little girl" role or the struggle to compete with men in the unconscious service of the dark, material side of the Great Mother. She links the transformation of modern women with their gradual awakening to their own "creative masculinity."

Marion Woodman is a Jungian analyst practicing in Toronto, Canada. A diplomate of the C.G. Jung Institute in Zurich, she is the author of three widely-acclaimed books on the psychic life and values of modern women: The Owl Was a Baker's Daughter: Obesity, Anorexia Nervosa and the Repressed Feminine *(1980),* Addiction to Perfection: The Still Unravished Bride *(1982), and* The Pregnant Virgin: A Process of Psychological Transformation *(1985).*

> Ourself behind ourself, concealed
> Should startle most.
> —Emily Dickinson

SOME years ago when I was traveling in the South Seas, I boarded a plane in one of the island ports. The women passengers were magnificent, massive Earth Mothers, most of them nearly six feet tall, weighing probably 300 pounds, their shining black hair coiled on top of their heads or falling in long braids over their brilliantly colored Mother Hubbard dresses. Their eyes sparkled with health and good spirits. I, who am not small by Western standards, cuddled in my seat feeling tiny, delicate, weightless, utterly at peace with so many big Mamas to protect me.

After some time in an island village, however, my romanticized image of these Great Earth Mothers changed. I saw their pain and the pain in those around them. Becky, for example, ruled her family with her insatiable appetite. Her twenty year old son, a mere wisp of a boy in appearance, was responsible for feeding his mother. He spent his entire day searching for breadfruit, tara, and coconuts, peeling, shredding, cooking. Terrified of "the voices" that shrieked at him in the coconut grove, "Faster, Becko, faster!" he nevertheless forced himself to go there in order to fulfill his sole responsibility in life—gathering food to feed his mother. Although he was educated, he showed no resentment. He lived with his family and the pigs that strolled in and out and about their home. He accepted his fate.

One day as she was sitting on the floor, steadfastly shoving breadfruit into her mouth, Becky said, "White people are lucky; they don't have to eat all the time. I have to eat all the time and Becko has to feed me."

Her attitude was as resigned as her son's: eating was her fate. She did not have the ego development which would permit her to assume any conscious control over her life; she could take no responsibility for the freedom of her own will. I shuddered at the ravenous appetite of the unconscious devouring mother, and shuddered equally at the senseless sacrifice of the young man's life to this gaping maw.

THE DEVOURING MOTHER

Since becoming an analyst, many times I have remembered Becky and Becko in their island home. I do not think of them as representative of their culture; possibly, they were an exception. But that particular mother was the living image of a woman blindly acting out an archetype, powerless to exert any conscious control over her abysmal appetite, powerless to release her enslaved son. Together they were enacting an unconscious destiny.

I remember them as I listen to some of my analysands who are, like Becko, feeding their unconscious devouring mother, their infantile masculinity driven to feed their unconscious, greedy complex. They frantically strive all day trying to fulfill her ravenous demands, and then, if their addiction happens to be food, they awaken at midnight to find themselves at their refrigerators "binge-ing" as voraciously as that island woman. I recall Becky sadly saying, "White people are lucky; they don't have to eat all the time," and I think how thin is our cultural veneer. We "whites" do our best to disguise our inner, unconscious devouring mother. Those of us who have recognized her are continually vigilant in our attempts to control her insistent cravings, but those of us who do not know her blindly live out her terrible aspects. She is manifested in our compulsive desires for more and more love, more and more PPFF (Prestige, Power, Fame and Fortune), more and more of whatever particular "food" our greed happens to fancy. The nightmare of Becko and his mother is the nightmare that drives many people into analysis.

While destructive behavior like that of Becky and her son is often manifested in the compulsive behavior of an individual analysand, it also emerges on a general social level in the materialistic ethos of our capitalistic society, the survival of which depends upon ceaseless economic growth and consumption. Although it has long been believed that capitalist society is a patriarchal arrangement because of the inferior roles and limited rewards granted to women, it is important to realize that Becky, not Becko, is in charge. The so-called patriarchy serves the dark side of the Magna Mater— what Phillip Wylie in *Generation of Vipers* (1955) called "Momism." This dark side is embodied in a materialism so pervasive that matter itself, in all its infinite variety, is the divinity we serve. Mater or matter ("the stuff of which a thing is made" [Oxford English Dictionary]) has become Western society's dark goddess.

From infancy, for example, perhaps even from conception, we are educated in the ways of technology. Like good little machines, we are expected, Becko-like, to perform as we are programmed, marching cheerfully toward the goals that are socially respected. "Don't stop! Tick tock! Get up! Tick tock! Work, work! Tick tock!" Driven by clocks, by "wasted time," by computers, by every conceivable kind of mechanical device, we attempt to be human beings in an inhuman environment. But what do our goals achieve? Where does our driven activity propel us? We end up buried alive under our own accumulated "mater."

Looked at from the inside, our culture functions in the service of a Great Mother Machine, a devouring Kali. Seen from this point of view, Becky and her son Becko provide an image of ourselves and our mater/matter-bound problem. So long as both remain unconscious of the impersonal dynamics governing their relationship, both remain the slaves of the archetype they blindly enact. While in Orwell's *1984* it is Big Brother who is omnipresent and omniscient, in reality it is the Great Mother who is omnipotent. Big Brother sees everything except the one that Big Brother serves, and that one, She Who is Omnipotent, is also blind, and is manifested in her ruthless, demanding, cold, and impersonal aspects. Moreover, she is angry, raging because her worshippers do not recognize her. She wants to be brought to consciousness.

The question is not how can we get out of matter, out of the womb of the Great Mother, but how can we redeem her—that is, how can we contact and release the light that is at the heart of her darkness? Becky, envying white women, whom she thought of as free from the necessity that governed her life, was, in her remark to me, unconsciously wondering how she could be released from her bondage to matter. Unfortunately, she did not have sufficient consciousness to formulate the question.

Many women who now demand equality with men in the professions are not struggling to overcome the tyranny of the patriarchal order. On the contrary, they are, in their long, regressive, unredeemed identification with matter, struggling to compete with men in the largely unconscious service of the dark side of the Great Mother. In this crucial respect, their behavior is far more regressive than their active rebellion would suggest. They are becoming the victims of the Great Maw in ways that release her particular fury. While men are as unconsciously victimized as women, this chapter is directed specifically to women who are now finding themselves enslaved to the Great Mother and are coming to realize that the way out offered by the more radical elements of the feminist movement only leads them deeper into her clutches.

The price we pay for our enslavement to matter, to the negative devouring Becky, is great. Take her out of her own society, translate her power into that of a superpower—Mother Russia or Mother America, for example—and the false security that I felt on the plane in the South Seas "with so many Big Mamas to protect me" assumes a very different shape. The I who felt "cuddled, tiny, delicate, weightless" now feels put upon, molested, violated. The terrifying voices that shrieked at Becko in the coconut grove, "Faster, Becko, Faster"—voices toward which he showed no apparent resentment—do finally take their toll when translated into modern technology, a toll well-demonstrated in Frank Coppola's film *Koyaanisgatsi*. Behavior that is directed by a force beyond our control, by a force that must be served, is driven or compulsive. Becky's son is a compulsive personality. Gathering food for a devouring mother who cannot get enough becomes a metaphor for a fully automated society in which human efficiency must aspire to the performance of an automaton. Psychic automatons are addicted personalities, governed by mysterious, irrational fetishes. To wean them from their addictions—to food, to alcohol, to sex, to drugs, to work—is to wean Becko from Becky. It is not easy. To wean Becko from Becky it is also necessary to wean Becky from herself. She is literally eating herself to death. Like her, our society grows on what it devours. It is destroying itself on what it manufactures. Economists call that self-destructive phenomenon "economic growth," and economic growth has become the chief measure of society's health. Anyone who weighs 300 pounds and is gaining 10 "pounds" a month on the stock market must sense that society's way of measuring its health is both perverse and crazy. A society that is devouring its natural resources is not becoming more healthy and more realistic. It is dying as surely as a patient who has gone from 300 to 400 pounds is dying. America at the moment is 200 billion dollars overweight. Many economists predict it will be 300 billion by the end of the century.

One day an obviously edemic woman arrived at my office. When I asked what had happened, she told me she could no longer stand the pressure and took a knife to herself to see if she could relieve it. Now that we have more or less given up on any arms reduction on the assumption that the more heavily armed we are the safer we are, we are driving ourselves toward the same kind of pressured desperation that drove that woman to thrust a knife into her own thighs. Whatever else it does, a hydrogen bomb can release a lot of pressure. Everywhere—from the individual, to the family, to the tribe, to the nation, to the global community—the pressure is too great. Becky's appetite growing on what it feeds on is Becky about to burst. Our hydrogen stockpiles, our nuclear warheads buried in the English countryside and all over Europe, are Becky's swollen stomach and massive, poisoned limbs. The Becky I have in mind, i.e. our global negative mother, weighs in the neighborhood of £300 trillion— roughly the price we are now budgeting worldwide for armaments. The Beckos of the world are feeding a ravenously destructive appetite and it is bound to explode unless Becko can be stopped, which is to say, unless Becky can be stopped. Becky's compulsive behavior must be redeemed if we are to survive. She not only controls with machine-like efficiency our waking "conscious" hours, but our sleeping, unconscious hours as well. She works both above ground and underground. Underground, she is worshipped, served, propitiated in fetishes, addictions, ravaging diseases, marital break-downs, premature deaths. Nothing can satisfy her hunger, which is uncon-scious, insatiable and autonomous. Her appetite feeds on its own power, endlessly giving birth to more and more and more, endlessly feeding on what is feeding on her.

How can we as individuals bring consciousness to the Great Mother? How can we allow our femininity to blossom, conscious enough to be well-grounded in our Great Mother Earth, at the same time conscious enough to redeem her destructive drives? What rites of passage can help us to make the transition from the icon of Becko and Becky to the icon of the redeemed feminine who is psychologically conscious enough to receive the Holy Spirit and psychologically strong enough to bear the divine child?

Contemporary feminists, recognizing the trap into which they might fall, i.e. becoming the enemy they sought to overthrow, have taken a positive approach. These women are genuinely attempting to reconnect with their own lost feminine roots. For such women the matriarchy that exists at the core of our technological culture is yet another demonic parody of femininity. The unconscious mother is, for them, no role model. They take no satisfaction in the state of nervous collapse to which Yves St. Laurent is annually reduced in his round-the-clock struggle to keep them clothed. It gives them no satisfaction that men willingly sacrifice their manhood to them even as they sacrificed their testicles to Great Mother Astarte. They are not gratified to see themselves in Vogue parading like so many queens. These women recognize that it is the negative mother who rules in Becky, that her son Becko is probably gay, and that it is not only his manhood that is being destroyed but their womanhood as well.

THE FUNCTION OF RITUAL

The distance between the unconscious Becky, for whom the world (including her son) is so much food to be devoured, and the psychologically conscious woman, is still too uncharted to be described with any precision. Many women, however, are creating their own rites, sometimes modelled on ancient rituals celebrating the ancient goddesses, sometimes modelled on rituals that have been guided from within by dreams, by body responses or active imagination. If the body is allowed to move as it wishes to move, it enacts its own feeling in ritualized movement. These rituals, however unsophisticated, are crucial in re-connecting women to their own instinctual roots. If the ritual emerges from their own authentic Being, well-educated women, superbly trained in the ways of technology and rational thinking, find themselves silenced in the presence of their own straightforward, non-negotiable, inner truth. For the first time in their complex lives, they feel their own *I AM*.

One young woman who had been in analysis for two years felt very discouraged because in spite of her growing understanding of herself as a woman (rather than a Daddy's little girl) she was rarely able to enact her own sense of herself in her university training. After months of irrational confrontation with her professors, confrontations which came dangerously close to releasing the hysteria of her locked-in little girl, Kathryn was preparing her oral examination for her Master's degree. She determined she would not fall into the trap of denying her own inner reality in order to "perform" as an "A" student should. She swung between propounding what she knew her professors wanted to hear and withdrawing into silence because she felt that anything she would say as a woman would be "childish, silly, stupid, and worst of all, unheard." Worse still, she might find herself rebelling against the humiliation of infantile feeling and over-react, turning questions into assaults upon her own womanhood.

On the day of her examination, Kathryn prepared an early morning ritual for our small group of closely bonded women. Although her dreams and two years of devotion to her conscious standpoint had prepared her inwardly to sacrifice her infantile attitudes, she knew she needed to experience herself as a woman among women in order to validate who she now was. An intuitive person, she had considerable difficulty attempting to stay with existential reality and thus had chosen the turtle as an important symbol of steadfastness, rootedness, and patience in achieving its goal. Kathryn owned a bronze candlestick shaped with four sturdy feet and a shell that provided a flat surface for a large candle—a balance of fire and earth, spirit and matter. While she told us of the powerful energy and symbolism of the turtle, she directed us in making our own origami mandalas, since our unpractised fingers were not dexterous enough to make turtles. As we crouched, creasing and folding and listening, the room became TURTLE, and each of us was walking on four stout legs carrying our own lighted candles, supporting Kathryn on her own feminine ground. The concentrated activity was important to the rite, but more important was the concentration of love which opened every heart in the room.

Then she told us about the growth process of the platelets on the shell— how the small must gradually give place to the large, how she must go to her examination and BE the person she now was, no matter what the consequences, instead of the performer who could certainly pass with honors. As a ritual food, she had prepared a large pineapple, its platelets still intact. With laughter and thanksgiving we ate the sweet flesh of the turtle-pineapple, and felt a new connection to the earth, to the Goddess, to the transpersonal in ourselves and each other. The integrated image of turtle became the foundation of a new world for Kathryn, even as turtle was the foundation of the world in the Ojibway creation myth.

There are many references to the turtle or tortoise in the mythology of different cultures such as in India, Japan and among the North American Indians. The turtle is safe from attack in its armored house. It is amphibious, that is, it lives in two worlds. Symbolically,

> the characteristics of the tortoise are characteristics of the transcendent function, the one that unites pairs of opposites. . . . The coming together each time *is* the transcendent function. . . . the functions of rational and irrational data in the functioning together of conscious and unconscious, of the differentiated function with the inferior function. It is the reconciliation of the pairs of opposites. From this reconciliation a new thing is always created, a new thing is realized. That is the transcendent function, and that is the tortoise (Jung 1984, pp. 647-648)

Kathryn had had a compulsive eating problem. Her unconscious drive to devour food carried over into unconscious drives concerning knowledge, money, men. In order to redeem her inner Becky, she had to transform Becky's unconscious behavior into sacred conscious activity. She had to connect her own ego to that archetypal energy without becoming identified with it. With the support of the other women, she was able to experience the transpersonal energy, integrate part of it into her own ego, and take that grounding to her examination.

The increased conscious awareness of herself which she achieved in the early morning ritual was carried into the examination situation. Holding that energy secretly in her heart, she put the chairs in the examination room in a circle and put a bouquet of flowers on the table. Because she was not coming from a place of power, the flowers did not suggest seduction. They were her way of making sure that she was resonating with her own femininity. Instead of the machine-like activity in which given questions would have received given answers, she was able to hear human voices and to respond from her own authentic center. She had the courage to act out of her own recognized inner necessity by creating an environment which acknowledged her presence as a woman conscious of herself, rather than falling back into the unconsciousness of Daddy's little girl. By doing this she overcame the role to which her upbringing would have assigned her. Her professors were open to what she as an individual could offer. Her answers fulfilled a human need on both sides. They were all attending an authentic dialogue, a real conversation in which human communion took place. Soul food was being digested, instead of intellectual jargon. "It was a real balancing act," said Kathryn afterwards, "balancing the constructive energy of the inner masculine without denying the gentleness of the feminine." It was a balancing act in which her little girl leapt into womanhood as the natural bride of her creative animus. She was conscious enough to Be and feminine enough to allow something unique to happen. Her capacity to resonate with her own truth brought a new dimension into the whole situation. She did graduate.

Not all rituals are so joyous. Sometimes our group brings the Goddess to consciousness through an abortion, a hysterectomy, the menopause, a terminal illness or death. The pattern is constant—the terror of separation, the death of the old, the sacrifice, the surrender through the rites of passage, the rebirth. Always the ritual connects each of us to our own inner depths where we are One with each other and the Transcendent Power; always we recognize when we are entering sacred space, ARE there, and then move out. The demarcation of the sacred and profane worlds purifies both. Because many women have never known what it is to cherish their own bodies, rituals involving their entire musculature can become powerful mystery rites. While the outward facts can be described, the inner transformation is veiled in silence. The power of transformative love cannot be articulated. Groups of women who love and support each other in attempting to find their own feminine rhythms and values are the touchstones of the growing recognition of the meaning of femininity.

In his essay on "Plato and the Primitive" (1960), Stanley Diamond provides further insight into the nature and relevance of ritual and drama, drawing on the broad perspective of his study of traditional societies:

> To clarify, let us consider those ceremonials which devolve upon personal crises, such as death, marriage, puberty, or illness. These can be considered

"existential" situations; that is, people die, marry, sicken, become sexually mature and economically responsible in all societies. In primitive societies, such ordinary human events are rendered extraordinary, that is, they are made meaningful and valuable, through the medium of the dramatic ceremonies. Here we confront man raising himself above the level of the merely biological, affirming his identity, and defining his obligations to himself and to the group. The ritual drama, then, focuses on ordinary human events and makes them, in a sense, sacramental.

At the same time, the ceremonials we are speaking of enable the individual to maintain integrity of self while changing life roles. The person is freed to act in new ways without crippling anxiety, or becoming a social automaton. That is, the person discharges the new status but the status does not become the person. This, I believe, is the central psychological meaning of the theme of death and rebirth, of constant psychic renewal, which is encountered so frequently in primitive ceremonials. It is an organic theme; what one is emerges out of what one was. There is no mechanical separation, only an organic transition, extending, characteristically, over a considerable time, often crowded with events, and never traumatic, but modulated and realistic in its effects.

Hence, the ceremonies of personal crisis are prototypically dramatic in two related ways. They affirm the human struggle for values within a social setting, while confirming individual identity in the face of ordinary "existential" situations such as death or puberty. These ceremonial dramas, then, constitute a shaping, and an acting out of the raw materials of life. All primitives have their brilliant moments on this stage, each becomes the focus of attention by the mere fact of his humanity; and in the light of the ordinary-extraordinary events, his kinship to others is clarified. Moreover, these ritual dramas, based on the typical crisis situations, seem to represent the culmination of all primitive art forms; they are, perhaps, the primary form of art, around which cluster most of the aesthetic artifacts of primitive society—the masks, poems, songs, myths, above all the dance, that quintessential rhythm of life and culture.

Ritual dramas are not automatic expressions of folk spirit. They were created, just as were the poems, dances, and songs that heighten their impact, by individuals moving in a certain cultural sequence, formed by the tradition and forming it. Whether we call these individuals "poet-thinkers," "medicine men," or "shamans," terms used by Paul Radin (1957), seems unimportant. Plainly, they were individuals who reacted with unusual sensitivity to the stresses of the life cycle and were faced, in extreme cases, with the alternative of breaking down or creating meaning out of apparent chaos. Let us call them primitive dramatists. The meanings they created, the conflicts they symbolized, and sometimes resolved in their own "pantomimic" performances, were felt by the majority of so-called ordinary individuals. There was, of course, magic here too; but, more deeply, there was a perception of human nature that tied the group together. The primitive dramatist served as the "lightning rod" for the commonly experienced anxieties, which, in concert with his peers and buttressed by tradition, the primitive individual was able to resolve. This is not to say that the primitive dramatist simply invented meanings promiscuously. It was always done within a given socio-economic and natural setting. But he shaped dramatic forms through which the participants were able to clarify their own conflicts and more readily establish their own identities.

There was an organic tie, then, between the primitive dramatist and the people at large, the tie of creation and response, which is, in itself, a type of creation. The difference was that the dramatist lived under relatively continuous stress, most people only periodically so. . . . The distinctions are a matter of degree. The very presence of the shamandramatist is a continuous reminder that life often balances on the knife edge between chaos and meaning, and that meaning is created or apprehended by man coming, as it were, naked into the world.

If the ritual dramas of passage rites are not enacted with personal introspection and discrimination, the individual does not emerge. The magazines that extol the new woman are replete with multiple choice questions with answers gauged from 1 to 5. By adding up her sum total, the new woman can estimate how well she is preparing herself to fit the new stereotype. But the questions are never formulated to help her to recognize her own values, her own personal strengths and limitations, her own uniqueness. Rather she is encouraged to spend her hard-earned cash on the rituals of expensive magazines, new punk haircuts, Ralph Lauren clothes, and Gucci shoes. She is a "new woman" because she is what a "new woman" is supposed to be. She has no sense of her own individuality. She is a walking mask. She has avoided the dramatic rites of passage that take long lonely hours of ruthlessly looking at herself and saying, "Yes, this is of value to me, that is of no value." These are the rites of passage that demand the courage to stand alone and say, "This is who I am."

The "new woman" who accepts the new stereotype may become anorexic in her attempts to fit into the Calvin Klein jeans that restrict her movement even more than her mother's Playtex girdle. Or she may become bulimic, vomiting out the collective poison she cannot recognize as poison because she cannot listen to her own body, her own Being telling her it can no longer digest what society is stuffing down her throat.

On the other hand, it is worth pointing out that in our culture, which is so schizophrenically oriented around eating, many young women, consciously, or unconsciously, refuse food as a way of saying, "Whatever that food represents, I reject." Starving, binge-ing, vomiting, and running as fast as they can away from life—they symbolize some basic self-destructive compulsion at the core of our collective psyche. Seen from this point of view, anorexia nervosa becomes an attempt to escape the tyranny of the unconscious mother.

Anorexics are the ones who are refusing to make the passover into womanhood as they perceive it, preferring to starve themselves into breast-less, hipless, amenorrheic skeletons. Looked at as a failed initiation rite, their self-enforced starvation is speaking loud and clear, and from the deepest levels of their psyche it is saying NO to cosmetic femininity.

MOVING TOWARDS WHOLENESS

Perched on the threshold of a new feminine consciousness, we are terrified to let the old values die because we are afraid to move into the unknown. Many of us are in what Victor Turner (1964) calls "the liminal state," caught between what is dead and what is not yet born. We find ourselves in a most dangerous period of transformation because we can no longer respect ourselves as we were, yet we have very little idea of who we may become. Our old support systems have crumbled but we have not yet found the new cornerstones. Mothers who have no time for *Being* themselves need to hear the whisper of an inner voice that erupts as they drop off the children, run to the supermarket, and dash to their exercise class: "If this is life, it's not worth it." However beautiful these woman may be, if they are obsessed by achieving and excelling, their center will become an empty hole and their instinctual femininity may unconsciously fall into despair. Worse yet, they may pass this despair onto their children, who may unconsciously pick up their mother's emptiness and sense of death. Any analyst working with an addicted patient is working within a shamanistic initiation rite, attempting to bring new life out of the bones, smashing the rigid stereotype in order to release the individual woman who can say Yes to life and herself as a feminine being.

People who are not in close contact with their own unconscious have great difficulty accepting the slow, unhurried, cyclic rhythms of nature, which allow time for birth, maturation, and death. When some part of us dies, there must be a time of mourning, a period of withdrawal and introspection, a period of allowing the tears to fall. Tears connect us to our hearts, our real values, our own inner Home. Without them, we become brittle, warped, prunes instead of plums. Born into a society in which rites of passage are not a consciously nor firmly entrenched part of life, we do not understand ritual. We hate death and we do not really believe in resurrection. The rituals which would connect us with these rhythms in ourselves we find "boring." Thus when the unconscious naturally tries to move us onto a new level of awareness, we feel violated because we are unable to enter the death experience; we experience ourselves as victims, rather than participants. We are half-aware that some life-threatening sacrifice has been made, something dead is inside us, something "crazy" is going on, but we do not take time to find out who the new person is, nor do we have the slightest idea what territory we have crossed into (see Trafford 1982).

The tragedy is that if we do not give ourselves space and time to find out, we attempt to live in the new era despite being inadequately equipped to do so, for we still have only the old concepts of ourselves. We are like confused butterflies just emerged from our chrysalises, butterflies who still think like caterpillars yet blame everyone else for damaging our wings, when the truth is we are afraid to take responsibility for the transformation that has taken place. Instead of taking time to let our beautiful wings unfold in readiness for new life, we fearfully draw back into non-existent cocoons, our protective coverings gone.

Once they have contacted their own Goddess energy, women are not satisfied in a relationship with a son-husband; consequently, their relationships undergo the fire of transformation with all the physical suffering and spiritual torment that transformation entails. Their male partners are forced into a choice: either to end the relationship and look again for an unconscious woman, or to open themselves to their own femininity and mature masculinity. Either way, the transitions in attitudes and behavior that are necessitated by the birth of a newly conscious femininity are precarious and challenging, demanding the finest honing of sensitivity and perception in both partners.

In the uncharted sea of re-emerging energies, there is one, huge, unmarked, undersurface rock that well-intentioned, conscientious explorers often strike. In their delight in experiencing their instinctual energy, they are indeed remembering the power of the Great Earth Mother. But if, in their *hubris,* they take that power as their own, and fail to recognize it as an impersonal authority flowing through them, then their ego becomes inflated because the Great Mother is in control. Far from being ignored, abused and left for dead, she suddenly turns her head, and, if she appears in her destructive, Kali aspect, women almost inevitably contact an inundation of transpersonal rage and revenge against men, probably the accumulation of centuries of repression. Its intensity can erupt like a fountain of black poison. Caught by this Kali energy, respectable matrons may suddenly be transformed into screaming maenads out for blood. If they are at all conscious, however, they recognize that their ferocity is more than personal. As individuals they do not hate the individual men in their lives. They do not really think that all the male sex is a conglomerate of insensitive baby boys who have no understanding of mature relationship. Rather, they move into their own strong ego position, take cognizance of their own personal feelings as distinct from the archetypal rage, and instead of attacking men, they help them to contact their own inner femininity in genuine relationship.

As a blind archetype without a strong ego consciousness to control her, the unconscious mother is as selfish and insatiable, destroying and self-destroying, as Becky. All the Beckos who come within her orbit do well to escape as furtively as possible. Their fear, conscious or unconscious, of being asked to make the supreme sacrifice of their testicles on her altar is well-justified. Without vigilant contemplation and inner dialogue a person is sucked into her vortex, and she will attack both the outer partner and the inner creative partner, so that the individual becomes driven to possess or contaminated with nameless fears. Succumbing to a blind archetype severs us from our own lives.

If we do not consciously recognize what is happening, raw fear and genuine anguish may be twisted into anger and the desire for revenge. A woman, for example, who is being pushed by her own unconscious to develop her own musical talents, may suddenly find herself enraged by her husband whom she now experiences as her persecutor. "He won't give me time to practice. He won't pay for my lessons. After all I've done for him! He finds every particle of dust, and won't eat packaged cookies." She is projecting her own inner, unconscious demon, the demon who tells her she cannot play and never will and asks who does she think she is anyway. Then it must follow as the night follows the day, as soon as that inner demon is projected, he finds the right target, usually her husband or lover who retaliates or succumbs, depending on his degree of consciousness. This transition situation is full of tears: the old relationship is dead; parts of both partners are dead. Tears are part of the healing that takes place from the depth of the wounding. They ensure a constant contact with the real feelings that are emerging from the genuine roots of the personality. They differentiate the real from the sentimental and false. They keep us in touch with the Goddess who is entering through the wound.

According to Jung's concept of psychological growth, the psyche by nature wants to move toward wholeness. Thus, when the structure that has been necessary for a given period of time becomes too small and inadequate for growing consciousness, we begin to feel ourselves banging into bars. One woman dreamed that she was tightly bound in swaddling bands that encased her like a mummy's shroud, and red blood poured out between the bands. She either had to break the mummy case or die within it. Because she was still projecting her jailer, she blamed her husband for binding her there, but as her analysis proceeded, she had to recognize that it was her own hostility to her own inner spiritual man that locked her in. Once that formerly unconscious inner component is contemplated, a whole new set of values, time and space evolves. Two different "realities" are operating. In the material world, life is still orderly, ticking by the clock, measuring itself by miles, goals and achievements; in the eternal world of inner images, paradox is queen: what was certain is uncertain; real time is timeless; nothing is but what is not; heart replaces head; and words mean their opposite. The anguish throbs at the point where the two worlds intersect—the point where divine crosses human—the mid-point of the cross. For a period of time the two worlds may exist in parallel lines, but inevitably, the underground throbbing becomes a geyser which erupts into the wilderness. Its eruption affects every life within its circumference, for better or for worse. If for worse, then the path taken is archetypal, such as the one followed by Macbeth when the eruption of the Self (the desire for Kingship) is placed in the hands of the unconscious mother—Lady Macbeth and the three witches.

In Jung's terms, the geyser erupting in the wilderness would be the transcendent function which brings together a new unity between conscious and unconscious poles. It is the living symbol which, if contemplated, helps the individual to bring that pregnant new energy from the abyss of unconsciousness into the conscious situation. Once that eruption takes place, the terrified individual may attempt to go back into the safe prison of her swaddling bands—but she does so at the cost of her own life. Even as the new baby, who did not understand the eyes, hands, feet, lungs (which were developing as potential necessities *in utero*), must put them into action once the umbilical cord is cut, so the new baby born from the psyche must be immediately nourished and allowed to adapt to the brave new world. The infant cannot climb again into the mother's womb (John 3: 1-21) but must emerge as a little child with all the energy, faith, hope, and love of the newborn. It is he or she who will be able to play, to dance, to see the Kingdom of God on earth. That child is the imagination, the creative energy that makes a person an individual rather than an automaton.

DREAMS OF PASSAGE

Very often before some passage there is a series of death dreams in which mother or father or some beloved older figure either dies or is killed. While some dreams are to be interpreted objectively, i.e. they foretell an actual death, more often they are to be interpreted subjectively, i.e. they foretell an inner death in the dreamer's psyche—a death which can transform energy locked in the complex into energy available to the ego. If, for example, the mother symbolically dies, the infantile need for security and dependence may also die. If the father symbolically dies, the woman's need to please men may suddenly turn into a desire to assert herself, may even release her rage against the beloved man who consciously or unconsciously has stolen her life from her. Violent feelings of release, grief, or hostility may erupt and physical symptoms may manifest in this state of imbalance. The dreamer may have heard a voice telling her that the sacrifice is necessary. Again, as *Macbeth* demonstrates, where the death is not properly understood because it remains in the maternal unconscious, the sacrifice, as in the killing of Duncan, is reduced to murder. Sometimes a beloved animal or even a beloved child is sacrificially killed. At any rate, there is always a sense of inevitability that this terrible deed must be done. The old has to go in order to make place for the new.

In a vision, one woman received instructions from her wise, old, inner Medicine Woman telling her that she must kill her beloved deer companion and teacher.

> *I panic, for in her hand is the dagger that pierced my son's heart in an earlier vision. I beg her not to make me kill this beautiful deer, but she stands firm and puts the knife into my hand. Begging her forgiveness, I take the knife and cut open her belly.*
> *'Find her heart,' says Medicine Woman. I reach up into her chest cavity with both arms. It is soft and warm. I cut into her heart and I offer it to the heavens, tears streaming down my face. The deer's blood*

drips down my white arms. I don't know why but then I put the heart into my mouth and as I eat it two visions suddenly appear.

I see the deer in the spirit world. She is free. I have freed her energy from matter. She wanted the spiritual freedom and that is why I was instructed to kill her. Now she is my spirit guide, and without being tied to the plane of reality she is free to connect me to the spirit world.

The second vision is of a golden cup in my heart and this cup is connecting my lines of energy to the deer. The cup is full of blood and the blood keeps spilling out of my heart, but it always remains full, for the deer's heart keeps pumping new blood into the golden cup. My heart is full; 'my cup runneth over.' The love I experience is not my love; it is the deer's love passing through my heart. I embodied her heart and in so doing I became a vessel for her love.

Medicine Woman hands me a bowl full of clear water. I wash the blood off my hands. She takes the bowl and then gathers the carcass of the deer into her arms.

'I will use the skins to make you moccasins so that your feet will be able to hear the heartbeat of Earth.'

This vision was this woman's initiation into her heart. It was the beginning of her move from conditional love (which was the only love she had ever received and therefore the only love she could give) to unconditional love. Before, she had understood love as a weapon of power to achieve what she wanted from those who were dependent on her. Now, through her incorporation of the heart of the deer, she assimilates the love that radiates through all living things. She experiences herself no longer as one tiny entity, attempting to control her tiny corner of the world by giving or withdrawing love; rather she recognizes herself as belonging to the whole of Life, and her individual heartbeat as part of the one great heartbeat. She is now a part of the cosmos.

As it often happens in fairy tales, the friendly animal must be sacrificed in order to make the passover into a higher form of love. The natural order is superseded by the spiritual through the conscious recognition that the sacrifice is being required, at whatever anguished cost, and the ego willingly or unwillingly submits. If unwillingly, it is tugged along like a squealing pig going to the slaughter. If willingly, then it moves into the new world with as much dignity as it can muster.

Another important milestone which the modern woman encounters on her road to maturity is her rejection of the patriarchy—whose devotion to the *status quo* reinforces the inertia of the unconscious mother. Many of us are unaware of our devotion to the values and standards which our "fathers" represent. We have unconsciously accepted ourselves as daughters, and unconsciously act out little girl roles in relation to men. One young woman with her partner was about to purchase a new home—when she had the following startling dream. Although her entire analysis had focused on differentiating herself from her mother, this was her first dream of her father.

> *My brothers and I killed our father. He was haunting us, terrorizing us. We pounded him with heavy stones in the alleyway. We put his body in the car trunk and buried him in a field. Then we went home and tried to act normally. What would Mother say? Would she guess? Would she be hysterical? It was hoped that with his death she would stop harassing us too. I don't know why we killed him and not her. She noticed blood on my nightgown and mentioned my period. I was on the period, thank goodness, but felt guilty and scared the cops would come and find us, and match the blood types.*

The dream illustrates the passover into mature womanhood that this young woman is attempting to make. In order to be the virgin bride (i.e. the psychologically conscious woman) in relation to her husband, she must symbolically kill her father. What "father" represents is closely related to her "phallic mother," i.e., the mother who domineers with pseudo-masculine power. Even in the dream she wonders why they "killed him and not her." Again the sacrifice is through the living blood. The dead father's blood on her nightgown could be her menstrual blood, the symbol of her womanhood. Death and resurrection are imaged in the same symbol. Although this dream gave her the strength to commit to the new relationship, she was still not free from her fear of "the cops," the guilt she experienced in leaving behind the life that her parents envisaged for her.

These feelings of guilt cannot be underestimated. If we ruthlessly attempt to cut ourselves off from our parental world, we cut out feelings and values that make us what we are. We are our parents' children, and most of us have inherited precious gold as well as dung. While negative feelings towards our parents are still alive, a long period of differentiation must ensue during which the wheat is separated from the chaff. The following dream makes this process clear:

> *I am working in the basement laboratory of a hospital. A woman is very ill in a ward above. Her life depends upon my staying awake to do my task. I have a tiny set of golden scales and golden tweezers and a little heap of red earth. It is my task to keep the scales in perfect balance—grain by grain—as her life energy ebbs and flows. A young man sits beside me, encouraging me to stay awake.*

In real life, the dreamer was attempting to give up a relationship that had reconstellated her relationship with her father. It was secure and without discord, but at the same time smothering her growth as an individual. To leave the security of this man's love seemed like choosing death. Over a period of months, grain by grain, the dreamer differentiated her feminine feelings.

Differentiation meant the slow agonizing process of looking herself straight in the eye, discarding what was not hers, taking responsibility for what was. Writing in her journal helped her to articulate her own truth. Guided by her dreams, she tried to answer questions such as: Who am I? What of my mother is me? What of my father is me? How many of their attitudes and responses am I blindly living out? What situations are no longer meaningful to me? Do my clothing and lifestyle reflect who I am? Why am I depressed? At what point today did I betray my own Being, thus turning my energy against myself? Am I trying to make my lover live out my talents? Can I take responsibility for what I feel?

The meticulous, grain-by-grain sorting was crucial in order to find the new balance that would restore the sick part of herself to health. Her tendency was to fall into unconsciousness, but a new inner masculine figure kept her awake. His task, as the analytical process evolved, was to learn to use his golden sword with love instead of hacking and sawing with his old butcher knife. Eruptions of fear manifesting in rage, jealousy or revenge had to be tempered with the conscious recognition of the purpose of the break. As the old life was carved away, the spirit of love within the sword was crucial to the dreamer's blossoming femininity. When the ego and the inner partner are working together, the masculine nurtures the feminine. He insists that she take time for herself, that she protect herself from the ravages of a world that would demand all of her time and energy. He cuts with a discerning sword in order to create a world where together they may BE.

I have mentioned a few of the birth canals through which women in our culture are being challenged to pass. They are hazardous and terrifying for the body and spirit because both must undergo transformative fire. It is my observation that as the psyche attempts to move into a new level of conscious awareness, the original birth trauma is re-enacted. A few healthy egos, untrammeled by fear of the unknown, reach out for new life, putting all their energy forward into new possibilities. Others, recognizing the dangers of the dark channel, yet knowing there is light somewhere at the other end, gird their loins and pass through. Others, for reasons which closely mirror the circumstances of their birth, stumble when they are confronted with the possibility of their freedom. When the authoritative voice of the dream says, "Go," they grit their teeth and say, "I won't, I can't, I will not move into life." The pain is too acute and they fall into unconsciousness. Then the analyst must decide whether to wait for the cycle to come round again, or to act as midwife and gently but firmly help the baby into the world without the deadening effects of the anesthesia to which the neurosis is addicted. Any addiction (food, work, alcohol, T.V., sleep, etc.) is rooted in the unconscious yearning to go back to the maternal unconscious.

CREATIVE MASCULINITY

I have mentioned the danger of being seduced into looking backward, a danger that is well-documented in myths. Where we are going, none of us knows, but it is obvious that an eruption is taking place in our culture. That eruption is mirrored in the dreams of countless women who are bringing their femininity to conscious birth, and with it a new concept of masculinity. The following dream foreshadows the spirit of what that new consciousness may be. It is the dream of a woman who has been through various thresholds during six years of analysis and body awareness.

> *My husband is a warrior, fighting afar. I am sitting for a portrait of myself with our new-born twin sons. I want him to share this miracle. I am sitting in a forest clearing, bathed in full sunlight, wearing a white velvet coat with a white wolf collar. I hold the twins, one in each arm, powerful baby boys, both named T. I am also aware that my maid has borne twin sons in the forest, and their names are both t.*

The woman awoke from the dream with an abiding sense of what Being is. While her warrior husband meets the challenge of her outer and inner worlds, she abides, serene, confident, cherishing the miracle that has happened to her. Throughout the early years of her analysis, a fiery, red wolf (symbolic of a devouring mother complex) had often roamed through her dreams, hungry, restlessly searching. That red animal now appears as a white wolf collar: the passionate, insatiable energy has been sacrificed and transformed into spiritual passion. She sits close to nature, knowing that her shadow maid has also given birth in a deeper part of the forest. The impact of the dream was so intense that the dreamer meditated daily on its feeling tone. After one meditation she wrote:

> I lie on the floor. I feel my bare feet on the warm earth. I feel its solid peace radiating with warm rays up through my dark legs and through my body, mingling with the warmer rays of the sun. I embody T. The energy of the cross bar shoots through my outstretched arms, wrenching them, opening my heart, my head is severed, my legs and torso writhe. 'Tension, Tumult, Terror, Trying, Tears, Tryst.' These words leap out with my sobbing. 'Tryst!' I scream, and all the shame and guilt and fear, the humiliation and vulnerability, the chaos of all the years of trying to find my own self roll through me, wave after wave of searing pain. Suddenly it is black. I am sucked into darkness. I am terrified. I am dying, I am being born. Then the torment ceases. I lie exhausted with Time.

Months later she dared to incorporate the "t."

> My body sings, 'tree, truck, torso, tongue, touch, tear, tender, trespass, torrid, trust, total, temple, triumph.' I re-member my exquisite body, its sinews, its skeleton, its perception, its obliterated suffering, childhood suffering locked in its muscles. I go into its darkness, my darkness, my unconscious identification with its density, this abandoned mound of flesh I have lugged around. I feel her grief. I

love her. I beg her to forgive me. Darkness comprehends Light. Her Light, her Wisdom, ancient, more ancient than I, SHINES. My body, my soul, my beloved enemy. My arms and chest ache with the pain of too much loving—HERE, NOW—forever, in this moment.

t opens, soft, flexible, yielding—yielding, yes, yielding to T, vibrant T. shimmering with Light. I let it happen—cell by cell my soul opens to my spirit. I lie silent in Truth.

Robert Graves in *The White Goddess* (1975) treats the letters of the alphabet as archetypes. He recognizes that the written letters reveal images of nature, and finds, inherent in these images, the energy and truth of the instincts:

> We may regard the letters D and T as twins: 'the lily white boys clothed all in green o!' of the mediaeval *Green Rushes* song. D is the oak which rules the waxing part of the year—the sacred Druidic oak, the oak of the *Golden Bough.* T is the evergreen oak [the holly oak] which rules the waning part, the bloody oak. . . . *Dann* or *Tann* . . . is a Celtic word for any sacred tree. . . .

Jung further amplifies the letter T in his *Seminars on Dream Analysis* (1984):

> In prehistoric Egypt we find the Tau, T, or gibbet form of the cross. This cross was used in its simple form and is thought to have been representative of the phallus. When the Tau cross is surmounted by a circle, or oval, we have the *crux ansata,* the magical key of life. The oval is thought to represent the sistrum (the musical instrument used in the worship of Isis, the goddess of the earth) or possibly to be a modification of the delta (those lands on which the gods played and produced all life, thus again connected with Isis, or Woman). the *Crux ansata* becomes in this way the symbol of creation. We find this cross on the most ancient Egyptian monuments, frequently in the hand of a god, priest or king; Amon-Ra, Kneph, Isis, Hathor, and Osiris are some of these. It was also placed on tombs, presumably having the same significance as the phallus, which signified resurrection. In the paintings on tombs it is evidently employed by divinities to awaken the dead to new life. We see it thus in a twelfth-century bas-relief, where a goddess is holding the *crux ansata* to the nostrils of a dead king, the inscription reading, 'I give thee life, stability, purity, like Ra, eternally.' It was also held out towards the living as a sign of vital power. Both the Tau, T, and the astronomical cross of Egypt, ⊕, are conspicuous in the remains of Palenque [ruined Mayan city in Yucatan]. The Tau was the sign which Moses instructed his people to mark in blood on their doorposts and lintels so that the Chosen People should not be smitten by the Lord.

If a letter which has appeared as a dream symbol is embodied (i.e. put back into the instincts) through active imagination, its healing power becomes numinous. As a symbol, T usually initiates the movement into the third eye, a movement into transformation, symbolizing specifically the differentiation of body and spirit. It is the letter of crucifixion which forcibly opens the body, at the same time keeping it flexible, so that light may penetrate the dark flesh.

This active imagination images one woman's experience of the rebirth of the feminine, the Soul, and with it, the constellation of the masculine Spirit, and the mystical union. Given the space and time, her body, her beloved enemy, reveals her Truth. Rooted in the firm ground of nature, the unconscious flesh eventually reveals its truth—its own Kore of Light, its Soul. In its joy it opens 'unawares,' and instantaneously the masculine Spirit comes to unite with it. Now the inner, creative process has begun, and while the warrior husband of the dream may continue to joust with his discerning sword both in the inner and outer worlds, his introverted side is ready to unite with the inner feminine, bringing life to the seeds in her virgin soil.

That creative masculinity which is so ready to unite with the mature feminine is manifest in the following dream of a middle-aged woman.

> *I am browsing in an old cemetery. The graves are above ground, mostly cement vaults. Suddenly I am aware that the top of one is moving. I stop in amazement about twenty feet from it. It is being pushed up from underneath. A powerful masculine arm thrusts the top off. An equally powerful leg swings out over the side, and a magnificent, blond, blue-eyed man rises out of the tomb, laughing and shaking himself. Light bounces off his skin. He opens his arms and strides toward me as if I were his long lost love. This is my royal Christ.*

The masculine spirit, freed from the dead stones of the patriarchy, rises up with the joyous energy of the instinctual masculine and unites with the radiant energy of the soul. The stone of the past is rolled away, and the vibrant new energy moves towards the feminine as if he had loved her all his life, if only she had known how to release him. Her own femininity is conscious enough to receive him—conscious enough and vulnerable enough, with all the strength that vulnerability demands.

In the Biblical myth, unconscious Eve is identified with earth, with matter. Because she succumbs to Satan, the serpent, and eats the fruit of the Tree of Knowledge forbidden by Jehovah, she and the equally unconscious Adam are expelled from the Garden of Eden. Cherubim and a flaming sword prevent their re-entry. In the *New Testament,* Mary, who comes from a lineage containing four harlots, consciously surrenders herself to her destiny, and allows her soul to magnify the Lord. The Holy Spirit enters. Matter is redeemed. Mary is the conscious Eve, and Joseph, in spite of his doubts, is conscious enough to obey the voice in his dreams, telling him to care for the pregnant woman to whom he is betrothed (Matthew 1:24). At the appointed time and place the child is born in a cowstable because there is no room in the collective inn. Mary, outcast from society, ponders the truth in her heart, and becomes the psychologically conscious feminine to whom the Divine Child is born.

Jung foresaw that a technological civilization hurtling toward its own destruction could eventually undergo an *enantiodromia,* and that Pope Pius XII's declaration of the *Assumptio Maria* in 1950 was the Church's way of "raising to a higher position the symbol of the feminine Godhead and with it matter. Since it is the Virgin Mary's body which is raised to Heaven, emphasis is on the physical, material aspect" (von Franz 1980). What is manifested by our society now, however, is a global obsession with unredeemed matter. Becky and Becko devouring and being devoured. Relationship to the devouring Goddess does not give us license for unbridled hedonism, nor mindless ecstasy in the rampant release of animal spirits. That route will abandon us to the density of our own dark bodies huddling in despair in our own dark garbage. To surrender our frail egos to the collective worship of concretized matter is to succumb to the opacity of evil, impervious to the grace of Light. True worship of the Goddess is to shake off our lethargy, confront our *hubris,* and submit to the rites of passage which will bring Her to consciousness. To love Her is to commit ourselves to the travail of creating our own ego container, a container strong enough and flexible enough to mirror Her divine receptivity.

It is possible that the Goddess, recognizing the danger of our annihilating ourselves, has decided that it is time to bring Herself to consciousness. Like the Old Testament Jehovah, She is allowing Her dark side to ravage the modern Jobs who would otherwise slip into the complacency of worshipping Her in Her materialistic form. Disdainful of such a demeaning level of consciousness, She ravages us with physical diseases and broken relationships in order to force us to a spiritual level of awareness—a recognition of Her as the container of divine creativity, and a recognition of our own bodies as the containers of divine wisdom.

If we blind ourselves to our own potential, we treat the symptoms. If we have the courage to face our anguish, we are thrown into the dis-ease of recognizing the rejected soul at the heart of matter. Are our dreams and body experiences suggesting that the emerging of feminine consciousness, and with it the emergence of a new masculinity, are the birth pangs of a new understanding of the Incarnation? Individually and culturally, something is trying to be born, if only we have the courage to breathe into the pain, and the consciousness to let it BE.

> Turning and turning in the widening gyre
> The falcon cannot hear the falconer;
> Things fall apart; the center cannot hold;
> Mere anarchy is loosed upon the world,
> The blood-dimmed tide is loosed, and everywhere
> The ceremony of innocence is drowned;
> The best lack all conviction, while the worst
> Are full of passionate intensity.
> Surely some revelation is at hand;
> Surely the Second Coming is at hand.

The Second Coming! Hardly are those words out
When a vast image out of *Spiritus Mundi*
Troubles my sight: somewhere in the sands of the desert
A shape with lion body and the head of a man,
A gaze blank and pitiless as the sun,
Is moving its slow thighs, while all about it
Reel shadows of the indignant desert birds.
The darkness drops again; but now I know
That twenty centuries of stony sleep
Were vexed to nightmare by a rocking cradle,
And what rough beast, its hour come round at last,
Slouches towards Bethlehem to be born?
                              —W. B. Yeats, "The Second Coming"

REFERENCES

Diamond, S. 1969. *Primitive views of the world.* New York: Columbia University Press.
Franz, M.-L. von. 1980. *Alchemy: Introduction to the symbolism and the psychology.* Toronto: Inner City Books.
Graves, R. 1975. *The white goddess.* London: Faber & Faber Ltd.
Jung, C. G. 1984. *Dream analysis: Notes of the seminar given in 1928-1930,* ed. W. McGuire. Bollingen Series XCIX. Princeton: Princeton University Press.
Radin, P. 1957. *Primitive religion, its nature and origin.* New York: Dover Publications.
Trafford, A. 1982. *Crazy time: Surviving divorce.* New York: Bantam Books.
Wylie, P. 1946. *Generation of vipers.* Norwood, Pa.: Norwood Editions.
Yeats, W. B. 1956. *The collected poems of W. B. Yeats.* New York: Macmillan.

MENSTRUATION AND SHAMANISM

Marilyn Nagy

"Menstruation and Shamanism" by Marilyn Nagy deals with meaningful aspects of feelings and emotions accompanying menstruation. Is there an unconscious psychic *factoring* process *accompanying the* physiological *structure of menstruation? There is "some evidence for speaking of the psychic cycle of the woman as contained within the menstrual cycle, at least as a model."*

In this study we discover unique components of women's initiation through the menstrual cycle. The author analyzes the development of feminine eros using women's dreams and myths and their relation to women's inner and outer relationships. Dr. Nagy presents a provocative hypothesis about taboos relating to the menstrual cycle in traditional cultures from a contemporary perspective.

Marilyn Nagy, Ph.D., is a Jungian analyst practicing in Palo Alto, California. A graduate of the C. G. Jung Institute in Zurich, she is presently a faculty member of the Pacific Graduate School of Psychology. She is also a professional member of the Swiss Society for Analytical Psychology, the Graduates of the C. G. Jung Institute, and the San Francisco Jung Institute, of which she is former secretary and chairperson of the Reviewing Committee. She has published in Psychological Perspectives, Quadrant, *and the* San Francisco Jung Institute Library Journal, *and* Voices.

I became interested in studying menstruation many years ago when I was suffering from horrendous depressions which went on and on, every month before my period came. The depressions must have begun sometime late in my teenage years. I don't remember exactly when. But I do remember a time in the 1950's, when I was in graduate school in Boston, going to the doctor for a yearly checkup and telling him about my symptoms. He gave me a prescription to take for pre-menstrual depression.

The whole idea of a pre-menstrual syndrome was very new at that time. I was relieved to think that my depressions had a physiological cause. Just what that cause was no one knew, but it seemed reasonable to think that medical researchers were on the way to finding out what kinds of hormonal changes might be causing this pre-menstrual distress. Well, as a matter of fact, this hasn't happened. We know now that endocrinologically, menstruation is a relatively quiescent interval, with the lowest body levels of estrogen and progesterone of any time of the month. At the same time, in the last 25 years we have gained much more clinical awareness of the emotional concomitants that surround menstruation. In Japan there has been much work done on periodic menstrual psychosis. In the United States we know quite a lot more about the depression, sleeplessness and emotional lability of the syndrome than we did before.

But this is nothing new. Women know that they are "not themselves" at their periods. A woman may be cold, or, on the contrary, unusually warm. She may every month suffer days of depression, or she may find herself unexplainably cheerful, only to have this mood swept away by a softly teary sentiment. Women are so accustomed to all this that they excuse themselves by saying, "Oh, it's just my period." *They direct their psychological behavior to a physiological cause.* But just what the physiological cause of our menstrual emotional symptomatology is eludes us completely.

But now let me go back to my own story. The next phase of the development of the idea, on the conscious level at least, came in Zurich six or seven years later. I was 2 or 3 years into my own analysis, and by this time I was well-initiated into Jung's point of view that not only the aberrations of my behavior, but also the apparently accidental meetings with people who became important to me, the seemingly spontaneous chain of events in my life, and, of course, my physical illnesses, all had a meaning—that is, a psychological reason for happening.

Now this is an important key to what I want to say, because I want to try to take you with me on the same journey that I've been on—a journey in search of a *reason,* namely the meaning of menstruation and especially of the emotional events which accompany it.

About this same time or a year or so later, while I was still mulling these things around in a very confused way, I started my analytical work. I happened to have two or three women analysands who were rather passive and didn't find very much to say during their sessions. They also did not bring any dreams. But at intervals, without anything very different happening in their outer lives so far as I could tell, they suddenly seemed to be dreaming more frequently, or perhaps their dreams were much stronger in affect. These women then became very active and brought in emotionally laden material, so we could really work. It occurred to me to ask them casually if they happened to be at their periods. The answer was so often yes that my interest in the matter became acute. *If an intensification of the emotional life is actually typical of the onset of menstruation, then why? What does this mean?*

This observation suddenly reversed my thinking. What if the depression or (as with my analysands) emotional alertness were not caused by menstruation *per se,* but by a psychological factor at work in the whole menstruation syndrome? It is after all only in modern western culture that medical knowledge about conception and menstruation has tended to depotentiate our valuation of the menstrual period. In pre-literate and traditional societies it is everywhere given the greatest attention as an important and extremely dangerous time. Our current collective view that normal bodily processes should not be emotionally disturbing does not prevent some women from highly singular behavior at monthly intervals. I had seen that in myself, and I was seeing it again in my analysands.

Of course, not all women complain of special moods at the menses. And some, who are often disturbed, have occasional periods go by unnoticed on the conscious level. But I have the impression that sometimes women do not notice because society expects them not to notice. One woman, who recorded her dreams together with her menstruation dates for me, wrote, "I don't know whether it was so before I started writing down these dreams, but now it seems that everything goes along and piles up till the end of the month and then explodes."

I decided to see what I could find out about menstruation, but not by dealing with consciously experienced moods and feelings at the menses. I wanted to look at unconscious material, to see if there might be an *unconscious psychic factoring process, an archetype, at work within the physiological structure of menstruation.* This meant I had to go to the mythology and folklore of primitive societies, since modern societies have suppressed such material as taboo. And I also had to study women's dreams.

MENSTRUAL TABOOS AND THE DEMON HUSBAND

In the beginning of my research I found a mass of confusing material. The mother of a menstruating girl in Malabar pours a jar of water over her head; a Javanese girl is powdered yellow; a Malaysian girl has her front teeth filed away. Out of the ancient world, Pliny reports that "contact with menstrual blood turns new wine sour, crops touched by it become barren, seeds in gardens are dried up, the fruit of trees falls off, the bright surface of mirrors in which it is merely reflected is dimmed, the edge of steel and the gleam of ivory are dulled, hives of bees die, even bronze and iron are at once seized by rust, a horrible smell fills the air, to taste it drives dogs mad and infects their bites with an incurable poison." What can we conclude out of all that? Apparently, menstruating women everywhere, except in our modern western societies, are in a very holy or taboo condition. And this taboo condition has something in it which is a strong force opposed to our everyday life.

I found out that menstruating women are very frequently separated out of their social groups. They live in menstrual huts outside the village and are sometimes secluded for as long as two or three years at the pubertal onset of menstruation. I wondered why that was, until I read that the Maori male lives in deadly fear of menstrual blood because he believes the evil spirit Kahukahu inhabits it.

Then I began to find in one text after another that at the time of menstruation the woman is possessed by an animal or a god-like spirit. Among the old Iranians it is the demoness Dshahi, the goddess of prostitution. It is through her works that menstruation was created, and each month during her period the woman is in the power of this evil spirit. The Siamese thought it was the evil spirits swarming in the air who entered in and caused the "wound," the monthly menstruation of their women. In Cambodia, unmarried girls were called the wives of Indra. Ancient Assyrian texts refer not only to the *lilith,* the ghoulish feminine spirit who could possess a man, but also to the *idlu lili* who possessed a woman when she became *niddah* (or menstruous).

Louis Ginzberg wrote about a Jewish tradition which says that menstruation is the penalty for Eve's sin, and "since sexual desire is considered as the result of the eating of the forbidden fruit, the Gnostics, as well as the Kabbalists, maintain that menstruation came to Eve with the enjoyment of the fruit." The fruit in question came from the tree of the knowledge of good and evil. Apparently there is a connection between (a) menstruation, (b) temporary marriage to the *idlu lili,* (c) sexual desire, and (d) knowledge of good and evil. The more I thought about this the more excited I became, because it seemed that here might be a clue demonstrating that all these strange customs have a meaning in common. But I could not really understand it yet.

What seemed to be the key was the idea among all these societies that menstruation was connected with being possessed or married to a demon or god. There is a folk legend stemming from a mountainous district in Japan which reflects the emotional stress and danger of the menstrual period, both for a woman and for her social group. The story is called *Otowa Pond*:

> Once upon a time a beautiful but humbly clad lady came to the temple of Cho fu ku-ji which stands beside this pond and asked for lodging. The priest pitied her and received her and she gave her name, Otowa.
> In the rice planting season, Otowa went gathering bracken and without noticing what she was doing, got too near to Mt. Konhoku, which hates the presence of women. On the way home at dusk she washed her blood-stained underwear in the pond and suddenly the pond grew larger and a voice came out of the haze saying,

'I am *kami* of this pond. I have been waiting for you to come for a long time. You must become *kami* of the pond in my place. This is the fate that has been determined since the fore-world.' Otowa begged for pardon but received only three days grace. She went home in a trance and when the priest asked her the reason she told him, weeping bitterly. The priest preached the way of Buddha to her until she conceived faith as though reborn, and on the third day at dawn a voice called outside her door. She said farewell to the villagers and rode toward the mountain. There was a sound of hoofs, a strange wind and a bitter rain. Then a noble man on a white horse appeared, picked Otowa up on his saddle and disappeared into the morning mist. He was the *kami* of the pond. Still today the village people give offerings to the pond, commemorating the day when Otowa wed the former *kami*.

In this story we can see clearly the connection between the affective state of the heroine and the image of the demon husband. That is to say, we do not see why they have to be connected, but only that they *are* both part of the situation, like *a priori* factors belonging to menstruation. The strong attracting power of Otowa's menstrual-blood stained clothes delivers her into the power of the demon of the pond and forces her to marry him. The weak emotional state of the heroine is also entirely typical of other legends of menstruating women. She is so forgetful of the protective taboos as to go near the forbidden mountain, then to wash her clothes in the pond. She returns home in a trance, gives herself over to weeping and on the appointed day accepts her rendezvous with death in the pond. She is completely in the power of her demon husband. The fateful violation of the taboo also results in a religious conversion, but not in remission of the penalty. Otowa is "reborn" but not into life, so that her religious experience is not psychologically integrated. If the menstruating woman in traditional societies is really in such a state of possession, then it is understandable that she is taboo; both she and her social group have to be safeguarded.

By this time I felt fairly certain that the common image which keeps appearing in the folkloristic traditions is that of the demon lover or spirit husband. But the prevalence of this image is not confined to ancient and primitive sources. In the twentieth century, Freudian theory about what a woman experiences at the menses is strikingly similar.

Basically it is this: a woman experiences her menstruation (a fully normal phenomenon) as an unnormal wounding of her inner parts; hidden behind the bleeding is the secret belief that it is the bleeding from a wound, namely the wound of her castration. The fantasy says, "I have neither child nor penis." Failure to menstruate may represent an attempt to heal the wound and to have an undamaged sexual organ like men have.

In this mythologem there is the sense of being inwardly wounded, just as the Siamese believed that evil spirits entered into the wombs of their girls and wounded them. The suggestion is that women want to be men and feel the loss of their masculinity in the form of the penis most keenly each month at menstruation. Let me anticipate my own conclusion: what *I* suggest is essentially the same thing. A woman is "wounded" each month by the painful encounter with her inner lover or with her spirit husband. *The pain arises out of the experience of the two sides of her own nature.* "I have neither child nor penis," means "I have both a masculine and a feminine spirit in me."

Freud's contention that a woman's ego remains incomplete because she is caught in permanently unfulfilled longings for her father ought perhaps not to be rejected out of hand, though I might wish to translate the terms in which his clinical observation is expressed. The sense of loss, of wounding, of desire (loss and desire are paired opposites), corresponds in a surprising way to the affective character of the images of the lover which appear as menstrual motif in traditional societies and in the dreams of modern women. Women may be, not so much "incomplete," as marked by *eros* as the connecting principle to the opposite sex, with "relatedness" as the central factor of the feminine ego.

THE DEMON LOVER AND THE STRANGE MAN IN MENSTRUAL DREAMS

While I was doing research on this subject, I collected women's menstrual dreams. Would there be a correlation between whatever I found through historical research and the content of modern western women's dreams? Originally I had no idea that I would find this image of the menstrual lover. I thought there might be something about the mother. I did a small pilot experiment obtaining 500 dreams which occurred just before and just after the onset of the menses, when emotional tension appears to be at a high point. Since that time, two doctoral dissertations have much expanded the design and repeated the experiment. However, the matter still seems unsettled, since the results of one experiment, done with adolescent girls, differ from the results I obtained; while a second experiment agrees with my conclusions. In my own sample, I was struck by the statistical frequency of the recurrence of an image which I finally called the Strange Man.

Many of these dream images sound remarkably like the images of the other-worldly lover of so much of menstrual mythology. The Strange Man is an intruder in the established order. We would not be very surprised if a woman dreams of her mother, or even of her father, or of marriage. They all belong to family life and to a traditional feminine role in society. But the image of the unknown man who appears on the scene, often in a highly threatening and dangerous pose, disrupts the harmony and suggests an opposition to the present state of things. This "opposition," personified in the image of the stranger, appears to be the new factor in the psychological situation. The attributes of the image, *together* with the affective qualities attached to it, may indicate the direction along which a change in consciousness is taking place.

Here is a sampling of fragments of dreams from that experiment. Of course they cannot be interpreted in any way, since the dreamers are completely unknown. What I hope one can hear through them is how the emotions of love, sexual arousal, fear, aversion and fascination are inextricably bound together with the image. Here we are beginning to make a connection between an inner image and some of the outer behavior so typical of menstruation. The dreams:

(a) *Our choir director was also there, and I was somehow close to him. It was a beautiful, erotic feeling, which made me very happy.*

(b) *I got left alone at a subway station and couldn't get out. Men started coming around me and saying rude things and laughing. I had feared this and tried to reason with them.*

(c) *I travel in a train at night. An asthenic looking man climbs through the window into my compartment. He speaks to me, kisses me, throws a flaming red blanket over us in order to protect us from the glances of other people. He says I should go with him. Almost without any will power I follow him. We go across a meadow where we have to be careful of dangerous hornets in the grass and then come to a lake where we want to go swimming.*

(d) *A terrible, angry man bursts into the house where my sister and I are alone and rapes both my sister, who is married, and me, a virgin.*

(e) *It is late in the evening. I have just finished taking a shower and putting on a pale pink nightgown. I open the bathroom door which opens onto my bedroom. The bathroom light is on but the bedroom is in darkness. I barely discern the sleeping figures of my husband and three children in the bed. They all seem to be sleeping face down. Now I become aware of a figure standing in darkness in the hall doorway. I can see only his leg. Somehow I know that he is not going to do anything. He only wants me to know that he is there. There we stand in two doorways, side by side like a medieval diptych, and visually we are opposites. He, in darkness, male, dressed in rough dark clothes, and I, female, in the light of the bathroom, all pink, light, soft and moist.*

How can it possibly make sense to lump together such disparate images under one heading? Can the images of a subway rapist, a choir director as lover, an unknown stranger in one's home, be described in common terms? Shouldn't we guard against the unknown man and welcome only men we know to be safe for us? The answer to these questions devolves from our characteristic response to events in life. Surely we can suppress new experiences for a certain amount of time. But no one can master his life so as to prevent all change, and still live. Whether a new event is greeted with hope or cursed as a dark fate may depend not entirely on whether it is good or bad but also partly on the inner attitude of the person to whom it happens. Love is like that too; every lover comes first as an unknown stranger and promises a woman both great joy and great danger. Perhaps these menstrual dream images of the strange man have a psychological purpose pertaining to just those inner attitudes.

CONCEPTION AND SEXUAL DESIRE AT MENSTRUATION

In the face of widespread prohibition separating a woman from her husband at the time of her menstruation was the almost equally widespread belief that conception takes place most easily, or exclusively, just before, just after, or even during, the monthly bleeding.

The ancient Chinese said the last day of menstruation was the best time to conceive. Susruta, the great Indian physician (c. 100 A.D.) agreed that at this time pregnancy most readily occurs because then the mouth of the womb is open, like the flower of the water-lily to the sunshine. Aristotle, Pliny and Galen all thought that women conceive at the menses.

The *Talmud,* although strictly forbidding the man from approaching his wife until seven days after the conclusion of her bleeding, nevertheless admits the possibility of conception during the prohibited time. But the children born of union during the menses will be "scrofulous, feeble-minded, crippled, epileptic, or insane." And later on, in the Christian church, Thomas Aquinas held that not only was intercourse during menstruation a deadly sin, but that children born of it would be leprous or monstrous.

As late as the beginning of the twentieth century, the great German gynecologist Hermann Ploss and the American gynecologist Havelock Ellis thought that all the evidence pointed toward menstruation as the time of conception.

Margaret Mead, in an early study of cultural patterns in a North American Indian tribe, describes the falling into disuse of the old prohibitions during menstruation. An old Indian woman says: "When we were young we kept away from our husbands for four days, now this is no longer done and look at the young women today, they have a child so high, and so high, and so high, and one hiding in their skirts, one on their backs, and one in their bellies." Conception therefore clearly occurred during those four forbidden days.

The observation that sexual desire among women is often heightened just before and even during menstruation has been made since ancient times. That was partly the reason why physicians thought conception must take place then. But since the discovery of the fertility cycle in 1937 by Knaus and Ogino, this factor has been disregarded, since it clearly did not fit the "procreative purposes of nature." Yet Havelock Ellis, in two essays, "The

Phenomena of Sexual Periodicity" and "The Menstrual Curve of Sexual Impulse," amassed a great body of evidence to show the "tendency of the female to sexual intercourse during menstruation." He used two cases, in one of which the incidence of masturbation and in the second of which the erotic content of dreams were correlated in the menstrual cycle. In both cases he found a positive harmonious curve which supported his conviction that the time of conception is coupled with the period of desire in women and with the menses. It represented a remnant of her former "animal nature" in which oestrus was the normal time for receiving the male. The taboos against intercourse at menstruation were only a cultural overlay with which an enlightened knowledge could well do away.

Today we know otherwise. Children are not conceived at menstruation. Yet the long-held belief that conception takes place at menstruation is a *psychic* fact, if not a physiological one, and points to the *psychic* presence of one who can give the woman a child. The stringent warnings from medieval pulpits against intercourse during menstruation would not have been necessary were there not some powerfully attracting force toward doing it—neither would the death penalties in Semitic societies nor the death-producing shock of even seeing a menstruating woman among some primitives. Either the woman is somehow especially desirable at this time, or she is especially desirous, which is to say the same thing.

MENSTRUATION AND SHAMANISM

We are still on our journey in search of a meaning. If women, in fact, do not conceive at the menses, although for thousands of years it has been believed they do, this belief is a fact which must have a reason. If women are often sexually aroused at menstruation, then we are observing an instinctive reaction which does not serve a procreative purpose. But then, what purpose?

I began to find some of my own answers when I came across descriptions of shamanistic initiation practices for women, both in rituals which have been culturally preserved and in North American Indian legends. In Mircea Eliade's book, *Shamanism* (1964), he describes how girls become shamanesses among the aboriginal tribes of India. First, the girl has a dream in which a suitor from the Underworld appears and asks for her hand in marriage. The girl at first refuses, with the result that she is plagued by nightmares. The divine lover threatens her with attack or with fall from a high place. The girl may then fall ill or be dissociated for a time. She wanders about alone in the woods or fields. Finally she accepts the call to be a shamaness; the family arranges her marriage and afterwards her tutelary husband visits regularly; takes her into the jungle for days at a time. She bears him a child, but the relationship is not primarily sexual. She is instructed by him through her dreams and thus fulfills her tribal duties.

Almost exactly the same thing is described in a myth of the Kwakiutl Indians of the Northwest coast, called *K. almodelanaga*:

> The tribe was at its winter quarters. Their chief was named Q.ade, and he was giving a winter dance. Then his sister, Q.walanenega, disappeared. She had not long disappeared when she became really sick, at the place where the women stay when they disappear. But after two nights she was heard talking with the spirit, who is called Helemil, asking him to give her a sacred song. Then she disappeared again, but at night they heard her song from far away.
>
> Then when night came they all went into the dance house and began to beat quick time on their boards. And then Q.walanenega uttered the cannibal cry at the door of the dance house. And as soon as she came in she turned into a shaman. She sang her sacred song, and then she bit four men and she said, 'I have been brought back to life by our friend Helemil, and he said to me that if any one should make love to me inside of ten years, he would immediately kill him. Thus said our great friend to me. And for ten years I shall cure the sick ones among you.'

The "place where the women stay when they disappear" is the menstrual hut, located outside the tribal area. The sister of the chief goes away for her usual separation period. But then she receives a call to become a shamaness, and *really* disappears, meets her tutelary spirit, Helemil, spends a period of time with him in the woods, and then re-enters the tribe to take up her shamanic duties. How similar, and yet how different is this story from the tragic Japanese Legend of Otowa, who met her death with the *kami* of the pond. Here the meeting with the spirit at menstruation leads to a vocation as teacher and healer.

Another tale, of the Kathlamet Indians, is called "The Gila'unalX Maiden Who Was Carried Away by the Thunderbird." It tells the story of a tribe which used to go hunting elk high in the mountains. But there was a narrow trail through which they had to pass, which was possessed by the Thunderbird spirit. There was a young girl who was menstruating for the first time, and she was not allowed to go. But she did not like to stay alone by the tents, and one day a woman said to her, "We are going to dig roots. I went up there, although I was menstruating, and nothing happened to me. Perhaps they deceive you only." So on the next occasion the young girl went with the women, but then when they were on the mountain, the other women lost her. They searched for her but could not find her. A mist covered everything. Then they went to the high trail possessed by the Thunderbird, and there they found her, near the rocks. They called her, took her hands and tried to pull her, but she did not move and did not speak. Her face was changed. So the women finally left her and went back to the tribe and told the people that she had become a monster and they were all weak with fright. The next day the tribespeople went to search for her but could not find her. The tale concludes:

> When it becomes foggy, she is heard singing shaman's songs in the rocks. Thus she did: When they came to the place where she was, she sang shaman's songs. Then the people gave up the search and went home. The chief of Gila'unalX went home. Therefore it is forbidden to take girls who are just mature up Saddle mountain, because that girl was taken away. The Thunderbird took her.

It seemed to me that with the discovery of these legends my search for a psychological, rather than a physiological explanation of those peculiar emotional states accompanying menstruation had finally found an answer which could satisfy my desire for a meaning. That meaning focused on the image of the strange lover or the spirit husband which appears in the myths, legends and dreams of menstruation. The union of the woman with this lover cannot have to do with the bearing of children in the outer world. Yet the character of the imagery bears all the marks of a truly instinctive and therefore purposive phenomenon. The Indian shamanic legends show that it may have an inner, spiritual purpose. In that case the problematic affective condition of the woman at her period may indicate an inner pre-occupation. That is what it really means to be possessed.

In neither of these myths does the fact of becoming a shamaness have a very happy result for the personal development of the young woman. In the Kathlamet myth the girl falls into a psychotic state (a cataleptic or fugue state, if we take the text literally). I suspect that the ego-consciousness of the relatively primitive groups out of which these stories come was not differentiated enough to permit a real confrontation with so powerful an archetype, nor an integration of its contents. Therefore the women who fall into possession of the Spirit are really lost to all further life in the tribe. Perhaps that is why the menstruating woman was regarded as so terribly dangerous; because her state of possession at this time threatened the collective ego of the tribe. Only in modern western culture has consciousness become strong enough to give even the possibility of assimilating the appearance of the Spirit-lover at the menstrual period.

REFLECTIONS ON SHAMANISM AND FEMININE PSYCHOLOGY

What do we mean by an ego consciousness that is differentiated enough or strong enough to permit assimilation of an inner figure? And how do we pass from a stage of culture, personal or collective, where assimilation is not possible, to one where it is? It should be remembered that menstruation appears only in the highest of the species—from the primates on upwards. In most lower animals, the moment of ovulation is simultaneous with heat or oestrus, and with coitus. The female is therefore absolutely identified with her instinctive nature. Among humans, mating is not limited to the period of heat. There is a distinct difference between ovulation and the moment of physiological conception and menstruation, which ends the post-oestrum and begins the new cycle. The human female is not bound to accept her lover only when she can conceive a child, as with other female animals. She can take him at any time she wishes. And this fact represents also the beginning of psychic differentiation.

It marks a moment where choice, or *personal* eros, intervenes in the biological scheme. Instinctive desire is split off from a necessarily procreative goal. The primary unconscious identity between subject and object is broken when the object can be perceived and valued. Where a woman can choose, the existence of an other than herself becomes subjectively real for her. This provides a polarity in which differences, and thus psychological consciousness, are possible. Thus the energy which is released toward the onset of menstruation and which the unconscious presents in image form as the strange lover or god-husband, may have as its purpose the psychic development of a woman. It is not the *physical* child which is conceived at menstruation, as was so long thought, but the *spiritual* child.

Yet it is the same instinctive eros which leads to the conception of a child at ovulation. We have then some evidence for speaking of the psychic cycle of the woman as contained within the menstrual cycle, at least as a model. Half of it, the time leading up to ovulation, belongs to her collective and instinctive life as mother and procreatrix. The second half, leading up to menstruation, belongs to her psychic life as an individual, with a personal destiny to understand and fulfill.

Of course, seen from the outside, things are just reversed. In the days after her period the woman is often released from confusing emotions. She is open and energetic and capable of much creative work. And in the days approaching her period she is quite obviously in a regressive state. She is apt to suffer alienation from others; conflicts which can usually be contained assume monstrous shapes. Daily duties may be suddenly altogether impossible. And we have seen in legends how really dangerous this regression can be.

But the introverting libido of the second half of the cycle seeds the extraverting libido of the following period. I think that is why the figure of the shamaness appears in the legends of women at the menses. She represents the inherent possibility of the woman not only to bear children, but also to understand, to teach and to heal. It is the mysterious interweaving of both phases which gives meaning to the whole.

At a still deeper level, the possibility of personal eros which is contained in the separation of ovulation from menstruation in women also opens out, in the fact of desire made conscious, the whole realm of the shadow, of conflict and the problem of love. We are back now to the Kabbalist legends about menstruation as Eve's penalty for enjoying the fruit of the tree of knowledge of good and evil. Desire wants to *possess* what it desires, yet never succeeds. The reality of the shadow is born, together with eros, when the image of the lover is constellated, within or without. The creative tension of these dual aspects of instinct libido makes it possible for the true individual to emerge. Eros creates an energetic continuum along whose path all creative activity takes place, but it is maintained only because of the dark fact that eros never stops wanting and is never finally fulfilled. The tension of eros obviates true altruism. Yet without that tension life is also flat and unreal—and unconscious.

If the love problem (the union of opposites) is insoluble in outer life, so is it also insoluble in inner life. This does not mean that there is no way to go. It means that the way to go is back and forth, from inner to outer and then again inwards. The meeting of the woman with her lover at an inner level where conscious understanding of her life is developed, where personal creativity finds its expression, where spiritual values can be affirmed—that is, where the whole difficult process begins to make sense and be worth doing—is a mere preparation for the shattering demands of love in real human relationships.

We never come anywhere near coping in a responsible way with the need for intimacy and tactful distance in friendship, with the "me" and the "you" in our roles as parents. We fail in our capacity to carry both the suffering and the companionship of marriage relationships. We are in love and out of love, filled and empty, hungering and devouring, affected so deeply that we are engulfed, or so little that nothing happens. We defend our personal integrity against the invasion of love. We use power techniques to avoid exposure, and power to catch and limit the freedom of the loved one. Yet the demand for union is so compelling that we are forced to improve on our failures. It is a false dichotomy to speak of the resolution of the problem of love on either the "outer" or the "inner" level. It must be worked on, though it cannot be finally resolved, at either level. Otherwise life has no meaning.

This is the model that we see in the menstrual cycle, where we find evidence of bi-phasal patterning in feminine psychic life—a phase in which energy progresses into outer life; and a phase where adaptation breaks down, where affectivity predominates, and the image of the lover is presented in unconscious material.

Does this mean that we succeed in the progressive, less emotional phase of our lives, only to fail in our emotional times? No, I think not. This is just the danger of the rationalistic temper of much current thinking. It is precisely the psychology of the woman to succeed where she is failing. Her capacity to submit to being in love both on the outside and the inside, to be involved with an other than herself, marks her capacity for change, for experiencing what she did not experience before, and thus for both true consciousness and for conscious loving. The capacity to *accept* emotion is the condition of conscious psychological and intellectual development, not its antithesis.

Jung's concept of the animus as an inner male component of the female personality which is the carrier of her potential for psychological development is repugnant to many women nowadays, who consider that men and women are in fact much more similar than culture until now has allowed them to be, and that a strong ego and capacity for achievement in the world are certainly not male perquisites. It may well be that Jung's descriptions of the animus were relatively undifferentiated and depended largely on the type of transference projections he was apt to constellate in his women patients. Yet anyone who has worked extensively with women's dream material and listened carefully to what makes their lives move, cannot avoid realizing that women's dreams about men and relationships with men have an enormous effect, whatever their stage of maturational development. Why should we be surprised at that?

Biologically it is simply a fact that the sexual libido reaches a level where it is useful for the preservation of the species when it is focused on heterosexual relationships. This fact has symbolic and psychological as well as biological significance. Whatever the life of woman is all about, it must not be different in kind from her biological determinants. It must also be fruitful for the life of the species. The symbolic imagery which expresses the extension of the biological into psychological functions will surely not lose track of body imagery and instinctive libido. How inhuman if it did!

The unconscious appears to ignore the fact that women today are experimenting with great freedom in all sorts of love arrangements and goes on producing endless dreams of the male lover. Perhaps such dreams are even exacerbated, because of our tendency to resist a compensatory, unconscious viewpoint, or because collective attitudes in the western world have become rationalistic, ignoring the presence in psychic life of a contra-sexual "other" which cannot successfully be integrated into ego consciousness.

What I pay attention to, more than the arguable content of what the image of the lover is, is the quality of what is happening in the relationship between the woman and her opposite—the one who is the "not I" in her life. The mystery of love is that the loved one can be received but not won, or else love fails. Desire may be fulfilled in a moment outside time, but is never finally satisfied, so long as life lasts. The loved one remains different and unattainable. What does happen is that increasingly the need for a personal and productive relatedness—to people, to general goals, to the world of ideas—is embraced and accepted as the goal of life.

Insofar as what I have just been saying has to do with the relationship of the feminine ego to the unconscious and thus with psychological development, the appearance of the figure of the "strange lover" in the menstrual cycle of women may indicate that the patterning of the individuation process in women is different than with men. Menstruation belongs to the first half of woman's life—not the second. Perhaps she is not so able to split her development chronologically into two halves, with collective duties in the first years and personal development later. Woman's collective duties with children and family are in any case highly personal, and her personal development is apt to have results for the collective. Perhaps her whole psychological development depends from the beginning on a dialectic between inner and outer relationships.

Individual differences among women must be respected; they surely cover a wide range. But if it is true, as I believe, that the psychology of women is reflected in biological rhythms (or vice versa!), and since it is clearly the case that women's biological functions fall into the same time span as the first appearances of the strange inner lover who beckons the woman to personal psychological development, then affective relatedness must all along be the key to feminine psychology.

REFERENCES

Boas, F. 1901. *Kathlamet texts.* Bulletin no. 26, Bureau of American Ethnology. Washington: Government Printing Office.

Condrau, G. 1965. *Psychosomatik der Frauenheilkunde.* Bern: Verlag Hans Huber.

Crawley, E. A. 1902. *The mystic rose: A study of primitive marriage and of primitive thought on its bearing on marriage,* 2 vols. London: Methuen & Co., Ltd., 1927.

Ehrenreich, P. 1910. *Die allgemeine Mythologie und ihre ethnologischen Grundlagen.* Leipzig.

Eliade, M. 1951. *Shamanism: Archaic techniques of ecstasy.* London: Routledge & Kegan Paul, Ltd., 1964.

Ellis, H. 1905. *Studies in the psychology of sex.* New York: Random House, 1942.

Fenichel, O. 1946. *The psychoanalytic theory of neurosis.* London: Routledge & Kegan Paul, Ltd.

Ginzberg, L. 1911. *The legends of the Jews,* 7 vols. Trans. P. Radin. Philadelphia: The Jewish Publication Society of America, 1947. 1959.

Mead, M. *The changing culture of an Indian tribe.* New York: The Viking Press.

Pliny. *Natural history,* 10 vols. Loeb Library.

Ploss, H. and Bartels, M. 1887. *An historical, gynecological and anthropological compendium,* ed. E. J. Dingwall. London: William Heinemann Ltd., 1935.

Roth, W. 1908-09. *An inquiry into the animism and folk lore of the Guiana Indians.* 30th Annual Report of the Bureau of American Ethnology. Washington: Government Printing Office, 1915.

Swanton, J. R. 1909. *Tlingit myths and texts.* Bulletin no. 39, Bureau of American Ethnology. Washington: Government Printing Office.

Winter, G. F. 1955. *Historisches zum mensuellen Zyklus.* Berlin: (aus der Universitats-FrauenKlinik) VEB Carl Marhold Verlag.

RECENT PUBLICATIONS

Hoffman, C. 1976. Menstruation and the unconscious: a content analysis of dreams. Unpublished doctoral dissertation. Los Angeles: California School of Professional Psychology.

Smith-Marder, P. 1978. A study of selected dream contents in the dreams of adolescent and mature women during menstruation. Unpublished doctoral dissertation. Los Angeles: California School of Professional Psychology.

Shuttle, P. and Redgrove, P. 1978. *The wise wound: Eve's curse and Everywoman*. New York: Richard Marek Publishers.

Reprinted from *Psychological Perspectives,* vol. 12, no. 1, Spring, 1981, with permission of the C.G. Jung Institute of Los Angeles.

$\left(\!\begin{array}{c} 14 \end{array}\!\right)$

SINGING FOR LIFE:
THE MESCALERO APACHE GIRLS' PUBERTY
CEREMONY[1]

Claire R. Farrer

*In "Singing for Life: The Mescalero Apache Girl's Puberty Ceremony,"
Claire R. Farrer, Ph.D., describes this annual rite not only as a rite
celebrating Apache girls' attainment of womanhood, but as a "reenactment of
events from the beginning of cosmological time and a recitation of ethnohistory." Her meticulous essay demonstrates the appropriateness of
concrete detail—how seemingly insignificant data reflect metaphysical and
cosmological truth and value to the Apache celebrant. The continued practice
of this rite in the modern world testifies to its strength and importance as* "the
crucial factor in [Mescalero Apache] ethnicity and their success in coping
with the rigors of survival as a people in a pluralistic society not of their
making."*

*Note: the reader might contrast this native model, an old, yet living "rite
of confirmation" or "intensification," with the vision quest model described
in the chapter by Foster and Little. The modern vision quest ceremony has
been "re-introduced" into modern culture and lacks the social sanction of
centuries of use. The vital, health-engendering function of the Apache
ceremony is an indication of how culture at large might benefit if, in time, we
had a culturally-sanctioned rite of passage among the young.*

*Claire R. Farrer, Ph.D., received her master's and doctorate degrees in
Anthropology/Folklore from the University of Texas. Both her master's thesis
and her doctoral dissertation were written about the Mescalero Apache
Indians, among whom she spent considerable amounts of research time
during the 1970s. At the present time she is Associate Professor of Anthropology at California State University, Chico. She has authored numerous
papers presented at professional meetings and is now working on a book,*
Living Life's Circle: Mescalero Apache Cosmovision.

INTRODUCTION

All our actions are based on our religion—if that goes, we go as a people.
—Bernard Second[2]
Mescalero Apache Singer

THE Mescalero Apaches have increased from fewer than 500 people (by the Army's 1873 census) to over 2,000 formally enrolled members on the tribal rolls (1975 tribal figure). Within the last 20 years they have moved to an enviable position of prestige and relative wealth. These people, who were hunted, beaten, decimated, and finally incarcerated, have within 100 years—more than quadrupled their population and raised their standard of living almost beyond imagination. What caused the rejuvenation?

Whenever the question was asked, the same answers were given: "our feast" and "tribal leadership." This chapter concerns the former, the "feast," as the Girls' Puberty Ceremony is often called in English. It is the Singers who have sung the tribe back to viable existence.

History, in the form of census records, supports the folk explanation that the Girls' Puberty Ceremony contributed to tribal increase, since the population did not increase substantially until after 1912, when ceremonial activity resumed following the government-enforced hiatus from 1873 to 1911.

Similar ceremonies have captured the interest of anthropologists. M. E. Opler (1965) wrote in detail of the Chiricahua version; he also described the Jicarilla practices (1942, 1946). The homologous Cibique Apache rite has been the subject of a monograph (Basso 1966), while Clark (1976) has described the San Carlos Apache version. The full Mescalero Apache rite has yet to be discussed, although portions of it have been considered by Breuninger (1959) and Nicholas (1939), both Mescaleros.

At Mescalero the Girls' Puberty Ceremony is an annual event celebrating the initial menses of selected girls, as well as the perpetuation of the tribe. During the event, the Singers recount tribal history from the time of the beginning by the shores of a big lake far to the north.

While the Ceremony celebrates womanhood and focuses on women, it is conducted by men; not just ordinary men, but powerful holy men who are beyond reproach. Each Holy Man/Singer (*Gutqqł*, One Who Sings) must be intelligent and able to memorize and interpret songs in a special form of Mescalero Apache. Each must sing 64 different songs on each of the four nights of the Ceremony. Additionally, the Singer must memorize long stories of the people, their travels, and accounts of tribal interactions from the beginning to the present. The Ceremony is thus a re-enactment of events from the beginning of cosmological time and a recitation of ethnohistory.

The Ceremony and its attendant rituals are seen by the Mescaleros as *the* crucial factor in their ethnicity and their success in coping with the rigors of survival as a people in a pluralistic society not of their making. The Singers sing women into their adult roles, sing tribal history, and sing the people into their concerted existence.

> Our Ceremony, the puberty rites, is the most important religious rites that we adhere to today . . . . The female - - - - the woman of the tribe, when she reaches womanhood, this elaborate Ceremony is held over her. Not, not because she has reached puberty, but because she is a *woman*. And, then, everything is done - - - - for her that a people might live. That a people will *always* live. Every year we have this to regenerate ourselves as a people. - - - - - - - - That we will make her strong, and generous, and kind, and proud so that she will bring forth *strong* warrior child that . . . will protect the people. - - - - - - This is the way a people perpetuate themselves.

Not only do the rites celebrate the achievement of womanhood for girls, but also they serve a sociability function. Each summer the parking lot adjacent to the Ceremonial grounds boasts cars with license plates from several states, attesting that friends and relatives from across the country have arrived.

At the same time, the Ceremony is a reunion with the primary life force, the Creator God (*Bik'egudindé,* Because of Whom There Is Life), and his consort, Mother Earth or White Painted Woman (*Isdzanatł'eesh,* Woman Painted White).

> CRF: Tell me when you first had this.
> BS: When we were created as a people and we became a people . . . in order for us to return respect for our Mother, we organized this ritual. We, as men, organized this religion to give thanks back and also to our hopes and aspirations in this life. . . . [We say,] 'Give us strength to live on this earth—that we will live as strong and good and holy people and that our womenfolk will continue to bring forth strong and healthy children and that we will continue to live as a people.' . . . This is a re-enactment of our creation as a people.

The Girls' Puberty Ceremony, then, is a ritual drama, a reenactment of creation. The Ceremony is also a cultural performance (Singer 1958, 1972) during which time those things of value to the people are displayed for themselves and for outsiders.

Cultural performances communicate what is of importance to a people; however, that communication is not always readily grasped, as Singer observes:

> . . . these were the kinds of things that an outsider could observe and comprehend within a single direct experience. I do not mean that I could, even with the help of interpreters, always understand everything that went on at one of these performances or appreciate their functions in the total life of the community (1972).

The difficulty in understanding is compounded when the cultural performance spans several days and includes various performance genres. The interpretative task is facilitated by following a base metaphor through its many guises or transformations and recombinations during the cultural performance.[3] Balance, circularity, directionality, the number 4, and sound/silence are all components of the Mescalero Apache base metaphor.

The various subsystems constituting a culture are unified through a shared set of organizing principles, or a base metaphor. Such sharing produces the patterns that allow recognition of particular kinds of behavior and beliefs as being characteristic of a culture. For the Mescalero Apaches the components mentioned above produce patterns that begin to make the cultural performance of the Girls' Puberty Ceremony intelligible. What the patterns and their significance are form the burden of what follows—the singing for life.

THE CEREMONY

The First Day

The few spectators who have braved the predawn chill sit on the north side of the ceremonial area directly opposite the large cooking arbor. Several Singers and Painters (*Anaagu'łiin,* One Who Makes Them) emerge from behind the cooking arbor. They have been singing and praying near the girls' quarters while each Godmother (*Naaikish,* They Who Direct [the girls]) begins to dress her charge from the left, the side of the heart and, therefore, the side closest to the Creator God. First comes the left moccasin, then the right. Next comes the soft buckskin skirt made heavy with its fringe, each strand of which ends in a handmade tin cone. The buckskin over-blouse with its elaborate beading and more tin cones follows. Finally, the scarf is added, attached at the shoulders and falling down the back. Finishing touches are provided by jewelry: beaded work, porcupine quill work, turquoise, and silver. The process is reversed and the girls are undressed from the right toward the end of the four days and nights of the public ritual.

As the final items (scratching stick, drinking tube, pollen bag, and sometimes a medicine bundle) are put in place on the dresses, the Singers come to the northwest side of the Ceremonial grounds and stand near the spectators. The Painters array themselves behind the Singers. The lead Singer begins to chant a prayer to the Powers.

Strong, young men assemble the poles for the holy lodge (*Isgqnebikugha,* Old Age Home), inside which the actual ritual will take place. The 12 evergreen poles are arrayed in a circle, bases toward the center, behind the Singers. Grasses are tied to the tops of the four primary poles, the Grandfathers; they are then blessed with cattail pollen *(teł, Typha latifolia).* The circle opens to the east and has a basket at its center. The Singers pray as they sprinkle pollen from the base to the tip of each Grandfather.

Prayers continue as the mothers, grandmothers, and Godmothers of the girls join the Singers. As the Singers chant to each Grandfather, the women "send forth a voice," a high-pitched ululation of reverent praise and pride. Meanwhile, the young men who are raising the poles pause four times, once for each cardinal direction, before bringing the poles to their full upright position.

The first Grandfather represents the moon and the stars; he stands in the east. The second Grandfather represents the sky elements (wind, rain, lightning, clouds, thunder, rainbows, mountains) from his position in the south. The third Grandfather represents the animals; he stands in the west. And the fourth Grandfather represents man, humanity; he stands in the north. "And since man is a frail being, it takes all the other three to hold him up." The four Grandfathers remind the people of creation.

> CRF: Tell me about the beginning time. What happened then?
> BS: When my grandparents started off these stories, they started it off with the word '*niaguchilaada*,' when the world was being made. At that time there was nothing in the universe except—for the Great Spirit God. And He—*He* made the world in four days. First came Father Sun and Mother Earth; then the sky elements and Old Man Thunder and Little Boy Lightning. Next came animals and on the fourth day came man, the Apaches.

When the 12 evergreen poles are in place and lashed together at their tops, a young man climbs up the frame to secure the lashing and then cover the top third with white canvas.[4] Other men cover the bottom two-thirds with freshly cut oak branches. Soon the holy lodge is completed on the outside. At the very top are tufts of boughs left on when most of the trunks were stripped of their branches and greenery. In the middle is the white canvas and, finally, the bottom is composed of tightly interwoven oak boughs.

> The main Ceremonial lodge is made of 12 evergreen fir trees. These poles . . . represent eternal life for us. And the 12 represent the 12 moons of the year. . . . The 4 main structure poles . . . correspond to the 4 directions of the universe, the 4 seasons, the 4 stages of life—for in the natural world everything is based on 4. . . .
>
> These 12 poles that form the tipi, to us represents the balance of Power, goodness, generosity; all that is good in this world comes from this tipi, this holy lodge. . . . It says to us, "Come forth, my children, enter me. I am the home of generosity, pride, dignity, and hope." . . .
>
> The 4 Grandfathers hold up the universe for us. . . . These poles are heavy; it takes many men to lift them. . . . When these poles are being raised, the mothers of the daughters put their hands on the poles. And that signifies that the home is not a home without the woman; and even though this Ceremonial structure is going up, it also has to have the help of the woman even though she is physically not able to put it up.

The basket that had been in the center of the circle formed by the poles is now brought out in front of the holy lodge. It is a handmade basket containing gramma grass, pollen, eagle feathers, and tobacco.

[The] basket represents the . . . heart of a people: it has all the important things. It has grass in there: food for all that we live on, the animals. The feathers represent eagle. . . . We get our authority to live as a people from Eagle. He is God's earth authority. That's why we wear the feathers . . . feathers are our authority and pride. . . . Tobacco is man's hope and his prayers . . . the basket is industriousness.

Activity intensifies as men labor to form a runway of fully boughed evergreen trees, four on the south and four on the north of the east-facing entry to the holy lodge. Other men begin to bring in freshly cut tules *(Scirpus lacutris)* to carpet in front of and inside the tipi. Simultaneously, a fire-pit is dug in the tipi's center.

The fire-pit . . . signifies the woman and the poles represent the man. Men are the shield; they protect. The woman is the center, being protected. . . . Everything revolves around the tipi . . . it's a people. The cover is men. The fire is woman, warmth, love, and perpetual labor for a family to live. If there's no woman in here, there's no rhyme or reason to it. . . . Everything is male in that lodge except the women and the fire.

Outside the holy lodge the Singers are facing east and praying. The lead Singer slowly raises his left hand as he sings. His palm faces outward; painted on it, in red, is a sun with rays emanating outward to the four directions. The Godmothers lead the girls to their places on buckskin mats placed on the quilts and blankets on top of the tules just as the Singer completes his last song and his arm is fully extended. As if on command, the sun tops East Mountain, striking his upraised palm. It is a moment of breath-taking beauty, requiring an exquisite sense of timing and precise attention to minimal light cues as well as the manipulation of the songs so that the last line of the last song coincides with the sunrise.

When men offer red paint to the sun—red signifies male and men. That's the background of the sun. The two basic colors of the universe is yellow and red, yellow for women. . . . And the sun is the physical representation of God. . . . [As the sun rises] goodness washes over you.

The girls kneel, facing east, on their skin mats while a line forms to the southeast of them. The girls' mothers stand behind them holding burden baskets filled with food; their fathers and uncles stand to either side, inside the runway and directly in front of the holy lodge. Each Singer applies the yellow cattail pollen to the girl for whom he is singing: a tiny sprinkle to the east, south, west, north, thence from the west to the east (from the crown of her head to her forehead), to the south (on her right shoulder), to the north (on her left shoulder), and from south to north (across her nose). The movements form a cross, linking the four directions with the girl as the center.

Pollen is applied to them. They are blessed with pollen. Pollen is the color of yellow. The yellow color represents God's generosity. It also represents the south, from which the warm winds bring rain that a thirsty land might drink and bring forth its bounty of fruit and meat. And they are . . . blessed that they will be fruitful and bring forth strong sons that they will be mighty warriors . . . that they will bring forth strong daughters that will become the mothers of a warrior race; that they will perpetuate themselves in a good way, a holy way, with the Powers of the four directions.

The Singers step to the front of the line that has formed and are blessed by each of the girls, beginning with the one kneeling on the south and proceeding to the northernmost girl. Then the people in line pass before the girls. As the girls complete the blessing sequence for those kneeling in front of them, they are; in turn, blessed by the person's reaching into the pollen bag and repeating the sequence that the Singers had performed. Babies too small to move their own hands have them moved by the parent or relative bringing them through the line. Those who have specific complaints linger to rub some of the pollen on the afflicted area. Anyone who is sick or troubled will go through the line as will those who seek to remain well and partake of the blessings of God as mediated through the girls.

Singers and Godmothers keep a careful watch for signs of fatigue on the part of the girls, for there is still more strenuous activity to come. Sometimes the line is so long that not all waiting will be blessed in public. Those remaining will go to the homes (tents, arbors, and a tipi) behind the cooking arbor after the morning's public activities, there to be blessed privately.

The lead Singer motions away those still in line as the Godmothers assist the girls in going from their knees to their abdomens. Each girl lies face down with her head to the east as her Godmother presses and "molds" her into a fine, strong woman. The hair is smoothed over the girl's shoulders and back before molding begins: first the left shoulder, then the right; next the left and right sides of the back; the left hip and the right hip; the left then right thigh and calf; the left and right foot.

As the Godmothers near the feet, a man takes the basket, that had been present since the morning began, out to the east. While the Singers chant and the Godmothers ululate, the girls run along the north side of the dance arena, around the basket, and back on the south side of the arena. The basket is moved closer to the holy lodge three more times; and the running girls encircle it three more times.

The four runs around the basket symbolize the four cycles of life: infancy, childhood, adulthood, and, as the basket nears the Old Age Home in the west again, old age. As the primary characters in the ritual drama, the girls reenact the legendary journey of White Painted Woman who walked to the west as an old woman only to return from the east as a young woman once again.

At the conclusion of the fourth run the girls return to the entranceway of the holy lodge where their uncles or brothers invert the burden baskets, spilling tobacco, candy, piñons, fruit, and money over them.

The spilling from the baskets signals the end of the public rites and triggers massive give-aways by matrilineal members of the girls' families. Relatives throw candy, oranges, apples, and cigarettes from the beds of pickup trucks. People of all ages dash to pick up the gifts, for this is special food and tobacco that has been blessed.

While the assembled crowd, many of whom arrived with the sunrise, scampers for the distributed gifts, the girls return to their camp-out homes. There each girl's Godmother talks to her of sex and her responsibility for motherhood. The Singer gives his "daughter," as he will refer to the girl for the rest of her life, Indian bananas *(husk'ane, Yucca baccata)* and says, "Be fruitful all the days of your life; obtain food and not be lazy." He repeats this, and the feeding twice more. The fourth time, the Godmother feeds the girl; as she does so, she tells her, "May you bring forth in this world strong male children so they will protect your people."

Even before the Singer and Godmother finish, those who were not yet blessed form a line outside the camp-out home. At the conclusion of the feeding, they are admitted. Each kneels in front of the girl, who is sitting on a bed or a chair, and pollen blessings are exchanged.

The cooking arbor is also the scene of lines. Each girl's family has a fire in the arbor where food is cooked for all who come to the Ceremonial. A breakfast of fry bread and coffee is available; some families provide a meat, potato, and chili stew as well. In the camp-out homes, relatives and close friends eat traditional foods blessed by the Singer as well as bread, coffee, and stew.[5] Everyone who comes to a Ceremonial is fed all meals free. It is an embarrassment, and a rarity, to have the food run out before all have been fed. After breakfast participants and spectators alike rest at home; some go to their year-round houses and others to their campsites on the hills and mesas near the Ceremonial grounds. After lunch is served, preparations are under way for the supper to be served around 6 P.M.

While Ceremonial participants rest in the afternoon, the spectators are entertained by contests. Some members of the audience of the ritual drama become performers in these events. An all-Indian rodeo, with competitors from many states, takes place on a mesa to the northeast of the Ceremonial grounds. Prizes are generous and points are earned for the annual all-around Indian cowboy championship.

> [We had] horse racing and gambling [hand-game] in the old days. . . . Government outlawed it. Now, rodeo takes its place.

Meanwhile, in the dance arena there are dance contests in the pan-Indian Powwow style.[6]

The mounting tension is almost tangible as darkness begins to descend and the huge bonfire is prepared and lit in the center of the dance arena. When the sun no longer colors the mountains and deserts to the west and when the fire is roaring, jingling noises can be heard from the east as the Mountain God dancers *(Gą'hé)* prepare to enter the dance arena. Their Painter and his assistants have been busy for the past few hours praying, drumming, and chanting while the entire group of Mountain God dancers *(Baanaaich'isndé)* has been painted and dressed.

Each dance group is identifiable by its design set, distinctive sashes, and headdresses. The general costuming is the same—kilts, paint, head covering, headdresses, and red streamers with four eagle feathers attached and tied to each upper arm. There is no mistaking a Mountain God dancer or the group to which he belongs.

Each dancer wears an A-line wraparound buckskin kilt that is fringed and fitted with beaded or skin decorations as well as "jingles" cut and shaped from tin cans, which jingle each time the dancer moves. Worked leather belts, often with bells attached, and red sashes hold up the kilts. The mid-calf length buckskin moccasins are decorated with bells either at the top or at the ankle. If there are no bells on the moccasins, leather straps with bells are worn around each leg.

A head covering of black fabric (canvas, heavy cotton, dyed buckskin, or heavy doubleknit), with round openings cut for each eye and the mouth, is topped by a bilaterally symmetrical headdress[7] made of yucca and wood. The headdress of each group member is the same and is painted with designs matching or repeating an element of the design painted on the dancers' bodies. Thus, with the exception of the palms of the hands, a dancer is completely covered with clothing or paint from the top of his head to the soles of his feet. He becomes the anonymous personification of a Mountain God.

Usually there is a dance set (four Mountain God dancers and one or more clowns) for each girl, although at times two girls will share a set of dancers. Sharing is most apt to occur when the girls are sisters or first cousins.

The spectacle is awesome as the fully costumed Mountain God dancers converge on the dance arena, jingling rhythmically as they move, their headdresses piercing the darkness above them. The dancers pause from a trotting step just outside the dance arena. There the lead dancer gets the others in step by striking the sticks he carries in each hand against his thighs. The clown *(tibayé)* mimics each movement of the lead dancer, but always a bit late. All being in step, and all noises from the bells and the tin cones—as well as the strident note from the cow bell slapping against the clown's derrière—being in synchrony, the lead dancer moves his group into the dance arena. They raise their arms and sticks as they approach the fire and emit a hooting sound resembling that of an owl or a turkey. They are said to be praying as they make this noise. Their movements and vocalizations are said to be "blessing the fire." When the lead dancer is within a few feet of the fire, he lowers his arms and sticks and bows his head before the line steps backward still facing the fire. The approach, hooting, lowering, and retreating sequence is repeated three times. On the fourth approach the dancers dip their bodies first to the left, then to the right as they approach the fire; they move so quickly in their four dips to each side that their arms seem like windmills. This time as they retreat the lead dancer again slaps the sticks on his thighs as he guides the group once around the fire to the south side of the dance arena. The blessing sequence is repeated again from here, thence from the west and north each time with one complete circuit of the fire between stops for the cardinal directions.

After the fire has been blessed, the group moves to the holy lodge where the sequence is repeated from each of the directions in order (east, south, west, north).

When the blessings are completed the Painter begins his drumming and chanting from a position in front of the holy lodge. The Mountain God dancers and their clown now dance with dramatic posturing, stamping, and gesturing around and around the bonfire, always moving in a clockwise direction. Even when there is no singing or drumming, they keep moving; they are never still the entire time they are in the dance arena.

As the Painter begins his drumming a large cardboard is placed on the ground in front of the benches where he and the chanting men sit. Young boys congregate around the cardboard carrying evergreen sticks they have gathered from near the holy lodge. They join the adult drummers and chanters by beating in rhythm with their sticks and, occasionally, also join in the singing of one of the choruses of a song. Once again, a part of the audience becomes performers.

The regular dancing of the Mountain Gods signals the women to join in the dancing as well. Their dance path is several feet away from the bonfire and the path of the Mountain Gods. Some of the first women to dance are the girls for whom the Ceremony is being held; they are accompanied by their Godmothers who dance in front of them. Their mothers and close female relatives dance behind them: ". . . while the men are dancing, the women dance around them. There again, we can't separate the male from the female in our religion."

The girls for whom the Ceremony is being held wear their Ceremonial attire. All other women wear everyday dress without jewelry that might make noise. Only the Mountain God dancers, the clowns, and the girls make noise in the dance area; those sounds are perceived as music. Added to the everyday dress is a shawl, a piece of fabric approximately two yards long that is worn folded in half lengthwise and draped over the shoulders in such a fashion that the hands are covered and the 12-14-inch fringe hangs down on the sides and in back. Only the women's legs move in performing the dance steps used; however, the execution of the steps moves the body toward, then away from, the fire; and that movement produces a swinging motion of the fringing on the shawls: it is said to be beautiful.

The girls make only a few circuits of the fire before retiring to their arbors to rest before their strenuous dancing begins. As they retire, other women begin to dance "in support" of the Mountain Gods. Mothers encourage their very young (four- and five-year-old) daughters to dance, too. The women dance in groups of matrilineally related kin. Women of all ages dance, although those who dance longest are those between 15 and 50.[8]

While the Mountain Gods and the women dancing in support of them hold the attention of the spectators, the girls are led into the holy lodge by their Godmothers. During the leading-in portion of the Ceremony, the girls are said to be inviting in life and magnanimity for their people and for themselves.

Cowhide dance mats are awaiting the girls around the inside periphery of the holy lodge. The Godmothers spread blankets for themselves and the girls to sit on while resting; it is here that they await the arrival of the Singers.

Before recounting the tribe's history through chants accompanied by the deer hoof rattles, the lead Singer offers smoke to the Powers. The other Singers follow his lead. As soon as the Singers begin to chant, the girls rise to dance.

Two dance steps are used by the girls. The more common one involves keeping the body rigid while only the feet move. By pivoting alternately on the balls and heels of their feet they take four "steps" to the left, then four to the right. The cowhide on which they dance is just wide enough to allow four lateral movements. They hold their arms in front of them by bending their elbows, raising their forearms, and making their hands form relaxed fists with the palms outward while the knuckles rest lightly on the shoulders. The position and step create movement of the girls' clothing and cause the tin cones to strike one another, adding another sound to that produced by the men's voices and the percussion of the rattles. The other dance step the girls use is designed as a rest; it, too, however, is strenuous. Again the body is held still while the feet move. With their hands on their hips and while standing in place, they kick one foot and then the other straight out in front. Between songs the Godmothers will massage the girls' shoulders, backs, or legs if it appears they are showing signs of fatigue. Alternating the two steps with short rest periods, the girls will dance for several hours while the Singers chant.

> They're dancing . . . it used to be buffalo hides but now it's beef hides. They are dancing on it, gliding. They glide back and forth on these hides, shuffling. The . . . men sing to them and tell them, "These sounds that you make on this hide are the songs of a people walking and living. Dance on this hide—for it is your home. It is your food." The sound that it makes as a girl dances back and forth on it, it says, "This is the sound that a people will make on this earth. It is a pleasant sound, a good sound. Abide by it."

The girls dance while 64 songs are sung. During rest periods the Godmothers interpret the meaning of the Singers' "classical" language songs.[9]

The girls dance from about 10 P.M. to midnight before retiring to their camp-out homes. Social dancers replace the Mountain God dancers between 11 P.M. and midnight. Sometime between 2 A.M. and dawn the social dancers leave the dance arena. The first day ends.

The Second Through Fourth Days

There is no morning ritual on these days. Afternoons are filled with Powwow-style dance competitions and the rodeo.

After supper, but before the bonfire is lit for the Mountain God dancers, the war dancers appear in the Ceremonial arena. They carry rifles loaded with blanks or bows and arrows. Their hair is usually long, held in place with a plain headband. They wear loose shirts or are bare chested; each wears moccasins and a long G string, often over Levis. In the old days, I am told, they wore only buckskin and carried weapons. They danced in front of the girls' tipis to protect them. Now they dance in the dance arena and seemingly take delight in frightening the audience by aiming at the people with their arrows or shooting them with blanks, thus again giving the audience a performer role.

The bonfire, several feet in diameter, is lit at dusk in preparation for the Mountain God dancers and the social dancing that will follow them. Around 10 A.M. the girls will again dance for two hours or so in the holy lodge as the Singers continue their chanting recitation of tribal history, keeping track of the songs with sticks placed in a circle around the central fire-pit.

The Fifth Day

Since time is reckoned from sunrise to sunrise and since the fifth day's activities begin when the fourth day is almost complete, the activities are considered to be a part of the fourth day: this despite a fifth sunrise coming in the midst of the fourth days' final activities.[10] They may also be viewed and indeed are, as the beginning of the second four days when the girls will remain on the Ceremonial grounds with only close female relatives and their Godmother—when the public aspect of the ritual is over and the private aspect begins.

Again, people assemble before dawn for the final ritual activities just as they did for those on the first day. This time there are many people present for some of the social dancers have been there dancing all night, as was the custom in the old days. The girls' families distribute presents (cloth, dippers, knives, tobacco) to the dancers just as the sky begins to lighten. The presents are a tangible reminder of the endurance of the dancers and their dedication to tradition.[11]

The jingling of the girls' dresses and the percussion from deer hoof rattles are also heard just before dawn on the fifth morning, for the girls have been dancing all night while the Singers sang and the Godmothers counseled.

> These girls have been dancing for four nights. On the fourth night they dance from when it gets dark to daylight with a break around midnight. It is a physical ordeal for them. But they must go through it. . . . It is a sacrifice they make . . . their physical contribution that they make that a people can be strong and healthy.

On the previous three nights the lead Singer placed song tally sticks in a circle around the fire; this morning the sticks make a pathway replicating the form of the holy lodge and its runway. As the last stick is planted, the Singers rise, signaling the Godmothers to take the girls back to their living quarters where their hair and bodies will be washed in yucca-root suds, repeating the actions of the first day when the girls were cleansed and dressed. This ritual foreshadows activity which will take place at the end of the eighth day.

All tules are taken out of the holy lodge and replaced with fresh ones. The folding chairs for the Singers are placed so they face east and are behind the girls, whereas previously they had faced west toward the girls.

Before the girls reappear in the holy lodge they will have their faces painted with white clay by the Singers. Their arms, from fingertips to elbows, and their legs, from thighs to feet, will also be painted.

> The girls' faces are painted white signifying that they have achieved; they have done their ordeal. They have lived four good days and they will be running. Running signifying a physical effort that they must do in order to prove themselves that they are worthy mothers. . . . That white paint is the sign of purity and of the Mother Earth. . . . They are called White Painted Woman, because white is the color of purity, these four days.

But before their final ordeal, that which was given form by the males must be destroyed by them.

The young man who had placed the white covering on the holy lodge once again shinnies up the poles to disengage the lashings and lower the covering. While he is working, other men on the ground take away the oak boughs that had covered the bottom of the lodge. Meanwhile, inside, the girls are being blessed and sung to. People crowd in, even though the poles are beginning to fall. As the last of the poles falls, save the Grandfathers, the girls are revealed sitting on the ground, each with her Singer and Godmother kneeling in front of her. People form lines in front of one or another of the girls; the Singers take seats to the left of the girl for whom they sang while the Godmothers stand to the right. The girls sit with their eyes downcast as the Singers bless each one in line; this time there is no hurry—all who so desire will be blessed. Rather than pollen, the blessing is performed with white clay and red ochre. Each Singer paints the faces of those in line a bit differently from the other Singers. Males are painted on the left side and females on the right side of their faces; each Singer uses his own marks. When all have been painted and blessed, each girl is led out of the holy lodge with an eagle feather by her Singer.

Now they have been brought out of the tipi after the four days of religious functions.—They have been brought out. They have been brought by an eagle feather. They tell them,

Four days you have walked your land and done good.
Now hold this eagle feather, the symbol of authority
And walk out of your home.
Go forth into the world.

The girls are escorted to a white buckskin that has been placed on the ground in front of the runway, now lined by their fathers and close male relatives. Four crescent moons, painted with colors evoking the directions and said also to represent life's stages, form the stepping-stones each girl walks on, left foot first, before her final run. As the girl under the tutelage of the lead Singer steps on the first crescent, the first song is sung; one additional song is sung for each of the other three crescents.

And she will be told,

Now you are entering the world.
You become an adult with responsibilities.
Now you are entering the world.
Behold yourself.
Walk in this world with honor and dignity.
Let no man speak of you in shame.
For you will become—
The mother of a nation.

At the end of the final song, she is pushed off the buckskin by her Singer and Godmother. The other girls follow the first one by quickly stepping on each of the four crescents and, like her, running to the east around the same basket that was used on the first day's run.

They are singing to them as [they are] running and they are telling them,

You will be running to the four corners of the universe:
To where the land meets the big water;
To where the sky meets the land;
To where the home of winter is;
To the home of rain.
Run this! Run!
Be strong!
For you are the mother of a people.

Three times the girls run around the basket; each time it is placed farther from the frame of the holy lodge (the four Grandfathers).[12] On the last run, each girl takes from the basket the eagle feather with which she was led into and out of the holy lodge, and, instead of returning to the holy lodge as she had on the three previous runs, she runs to her quarters behind the cooking arbor. Simultaneously, the four Grandfathers crash to the ground.

> During their last run they are running to their destiny; they are running into the hard world of adulthood . . . the hard world of a hunting world, a war world. . . . When the last run is completed, food will be thrown out that a people might be fruitful and multiply to many.

What began five mornings ago with the erection of a holy lodge and the distribution of food, ends with the destruction of the holy lodge and the distribution of food. In between have been goodness, holiness, the affirmation of the essential rightness of the world, and the place of humans in it. As the last of the Dance Songs states,

In your country
In your plains and green mountains
You have lived four days
In holiness and goodness.

In your country
In your plains and green mountains
You have existed four days
In holiness and goodness.

In your country
In your plains and green mountains
You have walked four days
In holiness and goodness.

In your country
In your plains and green mountains
You have danced four days
In holiness and goodness.

Naaishá.
I have done this.
Here
It ends.

DISCUSSION

A Puberty Ceremony, by definition, is a ritual recognition of sexual maturity. Were it only that, it might be exotic, but would be rather uninformative. Among the Mescalero, however, the physical event of puberty forms a nucleus around which many attributes—believed to be essential for describing and defining what constitutes Mescalero Apache ethnicity—coalesce. Native exegesis, such as that provided by Bernard Second, is necessary for insight into the meaning of the Ceremonial, but is insufficient for outsiders to understand fully the ramifications of the total event. But modesty prevents Mr. Second from stating what becomes obvious through observations spanning several years: the Singer orchestrates the various segments that form the recognizable society.

The Ceremony may be thought of as possessing several layers; each layer is complete in itself, each has its own integrity. Yet recognition of the totality as a Ceremony depends upon the layers being in proper relationship to each other. The Singer provides the integrative force to bring together those things that allow the label "Mescalero Apache."

> . . . the four laws of our people are honesty, generosity, pride, and bravery. And a great people, they cannot be great if they have no sense of generosity about them. For it is out of generosity that a man sees the world and what a man is worth in this world. He cannot be proud if he is not generous, as he has nothing to be proud for and brave for. He cannot be honest, for honesty has no basis if it is without generosity. So generosity, at the end, is the most important law that we have. It is the value we have cherished from the day we became a people to today.

And generosity is certainly in evidence at the Ceremonial, from the massive food give-aways through the altruistic self-sacrifice of the girls, as they run for strength and endurance for their tribe, to the generosity of the Creator God.

The laws and values rest upon a layer I call the base metaphor; this layer is characterized by the number 4, balance, circularity,[13] directionality, and sound/silence. The Singer integrates the layers through his recitations of tribal history; in song, explicitly and implicitly, he forges the union which ensures that Mescalero Apache life will continue as it has in the past.

Directionality gives rise to both the concept of "four" and its related concept of balance. Together the latter two may be said to establish the harmony essential to existence. The Creator God created the world in four days; examination of the creation sequence reveals that not only did he *call* entities into being, but also that balance was present. Two days were devoted to the creation of the inanimate (sun, earth, sky elements, and earth elements) and two days to the animate beings (winged insects, crawling things, four-legged animals, humankind). Four sets of entities occur within each of the two sequences, as balance is further present in the juxtaposition of the above and the below.

Creation is recapitulated in the holy lodge as the Singers sing the first night to the first Grandfather and what he represents, the second night to the second Grandfather; and so on. The singing is structured to bring together male principles (the structure itself, the dancing hides, the Singers) with female principles (the fire-pit, Godmothers, those impersonating White Painted Woman)—balance again. Within the holy lodge, then, is the visual and verbal manifestation of balance and four. It is a visual and oral transformation of the base metaphor.

Both concepts are given further visibility in the costuming of the portrayers of both White Painted Woman and the Mountain Gods. The girls' costumes consist of an overblouse and a skirt. Each item of clothing has two areas, front and back, on which decorations are placed. Thus, there are four fields; blouse front, blouse back, skirt front, skirt back. The beaded designs balance: that is, what appears as decoration over the left shoulder will also appear over the right shoulder. What is painted on one side of a girl's face will be painted on the other side. Similarly, the designs on the moccasins balance each other and, most of the time, they are composed of four elements. When not composed of four elements, balancing each other in sets of two, the design is composed of two elements, each of which is seen to balance the other.

The Mountain Gods provide an even more striking reminder of the importance of balance and the number 4. A Mountain God is quadrilaterally symmetrical both above and below the waist. The design, in evidence by facing him forward and dividing his painted areas on both midsagittal and lateral planes, can be replicated four times to reconstruct his image front and back. Likewise, by so dividing his costume from the waist down, he can again be seen to present a quadrilaterally symmetrical picture. His back is perceived as being in balance with his front, as each side of his front and back balance each other. Each of his arms balances the other. His sash, headdress, and even his kilt and moccasins present a balanced picture. It is number and arrangement that create this balance rather than area, just as it was number and taxonomic equivalence that provided the balance in the creation.

The basket around which the girls run contains four items: grass, pollen, tobacco, and eagle feathers. Both grass and pollen are earth items while feathers and tobacco are sky items: that is, they mediate between the below and the above in that both eagle and tobacco are viewed as communication channels to the Powers. Thus, the four items in the basket are seen as being in balance and hence contributing to the harmony and rightness of the world.

The girls take four steps on the painted skin before running around the basket. Each step represents a stage of life with the first (infancy) and the last (old age) balancing the two in the middle (childhood and adulthood). Infancy and old age are seen as times of dependence when one must rely on others to fulfill needs and often to help one move about. Childhood and adulthood, in contrast, are times of free movement, independence, and self-reliance.[14]

Eight evergreen trees balance each other as four line each side of the runway/entrance for the holy lodge. The lodge itself is balanced with the four powerful Grandfather poles balancing the other eight poles.

The Ceremony abounds in additional examples of four and balance: activity spans four days with the two middle days presenting the "same" picture and the two days on either end balancing each other, partially by reversal. Four varieties of dance are performed with the dancing of the Mountain Gods (and the women dancing in their support) balancing that of the girls; the two kinds of social dancing provide balance to the two kinds of ritual dancing. Even the physical site is balanced in that the dance arena for the girls is balanced by the dance arena for the other dancers; and the girls' camp area balances the general camp area.

While directionality, four, and balance permeate the entire system, the other set of components, circularity and sound/silence, are less apparent. Of the latter two, circularity is more easily recognized and has already been discussed in regard to the cardinal directions.

Dancing provides the most obvious instance of circularity during the ritual drama. The primary dance pattern is circular and follows a "sunwise" circuit, clockwise, beginning in the east.

Traditional dwellings (tipis, arbors) are also circular. Today the rectangular pattern of a commercial tent is often appended to a more traditional camp-out home. But all ritual activity occurs either in a traditional, circular structure or outside in the world that is also perceived as being circular.

Perhaps the most pervasive aspect of circularity during the Ceremonial is time—cyclic and endlessly circular. Human existence has been so short in terms of time in general that we are unable to comprehend fully the magnitude of the wheel of time, it is believed. The girls provide a visual reminder of the circularity of time by running around the basket four times to symbolize infancy, childhood, womanhood, and old age. Simultaneously, this indicates human existence through time and time's ever constant cycle. Although each girl will die, she allows the tribe to live through her and her offspring: the tribe endures through the cycling of time as White Painted Woman herself endures by ever cycling from east to west and by ever appearing as an aspect of each girl participating in the ritual. The cyclical nature of time is said to be represented through the daily circuit of the sun, from which is taken the "proper" movement while in the holy lodge, or any ceremonial structure where entrance is from the east. Movement should properly follow the sun's circuit: east, south, west, north.

Circularity is engendered and maintained by following the "natural" order. Even salt sprinkled on food during the meals at Ceremonial time is distributed in a circular, clockwise motion.

Time is collapsed into symbols during the Ceremony. The girls are both symbol and icon of White Painted Woman. As it was with her in the beginning of time, so now it is with the girls in contemporary time. White Painted Woman had twin warrior sons who saved the people from all manner of tragedies; the girls are exhorted to be good mothers and bring forth strong sons, sons who will be the future saviors of the tribe. The girls' four days of exemplary existence and their journey through the four stages of life are emblematic of White Painted Woman's journey through the eons.

Of all the components of the base metaphor, sound/silence is the least accessible and the most difficult to discuss. During the Girls' Puberty Ceremony many distinctions are made between sound and its absence. In general, sound is for the Powers while silence is for humans during ritual times.

Women dancing in support of the Mountain Gods produce no sound. Even noisy jewelry is removed before they dance. Their dance steps, in contrast to those of the Mountain Gods and the girls, are executed in silence. Women make their statement through their presence and their participation. In the realm of ritual sound/silence, the place of humans is to be silent while Power's is to invoke sound.

The most holy ones present, save the clowns, are the girls impersonating White Painted Woman. Even when they are not dancing, their slightest movement produces organized sounds perceived almost as music. But again the sound is holy sound; the girls themselves speak little in public. The Power filling them is responsible for the noise; they, as humans, remain almost completely silent, as is proper when a human confronts Power.

Orally, aurally, visually, and kinesically a metaphor is proposed that links the Mescalero Apache people to their beginnings and to their future. On a very basic level the message is a sexual one, but it is sex in perspective and with respect for all life. As Bernard Second explicitly states:

> The four Grandfathers are the home; in the center is the hearth, the woman: this is completion. Neither is anything without the other. That is what our life is about.

The Ceremony accomplishes much more than the bringing together of the two biological elements; the Ceremony orders life as well.

The Ceremony is high context.

> A high-context communication or message is one in which most of the information is either in the physical context or internalized in the person, while very little is in the coded, explicit, transmitted part of the message. . . . The level of context determines everything about the nature of the communication and is the foundation on which all subsequent behavior rests (including symbolic behavior). (Hall 1977)

Observers not familiar with Apache culture easily misinterpret intended communications. Misattribution is exacerbated by local newspapers referring to the girls as "debutantes" and the Ceremony as a "Rain Dance," or the dancing of the Mountain Gods as a "Devil Dance."

The Ceremony can be appreciated by those who do not know the code, since the dancing alone is spectacular in form, movement, use of time and space, and setting. But in order to understand fully the cultural performance with its manifold messages, one needs to know the presuppositions which give rise to the performative statements being made. These presuppositions, or the base metaphor, are given oral, aural, visual, and kinesic currency during the Ceremony so that the code can be perceived by astute observers. The keys to the code are presented repeatedly.

Turner (1967, 1969), working from Ndembu native exegesis and building upon van Gennep's (1960) tripartite schema, developed an elegant model termed "the ritual process" wherein the subject(s) of a ritual event passed through states of separation, liminality, and reincorporation (cf. Turner 1969) to emerge into a new status. Before having spent a sustained time in the field, I believed the Mescalero Apache data confirmed Turner's expansion of van Gennep. Accepting native exegesis, I must conclude that the Ceremony is a rite of confirmation and a rite of intensification (Chapple and Coon 1942). This does not deny that it occurs at a life crisis; but a girl is said to *be* a woman immediately upon menstruation. She does not *become* a woman through the Ceremony; she already *is* one. Girls become women whether or not they have a Ceremony. It is possible to have a Ceremony several years after the initial menses, since a Ceremony makes one a better woman.[15]

My data suggest that a ritual drama image works better than does a rite of passage. Girls are characters in a drama—a life-giving drama. Costuming and behavior contribute to the message that a Mescalero Apache is good, kind, generous, proud, brave, and dignified. One gives of oneself by playing a demanding role for the betterment of the group. And the roles are indeed demanding for all participants: for the girls through a physical ordeal; for the Singers through prodigious feats of memory and performance; for the families through resource sharing,[16] to say nothing of the energy expended in food preparation; for the Painters and dancers who maintain a state of ritual purity during the four days and nights; and for the audience whose focused energies are essential whether as "good thinkers," partakers of the blessings, fearful targets of the war dancers, or as vital life forces in social dancing.

Rather than a rite of passage, then, it seems more accurate to consider the Ceremony a rite of confirmation and a rite of intensification. It is a rite of confirmation in that the main characters are already women—menstruation has made them so while the Ceremony publicly confirms the status of woman. It is a rite of intensification in that participants are viewed as having the potential of being better women for having experienced the good, holy, and proper and for having fully learned the vital importance of the woman's role: to become a mother and thereby perpetuate the people. Through song the participants are shown their relationship to the first woman; their role is sanctified through time and publicly acknowledged. Each learns the enormous power she controls through the proper use of her body.

The primary participants are never in a liminal state; they are children until the onset of menstruation when they become women. While impersonating White Painted Woman in the Ceremony, they are enacting a role. A girl does not become White Painted Woman; the girl *is* White Painted Woman, as is any woman who allows her body to be the vessel through which her people are continued. She does become infused with White Painted Woman's healing power while she impersonates her during the four days of the public Ceremony and the four days of the private one. As Schechner (1977) states, "Theatrical techniques center on transformation." This obtains whether the theatre is in an urban center or a Southwestern mesa. The girls comport themselves well not because their faces will wrinkle prematurely if they smile [this is just-so-logic], but because they are playing a character who was/is omniscient—White Painted Woman knew the result/end—and so need not worry or become distraught. Calmness characterized her. For the course of the drama the girls are transformed into White Painted Woman by playing her part.

Similarly, a man in a costume is not the Mountain God he plays. Each character is an icon of the supernatural being and each is temporarily infused with the power of the Powers. The actions each displays were determined in the beginnings by the actions of the first Mountain Gods and the real White Painted Woman. But the contemporary messages are every bit as arresting as were the original ones. The Ceremony states, "We are a proud, generous, dignified, and holy people. We have plumbed the structure of the universe and live in harmony with it. We demonstrate this to ourselves, the Powers, and to you, the audience, through our Ceremony."

In a very literal sense, then, as long as there is the Ceremony, there will be the Mescalero Apache people, Ndé. The Ceremony can occur only when the people live right, operate by and understand their philosophical system, and have respect for the Creator and all Power.

The Ceremonial activities constitute a cultural performance directed to two groups simultaneously: themselves and their audience of outsiders. If cultural performances do, indeed, communicate not only what the essentials of being Mescalero Apache are but also about other aspects of culture as Bauman (1976) indicates for a variety of cultural situations, then we can reasonably expect to find manifestations of these messages in other areas of social life as well. They abound at Mescalero. The stress on activities occurring in their appointed spaces in the Ceremony is evident daily in adult and children's activities.[17] The politeness-decorum system lays stress on not wasting words: this leads to an economy of speech that strikes outsiders as being conversation punctuated by silences. To a Mescalero it is conversation punctuated by time for reflection, framing the next statement, being sure that the previous speaker is finished, and showing proper respect for language. Formal meetings are arranged into four spatially distinct sections; speeches have four parts. When entering a tipi, even one raised alongside a house to provide guest quarters, a polite person always makes a sunwise circuit to her/his place.

Thus ritual—even a complex, many-day ritual—economically provides insight into the workings of everyday life and provides a template for organizing that life. When the ritual is cast in the form of a drama, individual society members have the opportunity to become personally involved in the affirmation of life as it should be. No matter what terms are used to describe this particular series of events, a rite of passage, of confirmation, or affirmation, the activities are seen by Mescaleros as being the essence of their uniqueness as a people.

As a ritual drama, the Mescalero Apache Girls' Puberty Ceremony celebrates (and ensures the perpetuation of) the existence of the Mescalero people through the balanced juxtaposition of the female and male forces that are seen to exist in the world. Simultaneously, the ritual dramatizes the essential rightness of life by its reaffirmation through chants, dances, music, use of space, and sharing of food. Concomitantly, the rules for proper existence and the ordering of the universe are given form. The daily social order is legitimized through its recreation in the Ceremony. Girls learn how to be better women by playing the part of the "perfect woman." The society is presented with a complex drama reinforcing ethnicity. Mescalero Apache life is dissected, explained, reaffirmed, and celebrated. In both literal and figurative senses, the Singer is singing for life.

NOTES

1. Intensive fieldwork from September 1974 through September 1975 was supported by the Whitney M. Young, Jr. Memorial Foundation and the Mescalero Apache Tribe. Time to think and write was made possible by Dr. Douglas Schwartz and a Weatherhead Resident Fellowship at the School of American Research. Grateful acknowledgment is tendered to all.

2. All quotes are from field notes and tapes made with the cooperation of Bernard Second, my friend and "brother," a holy man and one of only five Mescalero Apache Singers. All were made at Mescalero, New Mexico at various times between 1974 and 1978. The 1976 material was recorded in Washington, D.C. and Harpers Ferry, West Virginia. The Harpers Ferry material was "elicited" by slides, when Bernard Second

and I presented a seminar to National Park Service employees and townspeople utilizing slides I had made of Ceremonials. Those slides provided the visual stimulation for his extemporaneous commentary, which I recorded. Material gathered using standard field methodology is indicated by being preceded by my question; this style of reporting is what Barbara Tedlock termed "dialogic anthropology."

3. I use "transformation" in its geometric sense (see Goffman 1974 and Basso 1979). The term should not be equated with its use by structural anthroplogists after Levi-Strauss or by those linguists who follow Chomsky.

The base metaphor concept is given extended treatment in my dissertation (Farrer 1977).

4. The first Grandfather, the east pole, has a long rope secured to it immediately below the greenery at its tip. As the pole is raised, a man pulls the rope taut. When the four Grandfathers are upright, they are pulled in, one at a time, until they lean against the east one. They are fastened together by throwing and wrapping the rope. The process continues for all 12 poles. Finally, a young man climbs the tipi frame both to tighten and check the lashing and to attach and secure the fabric cover.

5. Traditional foods eaten at this time include mesquite beans *(Prosopis glandulosa)*, Indian bananas, mescal *(Agave parryi* or *A. neomexicana)*, various wild berries and seeds, nuts, dried meat, and the flowers from Spanish bayonet *(Yucca elata)*. It is as though there were an intermission in the performance of the ritual drama. Yet eating is also a logical extension of it, since mothers, including White Painted Woman who the girls represent, not only give life, but sustain it as well.

6. That is, straight dance and fancy war dance categories for men, buckskin and cloth dress categories for women as well as a junior (9-15 years) division, a tiny tot (1-8 years) division, and a division for men and women over 50. Dance prizes range from a minimum of $20 to a maximum of $200 (1975 levels). The master-of-ceremonies as well as the head singer and his drum and chant group are usually invited from other areas—most often the Plains.

7. The elaborate headdress with its "horns," as the upright projections are sometimes called, gives rise to the English colloquial names for the Mountain God dancers: horn (var. horned) or crown dancers.

8. These dances are discussed in detail elsewhere (Farrer 1978).

9. According to Bernard Second, "The real stories are told in classical language and you have to stop and explain the language. The classical language is full of allusion so that each word stands for a series of related concepts and it needs strict interpretation. The classical language is the root words of my language. Even a girl who speaks good Apache . . . has to have it interpreted; that's what that woman [the Godmother] is there for: my job is to sing—*she* interprets and tells them what I'm singing."

10. These are five days of ritual time. And, since time and space are collapsed in ritual drama, time is both here/now and then/ago while the space in which the drama occurs is both of this and the other world. Thus, days can be, and often are, cancelled. If, for instance, it rains during the day and the Ceremonial grounds become a sea of mud, the evening's activities will be postponed until the next evening. Or, if the sun does not visibly rise, due to fog, rain, or overcast conditions, on one of the days when it must wash over the girls, that day will be cancelled. The Ceremony consists of four full days of ritual events regardless of the number of times the earth spins around. Since days are reckoned by sunrises, there can be no day unless the sun rises over East Mountain; at least, there is no ritual day. On occasion, due to rains, days have been cancelled when people return to their jobs in the midst of the Ceremonial; when the weather is right again, they go to the Ceremonial grounds once again to resume the ritual events.

11. In the old days the men would pay the women for the honor of dancing with them all night; payment was money, a shawl, a blanket, or even a horse. As one old man said, "It was the gentlemanly thing to do."

12. On this final day, however, the basket is placed by a woman rather than by a man, as on the first day.

13. It is worth noting that while the Apache directional system generates a circle, the Anglo-American system of north-south and east-west generates a grid.

14. This provides at least a partial understanding of the freedom accorded Mescalero Apache children. They are free to choose with whom they will live (usually a mother's sister if not mother herself), whether or not they will behave as is socially acceptable, and so on. They are at a time of life when they are expected to be responsible for their own behavior.

15. In the summer of 1977 a young woman, several years past initial menses, requested and had a full, but private, Ceremony. She felt that she was not behaving properly, a situation she attributed to her not believing in the Ceremonial when she was younger and having refused to participate in it. She felt that, having attained a measure of wisdom and having seen a bit of the world, her earlier judgment was incorrect. In order to put her life in balance and to allow her better self to emerge, she felt a Ceremony was in order.

16. In 1974 a Ceremony cost a minimum of $1500. This is a prodigious amount of money in an economy where most workers earn only slightly more than minimum wage.

17. For a detailed look at spatial, kinetic, verbal, and nonverbal manifestations of the messages sent in the Ceremony, see Farrer (1977).

REFERENCES

Basso, K. 1966. The gift of changing woman. *Bulletin* of the Bureau of American Ethnology, no. 196. Washington, D.C.: U.S. Government Printing Office.

―――. 1979. *Portraits of "The Whiteman": Linguistic play and cultural symbols among the western Apache.* New York: Cambridge University Press.

Bauman, R. 1976. The technical boundaries of performance. *Form in performance: Proceedings of a symposium on form in performance, hard-core ethnography.* M. Herndon and R. Brunyate, eds. Austin: University of Texas, Office of the College of Fine Arts.

Breuninger, E. P. 1959. Debut of Mescalero maidens. *Apache Scout,* June, pp. 2-4. Mescalero: Mescalero Apache Tribe.

Chappel, E. D. and Coon, C. S. 1942 *Principles of anthropology.* New York: Henry Holt.

Clark, L. H. 1976. The girl's puberty ceremony of the San Carlos Apaches. *Journal of Popular Culture* 10:431-38.

Farrer, C. R. 1976. Fieldwork ethics. *Folklore Forum,* Bibliographic and Special Series, vol. 9, no. 15:59-63.

―――. 1977. Play and inter-ethic communication: A practical ethnography of the Mescalero Apache. Ph.D. dissertation, University of Texas, Austin.

―――. 1978. Mescalero ritual dance: A four-part fugue. *Discovery* 1-13.

Goffman, E. 1974. *Frame analysis.* Cambridge: Harvard University Press.

Hall, E. T. 1977. *Beyond culture*. Garden City, NY: Anchor Press/Doubleday.

Hoijer, H. 1938. *Chiricahua and Mescalero Apache texts*. University of Chicago Publications in Anthropology, Linguistic Series, Chicago: University of Chicago Press.

Nicholas, D. 1939. Mescalero Apache girl's puberty ceremony. *El Palacio* 46:193-204.

Opler, M. E. 1942. Adolescence rite of the Jicarilla. *El Palacio* 49:25-38.

_____. 1946. *Childhood and youth in Jicarilla Apache society*. Publications of the Frederick Webb Hodge Anniversary Publication Fund, vol. 5. Los Angeles: Southwest Museum.

_____. 1965. *An Apache life-way*. New York: Cooper Square Publishers.

Schechner, R. 1977. *Essays on performance theory, 1970-1976*. New York: Drama Book Specialists, Publishers.

Singer, M. 1958. *The great tradition in a metropolital center; Madras. Journal of American Folklore* 71:347-88.

_____. 1972. *When a great tradition modernizes*. New York: Praeger Publishers.

Turner, V. 1967. *The forest of symbols*. Ithaca: Cornell University Press.

_____. 1969. *The ritual process*. Chicago: Aldine Publishing Co.

van Gennep, A. 1960. *The rites of passage*. Chicago: University of Chicago Press.

TURNINGS IN THE LIFE OF A VIETNAMESE BUDDHIST NUN[1]

James M. Freeman

Professor Freeman's biographical essay on the Ni Su, *a contemporary Buddhist nun, describes many aspects of her various initiations to the Buddhist community. Then follow her experiences, literally in passage as a boat person fleeing Vietnam and the Communists. Finding her new life in America marked the crossing of a great threshold of her most recent initiation. Compassion, knowledge and involvement are essential to her teaching.*

James M. Freeman, Ph. D., is Professor of Anthropology at San Jose State University in California. His book, Untouchable: An Indian Life History *(Stanford University Press, 1979) is a pioneer work. More recently, his research and service to people from Southeast Asia newly arrived in America have been recognized as providing a new significance to anthropology.*

INTRODUCING THE *Ni Su*[2]

IN the Spring of 1982, while conducting a life-histories project involving Indochinese refugees, I attended a ceremony at a Vietnamese Buddhist pagoda, located in a predominantly Hispanic neighborhood in a West Coast American city. The most striking memory I have of this ceremony was the presence there of a slight, youthful-looking woman with a shaven head who wore a plain brown robe—the *Ni su.* Only later would I learn that she was over fifty years old. She projected a commanding presence, at once both lively and dignified, personal yet distant. The *ni su* was a mother-figure for children, a counselor for troubled adults, a mentor for older women, a ritualist for those celebrating weddings or funerals, a spiritual master for those wishing to enter the monastic life, and a narrator for the anthropologist.

When we met, I told her of my project, and she said she would be happy to tell me about the Buddhist way and her own experiences as a *ni su* in Vietnam and America. Here is her story.

Becoming a *Ni Su*, 1932-1952

I was born in 1932 in a village of about 400 people located in Hadong Province, North Vietnam. My father was a farmer and a seller of oriental medicines. My mother took care of my father, my elder sister, and myself.

My earliest memory is that of going to our village pagoda with my parents. I remember that I felt so comfortable there; the pagoda attracted me, I cannot explain why. I now realize that I was predestined for the pagoda. When I was five years old, I told my parents that I wanted to go and live in the pagoda. This was an unusual request from one who was so young; but they did not resent or resist my going there. They figured that I was too young to know what I was doing, and that I'd soon get tired of it. I never returned home again.

When I was young, my daily tasks at the pagoda, which housed six *ni sus*, consisted of house chores such as sweeping and cleaning the house, watering the vegetables, and watching the water buffalo to keep it from eating the rice. At the evening service, I would listen to the *ni sus* reciting the Buddhist canon. In this way, when I was very young, I learned it by heart.

One day, when I was still very young, I came home from school and found that lunch was unappetizing. A *ni su* said to me, "I'll give you an additional dish; it's a very special one for the master."

I replied, "If I have the right to eat it, give it; if you are doing me a favor, don't." I didn't eat.

Three hours later, the *ni su* took away the food, saying, "You didn't want the food, so now go hungry." That night I went to bed without food.

That incident taught me a lesson that has stayed with me all my life. I had become angry at first because the *ni su* hadn't served the special dish, then resentful when she brought it as a favor. It was an insignificant event, yet I attached too much importance to it. I failed to keep an even outlook, and the result was that I suffered for it. What I learned from this was never to be angry, nor disappointed; I use that lesson to teach others.

In 1944, when I was twelve years old, I moved with my master to another pagoda during the Japanese invasion of North Vietnam. In those troubled days, my master taught me one important lesson. "If you can do something of benefit for others," she said, "try to do your best not only for yourself but for them. Don't be disappointed if you fail; don't be overjoyed if you are successful, for success or failure depends on many circumstances. You may succeed because you are lucky. If you fail, don't feel bad. The main thing is devotion. Failure or success is of no importance."

When I was ten years old, I received my religious name. My master conferred it on me when I participated in the first of three ceremonies that we call "Acceptance of Restraints" *(Tho Gioi* or *Gioi Dan)*. At the first or lowest level, we are received as novices *(Sa Di* for males, *Sa Di Ni* for females). In the ceremony, we commit ourselves to sacrifice things, to follow the rules, to study the Buddha-teachings and canon every day, to wear Buddhist dress, to hold no property, to eat no meat but only vegetables, and to devote our lives for the benefit of others, with an attitude of disinterest, or rather, without self-interest.

For the same reason, we don't eat meat. The Buddha-teaching is that of cause and effect. If we do harm to somebody, it causes harm to us; we are responsible for our own actions. If we eat meat, we have lost love for the animals. We should show love; the more we eat meat, the more we destroy our love.

So we are taught to consider the seat of love. Our expression is *"Tu bi."* *"Tu"* means to bring happiness to somebody (not yourself); while *"bi"* refers to the relief of suffering of somebody else. This is a Buddha-expression—the combination of both. If somebody drives me downtown, it makes me happy, since it saves me from walking, so that is *"tu bi"* for the person who offers it.

Before I went through this first-stage ceremony, I was given formal preparation. I had to learn a prayer that I recited when washing my hands, "I use water to wash my hands. I pray for everybody to have clean hands and to understand the Buddha-teachings." When I washed my face, I uttered a different prayer, and so on.

Then I was subjected to a review and tests, not formal tests as in school, but observations through our normal routine. I had to learn the Buddhist canon and rules, but in addition, the master watched my behavior, and tested me to see how I would react. Once, she left a certain amount of money nearby when I was sweeping the floor. She wanted to see if I would keep it or return it, indicating that I was not attracted to desire. She watched to see if I took fruit from the trees in front of the pagoda. Sometimes she would create an incident such as accusing me of making a mistake, and would observe my reaction. She also evaluated how I conversed with other people, in a normal way, or with flattery to make them happy.

When my master decided I was ready, she announced, "My disciple deserves to be raised to a higher rank. I am responsible for her." The first ceremony marked my official entrance into the Buddhist religious community.

At the age of twenty, I went through the second-stage *The Gioi* ceremony, which raised us to the level of Bhiku *(Ty Kheo)*. The superior monk delivered a sermon on the meaning of the ceremony as well as ten rules we had to observe. The description of each rule was ten words long, and consisted of prohibitions such as not to lie, steal, or participate in sexual activities. Then we made our vows.

After this ceremony, I was sent to a nun-training school in Hanoi. This was a more formal, detailed and advanced training than I had received before.

Each year, we also went into a period of retreat for three months. To hold a retreat, at least four nuns or monks agreed to attend. This was an even more intense period for religious activity, with an even stricter regimen than our ordinary routine. On the retreats, we slept only five and a half hours a night. Unlike our ordinary routine, we spent more time in study and prayer, less time in work.

From this training, I have learned that we are responsible for our own deeds; nobody can be responsible for our own deeds but ourselves. The Buddha cannot make up good or bad; he can advise or show us, but then it is our own choice. If a medical doctor gives you a prescription and you throw it away, how can the doctor cure the illness? The Buddha is like a guide; if he shows the way and you don't follow it, the fault is not his, but yours. He cannot make us good, but he can help us. He loves people equally, and gives all people the same opportunity to use, to apply his help. Then it is up to the person, female or male, to develop their Buddha-nature.

EDITOR'S NOTE: LIFE OF THE NI SU, 1952-1978[3]

In 1952, the *ni su* accompanied her master to Saigon. Later, she was sent to Germany for five years of social work training, after which she returned to Saigon and was made director of an orphanage there. When the Communists took over in 1975, they removed the *ni su*'s authority, dismantled the cottage industries, dispersed the children to the countryside, prohibited her from conducting services, intimidated worshippers who visited the pagoda, and held "people's court trials" in which several senior monks were denounced and jailed.

Because of the loss of religious and personal freedoms, the great increase in corruption, and the development of widespread distrust and fear, in which strangers, friends, and even relatives denounced one another, the *ni su* decided to escape from Vietnam. On her fourth attempt, she succeeded. Her story now continues:

BECOMING A REFUGEE, 1978-1979

We escaped at twilight on August 19, 1978, with perhaps 150-200 people in our small boat. We were so crowded that we were cramped. As we pulled away from the shore, I thought, "Destiny, I have no control over it; what will be will be."

Because we slept crowded on the boat for several days, we soon recognized who is good and who is bad. We could not move around the boat, but we could turn around in one place.

On the second day, the boat reached international waters; now we worried about not seeing any commercial boats that might pick us up. Since we had no nautical map or compass, we feared that we might be lost.

On the third day, the boat owner and captain told us that for the past day we had been going in the wrong direction, and he didn't know exactly where we were. Now we began to panic. People complained, "We're lost, the boat is lost!" Some people talked of the dreams they had had the night before. Particularly disturbing were the dreams about owls, and those in which one person got others to follow him. Both of these are signs of death. Night birds, especially the owl, are considered inauspicious and are greatly disliked by the Vietnamese people. If someone in a family is seriously ill, and at midnight an owl sings, the family says that the person will die. We have an expression, "Wicked and ugly like the owl" *(Du nhu cu)*.

We felt that our situation was hopeless, that we would die. The passengers blamed the boat owner, "He did not know anything. We trusted him and he is incapable, and now we are lost." Most of these complaints were from women, but the men also spoke harshly, "I told the captain what to do but he didn't listen, so look at us now."

Near the end of this day, a Thai fishing boat approached us. Through an interpreter, our captain explained that we had lost our way. He asked that we be allowed to board their boat. The Thais offered some oil-fuel, along with cigarettes and drinking water.

In the meantime, after our captain pleaded with them, the Thais let two-thirds of our people transfer to their boat. Now began a mad scramble; those who understood the offer rushed over without consideration of women or children. Families were divided. It was everybody for himself. I ended up in the Thai boat, where we could circulate freely. The Thais provided food.

After another two days and a night, the Thai captain told us that we were close to Malaysia. He told us to return to our boat, and he showed us the direction to the shore. Early the next morning, we arrived, but we were immediately stopped by a patrol boat. We found out that we were near Kuching, Borneo.

A Malaysian came by and gave us a message written by Vietnamese refugees in the nearby camp. It told us that the Malaysians would tow our boat out to sea and send us away unless we destroyed the boat. The owner's brother made a big hole in the boat. When the owner started the engine, water rushed in and the boat collapsed. People jumped into the water, which was only about four feet deep, and waded to shore.

The authorities took us to a stable for cows, and we remained there for four days. The Red Cross provided rice and cooking utensils. I felt humiliated because they put us in an abandoned stable along the river—a place for cows and animals.

One morning, we were taken to a large barge and sent down the river on a journey that lasted about an hour. When we arrived at our destination, we were both surprised and discouraged. We had expected something better. We had left a country in which we had lived in brick houses; now we were put in makeshift huts of palm tree leaves and bamboo. We slept on the floor, and in some cases in the open air.

We were desperate; we never imagined that we would live in such an unbelievable place, surrounded by barbed wire, prevented from leaving or entering by armed guards. Every four days they gave us rice, but it lasted us only three days.

We had to stay too long in one place with no exercise. Life was monotonous: we had nothing to do; we had the same food every day; we had no water for bathing, just for drinking, so we swam in the sea.

In these circumstances, I had to struggle to show my real personality. In the refugee camp, everybody had lost their former positions, and their constraints. The refugees said, "All people act alike. Everybody is the same. If you strip the uniform off a colonel and a private, they are the same." But I disagree. It depends on one's true personality. I am different in the quality of my person. I show care to people, all people. I do not run after power. Some people if hungry simply grab food. If you really care, even if you are hungry, you still look and give the food to a person weaker than you.

My experience has taught me a lesson that if someone is in need, we have to share with them. Times may change, but don't act nasty; be nice, be helpful to everyone in all cases. According to the Buddha, charity should be done according to the following principle: Ignore the giver, ignore the receiver, ignore the quality (value) of the gift. If you want to help me, just do it, but without attaching value to the gift.

If we help people in a natural way, it is easy for the giver and the receiver, but if you attach too much attention, tell what we did, that is destructiveness of the relationship. It harms both the giver and the receiver. When we help somebody, he may show appreciation, but we should not pay any attention, or we'll be disappointed if someone doesn't show appreciation.

Each day, we would hear an announcement of people who would leave the camp. One day, the Red Cross announced my name as one who had been accepted for the U.S.A. Perhaps if that had happened after only a couple of months in the camp, I would have been excited. But by the time it came, after I had been there for one year, I felt no excitement. I knew it would happen. I left the next day for a transit camp. After a few days for health screening, I boarded a plane for America. When I landed, I was met by the monk who sponsored me. He took me back to his pagoda, where I remained for nine months.

BECOMING AN AMERICAN, 1979-1984

In February, around the Vietnamese New Year, the Vietnamese of a midwestern city invited me to visit them. They had a pagoda, but no full-time religious person, so they were happy to have me there.

For the elders, life was unbearable because it is not the way life used to be. Here they just worked every day without "relaxation" *(thoai mai)*. "In our own country," they said, "when we return home from work, we have friends, neighbors, sentimentality, the family, the environment: we feel secure, we feel relaxed physically and emotionally. In Vietnam, you work, but you also can ask to take off a couple of days. If you do that in America, you will be fired. Here you have to work, have to eat, have to run; you must, you have no choice."

We Vietnamese have grown up and lived in a period of continuous war— 120 years—ever since the French came to our country. I, too, was uprooted and forced to move many times because of war. That's why I and many others never had long range plans. We lived day by day. One government after another rose and fell, with no continuity. Family life, too, was not consistent. First it was based on Buddhism, then on Confucianism; when the French arrived we turned to the French, then the Japanese. When the Americans came, we learned American ways.

Despite all of this, we have an absence of pressure in Vietnam that you do not have here. In America, we are never free of pressure, never free of worrying. There is permanant pressure here because you don't feel *thoai mai* or relaxation. That's why you cannot enjoy life.

The concept of *thoai mai* does not mean not doing anything at all. You may work very hard day and night, but you enjoy working, you have an enjoyment of life. So it means, "free of worry" or rather, we may still worry, but we feel relaxed. If someone tells you how to do something, makes you do it his way, then you do not feel *thoai mai,* but when you do a task freely, when it is not another person's assignment, then it is *thoai mai.* In that sense, the term means "comfortable," and that is what is lacking in America. People frequently say, "Living here is not comfortable" *(Song khong thoai mai)*.

Now you can understand why people have left Vietnam after the Communists took over. What exists there now is not Vietnamese; it is a Russian import. It is inconceivable that *thoai mai* could exist when people control your life day and night, when your neighbors watch you, and your children spy on you, when you are controlled by the rationing of your food, by restrictions on your travel, and by prohibitions on what you are allowed to say. If we had felt *thoai mai* in Vietnam, we would not have passed through death to come here.[4] We came to America not for material life but for freedom.

We have another important belief, that of suffering *(kho)*. The Buddhists believe that you suffer if you do not have a cause or purpose. But if you believe, as do the Buddhists, that "nothing is permanent," that you are born, grow up, and die, then you see nothing abnormal when someone in your family dies, so why suffer? If something wrong happens, again there is no need to suffer if you believe in the Buddha-teaching of causality. If a bad thing happens to me, I realize that maybe I did a sin in an earlier existence. If good comes my way, I am not overjoyed, because that may just be a reward for my earlier good behavior in another life. So to understand is not to be too happy or unhappy.

There is also no need to feel hopeless. If we suffer, we can correct the cause of that suffering. We can redeem ourselves; we have that chance, for we are solely responsible for our acts. Nobody can save us but ourselves. The Buddha is like a medical doctor who can show us the way but cannot save us if we choose not to take the medicine.

Here, too, when refugees arrive in America, they experience a lot of hardship. If they sit down and think about their past, they suffer, they worry, and it does them no good. They destroy themselves after two or three years. Regret destroys the self. If they temporarily forget—not forever—and look forward to the future, they will not feel so bad. For example, unemployment is universal, but it is temporary. If you are unemployed, spend less money, manage, survive, until you can find employment.

And yet, people make themselves available. They have the ability and willingness to help, so I call them. They feel comfortable, not obligation. If they cannot help, they say so, and maybe the next time they can help.

That's why this pagoda was founded. Three to four months after my trip to the midwestern city, a group of people, mostly women, requested that I establish a pagoda for them in their city. To show respect to the monk who had sponsored me, I told the people to ask him. He agreed to their request.

We have no regulations. Those who worship and wish to give donations do so. Those who wish to help in other ways do so. Everybody is treated the same. Those who come to worship are completely free; nobody asks anybody anything. We have no president or organization, no fighting between factions. Even for big or great events (ceremonies) we have no organization. People come, they help as they will, spontaneously.

In the Buddhist family activities, we teach a three-word motto: Compassion (to others) *(bi)*; knowledge (to determine needs) *(tri)*; and involvement (acting courageously based on knowledge) *(dung)*. If you have no compassion, you will not treat others well; without knowledge you are blind; but without involvement, your knowledge is useless. Knowledge without action is useless; you cannot just sit.

I want all people to help others, to bring a cup of water to a child who is sick, to share a piece of cake, to help with chores, always with this spirit. When they get into arguments, I try to resolve them by reminding the children of those three words. If they have jealousies, I explain that they lack involvement; if they have rancor, I point out that they lack knowledge. In this way, I show them that events of their everyday lives revolve around these three words, all of which are concerned with helping people, sharing.

At the Buddhist family, the children study Buddhist teaching, they play games, and they learn camping skills and handicrafts. At the end of the lunar year, we have a big event for the children. They give musical performances and receive prizes, while their parents prepare a feast. Rather than hire professional singers, I prefer to encourage the children to perform and to make their own costumes and props so that they develop confidence in themselves.

For the adults, however, we have the main altar where they can worship. On it we have many images that are designed to remind us of the Buddhist teachings. These include representations of the Sleeping Buddha who reaches Nirvana, and of the Goddess Quan The Am Bo Tat, who helps those in distress.

Many people come to the pagoda, where they remain for two to three hours. They have many things in their hearts. They talk to me and I speak to them about the Buddha teachings, to set their minds at rest. In a sense this is like counseling therapy, and it clarifies and helps them to deal with their problems, marital and economic, as well as those of loneliness.

Buddhists come here for help because they feel at home here. Everything looks like their home in Vietnam, the atmosphere, the furniture. Furthermore, things here are informal and not expensive, so they are not too removed from their own experience.

Many young adults, ages 20-25, have no family in this country. They are very lonely. Often they come by themselves to the pagoda. I cook for them. I provide some family for them, like a sister. If they need something and I have the possibility, I help them to show that somebody cares about them, pays attention to them.

I see that my people have problems, so I try to give them the time. Most of their problems involve their adjustment in this country. For example, a relative comes to live with a family, but the family does not know how to tell the relative to share costs. Not to tell is bad, but telling directly also is bad. Sometimes children don't want to go to school, or they want to get married, or they want to live separately from the family. Parents worry about this because they fear the children are not mature enough, but also because it involves extra costs. Some of the elderly people complain that they are made to baby-sit over weekends; they do not want to do this, but they do not know how to say no. This is made more difficult because the children never say to their parents that they are going out for fun, only that they need to go out.

The problem for the elderly is that they want to go to the pagoda but they depend totally on their children, who are reluctant to take them. So the elderly are unhappy. In Vietnam they were not dependent on their children; they used taxis, pedicabs, or rode with friends, but here that is impossible.

People are very insecure. In Vietnam, a person could depend on parents and relatives, and so not go hungry. Here if you do not do everything yourself, you go hungry. People also send much of their earnings back to Vietnam. Two days of American wages enables a family to live for three months in Vietnam. If one's brother is in a concentration camp and his wife and children are starving, how can a person not send them money? Previously in Vietnam, people didn't have those worries; a person could earn and easily support a family of ten. So the time in America is not enough.

Sometimes people talk to me about some injustice they have endured. I usually tell them to forget it, not pursue it, or they will simply become more personally involved, but nothing will come of it. Everything is unjust. Instead of using their time for more useful activities, they will be wasting it on a lost cause. Injustice is greater now than it used to be because now that society is modernized, injustice is much wider. Missiles can kill many more people than do spears.

A lot of people complain that they are suffering and that they do not want to live. In one month, for example, ten people told me that they were considering suicide, and three people attempted it. I try to convince people that life is precious, and that others suffer much more. Often the complaints are not really serious, for example, when an old lady said to me that she wants to die because her children didn't treat her as well as they did in Vietnam. She always quarrels with her children, whom she says are disrespectful with her and ungrateful. Now she sees that her grandchildren treat their parents in the same way, and she says, "See, the cause and the effect!"

Although old people like that are depressed, they are not the ones who attempt to take their lives; mostly it is younger men and women in their middle twenties and early thirties, people who have no family and who have felt lonely; they have had no one with whom to talk. In Vietnam, it was much easier; you mix with your countrymen. But here people feel isolated. They have no support. Life has no meaning. Whether they die today or later makes no difference to them. To prolong life is simply to prolong suffering.

In Vietnam, we have had some unhappy and frustrated people, but at least when they came home, they saw their parents and relatives, who made them forget all unhappiness, and also made them feel some responsibility to their family. In Vietnam, if a person commits suicide, he hurts his family a great deal. People say that the family is very unfortunate, that they must have committed a sin in the past, so now they are paying that debt. People who commit suicide or have mental health problems are viewed as people guilty of religious sins in the past, so now the family must pay the price. This is a great stigma to the family.

But in America, people do not have any connection, they do not hurt anybody, so they feel free to commit suicide.

Particularly when people are suffering, they often misunderstand the Buddhist view of events. They expect that an immediate cause will produce an immediate effect, so they wonder, "Why did I receive unfortunate results when I did good?" Because of this they say, "Buddhism is not truthful.

Nothing is permanent in this world; everything changes, so why follow Buddhism; we are better off enjoying life because it doesn't last long."

Such a view distorts Buddhism. For an orange seed to grow into a tree, you need many causes: soil, sun, rain. The effect may be different at different times. We have to pay attention to different circumstances. When we were boat people, our seat on the boat was considered a good place to sit; when we reached shore, we no longer found the boat seat comfortable. In the refugee camp, we used small sticks with which to eat our rice. They were very precious to us, as were empty cans. But when we arrived in the U.S.A., do we use those things? Life in the refugee camp was better than in Vietnam, but who is satisfied with the camp? We expected to go to another country and have a better life. So too, this life is a false and temporary life, not a true life. If we would like to elevate ourselves to a higher one, we still must depend on our false life, our body.

Buddhism aims at something higher, but people distort that by saying our goal is disinterest. Not so, for our goal is to go for something that is permanent. So if we live here, we cannot do simply nothing. We should do something. The next twenty, thirty or forty years, we act, then we die. If we do nothing, it's just a waste of our life. We should do something, try to help, sacrifice our time because we believe that we can help. If we use our time just to enjoy, that's a waste. If we see a person is hungry, we should give him cake to satisfy his hunger, but it is not good enough if we did not also teach him to avoid sins, not to steal, but to earn the food.

We try to elevate ourselves over and above all the normal passions: anger, selfishness, greed. If we let our emotions disturb us, we are never happy, never elevated. So according to Buddhism, we must ignore all those passions, get rid of all passion and desire.

The person who achieves this is happy, enlightened *(giai thoai)*. Such a person does not regret this world, is ready to enter another world. This person is very rare, for he is close to being a Buddha. Several years ago in Vietnam, I heard a story about an old man who prayed and recited the canon every day. One day, he told his family to prepare to bury him in a big vase, and to invite a Buddhist monk to recite the canon. The big vase was buried in a big hole in the garden. After the monk recited the canon, the old man got up out of bed, ran to the large vase, jumped in, and sat sat down. The family placed tea and paper over him to absorb his bodily fluids. He expired in the vase. He knew in advance that his time had come.

My master also knew in advance that she would die. She told her followers who had come to see her to return after one week to see her die. They did not believe her, did not take her statements literally. One week later, she asked to be cleaned for death. After hot water was boiled and herbs were thrown in to make a scent, she died.

PERMANENCE THROUGH CHANGE: INFLUENCE OF THE MASTERS

In earlier Buddhist periods, many people became enlightened, but in our present era, of one million persons, not even one will gain enlightenment. I am not discouraged to see others fail, but am discouraged about myself. If you say something flattering, I am happy; if you criticize, I am sad. I become discouraged when I cannot control my emotions. I try to convince myself like the Buddha had done thousands of years ago, that the body is just temporary, that nothing lasts, that nothing is durable, all is temporary. The more we realize that, the more we can neutralize every passion, not become angry, overjoyed, or jealous. It is like food: it's delicious, we appreciate it, but after two or three hours of digesting it, do we dare to touch it? Three hours earlier, we took very good care of it. If someone takes some of it, and we have one piece less, we feel bad. But three hours later, who wants it?

My ultimate will is to become a religious person, a *ni su* with all the meaning of a *ni su*. I certainly try to participate in every activity rather than just sitting in one place. I pray that I can have wisdom and clear sight to guide myself to the correct way, not influenced by the exterior.

We know that sometimes a person has good ideas, sometimes bad. Sometimes an illiterate person has better ideas than a learned person. My master emphasized that we should not think our ideas are better.

We treat everybody with the same standard, not too close and not too far. If you are too close one day and too far the next, that person will become jealous and will develop hatred. The next time, he is your enemy. That's why we try to develop equal distance between all.

My master taught us to help people as long as we live, that we live to help others, not to enjoy life, not to drink, not to enjoy all the things of the world *(choi bai)*. "Do something useful," she said. "Don't do things and let time pass."

In conclusion, don't depend, don't be emotionally attached to others. Do everything the right way; don't be capricious, but modest. I try to follow that, but sometimes it is difficult to control. Even if one tries, it is impossible. But you cannot wait until you are perfectly successful. I follow my master, who said, "Start to do something; don't wait until you have all the necessary means—just do it."

SIGNIFICANCE OF THE *NI SU*'S LIFE-STORY

In this paper, I selected the three life-turnings that seem to be the most significant in the *ni su*'s life story. All three have initiatory qualities of the sort that Victor Turner has described in his well-known writings on processual ritual.[5] But the three turnings also differ significantly in the degree of unpredictability of their expected outcomes.

(1) *Becoming a* Ni Su. The *ni su*'s position in Vietnamese society is an ambivalent one. Parents often object and try to dissuade a son or daughter who wishes to choose the monastic life, for it removes them from family ties and commitments. At the same time, Buddhist monks and nuns are given great respect for developing those very traits that enable them to disengage from ordinary society.

In many respects, the life story of the *ni su* highlights the opposition between religious and secular spheres in Vietnamese society. Ordinary or secular society is hierarchically organized; at school, children traditionally were taught that their first allegiance was to their emperor, second to their teachers, and third to their parents. Within the family, statuses are carefully defined with a wide variety of personal pronouns and euphemisms that connote respect. This form of organization is what Turner calls "structure."

By contrast, the Buddhist monastic life represents what Turner calls "anti-structure", or the liminal-like phase of the ritual process, a transitional phase in which people prepare themselves for their transformation to a new mode of being—achievement of enlightenment. A characteristic of such phases is that they are reversals of ordinary structure and life styles. Ordinary social identities are removed. A monk or nun is known, not by his or her family name, but by the religious names conferred upon them by their religious masters, and later by the names of the pagodas in which they temporarily reside. A novice is shorn of hair, given plain food and garments, and is taught to devalue personal attachments, but at the same time is enjoined to be compassionate, knowledgeable, and involved for the betterment of other people, all of whom should be treated equally. While all persons are considered equal in their capacity to develop their Buddha-natures, all persons have not developed these qualities equally. This explains the apparent contradiction that certain monks and nuns are conferred with higher titles and are treated with great respect, yet they frequently avoid these titles when referring to themselves. Unlike Western religions, Buddhist female religious specialists—the *ni su*s, have greater equality with their male counterparts, even though they defer to them. The *ni su*s are fully empowered to conduct ceremonies for laypersons on virtually equal terms with the monks *(tu sis)*.

Within the Monastic community, there are initiation ceremonies which mark the spiritual journey of monks and nuns as they remove themselves further from ordinary society. For novices, the ceremony is simple: they may be asked if they are willing to undergo hunger, cold, austerity, and the removal of emotional attachment. Upon vowing to accept these or other conditions, they are brought into the pagoda. The ceremonies that transform monks and nuns into full-fledged members of the monastic community are more complicated, and may involve a large public audience of witnesses. Many monks and nuns are subjected to an ordeal in which three pieces of burning incense are placed on their heads. The resultant scars are symbolic reminders of the three pillars of Buddhism: (1) the Buddha; (2) the teachings; and (3) the society of monks and nuns. The ability to withstand pain, to recite the canon as incense burns into their skulls, is seen as a demonstration of sense-control which ordinary persons are unable to achieve. Not all monks or nuns undergo this ordeal, for according to some masters, the significance of Buddhism is symbolized not by external marks but by internal character.

(2) *Becoming a Refugee*. The Communist take-over of South Vietnam in 1975, and the consequent suppression of religious and personal freedoms, prompted the *ni su* to flee the country. Under Communism, although her activities were curtailed, her identity remained unchallenged. As a Buddhist nun who could attract followers, she was feared as a potential source of dissent.

As a refugee, however, she found herself to be considered powerless and worthless. Her social role changed from respected teacher to displaced boat-person. On the sea voyage, other Vietnamese refugees ignored her and even denied her water. In the refugee camp, she was treated without respect until the refugees found out that she received money and had connections in America that might help them be resettled. Suddenly these same refugees became solicitous and respectful.

In Vietnam, the *ni su*'s image of herself was reinforced by prevailing cultural values and practices, and by the society of monks and nuns of which she was a part. While she faced uncertainty regarding her success in spiritual development, the general direction of her quest was clear. As a refugee, she and others faced serious threats to their identities; their status, their social importance in Vietnam, was denied by fellow refugees as well as by refugee-camp guards. Frequently she heard people say, "All people are equal here; everybody is out for himself." She rightly comments that this was the most trying time of her life, when uncertainty and the potential for disintegration was at its greatest. In many ways this was an initiatory experience with no clear direction for resolution. The *ni su*'s unwavering faith enabled her to weather these ordeals, which lasted nearly one year.

(3) *Becoming an American*. Social and family patterns that were maintained in Vietnam are rapidly changing in the new American environment. The *ni su*'s description of this provides insights into the terrible dilemmas faced by Vietnamese people attempting to adjust in America. So too, those who wish to perpetuate the religious life often encounter great obstacles. Some Vietnamese Buddhist monks, faced with problems of survival in America, have abandoned their monastic activities. Not so the *ni su*. Her adjustive solution to this newest, most unpredictable, and most complex turning has been to provide a haven of Vietnamese culture where lonely refugees can retreat to rekindle old memories, maintain cultural traditions, and feel comfortable for a while before returning to the pressures of American life. The services provided by the *ni su* are by no means

traditional; they are themselves adjustments to a strange new environment. The *ni su*'s activities reflect her remarkable flexibility in adjustments that does not diminish her steadfast identity and commitment to seek what she calls, "permanence, not the impermanence of this world."

NOTES

1. This project was funded by a Fellowship from the National Endowment for the Humanities, 1983-1984, and by an NEH Summer Stipend, 1982.

2. Vietnamese-language terms are in italics, but for simplicity, tone and vowel marks have been omitted. Place names in America and the personal names of living people have also been omitted. Vietnamese place names have been Anglicized. *"Ni su"* and "nun" are used interchangeably.

3. An expanded version of the *ni su*'s life story, including the years 1952-1978, are in my book, *Hearts of Sorrow: Vietnamese Biographies*, Stanford University Press.

4. Over one million refugees have fled from Vietnam. Of these, at least ten percent have perished on the journey. Some people have estimated that the losses were two to four times higher than that.

5. See Victor W. Turner. 1969. *The Ritual Process: Structure and Anti-Structure*. Chicago. Aldine Publishing Co.

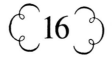

AN AFRICAN TALE

Helen M. Luke

Helen Luke's essay, "An African Tale," was originally a commencement address for the class of 1981, St. Mary's College, Notre Dame, Indiana. Retelling a Zulu tale told by Laurens van der Post, she derives from this symbolic story a modern parallel for young women entering adulthood. She advises her reader to follow the example of the young heroine in the story. Giving herself entirely over "to that which is greater than our egos, to the river of life itself," she licked her own psychic sores and healed herself with a woman's magic—"the compassionate heart." "Avoid being devoured by the demon of ambition," enjoins Luke, for it "kills the truly creative, masculine spirit in a woman . . . and all hope of equality of value in the world of men. . . . " She inspires the reader to be "obedient, not to convention or opinions or slogans, but to that voice from within that may be heard by us all at the crucial moments of life."

Born in England in 1904, Helen Luke, M.A., received a Masters degree in French and Italian literature from Oxford University. Twenty years later, she studied Jungian thought and analysis in Zurich and London, later establishing a counseling practice in Los Angeles. Since 1962, she has lived at Apple Farm Community near Three Rivers, Michigan, and has continued to counsel and to write. She is author of Woman: Earth and Spirit, the Inner Story, The Voice Within, *and an interpretation of Dante's* Divine Comedy, Dark Wood to White Rose.

A REAL *story* touches not only the mind, but also the imagination and the unconscious depths in a person, and it may remain with him or her through many years, coming to the surface of consciousness now and then to yield new insights. A great teacher of English at Swarthmore College, the late Harold Goddard, wrote in his book, *The Meaning of Shakespeare* (1965): "The destiny of the world is determined less by the battles that are lost and won than by the stories it loves and believes in." I heard the following story told a number of years ago by Laurens van der Post at a conference. He had heard it from a Zulu wise man in Africa, and he was retelling it as an offering of gratitude and respect to the women of the world. He has warmly approved my use of it.

All those stories that deal with basic human themes draw their power from the archetypal world that is common to people of all cultures and of all times, but the images in each culture will, of course, differ greatly, and it is for us to penetrate through these varying pictures to the universal wisdom that underlies them. I propose to tell the story first, simply, as it is told in its African context; and afterwards I will go through it again with a few indications as to how it may yield its wisdom in terms of our own lives. It is a story about young women on the threshold of their adult lives—and that is a rare thing to find. There is no hero in it at all—only one somewhat devastating male figure!

In an African village a group of young women had banded together to humiliate one of their number of whom they were jealous and whom they had rejected because she was "different," and especially because it seemed to them that she had a necklace of beads that was more beautiful than their necklaces.

These jealous young women ran down to the banks of the river and there they planned a trap for the envied one. When she joined them, they told her that they had all thrown their necklaces into the river as an offering to the river god. The young woman was a person of generous heart, so she at once took off her own necklace and threw it into the river; whereupon the others dug up their necklaces, which they had buried in the sand, and went off laughing and sneering.

The young woman, left alone, was very sad. She had been duped into a well-meant but foolish act, and she wandered along the riverbank, praying to the god to restore the necklace. There was no answer until at last she heard a voice, bidding her plunge into a deep pool nearby. She did not hesitate, for she knew it was the voice of the god. She plunged down into the unknown and found herself on the riverbed, where an old woman sat waiting. This old one was exceedingly ugly, even repulsive, for she was covered with open sores, and she spoke to the girl, saying, "Lick my sores!" At once the girl obeyed out of her compassionate heart, and licked the repulsive sores as she had been asked to do. Then the old woman said to her, "Because you have not held back and have licked my sores, I will hide and protect you when the demon comes who devours the flesh of young women." At that she heard a roar and a huge male monster came, calling out that he smelled a maiden there. But the old woman had hidden her away, and soon he went off cursing.

Then the old woman said to the girl, "Here is your necklace"—and she put around her neck beads of far greater beauty than any she had had before. "Go back now," the old woman said, "to your village, but when you have gone a few yards from the pool, you will see a stone in the path. Pick up this rock and throw it back into the pool. Then go on without looking back and take up your ordinary life in your village."

The young woman obeyed. She found the stone and threw it back and came to the village without a backward look. There the other girls quickly noticed her beautiful new necklace and clamored to know where she had found it—to which she replied that it had been given to her by the old woman at the bottom of the pool in the river. Not waiting for more, they all rushed off in a body and jumped into the pool. And the old woman said to each of them as she had said before, "Lick my sores!" But these girls all laughed at her and said they would not dream of doing anything so repulsive—and useless, too—and they demanded to be given the necklaces at once. In the midst of all this there came the roar of the giant demon, who seized upon those girls, one after the other, and made a mighty meal of them. And with that the story comes to an end.

I shall now look briefly at the images in the story as symbols of certain attitudes, conscious or unconscious, that are alive in each of us and influence us in often unrealized and subtle ways. Stories like this are not manufactured by the intellect; they are the symbolic dreams of humanity.

In Africa, the necklace is a highly prized symbol of a woman's identity and worth as a person. The group of girls in the story play a particularly unkind trick since it concerns devotion to a divine, transpersonal value. It is the product of group mentality, mass thinking, which so often covers and excuses hatred and cruelty. This is perhaps the worst menace in our society, requiring great effort and integrity to resist.

Notice the ease with which the simple girl falls into the trap. This is surely a warning of the dangers that lie in wait for the generous-hearted, who are so quickly induced by the slogans of some cause or crusade, fine in itself perhaps, and sponsored by people we long to please. We lose sight of our individual responsibility to reflect and to *choose,* and thus, as it were, we throw away our identity. Nevertheless, the story goes on to show us that such naive enthusiasms, *if* they truly involve the intention of a personal sacrifice to that which is greater than our egos, to the river of life itself, may indeed bring about the shock that leads us out of group thinking to the discovery of our meaning as individuals on a much deeper level.

The young woman in the story had a rude awakening from her identification with her peers. We may notice that she did not waste energy on resentment or remorse. She stayed alone beside the river of life, praying that she might rediscover her value as a person, waiting for an inner voice to bring her wisdom. And it came. She was to look for her necklace down under the water. Only by going *down,* not by striving upwards, would she find herself. She must plunge into the river of life *unconditionally,* risking mistakes or failure, not just throwing things, however valuable, into the river. Only by trusting herself to the unknown, both in her outer life and in her own hidden depths, would she find her unique way.

This young woman was now obedient, not to convention or opinions or slogans, but to that voice from within that may be heard by us all at the crucial moments of life, if we will truly listen.

She plunged down into the pool and there she found—not a radiant woman, symbolizing her potential beauty and power, but an old, ugly, repulsive thing with open sores. How shall we read this image for ourselves? When we enter with open eyes into the river of life, we find ourselves face to face with the ugliness, the suffering from which we have hitherto been protected in many different ways. And it is now that the story yields to us its specifically *feminine* wisdom.

We may take this image of the old woman on two levels. She may stand for the suffering that contempt for the feminine values has brought to all women through the ages—a contempt of which not only many men have been guilty, but also large numbers of women themselves, especially in our time. And secondly, the old woman is an image on the personal level of the most despised and repellent things in our own psyches that we refuse to acknowledge and from which we turn often in disgust.

The old woman's invitation is clear. "You can't bring help to me by any kind of technical, scientific, impersonal and collective panacea, or by *talk about* justice and freedom. Only with your own saliva can you bring healing to these sores in yourself and in the world." Saliva is symbolically a healing water that we are all born with. The licking of an animal is its means of healing wounds, and we may remember Christ's saliva on the blind man's eyes. So the girl is asked to give of her own unique essence—to bring healing to the sores, not by words out of her mouth, but by water from her mouth. Because she is on the threshold of true womanhood the girl at once responds out of that essential core of the feminine being—the compassionate heart. Here I would emphasize that true compassion bears *no* resemblance to a vague and sentimental pity. Compassion is not just an emotion; it is an austere thing and a highly differentiated quality of soul.

And now comes that universal threat—the demon of inferior masculinity that can so easily devour our womanhood. When this happens, we simply lose ourselves in an imitation of men, which kills the truly creative masculine spirit in a woman, and, however outwardly successful she may be, all hope of equality of *value* in the world of men disappears.

Had there been a male "hero" present, we might imagine the old woman telling him to take up his sword and fight the monster of greed and aggression. But to every woman she will always say, "Because of your compassion you will be freed from him."

So it came about that the devouring ambition and greed had no power over the woman who had the courage and humility to lick the repellent sores. It is at this moment that she receives her own individual and unique necklace—she does not just recover the old one that had come from her family before her initiation into life. This necklace is hers and hers alone.

It is time to return to her life in the world, to the daily, ordinary tasks and relationships. In her case, marriage and children awaited her and the building of a home; in our time and place, a career most probably awaits her, with or without the ancient way of woman in the home. But whether or not she marries or bears children, this ancient responsibility of woman remains. She is the guardian of the values of feeling in her environment, and if she remains aware of that compassion, that quiet, hidden nurturing that is the center of her feminine nature, then her skills in any kind of work whatsoever will grow in the manner of trees, well-rooted and strong, and her creative spirit will be free. The woman who has received the necklace from the old woman in the pool does not seek compulsively to achieve success after success, collecting necklace after necklace, so to speak. Always she will remember to "lick the sores" and to remain still and hidden when the demon of greedy ambition threatens, whether at home or in the public arena.

Now as to the stone that the girl was to find and throw back, I will give you one hint and leave you to work it out. The stone in all cultures is the symbol of the immortal self, and this is the true offering to the divinity in the river. Do not pick it up and put it in your pocket!

The last bit of the story speaks for itself. All those greedy girls who did not bother to reflect on the meaning of life went rushing off in a mob, all wanting more and better necklaces, which in our day would be more and more demands for wealth, or success, or men, or publicity, or security, or even for spiritual experiences. They refused with contempt the essential task of a woman, the compassionate "licking of the sores" in themselves and in their immediate environment. They were therefore devoured by the demon that rages around, assimilating such women to itself.

Charles Williams, the English poet and novelist who died in 1946, once defined the art of living as the ability "to live the ordinary in an extraordinary way and to live the extraordinary in an ordinary way." The story illuminates this beautiful saying. Dame Janet Baker, a great singer and a great woman, said recently in an interview, "I've found that the ordinary things are the important things. . . . We all—in life and music—have our backs up against the wall trying to preserve order and quality. . . . My gift is God-given and it must be given back. We all have a gift to give, and if you give it with a sense of holy obligation everything clicks into place."

Each of us, as we journey through life, has the opportunity to find and to give his or her unique gift. Whether that gift is great or small in the eyes of the world does not matter at all—not at all. It is through the finding and the giving that we may come to know the joy that lies at the center of both the dark times and the light.

This essay was originally published in the *Courier* (Summer, 1981), the alumnae quarterly of St. Mary's College, Notre Dame, Indiana. Reprinted from Helen Luke's *The Inner Story: Myth and Symbol in the Bible and Literature* (New York: Crossroads, 1982), with the author's permission.

PERSONAL
INITIATION

PART FIVE

17

PSYCHOTHERAPY, INITIATION AND THE MIDLIFE TRANSITION

Jan O. Stein and Murray Stein

In their recent research, Jan and Murray Stein have found that the psychological patterns of midlife transition and turmoil fall into three phases corresponding to the three phases of the social *process of initiation as described by Arnold van Gennep in his classic* Rites of Passage *(1960) and later by Victor Turner. The Steins indicate the steps that need to be taken to work through the psychological issues of the liminal or threshold phase at midlife which can lead to new purpose, direction and creativity. With the "reconstitution of the pattern of self-organization," an individual can develop ways of holding on to his/her new insights and direction. In other words, this process can protect and shelter new consciousness and lead to a new way of being, as an umbrella protects and shelters from the storm.*

Jan Stein, Ph.D., is a psychotherapist in private practice in Wilmette, Illinois. She is the author of a full length study of the mid-life transition. Murray Stein, Ph.D., is a member of the Chicago Jung Institute, editor of Jungian Analysis *(1982) and also editor of a series of books of Chiron Publications. He is the author of* In Mid-Life *(1983) and* Jung's Treatment of Christianity *(1985). He is a Jungian analyst in private practice in Wilmette, Illinois.*

> . . . I prefer to regard transition as a process, a becoming, and in the case of *rites de passage* even a transformation.
>
> —Victor Turner

"I noticed one day that I just felt I had a lump in my throat, and I felt out of contact with everyone and with myself. . . . It was as though I was standing in front of a blank wall . . . very much alone, totally alone, and nobody would understand how I felt." The speaker is Pat, forty-eight years old, a married woman with four children, reporting on her midlife crisis. "My external world was filled with accomplishments . . . and I tried to carry that [attitude] into marriage. We did appear as a very accomplished couple, but our internal world of relationships in the family was not what we wanted people to think it was."

Cecelia, another witness to midlife transitional turmoil, is now fifty years old. Twice divorced, she is the mother of three children. "It occurred to me that the house was going to hell," she says, referring to the beginning of midlife. "I had no energy whatever for that daily round, and no pleasure in it. From the outside, this is like the beginning of a depression, not caring about keeping things up . . . sitting and staring and wondering. . . . It felt like a question of life and death, really . . . I had no suicidal inclination, but I read . . . in those existentialists . . . Sartre saying, 'You can choose not to be.' Whatever his intent was in that passage, it just leaped off the page and I realized I wasn't about to do that."

Jack, now fifty-six years old, says of his midlife experience, "My whole world was collapsing . . . the whole map of the city was gone."

Sue, now thirty-eight years old, married, with two children, reports another feature of midlife crisis: "Maybe it was the need to be a sexual being again. It was the need to be . . . well, suddenly people were talking about how pretty I was, and I felt it was bringing out all kinds of things in me."

"I remember a dream of going down the stairs. My husband was upstairs. There was a sound and a golden glow that woke me early in the morning and I started going down these stairs. And there was this incredible force coming from this box and pulling me. And yet I couldn't move. My husband was sleeping, and I didn't know what I wanted to do. I woke up screaming. I felt so stuck . . . like in a bed of quicksand . . . like if I moved I would go down."

These statements are contained in a piece of recent research on adult development and midlife transition (Stein 1981). The last twenty years have seen a burgeoning of interest in these areas, and what had been more or less *terra incognita* to academic researchers before 1960 has now been mapped out in detail. Major explorers have been such well-known figures as Neugarten, Guttman, Gould and Levinson; more recently a host of other researchers have given this period in the life span a great deal of added definition.

One of the major results of this interest and research is that midlife is not what we had thought it was. What had been assumed by many psychological theorists and earlier researchers in human development, and certainly by the average man on the street, to be a relatively stable, even boring, period of the human life span ("middle age") is turning out to have a very different appearance. This body of recent research is revealing psychological life during the middle years to be full of major conflict and crisis.

From the staid picture of a blanket concept, "middle age," a much more complex view is coming into focus, a view that includes a tumultuous period of psychological reorganization known as the "midlife transition." This radical reversal of views may be only temporary, a somewhat excessive corrective of earlier misundertanding, but it seems quite certain that the assumptions about the nature of the midlife period will be permanently altered in many significant ways as the result of this accumulating body of evidence.

This paper follows this new view of midlife. Midlife as we see it is a period of upheaval and deep-going personality change. We rest our case on what we believe has not been seen before, namely a quite clearly organized transitional period made up of three phases.

We will begin with a brief summary of some recent findings in the area of life span research and of some observations about the structure of this transition period. Unlike some current research, our approach and interests are primarily psychological and focus on what happens intrapsychically (and to some extent interpersonally) during the midlife transition. We are interested especially in the *developmental meaning* of what takes place during this period of an individual's life.

Our main argument, in a nutshell, is as follows. Midlife is a transitional period within the life span as a whole. This transition can be regarded as homologous to transitions that the initiation rituals of so-called primitive peoples are designed to facilitate. The psychological purpose of this transition seems to be the transformation of consciousness, and, while modern society seems to lack a suitable ritual process for going through this transition period, psychotherapy is increasingly performing this function.

A few words of clarification, first, about some of the technical psychological terms used in this paper. In most cases the meaning of these terms is indicated in the text itself, but for readers unfamiliar with Jungian theory this may assume too much. So we will define several key terms more carefully here.

What we mean by a "dominant pattern of self-organization" is especially crucial. This phrase may be puzzling even to readers who are knowledgeable in Jungian thought, since it depends on a distinction between *Self* (capital "S") and *self* (lower case) that to us seems useful but does depart from classic Jungian usage.

We use the term *Self*, capitalized, to refer to the personality as a whole, conscious and unconscious aspects. Structurally, we understand the Self to be psychic totality and the container of the psyche's personal and non-personal contents. Dynamically, the Self governs, balances, and orders the whole personality and is responsible for its internal development, as well as for its instinctive adaptations to the surrounding world. (The terms *psyche, personality,* and *Self* have different nuances but in this paper can be considered interchangeable equivalents.)

Spelled with a small "s," the term *self* refers to a content within ego-consciousness. This is experienced as conscious selfhood, and the sense of it helps to shape the ego's decision and choices, its libido expenditures. The self is the "me" of consciousness. The ego, also a content of consciousness, is the "I": the center of conscious awareness and the source of a person's feeling of free will and intentionality. Together, the self ("me") and the ego ("I") are responsible for shaping and channeling the psychic energy that is available to consciousness. Both, too, are partial reflections of the Self: the ego reflecting its dynamic agency and its centering function; the self reflecting its containment and inclusion of contents.

The *pattern of self-organization* refers to an underlying structure of the self. This pattern is the psychological element that gives form to the contents of the self. This, in turn, is backed up by a deeper psychological structure called a *dominant*.

The term *dominant* refers to the archetypal basis of the patterns that structure the contents of ego-consciousness. The patterns that shape the contents of ego-consciousness, which in turn make up a person's character, typical emotional reactions, and sense of identity, are grounded in non-personal archetypal structures of the psyche.

The *archetypes*, following Jung's definition, are the basic building blocks of the human mind, its fundamental structural and dynamic forms. The archetypes are non-personal and innate to the human organism: they are inborn potential patterns of psychological functioning, i.e., of perception, of behavior, and of conscious attitude. Specific archetypes are constellated, or activated, both by innate development triggers and by cues and stimuli from the external environment.

The *dominant pattern of self-organization,* then, refers to the basic, archetypally derived form that shapes the self.

THE MIDLIFE TRANSITION AND INITIATION RITUALS

What some psychological thinkers have put forward intuitively and tentatively during the past seventy years, more recent investigators seems to have pretty well established: midlife is a transition period and is characterized by transitional phenomena. Assuming a normal life span of seventy to eighty years, the period between the ages of thirty-five and forty-five constitutes the middle. Midlife is a turning point from the first to the second half of life (Jung 1969, paras. 759ff.), and this shift creates profound effects in the psychological life of the individual.

In his study of generative psychologists such as Freud and Jung, Ellenberger refers to the experience of this transition period as a "creative illness." More recent empirical research, such as that of Levinson and a significant number of other social science investigators (cf. Cytrynbaum, Danielson, Gould, Guttman, Jackson, Jaques, Katz, Larsen, Livson, Merriam, Murphy, Neugarten, Rosenberg, Schoech, and Stein), has tended to establish the view that the years of the midlife period are psychologically turbulent in the lives of many people, not only of exceptionally creative ones. From these studies it is hard to avoid the conclusion that midlife is a major transition point in the life of normal individuals and that psychological turbulence and discontinuity during this period are not necessarily signs of psychopathology or serious psychic imbalance. "Creative illness" may therefore be somewhat misleading, insofar as it implies a psychopathological viewpoint. Transitional phenomena are to be expected at midlife as we expect them in other transition periods such as adolescence.

Granting, then, that midlife is a transition period within the life span of normal individuals, we want to link this up with the fact that in primitive and traditional societies transition periods are facilitated and marked by rites of passage. These are initiation rituals, and they function to move individuals through transition periods in their lives and to make these transitions actually transformative (Turner 1967, p. 94). They also give these transitions personal, social, and cultural significance. Transitions from childhood into adolescence, from adolescence into early adulthood, from single to married status, from non-parenthood to parenthood, from one level to another in the religious hierarchy of a people, from this life to the life beyond (or from life to death), and others are facilitated and marked by rites of passage.

We can learn a great deal about psychological transitions from observing these initiation rituals. Van Gennep found that *rites de passage,* as he named them, fall into three categories: rites of separation, rites of liminality, and rites of reincorporation. These, in turn, are linked to three phases of the transition process. In the first phase, initiants are ritually separated from the social group that had until then defined their roles and cultural identity, and they are removed to a special, and usually secluded, place. This inaugurates the second phase of initiation and its rituals. It is in the liminal phase that the most significant cultic and religious rites are practiced; here transformation is effected, as the internal structures of a person's former identity are dissolved and new structures are constellated. When this phase is complete there are rites of re-entry into society; the initiant is now reincorporated into the group, but as a "new person."

Victor Turner has taken up van Gennep's analysis and has added considerable detail to it, particularly to the phase of liminality. This phase is of particular interest to us because of its rich psychological content and the many parallels we find in it to the experience of the midlife transition and *its* liminality. Turner speaks of liminality as existence "betwixt-and-between" firm identities, and he delineates its qualities and contents as follows:

> The subject of passage ritual is, in the liminal period, structurally, if not physically, "invisible". . . .
> The symbolism attached to and surrounding the liminal *persona* is complex and bizarre. Much of it is modeled on human biological processes. . . . They give an outward and visible form to an inward and conceptual process. . . . the symbols

that represent them are, in many societies, drawn from the biology of death, decomposition, catabolism, and other physical processes that have a negative tinge, such as menstruation (frequently regarded as the absence or loss of a fetus). . . . The neophyte may be buried, forced to lie motionless in the posture and direction of customary burial, may be stained black, or may be forced to live for a while in the company of masked and monstrous mummers representing, *inter alia,* the dead, or worse still, the un-dead. The metaphor of dissolution is often applied to neophytes; they are allowed to go filthy and identified with the earth, the generalized matter into which every specific individual is rendered down. . . .

The other aspect, that they are not yet classified, is often expressed in symbols modeled on processes of gestation and parturition. The neophytes are likened to or treated as embryos, newborn infants, or sucklings by symbolic means which vary from culture to culture. . . .

The essential feature of these symbolizations is that the neophytes are neither living nor dead from one aspect, and both living and dead from another. Their condition is one of ambiguity and paradox, a confusion of all the customary categories. Liminality may perhaps be regarded as the Nay to all positive structural assertions, but also in some sense the source of them all, and, more than that, as a realm of pure possibility whence novel configurations of ideas and relations may arise. . . . We have no way of knowing whether primitive initiations merely conserved lore. Perhaps they also generated new thought and new custom.

. . . . We are not dealing with structural contradictions when we discuss liminality, but with the essentially unstructured (which is at once destructured and prestructured) and often the people themselves see this in terms of bringing neophytes into close connection with deity or with superhuman power, with what is, in fact, often regarded as the unbounded, the infinite, the limitless. . . .

A further structurally negative characteristic of transitional being is that they *have* nothing. They have no status, property, insignias, secular clothing, rank, kinship position, nothing to demarcate them structurally from their fellows. Their condition is indeed the very prototype of sacred poverty. . . . Undoing, dissolution, decomposition are accompanied by processes of growth, transformation, and the reformulation of old elements in new patterns.

(1967, pp. 95-99)

This anthropological description of liminality is useful for looking at what many modern people experience in the midst of the midlife transition. Spontaneous images appear of loss, death, and decomposition; fantasies of nakedness, anomie, and dying emerge; dreams of rebirth and renewal are common. These are characteristic phenomena in the experience of liminality at midlife.

The correspondences between what van Gennep and Turner describe as the structure and the contents of primitive initiation rituals and what empirical investigation has uncovered regarding contemporary midlife transitions are striking and suggest a common archetypal base. Some research (cf. Stein 1981) indicates that the midlife transition falls into three phases corresponding to the three stages of rites of passage, and that the phenomena characteristic of these phases correspond to the phenomena of the matching phases of initiation ritual. Hence the names we have chosen to use for these phases of the midlife transition are almost identical to van Gennep's terms: separation, liminality, and reintegration or reconstitution of a dominant pattern of self-organization. Since we are looking at the midlife transition as a psychological phenomenon rather than as a sociological or cultural one, the third term is different from van Gennep's more sociologically oriented "reincorporation." The contents and structures that interest us are psychological and the changes we look for are transformations of consciousness, but these are clearly mirrored in the external actions of primitive rites of passage.

To analyze and discuss the psychological contents and dynamics of the three phases of midlife transition we draw on Jungian theory.

The separation phase of the transition is chiefly characterized by a rampant process of psychological destructuring. This phase is dominated by the ego's separation from a psychological structure called the *persona,* a pattern of psycho-social identity and organization that was formed during adolescence and early adulthood.

The earlier pattern of self-organization itself also dissolves. Commonly this has been oriented largely by and toward the expectations and demands of family and society: it is directed by an individual's willingness to agree with others as to who one is and what one is like. Under the force of this dynamic, a person claims certain traits, impulses, personality characteristics, values, and qualities as "self," and disclaims others as "not-self." The "self contents" then fall into the frame of *persona,* and the "not-self contents" go into the *shadow.* When the ego identifies with these "self contents," it creates a state of psychological one-sidedness and imbalance, which is supported by primitive defensive mechanisms such as projection. When this pattern of self-organization dissolves, these neat distinctions come apart, and persons are left wondering who they are and what they are like.

This internal structuring, then, is transformed at midlife. The phase of separation sees a decrease in this pattern's power to organize the sense of identity and to channel libido into behavior. It is less and less able to shape psychological life.

The emotional and mental phenomena that signal the onset and continuing presence of this phase are various: strong and persistent feelings of boredom; disillusionment with life; the fading away of youth's "dreams"; bouts of depression filled with nostalgia and regret; a quickened sense of life's fragility and limited duration; new and unpredictable behavior. This state of affairs indicates the dissolution of the internal structures that had formerly held in place specific ambitions, duties, and interests, as well as commitment to specific self-images and to other persons. Loss of interest in a career, in a marriage partner, in family life, and in friends is typical. Feelings of defeat, of low self-esteem, of grief, and a deep sense of loss are inherent characteristics of the separation phase: since earlier images of selfhood and identity are being abandoned, an earlier self is now experienced as a "lost self," and no new contents have yet entered permanently to fill this void.

Fluctuations of mood and oscillations between inflated and depressed affective states also characterize this phase, and these swings seem to result from a combination of several intrapsychic dynamics: the ego is being separated from former identifications on the one hand, and this produces the feelings of emptiness and loss, the "downs"; but it is being fleetingly attached to newly emergent or formerly rejected aspects of the personality on the other hand, and this produces ego-inflations, the "ups." This complex combination of dynamics accounts for the mood swings and unpredictable behavior that are so often noticed by intimates of persons who are in the midlife transition.

As persons separate from the *persona* in this first phase of the midlife transition, they gradually enter a period that corresponds in feeling and tone and image to what van Gennep and Turner describe as liminality. Here the former sense of identity is further ground down and dissolved. Persons feel alienated from the social institutions in their environment. They find themselves, too, "betwixt and between" firm inner structures. They tend to "float" from one thing to another, and to feel invisible and insubstantial. They could as well be counted among the dead, so ghostlike is this existence.

The mood of midlife liminality is frequently expressed by adjectives like "lost" and "confused" and by images like "wandering alone in the desert," "lost in a city without a map," and "flatness, two-dimensionality." The mind is homeless, and persons feel themselves drifting in perilous waters.

Meanwhile the unconscious, which is highly active during this phase, produces dream images and symbols of great vividness and power. The psychic contents that typically appear in dreams, in fantasies, and in projections during this phase are: the *shadow*, a figure that sums up all of the rejected and repressed aspects of a personality, the discards of character formation (the "ghosts" of the past); the *anima* or *animus*, contrasexual figures who embody the opposite sex components of the personality and have the potency and authority of gods and goddesses; and the Self, often symbolized abstractly and representing a union of opposites within the personality (a mandala, a quaternity, a World Soul). The contents represented by these figures and symbols do not necessarily arise from the unconscious in this precise sequence, but this order does indicate the increasing "depths" of the personality from which these contents derive.

Dreams during this phase are quite often "numinous," as Jung terms this effect: that is, they inspire awe and leave a deep impression on the dreamer; they have a religious, symbolic, or mythic quality; they are impersonal and not easy to relate to everyday life. Liminality, as Turner points out, takes place in seclusion, out of the structures of ordinary life. In liminality a person is incubating the future, and these dreams are representations of the psychic structures and contents that will eventually coalesce to form a new foundation for the conscious personality. But during this phase they are still latent, deeply unconscious, and in flux.

To us, liminality seems to be the heart of the midlife transition and the key to understanding its nature and psychological function. Typically it lasts from eighteen months to two years, but it can continue longer, up to four years, according to our findings (cf. Stein 1981). What transpires psychologically during this period of flux and internal reorganization makes possible the structures of consciousness that will emerge at the end of the transition. Because the unconscious appears so vividly during this period and so forcefully engages a person's attention, it is legitimate to speak of midlife liminality as potentially transformative within the overall psychological development of an individual's consciousness. In the midst of the emotional flux and turmoil of midlife liminality, persons struggle with fundamental splits and dynamics of their personality and undergo internal structural changes that will affect their attitudes and emotional reactions permanently. The net result will be a transformation of consciousness.

As the phase of liminality comes to a close and a person begins moving into the final phase of the midlife transition, a number of psychological features stand out and give this interim period a distinctive character of its own. Persons report a gradually growing solid feeling of who they are and what they want to do, replacing their sense of loss over who they can no longer be. And what had been more or less aimless wandering during the liminal phase becomes more purposeful exploration of new possibilities for the future. This solidification of purpose and direction is accompanied by a conscious acceptance of formerly projected contents and aspects of the personality (shadow, anima/animus, and Self). What had appeared to be new or "foreign" during the separation phase, and had been struggled with during the phase of liminality, is now brought into the center of self-awareness and becomes a more explicit and integrated part of one's self.

The third phase of the midlife transition, which we call "reconstitution of the pattern of self-organization," continues what was begun toward the end of the phase of liminality and sees it to completion. This last phase witnesses a gradual firming up of a new dominant pattern of self-organization that is made up of an amalgam of former contents and images (the "psychological past") and new contents that appeared from the unconscious during liminality. These are structured by an underlying archetype (the "dominant") that was constellated during liminality. An individual's sense of identity will be shaped by, and will reflect, this new dominant. Characteristically this dominant is more Self-oriented and less other-oriented than was the earlier dominant that formed the underlying structure of the *persona*. The newly formed pattern of self-organization will demonstrate the degree to which the personality is integrated and now includes the repressed and denied aspects of the personality as well as the other unconscious psychological elements that appeared in the earlier two phases of the transition.

As this third stage develops, individuals gain a sense that conscious identity (the self) is now a more authentic and accurate reflection of the whole personality (the Self) than it had been before: they feel that their lives now express "fuller selfhood" than they did before the midlife transition began. People who report significant psychological transformation during the midlife transition emerge from this period with a sense of individuality and psychological complexity far exceeding what they had experienced or demonstrated before. They are better able to contain the opposites within consciousness and are less prone to psychological splitting and projecting. This gives them an increased sense of self-knowledge and a degree of healthy self-suspicion: they recognize that wholeness implies imperfection, and that no-one, no matter at what level of spiritual or psychological development, can ever leave behind human weakness, brokenness, and blindness. The shadow remains, but it is more conscious and held more accountable.

In retrospect these persons do not generally feel that they were in control of the psychological processes that transpired during the midlife transition period. While the ego may have more or less successfully coped with the process, and more or less completely come to terms with the results of it, it was clearly not a causative or controlling agent. The awareness of this fact gives these people a sense of the ego's relativity in relation to the psyche as a whole.

PSYCHOTHERAPY AS A MODERN INITIATION RITUAL FOR THE MIDLIFE TRANSITION

"Midlife crisis" is frequently seen as an unfortunate interruption in an otherwise rather static and dependable life pattern, just as adolescence must have been seen before the nature of identity formation during that period was widely understood. Until recently the psychological function and meaning of the midlife transition was opaque to contemporary social and cultural vision. If anything it was attributed to menopause or to other physical changes occurring during this time, but otherwise it remained irrational and therefore frightening. Even today a person who is going through this period of flux and internal change is held up to ridicule, an obviously apotropaic gesture on the part of the ridiculers, who are hoping to avoid this same disruption in their lives. The failure to value the phenomena of midlife transition results from psychological ignorance, but also from the absence of cultural authentication of midlife's transitional nature and meaning. With respect to adolescents and young adults we now generally accept the idea that an extended moratorium period is often an essential phase of their psychological development. But do we have the same tolerance and understanding for persons at midlife who are going through *their* identity crises and internal transformations?

If midlife is a transition to a new stage of psychological life and to a new dominant pattern of self-organization, and if this transition can be analyzed into structural and dynamic elements that parallel primitive initiation patterns, we are left with the question of whether there is anything comparable in contemporary culture to primitive "rites of passage," which function to facilitate, to honor, and to mark major life transitions. While it is clear that there is nothing in modern culture that *officially* performs this function, there does seem to be at least one "unofficial" culturally accepted framework within which this transformational process can be undergone, and that is psychotherapy.

Psychotherapy functions, or can function, to mark and to facilitate the midlife transition for persons living in modern societies. In this respect, psychotherapy is a modern version of an initiation ritual. In therapy the phenomena of transition are both understood and tolerated. But more than that, they are highly valued because they are seen as essential for a person's psychological development. Increasingly in our culture, people enter psychotherapy when the signs of midlife transition begin to appear. Typically these people are in the latter part of the separation phase, or well into the liminal phase when the reach the psychotherapist's office. What they find when they get there, one hopes, will be tolerance, understanding, and a sense of the significance of their present psychological struggle.

It seems critical to us that psychotherapists recognize what they are dealing with in these cases. The psychological nature and meaning of the midlife transition makes specific demands on the skill of the therapist and requires, for optimal care and treatment, specific attitudes, techniques, and psychological understandings. While therapists must naturally pay careful attention to the ego deficits of these persons in transition, it is even more important to grasp what is transpiring in the self and in the deeper layers of the personality, as one dominant pattern of self-organization is dissolving and another is forming. The transformation going on in the self often creates a distorted picture of severe deficits and damage in the ego, far in excess of what is actually the case. Methods of treatment and goals for these persons need to be adjusted to what is going on in the whole psyche, not only within ego-consciousness, if psychotherapy is indeed to function as an effective facilitator for psychological transformation within persons going through the midlife transition.

Our argument, then, is that psychotherapy is a possible modern cultural form for conducting persons through the stages of the midlife transition and for assisting them in what often amounts to the birth of a new self.

What we judge to be the most fitting attitude for therapeutic intervention during the midlife transition is indicated by the term "maieutic." "Maieutics" refers to the science and art of midwifery, of attending to the process of giving birth. Since the person in midlife transition is ultimately birthing a new self, the goal of the psychotherapist is to facilitate this process. Psychological maieutics, then, is the science and art of facilitating the psyche's transformation and the emergence of new psychological structures.

But first there is a death, and so there must be a burial. The former dominant pattern of self-organization is dissolving, and the self that was based on this archetypal structure goes through a process of decomposition. During the phase of midlife that we call separation, a gap opens up between the ego and the former self, i.e., between the "I" and the "me," such that the "I" can no longer attach itself as it has in the past to various specific internal images, memories, and ideas for its sense of identity and self-familiarity. This change in the inner world may be symbolized in dreams by themes, for example, of moving into new houses, destroying old buildings, changing furniture, or more radically in scenes of losing a child, a parent, or some other intimate who has represented a definer of selfhood. As the self begins to dissolve, the ego separates from it, and this is felt as loss or death. Consequently this phase is often highly disorienting to ego-consciousness.

The task of the maieutic therapist in this phase of the transition is to acknowledge the process of internal change that is taking place, to recognize its psychological meaning, and to maintain consciousness of this opening gap. The goal here is to help a person withstand the tension and even to open the gap wider, to increase the intensity of this process of disidentification.

The gap between a patient's former self and an increasingly free-floating ego may well stimulate anxiety in a therapist. This anxiety typically arises in reaction to the patient's emotional intensity and rapid oscillation between depressed and inflated states of consciousness. Is the patient going to collapse into psychotic depression, or suddenly take flight into a manically-driven new life based on a momentary identification with a new and unmodified archetypal content? This anxiety may lead a therapist to attempt a premature solution, which Jung calls a "regressive restoration of the persona" (1966), a retreat to former identifications and attachments. This strategy is fundamentally anti-maieutic, since it tries to resurrect a dead past and to stuff the emerging fledgling back into the womb, or to abort it. The maieut has become fearful of the process that is underway. The role of the therapist here is to facilitate the process, not to repair damage (that will come later, in the third phase). This is done by "containing" affect and behavior that derive from inner changes; a flexible yet firm attitude of tolerance and understanding is called for, and some encouragement to continue coping with everyday matters and ego demands as much as reasonably possible.

As the phase of separation blends into liminality, a person's emotional intensity often gives way to a kind of free, unattached, somewhat unrelated ego-floating. This phase looks more schizoid than manic-depressive. This is the key phase of the midlife transition, since the new psychological contents that appear during this period will make up the material that goes into the dominant pattern of self-organization. Here the role of the therapist is basically still maieutic: assisting consciousness to stay open and fluid throughout this ordeal; preventing premature foreclosure, either by regression or by identification with a newly discovered archetype; attending a soul that is both giving birth and being born.

What should a person be *doing* during the phase of liminality? Can the ego *do* something, or can it only suffer? One ego task does seem essential for this phase. It is one that helps rather than thwarts the aim of the midlife transition. We consider it to be a psychologically subtle and complex task because it involves neither action nor passivity, but rather what we call alert reflection. The goal is to become deeply acquainted with the contents of the psyche, its images, affects, and memories, and its personal and archetypal contents, as these appear during this phase, without identifying with any of them. For this, "the ability to be aware must be free from its usual tendency to attach itself to the object of awareness, thereby losing its ability to reflect on that object" (Watkins, p. 19). This combination of psychological awareness and detachment is the complexity of the attitude that we find essential for performing the task relevant to this phase.

Winnicott's concept of "transitional space" and of the value of "illusion" in this space, which is "unchallenged in respect of its belonging to inner or external (shared) reality" (p. 14), is useful here. For a person in midlife liminality, the therapist needs to create a transitional space and to enter this space with the patient. Liminality calls for transitional space, and the therapeutic attitude and ambience must reflect this if they are to be useful to these patients. In the liminal phase of the midlife transition, repressed or otherwise unconscious contents of the psyche need to be allowed to arise freely within consciousness without challenge as to their illusory and distorted perspectives. The non-critical attitude of the therapist towards these "illusions," as Winnicott refers to the psychic contents that emerge in transitional space, facilitates their flow into consciousness. Within this therapeutic "holding environment" (again, Winnicott's phrase), a person is able to face these often powerful contents of the psyche and to become intimately familiar with them.

For a person in midlife liminality, the ideal therapist is a maieutic attendant on the one hand and an empathic companion on the other, preferably one who has gone through midlife liminality and knows its major pitfalls. Therapists must know the great pressure that exists in the patient to "solve the problem" by taking action (getting married, or divorced; having another child; getting a different job) and by identifying with one or another aspect of the psyche. To a large extent, liminality is a period to be endured. Often it stretches from months to years, and often, too, both therapist and patient lose sight of where they are and where they're going. The therapist accompanies the patient on these wanderings, noting the features of the landscape as they appear in dreams, fantasies, emotional reactions and autonomous complexes; carefully observing memories of the past and images of the future; hearing and reflecting on plans that appear suddenly and disappear as rapidly; gathering all the pieces of the psyche as they flow into consciousness. If the therapist can contain this wealth of psychic material and keep one eye cocked to the perspective that sets liminality within the framework of psychological development, both partners can stay somewhat oriented and able to endure the tension of inaction, while they reflect on the appearances of unfamiliar parts of the Self, contain and honor them, and refrain from identifying with them. The comfort of this companionship may convert the experience of aimless wandering in liminality into a sense of actively exploring unfamiliar inner territories.

In the final phase of the midlife transition, a new dominant pattern of self-organization, rooted in archetypal structure, gradually takes form in the unconscious and magnetlike draws together many of the fragmentary pieces of the Self, both personal and archetypal, that were uncovered and experienced during liminality. Optimally, the sense of self that arises out of this congealing movement in the unconscious will reflect the psychological complexity that became conscious during the separation and liminal phases of the transition. As this newly won self-knowledge and awareness of unconscious contents and dynamics fall into place, there emerges into consciousness a coherent, but also paradoxical, pattern of psychological wholeness and continuity. This is a new "me," but it also contains all the old "me's" that preceded it.

Psychotherapeutic interventions during this last phase of the transition must be understood in the light both of what is happening psychologically during this phase and of previous interventions. Assuming that the therapist has been working with this person for some time, perhaps throughout most of the midlife transition period, therapeutic aims during this final phase will be focused largely on the integration of what has been uncovered and become conscious to this point, and finally termination. For stability, it is essential that this new sense of self be linked intimately to all other developmental periods, and so the therapist may function now more actively, linking new to old by interpreting the relation between what is happening in the present and what has happened in the past, providing insight into continuities often on the basis of transference and countertransference observations. In this way, new developments and contents are intimately linked to, if not altogether seen as deriving from, past developmental phases and conflicts, from areas where psychological complexes have been historically active and disruptive. By holding this complexity of new and old, personal and archetypal, factors of the personality intact, none of the psyche gets repressed by the emergence of a new dominant pattern of self-organization.

If the phase of liminality has been endured long enough and worked through at length and in depth, the new dominant pattern of self-organization will contain a complex amalgam of many archetypal and personal elements of the personality. It will not, as was most likely the case before the transition and the therapy took place, be based on one or two cultural stereotypes or introjected figures and their underlying archetypal patterns (the hero, the mother, the husband or wife, etc.). But if this is the case, the new dominant pattern of self-organization will not produce a sense of self that is without tension. Indeed, observation indicates the contrary. But now these are more conscious tensions, and this allows a person to suffer the paradoxes of psychological complexity consciously rather than blindly.

Throughout this final phase of "knitting together," the therapist serves to maintain consciousness of complexity and to prevent new repressions. While the therapist retains the maieutic attitude, the completion of birthing calls also for attention of a different kind. A new self has been born and now needs to be tended and nurtured in the outer world. Incubation is over, and the period of nurturing and rearing this new being now begins. Attention turns to adaptation to the social and interpersonal world, and while the therapist may continue in the picture as an advisor or consultant, the deep inner work of psychological incubation and birth is over and preparations for a new separation must begin. Optimally, the internalized image of the therapist continues always to represent the maximum containment of psychological complexity and paradoxical wholeness.

REFERENCES

Cytrynbaum, S., Blum, L., Patrick, R., Stein, J., Wadner, D., Wilk, C. 1980. Midlife development: A personality and social systems perspective. In L. W. Poon (Ed.), *Aging in the 1980's: Psychological issues.* Washington, D.C.: American Psychological Association.

Danielson, K. 1980. Assessment and characterization of midlife development among blue-collar men. (Doctoral dissertation, Northwestern University.)

Ellenberger, H. 1970. *The discovery of the unconscious.* New York: Basic Books.

Erikson, E. 1963. *Identity: Youth and crisis.* New York: W. W. Norton.

Gould R. L. 1978. *Transformations: Growth and change in adult life.* New York: Simon and Schuster.

————. 1980. Transformations during early and middle adult years. In N. J. Smelser and E. Erikson (Eds.), *Themes of work and love in adulthood.* Cambridge, Mass.: Harvard University Press.

Gutmann, D. 1976. Individual adaptation in the middle years: Developmental issues in the masculine mid-life crisis. *Journal of Geriatric Psychiatry, 9,* 31-59.

Jackson, P. F. 1979. Disruption and change in mid-life: An exploratory study of women in their fifth decade (Doctoral dissertation, University of Pittsburgh, 1975). *Dissertation Abstracts International, 39,* 4035B.

Jaques, E. October 1965. Death and the mid-life crisis. *International Journal of Psychoanalysis, 46,* 502-514.

Jung, C. G. 1961. *Memories, dreams, and reflections.* (A. Jaffe, Ed., and R. and C. Winston, trans.). New York: Vintage.

Jung, C. G. 1966. *Two essays on analytical psychology.* In Collected Works (Vol. 7). New York: Pantheon.

Jung, C. G. 1969. *The structure and dynamics of the psyche.* In Collected Works (Vol. 8) Princeton: Princeton University Press.

Katz, S. I. 1979. The relationships of the mid-life transition to death and self actualization. (Doctoral dissertation, Louisiana State University, 1979). *Dissertation Abstracts International, 39,* 4035B.

Larsen, G. C. 1977. A crisis of the developing adult: Mid-life transition. (Doctoral dissertation, Ohio State University, 1977). *Dissertation Abstracts International, 37,* 6953-6954A.

Levinson, D., et al. 1974. The psychosocial development of men in early childhood and the mid-life transition. In D. F. Ricks, A. Thomas and M. Roff (Eds.), *Life History Research in Psychopathology* (Vol. III). Minneapolis: University of Minnesota Press.

Levinson, D., et al. 1978. *The seasons of a man's life.* New York: Alfred A. Knopf.

Livson, F. B. 1976. Patterns of personality development in middle-aged women: A longitudinal study. *International Journal of Aging and Human Development, 7,* 107-115.

Livson, F. B. Feb. 1978. Personality development in men and women in the middle years. In *The life cycle: Development in the middle years.* Paper presented at the annual meeting of the American Association for the Advancement of Science, Washington, D.C.

Merriam, S. B. 1978. Coping with male mid-life: A systematic analysis using literature as a data source (Doctoral dissertation, Rutgers University, 1978). *Dissertation Abstracts International, 39,* 2690-2615A.

Murphy, P. 1977. The mid-life crisis in retrospect: An analysis of some recollections of specific emotional concerns experienced during middle age (Doctoral dissertation, Florida State University, 1977). *Dissertation Abstracts International, 37,* 5331-5332B.

Neugarten, B. L. 1968. The awareness of middle age. In B. L. Neugarten (Ed.), *Middle age and aging.* Chicago: University of Chicago Press.

Rosenberg, S. D., Farrell, M. P. 1976. Identity and crisis in middle-aged men. *International Journal of Aging and Human Development* (Vol. 7), 153-170.

Schoech, H. M. 1977. Androgyny in middle aged women (Doctoral dissertation, California School of Professional Psychology, 1977). *Dissertation Abstracts International, 38.* 2884-2885A.

Stein, J. 1981. A study of change during the midlife transition in men and women, with special attention to the intrapsychic dimension. Unpublished doctoral dissertation, Northwestern University.

Trafford, A. 1982. *Crazy Time Surviving Divorce.* New York. Harper.

Turner, V. W. 1967. *The forest of symbols: Aspects of Ndembu ritual*. Ithaca and London: Cornell University Press.
Turner, V. W. 1969. *The ritual process: Structure and anti-structure*. Chicago: Aldine.
van Gennep, A. 1960. *The rites of passage*. Chicago: University of Chicago Press.
Watkins, M. M. 1976. *The waking dream*. New York: Harper and Row.
Winnicott, D. W. 1971. *Playing and reality*. New York: Basic Books.

18

SELF-CREATED CEREMONIES OF PASSAGE

*Virginia Hine**

Several years before her death in 1982, Virginia Hine, M.A., social anthropologist and author of People, Power, Change *(1970),* Lifeway Leap *(1973), and* Last Letter to the Pebble People *(1979) began collecting material for a manuscript entitled* Rites of Passage for Our Time: A Guide to the Self-Creation of Ritual. *This project was put aside in 1980, when she sensed her own impending death and began work on her* apologia pro mortem sua, The Pearl of Great Price *(MS under consideration). With Luther Gerlach (University of Minnesota), Hine created the "network" concept of evolutionary social change (Segmented Polycephalous Integrated Network—SPIN), a concept now well-used by apostles of the "New Age." After her husband died, Hine shifted her interest to the area of self-generated life transition ceremonies, or modern rites of passage.*

She was convinced that people possessed an inherent ability to create and enact ceremonies that were confirmatory, healing and transformational. As she declared many times in workshops and lectures: "People do not need a priest or a holy man to be a mediator or intermediary between the Great Mystery and themselves. We all have a high priest or priestess within."

Except for the segment by Paul Kraska, "Matt's Rite of Passage," the following accounts of self-generated ceremonies and rituals are from Hine's collection.

> *Any affect or emotion which in its raw and unaltered form is too intense to be controlled by will alone may need its ritual. Without ritual, such energies may inundate the ego and force it into acting out or into obsessive behavior. Ritual brings about containment and acceptance, control of intensity, and "dosage." . . . Ritual offers us an alternative to repression for dealing with potentially overpowering affect.*
> —*E. C. Whitmont,* Return of the Goddess.
> *New York: Crossroad Publishing, 1982.*

---

*Edited from her notes by Foster and Little. Portions of this collection have been published in the *Pacific Sun* and *Mothering Magazine*. Printed by permission of Julia Hine-Gunnels.

CHILDHOOD TO ADULTHOOD

TRADITIONALLY, the passage from childhood to adulthood was marked by a series of ceremonies by which a child attained or earned the mantle of adulthood. Tribal cultures celebrated this passage with severance, threshold and incorporation ceremonies sanctioned by the community and conducted by acknowledged elders or leaders. Whether these ceremonies formalized physical maturation (onset of puberty) or social maturation (living as an adult), they provided for an orderly, meaningful transit of individuals through the personal, social and familial upheavals caused by the passage.

In modern society, this traditional passage is called "adolescence." An adolescent is one who is neither child nor adult, but in an "in-between" state. This interim life stage has only vaguely defined beginnings. Apparently, it ends when the adolescent has reached a certain age. Truly, the "adolescent passage" of American culture is a "holding pattern," a time of waiting that lasts up to eight years. To the not-yet-adult adolescent and the parents, this passage is often marked by chaos and upheaval.

Neither the onset of puberty nor most of the steps in personal and social maturation are celebrated by community sanctioned rites of passage. Maturational steps that do exist are hardly celebrated by rites of passage in any traditional sense. The old ways of marking the end of childhood and the beginning of adult life have "devolved" into gestures emptied of their content by the realities of modern experience. Many adults are unclear about when their adolescence actually ended. They continue to live as though they had never formally taken on the burdens and responsibilities of maturity.

Seeking experiential means of "earning" or marking adulthood, American youth sometimes generate their own passage ceremonies. Some of these ways of testing or proving themselves are socially unacceptable. Like flightless airplanes, they are allowed to taxi up and down the runway or to rev up their engines, but the control tower will not give them permission to take off. Those who persist in proving that they can fly anyway are liable to become entangled with the law. The restless searching of our youth for "grown up" experiences which satisfy their need to be "adult" often result in feelings and expressions of frustration, low self-esteem, or alienation, especially if peers and parents are as confused as they.

The following "self-generated" ceremonies of passing from childhood to adulthood illustrate the need of both adolescents and their parents to design and participate in rites that are relevant to their modern experience. These examples also demonstrate the ability of modern individuals to recreate within their own lives the wisdom and power of ancient, archetypal ways of severing and attaining adulthood.

Attainment of Puberty in a Small Community

A closely knit community of six professional families living in a rural area north of San Francisco designed and utilized a ceremony to formally mark the onset to puberty among the children of the community. Over a period of years, six children participated in this rite, which was designed to awaken the child's understanding of the meaning of the changes taking place in his/her body and psyche, to provide the child with a new sense of identification with the adult world, and to acquire a godmother or godfather as a wisdom guide. The ceremony, lasting two days and one night, was performed when the girl reached her first menses or when the boy reached his thirteenth year.

On a chosen evening, usually a Friday, all the family members of the community who were of the same sex as the child gathered at one of the homes. There the ceremony began and did not end until the following day. The ages of those who participated ranged from 14 to 60. If the initiate was a girl, her mother presided over the ceremonies; if a boy, his father.

The "chairperson" had prepared a list of questions pertaining to the child's future as an adult, such as: his/her sexual identity or role, relationships to parents and peers, relationship to work, plans for the future, and values or beliefs. These questions were written on pieces of paper and passed around in a hat. Each participant drew a question and, in turn, engaged the candidate in dialogue. While certain expectations were expressed regarding conduct, attitudes or beliefs, there were no "ought tos" or prescriptions. Discussion centered, rather, on how expectations were not like the realities of adulthood. Adolescent sexual experiences were shared, as were the relationships of the various community members to their own parents. Often, deep emotions were experienced, particularly between mothers/daughters and fathers/sons.

At the close of the discussion, the child spent the night alone, away from the house and his/her familiar bedroom, in a natural place close by.

Early the next morning, the initiate rose to perform a significant service for the whole community—usually to bake bread. If he/she did not already know how, he/she was taught by the community bread maker, who happened to be a male. The entire community, both male and female, then gathered for a bread and fruit breakfast.

When the breakfast was over, the company assembled for the ceremony of the naming by the initiate of the second mother or father. Although this person could be someone outside the community, he/she was in attendance, having been notified some time earlier. This adoption of a second parent was a matter of the deepest thought and the subject of many private consultations in the months before the puberty ceremony. When the name was announced, it came as a surprise to most of the community. The second parent presented a gift to the initiate. This gift was followed by other gifts from the natural parents.

Each member of the community then offered a statement, a song, or remark—remembering the initiate as he/she was as a child. These thoughtfully prepared expressions were gathered into a notebook and given to the initiate. A reading from scripture or literature regarding the meaning of adulthood by the chairperson formally terminated the ceremony and signalled the boistrous beginning of a community celebration and feast.

Matt's Rite of Passage

The following story by Paul Kraska, not a part of Hine's collection, was submitted independently. Mr. Kraska, a computer programmer living in Minneapolis, first published this account of his son's rite of passage in *In Context* (Spring, 1984). Without doubt, this encouraging story belongs here, among other accounts of self-generated, adolescent ceremonies of passage. Out of respect for the sacredness of Matt's own experience of it, Mr. Kraska has elected to keep certain details of the rite secret. As he says, "It is Matt's story, and you will have to ask him." Nevertheless, certain key elements of the rite are *connoted,* and hence accessible to the imaginative reader. Printed by permission of the author and *In Context.*

My son Matt was about to turn 14, and was already beginning to change in subtle ways. His two sisters, older by three and four years, were now young women, yet somehow I had not recognized their transition out of childhood until the contrast was staring me in the face. Now it was Matt's turn, and I did not want to let this important time slip by unnoticed again. To me, it was an event that clearly called for acknowledgment, celebration, and the creation of a gate/bridge to the paths awaiting him on the other side.

Yet I did not want to impose anything on him. Since the time my children and I were separated through their mom's and my divorce seven years ago, I had taken my own journeys into non-ordinary places and ways. Meditation, vegetarian eating, exploring the possible human, etc.—these are enough to make any kid from an upwardly mobile suburb suspect. But to Matt, nothing was so odd as my devotion to ritual long-dancing and pilgrimages for equinoxes, solstices, and quarter-points, and to bringing new ritual into my daily and person life. My friends talked about things, and in a manner that appeared a lot different from the things other adults were into. And yet, he had been asking questions about God and the context of life. Would he like to have a "rite of passage" trial, ritual, and celebration?

When he asked, "What's that, Dad?" I had no words or explanation that would lead him out of the dark. Finally I said, "It's like a *bar mitzvah,* but different." His eyes lit up as he said, "Sure! Wonderful!"

Now I was stuck. What is a rite of passage, anyway? I had done some exploring about adolescence and Native American rites, but not enough to tell me what to do for Matt.

Yet I did get an inspiration for how to start: I would ask five men to form a Men's Council for Matt and his passage. Jon, Mark, and Avram had known

Matt since he was seven. Tim and Michael plus Avram have been celebrating with me in our New Song Medicine circle here. Together we formed a special council for Matt.

At our first meeting, we sat in a circle around a single candle on my large carpet. We passed the talking staff, as is our way, and asked for each man to speak from the heart on the question asked. We did this three times. The first question was: "Who are you and how do you make life?" Until then, I was the only connection some had with each other.

Secondly we were asked, "What is a rite of passage"? Six different answers were told, yet they were all the same on another level.

The third question was, "Why do you want to be on this council and what in this experience will be for you?" We each agreed, in our own way, to make this a personal transition.

The staff was placed in the center next to the candle. I served tea and cakes while we sat in council talking of the forms a ritual such as this might have. We ended with a silent circle. All our meetings, from this first one in January, followed this form. We agreed to meet once a month, the next time with Matt, until May, and then end with a ritual and celebration in June.

At Matt's first meeting (in February), we asked, "What is your experience of being a boy?" and "What is being a man?" We spoke of boy's questions and knowings, curiosities, adventures; and the same things of men. We spoke of life (the giving and taking), sex, relationships, place, and being. At the end, I gave each member a copy of an interview with Robert Bly about "The Wild Man" from Grimm's "Iron Hans" fairy tale (*New Age Magazine*, May 1982).

At our March meeting we talked, from our own experiences, about the "wild man" energy in men (animus) that Bly discusses. We agreed that the article was not complete, and that we wanted the whole fairy tale to be read at our April meeting. [See Gustafson, "Fathers, Sons and Brotherhood"—Ed. note.]

It is a rich story, full of paradox and symbolism: the key to the cage kept under his mother's pillow, the golden hair, the mysterious wild man, the wild man energy and its relationship to excellence. In our discussion, we each remembered the story from our own experiences. Matt spoke of some of the ways he deals with fearful or challenging situations: lateral moves, willing to be outrageous, creative initiative.

We met a second time in April, since I was going to be out of town in May. The question, "What are the male archetypes?" came up. After we each spoke on this, I again borrowed from Bly and told the others about four that Bly discusses in his work on "The Great Father." They are: the statesman and the fool, who are on opposite poles on the vertical, and the shaman and the hunter-craftsman—poles on the horizontal. We had fun chewing on this over our potluck dinner.

While I was out of town, the council met once with Matt, and once without him. At the latter, plans were made about the tests to which Matt and I (to my surprise) would be put. We would camp out on the banks of Kinnickinnic River in Wisconsin on a Friday to Sunday morning in June. Sunday afternoon would be a public celebration-ceremony and feast—to acknowledge Matt's success in making this passage. I wrote an invitation letter to the celebration, but Matt thought it sounded a bit formal so we rewrote it together.

If I could give you an experience of the tasks Matt as given at the camp, I would tell all, but it is Matt's story, and you will have to ask him. What I can tell you is this: the men's council devised a task, as metaphor, for each of the four male (animus) archetypes. Matt took each to heart, one-by-one, and showed us his mettle on reason, innocence, vision, and skill. On Sunday morning we smoked our ceremonial pipe with Matt. In that council, he was welcomed into the community of men.

Present at the celebration were family, friends, and school chums. Elaine, a storyteller friend, told us all the Iron Hans story. We, on the council, publicly acknowledged Matt on his passage to his first paths of manhood. Matt completed his last task by giving each of the men in his council a gift which he designed and made that would be representative of who we were, as individuals. His gift to me was the Tai Chi symbol, which was wood-burned onto a maple branch segment end. I was not aware he even knew of this famous symbol, let alone the many meanings it has for me. We ended the ceremony with a wine toast to Matt, and a feast.

Now it's about six months later, and Matt has grown in many ways. I would not recognize him as the same person he was a year ago—and yet the boy is still present, as he always will be. Erik, our fourth child, will be 14 in August. I will be looking for men for his council soon and Matt will be one of the men I will ask.

Parents Whose Children Have Elected to Vision Quest

Since 1973, Rites of Passage, Inc., has provided a ceremony of passage for youth entering adulthood. This traditional rite, adapted to modern use, is called the vision quest, and involves a three or four day period of fasting and living alone in a natural setting (usually a desert place). Groups of high school students prepare over a period of two months to sever from their childhood and to step across the threshold into the "sacred world" of solitude and fasting. Thus they formalize or celebrate their passage from childhood to adulthood (see "The Vision Quest: Passing from Childhood to Adulthood," Foster and Little).

Under the guidance of Steven and Meredith Foster, Virginia Hine (anthropologist), Marilyn Riley (Youth Program Coordinator), Dinah Bachrach, MFCC, Tim Garthwaite, (Youth Probation Officer), and the participating parents, a ceremonial program was developed which addressed the need of parents to formally mark their children's attainment of adulthood and to utilize vision quest concepts within the family dynamic. With the active participation and understanding of their parents, the vision questers returned to a home and family prepared to received them. Many family difficulties created by the adolescent passage were righted and new privileges and responsibilities were conferred on the returnee. The parents were more able to encourage and ultimately to let go of their emancipating children.

Needless to say, the parents of these young vision questers became involved with their childrens' participation. In fact, many parents had a difficult time letting their children go alone to the sacred mountain. Assurance that their children would be safe was not the answer they were looking for. A large percentage of them responded eagerly to the opportunity to meet with staff members at Rites of Passage the same night their children would be keeping their all-night vigil in their "Purpose Circles" (see Foster and Little). On this last, long, lonely night of the threshold period, their vision questing children would be remembering their parents.

The meeting begins with the parents sitting in a circle, linking hands for three minutes of silence. They are asked to visualize their son/daughter alone on the desert mountain and to send them love, encouragement, or other kinds of moral support. These are strong moments. The parents are experiencing varying degrees of apprehension regarding their children and find this meditative focusing a help in reducing their anxieties.

A pile of stones has been heaped in the center of the circle. The parents are encouraged to select a stone from the pile which represents a significant quality in his/her relationship to the child. Once they have chosen their stones, each is invited to share with the others how the chosen stone reflects this quality. The parents speak in turn, without interruptions or outside comments. Nobody tries to solve anybody else's problem.

Then follows an hour of mutual sharing, at which time the parents discuss their own attitudes toward their soon to be emancipated children and the impact of this severance on their own life plans.

When the vision questers return to basecamp, at the conclusion of the threshold trial, they take part in a ceremony called "the tying of the knots." At this time, everyone ties a knot in a long rope and makes a vow concerning future responsibilities they are now ready to assume. When the rope has been knotted, a knife is passed around and each vision quester cuts his or her knot out. It will be kept as a reminder, or perhaps exchanged with parents who take part in a similar ceremony this first night they meet together. The rope is passed around the parent's circle and each parent ties a knot in it. The parents' vows, however, concern the letting go of particular responsibilities or attitudes related to their children. The knots are then cut out as symbolic reminders or exchanged with their returning sons or daughters.

The second, and final, parent meeting is also held at Rites of Passage and coincides with the "reunion" meeting of the returning vision quest group, usually two weeks later. In a room separate from their children, the parents reenact the stone ceremony, this time selecting stones which mirror any changes they have observed in, or in their relationships to, their sons or daughters. (On occasion, they are asked to pick a second stone to represent their relationship with their own parents). Again, each parent speaks in turn, without interruption.

Parents are then urged to share their experiences with their returning children with the rest of the group. Subjects of discussion range from "I remember when I was a kid leaving home" to observations regarding changes in the child or in the relationship. There is much appreciation of the difficulties of breaking free from outgrown parent-child habits and attitudes. Some parents want to describe what happened when they exchanged knots with their child.

An hour after the stone ceremony, the parents' meeting is adjourned to the room where the vision quest reunion is being held. Slides of the vision quest are shown and a pot luck feast culminates the evening. Spirits are usually so high at this point that an additional ceremony is added, to mark the end of the vision quest and the beginning of the vision quest of life. Vision questers and parents sit in a big circle together and a talking stick is passed around. As the talking stick comes to hand, each person speaks from the heart.

A High School Graduation

High school granduation is the nearest thing modern America can provide to an official, community sanctioned rite of passage into adulthood. The ordeal on the sacred mountain has been replaced by the academic procession and the switching of the tassel. Modern high school commencement "exercises" seem to elicit somewhat less than respectful behavior from those who are being "exercised." The graduation ceremony itself is notorious for a sort of ritual regression to "childish" behavior: sureptitious imbibing of booze and smoking of dope, irreverent and spectacular variations in expected dress, and other imaginative attempts at subversion.

"Graduation ceremonies are for parents," said one high school senior during a planning session for an "alternative graduation ceremony" in San Rafael, California. "I want a ceremony, but not theirs. The white gowns, the procession and all—it's like two lines of ants."

"Yeah," answered another. "Little ants coming out of a cage. I wonder—are they really letting us go or just cleaning the cage?"

This planning group, with the aid of trusted elders, parents and friends, designed a four hour ceremony to take place on a Pt. Reyes beach the day before their conventional graduation. They were willing to do both, but they felt that theirs was the "real" graduation.

When all the witnesses and participants had gathered on the beach, the ceremony began with impromptu dramatic enactments by the graduate of the most meaningful events of their high school years—the first date, scenes with mom and dad, being called to the principal's office, "getting busted," the death of a friend, "partying," taking exams, sports, and cheerleading. Their reason for acting these scenes was "to remember everything and then leave it behind."

After this dramatic exercise in severance, they enacted a symbolic threshold experience of rebirth. The elders and witnesses, varying in age from child to grandmother, formed into two long lines facing each other, creating a passageway across the sand and down to the edge of the surf. One by one, the graduates pushed and pulled their way through the "birth canal," hindered by the cross-linked arms of the elders and witnesses. Struggling, but making headway, they finally burst free of the passage and ran out across the tide line into the ocean, flinging themselves into the roaring surf. As they emerged from the water, they were symbolically reborn as adults. An elder met each graduate with a dry towel as he/she staggered shivering from the cold, gray water.

A ceremony of incorporation marked the final stage of the graduation. The entire company came together as equals in a circle around the campfire. A carafe of water was passed around. Each person held the water and put a vow, a commitment to the future, into it. When everyone had thus "promised the water," the carafe was passed around again, this time so that each could drink. In this way, all the vows were ingested, for the strength and well-being of those present. Small sticks were gathered by several children who then handed a stick to each member of the circle. These sticks represented the prayer of each person for the future of humanity and the well-being of earth. As each stick was committed to the fire, the prayer was spoken aloud. When the last prayer stick was given to the fire, there was a long moment of mutually agreed-upon silence.

The graduation ended with loud cheers, hugs and congratulations from elders and witnesses. A potluck feast ensued.

(Note: The local paper sent a photographer and reporter to cover this unique graduation ceremony. Not surprisingly, there were a number of letters to the editor in the ensuing weeks. The traditional graduation exercise at the high school had been disrupted by the satirical and outrageous behavior of many of the graduates. Prompted by the need to find relevant alternatives to the "traditional" commencement, high school officials altered certain elements of the ceremony and the conferring of the diplomas when graduation rolled around the following year.)

A Young Man Leaving Home

For modern youth, financial independence is often the last, formal act of severance from home. Prior to this break, hostility and resentment run strong. Communication may break down altogether. Ambivalence on the part of the parents regarding the readiness of their child to take on the adult world is quite common. Their child wants to be given the privileges and responsibilities of adulthood, but they are not certain he/she has earned these rights. A kind of running battle may ensue and last for years, during which time the child is not fully emancipated from the parents and the parents not fully emancipated from their child.

One family formulated their own way of dealing with this crisis. Their son, Tom, would be graduating from high school in several months—but did not plan on entering college right away. He was a strong and capable young man who had been given quite a bit of freedom in the last few years. He had vision quested for three days and nights and had been given, and took, new privileges for himself. Though he came and went as he pleased, he had little time for the family and expected that his "messes" would be cleaned up by his mother. Furthermore, the noise in his upstairs room was his own business. Conflict ensued.

Finally, after much discussion, the parents decided to give Tom one year to prepare himself for moving out on his own. When Tom first heard about this he felt angry, rejected and scared. Communication with his parents began in earnest, though it was not always comfortable. As the year progressed, shifting emotions were felt and expressed by Tom and his parents. Tom's anger and fear began to turn toward attention to the steps he needed to take in getting ready to leave home. He began to come to his parents for advice about a job and financial planning. They responded supportively and spent time talking with their son about tools and knowledge they felt he would need in the adult world.

By the end of the allotted year, Tom had gotten himself a job, discovering that he was a dependable and hard worker, respected by his employers. He had found an apartment to share with a friend. He was excited and self-confident, albeit anxious. His parents began to feel sad about his leaving, and savored his presence. Their pride in him began to grow.

To formally mark the end of their parenting and his childhood, and the beginning of a new relationship and living arrangement, the parents planned a simple ceremony. As Tom was leaving that night for a week-long trip before moving into his new apartment, the ceremony was planned to coincide with his actual departure from his childhood home, which heightened the drama.

The ceremony began with Tom tying a string to one finger of each family member (his parents, two siblings, an aunt, and two cousins were present). He secured all seven strings to his own left hand. As they sat, symbolically tied together, each family member addressed Tom, saying what was in his or her heart. Tom addressed each family member in turn, speaking his appreciation and mentioning special memories. Then he cut the string attaching him to that person, until all strings were cut. There were tears and laughter.

Next, the group moved outside on the terrace, where there was a small fire pit which held memories of many good times. A fire was started. Champagne was poured into a glass and each person toasted Tom, sipping from the same cup. Tom finished the champagne with a toast to his whole family, and then ceremonially smashed the glass in the fire. Then he stood up and walked off into the darkness. When he was gone, the remaining family members drew their circle a little tighter, symbolizing their smaller household.

DIVORCE AND SEPARATION

Modern American divorce, a major life transition, is not marked by meaningful ceremonies of passage. Divorce law is all too often empty of human content and blind to the consequences of its dealings. "Victims of divorce" inhabit the psychiatric couches and counseling centers of our culture. "Children of divorce" sit in every school classroom. In the popular imagination, divorce is a "failed marriage," a defeat of love, a family catastrophe causing wounds in parents and children that will never heal. Hence, when most Americans face the perilous passage of divorce, they expect to suffer through it, unable to find meaning in their experience.

There is probably no way of estimating how many "victims of divorce" continue to harbor anger, guilt, blame, revenge, pain, and confusion in their hearts even years after their divorce was final. Nor could any survey accurately register the effects of divorce on children, who must struggle with incomprehension, separation, and step-parents. The long term effects of divorce are aggravated by a self-indulgent clinging to the past, to hostility, self-pity, or even hope that somehow a reconciliation will be affected and all will be as it was before. Without the benefits of meaningful divorce ceremonies, many adults struggle through a long, dark passage without end.

To be sure, the separation of divorce is a form of dying. This severance produces many turbulent emotions and feelings. These feelings may be mitigated and given meaningful direction by formally marking the end of the severance period. A time of mourning must follow, as the individuals involved travel the passage toward the birth-light of new beginnings. When the dark passage is completed, there must be a celebration of incorporation, marking the resumption of life at a new stage.

In the absence of meaningful rites of divorce, individuals living in the modern world have found it necessary to design and participate in their own divorce ceremonies—thus creating meaningful ways of understanding their experience. The following examples illustrate different aspects of the "divorce passage" that have lent themselves to self-generated ceremony. These examples are not in any sense definitive, but merely suggest that there are self-generated ceremonial means available to individuals undergoing divorce.

A Unilateral Ceremony of Marital Severance

Frequently, one of a divorcing pair feels the need to formally mark the event—while the other does not. Mutual readiness is not common. One or the other may feel too resentful or vulnerable to agree to a bilateral ceremony. One or the other may not be willing to recognize the beneficial effects of ceremonializing such an event as divorce. In such instances, it is nevertheless possible for one ex-partner to go ahead with the business of officially (as opposed to legally) severing from the past marriage.

One woman living in the Bay Area expressed her need to celebrate her divorce from her former husband. When he refused to participate, she realized she would have to do it alone. She collected symbols of her and his former life together—the wedding dress and veil, picture albums, cherished objects and letters, etc. This process of collection (and selection) lasted many days and constituted a kind of life review. The woman said afterwards that this review or assessment of both the joys and pains of the former relationship helped her to prepare for her life as a single, older woman.

When these things had been collected, she invited her adult daughter and a close friend to witness a ceremonial burning. When the symbols of her marriage lay in ashes on the hearth, the only thing left was a wire ring that had held the flowers in her wedding veil. She took this tiny ring with her one day, when she met with her ex-husband to discuss final details of the divorce. She asked to meet for lunch at a particular restaurant with a balcony overlooking the sea. After lunch, as they were about to part, she told him briefly about her burning ceremony. She explained about the little wire ring in her hand, and told him what it meant to her. Then she threw it into the ocean.

This gesture received no response from her former husband. Nevertheless, she felt a sense of inner resolution. He had witnessed, albeit unprepared, this final act. Her sense of ceremonial completion required his witness. She had arranged the ceremony with grace and respect for his unwillingness to participate.

Bilateral Ceremony of Severance from a Love Relationship

The following account was written by a man who was willing to participate in a ceremony marking the termination of a long-standing love relationship with a woman. Though the couple had never married, they had been deeply involved and the decision to end the relationship was not easily reached.

"For me, the ritual of separation began ahead of schedule as I drove through traffic that was unusually heavy for a Saturday morning. An accident? No, a funeral cortege. It must have been 100 cars long. Not until I had worked my way around them and past the hearse in the lead did it strike me: I, too, was on my way to a funeral, a ceremony commemorating the life and death of a relationship.

My feelings at this point were mixed. Two weeks had passed since she said it was all over as far as she was concerned. I had reacted as people often do to a physical death in the family: denial ('She'll come to her senses'), anger ('How could she do this to me'), remorse, and the first stirrings of acceptance and resolution.

We had said our 'final' goodbyes a couple of times, but those partings had seemed tentative, incomplete. Maybe a formal ceremony of our own making would bury the corpse of our love once and for all, allowing us to get on with our lives as separate human beings.

It seemed only natural to build our ritual around fire. During the months we had known each other, we had spent a great deal of our time together beside fires, either outdoors or in front of the fireplace at home. The place we chose for the ceremony was the beach where we'd had our first date.

On our way, we talked, as we often had before, about my work and her work, past relationships, future uncertainties, what we wanted out of life. I was surprised at how easy it was under the circumstances to talk about these things—easier, in fact, than when we had seen ourselves on parallel paths stretching toward a distant horizon.

In the dunes by the beach, we found a shallow depression that offered some protection against the wind. The sun was hot, the air cool. We gathered driftwood, spilled a little wine on the sand as an offering, and she began the ceremony—invoking the spirits of the four directions, speaking to each in turn, asking for guidance. Then she stated what she hoped to gain from the ceremony—an end to our relationship as we had known it, an end to all expectations between us, and a clearer idea of how we might relate with one another in the future.

I had built the fire—my usual role in the past. We took turns adding sticks to it, using them to express thoughts and feelings about what we had meant to each other. In this way, speaking into the fire as much as to each other, we found it possible to say things—both positive and negative—that we probably would not have expressed face to face under ordinary circumstances.

For instance, she used a piece of firewood to represent the warmth I had brought into her life, and we watched it burn together. I talked about my anger at not getting my way, at losing her, at being rejected. The handful of dried twigs I placed on the fire crackled and flared in accompaniment to my thoughts.

As the fire began to die down, she laid a branch across it, saying that she would regard our separation as complete when the branch had burned in two. I chose a straight-grained piece of board for the same purpose. We ate our picnic lunch as fire ate through the wood.

My board, being thinner, burned through first. But instead of collapsing, one side reared up unexpectedly. It seemed to accuse me of harboring hopes that our love was not really over, and I had to admit the truth of this. So I offered the fire my confession and asked it to consume my last stray scraps of hope so I could go on my way free and clean.

When it was time to go, we heaped sand over the live coals. Then I put my hands on top of the new grave. It seemed cold already, but I knew the fire was still alive inside, for a time at least. As an after-thought, I drove a remaining piece of driftwood into the mound and left it there like a rude grave marker."

Incorporation of a Child of Divorce into His Father's Family

Children of divorce are often deeply confused by the family changes. They often fear they are not loved by one parent or the other, or that they were somehow the cause of the divorce. Even in the smoothest transitions the child may wonder where his "home" is, especially if he is sent back and forth from one parent to the other. Remarriages by the parents introduce further complications involving accepting, relating to, and loving step-parents.

The custody of an eight year old boy had recently shifted from his mother to his father. He had often visited with his father's new family but had not lived there for any length of time. He was joining a family with a half-sister, an older half-brother, a step-grandmother, a paternal aunt and two cousins—as well as his father's new wife. The family decided to hold a ceremony of incorporation welcoming Chris into the family.

On the appointed day the family gathered in the living room of his new home and arranged themselves in a circle on the floor. The father held a large ball of twine in his hands and explained that this ceremony would be symbolic of the family ties that would hold Chris secure in his new family. He then rolled the ball of twine to Chris, holding the end of the string firmly in his own hand.

"Now Chris," the father said, "you keep hold of the string. Let it run through your hand and you roll the ball to someone else." Chris chose his older brother who let the string run through his hand, holding it, and rolled the ball onto someone else. There was a good deal of talk about how the string, which was criss-crossing the circle by this time, was tangible evidence of each family member's relationship to each of the others.

As the pattern of linkages became more complex, Chris lay down on his side and stuck his head under the web of twine.

"What are you doing, Chris?" someone asked.

"Seeing how all this looks from underneath," answered Chris, delighting the adults with the apt symbolism. As he wiggled himself back out from under the criss-cross web, he happened to pull on the link between his hand and his brother's, who noted the tug.

"Hey, I felt that over here!" said the step-mother sitting on the opposite side of the circle. Everyone laughed at the obvious demonstration of how family relationships are interlinked.

Chris had chosen the menu for the feast dinner that followed the ceremony. After the feast of hot dogs and potato chips, a specially decorated cake was brought out. Chris lit a large candle and put it in the middle of the cake to represent his place in the center of his new family. Then he was given eight smaller candles which he distributed to each of the other members of the family. Each in turn lit a candle from Chris' flame, said something to welcome him into the family, and added the candle to the cake. Chris then blew them all out and cut the cake.

Several members of the family remarked on a subtle change in Chris' attitude that seemed to have occurred after the ceremony.

"He's always been a very pleasant little boy," said the grandmother, "but lately he seems especially affectionate, and he looks at me straight in the eye every time he passes. He used to just zip by on his way somewhere as if I were a rather comfortable but uninteresting piece of furniture! I feel such a person to him now—and he to me."

MID-LIFE

The "mid-life crisis" has become a predictable event in the lives of maturing men and women of our culture. This crisis marks the passage from "early" adulthood into "mature" adulthood and occurs somewhere in the middle of the seventy or more years of life span enjoyed by Americans in the twentieth century. Doubtless, one of the catalysts of the mid-life crisis is the relative good health and prosperity enjoyed by large numbers of middle-aged people. With thirty or more years ahead of them, they are challenged by the opportunity to reevaluate the values, symbols, beliefs, and habits of their "younger adulthood," and to grow into the fullness and fruition of their "greater years." If they do not respond to the challenge of personal growth at this crisis time of transition, their life purpose will be blunted. They may never escape the outgrown values of their youth.

The mid-life transition is usually accompanied by a variety of small and large upheavals. Values entertained from youth have outgrown their usefulness. The individual becomes aware that he/she will not be forever young. Old ideas about who he/she wanted to be are discarded in the light of the reality of the arrival of middle age. Old life styles and relationships may become limiting, inadequate, and burdensome. Job burnout, job change or relocation, separation or divorce from a spouse, death of parents, the "empty nest syndrome," drug or alcohol addiction, attempted suicide, "nervous breakdown," etc., are typical of the mid-life passage.

From the personal experience of such crises, new symbols arise from without and within. The rejection of old symbols and the self-creation of new, more meaningful symbols, is the task of middle age. These new symbols enable us to accept our own aging, to enjoy the fruits of middle age, and to find a meaningful death. The mid-life transition presents us with a "dangerous opportunity" to understand, accept, and let go of past symbols that no longer serve to draw our purpose toward a more rewarding and fulfilling life.

Mid-Life Passage of a Married Man

Mark, an associate professor, was experiencing difficulties typical of the mid-life passage. At the age of 44, he had begun to notice the inevitable signs of aging in his body. His professional position as a tenured faculty member of the Mathematics department at a large California university no longer seemed to challenge him. His marriage was not going well, for several reasons. For the last ten years he and his wife's interests had diverged to the point where they seemed to have little in common. He wondered if they were living together just for the sake of their almost-grown children. Although he enjoyed teaching, he had become weary of teaching the same subjects and having to grade large numbers of students.

When he looked seriously at the future, what he saw made him afraid. How could he leave his $40,000 a year profession, his wife, his family, his pleasant home—the very world he had built—and start a new life? It would be impossible! Yet he could not shake the growing conviction that his former life was somehow ending, that if he did not find new meaning for his life, he would suffocate in frustration and disappointment. He realized how little he trusted his own ability to survive apart from the way he had been trained to perform in the Ivory Tower. He wondered if he had any other skills or abilities with which to earn his way through the world. Certainly, he had dreams, dreams that were getting harder to ignore.

A bad case of prostatitis precipitated the crisis. At the emergency room of the hospital, he realized he had to make important changes in his life. He decided to put into effect a plan which he had been hatching for a long time. When summer break arrived, he would put his past life in order and take a leave of absence from it. For a period of two months he would not be who he was. He would go to a strange place and be a stranger, living as though he had no past. He would watch this stranger living his life and at the end of two months he would either return home to his wife, family and job, or he would begin a new life.

He began to prepare for his time of anonymity by informing his wife and children of his intentions. He warned his colleagues that he might not be returning for the new school year. He revised his will and went through his papers and accomplishments, throwing away everything that was no longer meaningful to him. He said goodbye to old friends, secretly wondering if he would ever see them again. His oldest daughter, married and in graduate school, supported his intentions and wished him well. His younger son, a senior in high school, was also supportive, remarking that his father had been quite unhappy lately. His wife, who expressed ambivalent feelings, nevertheless made her peace with his decision, and decided to travel in the Bahamas for the two months he would be away.

The day before he left, he bought a journal. Although he had never kept regular entries in a diary or journal, he was determined to do so, at least for the next two months. His first entry melodramatically began: "Tomorrow I die." The following day, he left the house with just a suitcase, a knapsack, and enough money to get him through his threshold time of anonymity. He walked to the Greyhound Bus station and bought a one-way ticket to a distant city.

For two months Mark lived as a stranger in a strange place, with none of the responsibilities or habits of his former life. He made regular entries in his journal, observing his behavior and attempting to make distinctions between what he had been and what he wanted to be. It was not an easy time for him. He was lonely and homesick and deeply depressed for nearly a month. In his journal he lamented how his past experiences had brought him to this point. Finally, however, he was able to accept his former life, mistakes and all, and to admit that he was hardly a stranger to himself. Nevertheless, he found himself even more strongly drawn, not towards a continuance of his past life, but towards what he termed "a world of wonderful, absurd, inexhaustible probabilities."

Two months after he left, he called his wife to say that he would not be returning home.

Mid-Life Passage of a Single Mother

N, a twice-divorced, single mother of two nearly grown children, had been living in Marin County for nearly 15 years. At the age of 39, she underwent a mid-life "crisis," due to disappointments with her professional life (elementary school teaching) and with aborted relationships. Finally, she was pursuaded by a trusted friend, an older woman, to "do something to change your life and make it the way you want it to be."

She decided to move to a remote island off the coast of Washington state where, in a rural setting, she would begin a new life. Her children encouraged her to make the move, feeling it would be good for her, and agreed to live with their father, who lived nearby. To this end, she gave notice at work and to her landlord, closed her bank account, withdrew her savings (a few thousand dollars) and sold most of her furniture at a garage sale. Over a period of time, she prepared herself for the move, acquiring what she would need to survive happily on her remote island. Finally, there remained one last step for her to take—to say goodbye to her close friends and loved ones, the living symbols of the life she was leaving behind.

On the eve of her departure, she threw a party for all her friends. An hour before the party began, she celebrated her severance from her former life with a simple, meaningful ceremony, or series of ceremonies, which, as she later commented, "I performed unconsciously, without thinking that I was ceremonializing a very important change in my life and in my life style." In her own words she describes what took place:

"When people came in, I asked them to join the circle that was forming in the middle of the living room. There were plenty of pillows and nobody seemed to mind sitting on the floor. While waiting for the other guests to arrive, we chatted and visited. It was easy to be together in a circle.

When it seemed that most of my friends had arrived, I asked for everyone's attention and told them that we were sitting together for a purpose . . . because I was leaving Marin after so many years and that I wanted to say goodbye, and to tell them thank you, that I loved them.

I had filled a box with specially wrapped and labelled gifts for each of my invited guests. These presents weren't anything big—just little things, like crystals, special stones, pieces of wood, jewelry, poems I'd written, etc. Each person had a chance to reply to what I said. Again and again, I could not keep tears from coming. Such a good life it had been—even though I was tired of it!

When all the gifts had been given out, I took out my guitar and played a song for everyone—one I had especially composed for the party. I can't play very well, but my heart was in the right place. In the song I told them about all the times I had needed and got their love and support, about all the good times and the hard times. . . . Everyone enjoyed the song and wanted to talk afterwards. . . . Where exactly was I going? They were sure going to miss me. How was I going to get along without a job? There were many expressions of good luck and love. But I wanted to get the formal part over with. I could hardly bear the feelings of joy and sorrow.

I took out a bottle of champagne, the best money could buy, held it up and said, 'There are the good years of my former life. Drink them with me.' I proposed a toast to our mutual past, its ups and downs, its triumphs and defeats. Everyone drank—with great satisfaction. . . .

When the bottle was empty, I held it up and announced: 'Goodbye, former life. I do not regret you. Now I make a clean break with you.' Then I threw the empty bottle into the fireplace. It smashed into a million pieces.

Then I yelled, 'Let the party begin!' It lasted long into the night."

Two days later, N said goodbye to her kids and drove a small U-Haul truck crammed to the gills with all her worldly possessions, all the way to a beautiful island in the San Juans, off the coast of Washington. Except to visit her children, she never returned to Marin County. She continued to teach elementary school, first as a volunteer and substitute, then on a regular basis. Several years after she arrived on the island she met and married a man who, for reasons similar to hers, had come to the island from the city of Seattle.

Aging

In our youth-oriented culture, the idea of aging is not popular. Ceremonies celebrating the passage into "elderhood" are rare. Our youth grow up in a world where young is beautiful, useful, and all that is to be desired. Old is a calamity, a never-never land, a "retirement" from social reality. The aging process must be hidden behind the miracles of makeup and modern medicine. The time comes, however, when each of us can no longer hide our age.

We may first become deeply aware of the aging passage when our first grandchildren are born, or our fiftieth birthday arrives, or our 25th wedding anniversary is celebrated, or the age of "retirement" is reached, or the aches and pains of a well-used body begin to plague us in earnest. Feelings of deep terror often accompany this realization that we are already descending the "peak" of our life span. Those who have avoided any meaningful thought about their own eventual deaths are particularly frightened. Their culture has not conditioned them for the shock.

As with other life passages, the aging crisis affects others as much as the one who is aging. Friends and family can be initimately involved. Anxiety, dismay, anger, resentment, and fear are emotions often felt by others as well as by the aging one. These feelings can hinder the individual from stepping purposefully into elderhood and accepting death. Nevertheless, this passage engenders new opportunities and symbols, and offers profound experiences of love and closeness within one's circle. The challenge of the aging passage is to assume the responsibility of personal power and wisdom, won from a lifetime of experience.

Some individuals have found ways to significantly mark, and embrace, their elderhood. They recognize that acceptance of their own aging was a liberating declaration of self-respect. They were able to enjoy the fruits of their life and to create a life-style appropriate to their life station. They freed themselves to look up their trail to where death waited. This freedom made them wise.

The Vision Quest as a Ceremony of Aging

A retired Marine three star general went on a vision quest to Death Valley to formally mark his "retirement" from an active life of military service, and, as he put it, "to master my fears of growing older." A large, robust man, a veteran of World War II and the Korean conflict and several times wounded in action, he was not afraid to speak of his fears. He body had begun to pain him more or less constantly. An old neck fracture plagued him and would not let him sleep peacefully. Having given most of his life for his country, his personal life had suffered. Bitter, often painful memories crowded his mind. Sixty-five years old, he had come to the twilight years of an extraordinarily full and passionate life.

Certainly, he had not given up. He had never been a quitter. He wanted to make the most of his remaining years. His life had been marked by a strong desire to serve his people, in whatever capacity. He particularly wanted to make peace with his children, from whom he had been estranged for long periods of time. His decision to go into the desert and fast alone for three days and nights was merely an extension of the aging crisis he was experiencing.

A week before he left for the desert with the vision quest group, he wrote and notarized his last will and testament. He put it in an envelope and left it on the mantlepiece, in the event he should not return. He brought all his current business affairs to a close and made phone calls to his wife and children. He thoroughly cleaned his home, putting everything in place. The day before he crossed the threshold into the sacred world of the vision quest, he pulled a large amount of food from his pack and asked that it be distributed among the others at the feast if he did not return. With this gesture, he fulfilled a final obligation to his former life.

Death Valley was caught in a late fall cold snap. The temperatures went down to 20 degrees in the early hours of the morning. By day, the sun shone bright and chill. Perched on a terrace above a wash in the Panamint Mountains, the General celebrated his first night alone by going out into the freezing wind to find rocks large enough to hold down his flapping tarp. He lost his footing at the edge of a dropoff and fell heavily, rolling and tumbling down into the wash. Bruised, dazed, and freezing, he pulled himself back up to the warmth of his sleeping bag. By morning, he could barely move his limbs.

Somehow, he hung on. He did not return to basecamp. He took care of himself, with the help of the cold sunlight and frosty stars. By the third day, he felt strong enough to build his purpose circle and to keep his vigil through the last dark night. All that night he prayed to the four directions for a vision for his life. In the coldest hour of morning, the dark heavens sent him a sign—a meteorite, or falling star—to answer his life's prayer. The meteor spoke to him. It said: "I am you. I am the fourth star you have sought. I am falling.

Soon I will be gone from the world. I go in glory and beauty. The three star general has become the four star general. And you have a new name—Falling Star."

Falling Star returned, battered but calm. Love for everyone glowed in his eyes. He had taken a bad fall, and had found insight there. The desert had assured him that his body would never be as strong as it had been. The falling star had told him that his heart would guide him on this last leg of his journey, and that the path would be full of beauty and honor.

A Fiftieth Birthday Ceremony

A divorced woman approaching her 50th birthday began to realize that she was experiencing a great deal of anxiety about it. She was living alone, her children had grown and gone, and she had begun to make changes in her life-style. Still, she felt vulnerable about her growth changes, even though the experience of coming out of her old "shell" was an exciting one. She realized that her 50th birthday was symbolic of a major life change.

She decided that she would do something special for her birthday to mark this life change. She knew that the ceremony would not resolve her anxiety, but would rather offer it a vehicle to carry her into the next phase of her life. The conflict that she felt most keenly was symbolized by her two sets of friends. She felt that her old friends wanted her to be "like she used to be" and that her new friends represented the different set of values of her life change. She therefore decided that she would invite both sets to help her celebrate this rite of passage.

The birthday party began with the two groups of people who did not know each other clustered at opposite ends of the spacious living room. They had been prepared to expect an "event" at the end of the cocktail hour, before dinner was served. Promptly at seven, the woman took her place at the top of two broad stairs that led down into the living room. She was dressed in the same old coat in which she had received her guests.

She explained that she had called them all together to celebrate a change in her life, and to witness what she was leaving and what she was going toward. She explained why she had invited both her old and her new friends and hoped that they might get to know each other. She then announced that part of her life change would include selling the house in which she had lived for many years. She also announced that she wanted to change her name. The Southern-style double name by which her old friends had known her she now wanted to shorten to the single name by which her new friends called her.

She then picked up an enormous pair of scissors, held out the first of three immense buttons that held her coat together, and cut it off. It fell to the floor with a clunk that sounded very loud in the astonished stillness of the room. Then she cut the second and third. She removed the coat to reveal a beautiful dress. She explained that the dress symbolized what she felt was emerging out of the old self, and that the old coat could now be shed.

The woman finished the formal part of the ceremony by reading a poem she had written. She then invited her guests to join in the feast. There was cheering and toasting and a general movement of people in the room towards each other, merging and mingling spontaneously in a dance of incorporation. Some of the guests noticed that everyone seemed more open with each other, even the ones who had never met, even to the point of discussing their own life-change experiences. Afterwards, the woman told her friends that her anxieties had not gone away but that the ceremony had somehow changed them. She felt she had more energy to do what she needed to do and found herself more willing to take the risks that her new life demanded.

A Family Ceremony for Impending Death

The final rite of passage for any individual is a simultaneous rite of initiation into bereavement for those most deeply affected by the death. If this double rite of passage is to provide the spiritual strength and facilate the psychological changes necessary in both the dying and the survivors, it must be linked to a mythology that gives meaning to the experience of death.

Some families reach a point where all members recognize the inevitability of death and can ceremonialize it together. In every good death there is some form of resolution of relationships before the final parting. In many cases where there have been old hostilities, buried anger, or guilt, the resolution comes in the form of reconciliation. Ceremonial expression of reconciliation and completion can ease the pain of parting at the final passage, and give deep meaning to this last transition of a loved one.

One family came to recognition and acceptance on the eve of their mother/grandmother's death. The dying woman suggested a ceremony of completion for them all, to ease the pain of farewells and to celebrate the "bond of eternal connection" between them.

The family formed a circle around a candle, symbolizing the illumination they believed came with death, and a box of Kleenex, symbolizing the tears that would come in the weeks ahead. They lit the candle and read selected readings from the New Testament expressing the concept of continuity of consciousness and connection beyond physical death.

The next part of their ceremony they called "litany of thanksgiving." The mother began with her eldest son by reading the first of seven prepared "statements of gratitude" beginning with "I am grateful to you, my son, for _____." They spoke alternately until all seven statements had been read. The same process was completed with each of the other family members. Then in unison they said: "Thanks be to God for the love we have shared."

Following this came the "celebration of eternal connection." The mother spoke a prayer for guidance through the final passage of her life and gave to each of her family a small natural gift (stone, shell, flower, etc.). Each of the others gave to her a small gift in exchange which she would keep until her death. They all agreed that the gifts they had given her would be cast into the sea with her ashes when that time came.

The physical severance that the mother's death required was symbolized by the "breaking of sticks." One daughter, who had been struggling with her feelings in trying to let go, had come to realize that her real task was in incorporating into herself what she wanted of her mother's essence. This fit in with the "breaking of sticks." The mother passed from one to the next, offering a stick to each which they then forcibly broke together. The mother then handed her half of the broken stick to the son, daughter, or grandchild "as symbol of the spiritual incorporation which is possible after the physical severance."

The ceremony ended with the "kiss of peace." The mother kissed each of the others on the forehead saying, "In a little while the world will see me no more, but you will see me with the inner eye and know that I am with you and you are with me and we are with the Father. Peace be with you."

The mother then turned on a special tape of music that was meaningful to the family and went out of the room, leaving her family to embrace each other.

PERSONAL TRANSFORMATION: THE INNER IMAGE OF INITIATION

James A. Hall

*In his essay, "Personal Transformation: The Inner Image of Initiation,"
Dr. Hall examines the psychic interface between inner and outer initiation as a
means of comprehending the dynamics of personal change and transformation in the modern world.*

*Using his own as well as his clients' experiences and dreams, Dr. Hall
draws an important distinction for all those who work with individuals passing through life transitions: "The outer ritual itself cannot produce the desired
inner change, which depends on subtle, inner forces of the psyche, forces that
. . . cannot be coerced by the outer process of initiation." He demonstrates
how dreams are indicators of initiatory readiness (or unreadiness) and
describes neurosis as the result of attempts to avoid initiation into the next
stages of life. His essay is highly useful for those who avoid formal ceremony
and seek ways of initiating themselves. He reminds us: "The quiet trials of life,
often requiring a heroism unseen by the world, mean something other than
meaningless pain. They are tests at the threshold of the temple. . . ."*

*James Hall, M.D., is Clinical Associate Professor of Psychiatry at the
University of Texas Health Center in Dallas. A founder and former President
of the Inter-Regional Society of Jungian Analysts, he is also a fellow of the
American Psychiatric Association and of the American Academy of Psycho-
analysis. Dr. Hall is a graduate of the Southwestern Medical School of Dallas,
and the C.G. Jung Institute of Zurich. He is the co-author of* Clinical
Hypnosis *(1975), and* Clinical Uses of Dreams: Jungian Interpretation and
Enactments *(1977).*

THE committee or job interview is a common form of initiation rite in our
society and is related to other rites such as those associated with
graduation, matrimony, parenthood, elderhood, or induction into clubs,
fraternities, or secret societies. What caught my attention during a trip to Los

Angeles for an interview to apply for training at the Jung Institute was how the *psyche* as dream-maker reacted to the outer initiation ritual of the committee interview. The night before the interview, when my anxiety was highest, I had the following dream:

> *I was in a restaurant or a room in a home where there were many tables. A number of Jungians were present. At the upper right corner of the room from the booth where I was sitting there was a small raised area, from which a closed door led into a large bedroom. In the bedroom Jung was ill—not a life-threatening illness, but one that kept him from being present at the meeting. The door opened, however, and Jung came out. He and several women came to the booth where I was sitting and we had a brief conversation. During the course of the conversation, when no one else was looking, Jung gave me a pill-box to keep for him. It was old, of carved ivory, and had the appearance of a sheathed dagger. Inside were a number of medicines in small modern containers. The carvings on the ivory case were of a stylized lingam and yoni, representing a combination of yang and yin, although anyone who did not know the symbolism would think it simply an abstract design. Jung went back to his bedroom to rest. A few minutes later he sent a message that he needed one of each of the types of medications in the pill-box. I arose to take them to him, but at the door of his sickroom I was stopped by a woman, one of his famous pupils, who had given herself the role of guardian of his threshold. She would not let me enter, but I kept the medications and resolved to find another way to get them to Jung in spite of her interference.*

You may surmise that I was as much concerned with the dream as with the waking experience of meeting the committee. It was as if the psyche was constellated by the approaching outer initiation ritual and used it in the dream for its own inner purposes, sensitizing me to an inner anima conflict that was the *real* problem to be confronted in entering Jungian training. Something in the unconscious, personified in the dream by Jung himself, was not only willing to help me but in a sense required *my* help to regain health. The "guardian at the threshold" was a real analyst whom I greatly respected. Yet I had avoided having an interview with her when it would have been easily possible. She subsequently appeared in other dreams that amplified the part of myself that had to be faced before "Jung" would be healthy. The working out of this problem in the outer world required a number of experiences and insights over a period of years.

This type of dream is not uncommon. I have spoken to many other analysts who have had similar dreams near times of outer ritual passages. My analysands often report two types of dreams concerned with initiation motifs:

(1) dreams (such as my own above) that seem to be constellated by outer collective initiation situations yet which seem to be more in the service of the inner process of individuation, and (2) dreams in which the outer forms of initiation are used by the archetypal Self, the maker of dreams, to symbolize inner changes in the psyche, particularly in the form of the dominant ego-image. Perhaps the most profound forms of the inner initiation dream motif refer to processes of alchemical transformation, motifs that occupied much of Jung's later thoughts. I have discussed some of these in an essay for the *Werner Engel* Festschrift (1983).

A second experience of the initiation motif in my own life occurred about a year later when I took the examination to be certified as a psychiatrist by the American Board of Psychiatry and Neurology. Since psychiatry covers an immense field (biochemistry, sociology, psychology, history, philosophy, religion, etc.) it is not possible for anyone to master more than a small area of psychiatric knowledge. I had studied intensely for the board exams, using all available time for six months. I bought review books and devoured them, often having night study sessions with colleagues. When it was time to drive to New York for the examination, I arranged to go with a neurologist who was also to take the exam. While driving he reviewed me in neurology and I reviewed him in the field of psychiatry.

The night before the examination I was deeply depressed, feeling that it was impossible for me to pass. The neurologist and I went out for a Chinese dinner. I remember he ordered squid in its own ink, the blackness of the dish reflecting my own depression and gloom. At 11:15 P.M. I went to bed while my neurologist friend was still reviewing his study notes. My last thoughts before falling asleep were how to explain my failure of the exam to my family and friends back home.

When I awoke, even before I opened my eyes, I knew that something had changed. I felt a deep sense of confidence and security in regard to the exam. During sleep the whole emotional structure of my mind had altered. Relieved, I decided to shower and dress for the exam, but discovered that it was only 2:30 A.M.! I went back to bed, slept soundly, and awoke refreshed at 7 A.M.

The day of the examination was most enjoyable. I felt relaxed and confident. It was not that I knew all the answers. In fact, I missed the diagnosis on one of the two psychiatric patients that I interviewed before a committee of examiners, but the interview itself was acceptable and my reasoning was sound.

What had happened between 11:15 P.M. and 2:30 A.M. that changed my whole sense of confidence in regard to that important examination in my continued professional growth? I do not know, but I suspect there was an unremembered *dream* that altered my ego-image in a way that gave me the needed confidence to remember and *use* all that I had learned. The objective examination the next day was pleasant and I passed. But the *real* initiation process was internal. I reached an *inner* judgment of my own competence as a psychiatrist in the middle of the night through processes of which I have no conscious knowledge. The initiation "took"—I achieved a sense of competency and self-reliance in the interior of the psyche itself. The outer examination was simply the occasion for me to bring my inner doubts about my competence into a clearer focus and overcome them more readily.

INNER AND OUTER INITIATION

These experiences, and those of others, have caused me to re-think our usual view of initiation rituals in terms of their inner impact on the psyche. I now consider the actual purpose of a ritual act to be the inner transformation of the psyche, particularly the dominant-ego of the person undergoing initiation. Much of the outer ritual is merely an attempt to make this inner transformation more likely, to increase the probability of real psychic transformation. The outer ritual itself cannot produce the desired inner change, which depends on subtle, inner forces of the psyche, forces that can be invited but cannot be coerced by the outer process of initiation. The outer ritual is necessary but not sufficient cause of inner transformation.

Such a process can be seen in the following dream, a significant developmental dream of a man in his forties who was successful in his career and (on the surface) in his relationship with his family and friends (although there was a curious insulation in his most personal relationships, as with his wife). He dreamed that he was in prison:

> *I am in prison with two other men, one of them a psychopath. The third man is unknown and unclear. There are three rooms in our quarters. I am in one of the rooms planing a big plastic sheet that I am holding on end. The planing makes beautiful curves of plastic in the shearings. It is a real work of art. The curves remind me of the female body. The plastic catches the light and is lovely. Somehow the artistic object I am working on is important in helping us to escape from the prison. The psychopath calls me to come back into another room because the prison policeman is making rounds to check and see if we are there.*

A second dream, reported at the same analytic session, was that the dreamer and his wife had been released from prison by a pardon; they had not finished serving their sentences.

These two significant prison dreams occurred almost immediately after the dreamer had been interviewed by an application committee for admission to advanced training. The interview had been the first in many years where he had felt himself to be bluffing and to have been "found out," although with a kindness and objectivity on the part of the committee that accepted him in spite of his persona.

This man's two dreams of prison showed the internal *use* to which his Self, the central archetype of order that is also the maker of dreams, put the external experience of the initiatory interview. The interview was successful in getting the man admitted into the training program that he wished, but it also revealed to his consciousness that his own state of alienation was visible to the committee members—although they did not reject him for his problems. His two dreams symbolized his state of inner discord as an actual imprisonment, and suggested there was a disassociation in his masculine image: himself (the dream-ego), the dream psychopath (who does not behave in a particularly psychopathic manner), and the unknown third man. If we also count the prison policeman, there are four masculine figures. Jung frequently cited the number four as a symbol of completeness, and in clinical experience with dreams important totalities are often broken into three units plus one unit. In this dream there are three men in the prison cell and one, the policeman, outside it.

The dream suggests a problem in masculine identity formation: how to reconcile the three imprisoned parts with the outer policing part (which indeed represents the way this analysand was accustomed to police himself—as if he were inherently guilty). It is striking that the solution suggested is not a thinking, judgmental solution, as might have been pictured by a trial. Neither is it simply rebellion, like overpowering the prison policeman. It seems to involve the creation of an aesthetic object, the planing plastic sheet, where curves of plastic, irridescent in the light, suggest the subtle curves of a female body. This theme is repeated in the second dream: his wife and himself (both prisoners of his neurosis) are pardoned without serving their prison terms. This suggests a feminine-like feeling function, a more aesthetic judgment against the harsh morality of his father-trained super-ego. Such speculations on the meanings of the dreams offered a pathway to pursue in his analysis as well as in his personal life.

As part of the personal research for this chapter, I spoke with an authority on initiation rituals in a number of secret old English societies. A man of great scholarly wisdom, he arranged for me to participate in some dramatic initiation rites, assembling a small team of friends for that purpose. I underwent three separate initiation rituals to determine their effects on my psyche. I wondered if they would evoke some of the same inner stirrings I had experienced at the time of the Los Angeles Jung Institute interview, or that I had discerned in the prison dreams of the professional man discussed above.

The rituals were elaborate and well-executed, and included appropriate costumes and symbols. But they caused not a single discernible ripple in my dreams or in my psyche. Perhaps they were too unconnected to my inner growth, although their symbols were meaningful and their enactments were dramatic. Perhaps they lacked the strong constellating effect of the committee interview or the board examination. In these I might have been denied a stage of career advancement that at that time was crucially important to me. The formal English initiation ceremonies, although performed in a ritually correct manner, failed to produce noticeable changes in my psyche, whereas the examination (not usually thought of as initiation processes) had evoked profound changes in my understanding of myself. In the case of the Jung Institute interview, a dream image was evoked that was useful in understanding my inner growth for years to come.

While doing research on the subject of initiation, I met a person deeply acquainted with the esoteric traditions that inherited the vitality of the old Order of the Golden Dawn, to which many Victorian students of the esoteric traditions belonged, including the poet William Butler Yeats. This person was kind enough to share with me several of his own dreams that occurred in connection with ritual initiations he had undertaken in various phases of his esoteric training. Before one of the most important initiations, he asked himself if he was ready for the personality changes that he expected would be the result of his ritual participation. He dreamed that he was on an immense plain of grass. In the distance there was a vague figure. As it approached at considerable speed, he saw that it was a knight in armour on a great horse much larger than ordinary horses. It rode right up to him. Stopping suddenly, the knight said "Yes!" and named the date of the impending initiation. To the dreamer it seemed that some figure in his unconscious psyche was telling him that the approaching initiatory experience was valid.

This same person, who has made extensive studies of lodge initiations, told of an elderly woman, now deceased, who had for years progressed along a path of personal development punctuated by various intentional initiatory experiences. At one point, however, she seemed to have rejected any further progress. Then she dreamed that she had travelled a long distance on a very rocky path, perhaps on Glastonbury Tor, but the dream showed her sitting beside the path in one of three rocking chairs, no longer striving. The reflection of herself in the dream re-motivated her to more energetically pursue her initiatory growth.

There is an important distinction between a person's intention to achieve initiation into a new state of being and the actual accomplishment of inner change—an inner change which may or may not be produced by an outer act of initiation. It would seem that the archetypal Self has its own intentions for the transformation of the ego-image. Moreover, it may utilize outer events that on the surface have little connection with consciously intended changes. Describing the inner content of a series of fantasies created by an analysand, Jung remarks:

> These fantasies are not so wild and unregulated as a native intelligence might think; they pursue definite, unconscious lines of direction which converge upon a

definite goal. We could therefore most fittingly describe these later series of fantasies as processes of initiation, since these form the closest analogy. (*Collected Works*, 7, par. 384)

Initiatory experiences might be seen as a threshold phenomenon that marks the intent of the ego to move from a former state of being to a larger, more comprehensive state. As Jung further states:

Conscious realization of the contents composing it [the mana personality] means, for the man, the second and real liberation from the father, and, for the woman, liberation from the mother, and with it comes the first genuine sense of his or her true individuality. This part of the process corresponds exactly to the aim of the concretistic primitive initiations up to and including baptism, namely, severance from the "carnal" (or animal) parents, and rebirth . . . into a condition of immortality and spiritual childhood, as formulated by certain mystery religions of the ancient world, among them Christianity. (*Collected Works*, 7, par. 393)

With this second statement, Jung highlights a subtle aspect of initiation that is often overlooked: initiation is not an end, but a beginning. It not only closes off a problem area, but moves the ego-image across a threshold into a new form, introducing *new* tasks and new goals of individuation. Jung points out that baptism is a rite of this sort—the "old" personality is submerged beneath the water and a "new" personality is "born" from the depths. New birth always means new possibilities, but it also means new tasks and responsibilities.

Outer events, whether intentional ritual initiations like baptism, or "accidental," may be used by the psyche to illuminate and further personal transitions. Such transitions are seldom achieved at one stroke. It is more usual for the movement to begin subtly in the unconscious, perhaps imaged in a dream, and for the actual working out of a transformation in the empirical personality to take a much longer time. The initiatory experience itself may be partial or flawed, but even this has the psychological advantage of preventing psychic inflation in the initiate. Joseph Henderson (1967) writes sensitively about the value of initiatory failure:

If the initiate had no further doubt about his status as an initiated man, he would either become an unbearable prig or else subtly return to the role of hero. The feeling that he has partially failed insures his humility and his human group identity, so that in his later life individuation will be real for both worlds, inner and outer, and will not deteriorate into empty individualism or eccentricity.

In fact, the idea of transition leads logically to the intuitive sense of a series of initiations, of an orderly progression of the ego along a coordinated path of transformations. There is no one stopping place. As in the *I Ching,* there are basic, underlying patterns of movement to which the superior person in us may respond to a greater or lesser degree. In this view of the cosmos, there is no isolated existence unrelated to the whole. The task, then, is not simply the heroic task of facing the ordeals and trials of an initiatory process, but facing also the new duties and responsibilities of each succeeding stage of existence into which one is consciously or unconsciously initiated.

NEUROSIS AND DREAM INITIATION

Neurosis would seem to result from attempts to avoid a necessary developmental change in life, an attempt to avoid (in the language of initiation) being initiated into the next phase of development. Jung (*Collected Works,* 4) suggests that the cause of neurosis in a patient can be better understood by asking "What is the task which the patient does not want to fulfill? What difficulty is he trying to avoid?"

The occurrence of neurotic behavior, therefore, may represent the need for an initiatory change—as well as signal its beginning. A professional woman having difficulty feeling her own maturity and authority in relation to two male supervisors, finally arranged a meeting with both of them. The meeting did not go well. She felt no relief: "It was like they were both against me, like trying to work things out with my brother when I was too small to fight back."

The night after the unsuccessful confrontation, she went to bed and awoke abruptly at 4 A.M., with a strong sense of anger. An hour later, she had a sudden surge of spontaneous imagery, a vision that "just happened to me." She remembered Jesus saying something like, "Jerusalem, how often have I wanted to gather you under my wings!" Then the imagery suddenly changed to one of her mother's red hens gathering her newly hatched chicks under her wings, settling into a warm nest. The chicks peeped for awhile and then settled down. A deep sense of peace followed this vision. She felt it all through the next day, even when talking to the two male supervisors. She felt spontaneous and whole: "I just moved and didn't have to think what to do." Partly because of this emotional experience, she began to examine more deeply painful childhood memories of her relationship with her parents.

This woman's experience, one of many associated with her initiation into expanded personal and professional capabilities, depicts how the initiatory experience often occurs only when there has been a failure to deal with the stress caused by ego fear of change. It also illustrates the spontaneous activity of the unconscious in producing meaningful dream imagery to bridge gaps in self-understanding—e.g., the images of Jesus and the mother hen, two previously unconnected images in her thoughts. The connection wrought an alteration in her ego, a sense of protection and peace, in which the conscious personality was able to more fully utilize its true potential. Note that in many initiation rites a heroic challenge *precedes* the initiatory experience, while a sense of peace (without ego inflation) *follows* the experience.

Each new initiation constellates another more advanced task of development. A college professor received tenure very early in his career, while many colleagues were being denied tenure altogether. But right after he achieved this new and outwardly more secure position, he began to dream repeatedly that he was not accepted by his older male colleagues, even those who had voted him the new academic position. "They think I'm the golden human being, but I don't know if they know what I really stand for; I'm afraid they'll just 'mouth' liking me but really undercut me." In response to this new inner doubt, following a major outward reassurance, he made a marked change in his appearance, apparently unconsciously, and grew a thick, black beard and mustache. When asked about the decision to grow the beard, he explained that his wife liked it and his parents didn't. It was therefore a symbol of moving away from the approval of parents (and the approval of paternal colleagues) and toward a more personal adaptation, his wife. Although his personal decision was *still* expressed in terms of what others wanted, he began to move toward responsibility for himself, more closely aligning his image of himself with his true abilities. Through repeated dreams concerning the flaws that yet remained in his interpersonal relationships, this man made a promising start in guiding his inner progress.

THEORETICAL REFLECTIONS

It is in the nature of the psyche to move through continual transformation. When the ego participates with this process in a responsible way, conscious ego-transformation occurs. As the dominant ego-image moves into more comprehensive forms of itself, each new movement may require a partial regression and struggle with residual, unintegrated contents.

At the threshold of each new transformation of the ego-image stands the formal or informal experience of initiation. The outer forms of initiation, such as those found in "primitive" societies still practicing mythological puberty rites, offer social and collective support for ego-transformation. In a diverse society such as ours, however, initiations are often informal, inner, hidden from public observation, and often revealed only to the psychotherapist— even then frequently only in dreams. Knowing that we are in a process of continual transformation, we may expect the recurrence of initiation motifs such as outlined by Henderson (1967): submission, containment-release or transformation, and the sense of immanence in the world. Intuitively we already know that there is meaning behind such otherwise painful experiences as isolation from a previously adaptive ego-image. The quiet trials of life, often requiring a heroism unseen by the world, mean something other than meaningless pain. They are the tests at the threshold of the temple, life-reviews preparing one for life-transformation. Outer passages become the occasion of inner change, mediated through the Self—the deepest layer of the personality that gives birth to dreams.

These inner initiations are part of what Edinger (1977) has called "The

New Myth of Meaning," the myth of the increasing embodiment of consciousness in the only carrier available to it—the individual human being who consciously undertakes the task of conscious individuation. Edinger sees the individual psyche as the Holy Grail, the container for increasing consciousness: "psychic substance which is produced by the experience of the opposites suffered, not blindly, but in living awareness." He adds, "This experience is the *coniunctio, the mysterium coniunctionis* that generates the Philosopher's Stone. . . ."

In alchemy, which Jung considered a forerunner of depth psychology, the Philosopher's Stone was the mysterious goal of the alchemical work. It was capable of transforming ordinary matter into gold. In psychological terms, the events of our ordinary daily lives are transformed into something of very high value—gold. The Philosopher's Stone, also described as the *elixer vitae,* the panacea, the water of life, would cure all ills. But if it was taken in the wrong state of mind, without the proper container of consciousness, it could also be deadly poison. The alchemist's work was not only on the transformation of matter, but upon his own deeper self as well.

In a previous essay, I examined strange types of dreams, which I called *Koan dreams* because of their apparent similarity of purpose to the classic Koan riddle of Zen Buddhism (Hall 1977, pp. 308-309). The purpose of these dreams seems to be the encouragement of the rational mind to relinquish its illusions of logical thought as a sufficient means of describing reality and to experience its own innate freedom and creativity. The first Koan dream that caught my attention was from a complex, painfully neurotic man who had studied Zen for one year in Japan soon after the Second World War. He had gone to graduate school in Philadelphia and frequently had been on the train between his home city and Philadelphia. He dreamed he was in the train station in Philadelphia desperately trying to find someone who could tell him which train to take to Philadelphia! He was attempting to get to where he *already* was, but required some outer confirmation to permit him to know in consciousness that what he sought was already present. He was seeking initiation.

In an ideal culture, socially sanctioned initiation processes would facilitate all significant stages of life transformation from birth through death. At present we are far from such a world, although I take hope from a dream reported to Jung (Edinger 1984, p. 11). This dream suggests that the foundation for such a culture is already in existence, but we are far from completing and inhabiting it:

A temple of vast dimensions was in the process of being built. As far as one could see—ahead, behind, right and left—there were incredible numbers of people building on gigantic pillars. I, too, was building on a pillar. The whole building process was in its very beginning, but the foundation was already there, the rest of the building was starting to go up, and I and many others were working on it.

Jung was told this dream and his remark was "Yes, you know, that is the temple we all build on. We don't know the people because, believe me, they build in India and China and in Russia and all over the world. That is the new religion. You know how long it will take until it is built? . . . about six hundred years."

REFERENCES

Edinger, E. 1984. The creation of consciousness: Jung's myth for modern man. Toronto: Inner City Books.

Hall, J. A. 1977. *Clinical uses of dreams: Jungian interpretations and enactments.* New York and London: Grune and Stratton.

Hall, J. A. 1983. Enantiodromia and the unification of opposites: Spontaneous dream images in *The arms of the windmill: Essays in analytical psychology in honor of Werner H. Engel.* New York: Jung Foundation.

Henderson, J. L. 1967. *Thresholds of initiation.* Middletown, Connecticut: Wesleyan University Press.

Jung, C. G. *Collected works.* London: Routledge and Kegan Paul.

Miyuki, M. Self-realization in the ten oxherding pictures. *Quadrant* (Spring 1982).

THE MEANING OF DEPRESSION AT SIGNIFICANT STAGES OF LIFE

V. Walter Odajnyk

*In his essay, "The Meaning of Depression at Significant Stages of Life,"
V. Walter Odajnyk stresses the need for, and the positive value of depression,
as part and parcel of the transitional process. Tracing the development of
Jung's ideas about depression, the author demonstrates how the contents of
the unanalyzed unconscious, the "shadow" or* nigredo, *regenerate the psyche
and develop the personality, particularly at adolescence and midlife. He
examines Jung's use of alchemy as a metaphor of psychic transformation.
Because "depression or mania follow on the heels of an initial contact with the
unconscious," the* nigredo *or* separatio *must be encountered and endured for
the sake of raising consciousness. Odajnyk reminds us that every significant
change in age, status, role, attitude, or personality is accompanied by the
demise and mourning of a former condition. Only through such "dark nights
of the soul" is the person reborn into a new way of being and living.*

V. Walter Odajnyk, Ph.D., *is a psychotherapist practicing in New York
City. He is a graduate of the C. G. Jung Institute of Zurich and author of*
Marxism and Existentialism *(1965) and* Jung and Politics: The Political and
Social Ideas of C. G. Jung *(1976).*

C. G. JUNG made a significant contribution to our understanding of the
psychology of depression. His most striking discovery was that in its
natural condition the unconscious is in a depressed state. The usual symptoms
associated with depression—the feelings of inadequacy, inertia, heaviness,
sadness, blackness, lack of interest in life and the pull towards death—are apt
descriptions of the lower depths of the psyche. It is no wonder that
consciousness, normally activated by the opposite principles—spirit, light,
energy, joy, curiosity, life—fights vigorously not to fall into the hands of the
unconscious. But by paying close attention to the unconscious, and with the

help of the disclosures that the psyche itself makes in the alchemical treatises, Jung discovered two other startling facts: that the unconscious deplores its depressed condition and longs to be made free of it, and that within its blackness it contains a germ of consciousness capable of unifying the conscious and unconscious parts of the psyche, thereby healing the split soul of man.

In what follows, I want to describe the evolution of Jung's ideas about the nature of depression. To begin with, he thought it was a compensatory response by the unconscious to one-sided or erroneous conscious attitudes and behavior. Next, he saw depression and mania as two possible reactions on the part of an ego-consciousness that has become aware of the powers of the unconscious and feels its stability and formerly assumed superiority threatened. In *Symbols of Transformation* (1956), he described depression as an aspect of the regressive tendency associated with the incest longing. The regression occurs because an obstacle is encountered in conscious development or social adaptation and there is a need for a renewal and a rechannelling of the flow of psychic energy. This is particularly true at two crucial stages of life: the passage from youth to adulthood and the passage from adulthood to the maturity of old age. Finally, with alchemy, Jung came upon the initially given black state of the unconscious and its desire to unite with consciousness. The manifestations and dynamics resulting from this urge of the unconscious parallel the process of individual maturation and involve a series of depressions as an integral part of such development.

DEPRESSION AS COMPENSATION

Noticing the similarity of symptoms in mourning and melancholia, Freud speculated that psychic libido withdraws into the unconscious because of the loss of a love object: if the loss is conscious, mourning results; if it is unconscious, depression. The self-deprecatory aspect of depression, absent in mourning, Freud ascribed to the basic love-hate ambivalence inherent in all intimate relationships and the turning of the negative feelings onto the part of the ego that had identified with the lost love object.

Jung's notion for the reasons of the withdrawal of libido into the unconscious during a depression was quite different. He thought it had to do with *compensation*. In *Two Essays on Analytical Psychology* (1953), Jung gives an example of what he means. He writes that while in America he was consulted by a forty-five year old man who for twenty-five years concentrated all his energy, in the one-sided way "peculiar to successful American businessmen," says Jung, to build an immense enterprise. He then retired, intent on enjoying the fruits of his labor. But instead of being able to "live," by which he meant the pursuit of sports, horses, women, and cars, he had a complete "nervous breakdown" and became a depressed hypochondriac. What happened? A compensation to his former one-sided conscious attitude set in. Having lived in a focused, mental way, his physical and emotional life was ignored. Unfortunately, our psychic energy is not always ours to command at will. Also, the psyche has goals that lie beyond conscious goals and can even by inimical to them. He was right—his body and his emotions needed attention. But the regulating center of the psyche (the Self) decided that this was to be done through introversion and not through the extraverted activities that he would have liked—extraversion being still part of his former conscious attitude. So he fell into a depression and his body started acting up with all sorts of psycho-somatic troubles.

Now usually, when the conscious world has turned cold, empty, and grey, the unconscious comes to life. But the unconscious does not inherently seem to care for human or conscious needs. Often consciousness can suffer, hunger, and freeze while the unconscious grows lush and green. This inimical stance of the unconscious normally has a meaning: it wants to restore a certain balance or bring some content to consciousness. And if the unconscious is extremely inimical to consciousness, it means that the conscious attitude was, or continues to be, false or pretentious towards the unconscious—ignoring it, overpowering it, manipulating it, and, in general, disregarding its needs and limitations.

The businessman's depression and hypochondria were signs that his psychic energy had receded into the unconscious and started a compensatory onslaught against the previous conscious behavior and attitudes. Having been ignored and repressed for so many years, now with the relaxation of tension, it began to pursue its own ends and make its own demands on consciousness. When this happens, it is imperative quickly to turn to the unconscious and establish a relationship with it. That means the businessman had to take his hypochondriacal symptoms seriously and pursue the unconscious energy of which they were an expression. This would entail his bringing the unconscious energy to consciousness through the fantasy images—images being the only way that psychic energy can be caught—that are usually associated with such symptoms. Had he succeeded in becoming conscious of the images and of their meaning, and incorporated all this into his conscious attitude he might have been cured—as well as changed. That, of course, is the problem. People often want to change but are terribly afraid, especially if they find that they will have little conscious control over the process and the results of the change, or if the change calls for a radical about-face in their ideological, moral, social, or professional lives. In the case of the businessman, the compensation that set in was extreme, and Jung was not successful in getting him to bring up his unconscious fantasies. "A case so far advanced," he concludes, "can only be cared for until death; it can hardly be cured."

The other example of a psychogenic depression that Jung gives in *Two Essays* is in the chapter entitled "Phenomena Resulting from the Assimilation of the Unconscious." Here, he speaks of depression as the result of an initial contact with the unconscious. Whether that contact is unintentional, for example when, the unconscious bursts forth into consciousness because of fatigue, drugs, stress, or some life trauma, or whether it is deliberately cultivated during analysis by bringing up fantasy images—depression or mania is the result. In some people, the contact with the unconscious leads to an "accentuation of ego-consciousness, a heightened self-confidence" bordering on "god-almightiness." In others, "their self-confidence dwindles, and they look on with resignation at all the extraordinary things the unconscious produces." The former assume a responsibility for the unconscious that goes much too far, identifying their ego with its powerful energy and extra-human contents. The latter give up all sense of responsibility in the overwhelming realization of the powerlessness of the ego against the fates that rule it. One becomes a god; the other, just a worthless worm. These are the extreme reactions. Most people fall somewhere in between. If looked at analytically, the conscious optimism is really a *compensation* for deep-seated feelings of insecurity and helplessness, while the pessimistic resignation hides a defiant will to power. In the latter case, therefore, the depression is caused by an unconscious, or consciously denied, will to power.

Marie-Louise von Franz (1980) writes that often behind a psychogenic depression there is an especially intense desire of some sort, whether for power, love, success, aggression, getting things one's own way, and so on, which the person for a variety of reasons won't allow to come to the surface. In many instances, the drive is so inordinate and irrational that, in fact, it has to be repressed. But often it has gotten that disturbed because it lies buried in the unconscious, where it becomes attached to one of the instincts or to a complex and then takes on the "all or nothing" reaction characteristic of unintegrated instincts or complexes. So part of the business of bringing these fantasy contents to consciousness is to humanize them, to give them rational and moral limits. But to start with, that too produces a depression; for losing a secretly cherished hope, hate, or drive, we feel disillusioned and diminished. "No, you can't have what you want—it's too late, or impossible!" How often that comes up in an analysis, in one form or another. Most of us don't want to hear that. We prefer to hold on to our "god-like" desires of getting the world the way we want it. This also applies to projections. How strenuously we, or rather, something in us, fights to maintain them in the face of all objective evidence. We just refuse to look at the facts staring us in the face—"It cannot be so!" And if a correction is forced on us by undeniable events, how often we withdraw into "a lofty sense of injury"—which is just another way of not giving up. "Well, perhaps it didn't work out this time," we say, or "You see, this always happens to me!" But even if the correction is made willingly and one really does give up, still a depression follows because the psychic energy that was invested in the projection no longer flows back to us but has been cut off. It then has to be sought in the unconscious, and if that is done properly, another bit of the unconscious is made part of the conscious structure, and the psychic energy formerly streaming out towards the world remains within. This is the case, for example, when men and women, after repeated disappointments discover that what their romantic fascinations are mostly about is the need for a relationship with the anima or the animus, or with some as yet unrealized characteristic or potential of their own psyche. It may make one depressed to realize these things, but at least this form of depression is inherently constructive. It can force us to focus on the necessary internal changes, and give up lamenting repeated disappointments, about which one can't do anything anyway.

Jung's early personal discovery that depression or mania follow on the heels of an initial contact with the unconscious was later confirmed by his study of alchemy where the *nigredo* is the product of the first alchemical operation. Even though the *nigredo* is usually depicted as a death-like state, it is also sometimes described as a condition of extreme agitation and restlessness. Here is a second century Chinese alchemical description of the sufferings caused by a "technical error" during the opus:

> Disaster will [then] come to the black mass [to the unconscious, to the psyche]: gases from food consumed [the contents assimilated by consciousness] will make noises inside the intestines and stomach [one must take all of this both somatically and psychologically]. The right essence will be exhaled and the evil one inhaled. Days and nights will be passed without sleep, moon after moon. The body will then be tired out, giving rise to an appearance of insanity. The hunched pulses will stir and boil so violently as to drive away peace of mind and body. . . . Ghostly things will make their appearance, at which [the alchemist] will marvel even in his sleep. He is then led to rejoice, thinking that he is assured of longevity. But all of a sudden he is seized by an untimely death. (Jung, 1954)

This is a description of a manic-depressive psychosis—an unfortunate assimilation of ego-consciousness by the contents of the unconscious. This form of the *nigredo* is not caused by an initial contact with the unconscious. It is said to be the result of an erroneous attitude or a mistaken intervention during the therapeutic process. Every analyst (like every physician) has his or her share of "technical errors," which sometimes end in tragedy. Fortunately, most mistakes do not produce reactions of such magnitude, but they do disturb the process and the health of the patient—and of the analyst.

The above is a description of a depression that passed into a psychosis and then death. More common are depressions, characterized by restlessness and agitation, that do not turn psychotic or fatal. It seems to me that the alchemists, and Jung after them, tended to emphasize the value of the heavy, black, death-like aspects of the *nigredo*, and to downplay its agitated, restless, frenzied manifestations. I think their emphasis is right. Agitated depression is not yet a real depression. It is an attempt on the part of the person to fight off the depression and to maintain the dominance of ego-consciousness. In this form the depression is useless for any psychological growth or healing. Only those depressions are useful and healing in which the ego stays intact but willing to compromise with the pressing drives and needs of the unconscious.

Mania, the other reaction to an initial contact with the unconscious, is also not emphasized by the alchemists, or by Jung, nor does it seem to be treated as a valuable or useful stage. This is probably due to the introverted bias of the alchemists, and of Jung—a bias for self-knowledge and inner development, as opposed to trying to improve others and the world. Yet a mania in which the ego remains intact and attempts to channel the energy streaming into consciousness from the unconscious can also be a healthy and life-giving phenomenon. (Many creative, religious, and humanitarian endeavors are fueled in this way.) By engaging in responsible interaction with people and with the external world, the manic-driven individual may also be led to inner development and self-knowledge. Therapeutically, it would be a mistake to try and force mania into a depression—even if that were possible. Mania is usually a compensation for deep-seated feelings of insecurity, helplessness, and worthlessness; it is probably preferable to a depression brought on by inferiority feelings of such magnitude.

But there is another form of mania that Jung does not mention. It is, however, implied in his concept of *enantiodromia,* and in the change of the *nigredo* into the *albedo* (whitening) as the second alchemical stage. When a depression has reached its nadir, a reversal sets in and the psyche moves into a manic phase. Everything is suddenly reversed: the symptomatology is directly opposite to that of depression. The previously hidden will to power is now in the open, while the formerly conscious feelings of inferiority fall into the unconscious. In most cases such an extreme swing denotes a weak ego or a severely disturbed and unbalanced psyche, hence the classification, *manic-depressive psychosis.*

DEPRESSION AND RENEWAL

Jung's initial ideas on depression were further developed in *Symbols of Transformation* (1956). *Symbols* is an expansion of the first of the *Two Essays,* "On the Psychology of the Unconscious" begun in 1911-1912. Jung was then thirty-six and had just broken with Freud. I mention this, because both his age and his break with Freud brought on a long-lasting depression to which he conscientiously devoted himself for many years. The creative fruit of that depression is analytical psychology.

In *Symbols of Transformation* Jung again stresses the compensatory nature of depression. "Depression," he writes, "should be regarded as an unconscious compensation whose content must be made conscious if it is to be fully effective. This can only be done by consciously regressing along with the depressive tendency and integrating the memories so activated into the conscious mind—which was what the depression was aiming at in the first place." But this time he examines, in some detail, the unconscious world into which the depression leads.

He begins where Freud ends—with the incest longing, the desire to return to the womb. He doesn't think that the longing should be taken literally. Instead, he sees it as an expression of a psychological longing for a return to the security of childhood and early youth, when the person lived without responsibility as an appendage of the parents and in blissful harmony with instinctive nature. The temptation for such a regression to the world of childhood takes place whenever a person is confronted with the task of adapting and growing psychologically and socially. But the other reason for the regression is a desire for renewal. For if the process of conscious adaptation has encountered an obstacle, a new attitude or channel for the flow of life's energy is required. This flow of energy can move only along certain given instinctive paths: as the example of the businessman shows, we are not at liberty to decide the flow of essential psychic energy. (The ego has some leeway with any "surplus psychic energy"—this is what we call free will: surplus psychic energy at the disposal of the ego. But in a depression where there is hardly any surplus energy at the ego's disposal there is hardly any choice in directing one's functioning.) Therefore it becomes necessary to return to the instincts, to pay attention to where they want to move, and begin a new journey from there. But this is easier said than done, and the process is fraught with great danger along the way. This is the other important issue Jung begins to stress:

> Regression carried to its logical conclusion means a linking back with the world of natural instincts, which in its formal or ideal aspect is a kind of *prima materia*. If this *prima materia* can be assimilated by the conscious mind it will bring about a reactivation and reorganization of its contents. But if the conscious mind proves incapable of assimilating the new contents pouring in from the unconscious, then a dangerous situation arises in which they keep their original, chaotic, and archaic form and consequently disrupt the unit of consciousness.

A severe psychosis is the result. In another place, Jung writes:

> Whenever some great work is to be accomplished [be it a task of life-adaptation or some creative effort], before which a man recoils, doubtful of his strength, his libido streams back to the fountainhead—and that is the dangerous moment when the issue hangs between annihilation and new life. For if the libido gets stuck in the wonderland of this inner world, then for the upper world man is nothing but a shadow, he is already moribund or at least seriously ill. But if the libido manages

to tear itself loose and force its way up again, something like a miracle happens: the journey to the underworld was a plunge into the fountain of youth, and the libido, apparently dead, wakes to renewed fruitfulness.

A good part of *Symbols of Transformation* is concerned with illustrating and amplifying the universal manifestation of this process with various mythological accounts of night-sea-journeys, descents into the underworld, and with stories, poems, and religious rituals of death and rebirth. In this book, Jung stresses two periods of life where an adaptation is required and a severe depression is likely to occur. One is at the stage where a separation must be made from the world of the parents, so that the libido can begin to flow outside toward the broader world. In this case, the regressive longing must not be encouraged beyond the point necessary to get things moving again. Here, not the courageous descent into the unconscious is required, but rather a courageous sacrifice of the retrospective longing, and a wholehearted dedication to life is what's called for. This, too, cannot be done without the aid of the unconscious. But at this stage it usually does help by throwing up the incest taboo in the form of various frightening emotions and terrifying images that threaten to swallow the still youthful ego. It requires an unusual pull of the parents, or a serious problem of adaptation, one often having its roots in inherent tendencies or in an earlier developmental stage, for the incest taboo on the one side and the pull of exogamous libido on the other to fail to get the person out of the unconscious parental milieu. Experimentation with psychedelic drugs, or the abuse of alcohol, marijuana, cocaine (and other "consciousness altering" drugs) are detrimental to the proper development of the ego at this point in life, for they tend to overpower the incest taboo, the natural fear of the unconscious, and support the retrospective longing that only wants "to resuscitate the torpid bliss and effortlessness of childhood" (Jung, 1956). Should a person fail to tear himself loose of his family fixations and of his unconscious fantasies and longings and so free his libido for social and other purposes, he will fall under the spell of unconscious compulsion. Wherever he goes, he will recreate the infantile milieu by projecting his complexes, thus reproducing the same dependence and lack of freedom that characterized his relation to his parents. The libido then remains fixed in a primitive form and keeps people on a low level where they have no control over themselves and are at the mercy of their affects. Needless to say, such a condition just leads to bouts of frustration, anger, rage, depression, a search for an escape from the intolerable situation, and, after a time, a fall back into another similar situation. Sometimes, unfortunately, the escape ends in a serious illness, a psychosis, or a suicide—all of which, in such cases, must be looked upon as unsuccessful attempts at self-healing and renewal.

The other place where a severe depression occurs is at mid-life, when a *metanoia*, a basic reorientation of one's attitudes and goals is called for. In this instance, just the opposite stance toward the unconscious is required. For by now, typically, the ego has become firmly established, the person is well-grounded in the material world, with parental, social, professional responsibilities. In other cases, the conscious attitude has become one-sided and then sterile: life seems to have run dry; enthusiasm for the things that once meant so much wanes or completely disappears; and the person falls into a stupor, questioning the purpose and meaning of all that she or he has done and should supposedly continue doing. At this juncture, it becomes necessary to follow the depressive tendency into the unconscious in order to bring up the "saving" contents and to discover where and how the libido wants to flow again into the world. This requires two things: (1) the willingness to let go of one's habitual conscious attitudes and assumptions, particularly one's so-called "reasonable" convictions about the world; and (2) the overcoming of the fear of incest, i.e., of the repulsion and anxiety that contact with the unconscious often calls forth. (This is what all those frog princes and princesses, the dragons and other ugly beasts of the fairy tales are all about.)

Jung gives a beautiful description of both the early and mid-life phases— in one of my favorite passages in all his writings. It is a long quotation but well worth the time and the space:

> The sun, rising triumphant, tears himself from the enveloping womb of the sea, and leaving behind him the noonday zenith and all its glorious works, sinks down again into the maternal depths, into all-enfolding and all-regenerating night. This image is undoubtedly a primordial one, and there was profound justification for its becoming a symbolical expression of human fate: in the morning of life the son tears himself loose from the mother, from the domestic hearth, to rise through battle to his destined heights. Always he imagines his worst enemy in front of him, yet he carries the enemy within himself—a deadly longing for the abyss, a longing to drown in his own source, to be sucked down to the realm of the Mothers. His life is a constant struggle against extinction, a violent yet fleeting deliverance from ever-lurking night. This death is no external enemy, it is his own inner longing for the stillness and profound peace of all-knowing non-existence, for all-seeing sleep in the ocean of coming-to-be and passing away. Even in his highest strivings for harmony and balance, for the profundities of philosophy and the raptures of the artist, he seeks death, immobility, satiety, rest. If, like Peirithous, he tarries too long in this abode of rest and peace, he is overcome by apathy, and the poison of the serpent paralyzes him for all time. If he is to live, he must fight and sacrifice his longing for the past in order to rise to his own heights. And having reached the noonday heights, he must sacrifice his love for his own achievement, for he may not loiter. The sun, too, sacrifices its greatest strength in order to hasten onward to the fruits of autumn, which are the seeds of rebirth.
>
> The natural course of life demands that the young person should sacrifice his childhood and his childish dependence on the physical parents, lest he remain caught body and soul in the bonds of unconscious incest. This regressive tendency has been consistently opposed from the most primitive times by the great psychotherapeutic systems which we know as the religions. They seek to create an autonomous consciousness by weaning mankind away from the sleep of childhood. The sun breaks from the mists of the horizon and climbs to undimmed

brightness at the meridian. Once this goal is reached, it sinks down again towards night. This process can be allegorized as a gradual seeping away of the water of life: one has to bend ever deeper to reach the source. When we are feeling on top of the world we find this exceedingly disagreeable; we resist the sunset tendency, especially when we suspect that there is something in ourselves which would like to follow this movement, for behind it we sense nothing good, only an obscure, hateful threat. So, as soon as we feel ourselves slipping, we begin to combat this tendency and erect barriers against the dark, rising flood of the unconscious and its enticements to regression, which all too easily takes on the deceptive guise of sacrosanct ideals, principles, beliefs, etc.

If we wish to stay on the heights we have reached, we must struggle all the time to consolidate our consciousness and its attitude. But we soon discover that this praiseworthy and apparently unavoidable battle with the years leads to stagnation and desiccation of soul. Our convictions become platitudes ground out on a barrel-organ, our ideals become starchy habits, enthusiasm stiffens into automatic gestures. The source of the water of life seeps away. We ourselves may not notice it, but everybody else does, and that is even more painful. If we should risk a little introspection, coupled perhaps with an energetic attempt to be honest for once with ourselves, we may get a dim idea of all the wants, longings, and fears that have accumulated down there—a repulsive and sinister sight. The mind shies away, but life wants to flow down into the depths. Fate itself seems to preserve us from this, because each of us has a tendency to become an immovable pillar of the past. Nevertheless, the daemon throws us down, makes us traitors to our ideals and cherished convictions—traitors to the selves we thought we were. That is an unmitigated catastrophe, because it is an *unwilling* sacrifice. Things go very differently when the sacrifice is a voluntary one. Then it is no longer an overthrow, a "transvaluation of values," the destruction of all that we held sacred, but transformation and conservation. Everything young grows old, all beauty fades, all heat cools, all brightness dims, and every truth becomes stale and trite. For all these things have taken on shape, and all shapes are worn thin by the working of time; they age, sicken, crumble to dust—unless they change. But change they can, for the invisible spark that generated them is potent enough for infinite generation. No one should deny the danger of the descent, but it *can* be risked. No one *need* risk it, but it is certain that some one will. And let those who go down the sunset way do so with open eyes, for it is a sacrifice which daunts even the gods. Yet every descent is followed by an ascent; the vanishing shapes are shaped anew, and a truth is valid in the end only if it suffers change and bears new witness in new images, in new tongues, like an old wine that is put into new bottles. (*Symbols of Transformation,* 1956)

DEPRESSION AND THE NIGREDO

Around 1930, soon after his own "descent into the underworld," Jung "stumbled," as he says, upon alchemy. At first he thought it was utter nonsense. Many people, including beginning analysts, are familiar with that feeling. But if one takes the trouble, one finds, like Jung, that the alchemical symbols and processes are so often encountered in analytical practice that, once mastered, they serve as guideposts along what is usually a murky and confusing journey. That was essentially what alchemy did for Jung: it enabled him to place his personal psychological discoveries in the context of a centuries old tradition that provided a non-personal, objective depiction of the stages of psychic development. For example, he knew a good deal about depression before he came to alchemy; but the entire phenomenon was placed in a much broader context with his studies of the *nigredo,* its various symbols, symptoms, and outcomes.

The alchemists, Jung writes, were like some modern men: they preferred immediate personal experience to belief in traditional ideas or dogmas. For many people, the Christian drama gave, and still gives, a satisfactory expression to the unconscious and its archetypal contents. Such people live contained within the Christian world, and Christ is their protective image or amulet against the unconscious powers that always threaten to possess or swallow the ego personality. "Jesus Saves!" And He saves one from evil, destruction, and death. Even when a Christian takes up his own cross and seeks his own death as a lived inner reality, he does so supported by a clearly defined tradition and the assurance of resurrection. However, once the Christian myth fades, as it has for many in our day, the individual is once again exposed to the powers of destruction—alone, and with no assurances of any kind. But even when the myth is intact, there are always people for whom the ruling expression of the collective religious life is not wholly satisfying. They set out on a search for direct individual experience. Following the lure of the unconscious psyche, they soon find themselves in the wilderness, where, like Jesus, they come up against the son of darkness. Then follows a fateful encounter leading either to their salvation or destruction.

On the whole, the alchemists were still safe, for they projected all the evil upon matter. Nevertheless, they were affected by it: "*Horridas nostrae mentis purga tenebras, accende lumen sensibus!*" (Jung, 1954). ("Purge the horrible darkness of our mind, light a light for our senses!") This was a prayer of an old adept who must have been going through the first stage of the work, "which was felt," Jung writes, "as 'melancholia' . . . and corresponds to the encounter with the shadow in psychology" (Ibid.). The alchemists dubbed this experience the *nigredo.* It not only brought decay, suffering, death, and the torments of hell visibly before an alchemist's eyes, but "it also cast the shadow of its melancholy over his own solitary soul. In the blackness of a despair which was not his own, and of which he was merely the witness, he experienced how *it* turned into the worm and the poisonous dragon" (Jung, 1964).

Here is the further development of Jung's understanding of the psychology of depression. There are usually four stages in the alchemical opus: *nigredo* or *melanosis* (blackening); *albedo* or *leukosis* (whitening); *xanthosis* or *citrinitas* (yellowing); and *rubedo* or *iosis* (reddening). One of the alchemists noted the association of these four colors with the four humors and the four temperaments: *nigredo* with melancholic; *albedo* with phlegmatic; *citrinitas* with choleric; and *rubedo* with sanguine (Ibid.).

Nigredo is the initial stage. Sometimes it corresponds with the *prima materia,* or is a quality of it. It is then described as the black earth in which the gold or *lapis* is sown like a grain of wheat. Another variation has it as the earth that Adam brought with him from paradise. This initially given earth is described as *nigrum, nigrius, nigro*—black, blacker than black. At other times, the *prima materia* is called *chaos* or *massa confusa;* in this case it represents the state prior to creation. In fact, it has a thousand names and characteristics, and they are all essentially synonyms for the unconscious in its initial, natural, raw, or we would say "unanalyzed" state. And an encounter with or a fall into this dark, chaotic foundation of our being inevitably produces a depression.

But the *nigredo* is not only or always a quality of the *prima materia.* It can also appear as a consequence of the separation *(solutio, separatio, divisio, putrefactio)* of the basic elements making up the *prima materia.* The opus is often likened to the creation of the world and *nigredo* is the dawn state. Looked at psychologically, the "creation of the world" has to do with the origin of consciousness. The fall from paradise, knowledge of good and evil, and the experience of shame and guilt, the curse of toil, suffering and death are all analogies to the *nigredo* that is the result of a *separatio.* A more contemporary and specific example would be as follows: many people come for therapy, more or less in good spirits, seeking to untangle some problem or conflict; in the course of the work, if it has to go deep enough, they become unsure of themselves, confused, disoriented and depressed. In other words, they have fallen from what appeared to them as a "whole" and healthy state into one where they are miserable and at odds with themselves.

The union of two opposed elements will also give rise to a state of *nigredo.* For example, say a person has already done some work on the unconscious in the course of his or her life or through analysis, but seeks a still closer union. Or suppose a person comes to analysis with a highly developed one-sided conscious attitude: let us say it is over-developed eros, to get away from the usual example of the thinking type. A union must now be brought about with the opposite principle, i.e., with the underdeveloped logos, which has probably become cold, unrelated and dogmatic, by way of compensation. The union of these opposites (called *coniugium, matrimonium, coniunctio, coitus*) is then performed under the likeness of male and female, either in actual life or in dream images. The union of conscious and unconscious, eros and logos having been accomplished, a "death" *(mortificatio, calcinatio, putreficatio)* follows and a corresponding *nigredo.* In alchemy this is called the *nigredo* of the first operation. Psychologically, one would say that a certain integration of the opposites has taken place and a better relation is established with the unconscious. But as time goes on, life, or a continuing analysis may again bring up certain problems or conflicts—and another separation and union must be brought about. This new union is again followed by a *morificatio*—a death. This would be the *nigredo* of the second operation. In fact, since there are usually seven or sometimes eight operations, there is a corresponding *nigredo* for each operation, so that one of the Greek treatises describes the alchemical opus as the "eight graves" (Jung, 1964).

Normally, the first *nigredo* is considered the worst, but there is no guarantee that this will always be the case. It depends on the nature of the personality and the difficulties that must be overcome along the way. In any case, some of the alchemists were optimistic about things. Maier, for instance, writes: "There is in our chemistry a certain noble substance, in the beginning whereof is wretchedness with vinegar, but in its ending joy with gladness. Therefore I have supposed that the same will happen to me, namely that I shall suffer difficulty, grief, and weariness at first, but in the end shall come to glimpse pleasanter and easier things" (as quoted in Jung, 1954). The first *nigredo* is seen as the worst, perhaps because with a person's first severe depression there is no sense that it has a useful purpose and no experience that one will ever come out of it.

Psychologically, the initial "*nigredo* corresponds to the darkness of the unconscious which contains in the first place the inferior personality, the shadow" (Jung, 1964). In a man, this then changes into the feminine figure that stands behind the shadow, and, in fact, controls it—the anima. In a woman, behind the shadow stands the masculine figure of the animus. The *nigredo* therefore leads to an encounter with the shadow and then with the animus and the anima, initially in their black, unredeemed, unconscious state. If the conscious mind allows itself to be influenced by these figures, it must inevitably become infected with their blackness and turn melancholic. But that is exactly how they are redeemed and made less black, while the conscious mind becomes less clear and bright, and less cheerful. But this is putting it much too simplistically. Here is how the feminine personification of the *prima materia* laments being in the state of *nigredo:*

> Through Cham, the Egyptian I must pass. . . . Noah must wash me . . . in the deepest sea, that my blackness may depart. . . . I must be fixed to this black cross, and must be cleansed therefrom with wretchedness and vinegar, and made white, that . . . my heart may shine like a carbuncle, and the old Adam come forth from me again. O! Adam Kadmon, how beautiful art thou! . . . Like Kedar I am black henceforth, ah! how long! O come, my Mesech [mixed drink], and disrobe me, that mine inner beauty may be revealed. . . . O Shulamite, afflicted within and without, the watchmen of the great city will find thee and wound thee, and rob thee of thy garments . . . and take away thy veil. Who then will lead me out from Edom, from thy stout wall? . . . Yet shall I be blissful again when I am delivered from the poison wherewith I am accursed, and my inmost seed and first birth comes forth. . . . For its father is the sun, and its mother the moon. (Jung, 1964)

Jung gives a detailed interpretation of this passage in *Mysterium Coniunctionis*. It is full of Old and New Testament allusions. Adam Kadmon is the original Adam, before the creation of Eve and before the Fall. He is the "first birth" whose father is the sun and mother the moon. Symbolically, he represents the Anthropos, the primordial universal being—hermaphroditic, whole, and immortal. He corresponds to the Atman of the Vedic tradition. Like the Atman, he is the paradoxical individual *and* universal soul of man.

The psychological implication of the passage is that after the unconscious undergoes a series of painful analytic procedures it can give birth to a completely transformed and integrated personality, the germ of which lies hidden within its depths. The other striking thing is that here we see how the unconscious feels about its own depressed condition. It longs for deliverance and promises a rebirth of the entire personality to anyone who takes the trouble to help. This is another example of the importance that alchemy has for an understanding of the human psyche and of the psychology of depression. In the alchemical treatises the collective Western psyche describes its own condition, its dynamic processes, and its ultimate goal.

Another way of seeing the *nigredo* is as a description of the original half-animal state of the unconscious, the inextricable interweaving of the soul with body which together form a *dark unity* (the *unio naturalis*). The aim of the entire alchemical opus was to rescue the light spirit *(Nous)* that had fallen into the embrace of dark matter *(Physis)*. Similarly, analysis works to free the soul from its enchainment in instinct and matter in order to establish a spiritual-psychic counterposition that will prove to be more or less immune to the influences of the body and of the external environment. (This is Jung's way of speaking in the context of alchemy, and it is not to be taken as referring to some metaphysical liberation; it refers to the freeing of the psyche from its blind attachment to instinct, objects, and people.) The establishment of such a counter-position is possible only if the projections that veil the reality of things are withdrawn. Once this unconscious identity comes to an end, the soul is "freed from its fetters in the things of sense" (Jung, 1964). This, of course, can be said in a sentence, but to accomplish it takes a lifetime.

In *Psychology and Alchemy* and in *Mysterium Coniunctionis* one can look up most of the synonyms and symbols of the *nigredo*. This is not just an idle game. These symbols come up in dreams and fantasies more often than one would suspect: we just are not always able to recognize them. Churchill, for example, was plagued during his entire life with bouts of depression. They were so familiar that the called them his "black dog." Now the black dog is one of the symbols of the *nigredo,* as is the mad or rabid dog. The black earth we already mentioned; at times it appears as black, heavy, oily water, or mud, or manure, or feces. There is Mercurius as the dragon eating its own tail. This motif comes up often enough as a fleshy circle of some kind. There is the black sun—*sol niger*—or the eclipsed sun, and also the dark crescent new moon.

One sees these in a lot of pictures by analysands. Then there is the raven, the black bird ("the black soul"), or the raven's head—*caput corvi*. The raven is a symbol of the Devil and of Saturn. I've never encountered the raven's head, but black birds are common enough in dreams. Then there is the skeleton, or the skull, or the head of the black Osiris. Again, with the exception of the head of black Osiris, the skull and skeleton come up frequently (Edinger, 1986). A very common motif is that of a crippled, sick, or dying old man—the dying or sterile king of myths and fairy tales. Then there is the buried man, Osiris, Christ—tombs, and coffins. Any black man or black woman is a symbol of the *nigredo;* in alchemy they often go under the names of the Ethiopian, the Moor, the Egyptian, or the Shulamite of the *Song of Songs.* In the United States these come up so often as blacks and Hispanics. The state of incubation, meditation, pregnancy are all *nigredo* analogues—so is the suffering of Job and the passion of Christ. Salt with its bitterness is an infrequent synonym, so is lead: "so bedevilled and shameless is lead that all who wish to investigate it fall into madness through ignorance," writes an alchemist (Jung, 1964). Lead fumes are poisonous and give rise to psychotic symptoms, hence the projection of the devil onto it and its use as a symbol for the *nigredo*. (Incidentally, lead poisoning is still called "saturnism.")

I hope this brief list and the above discussion demonstrate what a rich source alchemy is for a comprehensive understanding of depression—its symbols, causes, phases, and aims. In conclusion, I think it appropriate to give the *nigredo* the last word:

> Be turned to me with all your heart and do not cast me aside because I am black and swarthy, because the sun hath changed my colour and the waters have covered my face and the land hath been polluted and defiled in my works; for there was darkness over it, because I stick fast in the mire of the deep and my substance is not disclosed. Wherefore out of the depths have I cried, and from the abyss of the earth with my voice to all you that pass by the way. Attend and see me, if any shall find one like unto me, I will give into his hand the morning star. (von Franz, 1966)

The morning star is Venus. It heralds the coming of the light—the rebirth of the sun from its sojourn in the underworld. In the last chapter of *Revelation,* which anticipates the coming of the Kingdom of God, Christ says of himself: "I am the root and offspring of David and the bright and morning star." The Kingdom of God and the risen sun are symbols of completion and enlightenment. Psychologically, they indicate the attainment of wholeness and self-realization.

REFERENCES

Edinger, E. 1986. *Anatomy of the psyche.* La Salle, IL: Open Court.

Franz, M.-L. von. 1966. *Aurura consurgens: A document attributed to Thomas Aquinas on the problem of opposites in alchemy. Mysterium coniunctionis*, vol. 3. New York: Pantheon Books.

———. 1980. *Projection and re-collection in Jungian psychology: Reflections of the soul*. La Salle, IL: Open Court.

Jung, C. G. 1953. Two essays on analytical psychology. *Collected works*, vol. 7.

———. 1954. Psychology and alchemy. *Collected works*, vol. 12.

———. 1956. Symbols of transformation. *Collected works*, vol. 5.

———. 1964. Mysterium coniunctionis. *Collected works*, vol. 14.

Originally published as "Jung's contribution to an understanding of the meaning of depression" in *Quadrant*, Spring 1983. Reprinted with permission of the C. G. Jung Foundation for Analytical Psychology, New York.

INITIATION
INTO
OLD AGE
AND
DYING

PART SIX

21

"DO THEY CELEBRATE CHRISTMAS IN HEAVEN?" TEACHINGS FROM CHILDREN WITH LIFE-THREATENING ILLNESS

Tom Pinkson

In this article, Tom Pinkson, Ph.D., explores the ultimate, sacred passage of dying and death. He works with children having terminal illnesses who ask questions like "What is it like to die? Do they celebrate Christmas in heaven?" The author's remarks fulfill an "assignment . . . to share these lessons with others." As one of his dying patients, a 14 year old boy, put it: "That's why we're here, to work on our assignment. And when we're finished, we get to graduate."

Pinkson's treatment of the subject is doubly valuable, for his article is about death counseling just as much as it is about dying; in giving examples of how he has actually worked with dying youngsters and their families, he provides excellent guidelines not only for those of us who are concerned about our own deaths, but who are also concerned to help others to die peacefully and with dignity. He likens the role of death counseling to that of midwifery, as he helps these dying youngsters "give birth to themselves" by "actualizing their own symbols and myths to carry their spirit onward" through the portal of death. "People who are dying are on a vision quest. They may not articulate it that way, but they are."

Tom Pinkson, Ph.D., is clinical consultant to the Center for Attitudinal Healing (Tiburon, California) and a psychologist in private practice in Marin County and the San Francisco Bay Area. In 1971 he created the Marin Open House Wilderness Project, a unique and effective treatment program for heroin abusers, using Outward Bound techniques and vision quest forms and teachings. At the present time, much of his work is with children, families and adults facing life-threatening illnesses. He also consults with business and corporate groups on health promotion and conflict resolution. He is author of A Quest for Vision *(1976),* Do They Celebrate Christmas in Heaven? *(1985), and numerous articles on his work with cancer patients, rites of passage, and death and dying.*

Dedication

This chapter is dedicated to Bryan Bradshaw, Erik Renlund, Mary Beth Harder, Adrian Padilla, Tommy Fitzmaurice, and Barbara Eversole, for their lives, their teachings, and their spirits, which live on in the hearts and memories of their families and friends.

A PERSONAL ASSIGNMENT

BRYAN was eight years old and bedridden with cancer. He had been fighting a hard battle that included an amputation of one leg from the hip down, several lung surgeries, and intensive sessions of chemotherapy and radiation. Still the cancer had spread throughout his body. There was nothing else that could be done medically and Bryan's parents brought him home to die. I met Bryan through his involvement in the Children's Group of the Center for Attitudinal Healing in Tiburon, California, where I served as a clinical consultant. Over the years I had frequently visited him at home and during his numerous hospital stays. It looked as if this might be our last visit.

Bryan's mother told me he was upstairs and probably would not talk much because of the sedative effect of the pain-killing drugs he was taking. I went upstairs to his room. Bryan was lying very still with his eyes closed. The nearby TV was blasting away. I sat down next to his bed and greeted him. Several minutes went by as I sat in silence watching his indomitable spirit struggle for breath in his pain-wracked body. Then Bryan opened his eyes and sat up. He could barely muster enough strength to set up his pillow to support an upright position. I leaned over to help him get comfortable. He looked at me, suddenly clear-eyed and earnest, and asked, "Do they celebrate Christmas in Heaven? And, what about Easter, do they celebrate that too? Will there be a house for me like my house here?"

I was struck dumb by the suddenness and impact of his questions. My mind raced inward for answers, but there were none to be found.

"What's it like to die?" he asked, "Does it hurt?"

It was six weeks before Christmas and Bryan knew he probably would not make it to this important holiday. He would miss celebrating it with his family as he had done all of his young life up to now. What was to come for this valiant little fighter soon to die?

Bryan was one of many important teachers for me over the past fifteen years of working with people facing life-threatening illness. His blunt, heartfelt questions triggered a powerful confrontation within my psyche, similar to my previous reactions experienced with other children and adults on their passage into death. These confrontations have enriched my life immeasurably through the lessons they have provided. This chapter fulfills an "assignment" to share these lessons from several children and adults on their final passage, for I know they were given not just for me alone. The concept of assignment-fulfillment comes from a 14 year old boy as he lay in bed two days before his death from Ewing's Sarcoma. "Everybody has an assignment in life," he told me. "That's why we're here, to work on it. Sometimes they're longer and sometimes they're shorter, like with me," he added. "But that's why we're here, to work on our assignment. And when we're finished, we get to graduate."

The experience of "graduation," or death, is one transitional passage we all face; it is the great equalizer. Unlike other times of transition in the life cycle which might be ignored, repressed or unacknowledged, death demands our attention. I was painfully introduced to this fact at the age of four when my father died. Years later, while finishing my doctoral work in psychology, I received a suggestion that led me beyond my personal involvement and into the field of thanatology professionally.

I asked a member of my doctoral committee, Dr. William Lamers, what kind of client population he thought I would be most effective working with. I was shocked at his response: "People who are dying are on a vision quest. They may not articulate it that way, but they are. You've been taking people out for years now, guiding them on vision quests and this is what you could do for the dying."

The vision quest is a rite of passage into spiritual adulthood practiced by numerous Native American tribes in which a questing person enters the wilderness for a period of isolation and solitude, to seek guidance from the Great Spirit for their life path. In my book, *A Quest for Vision* (1976), I describe utilizing the vision quest as a model for a successful substance-abuse program I developed in 1972. Both the original vision quest as well as the program I developed, include the process inherent in all traditional rites of passage. These are severance, or letting go; transition/transformation; and return or incorporation. Rites of passage, as psychologist Dr. Jean Houston notes, are "doors through which one passes into larger life." They provide a form and support structure for powerful psychological processes during times of transition that, left unchanneled, might otherwise prove overwhelming to the psyche. The rituals and ceremonies of effective rites of passage provide a protected space where strong emotions can be openly experienced, thereby leading to transformation into new identity and developmental stages of growth. Participants need to surrender to the full psychic/emotional dimensions of the experience which includes, via the ritual, a joining of the personal with the collective, the inner with the outer, and the unconscious with the conscious.

Essential to all rites of passage is symbolic death and rebirth. The movement into and birth of the new, cannot take place without the release, or death, of the old. Severing the security of the known, such as leaving the comforts and safety of home to enter the unknown in the wilderness, as one does on a vision quest, dramatically elicits these dynamics. Rebirth is the return and incorporation back into the social collective with a new identity based on new consciousness acquired during the quest outing. When I reflected on the quest dynamics and the process of dying, I saw that Bill Lamers' assessment of their similarity was correct. When he asked me several months later to join with him and a team of others in starting the second Hospice program in the United States, I accepted the invitation.

During my experience with Hospice patients I found a paucity of effective psychosocial/emotional and spiritual support systems for the dying and their families, especially when they were not practicing members of a specific faith. Another observation was the significant role the patient's belief system and attitudinal mindset played in affecting the quality of their experience during their final stage of life.

Virginia Hine, anthropologist and author of *Last Letter to the Pebble People* (1979), describing her husband's death from cancer and its effect on family members, comments on the importance of these factors. She feels death forces us beyond the rational mind into a confrontation with spiritual reality. How we handle this confrontation helps determine whether "death is dehumanizing or transforming." Our attitudes, states Hine, can "enhance or detract from death's power to transform and spiritualize."

"It is quite possible," she goes on, "that a gradual spiritualization of consciousness is what life is all about." The altered states of her husband, described in her book, as well as many I witnessed through my hospice work, did indeed appear to be an acceleration of the "spiritualization of consciousness" process that she suggests. I left the hospice after a year to focus on working with children facing life-threatening illness at the Center for Attitudinal Healing in Tiburon, California. This Center was just getting started and, to my excitement, embodied a philosophy that recognized and validated the spiritual dimension of being.

My learning process intensified at the Center and led to a re-evaluation and subsequent transformation of my own "death myth," that is my conscious and unconscious beliefs and assumptions on the meaning of death and what happens afterwards.

For many people nowadays, there is little, if any, room for notions of soul, spirit, or the transcendent. We have lost touch with the numinous ground of our deeper being which is something more than the sum of the physical properties of the body. Sitting next to a lifeless body forcefully brings this into awareness. The physical body lies there before you with all its parts and components completely intact. But something has gone out of that body which was the real essence of the person. What remains is an empty shell, yet that essence-quality of life-force cannot be measured under a microscope or weighed on a scale.

In the dominant culture death myth, death as the Grim Reaper is sometimes seen as an enemy coming to get you. Bryan's bedside questions opened a door to the exploration of our mutual death myths. A "prime function of mythology and rite" states Joseph Campbell (1973), "is to supply the symbols that carry the human spirit onward," and the "common denominator of all mythic systems is their meaning-provoking capacity." Looking into the face of his own oncoming death, Bryan reached out for meaning and symbols to carry his spirit onward.

I had no definite answers for Bryan. Truth was all I could give him now. I told him I did not know if they celebrated Christmas in heaven. Then, without thinking, I said, "But if they do and you find out before me, let me know and I'll tell the other kids at the Center." Bryan nodded his head in agreement. We then went on to share our fears and anxieties about dying, along with our hopes and fantasies of who we would like to welcome us on the "other side," should that turn out to be what happened. I felt total joining and equality with Bryan, even with our thirty years' age difference, because in the areas that concerned us, there are no final answers, only our own thoughts and feelings which we shared freely without fear of judgment or pressure to believe in someone else's program.

Bryan thought that when we die, we go to heaven, and can choose whether to stay there, or return to earth as a helper for someone else.

"I think I'd choose to stay," I told him. "What about you?" I asked.

Bryan thought long and hard, his face grimacing in concentration. "I don't know. I guess I'll just have to decide when I get there," he replied.

I told Bryan of children I had seen die and that the actual process of dying did not appear to be painful. Perhaps there had been pain previously, as with Bryan himself, but the act of leaving the body seemed to be very peaceful—from what I had seen. Bryan had more questions and feelings to explore. We went on until suddenly he paused, sat up from his pillow, and said enthusiastically, "I feel better!" His face lit up in a big smile.

"I do too," I added, and we gave each other a big hug. I knew my work with Bryan was finished and we said our goodbyes. Then I went downstairs to be with his mother and younger sister who also needed time to express their feelings.

The next day Bryan's mother called the Center to report that Bryan had just died. He answered his own question about the painfulness of death by dying very peacefully. He had just finished a relaxing warm bath and was lying in bed with both parents present. I thought back to my conversation with him the day before and reflected on Bryan's "teaching lessons." I saw that more important than what actually happened after death, was what the person believed happened. The belief held in the moment determines the person's immediate experience. It was a teaching related to the Buddhist notion that the mind state creates one's phenomenological world. Bryan was showing me the power of the focused mind in helping to realize a death with dignity.

OLD PROPHETS IN YOUNG BODIES

Another powerful teacher was Erik, who had leukemia, a ten year old friend of Bryan's and mine from the Children's group at the Center. Erik was angry and in pain when his mother asked me to visit him at home. Six weeks earlier, Erik and I had traveled together to Oregon to address a conference on attitudinal healing. Erik's illness had just returned and he knew that, without a miracle, his chances of living much longer were very slim. "Why does this happen to me?" he asked. "Half of my life I've been sick with leukemia. Just when I started getting better, I get sick again; it's not fair."

He admitted he was angry at God. He also felt guilty for this and had been keeping it inside, adding more stress to his pained body. I suggested that it was OK to be angry with God and to let it come out, that God did not need our protection. Erik thought for a while then agreed and was able to talk out his anger and frustration. We then did some relaxation and guided imagery to lessen his pain (using imagination to see the pain as sharp, hot swords sticking him, which he then proceeded to visualize himself pulling out and releasing with his out-breath. Then, with the in-breath, he visualized a soothing presence bathing the wounds in a healing light). After these exercises Erik continued with his questions.

"Why is this happening to me?" he pleaded.

"I don't know why, Erik, and I wish it weren't happening to you or anyone else," I said. "But what I do know is that when you ask the 'why questions,' I notice your pain gets worse again." He nodded in agreement with my observation.

"It does look like death is coming closer, but it's not here now, and right now is all we've got." I reminded us both.

"What do you want to have now, Erik?" I asked, "Peace or pain?"

"I want peace," he said with conviction.

"Then we need to stop asking the 'why questions'," I stated.

The next step was over an immense cavern of darkness that, when taken successfully, brings liberation. I knew from previous conversations that Erik believed in a reality beyond the material world. We had talked about ESP experiences we had both had and our belief in mystery underlying the observable world of physical phenomena. I reminded Erik of our mutual belief that there was more going on here than what we could see with our eyes or know with our minds: "Somehow, in some way, if we can open up to having trust and faith that through all this terrible stuff that's happening, in a way we can't see or understand and that we don't have to like, but still it's happening—that something is working for the good—maybe it can help us feel peaceful."

Now this is a great deal to ask of anyone, least of all a ten year old boy dying of cancer, who hasn't had a chance to do half of what he had dreamed of doing with his life. I reminded Erik that he did have the power to choose what he put his attention into and that this choice would determine his experience in the moment. Erik was silent for several minutes. Then he looked directly at me and sat up on his bed. I remembererd times at the Center when we'd start the Children's Group by all of us holding hands in a circle and sending love to each other and to those of our group who were not there with us that night. Without speaking, we both reached out and took each other's hands. Our eyes closed. I suggested that we send our love to his parents and younger brother in the adjoining room. We focused on our own hearts opening and a beam of love flowing into Erik's family. I do not know how many minutes passed because all measurement of time stopped. I experienced a feeling of unification with Erik, myself, his parents and his brother. When we opened our eyes Erik was free of pain and ready to see his family.

Erik's mother called several days later to report that Erik had died. She asked if I would speak at his memorial service and then spoke of a great gift Erik had given them in the last days of his life.

"Erik brought God's presence into our home," she said. "It was so filled with peace, so special," she added, "a blessing" that helped them release Erik into his peaceful passage. Erik and Bryan each demonstrated the power of inner peace to transform an otherwise tragic situation into a sacred opportunity for spiritual joining.

A seventeen year old girl with cystic fibrosis, Mary Beth, shared with me a discovery that also transformed her last few days on earth. She had prayed as a little girl for God to take away her fatal illness. When he didn't, she stopped believing in Him. During her last hospitalization before coming home to die, she reopened the relationship and had a conversation with God.

"I realized," she said, "that God isn't necessarily a force that will take things away that you don't like. But He'll be there with you as you go through them."

Rites of passage, such as the vision quest, are vehicles of experience in traditional cultures that supported and empowered the release of the old and the birth of the new. They offered a "little death," which in turn helped prepare participants for the bigger death awaiting them when their "assignments" were completed. Repeated involvement in rites of passage throughout the life cycle helped strengthen trust and confidence in surrendering ego control to the mysterious unknown. The successful outcome of previous rites of passage gave participants psychospiritual strength and confidence with which to face their physical death. They were able to die with dignity, a "humanizing death," as did Erik, Bryan and Mary Beth.

The experiences with Erik and others suggests that death is something we actively participate in, it doesn't just happen to us. Just as Dr. Frederick LeBoyer introduced a more loving process into the labor and delivery of newborns, so are Bryan, Erik and others like them helping us to see that physical death is a birthing as well. It is a birthing back into spirit that also deserves a loving process. "The body is placenta to the soul," states philosopher/anthropologist Terence McKenna.

I see now that my work with Bryan and Erik was analogous to that of a labor coach with a woman giving birth to a baby. The birth process associated with death of the physical body brings the soul back into union with the ongoing flow of the cosmos. From this perspective, the deterioration of left-brain faculties that frequently occur during the dying process—confused and impaired logical and linear thought—may warrant new evaluation. Rather than merely pathological disorganization or hallucination, it may indicate a shift from the rational mode into a visionary state usually associated with right-brain functions. As such, it offers opportunity for exploration and growth for the dying person that merits our support and reassurance.

Active letting go is integral to this birthing with dignity, just as it is with the letting go into labor contractions that push the infant out into the physical world. Barbara, who was 36 years old when she died of metastasis from breast cancer, taught me a great deal about this kind of "doing." She had also undergone lengthy and painful bouts with surgery, radiation and chemotherapy. Barbara felt ready to die when I visited her at her apartment. She had suffered long enough, had said goodbye to her family and loved ones, and now wanted to be alone as she waited for death. Barbara had her own vision of what death would be like, and she felt ready to meet it through her preparation work of meditation and prayer. The only problem was that death did not come when she wanted it to.

For days she waited in her darkened bedroom, growing increasingly impatient and frustrated. Her faith in what death would be like began to crumble. When I saw her, she was cursing and yelling, amid violent coughing fits, for death to finally take her. Angry and defiant, she did not understand why this was happening to her when she felt she was so ready and well prepared. Sitting down next to her on the bed, I sat silent while she continued her bursts of anger. Her strength was ebbing, but her suffering was not. As Barbara and I looked at her experience, we gradually saw that she was still holding on to her expectation of how death would be for her. Her anger was itself a holding on. We saw together that she needed to let her expectations die. Each shallow breath brought in something new.

"Open to its presence," I urged her. "Follow it to wherever it takes you. Release expectations as you breathe out. Let them go. Let them die. Open to the new while releasing the old. Let the old breath die until your last release gently carries you on," I whispered. Barbara was calm now, and I took my leave. She died several hours later. Her death taught me that in the process of dying, our preconceptions may be excess baggage which interfere with the impending journey. They too, must be allowed to die for the greater birth to occur.

Another teaching of letting go into death involved a family and their doctor, who had become close friends through his loving care of their 13 year old son Adrian. I knew Adrian from the Children's Group at the Center. His family called when Adrian lay dying at a Bay area hospital. I drove over to be with them. Adrian's hospital room was filled with family, relatives and hospital staff. He had been an outgoing youngster with a zest for life that had brought joy to all who knew him. Eddie, his father, explained that Adrian had been in a coma for 13 hours. Each breath was accompanied by a spasm that shook his entire body.

"I wish he could just let go," Eddie said tearfully. We walked outside to talk, and Eddie explained how his son's suffering had brought him to the point where his only wish was for Adrian to be out of his pain. For years Eddie had urged Adrian to be strong in his fight for life. Adrian had responded and had far outlived his prognosis. But now Adrian's fighting on was only prolonging suffering.

I asked Eddie if he had told Adrian that it was all right to let go now. I knew Adrian worshipped his father and would never want to let him down.

"Maybe Adrian thinks he's failing you if he dies. Maybe that's why he keeps fighting so hard."

Eddie burst into tears. "But I want him to stop fighting now," he said. "He's been such a good boy, and fought hard enough."

At that moment I recalled a Native American elder who had taught me the difference between quitting versus surrendering, or giving over to something higher than yourself. I told Eddie of this differentiation, and that maybe it would be helpful to Adrian. Adrian was not giving up or quitting. He had fought courageously and could now release victoriously into the heaven he had dreamed about the night before he had slipped into the coma. Eddie responded with enthusiasm. He was proud of his son, and while saddened and already mourning his loss, wanted Adrian to go on now to the release he so desperately needed and deserved. Eddie believed that even though Adrian was in a coma, we could still communicate with him through the love in our hearts, and that he would "hear" us. We walked back to the room and told the doctor of our plan. He agreed with us on the need to let Adrian know he had not failed anyone, and could now let go, with his family's blessings, into a higher state of being that he had justly earned. Eddie, the doctor and I re-entered the jammed hospital room. We silently extended our "release message." I focused all my attention on supporting Adrian in knowing it was all right to let go.

Time wore on and still he struggled. To my dismay, I began to get frustrated because Adrian was not letting go. Then I realized that it was I who needed to let go. I was holding on to having Adrian die on *my* timing, to meet *my* agenda. Adrian had his *own* timing that needed to be respected. My role was not to project my needs and timing onto his, thereby interfering with whatever he might be dealing with in the mystery of his dying. I had to refocus on extending my love to him unconditionally, and release him into his own experience. Slowly I realized that Adrian was teaching me the importance of really letting go, cleanly and with clarity, and with love that wanted nothing in return. I smiled inside, and thanked him for his gift. Adrian died shortly thereafter. I could almost hear him chuckle a congratulatory "I'm glad you finally got the message, Tom," as the last breath left his body.

Richard Boerstler (1982), a modern death education specialist, asks a question relevant to situations such as the one with Adrian: "What state of consciousness do you wish to be in at the moment of passage?" My experience with Adrian raises an additional question: "What state of consciousness do you wish those around you to be in as you move through your dying process?"

The teachers I have been fortunate to experience all suggest the need for an open heart and an enlightened mind, i.e., a mind filled with light and free of all baggage save the quality of light, as being the best qualities for the birthing process we call death. How do we develop these qualities? Can we learn them, and must we wait for our own death for the spiritualization of consciousness they foster to occur?

"No," answers Dr. Salvadore Roquet, Mexican psychiatrist, who utilizes shamanistic ritual and rites of passage in his innovative work with patients. "We need to face death to come to life and live it, which is to love." He asserts that we need to deal with the fears that keep us from living and loving. We need to acknowledge and use them in a positive way, for they can sink or save us. Roquet believes there is a potential for spiritual realization within all human beings. "It is only a matter of liberating it, of freeing it from our subconscious," he says. "We have only to let it out and see it." In our fears about death and our attempts in "not dying, we die," he states—because "we imprison ourselves in fear and weaken our capacities to live full, creatively-productive, and loving lives."

In taking death as our companion, the goal is not to encourage despair and sadness. Instead it is to activate an awareness that this very moment is all you have. Face the truth that the act you are performing now may be your last one, so do it well with full consciousness. In facing the reality of death in such a manner, we come full circle back into life again. Only now we can live it with a fullness and vitality that was not possible when we did not face our fears directly.

Facing death directly brings forth a sense of humility. Yesterday I spent several hours with a middle-aged man prior to a major operation. He had a vague abstract belief in God, but had been living his life based on his own gratification with little regard for others. He had been impressed with his own power to achieve these ends. But now, fearful that he might die in surgery, of which there was a good chance, he suddenly saw how small his power really was, and the myopic vision that had characterized his previous activity.

Modern western society, with its emphasis on technological power and material riches, has become impoverished in spiritual riches, which are all that count when death comes to call. Aboriginal rites of passage provide opportunity to practice the art of releasing into the great unknown. This, in turn, can strengthen the development of humility and other spiritual riches such as patience, trust and the ability to be open, honest and present in the moment.

In the seeking of vision from the Great Spirit for guidance in one's life path, Native Americans were instructed in the importance of a humble attitude. Sacred knowledge, they learned, cannot be attained while one is arrogant and prideful. You cannot pour water into an already filled pitcher—all you get is a mess. To open to the numinous state of our deeper being requires humility. Black Elk, a Lakota Sioux medicine man, teaches that unless one humbles oneself before all of creation, before even the smallest ant, one cannot gain peace (Brown 1953). Peace comes only from seeing and knowing our relationship and oneness with the universe and all its powers, and realizing that at its center dwells Wakan Tanka (translated as Sacred Mystery), and that this center is within each of us. "Only in being nothing may man become everything," he says, for "only then does he realize his essential brotherhood with all forms of Life." Without this expanded vision and recognition of the sacredness of humankind's deeper being, we get lost in the darkness of the ego.

The person questing for vision had further training in humility in the purifying rites of the sweatlodge ceremony preceding the quest. The sweatlodge is somewhat similar to a steambath. You go inside a special lodge and sweat. Every part of the construction of the sweatlodge has symbolic meaning as do the prayers and rituals that take place inside it (Brown 1953). Death preparation is evident in Black Elk's explanation of the willow branches used in its framing:

> These too have a lesson to teach us, for in the fall their leaves die and return to the earth, but in the spring they come to life again. So too, men die but live again in the real world of Wakan Tanka, where there is nothing but the spirits of all things. This true life we may know here on earth if we purify our bodies and minds, thus coming closer to Wakan Tanka who is all purity. Thus we may see not only with our two eyes, but with the one eye which is of the heart, and with which we see and know all that is true and good. (Brown 1953)

Experiences such as the sweatlodge ceremony and the vision quest emphasize the importance of self-discipline, concentration, patience, focused will, and intent. These, in turn, encourage listening to the "looks within place," or inner attunement, as a source of knowledge. These qualities are instrumental in the positive utilization of altered states of consciousness precipitated by these rites where the Native American people sought spiritual renewal. The expanded consciousness provided opportunity to explore levels of reality beyond the observable world of sensory-based perception and ego control. Some reports of near-death experience also describe the dissolving of ego into an expanded state. People who experience temporary "ego-death," through rites of passage, or a near-death experience, enhance their ability to surrender control to the mysterious unknown with faith and trust. Greater familiarity and knowledge with a level of existence deeper, broader and richer than the one known in our normative state of consciousness, brings forth more confidence in the idea of total release into it at the time of physical death.

All the great religions of the world attest to Joseph Epes Brown's statement that "there is no greater error to which man is subject than to believe that his real self is nothing more than his own body or mind." The impact of this error of perception and identity manifests with full force when death approaches, especially if it has not been previously addressed. How the dying person and those around them respond to it, as Virginia Hine reminds us, helps determine the quality of the death experience.

Tommy was a dynamic youth of 14 years who lay dying of leukemia. His father, whom I knew from the Parent's Group at the Center, phoned to tell me of Tommy's condition. Then he called again to describe the transformational teaching his son gave him in his final passage.

Tommy was in and out of a coma the last few hours of his life. His death myth involved a belief in an afterlife that included a journey to Hawaii. I had given Tommy some coral I had obtained on a diving trip to Hawaii when I visited him in the hospital several days earlier. His father told me later that

Tommy kept it by his bedside throughout his hospital stay. Tommy was concerned that when he died he would not know how to get there, and this was a major worry for him.

Tommy was in an altered state as he approached death. He reported seeing two butterflies moving in the room. Then he asked his mother if she knew how to meditate. When she said no, Tommy had her, his step-mother and his father sit next to one another in a circle on his bed. He had them all join hands together. His father later reported feeling a burst of light come out of Tommy and go around the circle. "It was a circle of love," he said. "It had no beginning and it had no end. When Tommy had that love going just right, because that's what he wanted to teach us about, then he stepped out."

Tommy's father then described seeing the now-healthy image of his son emerge from the emaciated body lying on the bed. Two hands held his son's hands. They were the guides to help Tommy on his journey, two friends who had just recently died of cancer themselves. Together the three boys rose up above the bed. Tommy had his long blond hair that he had lost in the chemotherapy treatments. He shook his head, smiled, and rose on up and out of the room. Tommy's father explained somewhat sheepishly that he had not really seen this occur with his eyes. He saw it, he said, with his heart.

Tommy's passage over the threshold of death initiated his father into an expanded level of awareness with a new and deeper way of knowing. The circle without beginning or end, available to us all whenever we open our hearts to touch and be touched and to give freely of the love within, unites us as one. It is a birthing of a fuller and richer state of being, one that empowers our experience of the here and now wherever we find ourselves on the great universal wheel of life and death.

When Tommy's father spoke with embarrassment of his heart vision, I told him of psychiatrist C. G. Jung's experience in the American southwest (described in *Memories, Dreams and Reflections*). A Taos Pueblo elder confided to Jung that he thought white people were mad. When Jung questioned him on his reasons for this statement, he replied that white people were mad because they thought with their heads. "What do you think with?" asked Jung in surprise. The old man raised his hand and silently pointed to the middle of his chest. We can all benefit from the response of the Taos Pueblo elder who was known as "Mountain Lake." "We think here," he said, indicating his heart.

REFERENCES

Beck, P. and Walters, A. 1977. *The sacred: Ways of knowledge, sources of life*. Tsaile, Ariz.: Navajo Community College Press.

Boerstler, R. 1982. *Letting go*. Watertown, Mass.: Associates in Thanatology.

Brown, J. E. 1953. *The sacred pipe*. Norman, Okla.: University of Oklahoma Press.

————. 1964. *Spiritual legacy of the American Indian*. Lebanon, Pa.: Pendle Hill.

Campbell, J. 1973. *Myths to live by*. New York: Bantam Books.

Castaneda, C. 1981. *Journey to Ixtlan*. New York: Pocket Books.

Evans-Wentz, W. Y. 1960. *Tibetan book of the dead*. New York: Galaxy Books.

Gennep, A. van. 1960. *Rites of passage*. Chicago: University of Chicago Press.

Goleman, D. 1975. The Buddha on meditation and states of consciousness. *Transpersonal Psychologies*, ed. C. Tart. New York: Harper & Row.

Grof, S. 1976. *Realms of the human unconscious*. New York: E. P. Dutton.

Grof, S. and Halifax, J. 1978. *Human encounters with death*. New York: E. P. Dutton.

Hine, V. 1979. *Last letter to the pebble people*. Mill Valley, Cal.: Orenda Publishing/ Unity Press.

Houston, J. 1982. Psycho-historical recovery of the self. *Association of Humanistic Psychology Newsletter*.

Jung, C. G. 1961. *Memories, dreams, reflections*. New York: Pantheon.

McKenna, T. 1982. New and old maps of hyperspace. Audiotape. Available from Dolphin Tapes, Box 71, Big Sur, Cal. 93920.

Moody, R. A.; Grof, S.; Pahnke, W. N.; Kurland, A. A.; and Goodman, L. E. 1971. LSD-assisted psychotherapy in patients with terminal cancer. Presentation at 5th Symposium of the Foundation of Thanatology, November 1971, New York.

Ornstein, R. 1973. *The nature of human consciousness*. San Francisco: W. H. Freeman.

Pinkson, T. 1976. *A quest for vision*. Novato, Cal.: Free Person Press.

————. Turtle Island speaks: Native American consciousness as modern survival paradigm. Available from author at 240 Miller Ave., Mill Valley, Cal. 94941.

————. Tommy's crossings. Audiotape. Available from author at 240 Miller Ave., Mill Valley, Cal. 94941.

Roquet, S. n.d. Radio interview with Will Noffke, KPFA, Berkeley, Cal.

Underhill, R. 1965. *Red man's religion*. Chicago: University of Chicago Press.

22

TRANSFORMATION OF THE IMAGE OF GOD LEADING TO SELF-INITIATION INTO OLD AGE

Lionel Corbett

The initiatory dream presented here is of a woman about the age of 60 who never had analysis. This woman's dream can be seen as

> an authentic modern revelation of the objective psyche which makes a contribution to the "New Myth." The dream demonstrates clearly the reciprocal relation between the ego and the Self. They help each other and carry each other's burdens. In a letter Jung writes, "I consciously and intentionally made my life miserable because I wanted God to be alive and free from the suffering man has put on him by loving his own reason more than God's secret intentions" (Psychological Perspectives Spring 1975, p. 12).
>
> Primarily, the dream concerns the transformation of deity through incarnation, i.e., individuation. The incarnation is also a coniunctio which refers not only to a reconciliation of the male-female polarity but likewise to the union of all opposites. To me the most important feature of the dream is that it informs the dreamer that she is a partner of God and a participant in the drama of divine transformation. This gives her suffering and sacrifice archetypal sanction and roots her in a living myth.
>
> —Edward Edinger, M.D.

Lionel Corbett, M.D., is Assistant Professor of Psychiatry at Rush Medical College and Clinical Director, Department of Psychiatry, Rush-Presbyterian-St. Luke's Medical Center in Chicago, where he combines an academic and teaching practice. He is a graduate of the C.G. Jung Institute of Chicago.

> . . . the same initiatory patterns are found in the dreams and in the imaginative life both of modern men and of the primitive.
>
> —Eliade, 1958, p. 131.

INTRODUCTION

TRANSITION into old age has no clear social, psychological or biological demarcation, and like all developmental crises may produce emotional distress. If the individual accepts the challenge, this time provides an opportunity for growth, provided one feels the possibility of mastery and the ego is able to make the necessary sacrifices. Some missed opportunities for development in earlier life can also be reapproached at this time. However, if the additional demands of old age cannot be met, psychosocial decompensation may occur and the personality misses its fufillment.

Jung points out that old age would not occur unless it had some meaning for the species. Whereas the meaning of the first part of life has to do with ego, career and family development, new and different goals are required in the second half, namely the pursuit of meaning, wholeness and the further creation of consciousness (Jung 1969). Early developmental demands inevitably lead to partial, preferential unfolding of only some aspects of the personality. Ideally, later in life, family and occupational restrictions become less rigid, time is more available, and progressive emotional maturation leads to the relaxation of immature defenses and methods of adaptation. This provides the potential for widening of identity, brought about ultimately by reconnecting with more of the latent potential of the Self which was present at birth, but which had to be sacrificed for the sake of adjustment to circumstances. This period, of crucial importance, is often a difficult time to both enter and adapt to.

Hitherto, the individual has grown accustomed to sequential advancement in social status, with increasing prestige and authority. Now one is asked to accept a role which society devalues, which may have long been dreaded, with new norms and values and the risk of a fall in social status and self-esteem. This crisis is sometimes precipitated by retirement. The so-called "young old," who remains vigorous and engaged, resist the negative social stereotype of deterioration since this is not their experience. In fact, they exemplify exactly the long pre-terminal relatively steady-state period during which decline is minimal and energy and time are available for paying attention to further development. Unfortunately, however, those who are unable to differentiate themselves from our cultural bias may depreciate the very idea of old age and ignore its specific meaning, which simply postpones the transitional crisis for them.

The Need for Initiation into Old Age

A major difficulty facing the individual about to move into this period is that there are no adequate social provisions to help with the transition. At a time of turmoil and ambiguity, no clear expectations are defined and many of the skills the person has painstakingly acquired are suddenly much less relevant. The fact that help with major life transitions is often necessary is evident from pre-technological cultures, where movement into new developmental periods is marked by initiation ceremonies or rites of passage (van Gennep 1960). Although these seem primitive to modern eyes, they perform profoundly important psychological and social functions. For example, such rituals overcome resistance to change, preventing regressive dependency. The culture thereby validates the transition, which impresses the significance of the new status on the initiate and his clan. The rites offer the initiate protection during the uncertainty of the threshold (liminal) period, help predict what to expect, give a new set of symbols for the next part of life, and connect one with the history and tradition of the culture. Finally, the "reborn" individual is re-incorporated into the group with a new role, and with new rights and duties. Biological, social and personal necessities are then integrated. The rites thus protect the emotional health of the initiate and his society by ensuring safe psychological and social development. Successful initiation is essential for spiritual rejuvenation and the attempt to attain a "sanctified mode of being." When this process is successful, the new status has meaning to the person, which helps to mitigate life's harshness. It is no coincidence then, that without such cultural sanction and protection the move into old age may exact a heavy emotional toll; the individual may be unable to emerge from a state of chronic liminality. Jung believed that fear of meeting developmental tasks (failed initiation) is an important cause of emotional disturbance. When transformation is necessary but not forthcoming, when the only security lies in change which cannot occur because of fear, or because no helpful initiation into the new mystery is available, neurosis may supervene. Clinically, one often sees an exacerbation of early neurotic or characterological problems during such threshold periods. The therapist then has to understand the need to be a ritual elder and help initiate the patient into the new status as well as simply working on earlier developmental material. When such outside help is lacking, the developmental imperative may come from within (Henderson 1967).

Auto Initiation: "The Archetype Motivates from Within"

To illustrate the existence of Self-initiation into old age, the dream of a 60 year old woman is presented (with her consent), in which she is confronted with startling notions about the nature of God, the meaning and purpose of old age, and the relationship between these two. Personal details are unnecessary except to say that she had a puella "psychology": though she was reluctant to grow, another part of her was struggling to mature, aware of her impending old age. In this situation of tension between two opposing inner claims, the Self provided the necessary, transcendent, symbolic impetus, in the form of this dream—so that the dreamer's individual consciousness could be "reconciled with universal will." The dream illustrates one way in which contact with the numinous may be healing—the individual feels part of the whole, in a manner which simultaneously resolves her personal inner polarities by including them in a much greater synthesis.

The Dream

An authoritative male voice informs me that it is going to teach me about the process of aging. A black and white illustration appears before my eyes. It represents the rejuvenated Godhead. Underneath it, alive, is the head of a very old man. A connecting line is drawn from the old man's head to the diagram of the divinity, which consists of an outer elongated square enclosing an inner circle. At the bottom of the circle is a crescent, convex upward. Out of the crescent arise two heads on two almost identical long necks. I know that they share the same body which is not shown. The voice explains that this is an abstract of the rejuvenated Godhead. The right head represents the male aspect and the left the female. I want to know more about it— particularly, more about the feminine aspect of God. The voice ignores that except to remind me that this has been partly explained in a previous dream and would I please now focus on the old man. But I find the Godhead(s) a lot more interesting and I think to myself "God is one, two heads, but one." At the same time, what I have learned in a previous dream flashes through my mind—the awareness that what I am shown here is not God as ultimate reality—which we are not equipped to understand—but either an oversimplified version of that reality or an aspect of divinity that we are able to relate to.

The two heads are in absolute harmony with each other. They look like spirits, ethereal. I perceive their facial expression as autocratic,

blithe, somewhat curious, unemotional. They do not look authorita-
tive, but the voice is. The tops of their heads are shaped like an
indented crown with three prongs that I can see on each head. The old
man looks quite ordinary and sort of earthy, with reddish skin. The
voice explains that in our society we still do not understand the process
of aging. The purpose of maturation is to enable the Godhead(s) to
rejuvenate. If we could only understand that! When we are born, God
is old; when we grow old, God becomes young and when we die, God
experiences rebirth. This goes on and on, not in the sense that God is
feeding on us but that the whole thing is a natural process which is not
yet too well understood. It is absolutely essential that, particularly in
old age, we do not lose our connectedness with the Godhead, for
otherwise we not only deprive God of our share in His rejuvenation,
but may actually disturb the cosmic ecology, which in turn affects us.

The voice makes me understand that whereas ideally we gain
wisdom as we grow older, only a few people in fact do so. In the dream,
I understand wisdom to be a conglomeration of life experience, a
priori *and acquired knowledge, and the awareness and acceptance of*
one's inner child. Only too often the inner child has been lost in the
jungle or drowned in the flood or simply forgotten and left behind. To
accumulate knowledge per se is not all that important. What is
important is that we are connected with divinity and let it live within us
even though it is also outside of us. Belief in the supreme being
constellates the inner child and thus furthers the process of divine
rejuvenation. If we ignore the divine element—as is man's tendency
today—it sinks into itself and ceases to be conscious of itself.

As we grow older, we often "lose the child," and as we do so we are
apt to simultaneously sever our ties to the divine. Or, we lose our belief
in divinity and starve the child. It sort of goes hand in hand.

I think of some old people I know who have become childish and
irritating. The voice picks up on that and says that even though such
people have obviously not gained wisdom, their very childishness yet
reflects the rejuvenating God. This too is not too well understood but
instead of having a condescending attitude towards the child in old
people, we would do better to let it be and to have a positive attitude
towards it no matter how it manifests. Even if we perceive it as distorted
or wounded, we should be aware that it expresses and is linked to the
rejuvenation process of the Godhead(s) and that the process should
not be interrupted.

The dream voice also indicated that the birth and death process
are actually the same, except that as little children we seem to be
contained in the divine element while in old age we are apparently

expected to be a container for divinity. I reflect in the dream that old people ought to be less subject to the tension of the opposites— particularly of the masculine and feminine principle—and therefore more apt to reflect (unperturbed) the divine image that has been presented to me.

This dream is both a miniature description of the individuation process in late life and a visual mandala of aging. On the level of the collective, it imbues aging with considerable spiritual, psychological and social significance. The dream is composed of multiple, intertwined themes.

Themes Characteristic of Initiation Ceremonies (Eliade, 1958)

The dreamer is brought into relation with an image of divine unity, which is one of the purposes, meanings and effects of initiation. Knowledge of the sacred is revealed; a heirophany occurs. Like Job, the dreamer actually sees. Thus related to divinity, the individual can transcend the personal, and at the same time experience her individuality. The dream illustrates Eliade's point that initiation gives death a positive value. Death prepares for spiritual birth into a mode of being not subject to destruction by time. Being reborn indicates the attainment of another mode of being—becoming new and consecrated. Psychological transformation is often depicted in dreams and rituals by death—rebirth imagery, which is also a powerful image of healing. At the same time, the dream emphasizes the transitory nature of chronological time and images an ongoing relationship to sacred time and eternity. The individual's life becomes a necessary part of sacred history. Should the aging dreamer suffer from death anxiety, her existence is now placed *sub specie aeternitas*. Psychologically, the dream's overall effect should be to move the dreamer into a new consciousness, one more adaptive for later life.

Bisexuality and Androgyny

Androgyny is visually the central theme of the dream, and is clearly of major importance in its overall message. Accordingly, some aspects of androgeny specifically relevant to the dream image are reviewed and enlarged upon here. (Following Jung in various papers [e.g. 1970a] fuller discussions of the subject have been provided by Singer [1976] and from a Taoist viewpoint by Colgrave [1979].

Initiation ceremonies often include ritual transformation into the opposite sex. Among shamans such transvestism is common, sometimes with a relationship to a celestial spouse. The combination in one person of earth (femininity) and sky (masculinity) enables the individual to act as an intermediary between these realms (Eliade 1972). Hermaphroditic representations of mythic gods are common in many cultures and may be an archaic form of the idea of divine bi-unity (Eliade 1958). In fact, Dionysus was not only bisexual but is often represented as a divine child, which is interesting in view of the emphasis on the connection of the child to God in this woman's dream. Astrologically, bisexuality is depicted as Gemini. Those born under this sign are said to suffer from the tension of internal polarities such as rational-intuitive, male-female, transpersonal-earth bound, light and dark. Intellectually, they are "mercurial." In alchemy Mercurius (sometimes as an androgynous figure) symbolizes the making of bridges—he connects male and female and other apparent opposites, assisting in transformation. In Plato's *Symposium* man is initially created in the form of a sphere with two bodies and two sexes, and is separated, interestingly, because of hubris—suggesting that appropriate humility needs to be developed for full humanity to be experienced. In the *Kabbala,* not only does divinity have masculine and feminine aspects, but the original Adam is androgynous. This suggests that the masculine and feminine potentials of divine man were in equilibrium in the soul, but when Eve was removed their divine completeness was lost. In the Christian mystical tradition, Christ is also depicted as an androgyne.

The hermaphrodite and the androgyne are not synonymous. Jung (1976) notes that the hermaphrodite precedes individuation. This is an important psychological statement. As elaborated by Poncé (1983), the distinction is that the hermaphrodite is an image of masculinity and femininity joined in a sexual body, of the unconscious union of opposites, while the androgynous state is an image of their union in the archetypal realm of the subtle body, and of differentiated, conscious access to both modalities. (Note the dream image of the heads without a physical body rising out of the moon.) Poncé points out that the hermaphrodite (with its emphasis on sexuality) is given, whilst the androgyne is achieved. This process is reflected in several creation myths, as well as in the development of the individual. Its intermediate stage is of divided masculine and feminine consciousness. The baby is born with relatively undifferentiated sexuality; maturity separates the opposites in the physical body whilst old age demands their conscious psychological integration in a body which has become less clearly differentiated.

The concept is further found in the Gnostic Gospel of Thomas: "For every woman who will make herself male will enter the Kingdom of Heaven." This is not a sexist remark; rather it points out the need to develop androgynous consciousness. Several other gnostic writers emphasize the masculine and feminine characteristics of divinity, that self-knowledge is knowledge of God, and that humanity itself manifests the divine life. The Gospel of Thomas further reports that Jesus says that the Kingdom of God is not a physical place and does not occur at a future time but is found inside the individual. The "kingdom" is actually an image of transformed consciousness. According to this account, when the disciples said: "Shall we as children enter the Kingdom?" Jesus replied, "When you make the two one, and when you make the inside like the outside and the outside like the inside, and the above like the below and when you make the male and female one and the same . . . then you will enter the Kingdom" (Robinson 1977). In like manner, Lao-Tzu says: "He who knows the male and yet cleaves to what is female becomes like a ravine receiving all things under heaven. Being such a ravine, he has the eternal power which leaves not and he returns to the state of infancy." Being in the Tao resembles the state of infancy (Jung 1971).

The alchemists were also preoccupied with the problem of uniting the masculine and the feminine. The culmination of the great work (psychologically equivalent to individuation) consists in the production of the perfect androgyne, an image of wholeness and the "coniunctio oppositorum": a sacred marriage represented by the union of opposites such as heaven and earth, sun and moon, mercury and sulphur, masculine and feminine—often symbolized by joined male/female figures, the two-faced head of the king and queen or the red man and his white wife. To produce the philosopher's stone represents the conscious realization of the Self—the opposites united, the sum of all things and the key to knowledge. The work requires that these inner opposite qualities be purified (made conscious) and related to each other within the individual. Perhaps the dreamer has difficulty with some aspect of the masculine-feminine polarity, and needs to become aware of the androgynous nature of the Self, portrayed in the dream as a male-female coniunctio with two heads in "absolute harmony" with each other.

In various traditions androgyny symbolizes supreme identity, the level of nonmanifest being or the source of manifestation (Zolla 1981). Clearly, in this context "masculine" and "feminine" are not intended to be identified with male and female. They represent psychological and spiritual principles in their own right. Of all possible opposites which might have been represented in her dream, the fact that these are chosen suggests that they are of major, possibly supreme, importance, at least to this individual. The dream image supports the idea that both are found in the soul of individuals of either sex and have their divine analogues. Their essential nature, however, is not easy to grasp, and since they are aspects of divinity we may never be able to articulate them. Years of cultural conditioning may have obscured our vision and preferentially conditioned us to associate certain attributes with men or women. On close examination, however, the usual stereotyped descriptions do not coincide with experience.

Typically, generations of tradition ascribe to masculinity such decisive and goal-oriented properties as penetrating, initiating, classifying, organizing and discriminating, and to femininity the attributes of receiving, accepting, relating, harmonizing and nurturing. Another cliche is that masculine consciousness is sharply focused, in contrast to the diffuse awareness of the feminine, and so on. We should be less ready to accept such concretizations, since it is perfectly possible that each of these processes may be bipolar, possessing both masculine and feminine forms, each with specific qualities, which need to act in unison for their optimum expression. For example, only (patriarchal) convention and tradition tell us that when a woman is being assertive and logical this is her "masculinity"—perhaps such behavior is authentically feminine if it comes from her own essence and is not simply the result of introjects. (I am indebted to Marion Woodman for this insight.) Witness the enormous variation in the behavior of mythic gods and goddesses. To equalize the core metaphors, symbolically women may inseminate and men may gestate. It seems unnecessary to always differentiate between masculine and feminine behaviors. Furthermore, the unconscious of men is commonly said to be essentially feminine and to be so personified (Neumann 1954). However, surely men also possess profoundly authentic, unconscious masculinity.

Perhaps the most subtle definitions are provided by Miriam and José Arguelles (1977). They describe the feminine as the quality of all-accommodating space, which is "simply there, without conditions, either positive or negative. It is open, all pervasive and without origin." It is the unborn quality within experience; its essence is the cosmic womb in which all things may exist no matter how mutually contradictory. The feminine provides the "open and uncreated ground for the constant revelation and display of the phenomenal world." The masculine principle operates within this space, provoked to respond by the openness of the feminine. The masculine is form and content, encompassing the total range of personal experience and emotion. It is the essence of everything related to and contained by the unceasingly fertile, "unborn" feminine, which explores its spaciousness and articulates its endlessness. "The play of unborn feminine space and unconditional masculine response describes two cosmic principles. The unceasing interpenetration of these principles allows communication and meaningful activity to take place." From this interplay arises creativity. In the Arguelles' highly evolved model, the union of masculine and feminine is imagined as the inseparability of discriminating awareness and skillful compassionate behavior. It allows us to grow old without an ultimate resting point, or attachment to fixed ideas, by accepting confusion as "the working base for discovering greater warmth and intelligence."

Another oversimplification equates spirit with masculinity and soul with femininity. However, any archetype (including those considered feminine) is an ordering and hence spiritual principle. In the psychoid realm from which they emerge, the archetypes may be beyond such divisions, only taking on masculine or feminine characteristics in the human psyche, in this time and

space. Spirit is experienced within the individual soul, which is the organ or
(feminine) space of receptivity; but soul also transduces spirit, that is, soul
detects and transforms the energy of spirit into meaning and value. It does so,
for example, by casting the experience of spirit into image, metaphor and
language, or by its response to the numinous. Soul therefore also has active,
"masculine" qualities. Jung in fact suggests (1966) that the anima, linking
body and spirit, is hermaphroditic. In the realm of the body, structural
differences define sexuality, although body itself—being matter—is thought
of as feminine. It is certainly the container for experience. But the fact that our
bodies are either male or female may be simply because our evolution is as
incomplete physically as it is psychologically. Perhaps what ultimately
confers psychological masculinity and femininity is the quality (state of
development) of the embodied soul, which is able to act as a resonating end-
organ for spirit because of its similar nature (but to the extent that the soul is
not yet androgynous, one side of spirit's yin-yang polarity predominates in the
soul's experience). The net affect of these interactions is that in any given
aging individual certain spirit-soul-body harmonics predominate, and are
typically broadly masculine or feminine; there is clearly a spectrum of
possibilities between these extremes. Masculine and feminine can only be
described in relation to each other, and do not exist individually. Perhaps any
process in the psyche has both masculine and feminine aspects which need to
be integrated to give birth to the full expression of that process. These
principles behave like parents, and only in the realm of the transpersonal are
they undivided. Anima and animus not only have the same root, but are part of
the same tree. They complement and compensate for each other within each
individual.

     In spite of such problems of definition and mechanism, we remain in
intuitive agreement with the notion of a dialectic polarity, yin and yang, both
psychologically and in nature. All of life, not simply humanity, has masculine
and feminine energy. Their union in this dream seems to occur within an
individual psyche rather than between individuals. This birthing leads to the
production of an inner "child"—a new potential. Indeed, the tension between
such polarities seems necessary for the creation of consciousness. As we age,
if we continue to create consciousness, we birth more of this child inside us.
As Edinger (1984) explains, etymologically consciousness means "knowing
with"—"withness" implies coniunctio, perhaps of any opposites—logos and
eros, masculine and feminine, matter and spirit, *senex* and *puer*. Part of the
power of the dream described here is created by its uniting of several
opposites, a process which creates consciousness, which in turn allows
further discernment, or (paradoxically) separation of the constituent parts of a
situation. The dream image illustrates that there is no antagonism but rather
mutuality between the sacrality of masculinity and femininity in developed
androgynous consciousness. This may be yet another way in which the

numinous heals. What is missing in the personal is provided by revealing its divine counterpart to the individual's consciousness, which is thereby expanded. This makes it more complete and improves its balance. Discovering aspects of God leads to self-discovery.

A practical, incarnational aspect of the development of androgynous consciousness is described by Colgrave as the capacity to really love. This is a poorly understood process consisting of both personal and transpersonal aspects which have to be integrated and mediated by the individual, although it is not within individual control. Love happens to us, and comes and goes for no obvious reason. On the personal level, for love to be mature we have to find in ourselves what is otherwise only experienced in or via the other person. He then becomes needed in a different way. We see him for what he really is, instead of constantly seeing an unknown or otherwise unavailable part of one's self (narcissistic love), or an aspect of our parents that still possesses us (neurotic love). Although projections themselves are not love, they seem to act as vehicles which carry love, allowing us to experience it consciously. When they are withdrawn the potential for love still exists independently. As Jacobi (1973) puts it, when we do not project we then love realistically with conscious devotion to the other, without possessiveness. This requires considerable conscious work, but when the projections are integrated our own strength is discovered, and we can deal with the contrasexual in its more powerful and evolved form. To use Chardin's analogy, union is different from adolescent absorption (or, psychodynamically, a state of fusion). Real love differentiates the aging individual. At the same time, it opens one to increased consciousness. Singer correctly suggests that whereas romantic love is enclosed within the personal relationship, transpersonal love is essentially androgynous in nature. Only through love can these opposites of masculinity and femininity be transcended. In the androgyne masculine and feminine energies are (in Singer's terms) combined but not confused. As we grow older we realize our individuality through androgyny.

Perhaps such intermingling of the personal and the transpersonal aspect of love is another way of understanding: ". . . let us love one another; for love is of God, and he who loves is born of God and knows God . . . for God is love" (1 John 4:7-8). The necessity for human consciousness to bring divine love to fruition is also indicated by: ". . . if we love one another, God abides in us, and His love is perfected in us" (1 John 4:12). For the ego to achieve the difficult task of becoming a channel for divine love, it must try not to interfere with or handicap the process with its own needs.

Obviously, there is no direct mention of love in the dream. Therefore, if this particular amplification of the meaning of androgynous union is correct, and not due to personal distortion, finding love in the image is a further example of the result of adding human reflection to what is divinely given. Then not only is the classical notion correct that love leads to enlightenment, but knowledge

knowledge of God (enlightenment) leads to love. Such knowledge is here obtained by direct experience (as revelation) rather than by adherence to a particular dogmatic system. Those aspects of divinity are revealed which are most relevant to, or needed by, the dreamer's personal psychology.

The subjective experience of androgynous consciousness has been described by Grof (1976) as one which may occur to individuals undergoing LSD experiences. Since these are known to amplify our intrinsic psychology, the experience clearly exists as a potential in the human unconscious. Apparently, therefore, the archetype of androgyny was activated in the aging dreamer when it became necessary to further her development. Perhaps her concept of God was excessively tied to a traditional masculine—*senex* idea, and she had undervalued both her own femininity and the divine feminine, for which lack of awareness the dream is compensatory.

The Geometrical Forms

Since antiquity, geometrical forms have been invested with psychological and symbolic meaning (Pennick 1980). They are images of the structure of creation and their qualities can be understood as representative of aspects of the universe. Each form has been endowed with unique properties in esoteric symbolism, predicated on the Hermetic notion of "as above, so below," the correspondence of the macrocosm with the microcosm. Nature is created in an infinite hierarchical series of analogous structures, a continuum differing in size but not in principle and quality, so that the whole can be found in any part. Thus is man in the image of God—an implicit overall meaning of the dream image.

The square is an expression of quarternity, firmness, stability, honesty, integrity and an image of organization and construction. It refers to matter and rationality and is an old image of the order and stability of the world. Four elements, four seasons, four stages of life, and the four corners of the earth suggest God made manifest in creation. It may also represent the fixity of death as opposed to the dynamic circle of life and movement. Because the square has limits, it represents form, permanence and stability. In the dream, the square has limits, it represents form, permanence and stability. In the dream, the square is elongated vertically—perhaps to indicate the connection upward, to spirit, in the dreamer's psychology.

The circle is often an image of the sun, of heaven and perfection and hence of the deity or of the Self in its impersonal or potential aspect. According to Jung, the circle corresponds to an ultimate state of oneness, in contrast to the square which is an image of the plural state of man without inner unity. The circle is also an image of time in the sense of cyclicity, recurrence, birth and death, infinity or eternity, time enclosing space, timelessness with no beginning or end, and of spacelessness (since it has no above or below). It is zero, the origin, emptiness and totality. As the sun, the circle is masculine and spirit, but as the soul and the encircling water, it is feminine and maternal. The dream picture also has a crescent-moon image from which the necks arise, suggesting body and the feminine. Yet another coniunctio *(solis et lunae)* can thus be discerned.

Squaring the circle was an alchemical preoccupation about the relationship between the circle, or cosmic symbol of heaven, and the earth as square. It depicts the union of opposites into a higher synthesis—the material realm contained within totality. As the Rosarium puts it, "make a circle of the man and the woman, draw out of this a square, and out of the square a triangle. Make a circle and you will have the philosopher's stone" (Jung 1968b). Squaring the circle produces the philosopher's stone, and in the process the two sexes become one, which is necessary for the achievement of Selfhood. Although other images of coniunctio suggest a kind of shared Self, the totality image of the dream diagram (with its separate crowns which are integral parts of the heads) implies the maintenance of the height of individuality within unity—part of the paradox of the androgynous Self. In the hermetic tradition, a squared circle represented salt, among whose symbolic meanings are soul, understanding, wisdom and relationship (Jung 1970b).

The Triangle: the diagram's dotted line indicates an implicit triangle which is a symbol of the Godhead in many traditions, for example, of the Trinity in Christianity. For Pythagoras it represented wisdom. Traditionally, since it was firmly based below yet points upward, it was an image of femininity. It indicates a relationship between the contents at its corners. The empty space on the right presumably implies the presence of the dreamer. "The right is the male and the left is the female"—each connected to its appropriate human head. Spirit and body (or body and subtle body) are depicted with no split between them.

Alchemically, the triangle apex represented fire, an ancient symbol of spiritual energy, the energy of life, the presence of God and the means by which matter transforms, regenerates and purifies. Fire is needed to transform male and female into the androgyne. The alchemists also thought of fire as a unifying and stabilizing factor. In the shamanic and yogic traditions, religious energy (sacred power) burns. Both the shaman and the alchemist are masters of fire. Mystics of all traditions are "apt to feel the supernatural warmth to the degree that, each upon his appointed plane of being, they surpass the profane human condition and become embodiments of the sacred" (Eliade 1967).

Therefore, the dream image unifies body, soul and spirit and is probably an indication of the relationship between humanity and divinity, depicting what is usually called the ego-Self axis, although ego-Self analogue would here be a better description. Apparently the wisdom of the feminine, or inspiration by the holy spirit, relates the two. Interestingly, the apex of the triangle is precisely at the point where the two spirit heads are joined, perhaps at the center of the entire mandala. The human appears to be an emanation from this divine center, experienced as masculine or feminine as it incarnates within the human soul. Humanity cannot yet contain the divine opposites in their undivided state.

The Child

The child is often described by Jung as an image of the Self (Jung 1968b), expressing the idea of psychic wholeness. It conveys a sense of the future and of becoming, of potential and new hope. The dream defines wisdom in part as "the awareness and acceptance of one's inner child." An immediate meaning is the need to retain open and fresh vision, to be able to see things for the first time, to be open to new experience, to retain the capacity for naivete and learning, and to know truth when we see it. Without a relationship to the inner child we cannot experience excitement, wonder and awe, which we sometimes need to experience the numinous. The child in us is not bound by time and if healthy is not too obsessively disciplined. It acts out of spontaneous love and not power motives. The healthy child has ready access to fantasy, the imagination, and archetypal reality. It helps us to bridge that world and everyday reality. Without relation to the child we tend to be disconnected from the unconscious. It does, however, need help with boundaries. Like all children, this inner child may become destructive if ignored or maltreated and may die if it is not loved. According to the dream, childish (instead of child-like) old people have been overwhelmed by the inner child. It is living them out, its intensity too great for their insufficiently developed ego consciousness. Even this poorly understood process is of value as an illustration of the concept that the archetype insists on its own process with or without our conscious cooperation. In the latter case, what results often looks like pathology. Perhaps the severe regression of *senile dementia* is the ultimate example of the consequences of ignoring the inner child. This illness is always experienced as a terrible catastrophe. However, there is a hint in the dream that, if understood in a certain light, dementia too expresses an archetypal reality, albeit in an unconscious form.

Children are common images in the dreams and imaginal life of the elderly. Often such figures behave like long forgotten aspects of the personality, left-behind inner figures who were never given the opportunity to develop. To rediscover this child is to reconnect with childhood wounds. As at any age, dealing with them usually proves painful but is necessary for growth to continue. These early wounds remind us of our parents, and our early attempts to take care of their difficulties and struggle with their unconsciousness. As children, this was often too difficult, and sometimes we sacrificed important aspects of ourselves in the process of meeting their needs.

Late in life, we not only may be able to parent our own wounded inner child, but also understand our parents much better, and deal with their suffering at less cost to our adult personalities—that is, become a parent to the inner sick parent. When this is achieved it has a redemptive, healing quality.

Connecting with the inner child is considered so important that "as we lose the child we are apt to sever our ties to the divine." This is also because child-aspects of the psyche represent part of the potential of the Self which were present at birth and which have never been realized. If the ego crystallizes around a fixed level of defensive development, it loses its permeability to new revelations and to the pressure of the Self. By contrast, "belief" implies an attitude of openness, and results in behavior and feelings which would not otherwise occur. Jung emphasizes the fact that God needs man to become conscious of him. This dream also suggests that our attitude is all important for the furtherance of this process. If the ego loses its belief in the transpersonal, and its capacity for play, it is not likely to experience the continuing unfolding of the personality which otherwise occurs in later life. Thus the dreamer is urged to move on but at the same time to retain her connection with the child. This will prevent her from falling prey to fixed rules, rigid thinking and all the other *senex* characteristics she fears. Just as there is an inner child (or archetype of the divine child), so there is also an inner elder (or archetype of aging and wisdom). Just as the child can be understood as hemaphroditic, so the old person becomes androgynous. This may be another meaning of the phrase "God gets younger": the Self in late life becomes as bisexual as the Self of childhood, but now with the addition of consciousness.

The Creation of Consciousness in Late Life

"God gets younger" further refers to the fact that the Self in late life becomes more similar to the primal Self which originally existed, containing all potentials, at birth—without the boundaries or categories which later ego-consciousness found necessary. They both represent the union of opposites, but in late life the Self is more fully incarnated (actualized in the world) and transformed by consciousness. Individuation means both incarnation and differentiation; both are enhanced by progressive Self-revelation giving birth to new consciousness, which is itself necessary for individuation, in a circular process. Whenever an ego position dies, a little more of the Self is born ("when we die, God experiences rebirth"). Whereas the Self in the baby is old (Jung's "2 million year old man") it is unconscious. The developing ego allows the Self to be born constantly by realizing its potential. This may be a psychological understanding of Eckhart's idea that God is born in us (Jung 1966). The Self births ego in childhood, and ego returns the compliment in old age: "I am God's son and He is mine" (Silesius, quoted by Jung 1970). The rejuvenation of God seems to be equated with the birth of new consciousness, which according to Jung (1966), is equivalent to the renewal of life. According to the dream, this process is so important that its failure "disturbs the cosmic ecology," emphasizing the importance of mankind in the overall scheme of things. It is noteworthy that the diagram represents the rejuvenated God-head—the result only of the successful application of the process. Therefore, if we take old age seriously, it confers an enormous responsibility. For, according to the dream, without man's efforts God's energy is diminished, and divinity "sinks into itself and ceases to be conscious of itself." In Jungian terms, we need to help the creator become conscious of His creation. The ego can then become a model of the Self—and man thereby becomes deified. Relevant to this process is Dr. James Hall's suggestion to me that as the Self presses for the ego to individuate, the Self becomes simpler—i.e., more "schematic"—because less and less of it remains to become actualized. Perhaps this is why it is able in later life to represent itself in such a relatively simple way. The dream illustrates Jung's notion of the "relativity of God"—that is, "a reciprocal and essential relation between man and God, whereby man can be understood as a function of God, and God as a psychological function of man" (Jung 1966).

For those interested in the theory of reincarnation, "when we die, God is reborn" also refers to the idea that the Self (Atman) reincarnates in order to regenerate itself. It chooses its particular lifetime for further development to occur. The ego's responsibility is to realize who it is, and this furthers the process.

THE DREAMER'S SECOND BIRTH: HER PERSONAL JOB-EXPERIENCE

Apparently in response to his suffering, Job experiences God in a whirlwind, and hears His voice, and is initiated into a deeper understanding of the mystery of good and evil. Raine (1982) points out that, for Job, God is now no longer hearsay but actual vision—an experience, not just a belief. Job had hitherto been unconscious of the nature of the God existing within him. Now, through vision, deity becomes conscious, at the same time uniting his inner and outer worlds. Quoting William Blake, Raine points out that good and evil are transcended in Job's realization that God is beyond his personal categories, and that nature is alive with God. This, then, is Job's second, or spiritual, birth, which abolishes the spiritual pride (or unconscious grandiosity) that, according to Blake, was the original cause of his suffering. His vision of God makes questions irrelevant. His inner conflict, coinciding with painful outer events, is healed by contact with the numinous.

Analogously, the dreamer experiences a paradigmatic, quantum shift in her consciousness. She sees a transformed image of God, which resolves various antinomies which are of personal importance. To see on this higher level is to be at that level of consciousness: "Seeing provides a nondual basis of communication in which the awakened masculine responds to the self-existing feminine" (Arguelles 1977). Curiously, the purely visual elements— the "spirit" heads—are not especially powerful, perhaps because they are so diagrammatic. But the dream voice carries a level of authority beyond all doubt (Jung 1986b). The dreamer sees and hears that God includes and transcends masculinity and femininity, that youth and age are inseparable, that birth and death are two threshold aspects of a unitary process which endlessly renews itself, and above all that human consciousness is an integral ingredient of the entire opus.

In 1959, Jung wrote: "we are going to contact spheres of a not yet transformed God when our consciousness begins to extend into the sphere of the unconscious. . . . Individuation and individual existence are indispensible for the transformation of God. . . ." I suggest that the elaboration of the dream image in this paper is just such an example of how conscious work on any image of God that we discover in the unconscious transforms that image. Such work enables us to partake in the continuing incarnation (Jung 1959). In fact, human consciousness either brings about or is essential to incarnation. It is even arguable that consciousness is synonymous with incarnation—the more we have of it, the more we realize our divinity.

REFERENCES

Arguelles, M. & J., 1977. *The feminine*. Boulder, Co.: Shambhala.
Colgrave, S., 1979. *The spirit of the valley*. Los Angeles: J.P. Tarcher.
Edinger, E. F., 1984. *The creation of consciousness*. Inner City Books.
Eliade, M., 1958. *Rites and symbols of initiation*. New York: Harper & Brothers.
———, 1967. *Myths, dreams and mysteries*. Trans. Mairet, M. New York: Harper & Row.
———, 1972. *Shamanism*. Princeton: Princeton University Press.
Gennep, A. van, 1960. *The rites of passage*. Transl. Vizendom, M. B., and Caffee, G. L. Chicago: University of Chicago Press.
Henderson, J. L., 1967. *Thresholds of initiation*. Middletown, Ct.: Wesleyan University Press.
Hillman, J., 1972. *The myths of analysis*. Evanston: Northwestern University Press.
Jacobi, J., 1973. *The psychology of C.G. Jung*. New Haven: Yale University Press.
Jung, C. G., 1959. Letters. Ed. Adler, G., Vol. 2. Princeton University Press.
———, 1966a. The psychology of the transference. *Collected works*, vol. 16. Princeton: Princeton University Press.
———, 1967. *The visions seminars*. Zurich: Spring Publications.
———, 1968a. The symbolism of the mandala. *Collected works*, vol. 12. Princeton: Princeton University Press.
———, 1968b. The psychology of the child archetype. *Collected works*, vol. 9,i. Princeton: Princeton University Press.

―――, 1969. The stages of life. *Collected works,* vol. 8. Princeton: Princeton University Press.

―――, 1970. The personification of the opposites. Collected works, vol. 14. Princeton: Princeton University Press.

―――, 1970a. Rex and regina. *Collected works,* vol. 14. Princeton: Princeton University Press.

―――, 1971. *The type problem in poetry. Collected works,* vol. 6. Princeton: Princeton University Press.

Neumann, E., 1954. *The origins and history of consciousness.* Princeton: Princeton University Press.

Pennick, N., 1980. *Sacred geometry.* Wellingborough, U.K.: Turnstone Press.

Poncé, C., 1983. *Papers toward a radical metaphysics: Alchemy.* Berkeley: North Atlantic Books.

Raine, K., 1982. *The human face of God.* Thames and Hudson.

Robinson, J. M., 1977. The Nag Hammadi Library. New York: Harper & Row.

Singer, J., 1976. *Androgyny.* New York: Anchor Press.

Zolla, E., 1981. *The androgyne.* New York: Crossroads.

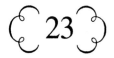

OLD AGE AND DEATH

Jane Hollister Wheelwright

In her essay, "Old Age and Death," Jane Hollister Wheelwright, a Jungian analyst for over forty years, reaps the fruit of an active life. Even in her old age she advises herself: "Never let an old horse lie down." Self-aware, candid, anecdotal, salted with wisdom and gentle humor, her remarks manifest the wisdom of feminine elderhood. Although she protests, "Don't expect me to be able to speak for you, for I am not an expert in this field," you will be not only sympathetically lured but also intellectually enlightened by her personal observations regarding the 'twilight years.'

Wheelwright stresses the need to let go of one's ego as one enters old age, because preparing for death is like preparing for a journey to a foreign country where one doesn't know what to expect, but where one knows somehow that it is necessary to cut down on the sheer quantity of one's "baggage" in order to make that trip a success. One must decrease one's stress-laden concerns in favor of a greater concentration on what she calls the "long view." Her article gives apt advice not only to those of us who are approaching old age but also to those of us who must still face the possibility of dying young; we do well to listen carefully.

Jane Hollister Wheelwright is a member of the San Francisco Jung Institute and the Inter-Regional Society of Jungian Analysts. She is the author of The Death of a Woman *(1980),* For Women Growing Older: The Animus *(1984), and* Men and Women *(no date). She is also co-author of "Analysis with the Aged," a chapter in* Jungian Analysis *(1982) and "The Ranch Papers" in* A Testament to the Wilderness *(1985).*

MY aim in this paper is both to convey to you some personal experiences of my old age, as well as thoughts about death. Certainly experiences vary enormously, and there must be about as many versions of old age as there are old people. Yet perhaps out of our pooled experiences we might pin down a few generalizations. Also, we should consider that our fantasies about what is to happen to us when we cross over may be valid. After all, on the subject of death there can only be speculation, as no one—so far as I know—has come back from the dead to tell us what happened. For each of us, our fantasies have an important personal validity as communications, perhaps hints, from the unconscious and (possibly all-knowing) area of our psyches. And hopefully our exchange of views of death and the afterlife will serve to open us up to further explorations and intuitions in this area.

To start the ball rolling, I will begin with notes jotted down and collected over the last ten years or more and elaborate on them briefly. In general they cover my thoughts about the significance of old age, life and death; observations of myself and my ever-changing attitudes in this stage of life, especially with regard to the relationship of the ego and the archetype of the Self; dreams, mine and those of others approaching death; speculations about the process of departing this life; and fantasies about what comes next. But please keep in mind that I am limited by my own make-up, as perhaps everyone is. Don't expect me to be able to speak for you, for I am not an expert in this field. No one can be an authority or semi-authority for someone else in so individual a matter.

For myself and for several other people I know, the sharpest concern about death came, most forcibly, in my fifties. Now, in my eighties, I feel that old, old age is not so crucial a concern—possibly because every year, every week, I am more and more aware of my deterioration. I do not need reminding. It also has occurred to me that since for millennia a person's life-span extended not much beyond twoscore years and ten, there has been laid down in the human psyche millions upon millions of times the expectation or habit of thought that life would come to an end in one's sixth decade. With unconsciousness of the ancient conditioning, it is perhaps not too surprising that some archaic messages about death would surface, as they did for me, in the fifties, even though now age fifty is too young to die.

At this time in my life, in my fifties, death loomed in my thoughts, and death dreams and occasional spasms of fear followed me around for some months. It was not, however, so much concern over the fear of death as it was a deep curiosity and interest, that led me finally into taking on in my analytic practice several terminal-illness cases. Through the experience of working with these individuals, I gradually outgrew my need to explore the subject. No doubt I was merely catching up on the problems of death, to which until recently modern society's attitude has been one of avoidance. (In earlier times, of course, death was a familiar event from childhood on.) I also discovered that the more I witnessed death, and the more contact I had with the dying, the less threatening death became to me. However, except for people like Kubler-Ross and the hospice movement, this does not seem to hold true with the medical profession.

Among the aforementioned patients was a woman I will call "Sally" with whom I worked during her final months of life, listening carefully to what she said about her own dying. (With Elinor Haas I have recorded this experience in *Death of a Woman*.) Besides working with these terminally-ill patients, I have read samplings of the current literature on death and old age but have found them disappointingly superficial. However, Florida Scott-Maxwell, the late Jungian analyst, in her book, *The Measure of My Days* (1968), had some provocative things to say. And Jung's chapter concerning life after death in his autobiography, *Memories, Dreams, Reflections* (1961), gives one a lot to think about. A book by Rosemary Gordon, *Dying and Creating: A Search for Meaning* (1981), is also well worth reading. And so is Jung's "Seven Sermons to the Dead" which I am at last understanding a little.

A book written in 1977 has perhaps influenced me the most; or at least it firmed up my own thinking about eternity, essence, infinity, and meaning— these aspects of life that old people, especially those who have lived fully, try to understand. It made me articulate what I was vaguely groping for. It is called *The Last Letter to the Pebble People* by Virginia Hine, an anthropologist and therefore a woman aware of the need for accurate observation and objective reporting. (See Hine's chapter on "Self-Created Ceremonies of Passage".) She described step-by-step her husband's dying from the moment he realized he had cancer to the moment of his last breath. In his fifties, and in the months he had to live, he achieved to my mind what most people take a life time to achieve. He experienced his struggle to stay alive; a year's remission; the many ups and downs of life; and finally a positive surrender to his fate as opposed to going down in defeat to the disease. He sorted out from months of alternating spells of elation and depression many basic truths: among them the psychological fact that disease is not the issue: it is instead a struggle between darkness and lightness. He also was able to find a deeper, more profound center by letting go his ego. Towards the end when the pain was at its worst, he refused morphine in order to go into his death consciously and retain his faculty for communicating to the extended family around him his subjective experiences. At the very end he had a long inner dialogue with death but, most significantly, also a realization that the figure of God stood directly behind the figure of death. His visions included other figures, among them especially a personification of love. He finally recognized his lifetime achievement was not academic; it was, instead, in the many relationships he cultivated: his creativeness thus lay in the area of relationship. The people around him, and there were many, changed, each one uniquely in himself and herself. His way of dying and his final victorious acceptance of Death as a friend became an inspiration for them. Their individual interpretation of his dying put them afterward on their own tracks. His wife's final comment in the "Afterward" of her book is most impressive, and it fits the archetype to which we shall refer later in this paper. She wrote: "love fulfills itself in death," thereby implying that love and death are two aspects of the same phenomenon. The thread in this man's life and in his dying was manifested in an attitude that changed consistently and constantly with his ever-widening subjective experiences. He was throughout in a state of transformation. It became his *raison d' être,* and possibly also the meaning of his death. Transformation for him transcended life and death. This story portrays what it is that we try to understand in our old age by bridging over from life to death. It gives us a glimpse of what is meant by eternity, essence, infinity, and meaning. For this man the life flow of his transformation achieved his victorious death. In Jungian terms: his individuation was the other face of death.

PERSONAL OBSERVATIONS ON OLD AGE

A central experience of old age, I have found, is that the opposites are close together. Take, for instance, wakefulness and sleep. The swing from one to the other happens to me, and to others I know, with enough frequency that now I usually expect when I sleep deeply one night to lie awake the next, for no particular reason. So I deliberately arrange to read or in some way to pass the sleepless nights constructively, if only in wakeful reflection. Because these exaggerated rhythmic swings do not happen when I am in a nature environment, I have wondered if such a syndrome is a product mainly of human civilized environments. Perhaps the effect of nature, which incorporates the opposites of life and death, helps to integrate the related opposites of wakefulness and sleep, thus perhaps eliminating the conflict.

Another way in which the closeness of the opposites makes itself felt is in the rapid alternation of opposing states of being. My experience of old age is an almost continuous movement from one extreme to another with practically no warning. Spells of efficiency shift to inefficiency and ineptitude from one day to the other. One day I am full of vitality and interest in life, and the next I have less will to live. I may have a feeling of being very present and focussed, and then suddenly an hour later I am lost in vagueness. One minute I am sound asleep, and the next minute so wide awake that sleep is out of the question. This proximity of opposites accounts for many happenings, odd feelings, odd sensations, and images difficult to understand. Death can appear imminent one moment, and life seems vibrant the next. One can be feeling unusually well, then suddenly all the aches and pains due to tension and over-extension return to plague one. Of course, these swings are not unknown in youth and middle-age, occurring exaggeratedly at times perhaps, but normally then they are less abrupt and spaced farther apart. In this regard, old age is simply a heightened counterpart of the rest of life. In any case, the problems of old age seem to center around the need to steer between these opposite conditions and states of being. I like to think that now I have finally learned to say "No" to many of society's demands that seem to add to this play of opposites.

Physical well-being in the old person seems to parallel—or occur in the same pattern as—mental well-being. Or so it happens for me. If for a few days I do not engage in any physical exercise such as taking a walk, the subjective need for exercise seems to diminish. Just the necessary getting around to take care of daily chores seems to tire me as much as actual physical exercise. But it becomes clear before too long that if one does not exercise, bodily discomforts soon become more and more noticeable. The danger then is to think either that one is on the way out after all, and so what is the use in exerting oneself, or that this state of discomfort is an inevitable part of old age.

On the ranch where I was raised, we had a dictum which applies here: "Never let an old horse lie down." It was indeed true that no matter what its age or illness or injury, a domestic animal was, if at all possible, kept on its feet. It is perfectly logical when you think of the wilds, where old or injured animals instinctively keep on struggling somehow to find food and water and to remain alert in order not to fall victim to predators.

This instinctual principle, to my mind, fits us to a tee. I often look at animal life to find guidelines for the basics of human life—not just physical, but mental, spiritual, and character guidelines as well. After all, animal instincts are also on our ground plan, along with the archetypes. To avoid "starving" psychically, we must go on making an effort, no matter how tempting at times it might be to give up. I say this because at the end of one's life one sometimes tends to feel that one has earned the right to retire not only from the demands of middle age, but for the entire business of living. One has shot one's bolt, and that is that!

Scientific studies are said to reveal that very small children are concerned with death, and I have found this to be true in my own experience. My granddaughters, when they were little, often asked me when I was going to die, and something told me their queries were not based entirely on the worry that they might lose their grandmother. Rather, I detected an interest in the subject itself, based perhaps on their private fantasies. It is not too difficult to understand why this should be so. Small children, with their as-yet-undeveloped egos, are in connection with the collective unconscious where, in this deepest psychic stratum, life and death—as well as past, present, and future—are not differentiated. There is also in the collective unconscious a certain disregard for the importance of an individual life. I saw this, by the way, in Sally's dreams when, faced with death, she was driven into contact with these deep impersonal levels. In her long series of final dreams, death was mentioned specifically only twice, possibly because she talked of death in nearly every interview. On the other hand I had the direct impression that her impending death was regarded as relatively insignificant by the collective unconscious. Children, still not as yet fully propelled into life, in connection with the collective unconscious, their egos not yet their centers of gravity, are bound to have fantasies of perhaps not ever making it all the way out of those depths.

It may have been from the perspective of this deep level that Jung was speaking when he advised old people to proceed as though they would live forever. The timelessness of the collective unconscious, if that is to be our final destination, as it may have been our origin, would warrant such advice. Certainly I have found that this advice has been good for me. It helps me to push aside the temptation to be lazy. Diminished physical strength and stamina, poorer concentration, less will to study, lapses in focus, and other diminutions of our powers all make us tend to not bother to exert ourselves. On the other hand, if I feel that what I do today may have a place in the long-range scheme of things, I am going to make the effort. Besides, for me at least, it is not too hard to believe one will live forever if one thinks in terms of some non-ego form of existence. And this leads me into the subject I want to touch on next: the ego-Self axis in old age.

The Ego-Self Axis in Old Age

One of Jung's comments, to which I referred in my opening remarks, was that in old age one tends no longer to have problems. While he did not elaborate at that time, I believe he was referring to problems caused by the ego. If this is the case, his statement has proved accurate for me and for other contemporaries of my acquaintance in recent years. Those of us who were in youth disturbed and conflicted enough to seek analysis, and who were unable to find a safe harbor in the conventions, found the ego a continual focus for conflict. However, now in old age, if all goes well, the deeper, impersonal, all-inclusive archetype of the Self, in which the ego has its roots, gradually supercedes the rule of the ego and many ego-related problems tend to disappear. The ego of course, up to the day of our death, never should entirely lose its hold. If it were to do so we would be inundated by the unconscious—perhaps become senile.

This ties in with Jung's second comment, actually a corollary to the first: when asked whether he was, in his seventies, individuated, he replied that he would be neurotic if he were not. His implication was that an untroubled old age is an individuated old age, and vice versa, for to be individuated means that the ego has become largely subordinated to the Self in the conduct of life. (I do not think of myself as being individuated.) The Self, being a phenomenon closer to nature than the ego, has a certain innate logic of its own which is derived from its incorporation of the opposites. This is reflected in an old person by the ability to see two sides of a question. Those who have struggled with their lives will find that the nagging self-concern of the past fades away, and it becomes possible to simply brush off many things that might once have been disturbing. Lessened energy and faltering memory may also help in the process, but the end result is sometimes that one comes to be looked upon undeservedly as wise and philosophical! Of course, one does see people who are troubled and despairing in their old age. They may be, for the most part, those who remain locked in the ego or who have lived an untroubled, outwardly successful ego existence and are faced with conflicts only at the end of life.

However, for those who have sought meaning in their conflicts, ego concerns seem to become progressively less important with the onset of old age. Ambitions, desires, efforts, decrease, while willingness to go along with what is around one increases. Those, on the other hand, who were over-willing to go along will come to stand their ground. The attitude is one of fatalism, rather than of *laissez-faire*. One accepts how things are and stops trying to change them. Defeats and disappointments are taken in stride (no telling, of course, how much poor memory for recent events has to do with this!), and victories are survived with less danger of inflation. It appears that one's ego has somehow come into a better relationship with the Self. It may be that this relationship is what nature intended in the first place, but which a lifetime of Western emphasis on ego development may have thrown off balance. It is hard to know.

On looking back on my life, I am struck by how much misery I experienced because of the ego. Being an analyst, I had ample opportunity to see the same phenomenon in many of my patients. For some people ego conflicts are so devastating that they are tempted to give up, and indeed some do. For those who are conflicted, the ego life is one riddled with doubts and ever-changing attitudes, relieved occasionally by temporary—or sometimes lasting—glimpses or experiences of one's true personality and brief reprieves from conflict. Too much time and energy seem to be consumed by relentless, nagging disappointments, agitations, apprehensions, although in actuality the solid, real accomplishments often balance out these long series of small deaths leading to small rebirths, as well as the struggles to satisfy the demands of ambition, and so on.

One wonders about the rationale of such a life of conflict and strife. It was caused no doubt by a too-prolonged, close connection with the deep unconscious, a hangover from a maladjusted childhood in which the satisfactory evolution of the ego was not possible. As I see it, if the connection to the deeper unconscious is not sufficiently closed off early in life, and at the same time the individual cannot take advantage of the protective screening of social prejudices, which tend to block out disruptive unconscious phenomena, then the ego gets tossed about on a sea of endless possibilities of conflicting drives. The personal human ego with its roots too directly connected with the non-human psychic strata, can become, in youth and middle age, a catch-all for the diverse elements of existence arising from below. It may be that the negative aspect of the Self takes over more than nature intended.

In my experience, finally in old age, once the ego gave way to the Self, all that past distress came to an end. As Jung had said, in old age the problems become minimal. Apparently individuation is what nature always intended for the conflicted, but it is strange that it can be achieved only via the long, hard road to consciousness paved with distress and conflict. Perhaps for those spared these conflicts there is an unconscious individuation process. I hope so. In any case, those destined to attain a conscious relationship to the Self are forced in youth and middle age to find any sort of psychological palliative, including formulations of a *raison d' etre*. They have to create a psychological theory or a philosophy, even a spiritual ethic, to explain and justify their existence—as many psychological leaders, for instance, have. They are required to struggle with the necessity of satisfying ego demands until, in old age, they can come closer to the psychic area of the Self. There they will find a certain satisfying acceptance of life—perhaps for the first time.

During a trip to China one summer several years ago, I had some interesting reactions which gave me a few clues about this ego-self problem. For one thing, reflecting on the fact that I found myself seeing eye-to-eye with the Chinese in a way I hadn't when my husband and I lived there for over a year in 1931 (nor, as a matter of fact, in my lifelong association with the Chinese), it dawned on me that my recently-acquired old-age view had something to do with it. As I thought more about this and observed the frustrations of the younger members of our tour, it came to me that the present-day Chinese culture is the product of centuries of conclusions arrived at by the senior members of their society. The fact that old age has always been venerated in China, and still is, has given the old-age point of view, especially with regard to downplaying the ego, a validity and influence it does not have in our culture. In the West, at least in our more recent history, the attitudes of the young have prevailed. The result has been that exaggerated emphasis on the importance of the ego, which properly belongs wholly to youth, and less so to middle age, is extended throughout the whole of our lives. Possibly such a disparity in outlook accounts for many of the differences between our two societies. In any case, these insights verified my personal impression that in old age the ego becomes less important. They also explained why I now found myself very much at home in a culture which assigns the ego a back seat, whereas in my earlier life I, like the younger people on our tour, did not experience this level of compatibility.

Parenthetically, some people have defended to me the youthful bias of our society on the grounds that it keeps old people young. But I would disagree with this line of reasoning. In my opinion, what makes an old person seem young is rather the emergence after middle age, of latent abilities and openess to new attitudes—especially the fourth function in its positive aspect. When these assert themselves they are bound to appear at first in the awkward, clumsy characteristic of youth. People who resist the demands of these new impulses pushing up from the inside and who cannot allow themselves to be temporarily awkward and unsure are, I believe, likely to become unnaturally rigid and fossilized as they age.

To get back to China, when I am asked what specifically I had in common with the people of that country, my answer in a nutshell is *the long view*. At my age you tend to see events in their long-term historical aspect. Geographically, too, you seem to lose interest in local happenings. You focus more on larger areas of the world, take an interest in cultures which are historically and geographically distant, and look everywhere for useful generalizations. Your reading takes in speculations of more cosmic nature. I, for instance, am absorbed in how the universe originated, how human beings got their start, and where they may be headed. The so-called "food chain" of nature with its interlocking life systems is also of keen interest to me. With a deep interest in ecology, I am intensely concerned with what is going to happen to our planet. These are all questions of the long view.

Something else that struck me about the Chinese was their attitude of "no hurry, things will work out given time." This outlook is a *must* for old people. They cannot afford to be hurried, or they will suffer physical and psychic tension. In 1931, when I asked our Chinese-language tutor where he came from, he named some place far in the interior. How long since he had visited his home? "I was there two generations ago," he answered in a totally matter-of-fact way, as though he might have been saying "two years." The three generations of a family—child, parents, grandparents—are seen as a whole, as a span of time. As far as I could see during our trip, in China there is little rift between the generations.

Another thing was that many of our tour members were keen to find out about the sex lives of the Chinese but could get nowhere. They received conflicting, contradictory answers to their questions and finally gave up. I felt the Chinese were confusing in their replies because they were trying to give our people the answers they thought they wanted to hear. It seems that either the truth of the matter actually is conflicting, or else the Chinese, being less hitched to the ego than Westerners, place less importance or perhaps a different emphasis on sex. Ancestor worship has not been eradicated by the revolution, and it appeared to me that the average Chinese regarded sex not only as too private an affair to talk about, but also as a service to the family, that is, a means of insuring the reincarnation of the individual. To my mind sex belongs psychologically primarily to the realm of the ego and hence to the young and middle-aged. I believe this in spite of the great promises which are now being held out to old people. These promises may, in fact, be helpful for those who are still living primarily through the ego and who, due to our society's youthful bias, are possibly quite numerous.

The one time in China that I got an unmistakably approving reaction to something I said was when I told Madame Wu, our guide, that China reminded me of one great family. She agreed with great enthusiasm. This brief exchange told me a lot: not only that the modern Chinese social life is an extension of their age-old family communal life, but that it fits easily into the individual's sense of continuity. Love and caring for children, as well as for old people, as it was before the Revolution, seems to be universal in China, if the condition of the very young and the very old is any criterion. It is as much a collective effort as it is an individual one. Incidentally, they have now added another dimension that is impressive: a new freedom for women which, because of vulnerability to pregnancy, was never before possible.

To return to the experience of the ego in old age, I have noticed that if my ego gets out in front, for whatever reason, at this stage in my life, I am threatened by tension. This would seem to be a logical reaction if one looks on old age as a gateway to death, for it appears fairly certain that the ego, like the body, is eliminated when we die. Therefore, if the ego does not gradually give way to the real center, the Self, it becomes an obstruction. It goes against nature and creates tension. For me, this condition is as much a bodily phenomenon as a psychic one; this is not surprising considering that the body exits with the ego at death and in this way is associated with it.

When the "I" in me takes over, I find myself countering a deep inner pull toward blending into the context around me. (Gregory Bateson said that without context there is no meaning, and I think he is right.) If my ego tells me to stand out, and the animus provides the means, the "I" part of me gets in the way of my instinctive, archetypal old-age needs. I am thrown back into a youthful state, absorbed with my ego life. I no longer fit into the inner environment from which comes the meaning in my life. I become like a *prima donna* who tries to make a comeback and botches it. I overlook the old-age need to sit back and let the Self speak through me if it so chooses, or be content to stay inactive and silent if it does not. If my "I" insists on being noticed, if it gets in the way of my relaxed journey into death, my gradual stepping across the border into the invisible world (Hades, by the way, originally meant "invisible") to which my present dreams may be referring, I may very well experience a growing fear of death or a sense of imminent calamity—or at least manage somehow to spoil my ego efforts. My old person's objective sense of humor or philosophical attitude would also be impaired. (Incidentally, this natural attribute of the old is personified in the Chinese Laughing Buddha.) It is my experience that old people are able to laugh, at least among themselves, at the failings of the old and at the prospect of death. A recently published collection of epitaphs written by famous people before their deaths gives evidence of this ability. Robert Benchley, for instance, wrote: "Pardon me if I don't get up!"

To some people the idea of letting go one's ego in preparation for death may sound defeatist, but I believe it is instinctive. In the sense of ego being the drive to stay alive, this same abdication occurs in animals when they are ready to die. They take themselves off to an isolated place. The Naskapi Indians do the same, exposing themselves to the dangers of the wilds. An instinct, even when its goal is death, is rarely negative. There must be residues of such an instinctive impulse in us. And we should never forget that death is normal!

Of course, just as one cannot neglect the needs of the body in old age on the grounds that it is destined to deteriorate, one cannot neglect legitimate demands of the ego on the theory that it is bound to be eliminated. One must have a sensitive ear for just how far to go. However, in a busy, demanding environment, it is hard to develop this ear. For me it is necessary to periodically submerge myself in a wilderness setting to restore my judgment, occasionally even my sanity. When this is not possible, I sometimes have to drop everything and take long walks in nature.

Perhaps because it was my childhood environment, I believe that wilderness is the most basic context, essential at times for anyone at any age, and that it is unfortunate not everyone can have access to it or at least to some physical setting which is in harmony with the Self, where the outer context correlates with the inner. A spell in the healing ambience of our isolated mountain ranch house enables me to recover my sense of the meaning and direction of my life and is especially helpful in keeping me focused on old age. The following quote from the naturalist Ann Zwinger in her journal, *Even the Sky is Hard,* points up what I am talking about:

> Many of us need this wilderness to listen to the quiet, to feel at home with ancient rhythms that are absent in city life, to know the pulse of a river, the riffle of the wind, the rataplan of the rain on the slick rock. Romantics, perhaps, but realists too. Here in the wilderness is a safety valve for our civilization, an environment that can absorb our pollutions and, given time, cleanse itself.

Incidentally, I find the wilderness also absorbs our psychic self-pollutions.

Walking or hiking in isolated places brings head and body (psyche and soma) together in an equilibrium which matches the equilibrium in nature. For old people in particular, achieving this physical wholeness makes it possible for them to discern more clearly the legitimate extent of their ego-body needs.

Take my case, for instance. Undertaking to lead a seminar on old age and death certainly meant I would have to exert my ego in order to prepare for it. Although it somehow seemed wrong to refuse to share my reflections upon and experience of my own old age with others who might be interested, I was reluctant when asked to do it. Yet making this ego effort proved beneficial for me. Having to gather my wits, think over my old-age experiences, look up notes, and so on, brought a renewal of strength. It was not a reversion to youth, but rather a verification of a satisfactory old age that insists on the ego being lived out to its end. Nevertheless, I had resisted this task until an inner voice seemed to say, "Go to the ranch; get with it, and take a chance—do it!" I believe this inner voice was the Self.

Rosemary Gordon has a different emphasis on the ego-Self axis that, because it broadens our concept, I would like to include here. She links ego to life and Self to death. She sees the ego as the separating, individualistic unique aspect of our lives and the Self as representing love, passion, fusion, belonging, submergence of the ego in a state of wholeness. The loss of ego, she says, can be real death or psychological death. If real death is not intended I call it "time out for recharging the batteries." By that I mean a condition of depression, immobilization sometimes, a period for psychic rest—a time to go into the wilderness. It is when the ego loses its clarity and the animus, for a woman, disappears into the unconscious to collect: new ideas and new understanding for a thinking person, new patterns, new inspirations for the artist, and so on. Gordon calls this a "state of fusion." The crux of her theory is that this state of fusion is not only the preparation for creativity but is also in the pattern for dying. The similarity of the process therefore indicates that normal dying is the same in principle as creating. One might speculate that the unconscious intends us to come up with something new in the next life.

The third of Jung's comments regarding the end of life had to do with the experience of the opposites, which I mentioned earlier as a central problem of old age. His remark referred to the period following his heart attack in 1944 when, as he says in his autobiography, he "hung on the edge of death." For several weeks he experienced a series of visions of mystic marriages culminating in the *hierosgamos,* or sacred marriage, a symbolic representation of the coming together of the opposites in the shapes of goddesses and gods or other archetypal figures. Jung's nightly visions were as real to him, or more so, than his daytime existence, and what he said was that at the time he had not wanted to return to this world. (For what it is worth, Jung is supposed to have told Dr. Bali that in his vision of soaring skywards there was a rope attached to him, and the Americans, catching hold of it, returned him to earth.)

Constellation of the *hierosgamos* is said to bring with it the feeling that all of life has been experienced, and hence there is no need to continue on in the earthly existence. This phenomenon is not confined to the approach of death in illness or old age. It is manifested also in the suicide pacts of lovers, such as Romeo and Juliet. Death and love are connected. Certain love experiences approximate the experience of the *hierosgamos,* giving the illusion there is nothing more to be lived. The death pull at these times of *coniunctio* is, according to Jung, a final state and comes also with death. Conversely, the struggle to stay alive, especially under adverse circumstances, comes from the feeling that there is more of life that needs living. Naturally I do not know what is in store for me, but I like to think Jung was right. I had some evidence that he was when my cancer patient, Sally, towards the end of her young life, dreamed she was God's partner. After the dream she said, "Now I can die."

Experiencing the pull of the opposites and discriminating between them is life, and it can also be conflict. In old age this conflict can sometimes make one feel sterile, as though in a disagreeable state of suspension, in a void. In my own old age I have found that being at our mountain hideaway helps with the problem mentioned earlier, of steering between the opposites. To me, encompassing as it does the entire spectrum of life, nature represents a milieu where the distracting, splitting-apart effect of "civilization" is eliminated. This condition is the essence of divinity, and to my mind puts wild nature in the role of goddess to our Christian god as the personification of the female principle, which has been downgraded in the West for well over two thousand years. It may be that nature, on the basic underlying level of existence, as manifested in the food chain, both includes and goes beyond the concrete reality of human beings and is for us, potentially at least, a divine reconciler.

In all this I am not forgetting that the problem of the clash of opposites is the hammer-and-anvil condition that makes for consciousness. If it had been the sole environment from childhood, nature would not help toward consciousness in old age, any more than would, for instance, a lifetime identification with a goddess. However, there are long-established alternative possibilities, apart from nature, of surmounting the dichotomies of civilization. For example, I know of a highly-educated, worldly, rich French couple who some years ago separated amicably in their old age, he to join a monastery and she to spend the rest of her days in a convent. There are now many kinds of retreats for people of all ages. I believe that these, like our mountains, are places designed to heal humankind's psychic split. To die the way nature intended, the way animals do, a relaxed state is indicated.

DREAMS

The lessening importance of the ego, about which I have been speaking shows up for me most clearly, so far, in the types of dreams I now have. Always heretofore my dreams were specific and concrete, so much so that I relied on them heavily as guidelines for my ego efforts. In the last years, however, they have seemed more unreal to me and more shadowy. People are mostly anonymous, animals and objects rarely any longer familiar. The dreams seem to have less and less to do with my everyday life. Recently Marie-Louise von Franz told me that old peoples' dreams in general are hard to analyse for this reason. The unreal, shadowy quality of my dreams makes me think of Patricia Berry's account of pre-Christian descriptions of the underworld. At that time, like Heaven, it was considered a good place to go. In her paper called "What's the Matter with Mother?" she quoted from pagan descriptions of the underworld place Christians call Hell:

> The underworld was a pneumatic, airy realm. The beings there, called "Shades" *(Skia)* or "images" *(eidolon),* were unsubstantial like the wind. It is a realm in which objects cannot be grasped physically, i.e., taken literally, but only felt in their emotional essences, the invisible counterpart of the upper world . . . that realm deep beneath the concrete world and yet somehow within it.

In those days, as I mentioned earlier, Hades meant "invisible," referring to the underworld as a qualitatively better world than ours in the same sense that we associate the word "spiritual" with the sky world. The underworld was the "highest" and the "lowest," the essence of the concrete world. It was the realm of the true mother, not the debased version of mother as matter *(materia).*

Some people have explained the change in my dreams by saying that in them I have finally become an intuitive; but I think there is more to it than that. I think that perhaps my dreams are now, in old age, coming more and more to reflect Persephone's underworld, as opposed to Demeter's upper world, or as I prefer to put it, wild nature rather than the Mother Earth about which we hear so much. (For me "the wilderness," which also refers to the unknown, is a more comprehensive concept than "the underworld.") The dreams may be referring to something Berry calls the "spiritualization," for want of a better word, of Demeter's concrete world. It is the refinement, the intangible essence, of the concrete world as we know it, and it may be a phenomenon of old age. It is different, as Berry points out, from the tangible concrete we urge people to get in touch with, by digging in the earth or some such advice when they are too high up in the head i.e., too spiritual, and need grounding.

A poem recited by Kiefer Frantz, not long before he died, at John Langton's funeral, may fit in here. The poem could be referring to the content and quality of my dreams, so I have added a line to include people:

> Where a home is not a home,
> Where a place is not a place,
> Where time is not time,
> Where people are not people,
> That is where the spirit goes.

Besides, "The Journey," whether by whale, or train, or plane, or on foot, is well-known as an archetypal motif relating to a psychological and spiritual process of adventuring into the psychic unknown, of reaching out toward the frontiers of personal experience. The roots of the timeless, universal meaning of The Journey go back to prehistory when early humans travelled great distances. They perhaps extend even further back on the evolutionary scale to the animal realm with the annual or semi-annual migrations of many species; and the awesome bird migrations are still regarded as near-miraculous phenomena by contemporary natural scientists. The long religious pilgrimages of the past, when travel was dangerous and tedious, as well as the tourist explosion of the present, are other examples of the compelling symbolism of The Journey. Also by no means insignificant are the current cruises and tours for retired people—people who, in their old age, are apparently living out an archetypal impulse that lies in their unconscious. With the ease and comfort of modern travel available to the average pocketbook, old people today have the means of acting out a process toward attaining a mature old age which nature may have intended them to go through subjectively. By translating the deep impulse of The Journey into actual travel, they may be living out their dying in a dramatized form.

Apropos of this, on a month's train trip through Mexico, which my husband and I took a few years ago, there was one man, a New Englander well into his eighties, who had been travelling this same route each fall for a number of years. During our trip, the old man died one night in his chair in the observation car. His going was swift and easy, as though he had been thoroughly prepared, that is, "packed up." So one cannot say for sure that subjective philosophizing or psychologizing of the end of one's life is the only right way. Considering that in the dreams of Northerners, especially New Englanders, the warm, emotional, southern country of Mexico often represents the unconscious, it is not surprising that the elderly gentleman from the North should have chosen this particular route. His instinct must have been guiding him.

In my old age I have had many travel dreams, occurring almost nightly at times—especially in 1979 while I was writing up my thoughts about old age and death. The frustrations of packing appeared in the first of that series. In that dream I was faced with an immense mess of things that needed to be sorted out and organized and put into containers before I could join my parents for dinner—although in reality they died a long time ago. Fortunately, under all the stuff I found sturdy chests. Considering my daytime activity, the dream must have been referring to my sorting out and putting together my thoughts on the subject of this paper and, therefore, certainly alluding to death.

However, this type of dream has appeared many times before, particularly in my middle age. For years, whenever I felt out of sorts, or unable to cope, or generally inept, it was not unusual for me to dream of frustrations about packing an excess of things that were supposed to go with me to some unknown destination. I have travelled all my life, and packing was always a bugbear because of not knowing what conditions to expect in strange countries, especially in the days when not much travel information was available. So it is possible the unconscious continues to use this packing motif because it is familiar to me. But the theme also fits the contemplation of death. In other words, the problem is how to "pack" for the next world without knowing what to expect. In the past when there was an obstacle to travel, in my dreams, I realized I had to clear away some wrong attitude. When travel was no problem, I was assured of being on the right track. (I should add that in the last dream of my 1979 series, packing was no trouble at all. My husband and I were planning to spend two weeks in some idyllic place, and I could not see why we should not stay longer.)

In my seventies, when the packing dreams occurred so persistently, the message, i.e., warning, finally got across to me that I must slow down in my activities and organize my life in a more orderly fashion. I must reduce my baggage. To use the language of the dreams, I began to sort out my "belongings," packing only what I could conveniently "carry." I ended up having to cut down on interests, duties, and even physical exertion. I also had to learn how to not be too responsible. While I recognized that the "things" in the dreams probably represented ties to the material world and to the world of ideas rather than my personal belongings, there were nevertheless times when I felt like putting a match to the actual clutter of possessions around me, a houseful of objects gathered through a lifetime of living.

Finally, in 1975, my husband and I completed the building of our hideaway in the mountains overlooking the Santa Barbara channel. Perhaps not entirely by accident, it looks out over the exact spot, Point Conception, which the Chumash Indians call their "Western Gate." They believe it is the threshold across which pass the souls leaving this world and those about to enter. In short, it is their burial ground. Our home is in total isolation, especially when it rains and the dirt roads are too slippery for travel. As I have said, weeks in this place seem to slowly put us back into our rightful, individual grooves. We are free from interruptions—phones, people, duties, even "pleasures." After some time there, the packing dreams gradually subsided. (They returned, however, on that visit when I was putting together these thoughts.)

For the most part, though, my dreams, including those about travel, have been the impersonal, unspecific type I mentioned earlier. I like to think this indicates improvement. By improvement I mean going more with life in the way nature intends for the old and proceeding with as much grace as possible towards my end on this planet. It may be that these vague dreams reflect the new fatalistic, "anything goes" attitude I have felt growing in me in recent years. I wonder if old people who resist this inner shift have to become rigid as a means of (or result of) defending themselves against it?

Possibly as a phenomenon related to the packing motif of the dreams, I have found in the last few years, in spite of deliberate streamlining of my activities, that my former interests, one by one, are fading away; personal enthusiasms have petered out; things that used to make an impression no longer do; what was once beautiful no longer is; and so on. Moreover, except for my increasing preoccupation with certain matters, such as universal truths or generalities, philosophical explanations of life in general, and problems of death, new interests tend not to appear in place of the old ones. "Interesting" books are dropping away at an alarming rate.

As with the need to cut out nonessentials when preparing for any journey, nature apparently assists us in preparing for death by severing our ties and projections to the outer world, thereby helping us to be as psychically unencumbered, or as self-contained as possible, for our exit. I have to look on myself in my old age the same way I look on my irreplaceable, prized possessions, as one by one they break or are marred. Each time one goes, I have to say, "There goes a part of me." But as possessions go, there is also relief. I need to know that once I get to the point of no longer having the elasticity or energy to accept or understand the new generations, new technologies, new ideas, new styles, new designs, new people, it will be time for me to go. My usefulness and my value will have passed. I can then contribute to the world only by gracefully bowing out, knowing that I am leaving my place in the scheme of things for whomever is to follow me, and being glad that by the process of my death a descendant, or someone who has benefited by my existence, is now free to go beyond me. Life, at least when nearing its end, is a process of making a place for those who can and must come next. I can never have the last word.

In the meantime, I am very much here. With me still, in fact more than ever, is an interest in the question of what is basically female, that is: what is a woman really made of? Also, as I have said, I care deeply about what happens to nature and to our wilderness areas. Of course, it could be that these interests are, in disguise, part of the process of my individuation, or that they camouflage a search for the missing female half of our Christian godhead. Or, on the other hand, my ego now being less insistent, I may be more sensitive to new forms pushing up into the general consciousness from the deep layers of the collective unconscious. If these concerns of mine have only to do with the personal, they may at least be connected with that part of individuation which is female.

However, I did find in the dreams of my dying female patients that a final love affair or marriage with the animus (or death) was implied. The male component is indeed crucial for a woman, although some dreams suggest that it is another woman who comes to complete the dying woman. I would just like to quote something attributed to Pope John the XXIII shortly before he died, which I think wraps up the matter quite dramatically and tells the man's side of the issue. In answer to some question about his health, he replied, "My bags are packed, and I am waiting for her." By deduction I suppose that I, too, must be ready with my bags packed, but that, as a woman, I must wait for *him*.

Or will it be *her* for me also? I know that archetypal woman is said to be concerned not only with life but with its opposite, death, as well. There is a great amount of symbolism pointing in this direction. For instance, in Africa the lioness has always represented both love and death. Perhaps this is so because, as we know, the lioness not only raises her young but also kills to provide food for her mate and cubs. The earth, symbol of woman, receives the dead in the form of seed in winter and sends up new life in the spring. As Virginia Hine wrote: "Love fulfills itself in death." (See von Franz, *On Dreams and Death 1986*)

In addition to my travel dreams of past years, which seem to relate to preparations for departing this life, I have some which may refer more specifically to the end of my life. For example, in one such dream I was scheduled for an 11:00 A.M. flight to my parents, that is, to join my ancestors, but I had to postpone the flight to the next day because my bags were not packed! A dream of Sally's also had to do with the 11th hour.

Speaking of the 11th-hour motif, I would like to insert here a warning against interpreting it as an inevitable prediction of death. As we have seen in the two examples I gave, this motif occurred under very different circumstances. It appeared in Sally's dream several months before she died. For me it came several years ago when I was conducting a seminar on death, and I have not been ill in the interim nor, to my knowledge, am I now, and I feel as though I could live a few more years. As a matter of fact, it is an important rule of thumb to regard dreams not as prophetic in character, but rather as compensatory to the conscious state and attitude. In my case I was not focusing on the possibility of my own death, so the unconscious jogged me into realizing that at my age it is not out of the question. Whereas Sally, who was wanting death and expecting it at any moment, needed to be distracted from her preoccupation with her imminent death. Her need was to focus on a time beyond her immediate condition so that she could fill in the months she had left with coming to a better understanding of herself—in spite of the fact that she had to struggle daily to live at all.

In a related vein, it is not uncommon for people who are mortally ill to have, as Sally did, dreams in which they appear healthy and well. Von Franz has told me she thinks that these "well" dreams are referring to life after death, not to recovery on the earthly plane of existence. This proved to be true in Sally's case, for due to the extent of her physical deterioration and the unlikelihood of her experiencing a spontaneous cure through a religious conversion, it was quite apparent that she had no hope of recovery and was going to die. In view of this, her numerous "well" dreams stood out as a most impressive phenomenon. In *The Last Letter to the Pebble People,* the man nearing the end of his life described himself as being well in visions of the next world, and as being miserably ill in this life. He had inner experiences of going from one to the other.

Dreams in which I am interacting with people who have long since died are always difficult to interpret. But if it is true that the "well" dreams of dying people point to their futures, and that deceased relatives and friends are

presented in the dreams of old people—and often of younger people as well—
as being healthy, usually younger than at the time of their deaths, or at the
prime of life, or ageless, then there very well may be a land of the dead. I do
not know, but it is a satisfying thought to me, and one in which Jung advised us
to indulge ourselves. We can never solve the mystery of life, so we might as
well follow the fantasies that allow us to function at our best. As far as death is
concerned, fantasy is our only reality!

Speculations and Fantasies

Speculating on what it will be like to die, and on the relationship of life and
death, brings me back to my earlier observation that in old age the opposites
are closer together, just as they are at times of depression and withdrawal
throughout our lives. I have come to suspect that this situation is not entirely
coincidental and that our periods of depression, which are like small deaths,
can be used in a sense, as practice times for our exit. I believe that, as
Castaneda's Don Juan said, we go along side by side with death all through
life.

Parenthetically, in my opinion it is a misinterpretation of this process
which, more often than not, leads people into suicide. The downward pull and
immobilization that accompany deep depressions are mistaken for sensations
of physical death rather than of the psychic death which, as a matter of course,
precedes psychic rebirth. Suicidal people often fail to recognize that it is
nature's demand for a change in attitude or an increase in self-awareness which
brings on the depressed state. They do not realize that to bring about a change
in their lives, they have to experience despair and to face the black night of
their tunnelled state of mind in order to come out into the light of change. It
does seem that nature, however, intends for certain people to bow out, and
these have no alternative. They will have too little will to tolerate the un-
understandable. Their egos are overpowered and lost, and they are helpless to
save themselves. But those who are willing to at least make the effort of
coping with their suicidal feelings stand a good chance of coming out ahead,
for it is my firm belief that trying helps more toward growth than actual
achievement. But this is a subject that needs to be elaborated on at another
time.

Our lifelong alternating pattern of depression and immobilization, in
varying degrees, followed by the customary aftermath of exuberance and
renewed creativity, resembles a series of minor death-and-rebirth experiences.
It does not seem illogical, therefore, that this pattern might mirror, on a lesser
scale, the final life-to-death transition experience, thus implying the possibility, at least, of some kind of rebirth into another form of consciousness.

The older one grows, and the nearer to the finality of death, the more
heightened life becomes. Florida Scott-Maxwell, in the book I mentioned,

expressed surprise at this development herself. She wrote, "Age puzzles me. I thought it was a quiet time. My seventies were interesting, and fairly serene, but my eighties are passionate. I grow more intense as I age." To my mind, however, it seems only natural in the face of threatened loss, and it is true not only for the old. Soldiers in wartime are noted for their zest for life, as is easily observed when they are on leave. Also, it is known that suicidally depressed people often become suddenly euphoric once they have made a definite decision to end their lives.

On entering into the process of dying, then, one moves from the climax of life to its opposite, the climax of death. At least I fantasize it will happen this way. I have been close to several people who, the very day before they died, commented they had never felt so well. Sooner or later, I imagine, there will be sleeplessness (illness, perhaps, or a sense of being in no-man's-land, of suspension, of being in a void, in unreality—all disagreeable sensations). After that, and probably with pain, will come the long, deep sleep of physical death. As I have mentioned, this happens on a minor scale throughout one's old age, and therefore, may be an indication of what to expect in the final experience of this world as we know it now.

Jung tells us to fantasize about where we go when we die. Zen masters tell us to fantasize from where we came, and that will be where we go. I like to think our destination is the deep layers of the unconscious, that being the source of superior wisdom, insight, and psychic and spiritual development, if not also of our origin. (Jung has referred to the unconscious as synonymous with God.) Besides, it is for me a familiar psychic place, and thus something I welcome the thought of in so unpredictable an experience as physical death.

I also like to think that when I go, I will become part of nature. I know of no more miraculous, fantastic scheme, no more perfect design for life and death, than nature. In nature, life and death are equally important. If we were to experience only life, we would be faced with the grotesque prospect that life, unchecked and unbalanced by death, would proliferate like cancer cells until all of life was destroyed. So, my fantasy, as of this point anyhow, is to melt into nature when I die: to become part of the trees, part of all vegetation; part of earth and rocks, also animals, birds, even the reptiles and insects or anything else that moves—in short become part of the goddess nature who, if we would only realize it, could be standing side by side with our Christian god.

A more lofty ambition might be to melt into the divine syzygy this pair represents. I may not as yet be honoring sufficiently the huge achievements of consciousness made under the aegis of the Christian god. But as a modern woman, I am more concentrated on establishing in my imagination the guiding force of the female deity before contemplating the male. Modern woman at any age has to anchor herself firmly in the female before she can give due respect to the male, or so I believe.

Jung's injunction that we should carry on as though we expect to live forever indicates he must have had some inkling that we do go on, and certainly his dreams point that way. I am not sure mine do so far. I am biased in this direction to the extent that I like to think our lives are purposive beyond the confines of our earthly existence, and that this is the reason one keeps on making an effort. This is my interpretation of Jung's counsel. But for the moment, I am content with my focus on living out what wants to be lived—and so experiencing the creative other side of death.

Nevertheless, I do find intriguing an idea of Jung's based on his and other people's dreams, which he discusses at some length in the "Life After Death" chapter of his autobiography. It is the idea that work on one's spiritual or psychological growth continues after death, but that the dead can acquire new insights and knowledge of psychological advances only from the living who join their ranks. This thought, although I personally have not had such evidence in my dreams, encourages us to remain alert, open to new developments, and to continue pushing toward consciousness as long as we are alive, so that when we die, we will bring with us something of value for those who went before. It adds to the belief in the importance of our earthly lives.

I see death, in this scheme of things, as a positive process of making room for further efforts in the progress of humanity, on the part both of those who come after us and those that have preceded us.

It is a chain built with greatest care and fantastic order in which a life may be obliterated at a moment's notice by the needs of another life, spaces filled and emptied for the flame of life to continue. Human beings, when they come to the end of their usefulness, like all lives, I feel, are not wiped out totally by another's physical needs, but are displaced temporarily, and this is as it should be. Otherwise we would interfere with the purposefulness of life.

Without one's having lived, and died, that small further effort of each individual might not come off. This concept presents, of course, an ideal view of the relations between the generations and is one which gives me personally another *raison d' etre*. A note of warning, however, against old people being too open to what the younger generations bring us. We must not be distracted from our efforts to find the timeless and the universal essence of our own generation's contributions.

In all this I am taking for granted that life moves on toward more and more highly, perhaps fewer, evolved systems. The direction may be toward smallness. For instance, the smallest birds are apparently the most recent on the evolutionary scale. Yet we humans are growing bigger and bigger—perhaps toward our extinction. I cannot believe we will go on becoming bigger and more numerous. We have to be stopped, and I am almost glad to add my own death to the slowing down, or even the demise, of our race. We also cannot forget that the ecological crisis of our time is directly caused, not only by the prolongation of human life, but by our present over-population.

Perhaps some of us see death as our becoming nothing and wonder how so long a life of striving and experiencing can go for naught. But if nothing is naught, or worthless, I wonder why nothingness is symbolized by zero, which is represented by a circle, the symbol of wholeness and completion? Hopefully one's death is the experience of that completion, a job of living well done. I am reminded here of a dream in which a Mr. Glass was driving a car with five zeros on the license plate. A male figure far from negligible, he was the bearer of a new attitude. Then, too, in my fantasy of melting into nature, I would no longer exist as myself and so, in a sense, would become a zero. I also remember my terminal-cancer patient whose only wish was, as she put it, "to be annihilated."

Furthermore, I think of the East Indians, who struggle for Nirvana (nothingness), and the Gnostics, whose loftiest deities were Silence (female) and Depth (male). Closer to our own tradition, there is the Christian god who has been called "The Void." And on the earthly level, there is the artist, who recognizes that spaces in a work of art are as important as the filled-in parts.

In the feminist movement we see the revolution of women against the traditional concept of being considered "nothing" in their own right. However, (and I would hope not to get caught saying this by women of that movement without having the opportunity of explaining myself!) women possibly have failed to appreciate and value their essential female nothingness—their ability to let live, to step aside for the benefit of others. Perhaps they need to recognize, and to tell men, that, like God the Void, they too are divine in their nothingness. (Granted, of course, that they have to assert themselves first as being everything before they can risk extolling their nothingness: "All *and* nothing!" might be the woman's cry.)

In this connection, I am reminded of a woman who underwent a severe mental breakdown, which in time became a death-and-rebirth experience. Her slogan as she recovered from the episode was, "Live by Letting Live." Before her breakdown she had been overactive, and as though living in a cocoon, totally involved with her affairs. The encounter with the unconscious gave her the first inkling of the other side of her true female nature, without which she had been headed for disaster. The slogan was to her an expression of the equally high value of inaction and concern for others. The saying reflects, too, of course, woman's fundamental concern with life—all life. Yet on the other side of the coin, as I pointed out earlier, the female has long, perhaps always, been associated with death as well. Because of this association, by the way, it seems to me that women in the medical and helping professions are the logical ones to pioneer new, more natural and satisfactory ways of dealing with dying people.

So, in a roundabout way, we come back from the female principle of nothingness to the subject of death. Nothingness and death and the female are, certainly in thought, linked. But this should not be surprising, for born of the mother, the sea from which all of life originated, we are destined to return to the mother, the unconscious, the sea. It is as the Zen masters say: if you wish to know where you are going, fantasize from whence you came!

REFERENCES

Gordon, R. 1968. *Dying and creating: A search for meaning*. London: Society of Analytical Psychology.

Franz, M. L. von. 1986. *On dreams and death*. Boston: Shambhala.

Hine, V. 1977. *The last letter to the Pebble People*. Mill Valley, California: Orenda Publishing/Unity Press.

Jung, C. G. 1961. *Memories, dreams reflections*. New York: Pantheon.

Scott, M. 1968. *The measure of my days*. New York: Knopf.

Wheelwright, J. 1981. *Death of a woman*. New York: St. Martin's.

———1982. "Analysis with the aged." In *Jungian analysis*, ed. Murray Stein. LaSalle, Illinois: Open Court.

———1984. *For women growing older: The animus*. Houston: Jung Educational Center.

———1985. "The ranch papers." In *Testament to the wilderness*, Festschrift for C. A. Meier. Zurich: Daimon Verlag.

Originally published in *Quadrant* (Spring, 1983). Reprinted by permission of the author and the C.G. Jung Foundation for Analytical Psychology, New York.

INITIATIONS:
ANCIENT
AND
MODERN

PART SEVEN

24

ANCIENT INCUBATION AND MODERN PSYCHOTHERAPY

C. A. Meier
Translated by R. F. C. Hull

In this essay, "Ancient Incubation and Modern Psychotherapy," Carl Alfred Meier, M.D., addresses not only analysts, physicians, and social anthropologists, but all of us. In this fascinating account of the pre-Christian Asklepieia of ancient Greece he not only finds parallels between ancient and modern healing practices; his descriptions of the rites of the Abaton also suggest comparison with the rites of dream questing common to many diverse cultures and times, including the "dream vision questing" of the American Indians. Those who take more than a passing interest in the initiatory rites and mysteries of their early Mediterranean ancestors will be gratified by the concreteness of Meier's document. His extensive research bears fruit in actual models of the Asklepian healing mystery, models which even today (see work of Jean Houston and Eugene Monick) are considered viable by those who seek to adapt them to contemporary culture.

Carl Alfred Meier, M.D., born in Switzerland, was Jung's pupil, assistant, and later his successor as Professor of General Psychology at the Swiss Federal Institute of Technology. He was one of the founders of the Jung Institute in Zurich, acting as its president for the first years. He also founded the International Association for Analytic Psychology and the Clinic and Research Center for Jungian Psychology in Zurich, and to this day directs the Clinic's Laboratory for Experimental Sleep and Dream Research. Dr. Meier has lectured extensively throughout Europe and the United States and has published over 150 papers and many books, among them a textbook, The Psychology of C.G. Jung *(1985) in four volumes.*

THE question of whether there are any ancient prototypes of our modern psychotherapy is one that has interested me for many years. As in ancient times everything to do with the psyche was embedded in religion, it was obviously necessary to look for these prototypes in the ancient religious cults. The first definite reference seems to be a passage in Galen,[1] where this most famous physician of late antiquity proudly styles himself the "therapeut" of his "fatherly god, Asklepios." What is the meaning here of the word "therapeut"? It can only be the name originally given to those who were the "attendents" of the cult, and who served the god by carrying out the prescribed ritual. From this point of view, therefore, psychotherapists would be people who had the care, or cure, of the soul. Erwin Rohde, in his still unsurpassed work, *Psyche,* has attempted to show how all ancient religion was a cult of the psyche, so that anyone who took an active part in religious life had no need to fear for his psychic welfare.

But what happened in the case of sickness? Here I got a second reference through a dream which was dreamt by an English woman patient at a critical phase of her treatment. It consisted of the laconic sentence: "The best thing he created is Epidauros." As is usual with such dicta or apodicta, no context was obtainable. I knew, however, that my patient had been to Greece, and I reminded her that there was a town of this name in Argolis. She thereupon remembered the theater which she had seen there—probably the most beautiful of all ancient theaters—and slowly the recollection of the local Asklepieion, to which Epidauros owes its fame, came back to her. The occurrence of this name in the dream was therefore a kind of cryptomnesia.

Then from a study of what was practiced in the ancient Asklepieia, I was able to obtain an answer to my second question as to what was done in ancient times for the care of the soul in case of sickness. And the answer was not, as we should be inclined to believe, ancient medicine or a physician, but exclusively a god or savior named Asklepios—not a human, but a divine physician. The reason for this was that ancient man saw sickness as the effect of a divine action which could only be cured by another divine action or by a god.

Thus a clear form of homeopathy was practiced in the clinics of antiquity, the divine sickness being cast out by the divine remedy *(similia similibus curantur).* When sickness is vested with such dignity, it has the inestimable advantage that it can also be vested with a healing power. The *divina afflictio* then contains its own diagnosis, therapy, and prognosis, provided, of course, that no one knows the right attitude to adopt toward it. This right attitude was made possible by the cult which simply consisted in leaving the entire art of healing to the divine physician. He was the sickness and the remedy. The two concepts were identical: Because he was the sickness, he himself was afflicted (wounded, or persecuted, like Asklepios or Trophonios), and because he was the divine patient, he also knew how to heal himself. We can apply to this god the oracle of Apollo: "He who wounds can also heal." The god sent the sickness, was the sickness, was sick, and healed the sickness. This is the widespread mythological motif used by Wagner, for example, in *Parsifal*:

"Only the spear that cleft can close the wound." The analytical need for a training-analysis has its ancient prototype in this mythologem, although to see in it nothing but a learning process would be a fundamental misunderstanding.

To come back to the dream mentioned at the beginning: I should like to say in advance that in the remarks which follow I shall deal with the amplifications of the key word "Epidauros," as I believe I have discovered in them much that illuminates, or allows inferences concerning, the ancient art of psychic healing considered as the prototype of modern psychotherapy. In the main, I shall leave it to you to think of the striking parallels with the existing psychotherapeutic situations, and in order not to overload an already highly condensed exposition with frequent interruptions, I shall make explicit mention only of the most important points of correspondence.

"Sacred Epidauros" is situated about five miles inland from the town of Epidauros on the Argolic peninsula. It dates back to about the sixth century B.C. and remained in use through several periods of prosperity and decline until the third century A.D. It represented a holy precinct enclosed by boundary stones, its chief deity being Asklepios. His cult did not die out in other parts of the ancient world until the fifth century A.D., so that he appears to have carried on his healing activities for over a thousand years. Nevertheless, Epidauros became, and remained, the center of the cult surrounding this god, despite the fact that every town of importance later established its own rival Asklepieion; for the priests of Epidauros were astute enough to affiliate all these new centers to themselves by strict retention of the translation-rite.[3] The transfer of the cult to another place was always effected by the conveyance of a holy snake from the Hieron of Epidauros, which represented the god in his theriomorphic aspect. Typically enough, it was only Kos and its medical school that refused to accept this filiation. The Koan Asklepieion, however, survived the famous Koan School of Physicians by at least two centuries. Over the whole ancient world there were finally more than 200 Asklepieia, all connected with Epidauros as the central authority.

I must remind you that I cannot give a complete picture of Asklepios, but can only mention those features which are of importance to our theme. Asklepios was originally a pre-Greek god, or rather, demon, as can be seen from the oldest forms of his name: Aischlabios, Aislapios, etc.[4] The oldest place of worship, unfortunately not yet excavated, was probably Trikka in Thessaly. He usually possessed an oracle which answered all manner of questions, and was thus of a decidedly mantic and therefore chthonic nature. This is born out by his animal attributes, the snake and the dog. Also, his places of worship were always associated with springs and groves (Asklepios Kyparissios on Kos and the Rufinic Grove in Pergamon). In the Greek myth, Asklepios was subjected to an interesting metamorphosis, being transformed from a mortal physician, described in Homer *(Iliad)* as the "Incomparable Doctor," into a chthonic oracle-demon or hero, and then into an Apollonian deity dwelling on Olympus. He finally developed into what could almost be called a Christian god or saint, as is evidenced by the striking similarity between the records of miraculous cures at Christian shrines and in the legends of the saints in late antiquity and the Middle Ages, and the reports of cures at Epidauros. The Emperor Julian even went so far as to draw a parallel between Asklepios and Jesus—but that lies outside the scope of our study. In his later statues, too, the dark demon develops into a Zeus-like, bearded figure whose most conspicuous feature is his "gentleness," which, according to the ancient etymology, can still be traced in his name, Askl-epios.[5] In this form he is actually the son of Apollo, who on that account bore in Pergamon the epithet, "he with the excellent son," and who had his own temple there in this capacity.[6]

Originally, then, he was a mortal physician who had learned the art of healing from the centaur Chiron. Carried away by success, he finally tried his hand at raising the dead, thereby offending divine providence, and for this impiety he was punished by Zeus who slew the reckless thaumaturge with his thunderbolts. Apollo was angry with the father of the gods and for a time left Olympus in protest, but not before he had liquidated the Cyclopes who had forged Zeus's bolts. For Asklepios, this had the unexpected and gratifying result that he was admitted into the Olympian circle, and a further advantage of his apotheosis was that, as a genuine god of healing, he could work a steady succession of miracles which were no longer dependent on his physical presence. He could now work epiphanies, and these remained henceforth his sole method of cure. But even here his original chthonic nature as a *genius loci*, or local diety, asserted itself, for he only performed his miraculous cures at his own shrines, despite the fact that he was now entitled to derive his mantic oracle-nature partly from his Olympian father Apollo, who had always been a god of oracles and healing, though his arrows showed that he was a god of disease as well. Mantic science and the healing art are still closely related, not only in the miraculous cures wrought by faith, but in the miracles of healing wrought by medicine—an ambigous and much disputed phenomenon which even today exhibits a certain local frequency. This is an entirely serious observation, and one explanation of the fact that many patients only have healing dreams when they live in a particular town or place (Zurich, for instance).

The metamorphosis of Asklepios which I have just described, and which consisted essentially in an *ascensus ad superos,* is especially interesting to me from the psychological point of view: The physician left the earth by divine intervention and was carried to a higher plane. Henceforth, the whole curative process was enacted on another, higher level. It is surprising, but extremely significant, that even at this height the god still retained his chthonic qualities, and that he worked his cures on earth below almost exclusively through his chthonic attributes—snake and dog—without this disturbing his Olympian image. In spite of the freedom of movement he enjoyed on Olympus, he remained true to the type of chthonians who were bound to their particular locality. One thinks involuntarily of this passage in the *Tabula Smaragdina,* which says: *"Ascendit a terra in coelum, iterumque descendit in terram, et recipit vim superiorum et inferiorum"* ("he ascends from earth to heaven, and descends again to earth, and receives the power of Above and Below"). Asklepios, therefore, unites in himself not only the human and divine opposites, but also the chthonic and the Olympian. Moreover, he is a boy and at the same time a bearded man.

We could mention many such pairs of opposites which are not so much united in Asklepios himself as represented in his attributes and in his family. To me, the most important fact is that it is hardly possible to imagine him without his female companions, who sometimes played the part of wives, and sometimes of daughters. There were, for instance, Epione the Gentle, Hygieia, Panakeia, Jaso, etc. Hygieia, the radiant virgin, to judge by her statues, seems to have enjoyed a particularly good relation to the Asklepian snake, which she is often seen feeding. Also represented in his family were men like his sons Machaon, the "Slaughterer" or "Wounder," Podaleirios, and especially Telesphoros, the "Perfector" and "Consummator," the Boy who brings the fulfillment of dreams and prayers. He is shown completely enveloped in his strange hood, the *bardocucullus,* looking just like a gnome in a cloak, a point to which we shall return later. In Copenhagen there is a statuette of Telesphoros, the top half of which can be taken off to reveal a hidden phallus. Harpocrates, another such ithyphallic infant, was as indispensable to Serapis, the Alexandrian god of healing, as Telesphoros was to Asklepios. All these manikins bear a marked resemblance to the Idaean Dactyls and the Cabiri. Telesphoros was first worshipped in Pergamon where there was an ancient Cabiri cult, and where he himself was described in inscriptions as "life-giving," "procreative." These Cabiri came into being when Rhea's fingers were poked into the earth, and therefore possessed spermatic power. For this reason they were also gods of healing, in the sense that they embodied the creative power of the divine touch. When Zeus cured the mad Io by holding his hand over her, she gave birth, while yet a virgin, to Epaphos, from which came the epithet, Zeus Epaphios, "the toucher." Healing in this case led to procreation. Similarly, Apollo was a god of healing, whence his cognomen Apollo Hyperdexios, "Holder-over of the hand."

As I have said before, very little reliable information is available concerning the ritual to be performed in the Asklepian sanctuaries. Only the following facts are certain: Patients came from far and near to those usually very remote sanctuaries in order to seek relief, especially when medical skill had failed, or seemed to offer no hope of success. If they were already moribund, or if they were women near their confinement, they were turned away from the sanctuary, as this had to be kept pure in accordance with the rules of the cult. This "cruelty," as can easily be imagined, was, of course, a godsend to the jealous doctors of antiquity, and later to the Church Fathers. (Japanese Shintoism is also acquainted with temple incubation and has, so far as we can judge, an identical ritual. Thus the holy precinct, the isle of Itsuku-Shima, had to remain undefiled by birth and death, and sacred animals were also kept in the sanctuary.)

After the performance of certain purificatory rites, ablutions, and preliminary sacrifices, the patient went to sleep in "the place not to be entered by the unbidden." Here we must make our first conjecture with regard to the ritual by assuming that the persons admitted to sleep in the Abaton were bidden or called. That, at any rate, must have been the original meaning, and it provides the first indication of the mystical character of the Asklepian cult. We know from the Isis mysteries that the goddess invited by means of a dream those whom she wanted to have in her temple, and that others had no access. Certainly, Apuleius was aware that he had to be called by the goddess, or else he would die if he set foot in the Abaton. We do not know whether such a call was sent to those seeking healing in the Asklepieia, but we shall soon hear more on this point. At all events, the most important thing was that one should have the *right* dream before sleeping in the Abaton. This was the actual process of incubation. The word *"incubare"* is aptly translated by Herzog as "sleeping in the santuary."

In Pausanias the Abaton is simply called "the sleeping-place." The question whether the dream was the right one was decided by its result, since in that case the patient woke cured. Apparently he was always cured if in his dream he experienced an Asklepian epiphany. The god then appeared to him "in the dream," to use the technical expression, or else "in the waking state," or, as we should say, in a vision: either alone, as the bearded man of his cult-image, or as a boy, or very often in the theriomorphic form, as a snake or dog. He, or preferably his snake or his dog, then touched the stricken part of the body (here I would remind you of what I said earlier about Zeus Epaphios) and disappeared. In early times the patient was probably regarded as incurable if he did not experience a dream epiphany on the very first night. This *"ex iuvantibus"* seems to confirm my supposition that one had to be bidden to the Asklepian healing mystery. We could then say: "Only he who was bidden was helped." But as we shall see, it is possible that auguries and haruspices were made during the preliminary sacrifices, and that the patient went into the Abaton to sleep only if the results were positive. At least this was so in later times when, as has been attested, the patients remained for a considerable time in the Asklepieion. Preliminary sacrifices were then continued until a favorable constellation occurred, a numen of the deity which indicated the "decisive moment." We shall come back to this point later on.

Here I would only like to correct some very widespread wrong assumptions about the practice of incubation in the Asklepieia. In the sanctuaries themselves there were no dream interpreters, for, as you have just seen, they were quite unnecessary. Even the priests could hardly have interpreted dreams. Nor were there any physicians in the sacred precinct, and no medicine of any kind was practiced there. On the other hand, every applicant for incubation appears to have been obliged to write down his dream, or have it written down, as we also require today. Then again, it appears that the patient, after making certain sacrifices—Asklepios had a preference for cocks (*Phaedo*), though he did not turn up his nose at a pig or a bull!—was under no further obligation beyond that of paying the fee. This, too, is a requirement which modern psychotherapy very definitely shares with its ancient prototype. There are even cases on record where the god administered a sharp lesson to tardy debtors by promptly ordaining a relapse. This payment of fees became, quite unjustifiably it seems to me, a great stumbling-block to the worthy Church Fathers, who maintained that Christian martyrs like Cosmas and Damien, or Cyrus and John, had wrought their miraculous cures as *anargyroi,* i.e., free of charge. So in this respect we modern psychotherapists are much more heathenish and faithful to the antique prototype than are the analogous ecclesiastical institutions such as Lourdes and others.

I do not propose to give you any archaeological information about the structure of the Asklepieia, as in spite of the multitude of excavated buildings, it is not yet clear what functions they fulfilled. For instance, in Epidauros itself we do not yet know for certain which of the many buildings was the Abaton. One of the most remarkable of these buildings, a rotunda of a type also found in Athens and Pergamon, with a labyrinthine crypt called the *tholos* or *thymele* (altar, or place of sacrifice), is still a complete mystery.[7] Nevertheless, it appears to be true, despite other assertions to the contrary, that at least in Pergamon the labyrinthine basement of the *tholos* was artificially flooded with water, as water in general played a very important role in the Asklepieia. It was almost as important as the sacred dogs and snakes.

Here again we must correct a widespread error: the springs and bathing-pools were never fed with mineral or thermal water; they simply belonged to Asklepios as a chthonic deity just as his snakes did, and the spring became a sacred spring, purely by virtue of its connection with the god. All chthonic gods had a spring near their sanctuaries. This peculiarity has been retained even by their Christian successors, the wonder-working saints, almost all of whom have a fount in their respective churches. With regard to the snakes, in many popular myths they are closely connected with the water of life[8] and were regarded by the ancients as symbols of regeneration, presumably because of their periodic change of skin. The fact that the so-called Aesculapian vipers can still be found in Schlangenbad ("Snake Bath": a spa in Taunus, Germany), clearly indicates the close connection between springs and snakes. It is not certain whether the comparatively tame snake kept in the Asklepieia was of the species *Elaphe longissima,* as it appears to have been a typical tree-snake, which *Elaphe* is not. But this does not affect the chthonic significance of the snake of Askelpios, for the trees in the Hieron were chiefly oriental plane trees, of which we are constantly told in the texts that sacred springs gushed from their roots, so that here again the close connection of the tree and and the snake with the water is preserved.

It is important for us to realize that the crucial experience took place at night, whether the patient was really asleep in the Abaton or unable to sleep from excitement. In the latter case, the cure was effected not through a dream, but through a vision. I take this fact as a further proof that the miraculous cure was considered a *mystery,* for all mysteries are celebrated at night.

Incubation, however, is a custom by no means peculiar to Asklepios. It is far older than his actual cult, and from its primitive forms we can gather a good deal of information that is lacking in the accounts of Asklepios himself. Homer tells us in the *Iliad* (16) of the Selles or Helles who, sleeping on the bare earth, received dreams and interpreted them prophetically. Herodotus (IV) says that the Nasamones slept on the graves of their ancestors in order to receive dreams. According to Strabo (VI), in order to receive healing dreams, people used to lie on the skins of sacrificial animals (black rams) at the oracle of Calchas on Mount Drion in Daunion, at the foot of which was a temple to Podaleirios (Asklepios' son). According to Virgil (*Aen.* VII) this was also true of the oracle of Faunus. The underlying idea seems to be that revered Mother Earth sends the dreams.[9] Strabo gives an account of the temple of Pluto between Tralles and Nyssa, where patients stopped at a village near the Charonic Cave. The priests invoked Hera Katachthonia on their behalf and received dreams stating aetiology and therapy. Sometimes they took the patients themselves into the cave, where they then had their own dreams but used the priests as mystagogues, i.e., as dream interpreters. No other persons were admitted. More detailed information about the ritual comes chiefly from the primitive incubation temples of the chthonic heroes, Amphiaraos and Trophonios.

Although we have a mass of literary evidence, from Plutarch among others, concerning the Trophonios Incubatorium in Lebadeia, I shall nevertheless keep to Pausanias, because he furnishes first-hand information based on the evidence of his own eyes, he himself having undergone initiation there. According to him, Trophonios had snake and staff attributes just like Asklepios. He was also called Zeus-Trophonios, like Zeus-Asklepios and Zeus-Sarapis, and his snakes lived with him in his cave. The sanctuary was therefore essentially a cave. Anyone who wanted to consult Trophonios by incubation had first to spend a number of days in a house dedicated to the Agathos Daimon and Agathe Tyche, during which time he observed the rules of cleanliness and abstained from warm baths. On the other hand, he had to bathe in the cold waters of the river Hercyna. (Note that Demeter was also called Hercyna.) Animals were plentifully sacrificed to Trophonios and his children, as well as to Zeus, Apollo, and Demeter, and the flesh was eaten. The priest then ascertained from the entrails whether or not the moment for the katabasis had come.

The decisive haruspicy was the one which was made at the final sacrifice of a black ram. If it was favorable, the consultant was fetched during the night by two thirteen-year-old youths, named Hermai, taken to the river Hercyna, and there anointed and washed. He was then conducted by the priests to two springs, Lethe and Mnemosyne, which flowed quite close together. Thus, on the one hand, he forgot everything that had gone before, and on the other, received the power to remember what he would see below. After being shown the otherwise unapproachable statue of Trophonios, he was clad in a white sheet and strapped around with bandages like an infant in swaddling clothes. He was then given a ladder with which to descend into the cave. Arrived there, he had to crawl feet foremost into a hole barely wide enough for a human body to squeeze through. When in it up to his knees, he was suddenly sucked downward as if by a tremendous whirlpool. In his hand he held honey-cakes with which to propitiate the snakes that dwelt down below. There he heard, or saw, his oracle. Sometimes he returned to the surface the following day, but he might be kept down there for several days on end. The *anabasis,* or expulsion from the hole, which Pausanias likens to a baker's oven, again took place feet foremost. On arriving at the top, he was placed on the stool of Mnemosyne, where he was able to remember the entire experience and tell it to the priests, who carefully took down everything in writing. He was then given over to the care of his friends, who carried him, still unconscious and trembling in every limb, back to the house of the Agathos Daimon and Agathe Tyche. There he slowly recovered and even regained the power of laughter. For obvious reasons, he had forgotten how to laugh down there, and this is understandable enough when we read Plutarch's account of the fate that befell Timarchos in the cave of Trophonios; his skull split open with a loud crack and his soul escaped through the sutures.

In this extremely primitive incubation ritual there are already, as you will have observed, numerous points of agreement with the highly developed consultations in the Asklepieia. I should like to dwell a little longer on three of these points.

First, the honey-cakes fed to the snakes: they are offerings which are typical of the cult of almost all chthonic gods. Here I will only mention Cecrops and Erechtheus, who were worshipped in the form of snakes and given honey-cakes to eat. In the Asklepieion the sacred snakes were likewise fed on these delicacies, and were thus characterized as chthonic aspects of Asklepios. We know from a *mimiambus* of Herondas of Kos that the cakes, when in the form of snake-food, were called "round cakes" or "barley-cakes," whereas after consecretion and when burning on the altar they were known as "holy bread" or "wafer." This distinction corresponds to that made in the Catholic Church between *oblata* and *hostia*.

The second point which is brought out very clearly in the Trophonios ritual is that the incubants were prisoners of the god. They were drawn down into his cave entirely at his discretion, detained there, perhaps against their will, for several days without food, and ejected again at his pleasure. This seems to me characteristic of the whole institution of incubation. As I have already remarked, there is only a hint of this in the Asklepios ritual, where we are told that the patients sometimes had to wait until they got the right dream. Naturally, this tradition applies only to later times. But in the case of Serapis, the most famous of Asklepios' colleagues, we do possess definite information regarding the imprisonment. The applicants for cure were obliged to remain in the sacred precinct as prisoners of the god for perhaps several days. Even Apuleius called himself "a fettered prisoner of the goddess." We know from the rhetor Aelius Aristides, or Aristeides of Smyrna, that the "prisoners" carefully noted down their dreams until a *"symptoma"* occurred, i.e., a coincidence with the dream of the priest. Referring to the Asklepieion, he says that the priest with whom he lodged outside the Hieron sometimes dreamt for him, or else the priest's slave. Apuleius sums up the imprisonment during the Isis mysteries in the apt saying: *"Neque vocatus morari, nec non iussus festinare"* ("don't hesitate when called, nor hasten when not commanded"), and the day on which he was bidden to initiation was *"divino vadimonio destinatus"* ("destined for him by divine guarantee"). Sometimes a definite vision was required as a sign that the applicant was ready for initiation. This corresponded to what was known in the Asklepian cult as the "effective dream," or "healing dream," which immediately brought about the cure.[10]

How skillfully the problem of transference was solved when the doctor happened to be not a human being but a god, can be seen from the following. Aristeides, who must have been as big a neurotic as he was an orator, and who spent twelve years of his life in and out of various Asklepieia, could write innumerable poems to the greatest glory of the god, which were sung throughout the whole of Greece, without doing the least harm either to himself or to Asklepios. Quite the contrary, he attributed all his personal successes to the god. Therefore, an inflation was impossible. He regarded his many illnesses as a benevolent fate which allowed him to make progress in "intercourse with the deity." I cannot but see this as an ancient prototype of the ideas of the great Romantic doctor, Christoph Wilhelm Hufeland, who, in his unjustly derided *Macrobiotics, or the Art of Prolonging Human Life*, 1797, writes much about the salutary nature of certain intermittent diseases. Do we not also frequently observe a profound meaning in intermittent illnesses during analysis?

I see the beginnings of our modern dialectical procedure in certain amusing anecdotes which have been handed down to us, as when Philostratus reports that Polemon, on being forbidden by Asklepios to drink cold water, replied: "What would you have prescribed for a cow?" or when a certain Plutarchus asked: "What would you have prescribed for a Jew?" when Asklepios ordered him to eat pork. Asklepios reacted amiably to these waggish objections and varied the treatment accordingly. But in other cases, when the whole point was to heal through paradoxes, and the forbidden thing was at the same time the remedy, the god remained firm, even if a Syrian should have to partake of roast pig, or a pious Jewess rub her child with an embrocation of lard, or a Greek Adonis-worshipper eat wild-boar's meat. *Contraria contrariis!*

Finally, I should like to deal with a special point which must have struck you all in connection with Trophonios: I mean the symbolism of death and birth. The process of being impelled and expelled through a hole is clearly a process of dying and being born. The incubant was, as you have heard, wrapped in swaddling clothes like an infant and was afterwards *"quasimodo genitus,"* like one reborn. We have statuettes of swaddled female patients of Isis. So we are certainly entitled to speak of a regeneration or rebirth, as in the Mithraic mysteries. In many cases the incubants were put on an infant's diet, chiefly milk and honey.

This swaddling garment is naturally also "the new man who is put on," the outward and visible sign of transformation, and hence the garment of the god himself, his very lineaments. At all events, we know that there was a very primitive image of Asklepios in Titane, where he was represented as a swaddled child. Once more we think of the infants Telesphoros and Harpocrates.

I have already referred on two occasions to the mystical character of the incubation cult: one in connection with the call which the patient received, and again in connection with the nocturnal nature of the cure. Also, the candidates were summoned by dreams. But quite apart from this, you must have been struck again and again by the underlying idea of a mystery. I should now like to substantiate this pet theory of mine a little more fully. It is in the first place essential to bear in mind what I have just said about birth symbolism, about being healed and reborn through a descent to the underworld. Is not this exactly what Apuleius tells us of the Isis mystery? Furthermore, when he comes forth from the mystery, he is himself a *religiosus*, a *cultor deae*. And when Aristeides has no compunction about calling his own case-history—an enormous affair of more than 30,000 lines—a "Holy Writ," he is saying with all possible plainness that he regards it as a mystery, since this was the technical term for the mystery myths.

Mysteries presuppose *epoptai*, who observe the *dromenon*. In our case, the incubant would be the *epopte*, the dream the observed *dromenon*, and the cure the mystery. That this is not just my personal observation can be proved out of the ancient authors themselves. You will remember that, according to Tacitus, it was a *eumolpide,* a priest of the Eleusinian mysteries, who played a prominent part in founding the first Sarapeion. An Orphic hymn to Hygieia says:

> Come, blessed goddess,
> To the seekers of mystical salvation.

NOTES

1. Galen: *Opera omnia.* Ed. Kuhn, VI, 41 and XIX, 19.

2. Earlier remains at the sanctuary dating from the Late Bronze Age are now known and reported briefly (with references) by V. Lambrinudakis, "Remains of the Mycenaean Period in the Sanctuary of Apollon Maleatas," as found in R. Hägg and N. Marianatos, *Sanctuaries and Cults in the Aegean Bronze Age,* Proceedings of the First International Symposium at the Swedish Institute in Athens, May 12-13, 1980.

3. There was long-standing dispute in antiquity about the true origin of Asklepios' cult. Only after the center at Epidauros was recognized by the Oracle at Delphi was the priority of the Epidaurian center set on a firmer ground. See E. J. and L. Edelstein, *Asclepius,* vol. II, part 2, Baltimore, 1945, pp. 238-57, for a thorough account of the history and spread of the cult.

4. Asklepios is first mentioned in Homer *(Iliad)* and it is there he first is referred to as a physician. In general, see Edelstein, *Asclepius* II, 2. Apollodorus and Pindar relate that Asklepios was the son of Apollo and a mortal woman (either Koronis or Arisinoe). He was raised by Chiron from whom he learned much of his medical craft. Asklepios was capable of reviving the dead, and for practicing this art, he was slain by Zeus with a thunderbolt.

5. The statue of Asklepios by Thrasymedes of Paros (Pausanias II, 27,2) in the early fourth century B.C. probably showed him as a bearded, gentle figure, as is apparent from some illustrations on coins. See G.M.A. Richter, *The Sculpture and Sculptors of the Greeks,* New Haven, 1970.

6. Aelius Aristeides: ed. Dindorf, B, 21.

7. The round building at Pergamon was perhaps a replacement of the earlier incubation room. It may have served as a great cure-hall. Most of the water installations in the building date later than its construction, so it seems unlikely that it was flooded. See O. Ziegenaus, *Das Asklepieion,* 3; Teil, "Die Kultbauten aus römischer Zeit auf der Ostseite des heiligen Bezirks," *Altertümer von Pergamon,* Vol. XI, Berlin 1981. Certainly archeological investigation has been able to demonstrate that the tholos at Epidauros did not retain water. See G. Roux, *L'architecture de l'argolide aux IVe et IIIe siècles* avant J.C., Paris 1961. For a general interpretation of the tholos form as a hero shrine, see F. Robert, *Thymélè.* Bibliothèque des écoles françaises d'Athènes et de Rome, Paris, 1939.

8. Frazer: Pausanias' Description of Greece, Vol. III.

9. Euripides: *Hecuba* 70, *Iphigenia in Tauris,* 1231.

10. A useful reference is C. Kerenyi, *Asklepios, Archetypal Image of the Physician's Existence,* New York, 1959.

This paper has been edited from Meier's Presidential Address read to the Swiss Society for Practical Psychology (S.G.P.P.) on March 3, 1945. Dr. Meier has since published a book with the title: *Antike Inkubation und Moderne Psychotherapie*, Studien aus dem C.G. Jung-Institut, Zurich: Rascher Verlag, 1948, and an American edition with the title *Ancient Incubation and Modern Psychotherapy*, Chicago: Northwestern University Press, 1968.

MODERN DREAM INCUBATION AS A
RITUAL OF INITIATION

Eugene Monick

Those who adapt ancient or primitive initiatory rituals to the context of modern life will recognize the necessarily experimental nature of the ceremony described in Eugene Monick's essay. His objective was not to re-enact the Asklepian incubation procedures, but to evoke and support the dream or vision as a guide to personal healing and new psychological growth. Monick and his co-worker, Eugenia Lee Hancock, introduced small groups of individuals to the concept of incubation and conducted a series of dream incubation experiences from 1979 to 1986. Although the results are difficult to assess objectively, many participants reported significant inner and outer experiences prompting changes in their perception of themselves and the world about them. These events succeeded, Monick notes, "insofar as they introduced the participants to knowledge of a reality that is not ordinarily perceived in daily life." He also came to the realization that "the unconscious emerges and can be integrated when an environment is established for this to happen."

Eugene Monick, M. Div., Ph. D., is a Jungian analyst practicing in New York City and in Scranton, Pennsylvania. A diplomate of the C. G. Jung Institute in Zurich, he is also a graduate of the Episcopal Theological Seminary in Virginia and the Union for Experimenting Colleges and Universities. He was, for ten years, vicar of St. Clement's Church, New York, an experimental theatre congregation. His book on phallos as the sacred symbol of the masculine will be published in 1987 by Inner City Books.

A friend who had successfully emerged from a series of serious physical disabilities proposed that we work together to develop a "ritual of healing" that might satisfy our mutual interests, that is, her experience as one who had overcome devastating illness as her *rite d'entré* into the Christian ministry and my interest in liturgical experimentation and psychology. It occurred to me that C. A. Meier's account of Asklepian healing might provide us with a model for what Lee was seeking, which might be adapted to use in a Christian context, but still permit its use by secular and uninitiated persons. We moved carefully and cautiously in our planning. We decided that the best way to use this model would be to hold a modern "incubation dream event," the focus of which would be the healing of physical or psychological "diseases" of a small group of participants.

The only prerequisites for participation would be (a) the individual's recognition of a personal need for healing, (b) a certain psychological "fitness," that is, ego strength,and (c) a desire or willingness to explore new dimensions in his or her personal growth. We used these criteria throughout our series of dream incubation events as the years went on, but we also found that more people were capable of gaining from incubation than we had first anticipated. Never once did we find that the experience constellated an unsettling or dangerously traumatic situation, something we quite properly worried about at the beginning.

Our first six dream events took place in the Central Presbyterian Church on Park Avenue in New York (later, we moved them to a church in Greenwich Village). The church has an eclectic neo-gothic structure, with a wall of glass in geometric design, a divided chancel, altar and reredos, and four great pillars on each side of the nave supporting a fan ceiling. Adjoining the church is a six-floor parish house built for use as a social center.

Our first incubation event began with a meeting in a comfortable lounge on the fourth floor of this building, in which we arranged the furniture in a circle, with a mandala-like plate on the floor in the center, surrounded by candles. We met the twelve participants outside the door, giving each a copy of two quotations. One, from June Singer, spoke of four main blocks to creativity, the most important of which was impediments to imagination stemming from fear of the disapproval of others. The other, from Jung, described the compensatory function of dreams in the development of consciousness.

We asked the participants to remove their shoes, deposit their belongings outside the door, and wash hands before entering the room where they could wait for the others in silence while listening to meditative nature sounds. As we explained when all had arrived Friday evening at 7:00 p.m., the removing of shoes and washing of hands were meant to aid in breaking the connection with the world outside. These things also suggested vulnerability and ablution. Separation and cleansing were integral parts of the Asklepian preparation.

Next we had a light meal of simple foods (bread, cheese, fruits, etc.) brought by the participants themselves. Lee helped us introduce ourselves by asking each person to tell the story of his or her name with anecdotes, some of which became significant autobiographical confessions. By the end of our meal the ice had broken and the group had begun its formation. Since we planned to share our individual incubation experiences on the following afternoon, such a beginning was important.

We then gathered around the central mandala, where I explained four important elements of dream incubations:

(1) Incubation is used to induce a dream that will speak to the dreamer about his or her problem and its cure, but one should not feel a failure if no dream is recalled. In the absence of a remembered dream, emotional images indicating fear, apprehension, intimidation, comfort, etc., are also of great value as are various associations and memories stimulated by the unfamiliar sleeping environment. We were preparing to sleep in the temple of the god and to invoke his presence, willing to accept whatever forms or images he bestowed. We could find a connection to him only if we accepted willingly the manner of his revelation: a dream, an affect, a memory, all are of value.

(2) Disturbing images, thoughts and feelings might emerge from the unconscious during the night of the incubation. These need not be taken as unusual nor need they cause undue alarm. Dreams are sometimes paradoxical; what is good for us sometimes appears as a negative experience.

We discussed the multivalent nature of unconscious material, the presence of shadow as well as light in the psyche and in divinity, and the strangeness of unfamiliar images.

(3) Judgments should not be made about the quality of one's experience. We were not competing with one another as to the "success" or importance of our experiences. Such a worldly, egocentric attitude had no place in the temple of the god. What he gives to us can aid our understanding only if our attitude is one of complete acceptance, and refusal to make comparisons among ourselves in terms of artistic ability, performance, or result.

(4) The incubation process is primarily psychological, not specific to a Christian background, even though our event would take place in a Christian church. The archetypes of the collective unconscious do not respect human theological distinctions. Religious concepts are relevant, however, in that the meaning of psyche is soul, the invisible, inner, central core of personality. Thus, although we would be surrounded by images from a particular religion, these images could speak to us in terms of who we are as soul persons.

After this discussion we moved our sleeping gear to the church proper. Each person was to find his or her own spot, a place that felt right and comfortable, but not so close to another as to interfere with that person's sense of privacy and space. We took time to get the feeling of the place, make our beds, and ensure we each had flashlight, paper and pen. Next we gathered again around the mandala plate which now held a chalice.

Lee then asked the participants to focus on their personal need for healing and to remember that healing requires a surrender, a sacrifice in order that the newness might have a place within us. We did some relaxation exercises that included an imaginary movement through our bodies where we visualized places of brokenness and confusion and concentrated on our need for healing. We then read the 23rd Psalm together.

Lee directed us to write our need for healing on a small piece of paper and, one by one, ignite the paper with a candle flame and place the offering into the chalice, watching as the flame consumed it. Next, we lit individual candles from this fire. We then began a procession through the darkened building down to the ground floor and into the church as we sang an appropriate hymn. We found our places in the church, extinguished our candles, and began the period of the great silence, which would end at noon on the following day.

In the morning, people arose as they wished and had a light breakfast of foods left from the night before. The participants then gave form to their images from the night by writing, sketching, painting, or modeling with clay. In the afternoon we worked through our experiences of incubation. As each person became ready, he or she spoke of the images received during the night and shared his or her creative expression of these from the morning. Listening was intense. With, I think, but one exception, everyone was willing, even eager, to allow the others to share their personal experience—so much so, in fact, that it was difficult to end the discussion on schedule. The incubation ended with a simple communion service, followed by heartfelt goodbyes.

What did these events accomplish? We cannot say with certainty that the incubation event cured or even significantly changed the problems or troubles the participants brought to the church that night. Even now, after ten group incubation experiences, it is difficult to evaluate results, because of the strongly subjective nature of each person's experience. However, we had conversations with a number of the participants and asked them for their responses:

(1) A woman in her forties who had two schizophrenic episodes in earlier years and now is a professional counsellor, spoke of the release she felt at the first of two events she attended. This came from "the other people around me," the feeling of "being in a terrifically safe womb," and sleeping in the church. There were hours of half-sleep for her during the night, during which she wrote poetry from time to time. She spoke of "being in touch with a deeper reality than I normally am" and of writing in a way she never had before. She experienced a "magical" quality to the night, strongly influenced by the preparatory ritual. For her it was "a time away from earthly time." She wrote:

> *Between the mounds of my mother's breasts*
> *I lie comforted.*
> *But what shall I do when she is gone?*
> *Who shall comfort me?*

Shall I find the strength of her help in myself?
I shall comfort myself,
Sharing with my beloved ones
The burdens of guilt
And the love I could not release to my origins.
Why must we go forward?
Do we not reach back to the depths?
Shall I not find you again, my mother?

(2) A woman in her twenties said, "Every time I participated in the incubation I saw new things about myself. I saw the continuing rage that I have. I saw my ambiguity and fear concerning my sexuality." She made a cut-out sculpture expressing her feelings about a major change in employment, feelings which had come to her in the night. On a black background, she placed an anxious confusion of zigzag colored lines intersecting with one another. During the discussion someone suggested to her that the lines also suggested energy. This gave the woman a new perspective and she came to understand and use the strength of her fears in a more positive way.

(3) Two men came to an incubation. One was gay, successful in his extraverted life and profession, but unsure of relationships. The other was unsure about his sexuality but capable of taking risks with another person. The two began a friendship in the incubation event, each helping the other break a barrier that had diminished him. The process began in the sharing which took place in the afternoon of the second day.

(4) I myself experienced what I consider an epiphany at one incubation event—a message from the unconscious which pointed me in a new direction in my research on masculinity. A voice came in the night, with accompanying visual letters above a small Greek temple, with the words, "The Indestructible House of Mary. The House not built with hands." Nothing more. Earlier, as I was falling asleep, I noticed among the shadows falling from the pillars of the church one which appeared to be massively phallic. On the opposite side of the church, falling from the pulpit, was another shadow forming the profile of an older woman. The juxtaposing of masculine and femine informed the issue I offered earlier in the fire and led to the later dream manifestation.

As Lee Hancock observed, the success of incubation events can be measured only in terms of the power they have in the lives of the participants. She called the steps of the incubation process "access buttons to the unconscious." The events succeeded insofar as they introduced the participants to knowledge of a reality that is not ordinarily perceived in daily life, a process within themselves, which gives vitally important information and which must be attended to and respected. In spite of the different backgrounds, the unconscious can be shared and understood by those who experience it if they do not impose an orthodoxy upon it. The incubation event demonstrates how it is that each person's experience is different and unquestionably unique in the form of its images and yet how universal is the ability to receive images and to understand one's own and another's on the basis of a common humanity and wellspring of symbolic energy.

The frenetic life of the city effectively blots out the reception of images from the unconscious, as well as our ability to connect the images we do get from constructive connection with the ego. The pathology of the domination of the unconscious by the ego and its concerns becomes obvious when one experiences the relative ease with which the unconscious emerges and can be integrated when an environment is established for this to happen. On an individual basis, psychoanalysis has become a way to counteract some of the psychologically harmful aspects of urban life. Small group dream incubation may be a way to begin the process at a collective level. A number of persons in analysis attended these events and found them helpful as an adjunct to their personal work. Several others began private analysis as a result of the incubation events.

During incubation, one might experience images from various myths or religions, but beneath the guise of any specific kind of experienced imagery is an encounter with heretofore unknown elements of one's own personality. It would be a mistake to think of the healing that takes place in modern incubation events as the precise and concrete elimination of one's spiritual or physical wounds; rather, the healing is more like a newly experienced relationship to those wounds and a new connection with the unconscious that promises to provide a wider context within which to understand the problem. The real wound upon which incubation pours an oil is the limitation of the ego's approach to the illness.

The inner image which comes upon one in incubation lies in the dark recesses of the sealed-off psyche, awaiting release. Lee Hancock observed, quite rightly, that "it is the *process* of manifestation that is divine." Jung called the capacity in human beings to connect that which is known and experienced in consciousness with the slumbering soul in the unconscious the "transcendent function."

The incubation event stimulates the transcendent function; but sometimes, in moments of contemplative silence and dreaming, it is the function itself. The divine, as Lee stated, is not only the specific image; it is also the process by which the image is realized. It is, as well, the subsequent use, after the fact, of the emergent images and insights. The issue, most of the time, is a matter of trusting the images that come from within. Only by experiencing the process can one arrive at that trust which produces knowledge and a new sense of soul. All of society benefits from a person who is alive and connected to the unconscious.

434 Betwixt and Between

REFERENCES

Kerenyi, C. 1959. *Asklepios: Archetypal image of the physician's existence.* Bollingen Series LX. New York: Pantheon Books.
Meier, C. A. 1967. *Ancient incubation and modern psychotherapy.* Evanston: Northwestern University Press.
Micklem, N. 1977. The Asklepion myth. *Harvest* 23:29.
Reed, H. 1975. Dream incubation. *The ARE Journal 10:00.*
Von Grünebaum, G. and Caillos, R. 1966. *The dream and human societies.* Berkeley: University of California Press.

WHAT HAPPENS
WHEN WE INTERPRET DREAMS?

Marie-Louise von Franz

In her essay, "What Happens When We Interpret Dreams?" von Franz examines the contents of a man's important dream about the very nature of dream interpretation. She emphasizes that "a good interpretation is an event, not a 'doing'," a self-initiatory event from which a growing relation to the large Self can emerge. In other words, the interpretation and understanding of a dream can become a form of inner rite of passage. The dream teaches the dreamer to relate to her/his own symbols. They are themselves thresholds to be crossed as the dreamer takes a journey of individuation. This remarkable dream is presented, in part, in a film series on dream interpretation with Dr. von Franz by Frazier Boa, Jungian analyst in Toronto.

Marie-Louise von-Franz, Ph.D., received her doctorate in classical languages from the University of Zurich and worked closely with Dr. C. G. Jung for 31 years. She was one of the founders of the Jung Institute in Zurich and is currently a training analyst there. She has lectured widely in Europe and North America. She is the author of many well-known books and articles, among which are: An Introduction to the Interpretation of Fairy Tales *(1970),* Patterns of Creativity Mirrored in Creation Myths *(1972),* The Passion of Perpetua *(1979),* Projection and Re-Collection in Jungian Psychology *(1980),* Puer Aeternus *(1981), and* On Dreams and Death *(1986).*

J UNG has developed an attitude toward dreams and also found some technical aids with which to approach their meaning, which are far more differentiated than anything known before him. Dream interpretation has thus become the core of an analytical treatment. We also know from Jung that the unconscious is a living reality, something which can react creatively to our conscious attitudes and proceedings. Therefore one may ask the question, what does the unconscious itself "think" about dream interpretation? In the following paper I will bring a dream which circles around this problem—it tries to interpret a dream about dream interpretation!

This dream was dreamt by a candidate of the Zurich Jung Institute. He was kind enough to allow me to use it here. This candidate had finished his first exams and was beginning to see control cases. He worried whether he understood their dreams and went on to ponder over the whole question of what happens in analysis. Then he had the following dream:

> *I am seated in the open square of an ancient city. A young man, wearing only baggy trousers, approaches and sits cross-legged on the ground facing me. His torso is muscular, full of life and vitality. The sun reflects on his blond hair. He tells me dreams which he wishes me to interpret. As he relates each dream, a large boulder falls from the sky striking the dream a tremendous blow. Chunks fly off the dream revealing an inner structure resembling a modern piece of abstract sculpture. With each dream, another boulder falls, fragments fly off, and more and more of the nuts and bolts skeleton is revealed. I examine the bits that have been knocked off the dream and find they are made of bread. I say to the youth that this demonstrates how one must strip away the dream until one comes to the 'nuts and bolts.' 'Dream interpretation is the art of knowing what to discard. It is like living.' The dream changes. The youth and I now sit opposite each other on the bank of a beautiful river. Between us the dreams have taken on a different shape. They now form a pyramid structure built up of thousands of small squares and triangles. It is like a Braque 'cubist' painting in three dimensions, but it is alive. The colors and tones of the individual squares and triangles constantly change and I explain that it is essential for one to maintain the balance of the whole composition by immediately compensating a color change by a corresponding change on the opposing side. (This color balancing is incredibly complex as the object is three-dimensional and the colors are in constant motion.) Then my eye travels up to the top of the pyramid of dreams, the apex. There is nothing there. It is the sole point of intersection at which the structure could be held together, yet it is empty space. As I look into this space it begins to glow, then radiate a white light.*
> *Again the dream changes. The pyramid shape remains but, instead of triangles and squares, it is now composed of shit. The apex is still glowing. I have the sudden realization that the invisible point is made visible by the solidity of the shit and vice versa, and the shit is made visible by the invisible apex. I peer deeply into the shit and somehow I grasp that I am looking at the hand of God. In a flash of insight, I understand why the apex is invisible. It is the face of God.*
> *Then Miss Von Franz and I are walking beside the river. She is laughing and says jokingly, 'I'm sixty-one, not sixteen, but they both add up to seven.'*

Let us look at the dream in our accustomed manner. Its drama takes place first in the open square of an ancient city, later it continues on the bank of a river. First it is more concerned with something man-made, the cultural side, namely the problem of interpretation, i.e., what we do or do not do with dreams. Later it shows a purely natural happening. The young teller of the dream is described as especially healthy, probably in order to show the normality and healthiness of what produces dreams (even in a "neurotic" patient). The dreams which he tells are something real—a sort of substance. The moment of interpretation is represented by a stone falling from heaven; the dreamer does not do the interpretation himself. This probably compensates for what he overvalued in his consciousness: the importance of his good or bad interpreting of dreams. It says that a good interpretation is *an event,* not a "doing." Things which fall from heaven, mythologically speaking, are thrown down from the gods, signs of the gods for man. Therefore meteorites were always and everywhere considered to be sacred. The Ka'aba of the Moslems also came originally from heaven. Dream interpretation is evidently a being *hit* by some mysterious active forces in the spiritual area of the unconscious (i.e., heaven). Those parts of the dream which are hit then turn into bread. If we understand a dream in the right way we are vitalized and nourished by its meaning. It is like manna or that "super-substantial" bread for which we ask in the Lord's Prayer. ("Our daily bread" is a wrong translation. The Greek word *hyperousion* means transcendental, above substance.) The other parts of the dream each turn into a "bolt with a nut" (or mother!), for every real understanding of a dream is simultaneously a *coniunctio.* The bolt and its mother represent the union of a masculine and feminine and are also something which serves to bind things together. Each time a dream is realized, the conscious and unconscious unite and something in us, which was autonomous before, becomes one with the rest of the personality and thus the structure of the Self slowly emerges.

The voice then explains that one must know—as in life also—what to discard and what to keep. Probably the "flesh" of the dream (the bolts are, as it says, its skeleton) must be discarded: it is the surface of many images which veil, so to speak, the deeper meaning of the dream. People often say that they had a "silly" or "disagreeable" dream, but when one analyzes it, it always contains a deep and helpful message.

After the period of seeking for the structural elements, there then comes a more "fluid" way of contacting dreams—contemplating them together with the stream of life. The structure has become a pyramid, which in Egyptian religion is a symbol of the Ba-soul, of the individual immortal kernel of man. Though the Self always already exists (it probably throws the transforming boulder onto the dreams), it is also "built up" by our attending to our dreams and thus becoming conscious of it. The pyramid consists of innumerable triangles and squares constantly changing in shape and color. In a more advanced phase of dream interpretation, all the different nuances of emotion and of feeling tones become relevant and also their constant complementary play of opposites and their paradoxes. The apex, however, consists of empty space. It is that emptiness or Nirvana aspect of the Self, its indescribable neti-neti—not this and not that!

Then comes a strange enantiodromia: the pyramid suddenly consists of solid shit. This reminds one of the old alchemists' saying that the philosophers' stone is found on the dung hill! When one gets older, one often feels more and more how much of our daily life is all shit—the dreary round of duties, the trivialities we have to attend to, the ever-recurring shadow-nonsense we have to look at in ourselves. But the hand of God is in it. It works secretly in all the sad, rejected aspects of oneself and of one's life. English insurance companies still call unforeseeable catastrophes "acts of God." There is nothing which does not reveal the hand of God. The invisible apex, on the contrary, is the face of God which "no man shall see and live." It is hidden from us but it is the ultimate reality. It is also—as the Self—the ultimate secret in the soul of the individual, a secret which also remains unexplained in every dream. Jung even went so far as to say, in a letter, that analytical understanding is destructive, and thus only useful in destroying the neurotic disease of the patient. So "healing is given to us in the incomprehensible and ineffable symbol, for it prevents the devil from swallowing the seed of life . . ." We must understand the divinity within us but not in the other, so far as he is able to go by himself and understand himself. Ultimately, there remains a divine mystery.

The end of the dream returns very much to the surface of things, to the dreamer's analyst. One and six add up to seven, which is the symbolic number of evolution. At sixteen one begins adult life, and at sixty-one the flow of life goes in opposite directions, but both are an evolutionary process. In youth one moves from the one to the six, which symbolizes sex, and the many things; in old age one moves away from the multiplicity back to the One. The dreamer himself is about forty years old; he stands in the middle of life where the flow has already begun to move toward individuation. His few patients were all young; probably his "inner" analyst has to realize this in order to understand the dreams of his patients, and his own attitude, better.

It seems to me that the unconscious is intensely interested in our interpreting dreams correctly and in our understanding what is happening when we do so. For only then do dreams turn into the "bread of life" and the immortal structure in our soul become visible, except for that ultimate secret which may be revealed to us only in death.

Reprinted from *A Well of Living Waters: A Festschrift for Hilde Kirsch,* C.G. Jung Institute of Los Angeles, 1977, with permission from the author and the editor.

INITIATION OF XHOSA INDIGENOUS HEALERS
(AMAGQIRA)

M. Vera Bührmann

In her essay, "Initiation of Indigenous Xhosa Healers," M. Vera Bührmann, M.D. (like Farrer in an earlier chapter) leads the reader into ancient traditional yet contemporary initiation rites practiced by native people. She describes the accreditation ceremonies for apprenticed healers of the Xhosa (a tribe of the Nguni nation) in South Africa, utilizing her experiences both as observer and participant in the ritual life of a small southeast South African village. Over a period of several years the candidates are initiated in a step-by-step process that requires rigorous preparation and ancestral approval. Dreams, spirits, visions, signs, offerings, sacrifices, seclusion, ablutions, purgings, dances, songs, feasts, relatives and friends, and, above all, the sacred ancestors, play a role in the initiation. Finally, the candidate is incorporated as a full-fledged healer in a series of powerful ceremonies that include the severance of the student from the teacher—and the teacher from the student. "Dreams serve to guide and direct all treatment procedures."

Dr. Bührmann is currently involved in medical-anthropological research and teaching at the University of Cape Town, South Africa, and at the Psychiatric Clinic of the Groote Schuur Hospital, Cape Town. Trained in medicine at the University of Cape Town, she has a diploma in Public Health from the University of Witwatersrand and a diploma in Mental Health from the University of London. She was trained as an analyst at the Institute for Analytical Psychology in London and as a child psychotherapist at Brixton Child Guidance Clinic and Great Ormont Street Hospital for Sick Children in London. She is author of many articles in lay and professional journals as well as an important book on South Africa, Living in Two Worlds *(1987).*

> It is clear you are not under yourself,
> but under your ancestors.
>
> —Tiso

IWANT to explain that I did not choose the Xhosa initiation research; it seemed, rather, to choose me. A psychology student had elected to do his honors thesis on the Xhosa indigenous healers of South Africa, but found that he required the assistance of a psychiatrist. He wanted to assess the mental health of these healers, as well as that of their patients, from the standpoint of Western psychology.

We had not known each other previously, and indeed, it seemed that our paths crossed merely by accident—but soon after our first meeting we arranged to visit the Xhosa together. At the time, I was completely unaware of the importance and direction-giving nature of that step.

The night before we set out on our proposed trip and my journey into the unknown, I had a dream:

> *I was sitting at the bedside of my dying mother in the hospital to which I was attached. My father was also terminally ill in the same hospital. My mother said to me, 'My child, it is time for you to leave us and for you to go and do your work.'*
>
> *I then found myself in a car in the front passenger seat, with a baby on my lap. The driver was a composite figure of several of my young, dynamic, enterprising male relatives.*

I could not fully appreciate the significance of this dream and its reference to my "work" and to my own immediate ancestors at that time, for only later did I learn of the Xhosa belief in the important role of their ancestors in their daily lives. The Xhosas' ancestors are their "living dead," deceased clan members who concern themselves actively with all facets of the existence of their living kin.

The specific group of psychic healers whose methods and ideology form the focus of this article practice primarily in a rural area of the Ciskei in South Africa. The tribe to which they belong forms part of the larger Nguni nation, and inhabits the southeastern coastal regions of southern Africa. Apart from Xhosa, they have little knowledge of any other language, and thus a bilingual interpreter was invaluable to me. My chief informants and teachers were Mr. and Mrs. Tiso, who are both senior Xhosa healers, and others whom they trained and helped to initiate to healer status.

The type of Xhosa initiation with which I am concerned is described by Eliade (1975) as belonging to the "third category," wherein the initiate experiences a mystical calling. The Xhosa initiates are on a quest which leaves them little peace and over which they have limited control. The object of their quest is to find the meaning of their lives as well as of life in general. The vision or truth that they seek cannot be found in an abstract "scientific" way, but must be lived or experienced.

The onset of the Xhosa quest is triggered by an "initiatory illness" which prompts the initiate, male or female (I follow the Xhosa use of the masculine pronoun), to "become what he must become." During his initiatory process, he develops an awareness of the meaningfulness of the world; he discovers his ancestors as transpersonal forces, some of whom are endowed with the ability to impart a power and numinosity which can lead to his experience of the sacred.

In both their healing and in their training of aspirant healers, Mr. and Mrs. Tiso utilize a variety of methods, depending on the problem. When dealing with psychological conditions they use purification, dream clarification, ritual dances, and ceremonies which sometimes include animal sacrifices. These procedures are employed in a meaningful and well-considered sequence, and are aimed at leading the initiate step-by-step to ever-closer contact with the ancestors, suprapersonal and numinous forces. The Xhosa do not distinguish between "inner" and "outer" or between "body" and "spirit." Theirs is a cosmic wholeness. The numinous ancestors may not be approached without special precautions.

To indicate the depth and meaningfulness of these procedures, I will have to include some of my own experiences and inner responses. During my stay with the Xhosa, I found that I was not only introduced to a culture very different from my own, but also that I could become acquainted with their mysteries, sharing in them to the extent that I became aware of aspects of my own psyche previously unknown to me. The practices espoused by the Xhosa healers stimulated many of my own dormant potentials. In a sense, I too became an initiate, and could share some of the Xhosas' experiences as both participant *and* observer.

Apart from real cultural differences, which are not always helpful, I arrived on the research scene with some helpful aids. Of these I would mention a few. My childhood was spent in close contact with the Zulu and Swazi speaking people of the Nguni nation, and I learned enough of their language for ordinary communication. The language and culture of these have many similarities to the Xhosa people. As a medical doctor, a large proportion of my practice were Zulu speaking because communication was easy. The most useful, however, was my training and practice as an analytical psychologist and child psychotherapist. Working psychotherapeutically with children requires entering and actively participating in their magical, archetypal world. The research at times required participation at a non-verbal and often pre-verbal level entering into an archetypal world where symbols are still alive and active.

My method of research is to shed my Western, scientific, logical mode of being (to the extent to which it is possible), and to merge with the group and participate in their ceremonies with a minimum of prejudice or criticism; i.e., I try to become an organ of perception. The research, in the first instance, is therefore subjective and experiential. On withdrawal from a ceremony, I immediately write down what I have experienced, observed and heard. The third stage is when I try to put these into meaningful terms of analytical concepts or the concepts of related fields of knowledge. Dicussion with the healers is not excluded but I do not use a questionnaire method, rather the dialectic of analysis.

To understand the healer's function in the Xhosa tribe, it is necessary to first know something about their cultural beliefs, their cosmology, and the vital role they give to their ancestors as determinants of health and of illness. The closeness of the individual Xhosa to the ancestors varies with his status in the community as, for example, an ordinary member, a mentally disturbed one (e.g., a *thwasa* person), a bewitched one, a novice in training, or a qualified *igqira* (a healer).

The ancestors are omniscient and omnipresent, but they also have particular areas around the homestead where they like to congregate and to linger. Two such places are the cattle pen and an area in the main hut of the homestead opposite the entrance door, called the *entla*. On the whole, the ancestors are kindly mentors and protectors and they have many human qualities. They need warmth and comfort; they experience thirst and hunger; they can be pleased and they can be angered. The ancestors communicate mostly through dreams, but can also manifest themselves in other ways. In dreams they can appear as people who are known or unknown; or, they might appear as animals, or as voices. They can be "experienced" in the body, as sensations of pleasure or pain and discomfort. They also make their presence known through omens such as the flight of a bird, the behavior of an animal, or phenomena of nature such as thunder, droughts, or floods.

The attitude of the living to the ancestors and the relationship between them, largely determines the health or ill-health, the happiness or unhappiness, and the good fortune or misfortune, of the living. One of the main concerns of the ancestors is that the customs be kept and the necessary ceremonies be performed. It seems as though a certain equilibrium is sought, the living and the non-living each attending to the needs of the other.

There is another category of ancestors, however, who are not clan-linked and "who we do not recognize by their faces." These are the Ancestors of the River and the Ancestors of the Forest. The former are white, have blond hair, live under the water, and carry on farming activities much as ordinary people do. They are powerful and numinous. The Ancestors of the Forest, however, are less clearly defined. They have the form of animals, but they are also vital and powerful. Of both, it is said, "We become ill by the Ancestors of the Forest, or by both, but mostly by the Ancestors of the River." The illness referred to here is a special kind of mental disturbance called "the Xhosa illness," or "the white illness," but most commonly, *thwasa*.

I will concentrate on this "Xhosa illness" because having it is a prerequisite for the treatment and training which could result in one's becoming an *igqira* or healer. That is, it can be seen as an initiatory illness.

THWASA AND THE PRELIMINARY STAGES OF INITIATION

The word "thwasa" means the emergence of something new, the season of spring, a new moon, or a new heavenly constellation; it seems very appropriate to a condition which has the potential for eliciting new aspects of the psyche or new personality factors. The initiatory significance of *thwasa* is well portrayed in some of the dreams which occur during the early phases of the illness. The following dream occurred during the preliminary illness of a now-practicing healer. For many years she was "sickly" and had many disturbing dreams:

> *The animals of the forest came strangely to me in my dreams. As I grew up in the forest, I knew them and was not afraid. As there are forest* amagqira *(healers) and river* amagqira, *my dreams showed me that I was to be a river* igqira as my father was.

The dream which led to her training was as follows:

> *I was in the river with a piece of plank, playing in the water. I played a long time. There came an old grandfather who looked at me and then asked, 'What are you doing?' I said, 'I'm playing.' He stayed and I played my games. Then there came another old man exactly like the first, but I knew the second one. He asked the first one, 'Why are you staying here watching this child at play?' He answered, 'I'm watching her and I've come to tell her that she's an* igqira *of the river.'*

She was regarded as being *thwasa* and was taken to a healer for confirmation, treatment and training.

Thwasa has many similarities to shamanistic states as described in the literature (Eliade 1974, 1975). These are particularly seen in the early symptomatology, but less so in the later healing practices. The person usually becomes solitary and asocial, withdrawn and given to wandering about aimlessly. He neglects his personal appearance, eats poorly, and his sleep is interrupted by frequent frightening and confusing dreams. He becomes "a house of dreams." He often "hears voices" and has visionary experiences. His ideation and behavior can strike the trained Western psychiatrist as bizarre enough to be called schizophrenic.

Such a person is usually taken to a qualified healer for a *vumisa,* i.e., a diagnostic session. If the finding is that he really is *thwasa* and not simply mad, it means that he has been called by the ancestors to serve them. To become worthy of such a mission, he is required to undergo prolonged treatment and training.

Thwasa can also be seen as a "creative illness" (see Ellenberger 1970). Its treatment and training consists of diverse forms of therapy (such as milieu therapy), but most important are the performance of healing dances, initiatory ceremonies (sometimes with animal sacrifices), and the interpretation of the dreams of both the novice and healer/teacher. Herbal extracts are used often.

As in other cultures, purification rituals are performed at various stages during training, but also by the healer as and when indicated for the good of his own health and healing powers. The training period can range from three to eight years, although many novices never reach the fully qualified *igqira* status. If the *thwasa* person shows evidence that he is really fit to become a healer, he also receives training in divination and diagnosis *(vumisa).* (I still have little understanding of this aspect, partly on account of my imperfect Xhosa. Mr. Tiso claims that he would be able to teach me to *vumisa* as soon as my Xhosa is word-perfect. Apparently some people can be taught but others are never very good at it.)

When the diagnosis has been accepted by the "patient" and his relatives, he leaves his parental home to live with the healer of his choice. Ceremonies and sacrifices are always performed at the family home. Living kin, as well as ancestors, must be active participants.

The training and initiation of the aspirant healers seems to be twofold. First, he acquires intimate knowledge and insight into the life of a healer. Only then is he gradually introduced to the ancestors. He must thus acquire the ability to communicate with them, to understand their messages, and to become a mediator between the living and the living dead. In time, he also acquires the ability to tolerate their closeness without feeling endangered as he did during his *thwasa* state. It is said, "Everything which is done during treatment and training is to improve communication with the ancestors."

In the healer/teacher's household, the *thwasa* person is taken up as a member of the family. He shares living and sleeping quarters, and assists with the household chores. He is given tasks which are appropriate to his state of health, and is given increasing responsibility as he progresses. This treatment gives him a feeling of being accepted and understood, decreases his isolation, and furthers his self-esteem (excellent milieu therapy).

The treatment starts with purification. It is the first requirement on arrival: "Any evil which could cling to him must be removed immediately." The only item he brings with him from his own home is soap. The cleansing is a ritual performance and is repeated frequently during the course of the training. It consists basically in the washing of his whole body with an herbal extract called *ubulawu,* and the drinking of it to the extent that it induces vomiting. It serves a double purpose: "to cleanse the body of evil" and "to open the mind to the messages of the ancestors." This herbal extract and home-brewed beer are two substances which are constantly used at all ceremonies, primarily because "they call the ancestors and open the mind."

DREAMS

We have already mentioned how initiatory dreams can lead the novice to begin his training. But dreams are also the principal means by which the ancestors communicate and make their wishes known. Thus dreams serve to guide and direct all treatment procedures. No important step in treatment or training is undertaken except under the guidance of the ancestors through the medium of dreams. Special measures are taken, such as the internal and external use of *ubulawu* and regular *xhentsa* (ceremonial dance) sessions, to stimulate dreaming and dream recall. The importance of dreams is reflected in Mr. Tiso's remark on our first meeting: "If they do not dream I cannot treat them" (Cf. Bührmann 1978).

Dreams must be promptly told to the healer/teacher in a setting of confidentiality. "Your dreams belong to you and may not be shared by just anybody." Occasionally, however, the healer may decide that a dream is to be dealt with at an *intlombe*, i.e., in a special group setting (Bührmann 1982). The Xhosas' general attitude to dreams, their belief that these come from the ancestors, and the uses they make of them, are strongly reminiscent of the Asklepian methods in ancient Greece (see Meier 1967 and Bührmann 1977).

INTLOMBE AND XHENTSA: THE CEREMONIAL DANCES

Dancing sessions are held as often as possible, that is, several times during the week, especially over weekends. Their function is to introvert libido and to stir up certain bodily functions for the production of *umbilini* (a physical feeling of anxiety), which "clears the mind, makes you see things clearly, enables you to say the right things at the dance meeting" (Bührmann 1981). Ceremonial dance sessions are ongoing activities which stimulate psychic growth and development, and acquaint the novice with the images and meaning of the unconscious. I have seen the stimulation of strong emotions in the participants, and have myself been deeply involved and moved during these sessions. (It should be noted that "dancing" is a very poor translation for the slow, rhythmic, earth-pounding movement of the *xhentsa*.)

THE CEREMONIES OF INITIATION

Ceremonies and sacrifices are interspersed during the years of training. The timing of their performance depends on a variety of circumstances, the most important being the messages of the ancestors portrayed in dreams. The readiness of the novice as assessed by his teacher is another important aspect. The teacher/healer watches the novice's behavior around the homestead, his ability to work and form relationships, his performance at the dance sessions, and his developing ability to diagnose. The final decision to conduct any of these ceremonies, however, rests with the initiate's family, for they must not only participate in them; they must finance them as well.

To me the ceremonies appear to be major encounters with the power of the unconscious. During the ceremonies an atmosphere of numinosity is created which touches one deeply. They are moving and meaningful at a level which is often beyond words; one becomes aware of suprapersonal forces which are shared by others in the group. I believe that the symbolism of these ceremonial acts is not contrived nor consciously perceived. This is borne out by what Mr. Tiso has often said to me over the years: "Working with you has helped me to think. We do these things because they come from the ancestors and we know they are right—you seem to understand them."

Each ceremony seems to be an introduction to the ancestors at a level appropriate to the psychic state of the novice. The healers frequently say, "One must be strong to take what the ancestors have to say. Even we have to take medicine from time to time to make us strong." In the same way the patient/trainee must get progressively stronger to cope with the ancestors as they are manifested in each particular ceremony. They are therefore initiated step-by-step, guided from within as well as by tradition, culminating with the final ceremony of qualification and graduation.

The guiding function of the unconscious in the Xhosa initiation process is exemplified in the dream of a female initiate. Her dream indicated that she had to go to her parental home to relate her dream to her uncooperative father and request him to act on the instructions of the ancestors. This resulted in the performance of the first ceremony which is customary in the treatment and training of a *thwasa* person (Bührmann 1978).

The First Ritual: The River Ceremony (Hlawayelela)

This ceremony can only be performed when everything indicates that the time is ripe and the relatives agree to its performance. As Mr. Tiso explained,

> When a *thwasa* person responds well to treatment . . . if I get the proper messages from my ancestors, and his people agree to his training, the first step is the River Ceremony . . . They will have to decide when they are ready to go to The River Place . . . the place where the River Ancestors live.

The actual ceremony lasts three days. A special hut at the parental homestead is set aside for the healer and his group. Meticulous attention is paid to every detail of the preparations. These preparations are done "to make the home ancestors [shared by the family] ready to accept the Ancestors of the River."

On the first day, beer must be brewed by women who are blood relations of the patient—they who must share the same ancestors. On the same night, the prepared beer must be placed in the cattle pen in the area where the home ancestors like to linger. Of this Mr. Tiso says,

> If my mission is accepted by the home ancestors at the cattle pen, it can be seen next morning by the foam which spilled over onto the ground, i.e., the manure. The most senior of the ancestors of the homestead will then come to my hut to form a relationship and to cooperate with my ancestors in the work for the trainee.

Not yet having been accepted by the River Ancestors, the trainee must remain with his people in their part of the homestead.

The second day is spent by the family with ordinary preparations to receive the expected guests on the third day. In the healer's hut, the preparations are of a different kind. Singing, clapping and dancing, and a discussion of the "white illness" takes place without much interruption. The healing dances are performed as a dancing mandala (Bührmann 1981). The aim is to channel libido to the task in hand, to get in touch with unconscious forces (conceptualized as ancestors), and to invoke their aid.

On the third day, before dawn, a silent procession sets off for the river. The party normally consists of four people, two from the healer's group and two from the trainee's family. As an observer of the River Ceremony held for a particular initiate, I was allowed to attend such a procession provided that I would conform to every detail, including having my face painted with white clay. All preparations were done in complete silence and semi-darkness.

With faces painted white, bodies well-decorated with white beads and beads well-covered, the group walked single-file in complete silence to the river, carrying offerings for the River People. The offerings consisted of items dear to the River People—a billy can of beer, white beads, pumpkin and calabash pipes, sorghum seeds, and tobacco. These are all thrown in a special sequence into the water of a particular pool. The movements of the offerings on the surface of the water are watched with intense concentration. From these movements and patterns the attitude of the River Ancestors can be assessed. If the offerings are accepted, their attitude is favorable and the candidate is received with approval.

The party then hurries back to the homestead to make its report to the waiting group. This must be done before sunrise. In the presence of the assembled people, in a place favored by the ancestors, a detailed account is given. If it is favorable, the acceptance of the candidate is sealed and celebrated by the drinking of beer or some other alcholic beverage. The ancestors are served first by pouring some on the ground.

The face of the accepted *thwasa* person is again painted white; he now becomes a regular trainee called an *umkwetha,* and he joins the group in the healer's hut. The rest of the day is spent in feasting and almost uninterrupted dancing sessions.

The Second Ritual: The River Ceremony with Brooding (Fukamisa)

At a later stage, again when indicated, the River Ceremony is repeated, but with important differences. The word *fukamisa* is descriptive of a brooding hen sitting on a clutch of eggs, hatching out chickens. The trainee is put into solitary confinement in a dark hut for two days. During this period the initiate is served salt-free, cold semi-solids, and there may be no verbal exchange of any kind. It is said, "He must have some strength before this ceremony can be done." Referring to my own abilities, Mr. Tiso asked if I would be able to take it, if I would not be overcome by fear!

At dawn of the third day, while the river party performs its ceremony by the water, the secluded one is brought out. His head and face are kept covered while he is given the herbal extract to wash his body and to induce vomiting. Then he is fed a specially prepared porridge to which the powdered bark of a tree which grows on the river banks has been added. All this is done under the supervision of his teacher, and in complete silence.

If, on returning, the river party gives a favorable report, the initiate's head and face are uncovered, and he joins in the procedings described above for the first River Ceremony.

This ceremony resembles a return to the womb and is followed by a rebirth experience. During the initiate's seclusions, he is plunged into intense introspection. Hopefully, this introspection will stir up archetypal images of the unconscious in him, which will lead to the emergence of new psychic knowledge and strength.

A further period of training and preparation is necessary before the next ceremony can be performed. The nature of the ceremony confirms my belief that a birth has taken place in the previous one, for only a more *whole* person, with considerable depth and integration, may have this ceremony performed for him. The previous ceremonies are "cool." The next is the first blood sacrifice, with historical, symbolic and archetypal implications. Incorporation of the ancestors and "god eating" is not to be undertaken lightly.

The Third Ritual: Isiko Lentambo

This is the third ceremony in the sequence of the Xhosa initiations, but it is the first in which an animal is sacrificed. The animal is "a spotless white goat." The name of the ceremony is derived from the fact that a frilled neck band, to be worn later by the trainee, is made from certain parts of the goat carcass and hair from the tail of a particular cow. The timing of the ceremony is indicated, as always, by dreams and external circumstances such as the ability of the relatives to afford the expenses it incurs. Again, however, the cardinal point is the psychological readiness of the trainee.

This is the first ceremony to be performed in the cattle pen of the homestead, in the presence of the ancestors. Since the animal was chosen by them for the purpose of the sacrifice, they are believed to reside in its body. The goat is caught and held down by assistants. Then the "stabber" starts the ritual slaughter. Having daubed the goat with herbal extract "to call the ancestors," he pokes it with the sacrificial knife to induce bleatings. The bleating signifies the ancestor's acknowledgment that the sacrifice is acceptable. When the goat has been killed, its skin is removed. The skinning is done carefully, for the skin will play an important role in the future practice of the trainee. It may never leave his home, and it may not be sold. He must sleep on it, and sit on it while diagnosing. It is a vital link with the ancestors: "The skin is taken as having been given to him by the ancestors."

A particular piece of meat from the right shoulder, *umsamo,* is roasted immediately on wild olive branches (the ancestors like the smell and the smoke). The trainee eats this in complete silence, and in a ritually prescribed way, followed by the drinking of beer and herbal extract. His relatives follow his example in order of seniority and relatedness. They communicate with the ancestors by eating them, by integrating them into the physical body.

The rest of the carcass is taken to the main hut. In the area consecrated to the ancestors, the *entla* (dry manure from the cattle pen) is spread. On top of that go the remains of the wild olive branches which were used at the slaughter, then the goat skin, with the carcass on top. This is flanked by two barrels of beer. All these items have a special meaning and are dear to the ancestors: "It feeds and calls them."

The sleeping arrangements for that night are considered to be very important. As Mr. Tiso explained,

> The [trainee] sleeps next to the carcass on the men's side of the hut, then the father, then the first-born (heir), then [the trainee's] paternal uncles, then brothers of the first born, then male relatives in order of seniority, and finally the male visitors. For the women it is the same order on the women's side of the hut.

On the following day, a rope or thong is made by someone who specializes in this work. Later, on the same day, the investiture takes place. During a ceremonial dance meeting in the main hut, the initiate kneels at the *entla.* The rope is dipped in herbal extract and tied round his neck by a senior clan member. The dance meeting continues for a while with songs which have bearing on the event. The assembled people then leave the hut for the cattle pen, led by the senior clan member who stops at the gate, addresses the ancestors, and introduces the newly-invested initiate to them. In the meantime, the carcass has been cooking in the cattle pen; now, general eating and feasting starts, and lasts until sunset.

The meticulous plaiting of the rope from parts of two beasts which have significant links with the ancestors is itself of ceremonial importance: each piece that went into its construction has symbolic meaning. By dipping it in herbal extract and tying it round the neck of the kneeling initiate, another link is forged between him and the ancestors.

The ritual eating of the goat's shoulder meat is an act of incorporation and communion with the ancestors. It is reminiscent of the Eucharist. The initiate participates in a mystery that he does not conceptualize intellectually, but which he *experiences* as meaningful and awesome. The atmosphere is quiet and dedicated, and each person performs his part with respect and veneration, as though he is really in the presence of a god. According to Jung (1954), two separate and distinct ideas blend in the Mass: the sacrifice or slaughter, and the eating of the consecrated food in the presence of the god. In the Xhosa ceremony, after the sacrifices, the meal is eaten in the presence of the ancestors, a very numinous experience for all. They think of the ancestors as many people think of God.

The *Isiko Lentambo* ceremony also bears a strong resemblance to the "god-eating" rites of the Aztecs: "And of this which they ate it was said, 'The God is eaten' and of those who ate it, it was said, 'They guard the God'" (Jung 1956). During *Isiko Lentambo,* the initiate can also be said to "guard" the ancestors.

Isiko Lentambo is regarded by the Xhosa as a "strong" ceremony, for in preparing for it, in performing it, and in absorbing its effects, the initiate has much to learn and to integrate. A more detailed description of this ceremony, as adjusted by the Xhosa for different circumstances and for a different purpose, can be found in "Isiko Lentambo: A Renewal Sacrifice" (Bührmann 1982).

The Final Ritual: The Godusa *Ceremony*

The *Godusa* or "Taking Home Ceremony" is the final qualifying and initiatory rite of the aspirant Xhosa healer. It is rarely performed earlier than one and a half to two years after completion of the *Isiko Lentambo,* although the interval may be much longer. Many trainees never succeed in reaching this final ceremony. Mr. Tiso has been in practice for more than 35 years, but has only twelve fully qualified healers who have completed all the ceremonies.

In the *Godusa* ceremony, the initiate is taken to his parental home by his teacher to be introduced to his relatives, the local community, and his clan ancestors as a qualified, competent and trustworthy healer. He has become what the ancestors had demanded of him during his *thwasa* state: he has "become what he must become," and he has answered the call to serve them. He is now a mediator between the ancestors and their living kin.

Apart from early preparations, the actual event lasts four days. Two days before the arrival of his teacher, the initiate must purify and strengthen himself by drinking the herbal extract. Mr. Tiso comments, "Once we arrive and start there will be no sleep or rest for him. He must attend to everything. No weak person should be *godusa*ed."

I attended a Taking Home Ceremony for a young man name Qadi. The ceremony can best be described by dividing it into two kinds of activities: (a) the separation of the animals; and (b) the sacrificial and induction ceremonies.

The separation of the animals. This activity deals with the severance of both the personal and archetypal transference. (The theme has been treated fully in a talk given at the International Congress [Buhrmann 1980].) Mr. Tiso formulated the Xhosas' beliefs about the significance of this act as follows:

> We believe that while we were working together and he was my student, our ancestors united. Now we are dividing (separating) them so that he may stand on his own, while leaving my ancestors with me. While we were together, even when he started practicing on his own, my ancestors were to some extent leaving me to assist him. We must now divide and test his animals to see if we are equal, and if he can work independently.

To portray the actual events and the subjective experiential nature of a Taking Home Ceremony, I will describe the one I attended in which I participated. It must be kept in mind, however, that there was much which is very difficult to put into words: such as the atmosphere of the seriousness and dedication combined with one of gaiety and sponteneity, the feeling of being an observer and yet a deeply involved participant, and finally, the general orderliness and camaraderie which prevailed everywhere during the whole period.

As all ceremonies are conducted over weekends, Mr. and Mrs. Tiso and their entourage arrived at the initiate Qadi's homestead early on Thursday. They moved into a large, round, thatch-roofed hut which had been put aside for their exclusive use during the whole period. Close to this was a newly-erected, round hut, firmly constructed of poles and grass, with a strong door and door posts. The hut is called the *intondo,* and is a place where the new healer's ancestors will reside. From this hut the new *igqira* will conduct some of his healing activities. To me, this hut is a symbol of the self. These two huts, and the area between them, will be the stage setting for the drama of the "separation of the animals," which will be conducted over a period of three days. Basically, it consists of a mock fight between the animals of the pupil and those of the teacher.

Every morning at dawn for three successive days the occupants of the Tiso hut (Qadi included) marched, armed with sticks and *sjamboks* to the new hut. They would circle around it, singing, "You are asleep, *igqira*; come outside! Wake up; come outside!" On each occasion Qadi separated from the group, entered the new hut, and stayed inside for longer periods every day. Then he would rejoin the group, and they would all return to the Tiso hut, singing and dancing and playfully fighting with sticks. As the group approached, they sang, "Wake up, wake up! Wild animals are outside your door!" Inside, Mr. Tiso was lying on his sleeping mat, feigning deep sleep.

The excitement mounted with each successive day, and culminated on the third day at noon. At about mid-morning the whole group divided into two factors, the Tiso supporters ("animals") and the Qadi supporters. Armed with sticks and *sjamboks,* dancing and singing warlike songs, the Qadi group left for his own hut. There they organized themselves for the oncoming "battle."

The Tiso group, with himself in the lead, advanced on the new *igqira*'s hut, singing, "We are coming, we are coming; beware, we are coming!" A fierce struggle ensued, with Mr. Tiso and some of his "animals" trying to force the door, which was held inside by Qadi and his "animals." The outside group indulged in fighting, cheering and singing. In spite of trying several tricks, the Tiso group could not force the door. Mr. Tiso eventually took to flight, with Qadi in hot pursuit! Mr. Tiso barely reached the safety of his hut, and then had to admit defeat.

All participants then gathered outside, and lengthy "peace negotiations" were started. It was agreed that the Qadi animals could not be overcome. Qadi was welcomed as Mr. Tiso's equal, to the satisfaction of both teacher and pupil, and was given a gift of money by his teacher. In doing this, Mr. Tiso symbolically acknowledged Qadi's status.

The sacrificial and induction ceremonies. These ceremonies were serious and moving, in contrast to the fun, laughter and joy of living which was evident in the separation of the animals.

On the first day of the Taking Home Ceremony, i.e., Thursday, Qadi's relatives were preoccupied with preparations for the coming event, such as the brewing of beer, preparation of food, and arranging of sleeping accomodations for the large number of visitors who were expected for the following two to three days.

By noontime on the second day, everything was ready for the ritual sacrifice of the animal that had been indicated by the ancestors for that purpose. The proceedings started with a dance session in the main hut of Qadi's homestead. Only fully qualified healers, dressed in their regalia, were permitted to dance to the singing, the clapping of hands, and the beating of two drums. Soon everyone was deeply immersed in what they were doing and experiencing. The singing and dancing was interrupted from time to time with brief statements by Mr. Tiso, such as, "I am bringing this boy back to his home . . . because he is now a man . . . . I am going out and this man is coming in . . . . " Following this session, Qadi took the lead. After praising and thanking Mr. Tiso, his relatives and his own ancestors, he said, "We will sing a song of this house." Several haunting songs were sung.

The next step was for Mr. Tiso to present Qadi with an *assegai*, a kind of javelin or throwing spear. Only fully qualified healers may carry these. Then, with Qadi's brother in the lead, the assembled people left for the cattle pen where beasts had been gathered. Qadi indicated which ox was to be sacrificed—his favorite. He stood quietly, holding his *assegai*, with a serious and brooding expression, as though he might be looking inward. What lay ahead was a crucial test, a sacrifice and communion with the ancestors. His future relationship with them, his health, and his work were at stake.

I was deeply moved by what was going on and, watching him, my mind went spinning back through the ages. Time, places and space ceased to exist. I had vivid images of participating perhaps in an ancient initiation ceremony as was practiced in Greece, or at the initiation of Isis and Osiris in Egypt. I heard the music of the Magic Flute, and saw Tamino in front of the temple of Sarastro. In my mind's eye I saw the Last Supper and present-day Holy Communion. The cattle pen, to the Xhosa, is a temple where the ancestors live. We were standing at its entrance, at the symbolic threshold of initiation.

I was pulled back to external reality by the loud bellowing of the ox, and all around me the resounding cries of "Camagu!," an expression of praise and thanksgiving. The bellowing was the answer of the ancestors, indicating their approval and acceptance of the sacrifice, and thus also of the initiate. The numinosity present at this time cannot be adequately described in words. Its reality could only be experienced sensually.

Qadi had to kill the sacrificial beast by severing its spinal cord at the occiput with a special sacrificial knife. The first blood had to soak into the manure as an offering to the ancestors. The tail was cut off immediately and pulled over a prong which would subsequently be decorated to serve as an additional insignia of Qadi's *igqira* status.

As described in the *Isiko Lentambo* sacrifice, the shoulder meat was cut off and roasted on a fire of wild olive branches. In the meantime an elder of the clan (Qadi's oldest paternal uncle) draped a white blanket round his shoulders. This was a gift from Mr. Tiso. Qadi then knelt down in front of Mrs. Tiso, who cut small pieces of the grilled meat, dipped these in a mixture of beer and herbal extract, and offered them to Qadi to eat. Complete silence reigned; Qadi's dedicated expression and total absorption were striking. To me, the similarity of this act to the taking of the Holy Communion seemed strong indeed. Thus Qadi incorporated his ancestors. He became identified with them. He shared in their wisdom, power, and numinosity.

After Qadi had finished eating, his blood relations followed suit in order of seniority and relatedness. They also had to kneel down, and follow every detail of the ritual. Finally Qadi had to drink the beer, the food of the ancestors, mixed with *ubulawu*, the herbal extract. He then handed it round in the traditional way to the oldest male relative, who in turn passed it on according to the dictates of custom. The entire family was included. These events of the cattle pen gradually merged into the singing and merry-making outside. Soon, an all-night dance session was begun in the Tiso hut, where only healers and patients were allowed to participate.

At noon on the following day, the final ceremony was performed. Another dance session was begun, this time in Qadi's own hut. Again, only fully qualified *amagquira* were allowed to participate, but now this included Qadi, despite the fact that some items of his regalia were still missing. The hut was packed with singers and clappers, and the customary mandala group was formed and dances performed (Bührmann 1981). Outside was a large audience. The importance of the proceedings became clear when Mrs. Tiso stopped the dance and spoke with great emphasis and authority. She ended by stating, "This ceremony is for this young man. The proper songs must be sung properly. Unless this is done properly it will spoil his future work." It must be remembered that one of the functions of the ceremonial dances, which are always performed indoors in the presence of the ancestors, is to get closer to them and to improve communication and communion. Nothing may be done, therefore, which is offensive or disrespectful to them.

After this interruption some visitors left the group and started singing on their own outside. I was later told that they were "from the cities" and "had the wrong attitudes." They "lacked respect" and were "ignorant about customs."

The vigor of the singing, clapping, dancing and drumming increased. All attention was focused on the dancing group. One had the feeling of libido being directed through all channels to the central point of the mandala, to Qadi, his future, and his ancestors. The songs certainly dealt with these aspects. After a considerable period of dancing, everyone left the hut for the space between the hut and the cattle pen. The proceedings now acquired an atmosphere of celebration. Speeches were made, and a praise singer performed his traditional song of praise to the departed clan members, the teacher, and his pupil.

Then, once more, the setting became more formal. The Tisos were seated on low stools. In front of them were Qadi's white investment blanket, his white goatskin, his new healers' skirt (which was made from strips of animal skin), and other insignia of his qualified state. White was used as a means of identifying with the numinous white Ancestors of the River. Around these the other healers planted their *assegais*, the erect symbols of their authority, in a semi-circle. This was done "to plant him here at his homestead . . . so that he should be [a healer] in this place and not wander around."

To my surprise, I was asked to bless the new *igqira*. I felt both honored and deeply moved. Qadi knelt in front of me. Putting my hands on his head, I spoke of the universal meaning of the ceremony, and asked for the assistance of his personal and our collective ancestors in his future work. After this solemn blessing, merriment again broke out. Many gifts were showered on Qadi, including money, household utensils, and even livestock. Each gift was acknowledged with clapping of hands and shouts of "Camagu!"

These mid-day proceedings were brought to a close by the performance of a very symbolic act. Qadi's *igqira* skirt of animal pelts was spread on the ground, inside uppermost. Mr. Tiso appeared, carrying a piece of freshly roasted meat, dripping with fat and juice, on the tip of an *assegai*. He streaked the inside of the skirt with this meat and then offered it to a dog of the household. When the dog took it, a loud "Camagu!" arose from the crowd. Mr. Tiso then fastened the skirt round Qadi's waist. With his other regalia, he was now fully accoutred as a qualified *igqira*, acceptable to the community and to the ancestors. The ingesting of the meat by the dog was explained as an assurance of the constant presence of the ancestors: "The dog is a shepherd of the home . . . like an ancestor of the home." The treatment of the skirt seemed to ensure constant communion and a fruitful relationship with the ancestors. The juice and fat from the sacrificial animal would always be next to Qadi's skin when he wore his skirt in the performance of ritual ceremonies. In a sense, Qadi and his ancestors had become one. A mystical union had taken place.

After final words of wisdom and advice from Mr. Tiso and other senior healers, the crowd dispersed. There followed a general feast for the relatives and all of the visitors.

That evening, at another dance meeting in the Tiso hut, Qadi, in a simple but touching speech, bade goodbye to his former fellow trainees, and joined the ranks of the qualified, where he was warmly welcomed. The atmosphere was charged with emotions of sadness and joy, with respect for the new healer and awareness of the new responsibilities which lay ahead for him. He had been finally initiated as a servant of the ancestors. From now on, he would have to live and work according to their wishes, a task not always easy: "It is sometimes difficult to take what the ancestors have to say to one—we have to take medicine from time to time to make us strong."

CONCLUDING REMARKS

The above is a description of the initiation of a Xhosa indigenous healer as an orderly sequence of events. In reality, initiation is rarely so orderly. The aspirant healer's training, and the sequence of initiation ceremonies that must be performed for him, are often interrupted by such realities of life as family and work commitments and lack of funds. Many people diagnosed as *thwasa* never get beyond the River Ceremony. When they experience symptomatic relief, they return to their former occupations.

There is an alternative way of becoming a healer which does not require the years of training and the customary ceremonies described above: one may become a healer by sudden revelation. Such healers claim that they disappeared and spent several days or even weeks with the ancestors under the water. The ancestors taught them how to heal directly, without the mediation of a living teacher. The external initiatory ceremonies are unnecessary. As I have not studied this matter in detail, I am reluctant to comment more fully.

From my research with the Xhosa, I cannot help but conclude that these are a people who both succeed and excel in establishing and maintaining a living, vital link to important archetypal forces which we, as modern, Western, "civilized" people have only begun to tap. From this research project and from others like it, I think there is much to be learned about initiation, ritual and dance as new sources of self-understanding. In writing this account, I have become acutely aware of the truth of C. A. Meier's statement (1967): "All conclusions in the realm of psychology have to be drawn by each individual from within his own psyche. . . . But to one question at least I will give an answer: If the facts that have been described are taken seriously, every physician must also be a metaphysician."

REFERENCES

Bührmann, M. V. 1977. Dream therapy through the ages. *Psychotherapeia* 3/1:16-18.
_____ . 1978. Tentative views on dream therapy by Xhosa diviners. *Journal of Analytical Psychology* 3/1:105-121.
_____ . 1981. The Xhosa healers of southern Africa. *Intlombe* and *xhentsa:* A Xhosa healing ritual. *Journal of Analytical Psychology* 26:187-201.
_____ . 1982a. A family therapy session with a dream as central content. *Journal of Analytical Psychology* 27:41-57.
_____ . 1982b. Isiko Lentambo: A renewal sacrifice. *Journal of Analytical Psychology* 27:163-73.
_____ . 1983. Archetypal transference as observed in the healing procedures of Xhosa indigenous healers. *Money, food, drink & fashion & analytic training,* ed. J. Beebe. Fellbach: Verlag Adolf Bonz, pp. 249-258.
_____ . 1987. *Living in two worlds: Communication between a white healer and her black counterparts.* Wilmette, Il.: Chiron.
Eliade, M. 1974. *Shamanism.* Princeton: Princeton University Press.
_____ . 1975. *Rites and symbols of initiation.* London: Harper & Row.
Ellenberger, H. F., and Allen, L. 1970. *The discovery of the unconscious.* New York: Basic Books.
Jung, C. G. 1954. Transformation symbolism of the Mass. *Collected works,* vol. 11, pp. 203-296. London: Routledge & Kegan Paul, 1958.
Meier, C. A. 1967. *Ancient incubation and modern psychotherapy.* Evanston: Northwestern University Press.

THE RITES OF CHRISTIAN INITIATION

Mark Searle

*In his essay, "The Rites of Christian Initiation," Mark Searle, returns to
the early Church to examine the traditional roots and dynamics of Christian
initiatory practice. Availing himself of van Gennep's classic paradigm
(separation, marge, aggregation), he describes early Christian rites of
baptism from the perspective of the fourth and fifth century ecclisiastical
writers. As the author follows a "catechumen" (initiate into Christianity)
through the three phases of the baptismal rite, the reader may find parallels to
earlier Greek or "pagan" rites. "Although the attitudes of Christian writers
in the early centuries towards the mystery rites would seem to have precluded
any direct borrowing," initiatory archetypes common to many and diverse
belief systems are found along the catechumen's journey.*

*Mark Searle, is Associate Professor of Theology at the University of Notre
Dame. A native of England, he received his doctorate at the Faculty of
Theology at Trier, Germany, and, after teaching in England, served as
Associate Director of the Notre Dame Center for Pastoral Liturgy from 1977 to
1983. He is past president of the North American Academy of Liturgy. His
special interests include the study of Christian ritual in the light of the human
sciences. He is author of* Christening: The Making of Christians *(1980) and*
Liturgy Made Simple *(1981).*

"CHRISTIANS," wrote Tertullian in the second century, "are made, not
born." It is not by birth from Christian parents, but by a special process
of initiation, that a person becomes a Christian. This distinction between birth
and re-birth, between generation and regeneration, lies at the basis of all
initiatory practice, even though it may happen, as it has tended to happen in
Christianity, that the more or less universal practice of initiation tends to
"naturalize" the new life of the initiates and rob it of its radical newness. Even
so, the traditional rites and symbols of initiation continue to speak of the
differences between the two orders and of the threshold that must be crossed.

As Levy-Strauss pointed out with regard to the ritual practices of so-called "primitives," the meaning of rites is best understood by attending to the rites themselves rather than to what their practitioners say about them. This caution would be equally applicable in our own society, where the actual practice of Christian initiation and popular understandings of the Christian sacraments are marked by a considerable impoverishment of meaning.

Moreover, actual practices of Christian initiation, ancient and modern, display a bewildering diversity and such seems to have been the case from the beginning. Attempts to discover a single original form of Christian baptism have failed and it is now commonly recognized that the New Testament writings themselves testify both to a rich variety of baptismal images and to remarkable diversity of practice.

For these reasons, and in view of the general purpose of this collection of essays on initiation, it seems best to suggest some of the imaginal wealth of Christian initiatory practices as a whole—rather than to offer a description of any particular rite, ancient or modern. In what follows, we shall bring together a diversity of data from documents of different places and epochs, though it must be admitted that the bulk of the data will be drawn from the Mediterranean churches of the fourth and fifth centuries. The reason for this bias is simple: it was in this world and at this time (mainly between 350 and 450 AD) that the rites of Christian initiation reached their fullest development and attained the classical forms which Christians of subsequent generations were content to reproduce with greater and lesser understanding of what they had inherited.

The question of the relationship between Christian baptism and the pagan mysteries has long been disputed. Though the attitudes of Christian writers in the early centuries towards the mystery rites would seem to have precluded any direct borrowing, we shall nevertheless avail ourselves of the useful categories of Arnold van Gennep's *rites de passage*.[1] This is made easier by the fact that, while not all Christian traditions understand baptism as a *rite of passage* in any anthropological sense, (i.e. as tied into a certain stage in the human life-cycle), still the images of baptism as a *transitus* was both original (e.g. I Peter 2:9-10) and, in the fourth century, enormously influential. It was then, if not a century earlier, that baptism came to be celebrated almost exclusively on Easter night, the night when Christ's new "passover" or *transitus* from this world to the Father, from death to life, was accomplished. Thus, as van Gennep suggests, we shall gather a representative sample of Christian initiatory practices together under the three headings of rites of separation, rites of liminality and rites of integration.

RITES OF SEPARATION

The earliest sources for Christian initiation, apart from the *New Testament*, present the predicament of the would-be Christian as that of choosing between the Two Ways: the Way of Life and the Way of Darkness. In the *Didache,* (probably a Syrian document, from late first or early second century), the two ways are presented in predominantly moral terms, but the *Epistle of Barnabas* (Egypt? Early second century?) hews closer to Essene and to later gnostic teaching in representing the ways of light and darkness in terms of cosmic dualism:

> There are two ways of teaching and authority: that of light and that of darkness. And there is a great difference between the two ways. For over one are appointed light-bearing angels of God, but over the other, angels of Satan. And the former is Lord from everlasting to everlasting, but the latter is ruler of this present time of lawlessness (18:1-2).[2]

Almost all the baptismal rituals of the early centuries reflect this awareness of the need to break with the past, to be set free from the demons which have previously steered one's life. Justin Martyr (c.160) explains:

> We were totally unaware of our first birth and were born of necessity from fluid seed through the mutual union of our parents, and were trained in wicked and sinful customs. In order that we do not continue as children of necessity and ignorance, but of deliberate choice and knowledge, and in order to obtain in the water forgiveness of our past sins . . . there is invoked over the one who wishes to be regenerated the name of God the Father . . . and of Jesus Christ . . . and . . . the name of the Holy Spirit.[3]

Hence, he gave the name "illumination" to baptism. The preaching of the Gospel, then, succeeds to the degree that it brings the hearers to awareness of how much their lives have been dominated by forces of which they were hitherto unaware. The decision to ask for baptism represents a break with such compulsive blindness, but it cannot be made by merely willing it. Baptism requires deliverance, or salvation, with which the candidate must cooperate by adopting a new lifestyle.

One major source of information about the baptismal process in the third century, Hippolytus describes the process by which a would-be convert is admitted to the "catechumenate," or period of prebaptismal formation:

> Those who come forward for the first time to hear the Word shall first be brought to the teachers at the house (of the church) before all people (of God) come in. And let them be examined as to the reason why they have come forward to the faith. And those who bring them shall bear witness to them whether they are able to hear.[4]

As the Apostolic Tradition makes clear, the ability to "hear the Word" consists of the willingness to undergo a radical change of life-style. The candidates are asked about their marital and social status, as well as their profession or occupation. A lengthy list of "forbidden occupations" includes such things as owning a brothel, serving as a magistrate (with power to impose the death penalty), being a priest in a pagan temple, or even working as an artist, actor, or school teacher—all of whom made a living by furthering pagan culture. If the candidate proves to be earning a living in such a way, he or she must either promise to abandon the profession or else be sent away. The ability to hear the Word involves a readiness to make whatever sacrifices may be necessary in order to live by the spirit of the Gospel. The sacrifices are not imposed arbitrarily; all require breaking with areas of life and spheres of influence dominated by spirits other than the Spirit of the Lord.

The ritual of enrollment in the catechumenate, or being admitted to the status of one under instruction, seems not to have been much developed in Hippolytus' time, but was firmly established by the fourth century. While different places had some variations, the essential ritual acts were those of the giving of salt and the signing of the Cross on the forehead of the catechumen. The giving of salt was probably taken over originally from the practice of giving salt to guests in the Mediterranean world as a sign of hospitality, but it quickly assumed further symbolic reference in the Christian world. The following, from a letter of John, a Roman deacon (c. 500), is fairly typical:

> Now that he is a catechumen, he will receive blessed salt, with which he is signed, because just as all flesh is seasoned and preserved by salt, so too the mind, sodden and soft as it is from the waves of the world, is seasoned by the salt of wisdom and the preaching of the Word of God.[5]

The same ambivalence, the reference to breaking with the past and turning to a new future, is found in the signing of the catechumens. In the Byzantine rite (c. 790 A.D.), the priest traces the sign of the Cross on the catechumen's forehead, praying:

> O Lord our God, we pray and beseech thee, let the light of thy countenance be marked upon this thy servant, and let the Cross of thy only-begotten Son be marked in his heart and in his thoughts, unto the renunciation of the vanities of the world and all the evil schemes of the Adversary, and unto the following of thy commandments . . . .[6]

Other rituals which may accompany the "making of a catechumen" include exorcisms and annointings, the multiplication of signs of the Cross upon the sense and limbs of the candidate, and the renunciation of magic and witchcraft. The cumulative purpose is the same: to draw a line of clear demarcation between before and after, outside and inside, the old self and the new that is coming to birth, both for the sake of the candidates themselves and for the community as a whole. For the rituals of initiation are never merely for those who undergo them. They are also intended to renew the imagination and sense of identity of all who participate.

RITES OF LIMINALITY

The person who has become a catechumen already belongs to the Christian community, but in a more important sense, such a person is in a liminal state, between two worlds. As always, the liminal state is one of great opportunity, but also of great danger:

> Great indeed is the baptism that is offered to you. It is a ransom to captives; the remission of offenses; the death of sin; the regeneration of the soul; the garment of light . . . the luxury of paradise; a procuring of the kingdom; the gift of adoption. But a serpent by the wayside is watching the passengers; beware lest he bite thee with unbelief; he sees so many seeking salvation and seeks to devour some of them. Thou art going to the Father of Spirits, but thou art going past that serpent; how then must thou pass him? 'Have *thy feet shod with the preparation of the Gospel of peace*' [Eph. 6:15] . . . . Have faith indwelling, a strong hope, a sandal of power, wherewith to pass the Enemy and enter the presence of thy Lord.[7]

The period of the catechumenate, then, is not merely a time for instruction, though it will include instruction. It is above all a time for facing and doing battle with the "dragon of the sea," as Cyril also puts it. For this reason, the instructional sessions either begin or end with the so-called "minor exorcisms" (in contrast to the "major exorcism" which is administered by the bishop on the eve of baptism). The following example, from the early medieval Roman liturgy, gives something of the flavor of the genre:

> Hearken, accursed Satan, adjured by the name of the eternal God, and of our Saviour the Son of God: thou and thy envy art conquered; depart, trembling and groaning. Let there be nothing between thee and these servants of God, who even now ponder heavenly things, who are to renounce thee and thy kingdom and make their way to blessed immortality. Give honour, therefore, to the Holy Spirit as he approaches, descending from the highest place of heaven, who shall confound thy deceits and at the divine fount (of baptism) shall cleanse and sanctify their breasts unto a temple and dwelling place of God; so that, being freed from all the inward hurt of past offences, as the servants of God they may always praise the everlasting God, and bless his holy Name throughout all ages. Through our Lord Jesus Christ, who shall come to judge the quick and the dead and the world by fire.[8]

Although this prayer has been used for centuries in the Roman rite of the baptism of children, it is clear from its contents that it was originally developed for use with adults ("the inward hurt of past offenses") and that it envisages a more or less lengthy process of transformation or purification.

If, as Kierkegaard suggested, purity of heart is willing one thing, then the purpose of the catechumenate in general and of the exorcisms in particular, can be seen as a focusing of the heart's desire and an overcoming of the dissipation of the soul's energies, wasted by following false paths of untruth and half-truth attributed to Satan, the "father of lies," and to his angels. This process of learning how to live in single-minded obedience to the Spirit of God and the Word of the Gospel was one that lasted a considerable period of time (as long as three years in the third century, as short as forty days in the fourth and fifth centuries) and consisted of a variety of exercises which fostered the sense of transition and liminality.

Ambrose, the 4th century bishop of Milan, exhorted his catechumens to "meditate, exercise, . . . be moderate in food, avoid intemperance of any kind and all impurity; eat poorer food, avoid getting drunk, guard the chastity of your bodies that you may win the crown."[9] Other bishops advised women not to wear bangles or talismans (which were associated with protection against spiritual forces) and sexual abstinence was commonly required for all candidates throughout the six or seven weeks leading up to baptism at Easter.[10] In these liminal practices, the candidates were joined by their sponsors and other members of the community. From the early fourth century, the "forty days" *(quadragesima)* before Easter became a time of asceticism for the whole Christian community, as bishops encouraged the faithful to associate themselves with the catechumens. Through an annual return to liminal status, then, the whole community was to be renewed. Such were the origins of Lent.

Priority was given, not to doctrine, but to what might be called an apprenticeship in the Christian life, or, to borrow a phrase from Aidan Kavanagh, to "conversion therapy." Conversion had to precede instruction for the simple reason that the mysteries of Christianity could not be intelligible to those who were not already amenable to the workings of the Spirit of faith. For this reason the *disciplina arcani,* the practice of not revealing the teachings and practices of Christianity to outsiders, was strictly enforced. Indeed, this was taken so far that the explanation of the rites of initiation—the water-bath, the anointings, the sharing in the eucharistic meal—was frequently only given to the neophytes *after* they had been through the rites. As Cyril of Jerusalem explained to the newly baptized.

> I long ago desired . . . to discourse to you concerning these spiritual and heavenly Mysteries, but knowing well that seeing is far more persuasive than hearing, I waited till this season; that finding you more open to the influence of my words from this your experience, I might take and lead you to the brighter and more fragrant meadow of this present paradise; especially as ye have been made fit to receive the more sacred Mysteries, having been counted worthy of divine and life-giving baptism.[11]

In preparation, then, for the climactic mysteries of Easter night, the catechumens prayed, fasted, were exorcised and instructed. The purpose of the instruction was less to render them theologically articulate, than to reveal to them the Story they were becoming involved in. The common practice was something like what Egeria, a fourth century Spanish nun, observed upon her visit to Jerusalem during Lent.

> The custom here is that those who come to baptism through those forty days, which are kept as fast days, are first exorcised by the clergy early in the morning . . . . Immediately afterwards, the chair is placed for the bishop at the martyrium (site of the crucifixion of Jesus) in the great church, and all who are to be baptized sit around, near the bishop, both men and women, their (god)fathers and (god)mothers standing there also. Besides these, all the people who wish to hear

come in and sit down—the faithful only however, for no catechumen enters there when the bishop teaches the others the law. Beginning from Genesis, he goes through all the Scriptures during those forty days, first explaining them literally and then unfolding them spiritually. They are also taught about the resurrection and likewise all things concerning the faith during those days . . . .[12]

The reference to the "literal" and "spiritual" explanations of Scripture is significant. By "literal" was meant a simple re-telling of Scripture stories which were to serve as the basis of the morning's lecture. As Augustine advised a catechist: "We ought to present the matter in a general and comprehensive summary, choosing certain of the more remarkable facts that are heard with pleasure and constitute the cardinal points in history."[13] From the general story of God's dealings with the human race from Adam down to the present time, the catechizer distills the "spiritual" meaning of the story: i.e., its relevance to the lives of the faithful. The story is to be unfolded as an example of God's love, manifest from generation to generation, discernible in present experience and calling for a response: "With this love, then, set before you as an end to which you (the catechist) may refer all that you say, so give all your instructions that he to whom you speak by hearing may believe, by believing may hope and by hoping may love."[14]

This kind of commentary would often be moralizing or exhortatory, but was also typological and eschatological. The stories of the acts of God in Scripture, or the ritual words and actions of the initiation rites, were expounded by reference to types from the past and antitypes of the future. The preacher would point to the meaning of the present situation by reference to stories of the Old and New Testament which had no literal connection with the present, but which offered illuminating analogies. The present, in turn, was interpreted as a mere foreshadowing of the glories to come. Theodore of Mopsuestia, for example, comments on the dressing of the newly baptized:

> As soon as you come up out of the font, you put on a dazzling garment of pure white. This is a sign of the world of shining splendour and the way of life to which you have already passed in symbol. When you experience the resurrection in reality and put on immortality and incorruptibility, you will not need such garments any longer; but you need them now because you have not yet received these gifts in reality, but only in symbols and signs.[15]

Conversely, the stripping of the candidates in preparation for their baptism is interpreted as a return to Paradise, to the unashamed nakedness that was the hallmark of innocence, as well as to the naked Christ crucified upon the Cross. The willingness to multiply and shift images reveals that the catechetical method was less a matter of "explanation" than an exercise of shared active imagination.

The sense of liminality intensified as the time for baptism drew near. "Those who are upon the point of entering upon baptism ought to pray, with frequent prayers, fastings, bendings of the knee, and all-night vigils, along with the confession of their sins . . . ." wrote Tertullian in North Africa at the turn of the third century.[16] The climax of all this preparation was the great three-day feast of the Lord's *pascha,* or passover, comprising Good Friday, Holy Saturday, and the long night vigil of Easter.

On Thursday, Hippolytus ordained that the candidates for baptism were to bathe and on Friday and Saturday they were to fast. This fast, in which the catechumens were joined by the whole community of the faithful, was the most solemn fast of the Church's year. Unlike the fasts observed at other times of the year, this fast was not strictly penitential or ascetical, but sacramental. That is to say, it was a participation in the death of Jesus himself, lasting through the hours of his death and descent into hell, concluding with the Easter eucharist in the early hours of Sunday morning. For the catechumens, this was (and is today) a time of stillness and prayerful expectation. On Saturday morning they gathered with the bishop for a final series of preparatory rituals. It was here that they "gave back" the Creed, reciting the profession of faith they had been taught and had learned by heart. It was here that the final, solemn exorcism took place. In fourth century Antioch, this took place on Good Friday, at the hour of Christ's death. The catechumens were stripped of their garments and, kneeling on goatskins, with hands outstretched like captives, they renounced Satan and professed their allegiance to Christ.

> Sacred custom bids you remain on your knees, so as to acknowledge (God's) absolute rule even by your posture, for to bend the knee is a mark of those who acknowledge their servitude . . . And after you have bent your knees, those who are initiating you bid you to speak those words: 'I renounce you, Satan.'
>
> I renounce thee, Satan! What has happened? What is this strange and unexpected turn of events? Although you were quivering with fear, did you renounce your old master. . . .? Whence came this boldness of yours? 'I have a weapon,' you say, 'a strong weapon.' What weapon, what ally? Tell me! 'I enter into thy service, O Christ,' you reply. 'Hence I am bold and rebel. For I have a strong place of refuge.'[17]

The anointing with oil followed immediately for, as Chrysostom pointed out, "when (Satan) hears those words, he grows more wild, as we might expect, and desires to assault you on sight. Hence, God anoints your countenance and stamps thereon the sign of the Cross. In this way does God hold in check all the frenzy of the Evil One."[18]

In Jerusalem, the renunciation took place immediately before baptism. The hour was shortly before dawn:

> First, ye entered into the outer hall of the Baptistery, and there, facing the West, ye heard the command to stretch forth your hand, and as in the presence of Satan ye renounced him . . . . Since the West is the region of sensible darkness, and he [Satan] being darkness, has his dominion also in darkness, ye therefore, looking with a symbolical meaning towards the West, renounce that dark and gloomy potentate . . . . When therefore thou renouncest Satan, utterly breaking all

covenant with him, that ancient league with hell, there is opened to thee the Paradise of God, which he planted towards the East, whence for his transgression our first father was exiled; and symbolical of this was thy turning from the west to the east, the place of light. Thou wert told to say, 'I believe in the Father, and in the Son, and in the Holy Ghost, and in one baptism of repentance.'[19]

In the Roman rite, the renunciation of Satan and the ensuing anointing of the whole body, took place on Holy Saturday. Later that evening, the great vigil, "the mother of all holy vigils," as Augustine called it, began. Twelve readings from the Old Testament, beginning with Genesis, recalled the great works of God in creation and redemption, and spoke through the prophets of the new world to come. Shortly before dawn, the catechumens and clergy left the assembled faithful and moved out to the baptistery, housed in a separate building usually shaped like a mausoleum. There, while the faithful stormed heaven with litanies, the water was blessed for baptism, the candidates removed their clothes in the semi-darkness, and were led one by one to the baptismal pool. As they stood in water, each was asked: "Do you believe in God the Father Almighty?" On responding, "I do," the neophyte was immersed in the water. Twice more this happened. Each time they were asked to profess their belief in Jesus Christ, the Holy Spirit and the Holy Church.[20]

The baptismal procedure was similar in all churches. Cyril of Jerusalem links the triple immersion to Christ's three days and nights in the tomb:

> O strange and inconceivable thing! We did not really die, we were not really buried, we were not really crucified and raised again, but our imitation was but in a figure, while our salvation is in reality. Christ was actually crucified, and actually buried, and truly rose again; and all these things have been communicated to us, that we, by imitation communicating in his sufferings, might gain salvation in reality.[21]

Given this universal conviction that the candidate who went down into the water was thereby conformed to the pattern of Christ's obedient death and was, with Christ, raised to life by the power of God, the practice of linking the action to a ritual question and answer on the Creed may seem redundant. It is essential, however, to appreciate the significance of saying "I believe", or *"credo."* As Wilfrid Cantwell Smith has pointed out in his book, *Faith and Belief,* however, both the Latin, *credo,* and the English "I believe" have a much stronger meaning than we currently give to them.[22] Much more than a matter of opinion, belief meant an act of self-commitment, a giving of oneself to another in commitment and trust. *Credo* is derived from *cordo:* "I give my heart"; and "be-lief" is etymologically connected with the German *Liebe,* or love. The profession of belief, then, equalled the act of allowing oneself to be immersed in the water. The act was a surrender of one's life (heart) to God who gave life to the dead.

The entire process of the catechumenate, as we have described it, led up to this climactic finale. Everything—the exorcisms, the instructions, the careful scrutinizing of the life and morals of the candidate, the prayer, fasting and vigil—prepared the candidate for this final surrender, this final act of conformity "to him who alone could save him out of death" (Heb. 5:7). The candidate lost his life, only to be raised to new life in Christ. This raising to new life, vividly expressed by the shiny, wet figures emerging from the font, marked the beginning of the process of integration into the Church—the Body of the Crucified and Risen Lord.

RITES OF INTEGRATION

As a babe from the midst of the womb he looks forth from the water; and instead of garments, the priest receives him and embraces him. He resembles a babe when he is lifted up out of the water; and as a babe everyone embraces and kisses him. Instead of swaddling clothes, they cast garments upon his limbs, and adorn him as a bridegroom on the day of the marriage supper. He also fulfills a sort of marriage-supper in baptism, and by his adornment he depicts the glory that is prepared for him.[23]

The reference to the marriage-banquet is not arbitrary. The earliest form of the Easter vigil, perhaps even before it came to be associated with baptism, consisted in expectation of the return of Christ. According to the parable of the wise and foolish virgins, the return of Christ would be like the return of a bridegroom who came home unexpectedly at midnight. Much of the imagery of this parable is derived from the Jewish Passover tradition. It was natural that early Christians should have observed Passover in their own way—i.e., waiting for the return of Christ. What the text of Narsai seems to suggest is that the risen Christ indeed appears in the midst of his church, in the form of the newly-baptized. While not using the marriage-imagery, John the Deacon says something similar about the newly baptized at Rome: "All the neophytes are arrayed in white vesture to symbolize the resurgent Church, just as our Lord and Saviour himself in the sight of certain disciples and prophets was thus transfigured on the mount . . . . This prefigured for the future the splendour of the resurgent Church, of which it is written, *Who is this that riseth up* [Cant. 3:6] all in white?"[24]

Thus the resurrection of Jesus is never an event merely to be commemorated. Wherever the Easter Vigil culminates in baptism, the resurrection of Jesus happens again, and new members are engrafted into his risen body, having passed with Christ from death to life. The final rites of Christian initiation celebrate this happening.

As we noted earlier, the actual baptism took place out of sight of the gathered community, usually in a separate building constructed for the purpose, in the presence of the ministers of the church and the godparents of the initiates. As each candidate emerged from the water, he or she was usually greeted by a deacon and his godfather, or by a deaconess and her godmother.

The Roman rite called for them to be anointed on the head at this time, in token of their sharing in the messianic anointing of Christ (*christos* = anointed) and in his mission as prophet, priest and king. This anointing was accomplished by a priest in attendance, and was followed immediately by the candidates drying themselves off and dressing in white garments. The *Missale Gothicum*, a ritual from France (c. 700), seems to see the anointing and the giving of the white robe as two symbolic expressions of the same thing:

> *While you touch him with chrism, you say:*
> I anoint thee with the chrism of holiness, the garment of immortality which our Lord Jesus Christ first received from the Father, that thou mayest bear it entire and spotless before the judgment seat of Christ and live unto all eternity. . . .
> *While you place the robe on him, you say:*
> Receive the white robe, and bear it spotless before the judgment seat of our Lord Jesus Christ. Amen.[25]

The effect of both the anointing of the head and the dressing in white robes is clearly intended to bring home the new identity of those who have passed through death and have now been raised to life again in Christ. Like the risen and transfigured Christ himself, and like the saints of the Apocalypse, they belong already to the world to come. They have put on immortality, having experienced the resurrection of the dead. In the Middle Ages, a further ritual developed at this point: the giving of a lighted candle to the newly-baptized. This was invariably accompanied with the admonition, "Guard thy baptism, keep the commandments, so that when the Lord comes to the wedding thou mayest meet him together with the saints in the heavenly hall . . . and live for ever and ever."[26] In this text (from the Sarum Rite), the ancient paschal image of the return of Christ as the coming of the bridegroom to the wedding-feast is not altogether obscured by moralizing.

Thus garbed as beings of the world to come, the newly-baptized were brought back to the congregation by their godparents and the ministers. In the Roman rite, the bishop once again assumed the presidency of the assembly of the faithful, having returned from the baptistery while the baptisms were still in process. Now he stood in the midst of the congregation to greet the newcomers. As they gathered as a group before him, with hand outstretched over their heads, he prayed:

> O Lord God, you made these people worthy of the forgiveness of sins through the bath of regeneration. Make them worthy now to be filled with your Holy Spirit and send upon them the grace to serve you according to your will . . . . To you is the glory, to the Father and to the Son and to the Holy Spirit in the holy Church, both now and ever and world without end. Amen.[27]

With this ritual, the newly-baptized were to be filled with that same Spirit which is of and with God, but which is also "in the holy church." Grafted onto the Church, the Body of Christ, by baptism, the newly baptized now began to breathe with the breath of the Church *(spiritus)*, to live with the very life of

God, which is the life of Jesus risen from the dead and the life of the community of the baptized. Then the bishop took consecrated oil, (usually perfumed oil or chrism) and anointed the head/forehead of the initiates. The Roman Catholic formula for this anointing or "confirming" of the baptized is the same as the one that has been in use in the Byzantine churches since at least the fifth century: "N., be sealed with the Gift of the Holy Spirit." With this admonition, the bishop embraced each candidate with the "kiss of peace," a gesture of intimacy hitherto forbidden the catechumens. As Hippolytus described it: "The catechumens shall not give the kiss of peace, for their kiss [is] not yet pure."[28] The same prohibition stood against catechumens and the baptized praying together and, of course, against admitting the unbaptized to the Eucharist. Conversely, no sooner were the candidates baptized and made partakers in the life of the Spirit, than they shared the kiss of peace with the faithful, joined in the community's intercessions for the world, and were admitted to communion in bread and cup.

Common prayer followed the anointing and embracing of the newly-baptized. This prayer was not for the newly-baptized alone, nor even for the Church alone; it was, as Justin (second century) made clear, an expression of the Church's vocation to pray "for all men everywhere, that, embracing the truth, we may be found in our lives good and obedient citizens and also attain to everlasting salvation."[29] Prayer for the world is part of the Christian's mission to share in the mystery of Christ, whom the Epistle to the Hebrews identifies as the great high priest who continues to intercede for humanity at the throne of God.

The neophytes finally reached the destination of their spiritual journey when, for the first time, they took part in the sacred meal of the Christian community. Their bond with the faithful in the Body of Christ is celebrated in the act of communion, the sharing of the bread and cup which represents the body and blood of Christ. The Christian Eucharist is seen here in its three essential dimensions: as a memorial of Christ, as present communion with Christ and one another, and as anticipation of the final communion of all the blessed, commonly spoken of in the Scriptures as the banquet in the Kingdom of God. The sense of having arrived is powerfully expressed in an ancient ritual which survives today only among the Christians of Ethiopia. There, as in ancient times, the newly-baptized are given not only bread and wine, but a cup of milk sweetened with honey. John the Deacon (c. 500), refers to such rites:

> You ask why milk and honey are placed in a most sacred cup offered with the sacrifice at the Paschal Sabbath. The reason is that it is written in the Old Testament and in a figure promised to the new people: '*I shall lead you into a land of promise, a land flowing with milk and honey*' [Lev. 20:24]. The land of promise, then, is the land of resurrection to everlasting bliss, it is nothing else

than the land of our own body, which in the resurrection of the dead shall attain to the glory of incorruption and peace. This kind of sacrament, then, is offered to the newly-baptized so that they may realize that no others but they, who partake of the Body and Blood of the Lord, shall receive the land of promise: and as they start upon their journey thither, they are nourished like little children with milk and honey, so that they may sing: *'How sweet are thy words unto my mouth, O Lord, sweeter than honey and the honeycomb . . .'* [Ps. 119:103].[30]

The journey of initiation is complete. Yet, for Christian pilgrims, baptism is the first stage in a longer journey. The journey of life is one for which they have been prepared by the discipline and formation of the catechumenate, and whose final terminus they have already glimpsed. In the course of this journey, the struggles with Satan will continue, as will the need to "listen to the Word," to pray, to practice self-discipline, to gather with the Church, and to celebrate the Eucharist. The initiation of the catechumenate is no substitute for the journey of life, but it trains the Christian to walk in the way of life.

NOTES

1. Arnold van Gennep, *The Rites of Passage,* tr. Vizedom and Caffee (Chicago: University of Chicago Press, 1960).

2. *The Apostolic Fathers,* ed. and tr. J. Sparks (Nashville and New York: Thomas Nelson, 1978), 297.

3. *I Apology, The Writings of Justin Martyr,* tr. T.B. Falls (New York: Christian Heritage, 1948), 100.

4. *The Apostolic Tradition,* E.C. Whitaker, *Documents of the Baptismal Liturgy* (London: S.P.C.K., 1970), 3. Henceforth cited as *DBL.*

5. *Epistle to Senarius, DBL,* 155.

6. *Barberini Euchologion, DBL,* 73.

7. *St. Cyril of Jerusalem's Lectures on the Christian Sacraments,* ed. F.L. Cross (London: S.P.C.K., 1960), 50.

8. *Gelasian Sacramentary, DBL,* 171 (8th century).

9. *De Elias, DBL,* 79.

10. For a masterly development of van Gennep's concept of liminality, see V. Turner, *The Ritual Process: Structure and Anti-Structure* (London: Routledge and Kegan Paul, 1969), 102-108.

11. *Mystagogical Catechesis,* Cross, 53.

12. *The Pilgrimage of Etheria, DBL,* 42.

13. Augustine of Hippo, *The First Catechetical Instruction,* tr. J.P. Christopher, *Ancient Christian Writers,* vol. 2, (Newman: Westminster, MD), 19.

14. *Ibid.,* 24.

15. "Baptismal Homily IV," E. Yarnold, *The Awe-Inspiring Rites of Initiation* (St. Paul: Slough, England, 1971), 207.

16. *On Baptism, DBL,* 9.

17. John Chrysostom, *Baptismal Instruction, DBL,* 37.

18. *Ibid.*

19. *Mystagogical Catechesis,* Cross, 53-5.

20. *Gelasian Sacramentary, DBL,* 184-190.

21. *Mystagogical Catechesis,* Cross, 61.

22. *Faith and Belief* (Princeton: Princeton University Press, 1979).

23. Narsai of Nisibis, "Homily 21," *DBL,* 55.

24. *Epistle to Senarius, DBL,* 157-8.

25. *DBL,* 162.

26. *Sarum Rite, DBL,* 247.

27. Hippolytus, *The Apostolic Tradition, DBL,* 6. In later Roman tradition this prayer was expanded to include the reference to the seven-fold Spirit of Isaiah 11:2ff: "the spirit of wisdom and understanding, the spirit of counsel and might, the spirit of knowledge and holiness . . . and a spirit of fear of the Lord." In this form it survives in the Roman, Episcopal and Lutheran rites to this day.

28. *Apostolic Tradition, DBL,* 3.

29. *I Apology, The Writings of Justin Martyr,* 104.

30. *Epistle to Senarius, DBL,* 157-8.

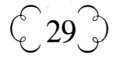

PSYCHOLOGICAL REFLECTIONS ON THE RITES OF CHRISTIAN INITIATION

Thomas Patrick Lavin

In his essay, "Psychological Reflections on the Rites of Christian Initiation," Thomas Patrick Lavin, Ph.D., reflects on the contents of the previous essay by his colleague, Professor Searle. Descriptions of baptismal rites by the early Church fathers are brought into contemporary focus through the dream of a Roman Catholic priest on the same night he had baptized five infants. Interpretation of this recent dream indicates the need for Christians to "go back to the archetypal roots" in order to fully understand the meaning of the rites of baptism. "If contemporary Christian baptism is to become alive and meaningful again, we must reconnect this rite to a deeper understanding of the basic human patterns of initiation."

Thomas Lavin is a Jungian analyst in private practice in Wilmette, Illinois. He holds a B.A. in philosophy and an M.A. in theology from the University of St. Mary of the Lake. He received his doctorates in clinical psychology and moral theology at the University of Innsbruck. He was awarded the diploma in analytical psychology from the Jung Institute of Zurich. Currently a senior training analyst, he has been director of training and vice-president of the Jung Institute in Chicago.

INTRODUCTION

A PATIENT of mine, a Roman Catholic priest, reported to me that he was accident prone one Saturday afternoon as he was trying to baptize five infants. He said that he kept spilling and knocking things over during the ceremony. That evening he had the following dream:

> There is a large vase in a room. It has ivory figures raised against a brown background. One figure is Christ being baptized by a large angel. I admire it. A man tells me he should have destroyed the vase

"because it shows that we are going backwards." Indeed the figures begin with the baptism and worked back to the apotheosis of some pagan figures. I suggest that it could be read from right to left and that would give a proper progression. But no, each figure is facing toward that final scene of pagan apotheosis.

Clearly, my patient had a conflict with what he was doing during his baptizing of infants. As Freud (*Psychopathology of Everyday Life* 1904) and Jung (*A Review of Complex Theory* CW 8) point out, accident proneness is an indicator of some unresolved complex or conflict in the unconscious. His own unresolved conflict about baptism and what he was doing was reflected in his accident proneness and an approach to the resolution of that conflict was suggested in his dream images that evening.

Since baptismal themes often appear in contemporary dreams, this dream is of particular interest here. Without elucidating all details, the dream points to the necessity for the dreamer to go back to the archetypal roots of universally human rites of initiation contained in the Christian ritual of baptism. The priest's dream has not only a personal meaning but a meaning for the community at large. Unresolved conflicts within the dreamer point to unresolved conflicts within the larger community.

In the dream, the "apotheosis of some pagan figures" indicates the necessity of the Christian community becoming more conscious of the archetypal dimensions of baptism. In other words, Christian baptism has its roots in rites of initiation practiced among humankind since the dawning of time. If contemporary Christian baptism is to become alive and meaningful again, we must reconnect this rite to a deeper understanding of the basic human patterns of initiation. We must come to realize, as did Andrew Greeley and Mary Durkin in *How to Save the Catholic Church* (1984), "that pagan customs were baptized and made Christian, and that this was done enthusiastically, if erratically, in the first centuries of Christianity, is beyond question." In the early Church, as in my patient's dream, some pagan images and patterns needed to be apotheosized in order that the sacramental actions of baptism might participate more fully in the depth and richness of human experience—and thereby become a greater source of energy and life to the newly baptized Christian.

In the preceding chapter, Professor Searle has presented rich images of initiation as seen through the prism of the early Christian experience of baptism. Searle's work here and elsewhere (see "The Journey of Conversion," *Worship*, vol. 54, 1980) is an excellent example of the meaningful and soul-searching scholarship with which increasing numbers of Catholic and Protestant theologians are refreshing Christian doctrine. Searle and others are leading us out of an essentialist and dogmatic fixture into the light of the freedom to examine and reflect upon the observable phenomena in Christianity's past and present. Their work seems testimony to the fact that Pope John XXIII did indeed open up the windows and allow the fragrance of spring air to freshen the dusty confines of tradition.

The phenomenological approach to the Christian mysteries, the pedagogical foundation of the early Church fathers cited by Searle, opens the windows and the doors of the treasury of Christian religious experience to all of the psychological types described by C. G. Jung. Theology and theological reflection are no longer restricted only to those persons in whom the thinking function, which is oriented to analyzing and classifying, is dominant. Professor Searle's historical/phenomenological approach unlocks the transforming energy of the symbolic, inviting all of us—within our gifts of extraversion, introversion, feeling, sensation, thinking, and intuition—to allow ourselves to reflect upon and to be touched by the numinosity of the living Christian tradition of initiation.

As in the catechesis of the early Church fathers, Searle does not "explain" the catechuminate or Christian initiation process to us, but instead holds before our eyes those images which gave new form to the lives of those early catechumens. He invites us to join him in an exercise of shared Active Imagination. A person's life is seldom given new form or turned around or upside down by dogmas. As C. G. Jung pointed out (*Symbols of Transformation* 1967), only images contain sufficient energy to give new form and meaning to life. Dogma and ethics, if they are to be meaningful and alive, are results of shared stories and/or images of religious experience. Therefore, the more conscious I am of my outgoing and deepening process of being initiated, the more wholly I participate in the Christian Church. One way of viewing the Church ("ecclesia" literally means "a calling out" or "rallying call") would be to gather all those "called out" of the collective, to share, amplify and ritualize within their community their own stories of initiation into the experiences of God's love.

At its best, the Christian Church is an inner and outer happening and "calling out" where a re-telling of stories about numinous spiritual experiences is encouraged and serves as a sacred ground (*temenos*) for the continuation of these mutual touchings between God and humankind in the present and in the future. The Christian is called to continually celebrate deeper and deeper levels of the mysteries of her/his initiatory experiences.

I would like to share the following five psychological reflections on Searle's excellent essay: 1) Baptism is an initiatory call to psychological wholeness and growth. 2) Baptism is a symbolic as well as an historic act of initiation. 3) Baptism means putting on a new persona. 4) Baptism, as initiation, is also personal affirmation. 5) Many of Jung's profound insights into the symbolic significance of baptism as a rite of initiation have both psychological and theological relevance for us today.

BAPTISM: CHRISTIANITY'S CALL FOR INITIATION INTO WHOLENESS

It seems to me that the call to initiation, as in the preparation for and the ritual of baptism, is the Christian way or modality of inviting a person to become a whole, mature, and fulfilled individual. All authentic religions in each age have demanded an initiation process of its members. As Jung reminds us in his *Two Essays* (1953):

> Initiations have survived among all cultures. In Greece the ancient Elusianian mysteries were preserved, it seems, right into the seventh century of our era. Rome was flooded with mystery religions. Of these Christianity was one, and even in its present form it still preserves the old initiation ceremonies, somewhat faded and degenerated, in the rites of baptism, confirmation, and communion. Hence, nobody is in a position to deny the enormous historical importance of initiation.

Baptism can be seen as a psychological process which invites us to grow—to grow out of and to grow into. In the baptismal process, a person is exhorted to grow out of the darkness of unconsciousness and collective identification and grow into a new dawning of consciousness in which he/she receives a new identity and a new persona. Baptism, as seen in the rituals and experience of the early Church, was not something that was routinely done to a newborn child. Rather, baptism was ritually lived and re-lived as a verb, and an active verb at that! As Searle points out in the preceding chapter, "The rituals of initiation are never merely for those who undergo them: they are also intended to renew the imagination and sense of identity of all who participate." Therefore, baptism must not be seen as a one-time ritual which happens to a person, but rather an ongoing, identity-giving and deepening process which affects the whole community and calls them as individuals and as a group to wholeness.

According to Professor Josef Goldbrunner (*Holiness Is Wholeness* 1964), living an authentic spiritual life and being committed to what Jung called the way of individuation or the symbolic life are the same existential reality. It is important to note that psychological growth and spiritual growth are parallel growths, and not, as some think, opposed to each other. A mature relationship with God demands and is supported by a striving for psychological wholeness. An honest relationship with a personal God requires a dialogue in which old images are given a new form and personal growth and identity are fostered. Baptism, as a call to wholeness, can then be seen as a process which initiates and ritually renews the dialogue: the ongoing, life-embracing, and re-informing conversation with one's multi-imaginal, personal God. Through the ritual of baptism, God, like any healthy mother and father, invites us to become more fully developed and whole.

BAPTISM: AN HISTORIC AND SYMBOLIC CALLING OUT

In our time, among many Christian denominations, baptism has lost its psychological energy. The ritual of baptism has degenerated from a bold, vital, and soul-shaking symbolic act into a socially expected sign. But a sign, like a stop-light, is a visible manifestation of a known reality. A symbol, on the other hand, is the visible manifestation of an unknown or mysterious reality, a reality that is filled with energies which can and should enliven our whole being. A sign points to external reality; but a symbol contains the reality to which it points. A symbol invites us to go deeper. Therefore, as a psychological reality, baptism can be seen as an ongoing process into which one continues to grow. My baptism is not only an historical fact, an event which can be marked on a space and time continuum; it is also a symbol which continues to call me to a deeper level of initiation and to cross yet another threshold. Because baptism is both historic and symbolic, the tension between generation and regeneration remains painfully real and calls us to transcend a myopic understanding of who we are and who we are becoming. Jung viewed the psychological process of baptism as being symbolic of a transformation by which man loses his archaic identification with material reality and is opened to the possibility of spiritual integration.

The symbolic core of the baptismal rite is the psychic energy which is released through the symbols to give a new, transcendent form to former identifications. Jung has described the symbol as having a "transcendent function," a means by which a person is able to make a transition between and beyond the many opposites and contradictions of her/his life. The images in the ritual of baptism give us the energy to begin to try to unite the opposites of spirit and matter within ourselves, to join the body and the soul into a meaningful wholeness.

An example might be helpful here. A symbol is like an electrical transformer which an American might bring to Europe. In Europe, electrical energy is 220 volts. An American appliance, which can only effectively operate on 110 volts, needs a transformer for that 220 energy or it will be destroyed. There is nothing wrong with the American appliance and there is nothing wrong with the 220 energy; but the raw 220 energy needs to be given another form if the hair dryer or razor is to function adequately. The archetypal energy contained in the archetype of initiation is too strong for a direct connection. Symbolic actions of pouring water and tasting salt, etc. are the transformers of the archetypal energy which enable us to live a radically new form of life. Just as dream symbols are transformers of energy, so the symbols in ritual help us to make the transition ("trans-situs"—movement from one place to another) from matter to spirit and from spirit back to matter. The initiation images of baptism can give us the useable energy to move from one place of identity to another. Thus, baptism has a transcendent/transitional function in our personal lives and in the lives of the Christian community.

The images which the Church has chosen to give to us in the rituals of baptism are related to the imagery which the psyche has used throughout the ages for the purposes of individuation. The images of the Church have a primal foundation in the human unconscious (see C. G. Jung, *Symbols of Transformation* 1971 and *The Symbolic Life* 1939).

Baptism: Putting on a New Persona

In the early Church, most rituals of baptismal initiation included the symbolic action of stripping the candidate of her/his clothing prior to immersion and of giving the baptized one new garments. This new clothing signified to the community that a dramatic change in the baptized person had taken place and that, as a consequence of this transition, the person was expected to perform a new role in the community. Even as circumcision signified the covenant with Yahweh, the new baptismal garments signified to the community that a new role and status must be given to one who has made a covenant with God. Baptism demands a new persona, a new way to face the outside world.

Jung defines the persona as a combination of who I really am and what society expects me to appear to be. An appropriate persona has four harmonious parts. It includes knowledge of:

1) Who I am (ego strengths and weaknesses)
2) Who I am becoming (ego-ideal based on religious experience)
3) Expectations of society
4) Where my energy is (attitudinal and functional types)

The word "persona" comes from the Latin, *per-sonare*, "to sound through." Thus, the persona is the way by which what has happened and is happening in the soul of a person can be shared with others. In ancient Greek and Roman theater, the mask or persona was meant to convey the actor's role to the audience and to amplify his voice. An adequate persona is meant to be the representation and amplification of realities of the soul.

The persona has three functions by which the Self is served:

1) It COVERS—The persona attracts that which I feel is superior and it shields that which I feel is inferior.

2) It CHANGES—The persona is a means of changing and enhancing one's personality. One grows into a persona; and the persona is thus an agent of individuation and growth.

3) It EMPOWERS—The persona in religious ritual has been thought to give the wearer a special power because it takes the wearer out of the collective and gives her/him the energy of the ancestral spirits.

The danger associated with wearing a persona is total identification with it. To identify with an archetype or archetypal image is psychological suicide. Thus we need to remember Theodore of Mopsuestia who tells the newly-baptized that they need their baptismal garments because "you have not yet received these gifts in reality, but only in symbols and signs" (Searle 1986). We may, as St. Paul suggests to us, put on Christ; but we may not identify the ego as being the same as the archetype of Christ in us. The identification of ego with an archetypal image is understood, in Jungian thought, as the basis of a psychotic condition. Paradoxically, baptized Christians are told to have and grow into a new persona, but they may not totally identify with this new Christ-persona. Perhaps this is the reason why some members of fundamentalist and/or charismatic Christian sects "rub us the wrong way." Some try to give us the impression that having a Christian persona means that by identifying wholly with the archetype of Christ, they have banished their own personal shadows forever. Both total identification and eternal sinlessness are humanly impossible. Developing a Christian persona is a never-ending process dependent upon and related to the development of a Christian soul. No one living will ever rise above her/his Pauline "thorn in the flesh."

In his letters to the early Christian Churches, St. Paul very clearly explains how a newly baptized Christian is expected to have a radically different persona (Gal. 3:27, Rom. 13:12-14, Eph. 4:22-24, Col. 3:9-12). In Galatians, St. Paul tells the new Christians: "All baptized in Christ, you have all clothed yourselves in Christ." In all of the references given above, St. Paul proclaims that baptism demands the taking off of old clothing and the putting on of the new Christian persona. Every facet of the persona is to be given a new form or image through the initiation of baptism. Initiation gives the initiate new images of who she/he is, who she/he is becoming, what the expectations of the Christian community are (Rom. 13:12-14), and an increase and consciousness of psychic energy.

The radically new persona of the baptized Christian is a reality which she/he can grow into; it is the result of an initiatory process. With long and hard preparation the new persona is earned with and through the Christian community. The Christian persona, therefore, is not a dazzling garment meant to further one's own narcissistic ends, but a role one wears and grows into within the context of a loving community. Baptism is the putting on and commitment of a new role in society.

BAPTISM: A PERSONAL AFFIRMATION

Jung found it important to go back to the primal myths of humankind in order to better understand the forms which patterns of human behavior can take and in order to understand the meanings of these patterns of behavior in our society. In other words, Jung studied mythology in order to understand the archetypal and imaginal support system of human behavior. Myths give us the earliest, best, and clearest images of the possibilities of human behavior. They are the building-blocks of human interpersonal and intrapersonal relationships.

In good Jungian fashion, it is important for us to go back to the primary story for Christian initiation, the baptism of Jesus, in order to understand what the transforming experience of baptism might mean for us.

It is necessary for the contemporary Christian to understand that Jesus' baptism in the Jordan was the beginning to Jesus' messianic mission. Both Jesus and John saw baptism as an essential part of Jesus' initiation, that it was necessary for Jesus to be publicly initiated if he were to fulfill the archetypally-based traditions of those he wanted to save. The prophets of the Hebrews had already established the importance of the ritual relationship between water and spirit (Ezech. 36:25-26; Joel 3:1-2; Isa. 33:15-18 and 55:1-10).

Luke's version of Jesus' initiation story tells us that while Jesus was praying (after he came out of the Jordan), heaven opened and the Holy Spirit descended on him, in bodily shape, like a dove; and a voice came from heaven: "You are my Son, the Beloved; my favor rests on you" (Luke 3:22). I have often wondered if the very basis of Christianity is not a father/son love story into which we have been asked to joyfully participate. It seems to me, as a Jungian psychologist, that the most internally significant aspect of the rites of initiation is that initiation is a process of personal affirmation. To be initiated is to be told that my existence is important and that my life has a meaning.

Every day in my consultation room I am painfully aware of how important it is in the life of a person to be affirmed by her/his parents. Many of my patients were never sufficiently told by their parents that "my favor rests on you." Their attainment of maturity was never validated by a loving parent. A major task of their analytical journey is to hear from within themselves those words of affirmation and validation which they never received from their parents.

At the conclusion of the story of Jesus' baptismal initiation, his Father says he loves him; He calls Jesus "the Beloved." It is interesting that although Matthew, Mark and Luke record this instance of paternal validation, John does not. However, at the end of the beautiful gnostic prologue of John's version of the Jesus story, John reminds us, "No one has ever seen God; it is the only

Son, who is nearest to the Father's heart, who has made him known" (Jn. 1:18). Perhaps "nearest to the Father's heart" is John's way of saying that Jesus was initiated because he was loved and affirmed by his Father.

We see that same love-affirmation of parent for child in the baptismal rituals of the early Church. After the baptism, "the bishop embraces each candidate with the 'kiss of peace,' a gesture of intimacy hitherto forbidden the catechumens" (Searle 1986). The bishop's embrace, a symbolic re-enactment of the Father's embrace of Jesus, was passed on to the new Christian. As psychologically significant as it is symbolically meaningful, the embrace and kiss hold out the hope that the Church is a place to be re-affirmed and nourished by a father and mother, even if one never received such primal regard from one's own parents. "Godfathers" and "godmothers" also have always been an important part of the Christian ritual of initiation. The godparents are present to receive the new Christian with regard she/he may never have received from her/his own personal parents. Christian initiation is meant to welcome a woman and man into a new family, into a new and perhaps deeper experience of parental affirmation. If more Christians could consciously participate in the affirmative realities of their baptisms, especially during Lent and Easter-time, some Jungian analysts would not have to "godfather" and "godmother" as much as they do. Jung believed that if Christians *really* lived their Faith, entering more fully into the transformational and affirmational symbols which their Faith offers, they would not need analysis.

BAPTISM: C.G. JUNG'S PARADIGM

There are many references to Christian baptism in Jung's writings (see Vol. 20 of his *Collected Works*). He demonstrates how the baptism dreams of his patients point to an initiation process taking place in their lives. In his *Symbolic Life* (C.W. 18), Jung describes baptism as an archetypally transforming ritual:

> You know that every church still has its baptismal font. This was originally the *piscina*, the pond, in which initiates were bathed or symbolically drowned. After a figurative death in the baptismal bath, they came out transformed, *quasi modo genti*, as reborn ones. So we can assume that the crypt or baptismal font has the meaning of a place of terror and death and also of re-birth, a place where dark initiations take place.

The place of baptism is not only the place of embrace, as mentioned above; it is also a place of terror and death. Thus, the Christian initiation ritual is an event during which the opposites of death and new life, terror and embrace, are united. For Jung, this bringing together of opposites constitutes a paradigm for wholeness and health and for him, the mystery of baptism was exactly that symbolic experience in which opposites could be brought together.

In 1913, the year of his famous break with Freud, Jung wrote *The Theory of Psychoanalysis*. Here he laid out a schema by which the experience of baptism could be better understood in a psychological sense. His explication must be included in any reflection on the psychological meaning of Christian baptism.

> Suppose, for instance, we did not understand the meaning of the baptismal rite practiced in our churches today. The priest tells us: baptism means the admission of the child into the Christian community. But this does not satisfy us. Why is the child sprinkled with water? In order to understand this ceremony, we must gather together from the whole history of ritual, that is, from mankind's memories of the relevant traditions, a body of comparative material culled from the most varied sources:
> 1. Baptism is clearly a rite of initiation, a consecration. Therefore, we have to collect all memories in which any initiation rites are preserved.
> 2. The act of baptism is performed with water. For this special form another series of memories must be collected, namely, of rites in which water is used.
> 3. The person to be baptized is sprinkled with water. Here we have collected all those rites in which the neophyte is sprinkled, immersed, etc.
> 4. All reminiscences from mythology, folklore, as well as superstitious practices, etc., have to be recalled, in so far as they run in any way parallel to the symbolism of the baptismal act.
> In this way we build up a comparative study of the act of baptism. We discover the elements out of which the baptismal act is formed; we ascertain, further, its original meaning, and at the same time become acquainted with the rich world of myths that have laid the foundation of religions and help us to understand the manifold and profound meanings of baptism.

Jung's interpretive model of baptism remains a challenge both to today's theologians and psychologists and to those of us who were baptized as infants. The paradigm invites us to a "collection of memories," a gathering of images and stories—both in the collective of history and in our own personal lives—about initiation. A deeper understanding of the meaning of baptism in our lives demands that we take the time to "re-collect" our images of religious experience. We need to recollect and reflect on our own experiences of being affirmed and loved in order to make our baptism a living reality.

CONCLUSION

Someone once said that contemporary Christian educators are not following Christ's pedagogical example. Christ blessed the children and educated the adults. We, on the other hand, bless the adults and educate the children. I think that our Christian churches need to spend more time and energy initiating adults, baptized as infants, into the meaning and celebration of who they are and can become as baptized Christians. Christian communities need to share, as adults to adults, their collection of stories and memories of the ongoing process of initiation into the mysteries of God's love for them. It is in the sharing of these mystery stories that Christians can become sacraments to one another. (The idea of sacramentality is not limited to only those rituals which are performed in a church.) By sharing our stories, the stories in scripture as well as our own personal stories, we, like the pagan figures in the priest's dream at the beginning of this paper, will experience an apotheosis. We will participate more fully and consciously in, what is for the Christian men and women, the greatest Father/son love story of all time.

REFERENCES

Freud, S. 1904. *The psychopathology of everyday life*. The Standard Edition of the Complete Psychological Works of Sigmund Freud. London: The Hogarth Press, 1960.
Goldbrunner, J. 1964. *Holiness is wholeness and other essays*. Notre Dame: The University of Notre Dame Press.
Greeley, A., and Durkin, M. 1984. *How to save the Catholic Church*. New York: Viking-Penguin.
The Jerusalem *Bible*. Garden City: Doubleday & Co., 1968.
Jung, C. G. 1967. *Symbols of transformation*. Collected Works, vol. 5. Princeton: Princeton University Press.
——— 1966. *Two essays*. Collected Works, vol. 7.
——— 1950. *The symbolic life*. Collected Works, vol. 18.
——— 1961. *Freud and psychoanalysis*. Collected Works, vol. 4.
Searle, M. 1980. The journey of conversion. *Worship*, vol. 54, 1980, pp. 35-55.

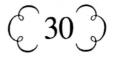

STORYTELLING

Elaine Wynne

In "Storytelling," Elaine Wynne reminds us that the hearing of tales (and the telling of them), is, in itself, an initiatory process, a bringing to consciousness ancient truths about the passages and initiations of heroes and heroines, villains and fools. We realize once again that storytellers, like poets, are one with the community, for their stories manifest the unfelt experiences, the heroic yearnings, the noble deeds, and the historic and mythic memory for the entire social body: "Poets [and storytellers] are the un-acknowledged legislators of mankind" (Percy Bysshe Shelley). Other yarn-spinners will profit from her references to collections of tales, legends and myths listed at the end of her remarks.

Elaine Wynne, M.A., a professional storyteller, studied Archetypal Psychology and Storytelling at St. Mary's College (Winona, Minnesota) and works with children, using imagery and storytelling, at Minneapolis Children's Medical Center. As a community faculty member, she teaches storytelling at Metropolitan State University, has served on the staff of the National Conference for Storytelling and the Religious Message, and has presented workshops for state and national hospice gatherings.

STORIES we tell about ourselves and the stories other people tell about us deeply affect how we live. If we want to change our lives, we must first change our stories. This realization came to me in the early seventies after I had been involved in and affected by several liberation movements, including my own with the dawning of the Women's Movement.

It was that awareness that propelled me into becoming a professional storyteller. I began writing, dancing, and photographing stories and made a videotape of storytellers. Friends began asking for stories at parties and spiritual gatherings. An early event I remember was a tree trimming party. I came to the party after spending three hours in a lawyer's office negotiating a series of renovation contracts for the clinic where I worked.

When I placed a wreath of Norway pine on my head and began telling stories, all memory of that hard factual language melted away into the language of story. I told "The Fir Tree" (Andersen 1976) and a Christmas scene from one of Dick Gregory's novels (Gregory 1964). Then I told the story of Pitys (Grant, *Hamadryaden*) who transformed herself into a pine tree to escape a marauding Pan. Ever since that time, the pine tree has symbolized immortality and eternal life. Children and grown-ups cuddled together around the stories and then trimmed the tree. The young ones fell asleep amidst the winter coats while adults sang, danced and drank glug. Since those early days, I have continued my path as a storyteller, a commitment which I treasure more each day. And as the years passed, I have come to see storytelling as a healing art.

In ancient times, the storyteller's drum would call people together at sunset. Shadows and the deep colors of the day's end signalled the time to listen to stories. This was an important way that cultures sustained themselves; the telling helped to maintain groups, to keep people healthy. A circle formed around the fire pit or flickering candles. Stories in the early evening were for the children (or for the "child" in everyone). As the children drifted off to sleep, the voice(s) of the storyteller(s) mixed with the dreams of the children and stories were told for the older ones.

There were tales of meaning, stories of how evil forces entered the world and had to be confronted, of heroes and heroines who embarked on Soul Journeys, of how the people would succeed, even when they seemed to be less powerful. Often the hero or heroine had to learn to listen, to accept magic, or listen to helpful spirits who appeared in the stories. Sometimes the helpers were animals, sometimes little people or guides from the Other World. But time and again, the dragons were subdued, the people renewed.

For some reason, storytelling lost its place and role. Some say industrial culture was responsible for its demise; some say it was the coming of the electric light bulb or the television. I cannot tell you why; I only know it happened. But in recent times there has been a renewed interest in storytelling, a renaissance, a re-membering. Perhaps it has been spurred by a desire for intimacy, perhaps by our disenchantment with television as primary storyteller.

When I began to recover my own interest in storytelling, I remembered telling stories as a little girl . . . . stories of loons, "shypokes" and wolves, as well as of cows, sheep and horses. My family encouraged these flights of imagination. Later, as a young mother, I told stories to my children. We travelled a lot when they were young and storytelling was a way to help them survive long rides in the car. I would make up stories, using names of people or places I wanted them to remember. The stories have long been forgotten, but the images linger.

Rites of Passage as Storytelling

The storytelling process carried us through the early years and later became a way for my children to pass from childhood into adulthood. During my training in Archetypal Psychology, I found many stories of other cultures which had created rites of passage into adulthood. I was struck by the lack of meaningful rituals for this emergence in our modern times. The Jewish Bar Mitzvah and Batz Mitzvah still seemed to hold meaning for some people; confirmation seemed to hold meaning for some of these within the Christian Church. Nowhere could I see a societal ritual; and besides, thirteen seemed too early to enter adulthood in a post-industrial society.

I began to wonder if we could construct a ritual strong enough to symbolize the passage from childhood to adulthood in our family. This pondering finally led to a family rite of passage for each child on his/her 18th birthday. The ritual involves both parents, the child, and a male and female guide. The role of the guides is to keep the ritual in process, to hold the three participants in the container of the rite, and to help them express themselves.

Starting with a simple form, the rite is a process of storytelling, from the child's conception, through the years of childhood, to this moment of passage into adulthood. Near the end, the child envisions a dark passage with light at the end. When he/she has reached the light at the tunnel's end, adulthood has arrived; a new relationship with the parents is acknowledged. Gifts are given to the newly emerged Life Journeyers in the form of riddles, stories or poems, and the Journeyer expresses his/her dreams, hopes and visions for life.

This process has been extremely important to our family, particularly since the children's father and I have been divorced. It has been important for the children to say goodbye to both parents together, even though they live with only one parent. It has been extremely helpful and meaningful for me to symbolize this change in our relationship, to re-orient myself to the role of parent of an adult child and to experience the grief of this enormous change.

This rite has lasted several hours each time and has been followed by a huge party involving friends of each of us. The stories we remembered and relived have been tucked away within our hearts, rarely spoken of again, yet never forgotten.

Since initiating this process, I have been asked to tell stories at other rites of passage into adulthood. I have told the Grimm's fairy tale, "Iron Hans" (Grimm 1972) and the Navajo story to celebrate Changing Woman's first initiation when she menstruated (O'Bryan 1956). I see part of my role as storyteller to be present at such rituals, to help people form them, to encourage them to assume the familial and community power to enact these ceremonies of re-membering as a way to go on with life.

SUPPORTING THE IMAGINATION

Several years ago, I presented many talks for parents on "The Effects of Television on Children" and "Supporting Your Child's Imagination through Storytelling." They are sponsored by Behavioral Pediatrics Program at Minneapolis Children's Medical Center. This program sees imagination as an important skill necessary to help children cope with or master illness. Children learn to regulate their bodies by creating images. Biofeedback and the teaching of self-hypnosis are tools for the children. Their images can be fed and nourished by stories. I developed a story there: "The Rainbow Dream (1982), a fairy-tale-like piece about a girl with leukemia. She learns to visualize herself feeling better and coaxing her body's immune system to help fight her illness.

When I began to work with children in the hospital I told them stories, played games, got them to tell stories, and tried to deepen my understanding of how their imaginations worked. They told me many things. "The Rainbow Dream" was a culmination of listening to their images and story motifs. I would tell the story to them and ask for their help in improving it. The story became a centerpiece around which to discuss feelings, their illness and life. Often, parents and family members would be in the room. I think the stories offered a moment of quiet, of relaxation, of comfort—a moment to travel into another world, a place that stands on its own, a place that has meaning in and of itself.

Telling the old stories is important work. We must wrestle with differing world views, with sexism and racism, with the lack of global perspective. Yet many of the old stories contain universal meaning and we need them to help us understand story language, to develop the stories of the future. I encourage parents to read and tell the folk and fairy tales. Some sources I recommend are *Tatterhood,* a collection of stories with women as central characters (Phelps 1978), *Black Folktales* (Lester 1970), and *One Hundred Favorite Folktales* (Thompson 1968). Jane Yolen (1981) and Diane Wolkstein (1978) write wonderful stories, taking old mythological symbols and re-weaving them into modern times. Of course, the American Indian tradition provides us with marvelous stories of North America, of the relationship between people and animals, of the conflict between Good and Evil forces, and of ceremonies that built communities.

THE KEY OF SEE-ING

After telling stories alone for five years, I began telling with a partner. Larry Johnson and I often perform as "The Key of See," playing songs on the keyboard, garden hose and water faucet to accompany our stories. In the teaching of storytelling, we have created a course/workshop called Storytelling for Personal and Planetary Healing. Participants pass a talking staff around in a circle and tell stories from their memory—about conflict and humor, about death, nuclear times, and stories to imagine the world as we would like it to be. It seems really important to tell each other those stories, to tell our children those stories.

A great deal is being said about the psychological impact of nuclear times and of the need children have for us to talk with them about it. Of course, we must. But the next step is finding ways to cope with the Terror and developing mastery over the Forces of Destruction. In the old stories, monsters and dragons do not go away if they are simply ignored. The people have to gather together, tell stories of how other people have survived. Someone among them will ride the energy of the community and with the guidance from helping spirits, the hero(ine) can bring happiness, play, and rest back to the people.

It is well to notice the face of the Dragon, to know its ways, but it is equally important to stay centered spiritually and to believe you will be given what you need to endure. In Jane Yolen's "Dawn Strider" (1974), a child who leads the sun on its daily path is stolen by a giant named Night Walker. There is no sun, so the plants are dying, the animals are freezing, and the people are afraid. They draw straws and one of the smallest children in the village is chosen to confront the giant. The giant is transformed by the smiles of Dawn Strider and that little child. The sun is again seen in the sky.

Children deeply wish to hear the stories of "how it used to be." When adults sit around and tell stories out of their past, they are deepened by those memories. So often I hear adults say, "Oh, I've had such a boring life; I have no stories to tell." But if they listen with an inner ear and dig down within themselves, stories begin to come . . . family stories, stories of close encounters, embarrassment, someone playing the fool, of resourcefulness, sadness, of favorite times of celebration. These stories are the glue, the essence that holds a people together . . . a family, a community, a nation, a planet.

TELEVISION

Culturally, our main storyteller has become television. Television has connected us as a planet; it tells many old stories in modern ways, but too much of what appears on the tube is connected to what will sell to the largest number; not enough programming is motivated by the values needed to sustain culture.

Because television has become such a powerful storyteller, we have begun to make the connection between stories and television. A course we have taught at the Minnesota Museum of Art and other places is based on "Be-ing Your Own TV." It helps children develop stories of the city, of their stuffed animals, stories using special effects—and these are imaged through the use of video. The story and the video tape are done by a group of 8-12 year olds; it is difficult for them to work so closely with a group of people to produce a finished product. The children have to put their own images into stories and then confront the difficult problem of how to visualize those images with video. We try to help them realize that television begins with a story that someone is telling. We want them to believe their stories are worth telling, that their stories can be visualized with a video/TV camera, and that the stories of ordinary people are important.

This approach to telling stories with high technology is necessary because television is a major part of our modern world. But we must never allow ourselves to stop telling simple stories to each other, and most especially, to our children. As George Gerbner of the Annanberg Foundation said last year on the "Nova" series, "The people who tell the stories control the way children grow up, and television has become our main storyteller."

My wish is that parents, grandparents, and members of our communities will find their own voices to tell stories, even if it is only once a week or once a month. Let us begin to seize the time to tell our children stories, live.

REFERENCES

Andersen, H. C. 1976. The fir tree. *Eighty tales*. New York: Pantheon Books.
Grant, M. *Hamadryaden*, P W 7:2 2287-92. *Dictionnaire des antiquites grecques et romains*.
Gregory, D., with Lipsyte, R. 1964. *Nigger*. New York: Pocket Books.
Grimm, The Brothers. 1972. Iron Hans. *The complete Grimm's fairy tales*. New York: Random House.
Lester, J. 1970. *Black folktales*. New York: Grove Press.
O'Bryan A. 1956. *The dine: Origin myths of the Navajo Indians*. Washington, D.C.: Smithsonian Institution, Bureau of American Ethnology, Bulletin 163.
Phelps, E. T., ed. 1978. *Tatterhood and other tales*. Old Westbury, New York: The Feminist Press.
Postman, Neil. 1985. *Entertaining ourselves to death: Public discourse in the age of show business*. New York: Penguin.
Thompson, S. (chosen by). 1968. *One hundred favorite folktales*. Bloomington: Indiana University Press.

Wynne, E. 1982. The rainbow dream. Minneapolis: Behavioral Pediatrics Program, Minneapolis Children's Medical Center. Audio tape.

Yolen, J. 1974. *The girl who cried flowers and other tales*. New York: Thomas Y. Crowell Co.

Zarambouka, S. 1977. *Irene-peace*. Washington, D.C.: Tee Lofton Publishers.

ADDITIONAL STORY SOURCES

Matson, E. (collected by). 1968. *Longhouse legends*. New Jersey: Thomas Nelson and Sons.

Spavin, D. 1977. *Chippewa dawn*. Bloomington, Minn.: Voyageur Press.

Wolkstein, D. 1978. *The magic orange tree and other Haitian folktales*. New York: A. Knopf.

Yolen, J. 1981. *Touch magic*. New York: Philomel Books (Putnam).

Reprinted with permission from *In Context: A Quarterly of Humane Sustainable Culture*, P.O. Box 215, Sequim, WA 98382.

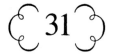

TRANSITION FILMS:
A SELECTED FILMOGRAPHY

Robert C. Hinkel

The following filmography consists of both feature-length films and shorter films, all of them reflecting, in one way or another, themes of initiation, rites of passage and life crisis or transition. These listings are of great potential use to students, parents, teachers, analysts, counselors, ministers, and others who deal with individuals in the midst of life-change. Each film, in its own way, may stimulate transformative inward processes or rewarding discussion among those who view it. A film, of course, is not necessarily an adequate "substitute" for the reality of the viewers' life experience. Life is one thing; celluloid is another. Nevertheless, a film may sow seeds that can be harvested later by individuals who seek to find meaning in their lives. The katharsis *engendered by viewing a good film can often mark the first step toward the resolution of life crises. The advent of videotape now makes it possible for educators, therapists and others to easily and inexpensively utilize film as a powerful tool.*

The following listings were selected by Robert Hinkel with an eye to their "excellence and relevance to the modern audience. Many are established 'classics' and others are of a more specialized nature, particularly suitable for certain age or interest groups. No attempt was made to include recent releases as such." It should be noted that most of the feature films would be especially appropriate for adult, college-age, or sophisticated high school students, while the shorter films are more likely to appeal to all age groups and families. Listings are alphabetized according to director and include brief synopses and mention of other films of similar genre or theme. The names of distributors and running times for each film listed are given at the end. Addresses of distributors can be found in two standard reference works published by R.R. Bowker: Feature Films on 8mm, 16mm and Videotape, *and* Educational Film Locater *(New York 1982). The Museum of the American Indian in New York has an excellent catalog of good films on Indian themes, feature films as well as documentaries.*

Robert Hinkel, Ph.D., an Associate Professor of English at Western Michigan University, has lectured for several semesters in Berlin. His most recent papers, "Berliner Christbaeume" and "Rudolf Rocholls Verlorene Landschaft," were published in Germany. Currently, he is studying the project of translating the works of C.G. Jung into English.

FEATURE FILMS

Ashby, Hal. *Coming Home* (USA 1978). Like Daniel Ford's *Go Tell the Spartans* (USA 1978), Michael Cimino's *The Deer Hunter* (below) and Francis Ford Coppola's *Apocalypse Now* (USA 1979), *Coming Home* is an anti-war film inspired by Vietnam. The central figure (Jon Voight) comes home as a paraplegic trying to make the passage into normalcy. Although the transition is incomplete, the healing presence of a woman nurtures the wounded man's growing ability to cope. Compare Ingmar Bergman's *The Seventh Seal* (Sweden 1957). In Bergman's film a knight is trying to return home after spending many years in the Crusades.

Bergman, Ingmar. *Wild Strawberries* (Sweden 1957). A series of dreams, visions and encounters during one day in the life of an elderly Stockholm physician (Victor Sjöström) enlightens him about his emotional isolation and makes easier the acceptance of aging. This is one of the finest of the many Bergman films in which the theme of "passages" dominates. After a career of more than forty feature films, Bergman made *Fanny and Alexander* (Sweden 1983), a five-hour celebration of a transitional year in the life of a ten-year-old artist-in-the-making.

Bogdanovich, Peter. *The Last Picture Show* (USA 1971). The senior year of high school and the first year after graduation is the time of transition for a young man (Timothy Bottoms) who is learning about the pains of adulthood from an aging cowboy (Ben Johnson) and a lonely middle-age woman (Cloris Leachman) in a small Texas town during the early 1950's.

Brown, Clarence. *The Yearling* (USA 1946). At the center of this highly-acclaimed portrait of a pioneer family in the South, a boy (Claude Jarman, Jr.) sacrifices his pet deer and a part of his own innocence as he struggles into the acceptance of the adult responsibility that will save his family. Two years later, in Brown's adaptation of William Faulkner's *Intruder in the Dust*, the same actor was to play a troubled Southern boy learning from and growing towards an understanding of a proud black man (Juano Hernandez).

Cacoyannis, Michael. *Zorba the Greek* (Greece/USA 1964). On his way to Crete, a quiet and reflective English author (Alan Bates) meets the passionate and impulsive Alexis Zorba (Anthony Quinn). The Dionysian

Zorba becomes a mentor initiating the Apollonian author into new dimensions of experience.

Camus, Marcel. *Black Orpheus* (France/Italy/Brazil 1958). The myth of Orpheus and Eurydice is transposed into carnival time in modern Rio as a black streetcar driver attempts to follow his Eurydice, a peasant girl, into the land of the dead. The modern Orpheus dies; and the life cycle continues as children, among them a new Orpheus and Eurydice, dance and celebrate the rising of the sun and the start of a new day. Compare Jean Cocteau's *Orpheus* (France 1949).

Capra, Frank. *Mr. Deeds Goes to Town* (USA 1936). One of the several Capra films depicting the initiation of small-town innocence into big-city experience, *Mr. Deeds* follows its hero (Gary Cooper) from Mandrake Falls to Manhattan. The innocent again in 1941, Cooper plays a bush-league pitcher who is thrust into a large-scale American proto-Facist organization *(Meet John Doe)*. In *Mr. Smith Goes to Washington* (USA 1939) James Stewart is the innocent who is initiated into political reality in the big city. In all three films, in one way or another, innocence is victorious and redemptive.

Cimino, Michael. *The Deer Hunter* (USA 1978). Fire, deer hunting and Russian roulette are the central metaphors in a 180-minute film which follows the development of a small-town steelworker (Robert De Niro) as he becomes a soldier and captive in Vietnam before his return to his hometown. His successful adjustments are contrasted with the failed passages of his friends.

Cocteau, Jean. *Beauty and the Beast* (France 1946). Cocteau's recreation of the well-known fable of the redemptive power of love presents an innocent's separation from his family, her residence in a monster's castle, and her growing realization of the meaning of beauty in an adult relationship.

De Sica, Vittorio. *The Bicycle Thief* (Italy 1949). Although the major figure in this prime example of Italian neorealism is a desperate father, the theme of a young boy's initiation into harsh city realities of post-war Italy emerges as the boy follows his father through Rome's streets in search of the stolen bicycle on which the father's job depends.

De Sica, Vittorio. *Umberto D* (Italy 1955). A classic portrait of aging, the film tells the story of an old man who is evicted from his apartment and ends up facing his remaining years with his dog as his only companion. A somewhat similar theme was developed two decades later in Paul Mazursky's more genial *Harry and Tonto* (USA 1974), in which a septuagenarian (Art Carney) and his faithful cat make a cross-country odyssey after being evicted from their New York apartment. In the 1974 film, old age is represented as a beginning.

Fellini, Federico. *Amarcord* (Italy 1973). The semi-autobiographical *Amarcord* ("I remember") is a lovely series of loosely-connected episodes that take place during a transitional year in the life of an Italian boy. The film follows his emergence from innocence—as do the films in which Giulietta Masina (Fellini's wife) plays the central role. In *La Strada* (Italy 1954) Masina is a waif cast into the harsh world of a brutish performer; in *Nights of Cabiria* (Italy 1956) she plays a simple soul in the world of prostitution; and in *Juliet of the Spirits* (Italy 1965) she is a naive, middle-aged housewife making excursions into a world of nightmare visions.

Fleming, Victor. *The Wizard of Oz* (USA 1939). This celebrated musical fantasy is about a Kansas farm girl (Judy Garland) who leaves home to roam in the fabulous land of Oz and who, allegorically, embarks on a vision quest and a circular journey that brings the young quester home with the insight that "there's no place like home."

Ford, John. *The Man Who Shot Liberty Valance* (USA 1961). This is the best example of a Western in which the development of the hero (James Stewart) counterpoints the growing pains of a country which is emerging from "wilderness" to "garden." John Wayne, an emblem of the Old West, is the craggy mentor facilitating the greenhorn's initiation. In Wayne's last film (Don Siegel's *The Shootist*, USA 1976), made three years before he died of cancer, Wayne acts out an aging gunfighter's alternative to a lingering death by cancer.

Hackford, Taylor. *An Officer and a Gentleman* (USA 1982). The story of a raw recruit who makes his way through an officer's training program and wins his wings in the Naval Air Corps makes use of and updates the formulas and archetypes of scores of typical and second-rate military initiation films such as Mitchell Leisen's *I Wanted Wings* (USA 1941).

Keaton, Buster. *The Navigator* (USA 1924). Keaton's silent comedies present miraculous transitions from incompetence to excellence. In *The Navigator* a helpless rich kid learns to cope singlehandedly with an ocean liner; in *The General* (USA 1926) a hapless locomotive engineer becomes a Civil War hero; and in *Steamboat Bill, Jr.* (USA 1928) a feckless Eastern dandy becomes a kind of savior-hero in the midst of an almost apocalyptic windstorm.

Kazan, Elia. *On the Waterfront.* (USA 1954). An ex-boxer (Marlon Brando) working for a corrupt waterfront union comes to know a tough priest (Karl Malden) who encourages his growth from "a bum" (as the ex-boxer calls himself) to an authentic, socially-responsible hero.

Kurosawa, Akira. *Ikiru* (Japan 1952). Variously translated as *Living, To Live* and *Doomed,* the film presents the experience of a lonely old man who is dying of cancer. During his remaining years he tries to create a playground for the poor children of his district.

Laughton, Charles. *Night of the Hunter* (USA 1955). Laughton and James Agee (who wrote the script) use Moses and Huck Finn archetypes to shape the nightmare-odyssey of two orphans escaping downriver from a menacing stepfather who represents the evil forces of an adult world. The film's almost idyllic ending works against conventional expectations about the transition from innocence to experience.

Lucas, George. *American Graffiti* (USA 1973). Like Robert Mulligan's *The Summer of '42* (USA 1971) and Peter Bogdanovich's *The Last Picture Show* (above), *American Graffiti* was part of a trend of nostalgic period pieces presenting boys growing into manhood. The actions of four friends in this low-budget film suggest variations on teenage rites of passage in a small California town after high-school graduation in the early 1960's.

Mazursky, Paul. *An Unmarried Woman* (USA 1978). A woman (Jill Clayburgh) whose identity has been built around her marriage of sixteen years must make the transition to being an unmarried woman when her husband leaves her for a younger woman. The celebrated drama about a modern woman's successful post-marital transition was followed in the next year by Robert Benton's *Kramer vs. Kramer* and Alan Pakula's *Starting Over*—American dramas suggesting the transitions that a man must make after marital breakup.

Mizoguchi, Kenji. *Ugetsu Monogatari* (Japan 1953). A potter in 16th-century Japan forgets his wife and child when he crosses a symbolic lake and begins a love affair with a sensuous apparition. Year later, when he tries to go home to the real world, he discovers that his wife has died. Yet her phantom presence sustains him, and new life can begin at the end of the circular journey through the potter's relationship with his young son.

Newman, Paul. *Rachel, Rachel* (USA 1968). The difficult but successful passage into approaching middle age is portrayed through a series of events, fantasies and flashbacks in the life of an outwardly-calm, spinster schoolteacher (Joanne Woodward) who finds herself in her "last ascending years."

Nichols, Mike. *The Graduate* (USA 1967). In this comic treatment of initiation, a young college graduate (Dustin Hoffman) grows up as he graduates from a summer romance with suburban mother-temptress Mrs. Robinson (Anne Bancroft) to a seemingly more "authentic" relationship with her daughter.

Parajanov, Sergei. *Shadows of Forgotten Ancestors* (Soviet Union 1964). The mythic story of a Ukrainian Romeo and Juliet follows its hero through a series of explicitly ritualistic transitions beginning in childhood and ending with his death and the ceremony immediately preceding his funeral.

Ray, Satjajit. *The Apu Trilogy* (India 1955-1959). Coming of age in India is the central theme of the films which follow Apu through childhood *(Pather Panchali)* and the adolescence which takes place between the deaths of his father and his mother *(The Unvanquished)*. In *The World of Apu,* the concluding film in the trilogy, Apu is a young man living alone in Calcutta. The life cycle continues as Apu's marriage and the death of his wife during childbirth lead to the beginning of a new life with his little son.

Reed, Carol. *The Fallen Idol* (Britain 1948). Using perspectives suggesting a child's point of view, Reed and Graham Greene (the writer of the story and the script) evoke a nine-year-old's observations of his mentor-idol (the household butler) and his growing awareness of corruption in the adult world.

Rydell, Mark. *On Golden Pond* (USA 1981). An irascible retired professor (Henry Fonda) celebrates his eightieth birthday and begins to come to terms with his fears of aging and death as he learns gradually to relate to his grandson and his daughter (Jane Fonda). An autumnal ending suggests the approaching end of the professor's life; and in the year following the release of the film, Henry Fonda himself was to die.

Roemer, Michael. *Nothing But a Man* (USA 1964). Set in the small-town black ghettoes of the deep South, this low-budget film offers a moving and almost documentary perspective on the transition of two strong black characters (Ivan Dixon and Abbey Lincoln) from the single life to marriage and parenthood.

Teshigahara, Hiroshi. *The Woman in the Dunes* (Japan 1964). A young man is trapped in an immense sandpit where he and a woman seem doomed to the task of endlessly shovelling sand. His attempts to escape are gradually replaced by his acceptance of the limitations and promise of his new world.

Truffaut, Francois. *The Four Hundred Blows* (France 1959). Evoking the experiences of an alienated twelve-year-old boy, this is the first in a series of films which depict the passages through adolescence, young adulthood (*Love at Twenty,* France 1962; *Stolen Kisses,* France 1968), marriage (*Bed and Board,* France 1970), and approaching mid-life (*Love on the Run,* France 1979) in the life of one Antoine Doinel. Jean-Pierre Léaud played Doinel during the entire twenty years of this unfolding epic of growth.

Weill, Claudia. *Girl Friends* (USA 1978). Working outside the commercial film world, Weill creates convincing portraits of friends passing from the roommate stage into two separate lifestyles.

Yates, Peter. *Breaking Away* (USA 1979). Bicycle-racing "townies" in a college town are shown in the process of "breaking away" from adolescence into adulthood.

Shorter Films with Transition Themes

Davenport, Tom. *Rapunzel, Rapunzel* (USA 1978). The 15-minute live-action adaptation of the Grimm's folk tale interprets a woman's transition from birth and abandonment through puberty and marriage. Davenport's other adaptations of German folk tales—*Hansel and Gretel* (1975), *The Frog King* (1981), *Bristlelip* ("King Thrushbeard") (1982), and *The Goose Girl* (1983)—all present archetypal plots based, in most cases, on a child's separation from parents and on the subsequent attempts to grow into adulthood. The rites of passage informing the Grimm's tales are represented in animated form by Sam Weiss in a series of Bosustow Production shorts: *The Fisherman and His Wife* (1977), *Tom Thumb* (1978), *Seven With One Blow* (1978), *Hans in Luck* (1978), *Three Golden Hairs* (1978), and *Beauty and the Beast* (1981).

Deitch, Gene. *Where the Wild Things Are* (USA 1973). Deitch's 8-minute animated adaptation of Maurice Sendak's famous picture book recreates a child's fantasy: a circular journey suggesting symbolic stages through which the growing child may eventually pass in his quest for self-realization. Deitch's adaptations of tales by Hans Christian Andersen (for example, *The Swineherd* [1974] and *The Ugly Duckling* [1975]), also offer curious visions of individuation.

Fields, Connie. *The Life and Times of Rosie the Riveter* (USA 1980). This 60-minute documentary poses the question of "a woman's place." Recent interviews with five women are intercut with (1) government propaganda films from the Second World War urging women out of their homes and into factories and (2) similar films from the end of the War suggesting that a woman's place is in the home. The study might qualify as a kind of reverse-initiation film, although the perspectives of the older women being interviewed reveal that they have indeed grown into a heightened consciousness of the modern world in spite of the war years in which they grew up.

Geller, Robert. Geller is the executive producer of *The American Short Story Series,* a series of seventeen short films released in 1977-80. Originally presented as a PBS television-film series, the films and video tapes are often used in high school and college courses dealing with the relationship between film and literature. Adolescent initiation is a dominant theme (for example, the adaptations of Sherwood Anderson's "I'm a Fool," Willa Cather's "Paul's Case," F. Scott Fitzgerald's "Bernice Bobs Her Hair," William Faulkner's "Barn Burning," and Richard Wright's "Almos' a Man"), although initiation into life's later phases is represented in the adaptations of such stories as Hemingway's "Soldier's Home," Henry

James' "The Jolly Corner," Stephen Crane's "The Blue Hotel," John Updike's "The Music School," and Katherine Anne Porter's "The Jilting of Granny Weatherall." Several years earlier, Britannica Films attempted similar adaptations with film versions of such stories as Shirley Jackson's "The Lottery" (1969), Hemingway's "My Old Man" (1969) and Joseph Conrad's "The Secret Sharer" (1973).

Hubley, John and Faith. *Everybody Rides the Carousel* (USA 1975). Eight animated sequences (67 minutes) illustrate Erik H. Erikson's theory of personality from birth to death.

McDermott, Gerald. *Arrow to the Sun* (USA 1973). A boy's search for his father leads him through four initiatory trials until he is recognized by his father, the Lord of the Sun. This 12-minute adaptation of a profound American Indian hero story—the fifth in a series of five short, animated films by McDermott—is based on the unique contours and colors of the Acoma Pueblo Indians in Arizona. The *Stonecutter* (1965) is based on a Japanese tale; *Sunflight* (1966) comes from the myth of Icarus; *Anansi the Spider* (1969) is an adaptation of a tale from the Ashanti of West Africa; and *The Magic Tree* (1970) is based on a tale from the Congo. Each one of these animated films offers an extraordinary interpretation of archetypal passage.

Preuss, Paul. *Our Totem is the Raven* (1972). An aging American Indian (Chief Dan George) leads his adolescent grandson on a journey of initiation into ancient tribal lands and customs. The ritualistic rediscovery of ethnic "roots" as a means of self-realization has been presented in any number of films (for example, the National Film Board of Canada's *Circle of the Sun*, directed by Colen Low in 1960).

FEATURE FILMS	DISTRIBUTORS	RUNNING TIME
Amarcord	Films Incorporated	127 Minutes
American Graffiti	Swank Motion Pictures	109 Minutes
Apocalypse Now	United Artists	146 Minutes
Beauty and the Beast	Films Incorporated	90 Minutes
Bed and Board	Swank	97 Minutes
Bicycle Thief	Audio Brandon	87 Minutes
Black Orpheus	Films Incorporated	103 Minutes
Breaking Away	Films Incorporated	99 Minutes
Coming Home	United Artists	127 Minutes
The Deer Hunter	Swank	183 Minutes
The Fallen Idol	Kit Parker	92 Minutes
Fanny and Alexander (Shorter version)	Films Incorporated	190 Minutes
Four Hundred Blows	Films Incorporated	98 Minutes
The General	Audio Brandon	90 Minutes
Girl Friends	Swank	88 Minutes
Go Tell the Spartans	Films Incorporated	114 Minutes

The Graduate	Audio Brandon	105 Minutes
Harry and Tonto	Films Incorporated	115 Minutes
Ikiru	Audio Brandon	140 Minutes
Intruder in the Dust	Films Incorporated	87 Minutes
Juliet of the Spirits	Audio Brandon	137 Minutes
Kramer vs. Kramer	Swank	105 Minutes
The Last Picture Show	Audio Brandon	118 Minutes
La Strada	Films Incorporated	107 Minutes
Love on the Run	Films Incorporated	95 Minutes
The Man Who Shot Liberty Valance	Audio Brandon	122 Minutes
Meet John Doe	Audio Brandon	123 Minutes
Mr. Deeds Goes to Town	Audio Brandon	118 Minutes
Mr. Smith Goes to Washington	Audio Brandon	95 Minutes
The Navigator	Audio Brandon	62 Minutes
Night of the Hunter	United Artists	91 Minutes
Nights of Cabiria	Films Incorporated	110 Minutes
Nothing But a Man	Audio Brandon	92 Minutes
An Officer and a Gentleman	Films Incorporated	126 Minutes
On Golden Pond	Swank	109 Minutes
On the Waterfront	Audio Brandon	108 Minutes
Orpheus	Films Incorporated	94 Minutes
Pather Panchali	Films Incorporated	112 Minutes
Rachel, Rachel	Audio Brandon	104 Minutes
The Seventh Seal	Films Incorporated	96 Minutes
Shadows of Forgotten Ancestors	Films Incorporated	110 Minutes
The Shootist	Audio Brandon	99 Minutes
Starting Over	Audio Brandon	105 Minutes
Steamboat Bill Jr.	Audio Brandon	60 Minutes
Stolen Kisses	Cinema 5	90 Minutes
The Summer of '42	Audio Brandon	102 Minutes
Ugetsu Monogatari	Films Incorporated	96 Minutes
Umberto D	Films Incorporated	89 Minutes
An Unmarried Woman	Films Incorporated	124 Minutes
The Unvanquished (Aparijito)	Tamarelle	108 Minutes
Wild Strawberries	Films Incorporated	90 Minutes
The Wizard of Oz	Films Incorporated	100 Minutes
The Woman of the Dunes	Kit Parker	130 Minutes
The World of Apu	Em Gee	103 Minutes
The Yearling	Films Incorporated	135 Minutes
Zorba the Greek	Films Incorporated	146 Minutes

SHORTER FILMS	DISTRIBUTORS	RUNNING TIME
*Almos' a Man	Coronet Films and Video	39 Minutes
Arrow to the Sun	Texture Films	12 Minutes
Anansi the Spider	Texture Films	10 Minutes
*Barn Burning	Coronet Films and Video	39 Minutes
Beauty and the Beast	Churchill Films	12 Minutes
*Bernice Bobs Her Hair	Coronet Films and Video	39 Minutes
*The Blue Hotel	Coronet Films and Video	55 Minutes
Bristlelip	Tom Davenport Films	20 Minutes
Circle of the Sun	National Film Board of Canada	30 Minutes

Everybody Rides the Carousel	Pyramid Films	67 Minutes
The Fisherman and His Wife	Churchill Films	10 Minutes
The Frog King	Tom Davenport Films	15 Minutes
The Goose Girl	Tom Davenport Films	20 Minutes
Hans in Luck	Churchill Films	7 Minutes
Hansel and Gretel	Tom Davenport Films	15 Minutes
*I'm a Fool	Coronet Films and Video	38 Minutes
*The Jilting of Granny Weatherall	Coronet Films and Video	57 Minutes
*The Jolly Corner	Coronet Films and Video	57 Minutes
The Life and Times of Rosie the Riveter	Clarity Education Productions	60 Minutes
The Lottery	Britannica Films and Video	18 Minutes
The Magic Tree	Phoenix Films	10 Minutes
*The Music School	Coronet Films and Video	30 Minutes
My Old Man	Tom Davenport Films	27 Minutes
Our Totem is the Raven	Britannica Films and Video	21 Minutes
*Paul's Case	Churchill Films	55 Minutes
Rapunzel, Rapunzel	Coronet Films and Video	15 Minutes
The Secret Sharer	Weston Woods	30 Minutes
Seven With One Blow	International Films	10 Minutes
*Soldier's Home	Weston Woods	42 Minutes
The Stonecutter	Churchill Films	6 Minutes
Sunflight	Churchill Films	12 Minutes
The Swineherd	Weston Woods	7 Minutes
Three Golden Hairs	Churchill Films	12 Minutes
Tom Thumb	Churchill Films	9 Minutes
The Ugly Duckling	Weston Woods	15 Minutes
Where the Wild Things Are	Weston Woods	8 Minutes

*Originally made for television.

INDEX

Printed in the United States
41078LVS00008B/1-45

9 780812 690484